Brothers in Arms

COLD WAR

INTERNATIONAL
HISTORY
PROJECT SERIES

James G. Hershberg

series editor

Brothers in Arms

The Rise and Fall of the Sino-Soviet Alliance, 1945–1963

edited by Odd Arne Westad

Woodrow Wilson Center Press
Washington, D.C.

Stanford University Press
Stanford, California

EDITORIAL OFFICES:
The Woodrow Wilson Center Press
One Woodrow Wilson Plaza
1300 Pennsylvania Avenue, N.W.
Washington, D.C. 20004-3027
Telephone 202-691-4010

ORDER FROM:
Stanford University Press
CUP Distribution Center
110 Midland Avenue
Port Chester, N.Y. 10573-4930

Paperback edition 2000
2   4   6   8   9   7   5   3
Library of Congress Cataloging-in-Publication Data
Brothers in arms : the rise and fall of the Sino-Soviet alliance,
  1945–1963 / edited by Odd Arne Westad.
     p.   cm. — (Cold War International History Project series)
  Includes bibliographical references and index.
  ISBN 0-8047-3484-4 (cloth : alk. paper)
  ISBN 0-8047-3485-2 (pbk. : alk. paper)
  1. Soviet Union—Foreign relations—China. 2. China—Foreign relations—Soviet
  Union. I. Westad, Odd Arne. II. Series.
DK68.7.C5B75   1998
327.51047—dc21   98-42422
                                                                CIP

Contents

The Woodrow Wilson International Center for Scholars

The Center is the living memorial of the United States of America to the nation's twenty-eighth president, Woodrow Wilson. The Congress established the Woodrow Wilson Center in 1968 as an international institute for advanced study, "symbolizing and strengthening the fruitful relationship between the world of learning and the world of public affairs." The Center opened in 1970 under its own board of trustees.

In all its activities, the Woodrow Wilson Center is a nonprofit, nonpartisan organization, supported financially by annual appropriations from the Congress and by the contributions of foundations, corporations, and individuals.

WOODROW WILSON CENTER PRESS

The Woodrow Wilson Center Press publishes books written in substantial part at the Center or otherwise prepared under its sponsorship by Fellows, Guest Scholars, staff members, and other program participants. Conclusions or opinions expressed in Center publications and programs are those of the authors and speakers and do not necessarily reflect the views of the Center staff, fellows, trustees, advisory groups, or any individuals or organizations that provide financial support to the Center.

The Cold War International History Project

The Cold War International History Project was established by the Woodrow Wilson International Center for Scholars in 1991. The project supports the full and prompt release of historical materials by governments on all sides of the Cold War and seeks to disseminate new information and perspectives on Cold War history emerging from previously inaccessible sources on "the other side" – the former Communist bloc – through publications, fellowships, and scholarly meetings and conferences. The project publishes the *Cold War International History Project Bulletin* and maintains a Web site, cwihp.si.edu.

In collaboration with the National Security Archive, a nongovernmental research institute and document repository located at George Washington University, the project has created a Russian and East-bloc Archival Documents Database at Gelman Library, George Washington University. The database makes available to scholars photocopies from Russian and other former Communist archives donated by the project, the National Security Archive, and various scholars. The database may be explored through a computer-searchable English-language inventory. For further information, contact the National Security Archive, Gelman Library, George Washington University, Washington, D.C. 20037 (Web site www.seas.gwu.edu/nsarchive).

At the Woodrow Wilson Center, the project is part of the Division of International Studies, headed by Robert S. Litwak. The director of the project is Christian F. Ostermann. The project is overseen by an advisory committee that is chaired by William Taubman, Amherst College, and includes Michael Beschloss; James H. Billington, librarian of Congress; Warren I. Cohen, University of Maryland at Baltimore; John Lewis Gaddis, Yale University; Samuel F. Wells, Jr., deputy director of the Woodrow Wilson Center; and Sharon Wolchik, George Washington University.

The Cold War International History Project was created with the help of the John D. and Catherine T. MacArthur Foundation and receives major support from it and from the Smith Richardson Foundation.

Series Preface

James G. Hershberg

It is a great pleasure to present *Brothers in Arms: The Rise and Fall of the Sino-Soviet Alliance, 1945–1963,* edited by Odd Arne Westad, as the first title in the Cold War International History Project Book Series. A collection of essays by Chinese, Russian, European, and American scholars presenting newly released evidence from Russian and Chinese sources on the advent, short life, and dramatic rupture of the alliance between the two Communist giants of the Cold War, it epitomizes the kind of collegial, international, institutional, multilingual, multiarchival, and interdisciplinary cooperation and collaboration that the project has striven to encourage and foster since it started operations at the Woodrow Wilson International Center for Scholars in Washington, D.C., in 1991. The project's primary mission has been to broaden, deepen, and otherwise enhance scholarly and public understanding of Cold War history by encouraging the fullest, fastest, freest, and fairest opening and release of historical materials by governments on all sides of the Cold War. It seeks in particular to disseminate new information and perspectives on Cold War history emerging from the previously inaccessible sources on the "other side" – the former Communist bloc – through publications of new findings (through the project's *Bulletin,* Working Papers, Book Series, and home page on the Internet at cwihp.si.edu); fellowships for young scholars from former Communist, quasi-Communist, and still-Communist lands to come to the United States to conduct archival research and meet American colleagues; and international meetings

James G. Hershberg is assistant professor of history and international affairs at George Washington University and editor of the Cold War International Project Book Series. From 1991 to 1996 he was the first director of the Cold War International History Project at the Woodrow Wilson International Center for Scholars.

and conferences for scholars to present and debate new research from former Communist sources.

What is "new" about the new international Cold War history, and how does it differ from previous accounts? One basic differentiation, of course, as John Lewis Gaddis has duly noted, is that the new "post–Cold War" Cold War history differs from the old in a temporal sense – in contrast to past authors, who wrote in the midst of an ongoing conflict, historians can now write from outside the period, knowing its duration and ending, which is in fact a more "normal" way to write history in the first place.[1] This would be true even if the East-bloc archives remained off-limits. But the unprecedented availability of Communist-side documents as well as additional Western sources (including materials such as intelligence intercepts whose release, or even existence, had been previously taboo), makes possible a different type of history in substantive and perceptual terms, transcending from the inevitable tendency, exacerbated by reliance on English language, preponderantly American, primary sources, to view the Cold War through the perspective of Washington. Recognizing the need for collaboration among scholars working in different languages, archives, countries, and for that matter, disciplines, the new Cold War history not only admits but requires a diversity of viewpoints as a basic precondition for attempting to describe international events involving multiple actors and multiple realities. To a great extent, this renewed attentiveness to utilizing the sources and appreciating the perspectives of competing sides in order to understand better their interactions simply marks a return to the traditional way diplomatic history was written before the secrecy of the Cold War era, on both sides, precluded such access. Like the U.S. government's Cold War classification restrictions, most of which originated during World War II and the Manhattan Project and never really "demobilized," the writing of Cold War history based on (partial) access to only one side's documents – what Gaddis Smith once aptly described as the diplomatic history equivalent of "one hand clapping"[2] – over time became accepted as normal, inevitable, acceptable "standard operating procedure" rather than the aberration from past practice it actually represented. While this multi-perspectival approach thus merely brings Cold War history closer to its roots in international diplomatic history, it also tries to exploit some of the insights of "postmodern" attention to text and culture. It recognizes, as Michael Hunt noted in his study of crises in U.S. foreign policy, that international events also represent an intersection of narratives, sometimes seldom overlapping narratives, when viewed from the often dramatically diverging perspectives of the various actors involved.[3] One may even argue that to a considerable degree the very idea of the "Cold War" as the descriptive term applied to post–World War II international relations represented an attempt to impose a single coherent narrative framework on what in fact remained an extremely complex multiplicity of interacting and intersecting narratives – national, regional, cultural, economic, technological, ethnic, etc. – which variously predated, postdated, and accompanied the global superpower rivalry that has usually been depicted in East-West, U.S.-Soviet terms. (The origins of the Korean War, as well as the Chinese entry into the conflict, now can begin to be understood in terms of a complex dynamic involving exchanges among Stalin, Mao, and Kim Il-Sung, rather than flowing from a bilateral "signaling" process between Moscow (or Beijing) and Washington. The Vietnam War (i.e., the Second Indochina War) emerges from Chinese and Vietnamese sources in a rather different light, as a chapter in the thousand-year history of Sino-Vietnamese relations as well as the culmination of a struggle for Vietnamese independence and unification, than it does in the framework of U.S. "containment" policy toward Soviet-backed communism.[4] Similarly, the war in Afghanistan can be read into the history of the latest rise of Islamic fundamentalism, epitomized by the Iranian Revolution, as much as it was part of a Cold War "system" or story.)

By integrating scholarly perspectives as well as sources and documents from the Communist and other non-Western actors of the Cold War era, the new history also seeks to view the period through a variety of cultural lenses, no longer taking for granted that policymakers and decision-makers on all sides adopted the same "realist" approach to power, international relations, and the concept of "national interest" that Americans tended to presume represented a common language.[5] Finally released from "party line" restrictions that forced scholars to conform to common interpretations, Russian, Chinese, and Central and East European scholars are finally free to contribute their intimate, internalized knowledge of their countries' culture, values, and historical experience to interpreting the more traditional forms of evidence emerging from archives and oral history witnesses. (Certainly, the rise and fall of the Sino-Soviet alliance that this book examines must take account of deep-rooted cultural patterns in relations between Russians and Chinese as well as the more recent ideological and geopolitical circumstances that gave birth to their Cold War cooperation.) With the benefit of previously-unavailable sources and perspectives, in many cases the "new" Cold War history devotes greater attention to domestic and intra-alliance (as opposed to inter-alliance) factors in explaining motivations of both sides, but especially among the Communist powers, whose interactions and internal tensions were often masked by secrecy, lack of access by Western observers, or public claims of unity.[6]

In no case were these factors more relevant during the first two decades of the Cold War than the rise and fall of the Sino-Soviet alliance, a development in international relations whose perceived import to U.S. policymakers was matched only by the murkiness, confusion, and controversy it aroused among those in the West charged with reacting to and analyzing it.

In this volume, young scholars breaking into the new sources and out of old interpretive shackles (imposed by lack of freedom, lack of access, or, as Odd Arne Westad points out in his introduction, lack of interest) cast new light on the most secretive and important of relationships within the erstwhile Communist realm. It is a story at the heart of the "other side" of Cold War history that CWIHP was created to help integrate with more customary sources and interpretations from the Western side. And the volume's appearance in the series reflects the exciting, exhilarating, sometimes somewhat improvised nature of the enterprise of ripping aside the secrecy that once veiled the Communist world's archives.

One morning in Beijing in the spring of 1994, at the Hotel Minzu, about a mile west of Tiananmen Square, Odd Arne Westad (then director of research at the Norwegian Nobel Institute) and I had a discussion over breakfast that ultimately led to this book. The two of us, along with a third scholar, David Wolff (later project director), had journeyed to the Chinese capital to meet with local scholars and archivists to explore the feasibility of organizing an international conference at which Chinese, Russian, and Western researchers could present new evidence on the history of the Cold War in Asia. I was then the project's director, making a first reconnaissance trip to Beijing, while Westad, who had just published his groundbreaking study of the intersection between the Cold War and the Chinese civil war,[7] had kindly agreed to show me the ropes, introduce me to his own cadre of contacts, and do what he could to facilitate my mission. Between slurps of congee (or was it mouthfuls of rice?), Westad and I discovered that we also had potentially competing – or potentially complementary – future plans. My own focus was on finding out whether it would be possible to organize a successful conference and commissioning papers from leading Chinese (and other) scholars; Westad, I found out, was already engaged in discussions with many of those same prospective participants regarding collection of essays for a volume on the Sino-Soviet alliance. Rather than gritting our teeth and rushing off to nail down commitments to contribute exclusively to one project or the other, or trying to extract two different chapters from each scholar rather than one (presumably better) effort, we quickly agreed that it would make the most sense if we coordinated our enterprises – the chapters for Westad's planned book would be presented at the project's proposed conference, then revised for publication.

In fact, although neither of us knew it at the time, the genesis of this work dated back more than a year earlier, to the deep freeze of a Moscow winter. There, in January 1993, the Cold War International History Project had organized the first major international conference on Cold War history since the collapse of the Soviet Union and the (still partial) opening of the Soviet archives. At that conference, held in cooperation with the archive holding the records of the now-outlawed Communist Party of the Soviet Union (CPSU), one of the many panels had featured reports from Russian archives and oral history sources on Soviet policy toward Asia during the Cold War and on the Sino-Soviet alliance and split in particular. These early glimpses from the formerly top-secret CPSU files captivated and excited the hundred or so scholars crowding the Russian Academy of Sciences conference hall, even the jet-lagged Americans. After hearing the panelists – who included Kathryn Weathersby, Deborah A. Kaple, and Constantine Pleshakov, each of whom presented early versions of the work represented in their chapters in this volume[8] – Westad, one of three commentators (along with prominent U.S. Sinologists Warren I. Cohen and Nancy Bernkopf Tucker), instantly voiced the most common reaction: now that, for the first time, high-quality Russian sources and scholarly analyses on the Sino-Soviet relationship were finally beginning to emerge to supplement Western ones, the logical next step was to complete the triangle and bring Chinese scholars and Chinese-language sources into the mix. Then and there the idea of bringing Russian, Western, and Chinese scholars and sources together for a three-way conversation jelled into a firm intention – and led, inter alia, to that breakfast at the Minzu on Fuxingmennei Dajie sixteen months later.

Despite the tensions over trade relations and human rights then clouding Sino-American relations on the political level, our talks with Chinese colleagues in May 1994 went well, as did contacts with historians at Hong Kong University (where Westad was spending a semester as a visiting scholar). We reached agreement to hold the conference the project envisioned – to be hosted by Hong Kong University, and with Chinese participation coordinated by the Institute of American Studies of the Chinese Academy of Social Sciences. Over the next year and a half, work went forward on research, conference papers, and book chapters (not to mention frantic faxes and e-mail messages on logistical preparations between the Wilson Center and Hong Kong University historian Priscilla Roberts), culminating in Hong Kong in January 1996 with four days of presentations, revelations, interpretations, and disputations relating to the history of the Cold War in Asia, with several panels devoted to the Sino-Soviet alliance and split. Westad, Chen Jian, Niu Jun, Yang Kuisong, Sergei Goncharenko, Weathersby, Kaple – indeed, all of the authors in this volume (with the exception of Pleshakov, who could not attend) – were among those giving papers, and the intense exchanges of those days and nights – not only in and between formal sessions but in long evening walks and sometimes queasy boat trips around the harbor – forged new bonds of scholarly collaboration and personal friendship and renewed old ones.[9] The findings also attracted broader popular as well as scholarly attention, receiving extensive media coverage in major newspapers and on CNN, and with Russian- and Chinese-language publications causing shifts in entrenched historiography.[10]

Typifying the kind of international community of scholars that the project has tried to foster, the editor and authors of this volume have in many ways besides their written work contributed to the expanding relationship among scholars from both sides of the former Sino-Soviet alliance and both sides of the former Cold War. Since the Hong Kong meeting, groups of scholars in Beijing and Moscow have banded together to form Cold War study associations to promote research and organize exchanges and conferences with foreign colleagues. Many contributors to this volume also took part in a project-sponsored workshop in Beijing in October 1997 to discuss additional new evidence on the Sino-Soviet alliance. In addition to this volume, other fruits of these coordinated research efforts have included publication of Russian and Chinese documents and findings on the Cold War in Asia in the project's *Bulletin,* where some of the documents in the appendixes originally appeared and which scholars may consult for additional materials.[11] Another result is a forthcoming volume in the Cold War International History Project Book Series containing additional research reports (from the Hong Kong conference and other project activities) on the Cold War in Asia – not only on the Sino-Soviet relationship but on the Korean and Vietnam wars, Sino-American relations, and other issues. And meanwhile, "the network" of researchers continue to collaborate to share the latest leads and findings and to try to pry loose archival materials still off-limits in Moscow, Beijing, and elsewhere. The hunt goes on, with each new discovery as prone to raise new questions as to provide long-sought answers to old ones.

For survivors and scholars of the Cold War – especially linguistically challenged ones such as myself – long dependent on (partial) access to one side's materials, the opportunity to delve inside the archives and memories of Communist world's giants, even vicariously through the reports of other researchers, offers an unparalleled and unexpected opportunity to relive, reassess, and reinterpret some of the most mysterious aspects of recent history. The authors would be the first to stress that these chapters are early and preliminary findings, subject to revision as further archives crack open and new materials emerge, in a search for understanding that will go on for decades. They have also frequently found that the newly available evidence has corroborated, at least to some degree, the analyses and speculations of scholars working at the time of the events in question or with far less access to materials than is now the case. But these findings are, nevertheless, significant harbingers of a new way of writing and understanding Cold War history – from contrasting national, disciplinary, cultural, and linguistic perpsectives – and representative, in quality and originality, of the scholarship that I look forward to presenting in forthcoming volumes of the Cold War International History Project Book Series.

Notes

1. John Lewis Gaddis, *We Now Know: Rethinking Cold War History* (Oxford: Oxford University Press, 1997), vii, 281–2.

2. Gaddis Smith, "Glasnost, Diplomatic History, and the Post–Cold War Agenda," *Yale Journal of World Affairs* 1 (Summer 1989), 50.

3. Michael H. Hunt, *Crises in U.S. Foreign Policy: An International History Reader* (New Haven, Conn.: Yale University Press, 1996), 425.

4. Stein Tonnesson, "Tracking Multi-Dimensional Dominoes," in Odd Arne Westad, Chen Jian, Stein Tonnesson, Nguyen Vu Tung, and James G. Hershberg, eds., "77 Conversations between Chinese and Foreign Leaders on the Wars in Indochina, 1964–1977," Cold War International History Project (CWIHP) Working Paper no. 22 (Washington, D.C.: Woodrow Wilson International Center for Scholars, May 1998).

5. For an example of this kind of comparative analysis, see Shu Guang Zhang, *Deterrence and Strategic Culture: Chinese-American Confrontations, 1949–1958* (Ithaca, N.Y.: Cornell University Press, 1992).

6. The author makes this argument at greater length for assessing one key Cold War juncture in "1958–1963 – A Cold War Turning Point: New Evidence on the Importance of Communist-Side Domestic and Intra-Alliance Politics during the Crisis Years," paper presented at the Norwegian Nobel Institute symposium "Reviewing the Cold War," Lysebu, Norway, June 17–20, 1998.

7. Odd Arne Westad, *Cold War and Revolution: Soviet-American Rivalry and the Origins of the Chinese Civil War, 1944–1946* (New York: Columbia University Press, 1993).

8. A revised version of Weathersby's paper for the Moscow Conference was published as CWIHP Working Paper no. 8, "Soviet Aims in Korea and the Origins of the Korean War, 1945–1950: New Evidence from Russian Archives."

9. For the program of the Hong Kong conference, see *Cold War International History Project (CWIHP) Bulletin* 8–9 (Winter 1996/1997): 220–2.

10. Perhaps the most striking indication of the latter impact is the rapid translation into Chinese of conference materials, especially Russian documents provided by the project, and the preparation of a new Chinese-language account of China's intervention in the Korean War reflecting the information contained in the Russian documents.

11. For findings published by the CWIHP on the Cold War in Asia, see, in particular, materials in *CWIHP Bulletin* 6–7 (Winter 1995/1996): 1–265; *CWIHP Bulletin* 8–9 (Winter 1996/1997): 220–69; *CWIHP Bulletin* 10 (March 1998): 149–82; and *CWIHP Bulletin* 11 (Winter 1998 [1999]): 155–99.

Preface

Odd Arne Westad

This volume introduces new multiarchival research on the history of the Sino-Soviet alliance – its rise in the late 1940s, high point in the 1950s, and collapse by the early 1960s – by a group of international historians from several different countries. It exemplifies a trend in post–Cold War writing of international history that underlines scholarly cooperation across borders as necessary for making full use of evidence available in different languages and within different cultural or political paradigms. It also underlines the challenges that a dramatic widening of the database and a sudden internationalization of research bring to post-1945 international history in terms of approaches and interpretations.

Until recently the Sino-Soviet alliance – the one major bid by the two most powerful Communist regimes to combine forces against capitalism – has been perhaps the most underresearched major topic in Cold War history. After a few early and very useful attempts at a postmortem of the alliance, written mostly during the early or mid-1960s, interest in the once so mighty compact seemed virtually to dry up.[1] In spite of the intrinsic importance of the subject, which most Cold War scholars acknowledged, the Sino-Soviet alliance received short shrift in all but a few general histories, and no more comprehensive treatments were forthcoming.[2]

There were many reasons behind the death of interest. Obviously, few scholars possessed either the requisite languages or cultural skills to deal with the alliance from both the Soviet and the Chinese angles. And even if a scholar did surmount these requirements, he or she faced the seemingly insuperable problem of gaining access to primary sources. Until only a few years ago, the Moscow and Beijing archives remained special preserves of the party elites, heavily guarded and shielded behind draconian laws on state secrets.

But as if secrecy and language barriers were not enough, the evident apathy appears also to have stemmed from the belief among many Western scholars of the 1960s, 1970s, and 1980s that they already knew and understood the reasons behind the alliance's rise and demise. In the first decades of Chinese and Russian communism, it was believed, sufficient ideological attraction existed between the two to make the countries they controlled natural allies. Then, as the new states came better to recognize their national interests, they drifted apart, and the traditional pattern of rivalry and mistrust between Russia and China recommenced. Often linked to general presumptions about modernization and state behavior, this realist paradigm dominated the field across political and parochial divides within the scholarly community.

In the late 1980s, however, as the Cold War drew to a close, the database for studying the foreign relations of Communist countries suddenly changed. Gorbachev's glasnost and the stunning liberalization that took place in China under Deng Xiaoping burst the shackles of secrecy and, for the first time, allowed Russian and Chinese scholars to begin serious work in their archives. Since then the trickle of new documents has turned into a flood. While ten years ago barely enough inner documents of the Sino-Soviet alliance existed for me to fill the normal space of a classroom lecture, today we have considerable access to a vast amount of archival documents, printed collections, briefing books, and manuscripts throughout China, the former Soviet Union, and the Eastern Bloc. In addition, as this volume demonstrates, wide-ranging opportunities have opened up to interview former policymakers and participants involved in the bilateral relationship.

While in no way unproblematic from a scholarly standpoint, the recent flood of documents has opened up possibilities for a reevaluation of the main issues of the alliance.[3] This reevaluation has been heavily influenced by new opportunities for scholarly cooperation across national boundaries. Working with colleagues from China and Russia has allowed European and American scholars to benefit from their insights into the mentalities of the Communist regimes. Likewise, scholars working from within the geographical space of the former alliance have learned to question their established truths and to employ new methodologies and approaches.

This volume gathers writings by some of the foremost younger experts on the history of the alliance from China, Russia, the United States, and Western Europe. Our cooperation began in 1994, when the contributors, on my invitation, agreed to write for the volume. Since then the project has developed in many different ways. We have shared information and documents, have helped each other gain entry to archives, and, of course, have read and commented on draft versions of the chapters. Some of us have met fairly regularly at conferences and meetings, while others have kept in touch mainly through that most wonderful of inventions for long-distance scholarly cooperation, the Internet.

We have frequently disagreed on the interpretation of much of the formerly top-secret material to which we have gained access. Although all the contributors to this volume distrust the realist paradigm, we point in very different directions in search of an alternative and comprehensive approach. For instance, in chapter 9, Chen Jian and Yang Kuisong emphasize the domestic policies and perceptions of the Chinese Communist leaders as the key to understanding the development of the alliance. Constantine Pleshakov, on the other hand, uses Soviet materials from the Khrushchev era to suggest, in chapter 7, that it was changes in the Moscow elite's worldview that presaged the rapid breakdown of the alliance in the late 1950s.

Beyond heated discussions among the contributors, we have made no attempts at harmonizing the differing views of the authors. Several of the contributors plan more comprehensive discussions of the Sino-Soviet alliance in forthcoming books, and the evolving historiography will no doubt see much debate on the central issues included here. This volume is by its very nature preliminary – a joint effort at a first assessment of massive amounts of new information. It provides new insights on many aspects of the alliance between Mao's China and the Soviet Union: its creation, its aims and instruments, and its final collapse. But it does not pretend to come up with any unified view of the causes of these developments.

The chapters are ordered in a rough chronological sequence according to the issues upon which they focus. My introductory essay presents the topic and some of the main issues of interpretation as well as a chronological overview for the benefit of new students of the alliance. It does not represent the views of all the contributors but argues strongly in favor of the tools I have found most useful in attempting to disentangle the history of the Sino-Soviet compact.

Chapter 1, by Niu Jun, deals with the origins of the alliance during World War II and the ensuing civil war in China. It emphasizes the close cooperation that developed between Chinese Communist Party (CCP) leaders and Moscow during the civil war, in spite of long-term differences between the two sides. Niu stresses the gradual increase in the importance of Soviet advice and models to Chinese Communists during this period. Although policy disagreements between the two parties persisted, the CCP in 1949–1950 was considerably closer to Moscow in word and deed than at any other time during the preceding twenty years.

In chapter 2, Kathryn Weathersby looks at the importance of the Korean War in the creation of the alliance and especially on how the negotiations to end the war influenced the Sino-Soviet relationship in the late Stalin era. Although both the general sense of purpose and the practical cooperation of the alliance was strengthened during the war, Stalin's ambivalent approach to the peace talks worried both the Chinese leaders and his own lieutenants and probably prolonged the war by months, if not years.

Chapter 3, by Deborah A. Kaple, reports on her interviews with former Soviet advisors who served in China during the 1950s. The interviews illuminate both the sense of solidarity and ideological purpose that imbued the young advisers and the problems, both political and personal, that sometimes hampered their work. The chapter also underlines the magnitude of the assistance program – by far the largest such program ever undertaken by the Soviet Union.

Sergei Goncharenko, in chapter 4, explores Moscow's programs of military assistance to the People's Republic. It shows one of the main Soviet predicaments throughout the lifetime of the alliance: On the one hand, the Soviet Union and particularly its top generals were cautious about providing the Chinese with the latest technology in offensive weapons, believing that Beijing's possession of such weapons would reduce Soviet leverage in forming joint strategies against the common enemy. On the other hand, Soviet political leaders of the post-Stalin period, driven by ideological motives or political expediency, often in the end agreed to provide the Chinese with exactly the technologies they wanted, including, in many cases, nuclear technology.

Chapter 5, by Odd Arne Westad, concentrates on the alliance's principal foreign relations challenge: the relationship with the United States. Throughout the alliance's existence, the desire to confront Washington and its policies formed a central part of its raison d'être. However, in spite of numerous attempts to integrate their views of the American threat, Chinese and Soviets tended not to see eye to eye in their Marxist understanding of U.S. intentions. As a result, Mao's view of the United States as a rapidly declining power in the late 1950s diverged from the more prudent thinking of the Soviet leadership and became an important reason for the alliance's collapse.

Shu Guang Zhang examines the development of Sino-Soviet economic cooperation and trade in chapter 6, and especially the role the American embargo of China played in this relationship. It concludes that the problems of both sides in managing their respective economies caused more friction than rational calculations of cost and benefit. Both sides generally profited from the economic cooperation, although China obviously was the main recipient of goods. But perceptions of each other's economic strategies, including trade, in the late 1950s exacerbated ties and helped foster the split, even more than specific problems of the bilateral relationship.

In chapter 7 Constantine Pleshakov discusses the role Nikita Khrushchev's leadership played in the advent of the Sino-Soviet split of the late 1950s. He finds that Khrushchev's changing geopolitical thinking prevented Moscow from seeing the opportunities that existed for continued cooperation with China despite Mao's radicalism. Khrushchev's emerging hopes for Soviet-American détente increased his, and other Soviet leaders', impatience with Beijing's unwillingness to subscribe to their view of geopolitical realities and prepared the ground for the final break with China in the early 1960s.

Chapter 8, written jointly by Chen Jian and Yang Kuisong, sums up the links the authors find between Mao Zedong's ideological development and the alliance's collapse. The authors argue that understanding Mao's mind-set is essential to grasp why the Sino-Soviet break happened when and how it did. Mao's view of the Chinese revolution grew increasingly pessimistic at the end of the 1950s. The chairman started to search for cadre within his own party who allegedly had sabotaged the progress of socialism in China and began to believe that their existence was connected to the advice China had received from the Soviet Union on its domestic policies. By 1959, after the first phase of the Great Leap Forward, Mao had become convinced that he needed to jettison the close alliance with Moscow if his ideas of a continuous revolution were to triumph in China.

Taken together, the individual chapters offer a collective snapshot of current scholarship with regard to the history of the Sino-Soviet alliance. The volume should, however, be used together with some of the earlier accounts, which—despite being based primarily on "open" sources—are still important for our understanding of what took place between the two Communist giants during the 1950s. The surveys that this volume presents also should be supplemented by more specialized works on important issues that cannot be presented in full here, such as the outbreak of the Korean War, the Taiwan Straits crises, or, for that matter, Sino-Soviet cultural or educational cooperation.

The editor and the authors wish to thank scholars and archivists in China and Russia who made this book possible. A special thanks is due to the former head of the Foreign Ministry Archives in Moscow, Dr. Igor Lebedev, and the head of the Institute of American Studies under the Chinese Academy of Social Sciences in Beijing, Professor Wang Jisi. Thanks also to the Cold War International History Project at the Woodrow Wilson International Center for Scholars, Hong Kong University (especially Priscilla Roberts), and the Louis Cha Fund for East-West Studies for organizing and funding a conference in Hong Kong in January 1996 at which several of the chapters were presented in draft. In Oslo, the Norwegian Nobel Institute provided a genial institutional base for the editor and, at different stages, for several of the other scholars involved. A special thanks to Anne Kjelling, the head of the Nobel Institute Library, who, in usual fashion, went out of her way to provide some of the harder to get at published sources for the volume.

The editor is also grateful to the Master and Fellows of Corpus Christi College, Cambridge, who gave him refuge during the last stage of the editing process. Special gratitude is due to James G. Hershberg and his two successors as heads of the Cold War International History Project, David Wolff and Christian Ostermann, who all, in innumerable ways, contributed to the publication of this book. Finally, I wish to thank the editors at both our presses, Joseph Brinley at the Woodrow Wilson Center Press and Muriel Bell at Stanford University Press, who did an outstanding job with an unwieldly and recalcitrant manuscript.

Notes

1. The most important early works are G. F. Hudson, Richard Lowenthal, and Roderick MacFarquhar, *The Sino-Soviet Dispute* (New York: Praeger, 1961); Donald S. Zagoria, *The Sino-Soviet Conflict, 1956–1961* (Princeton, N.J.: Princeton University Press, 1962); William E. Griffith, *The Sino-Soviet Rift* (Cambridge, Mass.: MIT Press, 1963); John Gittings, *Survey of the Sino-Soviet Dispute: A Commentary and Extract from the Recent Polemics* (London: Oxford University Press, 1968).

2. The recent works that come closest to providing a comprehensive survey are Gordon Chang, *Friends and Enemies: The United States, China, and the Soviet Union, 1948–1972* (Stanford, Calif.: Stanford University Press, 1990), and Lowell Dittmer, *Sino-Soviet Normalization and Its International Implications* (Seattle: University of Washington Press, 1992). Their main foci are, however, on the United States and on the 1980s respectively.

3. For some of the difficulties connected with research into new sources, see Odd Arne Westad, "Secrets of the Second World: Russian Archieves and the Reinterpretation of Cold War History," *Diplomatic History* 21, no. 2 (Spring 1997): 259–72, and Michael H. Hunt's introduction in *The Genesis of Chinese Communist Foreign Policy* (New York: Columbia University Press, 1996).

Introduction

Odd Arne Westad

One early morning in the fall of 1993, as all of Moscow was awash in rumors about the impending confrontation between President Boris Yeltsin and the Russian parliament, I came across a group of workers who were busy moving huge paintings from one of the downtown buildings of the former Soviet Ministry of Culture. Curious about the fate of Russia's art treasures and eager for a break from the street life of Moscow, I asked them whether I could have a peek at the unwrapped paintings lined along an interminable corridor behind the side entrance. "Please," they said, "go ahead, but these paintings are worthless, *ustarevshii* [outdated]."

The second to last painting – a work in the most ponderous social-realist style – depicted the signing of the Sino-Soviet Treaty of Friendship on February 14, 1950. In the Hall of Vladimir in the Kremlin, Andrei Vyshinskii is alone at the table, signing the protocol (while Wang Jiaxiang is watching him intently from afar, peeking over Molotov's right shoulder). But the attention of everyone else in the hall is toward the back, below the great statue of Lenin, where a grandfatherly Stalin, flooded in light, shakes hands with a swarthy-looking Mao Zedong, patting him on the back with his left hand. Behind Mao stands a small group of simply dressed Chinese, led by Zhou Enlai, while Stalin's companions – Molotov, Lavrenti Beriia, Kliment Voroshilov, Mikhail Kalinin, Anastas Mikoyan – stand around applauding. The scene is remarkably similar to those in many paintings in the same genre depicting Stalin presenting awards to Soviet or foreign prize winners – the leader bestowing the honor of recognition on a subordinate who has proved his worth.[1]

The author wishes to thank Frederick Teiwes and Chen Jian for comments on a draft version.

1

The Soviet public image of the alliance with China at the time and since has been that of an industrially advanced state helping a developing nation by transferring technology, resources, and social and economic models. The Chinese image, on the other hand, stresses shared security and economic benefits as well as cooperation in a global struggle against imperialist domination. These lasting images, stored in the memories of millions of Chinese and Russians, and in paintings, posters, and songs from the 1950s in both countries, need to be present in any attempt to reinvestigate this period. They help us see both the rise and the fall of the alliance. They also help us see the fervor that sustained and shaped it and that left important legacies in both countries.[2]

Marxism-Leninism – the theory of state-building and social change that framed both the Chinese and Russian revolutions – provided the language and the symbols that contained this fervor. Over the past decade, as another revolution – that of the market – has transformed both countries, the erstwhile intensity of the dedication to this theory among the elites and a great number of ordinary citizens has quickly faded from view. But for the purposes of this volume it is important to resurrect that fervor – the pride of having found a theory that combined rapid economic progress with social justice, a shortcut to modernity for backward countries, a way of showing that their people counted for something. For its adherents, the best proof of the theory's validity was the very scorn and hostility it engendered among Western leaders. In the view of the faithful, those powers that had looked down on Russians or attempted to dominate China – now they hated and feared these "new" states because of their strength, their independence, their communism. It is difficult to find more potent amalgams of nationalism with a specific social theory in any historical epoch.[3]

It was the invertionary policies of the alliance partners that made the union seem natural to most Soviet and Chinese leaders and that made it such a formidable enemy in the view of the West. The Sino-Soviet alliance was the greatest antisystemic power assembled so far during the capitalist era and probably the greatest power to challenge the political supremacy of the Western capitals since the final expansion of the Ottoman empire in the sixteenth century. The geographical space of the alliance covered nearly a quarter of the earth's landmass, and the size of its population made it dominant on two continents. It was intended to be and served as a threat that could not be ignored. With Cold War tensions already running high in Western capitals, the signing of the alliance set off acute alarms. General Dwight D. Eisenhower noted in the spring of 1950: "I believe Asia is lost with Japan, P[hilippine] I[slands], N[etherlands] E[ast] I[ndies] and even Australia under threat. India itself is not safe!"[4]

Throughout its existence, the men in charge of the alliance had to devise ways to translate the symbols, the sense of achievement and unity, into political aims.

This is a difficult process in any alliance formation, and perhaps particularly difficult in an alliance in which the elites have varying images of purpose but very similar political language and concepts. Still, the realist interpretations of the 1970s and 1980s, in which the alliance was doomed from the outset, find little support in the vast archives in Moscow and Beijing on which the chapters in this volume are based. At the end of the Korean War, the Sino-Soviet alliance was well moored in common policies as well as common symbols, and there was vigorous debate in and between the capitals on how to develop the relationship further. Indeed, for most of its life span – up to 1958 – the alliance was more dynamic and purposeful than its chroniclers have so far accepted.[5]

The vitality of the alliance during its first years makes the totality and the relative suddenness of its breakdown that much more difficult to explain. All contributors to this volume agree that in spite of the alliance having its ups and downs from early 1957 onward, the process of breakdown was not irredeemable until around 1960. The different perceptions of the alliance's domestic and international significance played a fundamental part in this collapse, as did the whole specter of cultural differences between Russians and Chinese that complicated day-to-day cooperation.

The perceptions of the world held by the Soviet and Chinese leaders were rooted in their ideologies. In spite of their common roots and the inspiration that Soviet Marxism-Leninism (or Stalinism) had provided for the ideology of the leading members of the Chinese Communist Party (CCP), it is essential for our understanding of the growth and collapse of the alliance to be able to distinguish between the two. Where the system of beliefs of Stalin and his successors underlined state construction, social order, and Marxist laws of development, Mao's thinking always returned to issues of individual will, human capabilities, and mass action. Where the Soviets wanted a state that first of all provided equality and social justice, Mao sought to create social instruments in which the creative abilities of man were released, often prompted by anger at tradition or foreign oppression.[6]

The tricky concept of *culture* in international relations does have the advantage that it slips past *ideology* to form general patterns of behavior, texts, myths, and symbols with an intrinsic value to a social or ethnic group.[7] The problem is, of course, to come to grips with how cultures play themselves out in specific international settings. There is no doubt that Soviets/Russians and Chinese, despite their long common border, have little in common in terms of cultural legacies. On the contrary, over the past three to four centuries negative stereotypes of the other have dominated the relationship, and negative opinions of the other's way of life – from food, to personal hygiene, to ways of conversation – continued to create trouble during the 1950s. But the October Revolution – the Soviet "invention" of the kind of modernity that the Chinese Communists wanted for themselves – made it possible to transcend the negative images and stake out common ground. *Sulian lao dage,* Soviet elder brother, was not an ironic form of address in China in the mid-1950s; it symbolized the role of the northern neighbor within a Chinese cultural scheme in which the elder brother should be treated with reverence as long as he fulfills his obligations to the family.[8]

A better understanding of ideology and culture is not sufficient to explain the breakdown in Sino-Soviet relations. In order to understand what happened, we also need to look more closely at the directions of Soviet and Chinese domestic politics and – even more important – at how their leaders viewed the interaction between the two countries on a whole range of specific issues. The main issues in economy (loans, technology transfers, border areas), military affairs (bases, weapons, intelligence), and foreign policy (Taiwan, Korea, Indochina, India, the U.S. threat) define the progress, stagnation, and breakdown of the alliance, particularly if we can show how these issues influenced the overall perceptions of the main leaders. In analyzing policies, however, we need to watch out for the sometimes spurious connection between different issues: Some policies are strongly interconnected, while others are deliberately or accidentally kept separate. This imbalanced relationship between issues, which political scientists often refer to as *issue escalation,* is no less true for the Sino-Soviet alliance than for other alliance formations.[9]

The chapters in this volume have no common background in terms of schools of interpretation. The authors are all somewhere near the center of the scale between hard-core realism and discourse-bound, antistructural approaches; there is more awareness of the subjective parts of international affairs – ideologies, perceptions, and personalities – and less emphasis on interests, borders, and grand strategies than in previous accounts. Undoubtedly this implies a move *away* from the realist dominance in the study of the Sino-Soviet alliance, although the authors exploit many insights from the realist school.[10]

Social realism in art and realism as a school of thought in the study of international relations have something in common. Their best practitioners can show a structure or a situation with perfect clarity and provide an image that convinces and, in some cases, inspires. But neither of them can penetrate the surface of the image and make us wonder about the complex ideas that uphold it. This is why we, at least at this stage, should emphasize multidimensional interpretation in history as well as in art.

Writing the Alliance

This volume is a very early attempt to make use of the newly available Russian and Chinese documentary sources to enrich our picture of the Sino-Soviet alliance. The individual chapters vary in approach and method and there are clear disagreements on some issues of interpretation. The group who has been working to prepare the volume consider its metamorphic base an advantage – "international" history needs heterogeneous approaches.

The authors in this volume come from four different countries, China, Russia, the United States, and Norway. The heterogeneity of the project undoubtedly has been helped by the diversity in traditions of historical writing. But more important in terms of conclusions has been the fact that although from different countries, all the authors come from the same generation. Born between 1950 and 1960, none of us has more than a fleeting recollection of the heyday of the alliance. We all have encountered it primarily as history, presented to us in widely divergent interpretative wrappings. Those conclusions on which we do generally agree may, at least in part, be attributed to all of us approaching the historical record intent on unwrapping those presentations that we have encountered.

This introduction provides a chronological overview of the period and brief looks into the main issues discussed in the individual chapters. The chronology that emerges from the new Russian and Chinese sources is different from the periodization so far employed by Western scholars – not only was the alliance effective for considerably longer than what has been believed so far, but the practical cooperation started earlier and was broader in scope than many of us thought. In some cases the conflicts that did emerge in the relationship had different backgrounds – or even different content – from what has been the general wisdom in the West. The new chronology shows a very complex set of connections between the two countries and shows how both domestic and international changes influenced the timing of their development.

The Past, 1917–1946

Images of the 1917 October Revolution – the Communist seizure of power in Russia – were at the core of the founding of the Chinese Communist Party in 1921.[11] The leaders of the fledgling Chinese party adopted the language, the symbols, and important parts of the worldview of the Russian Communists. Internationalism – which in practice meant subsumption under the political direction of the CPSU and the teachings of its first leader, Vladimir Lenin – joined Chinese nationalism in an uneasy ideological marriage that lasted for over forty years. Soviet control of the CCP was always tenuous, even during the 1920s, when the party could operate legally and when both it and its rival, the Guomindang (GMD), received Soviet advisors.[12]

In 1927 the head of the GMD main faction, Jiang Jieshi (Chiang Kai-shek), turned on his Communist allies and defeated them for control of the cities. The massacres of CCP members that followed marked a bloody turning point for the party and for Soviet China policies. The Chinese Communists who survived the 1927 defeats and did not defect in their wake had to start rebuilding the party almost from scratch. Some party members blamed the Soviet Union and the Communist International (Comintern) for having insisted on the CCP continuing its alliance with the GMD past the point when it served the interests of the Chinese Communists. In Moscow Joseph Stalin – who had been among the main promoters of a united-front policy in China – did his standing within the CPSU leadership no good by continuing to insist that his political "advice" had been "correct."[13]

During the 1930s, when the GMD pushed the CCP to the periphery of Chinese lands and politics, Soviet control over the party declined. Partly as a result of their fall in fortunes, the CCP went through a series of inner conflicts in which Moscow and the Comintern had only limited influence, and from which Mao Zedong emerged as the dominant leader around 1936. The party heads also started to have their own first experiences in directing protracted warfare and in civil administration, albeit in small areas in south or northwest China. In addition, Soviet preoccupation with East Asia declined dramatically as tensions in Europe grew during the early 1930s.[14]

The Japanese attack on China in 1937 rescued the CCP from political isolation and, probably, from territorial oblivion. Public opinion inside and outside the GMD forced Jiang Jieshi to make a temporary truce with the Communists in order to fight the invaders. Mao, while hailing the brittle truce as a Comintern-style "united front," made good use of the anarchy that followed from the war to expand his party's influence in north and central China. Partly because of the breakdown in state authority, partly because of the appeal of the party's radical program in a time of crisis, the CCP suddenly found itself in control of large territories, with a potential to operate almost as an independent state actor.[15]

With this sudden change in the party's fortunes began a slow and troubled reestablishment of Soviet interest in the CCP. On one hand, Mao ignored some key Comintern instructions regarding the conduct of the war against Japan, incurring the wrath of the secretary general of the Communist International, Georgi Dimitrov. On the other hand, Moscow was rather pleased with the party's "theoretical" development, seeing how Mao Zedong adopted the most recent Soviet and Comintern doctrines and slogans. The Comintern archives show that nearly all of Mao's concepts from the anti-Japanese war period – "protracted war," "new democracy," "three-thirds system," "antileftism" – were inspired and sanctioned by Moscow. But while there is little reason to question Mao's wish to implement Soviet theory in China, there are few grounds to doubt that he and other CCP leaders left their own mark on these concepts when they presented them to a Chinese audience.[16]

Mao regarded the 1943 dissolution of the Comintern, which Stalin carried out primarily as a tactical move to appease his wartime allies against Adolf Hitler, as a welcome sign that Moscow would agree to more independence for each party in the carrying out of Communist policies. The CCP chairman's main foreign policy aim at the end of World War II, however, was to encourage the Soviet Union to enter the war against Japan, defeating the enemy and supporting the CCP. Mao therefore tailored his party's policies to fit as closely as possible with Moscow's requirements, even in those cases when understanding Soviet motives was difficult, as in Stalin's negotiations with the Guomindang in the summer of 1945.[17]

Although Mao could accept Stalin's explanations of the August 1945 Soviet-GMD treaty as part of an international strategy that ultimately would benefit the Chinese Communists, the CCP leader still expected the Soviets to work closely with his party as soon as the Red Army entered Manchuria. Mao Zedong and other CCP leaders reacted with incredulity when Soviet forces offered no consistent support for CCP objectives in the Northeast, and, on the contrary, began blocking some of the party's aims. At the regional level, the confusion over Soviet actions was total. Peng Zhen, head of the CCP Northeastern Bureau, blasted the Soviets over their November 1945 order for the Chinese Communists to quit the Manchurian cities: "The army of one Communist Party using tanks to drive out the army of another Communist Party. . . . Can this kind of action be acceptable?"[18]

These first experiences of working with the Soviets taught the CCP leaders two important lessons. First was that the party had to work even harder to align its policies with those of the Soviet Union. Quite a few of the CCP leaders – including Liu Shaoqi and Ren Bishi – felt that their party had not been fully accepted by Moscow because they had been found wanting in terms of "socialist" and "internationalist" consciousness. But the other lesson learned from the events of the hard winter of 1945 was that the party could not, under any circumstance, depend on Soviet support to attain its ultimate goal of political control of China. This lesson would stick with the party leadership until Mao threw it overboard in agreeing to Kim Il Sung's attack on South Korea in the spring of 1950.[19]

Origins, 1946–1950

By the early summer of 1946, as Mao decided to counterattack against the GMD offensives in Manchuria, Soviet attention was directed squarely at the new Cold War tensions in Europe. Mao kept in close touch with Moscow on all important questions of military or political strategy, even after the complete Soviet withdrawal from Manchuria, but he was unable to secure any major long-term commitments from the Soviets to aid his revolution. Although Soviet material assistance to the CCP – Japanese arms, communications equipment, money – kept coming in, there is no indication that Stalin expected or intended this aid to help the CCP to victory in the civil war.[20]

On the contrary, Stalin was not interested in squandering scarce Soviet resources in pursuit of a revolutionary victory that he considered implausible, at least in the short term. The Kremlin preferred to continue dealing both with the CCP and the GMD government, thereby getting maximum leverage for its own short-term aims in China. Judging from Soviet contacts with both Chinese parties in this period, these aims consisted of controlling the Chinese northeastern provinces, Xinjiang, and Mongolia, or at least making sure that Western influence did not extend into these Soviet border areas.[21]

As the foundations of the Guomindang regime began crumbling in 1948, Stalin could not adjust his policy to the CCP advances. Not even after the September-October 1948 Liaoning-Shenyang campaign, in which the Chinese People's Liberation Army (PLA) broke the government's hold on north China, was Moscow willing to make a substantial investment in the CCP. Soviet aid remained very limited, although in some areas – such as radio communications, transport, and air defense – Moscow's contributions did provide a critical edge to the PLA's war effort.[22]

Stalin's doubts persisted well into the spring of 1949 and spawned the first crisis in the Soviet-CCP relationship since 1945. As the PLA was racing to the South and West, and as one city after another – Beijing, Shanghai, Tianjin – surrendered to the CCP, Stalin could not believe that some intrigue or intervention would not in the end thwart a complete Communist victory. The Guomindang could regenerate its strength in the South, Stalin feared. There could be local anti-Communist rebellions in central China and along the coast. The different armies of the PLA could start fighting each other. The Americans could issue an ultimatum not to cross the Yangzi River and threaten to use nuclear weapons. In Stalin's view, a full CCP victory was in no way assured, and the Soviet Union would have much to lose by allying itself too closely with the Chinese Communists.[23]

An at least temporary truce along the Yangzi, while Moscow and Washington talked about China's future, would serve Soviet purposes well. A truce resulting from international negotiations would take some of the heat out of East-West confrontation after the Berlin crisis and could even give the Soviet Union a permanent say in Chinese affairs. Such a truce would enable the Soviet Union to train and equip the Chinese Communists – who in Moscow's view were poorly prepared to govern a large country – while they were still alive to Soviet experience and not, like the Yugoslavs, too dazzled by their own success to take Moscow's advice.[24]

Stalin's attempts to promote international negotiations over China's future in January 1949 was received coldly by Mao Zedong. Moscow's approach, Mao said, would "make the United States, England and France assume that participating in mediation is an appropriate thing, and give the Guomindang a pretext for scolding us as warlike elements." The CCP leader accused Stalin's policy of "exact fulfillment of the U.S. government's wishes" with regard to China and claimed that such a policy would "bring much dissent among the people of China, the democratic parties and popular organizations, and even within the CCP, and would be very damaging for our current position."[25]

In spite of the quarrel – which ended with Stalin acquiescing to Chinese demands and refusing to participate in mediation – Mao remained convinced that a close alliance with the Soviet Union was the supreme foreign policy aim of his government-to-be. First and foremost, Mao argued, "we shall need economic assistance. We believe it possible only to receive this assistance from the USSR and countries of the new democracy."[26] The new CCP government also needed a large number of Soviet experts to give advice on how to gradually build a socialist society and a state directed by the party. Last, China needed security. Only an alliance with Moscow could provide the new revolutionary regime with the protection it needed from attacks by the United States, its ally Japan, and anti-Communist forces in China.

Mao's meetings with Soviet Politburo member Anastas Mikoyan in January/February 1949 in Xibaipo constituted the first step on the road to a formal alliance. Mikoyan's report to Stalin seems to have opened the way for an increased Soviet interest in dealing with the CCP as a partner. Soviet assistance grew in many vital areas, including heavy weapons, railway repairs, and money. Mao felt that it was time for him finally to go to Moscow – three Chinese suggestions for him to be Stalin's guest had been turned down by the hosts in 1947–1948 on grounds ranging from the urgency of the military situation in China to the Soviet grain harvest. But even after reading Mikoyan's report, Stalin was worried about inviting the unbiddable Mao to Moscow. The Soviets instead agreed to ask Liu Shaoqi, Mao's second in command, to visit in the summer of 1949.

The meetings in Moscow between June 26 and August 14, 1949 – in which Liu, Gao Gang, and Wang Jiaxiang were the main participants on the CCP side, primarily meeting with Stalin, CCP-Soviet Molotov, and Mikoyan – were breakthroughs for cooperation. Liu Shaoqi – temperamentally and politically more well tuned to Soviet socialist models than his boss in Beijing – managed to instill in the Moscow leadership some confidence in the Chinese wish for a close but subservient relationship with the CPSU. In his report to Stalin, Liu stressed that:

> the Soviet Communist Party is the main headquarters of the international Communist movement, while the Chinese Communist Party is just a battle-front headquarters. The interests of a part should be subordinated to international interests and, therefore, *the CCP submits to decisions of the Soviet Communist Party.* . . . If on some questions differences should arise between the CCP and the Soviet Communist Party, the CCP, having outlined its point of view, will submit and will resolutely *carry out the decisions of the Soviet Communist Party.*[27]

Avoiding all of Stalin's traps, Liu pushed through his agenda on military and economic aid to the CCP regime. In his efforts, Liu may have been helped by a growing sense in the upper echelons of Soviet bureaucracy – in military affairs as well as foreign policy – that a Communist China would be a valuable ally of the Soviet Union.[28] Even though Stalin himself insisted officially on treating the visiting CCP leaders as a trade delegation from Manchuria, in his first meeting with Liu he already made clear that he would provide direct support for "an all-China democratic coalition government" as soon as it was set up.[29]

Mao and his colleagues still could not be certain of the Soviet reaction as they formulated their plans for establishing their own government and their own state in late September 1949. Even though the Soviets had been pressing for a separate CCP government since January, Mao knew how difficult it was and had been for the East European Communist regimes to fit into Moscow's plans.[30] His new state had to conform to the Soviet worldview in terms of its domestic policies and, even more important, its international posture. There seem to have been numerous exchanges between Moscow and Beijing on the basic policies and organization of the new state between the end of Liu's visit in mid-August and October 1. At his very first meeting with the Soviet ambassador, General Nikolai Roshchin, on October 16, Mao still felt the need to use most of the time to condemn Yugoslav perfidy. Mao thought it vital that Moscow see that China's orientation was written in stone.[31]

The ultimate step up the ladder in the Chinese leader's search for Stalin's recognition was a face-to-face meeting in Moscow. After the People's Republic had been set up, Mao's inner-party prestige could no longer suffer snubs by the "boss" – as a "disciple of Stalin," Mao had to secure a rendezvous with his teacher. After having made Mao's intention plain to Roshchin, it still took substantial Chinese pressure and Zhou Enlai's diplomatic skills to arrange for Mao's train finally to depart for Moscow on December 6.[32]

Until recently our view of the Moscow summit – the only meeting between the two Communist autocrats – has been like a poorly made home movie: We see shadows moving about, we see people we think we identify doing things we think we recognize and comprehend, but it is all blurred, out of focus. The refocusing made possible by the Russian archives enables us to start pondering the significance of the meeting. What we can conjecture is the following:[33]

Mao's main priority was establishing a new relationship between the two countries. He wanted a treaty that validated his regime as a socialist government, regulated Soviet policy toward the Chinese border areas, and provided Moscow's support for China's development and national security. After much tergiversation on Stalin's part, Mao got most of what he wanted in terms of a formal alliance as well as economic aid and military assistance. The final treaties promised China Soviet military assistance in case of "aggression on the part of Japan or any other state that may collaborate in any way with Japan in acts of aggression" – implicitly providing Beijing with protection in case of a conflict with the United States. In addition, the Soviet Union would supply China with credits of around $300 million and expand the programs of military aid in essential areas such as the construction of a PRC air force and development of long-range artillery.[34]

Other bilateral issues fared much worse in the Chinese view. Mongolia was a main concern for Mao, who initially had hoped to unite the Mongolian People's Republic with (Chinese) Inner Mongolia as a part of New China. The Soviets would have nothing of it. Even worse for Beijing were the Soviet references to Xinjiang and Manchuria, Chinese provinces under CCP control. With his unflinchable ability to push wrong buttons in such talks, Stalin at one point asked Mao whether Moscow from now on should sign separate trade agreements with these areas, thereby forcing on the Chinese leader images of Soviet control of the Chinese periphery. There are no doubts that Mao had problems accepting the secret additional agreement that, among other privileges for Moscow, excluded all non-Soviet foreign citizens from the three Manchurian provinces and from Xinjiang, even though he appreciated Soviet willingness to transfer some of the Manchurian railways and to phase out the Soviet military presence on Liaodong.[35]

Mao hoped to discuss a fairly full foreign policy agenda with Stalin, with the problem of "uniting the revolutionary forces of the East" on top of the list. But even before the Chinese leader set out for Moscow, Stalin had made known that he did not want to consider regional problems. Because of Soviet resistance, the CCP had had to shelve its plans to send Chinese troops to fight alongside the Vietminh against the French in Vietnam. Korea, Mao's second priority in terms of foreign relations, was not on the agenda in any of the official talks in Moscow. On relations with the United States, Stalin recommended a moderate policy, even on the issue of Taiwan. "What is most important here is not to give the Americans a pretext to intervene," Stalin told Mao. He rejected Mao's request for Soviet "volunteer pilots or secret military detachments to speed up the conquest of Formosa" and suggested that an internal uprising would be the best way to liberate the island.[36]

The summit ended in a mixed result for the Chinese visitors. They did get aid and security guarantees. They did get Soviet promises to restore formal Chinese sovereignty in Manchuria. They did not get Mongolia, aid to conquer Taiwan, or a joint revolutionary strategy for East Asia. Worse, the Soviet side consistently forced the Chinese into the role of supplicants, and Stalin, especially, missed no opportunity to lord over his visitors. For those in the Chinese delegation who had not experienced Stalin's Russia firsthand, it was a rude reminder of the inequalities of Soviet socialism. For all the CCP leaders, embarked on a mission of national resurrection through socialist transformation, there were only two ways out of the dilemmas the Soviet slights posed: to prove one's worth as a loyal junior ally, or to stand up for recognition as an equal. The next two stages of Sino-Soviet relations were shaped by these mind-sets.[37]

War, 1950–1953

The Korean War provided the content for the Sino-Soviet relationship that the Moscow summit had failed to produce. Fighting the war gave the new Chinese regime a chance to stand up against imperialism and fitted Mao's sense of purpose as a regional liberator. The war linked the military establishments of the countries in a common task, in spite of frequent disagreements on how to conduct the campaigns. Through their efforts in Korea, the CCP leaders could prove themselves worthy of a prominent role in the world Communist movement. For Stalin the war became a surrogate for the all-out war with the West that he neither wanted nor was prepared for, a containable war in which he, through the Chinese war effort, could hit back at the United States for past setbacks in Europe, Japan, and the Middle East.[38]

It is unlikely, however, that this was a war which Mao or Stalin really wanted in the first place. Mao was ready to confront imperialism outside China's borders, but Korea was not his arena of choice. As he explained to his colleagues during the long and tortuous debate in Beijing in the fall of 1950 on whether China should intervene, Korea was right next to China's most important industrial areas and close to the center of the PRC government.[39]

North Korean leader Kim Il Sung pushed for an attack on the South throughout 1949, and Stalin promised to "assist" him in the matter of reunifying Korea
by military means already on January 30, 1950. Stalin and Kim discussed the
strategic plans for the offensive at meetings in Moscow in April. But the Soviet
leader may well have hoped that Mao – whose agreement he instructed Kim to
obtain before proceeding with the plans – would turn the Korean leader down.
A Chinese refusal to play along would have given Stalin a chance to back out of
the Korean challenge with his revolutionary credentials intact, while chastening
Mao's bothersome vigor on regional issues. But Mao could not turn down Kim's
request. His personality as well as his ideology blocked such an option: Kim
came to him to seek the liberation of his country – one of China's traditional
clients; he had Stalin's OK; and he had reasonable chances of success. Mao believed that "solely military means are required to unify Korea" and activated
Chinese support for the war effort as soon as the North Koreans attacked on June
25.[40]

As war broke out, the Chinese had not decided how far they were willing to
go to support Kim's crusade for reunification. Mao sent Chinese military and intelligence advisers to accompany the North Korean forces during their advance
and helped Kim's troops to cross over to South Korea from ports on the Shandong peninsula, thereby attacking Seoul's forces in the rear. But after the massive American counterattack in mid-September, Mao hesitated. He told Stalin
on October 2 that China would not send its army to fight in Korea, since such a
giant intervention meant that "our entire plan for peaceful reconstruction will be
completely ruined, and many people in the country will be dissatisfied."[41] It
took a direct request from Stalin to Mao, as well as a series of meetings between
the Soviet leader and a Chinese delegation headed by Zhou Enlai and Lin Biao
in the Crimea on October 9–10, to get the Chinese to change their minds. On
October 13 Mao told Ambassador Roshchin that China would send troops to
Korea.[42]

After the Chinese intervention began on October 19, the Soviet Union did
provide substantial support for the Chinese and North Korean operations. Soviet
air force units supplied air cover for the Chinese troops as they crossed the Yalu
River, destroying twenty-three American planes in twelve days. Over the next
two years of war, Moscow continued to provide military supplies and advisors
for the Chinese war effort, enabling the PLA first to roll back and then to contain the better-equipped United Nations forces. There are still no firm figures as
to the extent to which military aid to China reduced Soviet output in other areas,
but judging from Soviet documents, the expenditure must have made a considerable dent in overall production. Stalin promised Mao to arm and equip ten

Chinese divisions in 1951 and an average of twenty divisions per year in the years to come. Still, the Chinese rightly felt that they were bearing the brunt of the effort, with 900,000 dead or wounded by the end of the war, and Stalin's demand that China acquire the supplies on credit did not go over well in Beijing (chapter 4).

In terms of military strategy in Korea, Stalin agreed to let Mao lead the way but reserved the right to intervene as the ultimate arbiter of strategic sagacity. Except in two cases (both in 1951), Beijing followed Stalin's advice on overall strategy. On the battlefield the situation was very similar. When Soviet and Chinese military advisers disagreed – as they did frequently, particularly at the start of the war – the Red Army officers usually prevailed, even though it sometimes took Beijing's direct intervention to secure its envoys' agreement. Still, it is remarkable how fast the Chinese conformed to Soviet methods of fighting, even though those methods were very different from their own experience. By 1953 the cooperation between Soviet and Chinese military advisers seemed rather harmonious, with the two groups often jointly imposing their decisions on grudging Korean officers.[43]

As could be expected from the way the war started, Stalin and Mao quickly turned the issue of peace negotiations into a game of political posturing. Stalin seems to have wanted a cease-fire already in the summer of 1951 – to him, what counted was that the military situation had stabilized; an attempt to reunify Korea had been made, but the game was up and there were much more important matters going on in Europe. To Mao, who had invested so much of his domestic prestige in standing up to the Americans in Korea, the issue was not that simple. On one hand, he had to avoid defeat. On the other hand, he did not want to give Stalin, or his own Political Bureau, the impression that he was willing to call it quits. In the summer of 1951, Mao therefore followed a tough line in his contacts with the Americans while remaining on the lookout for ways to get out of the conflict.[44]

After months of inconclusive battles and stalled negotiations, Stalin's attitude hardened. With the front stabilized, the stakes in Korea were much reduced, and the Soviets could use peace in East Asia as leverage to get American concessions in other areas. Consequently, Stalin became increasingly unwilling to consider any real peace initiatives, even as the Chinese during 1952 started to make clear to him their desire for a settlement. Peace became possible only with Stalin's death in March 1953.[45]

The Korean War influenced the Sino-Soviet relationship by creating a sense of accomplishment on the Chinese side and a sense of fraternity with the Soviet Union that had stood by them. Mao felt very strongly that the Chinese Communists had proved their worth to Stalin and their Soviet comrades – and such a feeling was not uncommon even in Moscow. Yet Stalin's policy of keeping the war simmering could have created havoc in the alliance, as the terrible cost for China kept growing. Stalin, whose constant maneuvering had led to the Korean War, ended his reign with a fatigued policy of incessant low-grade war at China's expense (chapter 2).

Ascent, 1953–1957

Stalin's death altered the relationship between the Soviet Union and China in fundamental ways. The Kremlin successors – Nikita Khrushchev and Anastas Mikoyan more than anyone – realized that China was an extraordinary strategic asset in the Soviet confrontation with the West, an asset that Stalin had come close to gambling away through his reckless political games. But Khrushchev also was impressed with China in political and ideological terms – the Chinese party had, against all odds, won military victories against powerful enemies and established a People's Democracy, intent on learning from the Soviet Union. Moscow had to assist China and to prove to Chinese leaders that the Soviet Union was capable of offering assistance beyond Stalin's habitual stinginess (chapters 7 and 8).

The reaction to the news of Stalin's death in Zhongnanhai – the Beijing Kremlin, which the Chinese had set up within the old Imperial City – was disbelief and sorrow. For the CCP elite, Stalin was the leader of world communism who had guided the movement since the Chinese party started its climb to power. They respected and honored him, and it would take years before criticism of Stalin could be voiced openly within the party, even if the party leaders well knew, as Mao put it in 1956, that "if I had always followed Stalin's advice, I would have been dead."[46]

As the struggle for power in the Soviet Politburo was decided with the arrest and execution of Deputy Premier Lavrenti Beriia in the summer of 1953 and Khrushchev's gradual replacement of Premier Georgi Malenkov that fall and winter, Mao was careful to stand on the sidelines. He seems to have hailed Khrushchev's ascendancy, possibly because Khrushchev was not personally associated with any of Mao's past humiliations at the hands of the Soviets. But the Chinese leader also strongly believed that after Stalin's death he himself had advanced to a position of prominence in the world Communist movement – Khrushchev could not match Mao as a theoretician nor in his experience as a political leader.[47]

To the Chinese, Khrushchev's visit to Beijing in September–October 1954 signified a transformation of the relationship with the Soviet Union. Not only had the new Soviet leader chosen China for his first major foreign trip, but the very fact that the head of the Soviet party came to see Mao – and not the other way around – carried tremendous symbolic significance to most Chinese. It bolstered the image of the international position of the CCP leader, especially among those who had been puzzled by Mao's hurried departure for Moscow after the proclamation of the People's Republic in 1949.[48] Khrushchev's readiness to agree to Chinese proposals for the handing over of the Lüshun naval base and of Soviet shares in the joint companies in Manchuria and Xinjiang added to the Chinese satisfaction, as did the Soviet leader's granting further loans and technical assistance (chapter 8).[49]

Economic cooperation between the Soviet Union and China reached a new level after Khrushchev's 1954 visit. The 520-million-ruble long-term credit granted by the Moscow leaders enabled the Chinese to acquire new Soviet technology for their factories and plants, equipment for their mines, ships, and locomotives for transport. Unlike under Stalin, the Kremlin ordered its ministries to provide the Chinese with what they wanted, even state-of-the-art technology that had not yet been implemented in the Soviet Union. The aid to China had "highest priority," the Foreign Ministry reported to the party secretariat (chapter 7).[50]

The number of Soviet experts and advisors going to China and the number of Chinese students going to the Soviet Union increased dramatically during 1954. The Soviet experts – mostly engineers, technical instructors, or teachers – were spread all over China and in most cases received an enthusiastic welcome from the people. Although many had had no choice when ordered abroad, as a rule they were able to live a more privileged life than they ever would in the Soviet Union.[51]

For the Chinese students who were sent to the Soviet Union, life was considerably harder. Problems with language, food, and climate were common, and some of the students were sent to study at provincial colleges that had few facilities for receiving them and in which the level of training was low. Still, most of the Chinese excelled at their studies and returned home with necessary skills and with administrative and organizational ideas that would stay with them beyond their Soviet experience.[52]

The military cooperation between the two sides also flourished from 1954 on. Before Khrushchev's visit, Moscow and Beijing had agreed on a new comprehensive program of supplying China with new Soviet defense technology, including the MiG-17 jet fighter and short-range missiles. The Soviet leaders seem to have been somewhat more hesitant in supplying the Chinese with nuclear technology, but during his visit to Beijing Khrushchev did agree to help China with materials and technical support and to train Chinese scientists, so that China would be able to start its own nuclear research programs. Parts of this agreement were implemented immediately after Khrushchev's return to Moscow, well before it was officially announced on May 1, 1955.[53]

The Soviet technicians and nuclear scientists who were sent to China soon discovered that Beijing's main aim was to construct a nuclear weapon, not, as they had been told before departure, to solve China's energy problems. Still, Khrushchev decided to move ahead with the program, and the Soviet ministries involved already in 1955–1956 routinely accepted Chinese requests for technical drawings, designs, and measurements that could be used only to make a nuclear bomb. In October 1957 the Kremlin finally caved in to Chinese pressure and made a promise—later withdrawn—to supply Beijing outright with a prototype nuclear weapon and related technical data.[54]

The substantial upturn in the levels of civilian and military cooperation during Khrushchev's first years in power stimulated further growth of alliance cohesion on other issues. Chinese publishers translated large numbers of Soviet books and pamphlets and made them available to the public. Local authorities in even the most remote parts of the country screened Soviet films, put on cultural exhibits, and arranged language courses. Government officials at all levels studied the Soviet experience in economy, administration, and law (chapter 3).[55]

The successes of the bilateral assistance programs also helped solve potentially awkward problems in politics and diplomacy. The Soviets accepted Mao's 1954 purge of CCP Central Committee members Gao Gang and Rao Shushi, including the charges that Gao had attempted to subvert Mao's leadership by "undermining the CCP's relations with fraternal parties."[56] Moscow also decided to be careful in criticizing the rapid and enforced collectivization of agriculture on which Mao embarked in early 1955 against Soviet advice. The "excesses" that the Chinese committed should be interpreted as signs of their eagerness in building socialism, according to Soviet foreign ministry analysts. In an era in which the enthusiasm for socialist construction probably was at its all-time high in the Soviet Union – and in which Soviet leaders often despaired over hesitancy and skepticism in Eastern Europe – the Chinese ardor was a welcome addition to Khrushchev's ebullience.[57]

In foreign policy, too, there was increasing cooperation between the two allies. Beijing and Moscow negotiated the end of the Korean War and set the framework for the future policies of Kim Il Sung's North Korean regime by frequent consultations and substantial understanding for each other's views. The two highlights of this diplomatic cooperation were the 1954 Geneva conference on Indochina – in which the Chinese accepted, and brought Hanoi to accept, a de facto division of Vietnam – and the 1956 crisis in North Korea, during which Beijing and Moscow forced Kim to accept the inclusion of some of his former opponents in the party leadership.[58]

The Taiwan Straits crisis of 1954–1955 did not lead to a crisis in the Sino-Soviet relationship – on the contrary, Beijing kept Moscow informed of its plans and intentions, and assured the Soviets that it would avoid a direct confrontation with the United States. Moscow, on its side, made clear both privately to Mao and publicly that the Soviet Union would assist China in case of a conflict with the Americans. Although the Soviets were puzzled and not too pleased by the timing of the Chinese military operations, Khrushchev accepted Mao's underlining of Beijing's need to keep the issue of Chinese reunification in focus and to pressure Washington to open negotiations with China.[59]

In 1955, as collectivization transformed ancient patterns of production and ownership in the Chinese countryside, Mao began to regret the measured pace of socialist change during the first years of the People's Republic. Enflamed by what he saw as the creativity and energy of the masses, Mao believed that the introduction of socialism and increases in productivity should be speeded up, and he started to suspect that some of the leaders of his own party had been holding him back deliberately, because they feared relying on the masses and were too bound up by the stages of the Soviet experience. The post-Stalin changes that were taking place in the Soviet Union emboldened Mao in his new revolutionary optimism – just as Khrushchev had unleashed the full productive forces of socialism, Mao hoped to mobilize his party for a quicker and more thorough socialist transformation.[60]

Mao's response to the CPSU Twentieth Congress in February 1956 must be seen in light of these changes in his political attitudes. The chairman welcomed Khrushchev's denunciation of Stalin, noting to the Soviet ambassador in March that if the CCP had followed Stalin's advice, it never would have taken power. For Mao, de-Stalinization implied Soviet criticism of Stalin's China policy and Moscow's recognition of the achievements of the CCP and of Mao himself. Therefore, Khrushchev's criticism of Stalin would enable Mao to further his own visions of socialism in China.

But while welcoming Khrushchev's "secret" speech, Mao saw at least three problems with the way the criticism of Stalin had been presented. He resented not having been consulted before the speech was made. Also, Mao felt that Khrushchev's condemnation was too general and wanted specific criticism of Stalin's policies (including, to be sure, his policies on China). Third, Mao took exception to the fact that the speech had been leaked to the West and feared that Khrushchev's behavior would weaken international socialism.[61]

For Mao, the popular rebellions against Communist rule in Poland and Hungary in the summer and fall of 1956 confirmed his worst fears about the consequences of Khrushchev's behavior and made him turn violently against the process of de-Stalinization.[62] The East European crises arose just as Mao was receiving reports of resistance to collectivization and the party's control of culture and city administration. Expecting a full-scale confrontation with "counterrevolution" inside China, Mao convened all-night Politburo meetings – with the Soviet ambassador present – in which the chairman advised Khrushchev to crush the Hungarian revolution, while leaving the Polish party as much leeway as possible to solve its own problems.[63]

Mao still accepted that the Soviet Union was the "older brother" among socialist states and expected the Chinese involvement with Eastern Europe to strengthen Soviet authority inside the Eastern Bloc. But he was in no way blind to how Chinese missions to Moscow, Warsaw, and Budapest in the wake of the political upheavals also helped boost his own authority within the Communist world movement. "Now that the enemy is taking advantage of the criticism of Stalin to take the offensive on a worldwide scale, we ought to support the Soviet Union," Mao told a visiting Yugoslav delegation in January 1957.[64]

The year 1957 was to be the last time the Sino-Soviet alliance functioned well. With criticism of the CCP mounting in the Hundred Flowers campaign – a wave of political openness initiated by Mao himself to prove mass support for his party – the chairman drew parallels between mistakes made in the Soviet Union and mistakes made by CCP officials that had cost the party popular support and hindered the country's development. "We still need to learn from the Soviet Union," Mao said; "however, we shall learn from them in a selective way, only accept good things, while avoiding picking up the bad things."[65]

As Mao's doubts about the Soviets mounted, practical cooperation between the two sides continued. In some areas, such as military and nuclear technology, it even intensified. The secret October 1957 agreement on exchange of nuclear technology aimed at making China capable of producing its own nuclear weapons by 1960, and the many visits of high-level military delegations to each other's countries explored ways of extending Sino-Soviet cooperation in military production. Economic and educational cooperation also was extended in several agreements signed during 1957.[66]

Nikita Khrushchev's response to the trouble in his eastern alliance – China's meddling in Europe and its criticism of his foreign and domestic policies – was at first remarkably moderate. Khrushchev – with his earthy sense of politics – seems to have sensed that what the alliance needed was a perception of common purpose, of having joint strategies for dealing with the political and military situation in Pacific Asia. Throughout 1957 the Soviet ambassador was instructed to discuss American policies and the internal situation in Korea, Vietnam, and Indonesia in detail with Mao and the Chinese leaders and to pay special attention to China's defense needs. This belated Soviet attempt at foreign policy integration was obviously appreciated by Zhou Enlai, Liu Shaoqi, and the heads of the Chinese military and intelligence services. But to Mao the Soviet initiatives seemed suspect in view of the political gap between his own aims for

China and Soviet practices. When Khrushchev decided to turn to military integration, Mao's suspicions came out in full bloom.[67]

Descent, 1958–1960

Mao's November 1957 visit to Moscow for the fortieth anniversary of the October Revolution marked a watershed in Sino-Soviet relations. The chairman's official and unofficial remarks during his trip show that he no longer deferred to Soviet views on ideology and policies; on the contrary, Mao expected Soviet and East European leaders to learn from him. His lessons were clear: The Soviet Union, China, and socialist and progressive movements around the world constituted a stronger force than the United States and its allies: "The east wind prevails over the west wind." The Soviet leadership should confront the Americans with confidence in their own strength and without fearing war. These international policies should be underpinned in all socialist countries by a reinvigoration of socialist transformation and mobilization of the masses.

In his rambling speeches in Moscow – in which he demonstrated his agitation and his determination not to be humiliated as he had been during his first visit – Mao took care not to be accused of anti-Soviet attitudes. "The Soviet Union is the only country which is qualified to be a leader," Mao said, adding "I have been to Moscow twice, the first time made me very unhappy. 'Brotherly parties' – it sounded beautiful, but actually we were not equal. Now I feel some kind of equality."[68]

For Khrushchev himself and for many of the East and West European Communist leaders present, Mao's behavior could not have come at a more unfortunate time. In the summer of 1957 Khrushchev had defeated a Stalinist plot against his leadership in the CPSU Politburo, in which the plotters – Molotov, Lazar Kaganovich, and others – had argued for positions not unlike those of Mao. In the fall Khrushchev wanted to take advantage of his victory to redirect Soviet foreign policy toward a relaxation of tensions with the West. Most Communist leaders welcomed the new trend in Soviet policy and the beliefs in peaceful coexistence and nonviolent revolution that accompanied it.[69]

Mao and Deng Xiaoping, who had accompanied the chairman to Moscow for secret talks on Chinese complaints concerning Soviet aid, felt that the other Communist parties had taken note of the Chinese positions. In the spring of 1958 Mao repeatedly assured the Soviets of his intentions to follow the Soviet lead in foreign policy. "We completely support every one of the recent foreign policy initiatives of the Soviet Union," Mao told Ambassador Pavel Iudin on February 28. "[They are] distinguished by great flexibility and thorough thinking."[70]

Mao's concurrence with Khrushchev's early attempts at Great Power détente may have been a way of deflecting Soviet criticism of the Great Leap Forward, the intense campaign to raise production through mass mobilization that Mao promoted from 1957–1958 on. Soviet diplomats and experts noted very early on that production targets were inflated and that the sudden collapse in central planning and shifting of labor from agriculture to rudimentary steel mills and production plants were recipes for disaster. Mao did not respond to the Soviet criticism, even though he must have been very annoyed by it. According to his colleagues, he waited for the results of the Leap to prove the Soviets wrong.[71]

In late May and early June 1958 the Soviet Union started presenting a new set of proposals for military cooperation and integration between the two allies. These plans had been under preparation for some time in the Soviet ministries of defense and foreign affairs. The main points of the plans were joint technical intelligence facilities, Soviet-operated early-warning systems, and long-distance naval communications stations, all to be installed in China and paid for by the Soviet Union. Moscow would supply China with advanced equipment for amphibious operations and send instructors. In early July the Soviets also suggested setting up a joint force of nuclear submarines to operate along the Chinese coast and in the western Pacific. This latter initiative was intended as a positive response to the Chinese request to buy nuclear submarines from the Soviet Union.[72]

For the Sino-Soviet relationship, the Soviet initiatives came at the worst possible moment. Mao had called a meeting of the Chinese military leadership in late May, probably because he needed to shore up the army's support for his Great Leap initiatives, enthusiasm for which was flagging among several of his Politburo colleagues. During the two-month meeting of the Central Committee's Military Affairs Committee, Mao repeatedly stressed self-reliance, criticized "dogmatism" and excessive dependence on the Soviet Union, and underlined the "high tide" of the international revolutionary movement. Turning down or amending the Soviet proposals became a way visibly to demonstrate the correctness of Mao's positions.[73]

Mao's reaction to the Soviet proposals set off alarm bells in Moscow. In the summer of 1958 the Soviet leaders reviewed their aid programs to China and started to worry about how China would use the technologies transferred from the Soviet Union. After receiving a thorough report about the status of the Chinese nuclear programs and the effects further Soviet assistance would have on Chinese capabilities to produce nuclear weapons, Khrushchev decided to slow down the transfer of nuclear technology under pretext of technical difficulties. After learning in early July of the CCP's intentions to put military pressure on Taiwan to challenge U.S. resolve in the Taiwan Straits, the Soviet leaders worried that Chinese policy could lead to war, even though they never advised the People's Republic not to take military action.[74]

During Khrushchev's visit to Beijing in the late summer of 1958, the Soviet leader was on his diplomatic best behavior. After listening to Mao's monologues on how the countries of the world were turning against the United States, Khrushchev attempted to return to the plans for future military integration, which, he claimed, would be to the advantage of both allies. The Soviet leader believed that he had convinced the Chinese of the need to take great care not to involve the United States in any fighting around Taiwan, in return for a Soviet promise to take a tougher stand against American policies in the Middle East. Each leader came away from the meetings believing that he had convinced the other of the rectitude of his own view of international affairs, while refraining from criticizing the other's internal policies.[75]

The Chinese shelling of the GMD-controlled islands Jinmen and Mazu in the Taiwan Straits – which began right after Khrushchev's return from Beijing – set off a complex set of events that further undermined Sino-Soviet solidarity. The Chinese believed that the Soviet leaders had attempted to lessen their commitment to the defense of China after learning of the strong American response to the People's Liberation Army's attack, and that the Soviet offer of military experts, logistical support, and the use of Soviet bombers and artillery was an attempt to control the outcome of the crisis. The Soviets felt that the Chinese had been unwilling to coordinate policies with Moscow, even after the Soviet Union had publicly threatened the United States with nuclear retaliation if nuclear weapons were used against China. Khrushchev was particularly enraged that Mao had refused to comply with the notions of nuclear deterrence underlying Soviet messages to Washington. By claiming to be ready to absorb American tactical nuclear strikes without invoking the mutual defense obligations of the Sino-Soviet treaty, Mao had attempted to reduce Soviet influence on Chinese policy during the crisis and in effect poked his nose at the superpower status of the Soviet Union.[76]

The main issue for the Soviet leaders after the second Taiwan Straits crisis was not Mao's wish to confront the United States, a desire for which they had a great deal of sympathy, Khrushchev's "peace offensive" notwithstanding. The problem was the conspicuous and irresponsible Chinese behavior toward their Soviet allies during the crisis – no consultations on tactics, declining additional Soviet military support, and the bizarre ending to the crisis, in which Mao simply declared the Chinese would stop shelling Jinmen and Mazu on alternate days. Khrushchev, Mikhail Suslov, and other Moscow leaders started questioning Mao's mental stability and instructed Ambassador Iudin to provide more materials on the chairman's private life.[77]

Mao's spectacular retreat in the last battle of the Taiwan Straits and the faltering of the Great Leap campaigns made the chairman dampen his diplomatic criticism of the Soviet Union in the spring of 1959. Driven on the defensive internationally and with mounting problems at home, Mao spent much of this time finding reasons for the decline in the fortunes of the revolution. Reading what is available of Mao's writings, it is reasonable to suggest that toward the summer of 1959 Mao started seeing his problems as directly linked – many of his colleagues within the CCP had failed the masses during the Great Leap campaigns because they were wedded to the Soviet path of development. If not checked, these people would destroy the Chinese revolution. From roughly May or June 1959, the Soviet alliance seemed to Mao to be a hindrance and not a support for the development of socialism in China.[78]

Based on the evidence we have, it is likely that Mao from mid-1959 on was aiming at a dramatic reduction in Sino-Soviet interaction, albeit within the framework of the alliance. Mao's increasing stress on self-reliance was created out of political necessity – Soviet advisors, Chinese studying in the Soviet Union, political and cultural delegations were all potential critics of the CCP's disastrous development policies. As the full effects of the Great Leap Forward became visible in the summer of 1959, Mao started circulating reports critical of Moscow to CCP leaders at all levels. "At the beginning of the construction of the Soviet Union, the speed of industrial development was very high. Later, the speed of industrial development has decreased. Soviet planners constantly lowered the speed of development. [This shows] their right-deviationist thinking," said one report.[79] In the wake of the Lüshan conferences – a series of meetings held by the Chinese leaders from early July to mid-August 1959 – Mao accused his critics within the party, most notably Defense Minister Peng Dehuai, of conspiring with the Soviets to bring him down.[80]

Although the first Sino-Indian border incidents in the summer of 1959 probably were not instigated by China, Mao had no reason to seek a settlement of the conflict. For the Soviets, who had been building a close relationship with India during Khrushchev's time in power, both the timing and the character of the flare-ups indicated Chinese premeditation: The incidents came on the eve of Khrushchev's visit to the United States and were directed against India, a country that symbolized Soviet abilities to have a diplomatic impact outside the socialist world. Khrushchev was able to hold his temper on the American tour, although he had indicated to U.S. envoy Averell Harriman earlier that summer that relations with China were "special and delicate." But upon arriving in Beijing on September 30, straight from his meetings in Washington, Khrushchev was "furious."[81]

This time the Soviet leader spelled out his "proposals" so that the Chinese would be forced to respond. His first concern was Chinese policy on Taiwan; he called for restraint from Beijing in support of Soviet efforts to "ease international tension and eliminate war." He also accused the Chinese of aggressive behavior in the conflict with India and condemned Mao's allusions to the socialism that could be built after the Third World War as "irresponsible." China had to stop sabotaging the international policies of the Socialist bloc, Khrushchev said. As the Chinese responded with accusations of "sellouts" and "right-deviationism," the crucial meeting on October 2 deteriorated into a verbal slugging match.[82]

Mao's thinking on international affairs in late 1959 was finding the shape that it would maintain until the end of the 1960s. In a fascinating series of notes for a speech in December, Mao found that Soviet "revisionism" could "last for a long time (over ten years, for example)." He reminded himself of the mingled history of his contacts with Moscow, in which he underlined the many attempts by Stalin and Khrushchev to undercut him. "We resisted the fallacies of our friends . . . , [but now] our friends together with the imperialists, the counter-revolutionaries, and Tito's revisionists organize an anti-China chorus." He noted that China would be isolated for a long time but that it would "get support from many Communist parties, countries and peoples." And even in isolation, "in eight years, China will have finished the initial construction of [its] industrial system. . . . The Chinese flag is bright red."[83]

The reason why the full collapse of the Sino-Soviet alliance did not come as early as the winter 1959–1960 lies in Mao's perception of Chinese politics. Mao felt that his political position within the party leadership was still weak as a result of the failures of the Great Leap Forward, and none of the other leaders – although they all shared much of Mao's resentment against the Soviets – had yet arrived at a point in which he envisaged an open conflict.

Mao moved very cautiously to instigate public dissension between Beijing and Moscow, possibly hoping that the Soviets through some dramatic action would take the first visible step. "Long Live Leninism," the April 16, 1960, article in the Chinese journal *Honggi* that for the first time made the split perceptible to a general audience, centered its attack on Soviet unwillingness to admit that the danger of war went with the existence of capitalism. As Mao expected, the Soviet press shot back, saying that

> present-day leftists regard the policy of achieving peaceful coexistence, stopping the arms race, and friendship between the peoples of capitalist and socialist countries as a retreat from Marxism-Leninism. They take the slightest deterioration in the international situation as proof of the correctness of their sectarian views.[84]

Even though in public both sides still attributed "errors" to "Yugoslav revisionists" or "certain leftist elements," the foundations of the alliance were rapidly deteriorating.

Breakdown, 1960–1963

The congress of the Romanian Workers' Party from June 20 to June 25, 1960, in Bucharest provided the stage for the first public display of the split in the Communist movement. The Chinese delegation, headed by Peng Zhen, went there with a set of alternative instructions from Mao Zedong. Peng should listen carefully to the speech of the head of the Soviet delegation. If Peng deemed the speech to be an outright attack on the CCP, he should respond in style. Most important, however, the Chinese delegation should spend its time trying to convince members of the other party delegations of the correctness of the Chinese views. As Mao had expected that winter, "[Khrushchev] is afraid that the Communist parties in Eastern Europe and others countries of the world will not believe in them, but in us."[85]

The Soviets attempted to use the Romanian congress to surprise the CCP. Convinced of his personal ability to persuade and influence others, Khrushchev at the very last moment decided to lead the Soviet delegation himself and to deliver an overall defense of his perception of the international situation and Chinese behavior. "In present conditions," Khrushchev said, "when there are two world systems, it is imperative to build mutual relations between them in such a way as to preclude the possibility of war breaking out. . . . One cannot mechanically repeat what Lenin said many decades ago on imperialism, and go on asserting that imperialist wars are inevitable until socialism triumphs throughout the world." In order to illustrate Chinese fallacies, the Soviets circulated among the delegations a letter addressed to the CCP Central Committee setting out the Soviet case and complaining of Chinese factionalism.[86] The Bucharest meetings ended with Sino-Soviet relations in tatters, as Khrushchev lost his temper at a small session of party heads, calling Mao "an ultra-leftist, an ultra-dogmatist, indeed, a left revisionist."[87]

In the weeks following the Bucharest meetings, Mao's strategy produced even more dramatic results than the chairman had expected. On July 16 the Soviet government informed Chinese President Liu Shaoqi that it had ordered all Soviet technicians working in China to return home by the end of August. No Soviet act could have been better suited to unify the Chinese leadership and make it rally to Mao Zedong, as it always did during times of crisis (even those that Mao himself had created). "This is a big event, which will shake the whole of China," Foreign Minister Chen Yi told the Soviet ambassador on August 4.

"We are not Yugoslavia," said Chen; "if you want to treat us as Yugoslavia, then we will not accept it."[88]

The decision to withdraw the Soviet advisors was taken in haste, obviously as a result of Khrushchev's experiences in Bucharest. It was a policy mistake with far-reaching consequences: In one stroke Khrushchev had almost eliminated Soviet abilities to influence developments in China. Soviet Ambassador to Beijing Stepan Chervonenko later claimed that he tried to make Khrushchev change his mind, and supporters of Leonid Brezhnev in the 1964 leadership struggle saw the pull-out from China as one of the "impulsive foreign policy measures that damaged our own state interests." The Chinese had sown the storm and reaped the whirlwind.[89]

True to form, Mao attempted to lessen the genuine shock many Chinese felt at the Soviet actions. Already in August, he sent Zhou Enlai to see the Soviet ambassador to iron out in which areas practical cooperation could continue. Mao seemed particularly eager not to cut all ties on defense and military production. China's security needs and the possible political effects of the great disasters created by the "second wave" of the Great Leap made Mao send Liu Shaoqi and Deng Xiaoping to Moscow for the international conference of Communist parties in November 1960. After much haggling, Deng, who in the past had cooperated well with the Soviets and was critical of the excesses of the Leap, was able to reach a limited set of compromises at the conference. Liu went even further in his informal conversation with Leonid Brezhnev on the train between Leningrad and Minsk while touring the Soviet Union before his return to China. Both men looked forward to a time in which "ideological quibbles" could be resolved. Mao confirmed his support for the Moscow resolutions in a conversation with Ambassador Chervonenko in late December.[90]

The lull in the Sino-Soviet dispute lasted for almost a year and a half – a brief flare-up at the twenty-second Congress of the CPSU in October 1961 notwithstanding. In spite of continued polemics directed against "Yugoslavia" (by the Chinese) and "Albania" (by the Soviets), both sides made attempts to rescue parts of the bilateral relationship. In June 1961 the two countries signed a set of agreements on economic, scientific, and technical cooperation. Some Soviet leaders, both in the party and in the military, argued for a lessening of tension with China in order not to lose the strategic potential and the established economic interaction in the Chinese alliance. Inside the CCP, Mao had "retreated to the Second Line" and left to Liu Shaoqi, Deng Xiaoping, CCP Politburo member Chen Yun, and other leaders the thorny task of rescuing China from the famine created by the chairman's social and economic experiments.[91]

The food shortages in the spring of 1961 made the Chinese leaders launch an all-out appeal to the socialist countries for help. In March Zhou Enlai described the desperate situation in the Chinese countryside in stark detail in a talk with the East European and Soviet ambassadors. The Soviets, who had predicted large-scale starvation in the central and western provinces for almost a year, were ready and willing to provide emergency grain and other foodstuffs. Khrushchev had written to Mao on February 27 promising massive aid, and large amounts of supplies crossed the border from March to June 1961. Liu praised Moscow's effort, calling the Soviet aid "a manifestation of real support for China." In late March Foreign Minister Chen foresaw a new period of close Sino-Soviet cooperation.[92]

The continuing military cooperation beyond 1960 is of specific interest to scholars, since most accounts written before the opening of the Russian archives assumed that the military relationship in effect ended *before* the withdrawal of Soviet experts.[93] Although we still do not know the full extent of Sino-Soviet military cooperation from 1960 to late 1962, it is obvious that in some areas it was alive and well as late as January 1963. Moscow agreed to continue aiding the construction of a Chinese air force, including sending groups of Soviet instructors, and assisting in the production of the advanced MiG-21 jet fighters in China.[94] The Soviets continued to provide the Chinese with intelligence on U.S. military exercises and defense planning.[95] The two sides cooperated in setting up military communication systems in northeastern China.[96] Finally, there is evidence that the Soviets provided the Chinese with advanced military technology, including air-to-ground missiles, as late as December 1962.[97]

It was Mao's resurgence in Chinese politics in mid-1962 and the ensuing confrontation over foreign affairs that in the end laid the Sino-Soviet alliance to rest. At the CCP leaders' annual summer conference at Beidahe, Mao again went on the offensive, claiming that his associates had "capitulated to the bourgeoisie" with their "adjustments" over the past year and a half. He explicitly tied his criticism to Sino-Soviet relations by condemning Wang Jiaxiang, the former ambassador to Moscow who in the spring of 1962 had called for a reduction of tension with the Soviet Union (and the United States) "to try to win a long-term peaceful environment for the socialist construction of our country."[98]

Mao disagreed with Wang's fear of enemy attacks on an enfeebled China. The chairman saw the imperialist powers as increasingly at odds with each other and the Soviet Union as wishing to join the fray. China could therefore safely concentrate on intensifying the revolution at home and the criticism of revisionism abroad. To the chairman, events in the fall of 1962 confirmed his optimistic worldview. For Mao, the outcome of the crises in the Caribbean and the Himalayas showed China's growing strength and the increasing weakness of the imperialist powers and the Soviet Union. At the end of 1962 he instructed the party that "the struggle against modern revisionism would become more acute for a period of time in the future."[99]

Beijing viewed the Indian dispatching of border forces into the disputed areas of the Himalaya Mountains in early fall of 1962 as preparations for an attack on Chinese positions. Mao ordered the Chinese army to strike first. In two waves of attacks – starting on October 20 and November 16 – large Chinese forces routed the Indian units and advanced into Indian territory in the Northeast. During the first phase of the crisis, the Soviet Union reversed some of its earlier positions in favor of China while agreeing to sell MiG-21 fighters to India during the Chinese attack in mid-November. Mao later believed that the initial Soviet policy could be attributed to Khrushchev's opportunistic wish for Chinese support during the Cuban missile crisis that had taken place in the interim.[100]

The Soviet-American confrontation over Moscow's deployment of nuclear missiles to Cuba in October 1962 was the second external event that fall that pushed Sino-Soviet relations back into the downward spiral. Ever since the victory of the Cuban revolutionaries in 1959, Beijing and Moscow had watched each other's policies toward the island with great care. Both wanted to recruit Cuba's leader, Fidel Castro, to their view of the Sino-Soviet controversies. When President John F. Kennedy challenged Khrushchev's nuclear ploy, the Chinese press supported the Soviet position, while Mao, privately, was telling his colleagues that there would be no war, because both Kennedy and Khrushchev feared the consequences of an all-out conflict. After Khrushchev capitulated on October 28, Mao decided to swing the CCP propaganda machine into action, praising the Cuban comrades and condemning those "who were frightened in the face of imperialist aggression," who "bartered with the freedom and independence of another people," and who believed in "juggling nuclear weapons as the solution to international arguments."[101]

In spite of the open and direct polemics between the two sides that started in December 1962, Khrushchev made one last attempt at secret negotiations. Delegations from the two parties, headed by Deng Xiaoping and Mikhail Suslov, met in Moscow from July 5 to 20, 1963, but could not even agree on when to meet again. Immediately after the breakdown of the meeting, Khrushchev informed Mao that Moscow expected to sign a treaty on nuclear test bans and nonproliferation with the United States and Great Britain in spite of Chinese warnings. To Mao, this was final proof of Khrushchev's treason against the Communist movement and China, an undisguised attempt "at depriving the Chinese people of their right to resist the nuclear threats of U.S. imperialism."[102] As the polemics intensified that summer and fall, it became obvious both to foreign governments and to their own populations that the split between the two Communist giants was there to stay.[103]

The break with the Soviet Union and its allies left China in international isolation just as a new danger – the U.S. intervention in Vietnam – appeared at its borders. But to Mao, China's lack of state allies was a necessary by-product of the intensification of the class struggle inside China itself. The real allies of Mao's new revolution were "the peoples of the world" and especially "the oppressed nations and peoples of Asia, Africa, and Latin America."[104] "Peaceful coexistence between oppressed nations and imperialism is impossible," the chairman found. "Every Marxist knows that class struggle cannot be finally resolved except through war."[105] As China descended into the final chaos of the Maoist era, the Great Proletarian Cultural Revolution, Mao remade the leadership of his party in preparation for domestic and international confrontations.

Causes and Causalities

For Leonid Brezhnev and the Soviet leaders who ousted Nikita Khrushchev in October 1964, the final years of trouble in the Sino-Soviet alliance had left a legacy of mutual fear and distrust. What they saw as Mao's unpredictability and coarseness reminded them of Stalin, and they knew well what kind of damage Stalin had been capable of inflicting on domestic and foreign enemies. Chinese hints that they "had not yet presented the account" for czarist land acquisitions in East Asia during the nineteenth century, and, even more, China's testing of its first nuclear weapon the very month the new leaders took over in Moscow, created a perceived threat against the Soviet state of which Brezhnev and his cohort were never able to rid themselves. In the minds of the Brezhnev Politburo, Mao's diatribes against them reawoke fears of the Mongol threat from the East to form images of Chinese hordes invading Soviet territory.

As Soviet leaders grew increasingly concerned with security along the Chinese border, they kept asking themselves whether nuclear deterrence could work in their new and antagonistic relationship with Beijing. The Brezhnev leadership believed that the strategic nuclear power of the Soviet Union had provided the nation with a cover against Western attack unprecedented in Soviet history. But Mao's rhetoric on the futility of nuclear armaments at the 1957 Moscow meeting and thereafter left Brezhnev and his associates with lingering doubts about whether strategic superiority was enough to deter a Chinese attack. Believing themselves to be rational policymakers and the Chinese to be heavily ideological and under the spell of Mao's apocalyptic visions, the Kremlin had to fight the remaining part of the Cold War always looking over its shoulder.

The Soviet fear of a Chinese attack was mirrored on the Chinese side in Mao's belief from 1964 on that the United States and the Soviet Union jointly might attack China. The frenzied building of defense works and the relocating of vital industries to the interior joined the dislocations of the Cultural Revolution to weaken China's international position and ultimately defeat Mao's revolutionary project. But to Mao the vision of a growing external threat went well with his ideas of revolutionizing the party and Chinese society – it proved the correctness of his second revolution, and it enabled him and his associates to label those who resisted them foreign agents.[106]

Throughout the Cultural Revolution era there was opposition within the CCP to accepting the thatched-roof protection of the "solidarity of the world's peoples" and "revolutionary consciousness of the masses" as China's defense against foreign attack. As Mao's own belief in a speedy domestic revolutionary victory again foundered at the end of the 1960s, he turned for advice to the "old marshals" of the People's Liberation Army – men such as Chen Yi and Nie Rongzhen – who had been an important part of this opposition. In late 1969 he welcomed the marshals' suggestion that China should seek to reduce tension with the United States since the Soviet Union was the more dangerous enemy. Mao's own view of the Soviet Union had come full circle.[107]

The chairman's American romance at the end of his life often has been taken as the ultimate example of realist politics – in spite of a lifelong dedication to fighting Western imperialism, Mao turned to the United States when faced with a military crisis in his relations with a socialist neighbor. But to Mao, as indeed to most revolutionary leaders of the late twentieth century, ideology never contradicted the making of international alliances in defense of the revolution. His main aim was the survival and ultimate victory of communism in China, against which – in Mao's view – Soviet "social-imperialism," conducted by Brezhnev's "fascist dictatorship," had become the main threat.[108] In 1969, faced with what he saw as a new and particularly dangerous form of imperialism, he attempted to get support from the United States, just as he had done twenty-five years earlier when the Japanese threatened his movement with annihilation.

Although connected by common texts, language, symbols, and interpretations through the Chinese adaptation of Soviet Marxism, the CCP-CPSU relationship had shown visible evidence of strains from the very beginning. At times during the forty years of collaboration, the two parties had disagreed on organizational structure, military strategies, and class analysis; they had suspected each other of betrayal; and they had misunderstood each other's aims because of personal rivalries and cultural differences. Both sides had, at times, been led astray in their policymaking by their belief in a shared ideology.

The fact that ideology was crucial to both sides, while there was never a *common* ideology, is essential to understanding the rise and fall of the Sino-Soviet alliance. Without Marxism, there would be no alliance, no Chinese adoption of Soviet models in politics, economy, science, education, or the arts. Likewise, without Mao's dramatic turn to the left in the mid-1950s, there probably would not have been a collapse in the alliance around 1960.

Just as the differences in ideology presaged the breakdown of CCP-CPSU co-operation, the personalities of leaders on both sides contributed to the different stages of the alliance. Joseph Stalin's enormous prestige in the CCP was funda-mental to the idea of Sino-Soviet friendship in the late 1940s, just as the real Stalin's rude and contemptuous treatment of Mao in 1949–1950 left wounds that the CCP leader never forgot. Khrushchev's ebullience and impulsiveness at first strengthened and then added to the weakening of the alliance. But at the core of the relationship was Mao, and when he started to focus on some of those ele-ments in which Soviet and Chinese Marxism differed, the alliance was doomed.[109]

The explanations that emphasize *nationalism* as the foundation for conflict do have some connection to this interpretative framework. Both the Soviet and the Chinese party made frequent use of appeals to national cohesion when building their regimes. More important, both blamed foreign states for their countries' past miseries. But the *content* of Moscow's and Beijing's nationalisms was con-nected to Marxism and their revolutionary experiences, and without filling in this ideological content, the explicatory value of rival nationalisms seems very limited for Chinese and Soviet foreign policy during the 1950s.

Mao was right that the mid-twentieth century was a period of unprecedented global upheaval. The victories of national liberation movements in the Third World and the extraordinary doubt of purpose and achievement in Western Eu-rope and the United States left a wide playing field for China and the Soviet Union. But while Moscow tried, at least to some extent, to exploit the compar-ative advantages it had been given in the competition with the West at the global level, Mao made Beijing turn inward, away from foreign commitments and to-ward the intensification of the Chinese revolution. In terms of legacies left by the fall of the Sino-Soviet alliance, the CCP's inward turn is of immense signif-icance.

Of other legacies of the alliance, most are visible on the Chinese side. The transfer of Soviet models had a substantial impact on Chinese society, for in-stance in education, political organization, and the national economy. Although the Cultural Revolution was intended, at least in part, to remove the Soviet stamp from Chinese institutions and from ways of thinking within the party, many of the Soviet models still linger on, now besieged by the effects of the market revolution.

The most important effects of the alliance still cannot be evaluated in full. One such effect is the vital contribution of the Soviet Union to the socialist victory in China, which destroyed traditional society (and paved the way for a new society that has not yet come into being). The other is the political cohesiveness and the will to intervene that the perception of a massive Sino-Soviet threat created among elites in the West. The international effects of these two legacies of the alliance will be with us well into the twenty-first century.

Notes

1. I discovered later that the painting, entitled *Vo imia mira* [In the Name of Peace], by the Soviet artist Viktor Vikhtinskii, is now owned by the Committee on Fine Arts, Ministry of Culture of the Russian Federation, Moscow.

2. A very useful way of getting a look into issues of mutual perceptions is by reading the magazines published during the 1950s by the friendship societies in Beijing and Moscow, *SuZhong youhao* [Soviet-Chinese friendship] and *Druzhba* [Friendship].

3. Good overviews of the Western debate on the essential issues of the alliance are Steven M. Goldstein, "Nationalism and Internationalism: Sino-Soviet Relations," in Thomas W. Robinson and David Shambaugh, eds., *Chinese Foreign Policy: Theory and Practice* (Oxford: Clarendon, 1994), 224–65; Allen Whiting, "The Sino-Soviet Split," in Roderick MacFarquhar and John K. Fairbank, eds., *The Cambridge History of China,* vol. 14 (Cambridge: Cambridge University Press, 1987), 478–538.

4. Eisenhower notes, April 29, 1950, *The Papers of Dwight D. Eisenhower* edited by Alfred D. Chandler, (Baltimore: Johns Hopkins University Press, 1981), vol. 11, 1092. See also John Gaddis, "The American 'Wedge' Strategy, 1949–1955," in Harry Harding and Yuan Ming, eds., *Sino-American Relations, 1945–1955: A Joint Reassessment of a Critical Decade* (Wilmington: SR Books, 1989), 157–83; Jonathan D. Pollack, "The Korean War and Sino-American Relations," ibid., 213–37.

5. For two very influential and insightful works in the realist tradition, see John Gittings, *The World and China, 1922–1972* (New York: Harper and Row, 1974); Michael B. Yahuda, *China's Role in World Affairs* (New York: St. Martin's Press, 1978).

6. On Stalin's foreign policy beliefs, see Vladislav Zubok and Constantine Pleshakov, *Inside the Kremlin's Cold War: From Stalin to Khrushchev* (Cambridge, Mass.: Harvard University Press, 1996), especially 9–77; Vojtech Mastny, *The Cold War and Soviet Insecurity: The Stalin Years* (New York: Oxford University Press, 1996). On Mao, see Michael H. Hunt, *The Genesis of Chinese Communist Foreign Policy* (New York: Columbia University Press, 1996), especially 125–202; Yang Kuisong, *Zhongjian didai*

de geming: zhongguo geming zai guoji beijing xia de fazhan [Revolution in the intermediate zone: The development of the Chinese Revolution in an international context] (Beijing: Zhonggong zhongyang dangxiao, 1992); and Niu Jun, *Cong Yan'an zouxiang shijie: Zhongguo gongchandang dui wai guanxi de qiyuan* [From Yan'an to the world: The development of the Chinese Communist Party's foreign relations] (Fuzhou: Fujian Renmin, 1992).

7. For an overview of the debate on culture and foreign policy, see Iver B. Neumann and Thomas Hylland Eriksen, "International Relations as a Cultural System: An Agenda for Research," *Cooperation and Conflict* 28, no. 3 (1993): 233–64.

8. Some fascinating glimpses of these mutual perceptions may be found in Marie-Luise Näth, ed., *Communist China in Retrospect: East European Sinologists Remember the First Fifteen Years of the PRC* (Frankfurt-am-Main: Peter Lang, 1995).

9. For the International Relations literature, see Stephen M. Walt, *The Orgins of Alliances* (Ithaca, N.Y.: Cornell University Press, 1987); for the classical realist view, see George Liska, *Nations in Alliance: The Limits of Interdependence* (Baltimore: Johns Hopkins University Press, 1962); Arnold Wolfers, ed., *Alliance Policy in the Cold War* (Baltimore: Johns Hopkins University Press, 1959), especially pp. 1–15.

10. For instance, one contributor, the Russian scholar Constantine Pleshakov, does emphasize geopolitical concerns but interprets these preoccupations within a framework of ideology; see also his *Geo-ideologicheskaia paradigma: vzaimdeistve geopolitiki i ideologii na primere otnoshenii mezhdu SSSR, SShA i KNR v kontinentalnoi Vostochnoi Azii 1949–1991 gg.* [The geo-ideological paradigm: interaction of geopolitics and ideology in the primary relations between the USSR, USA, and the PRC in continental East Asia, 1949–1991] (Moscow: Rossiiskii nauchnii fond, 1994).

11. One of the first political positions of the young Mao Zedong was as secretary of the Russia Studies Society in his native Hunan; see Takeuchi Minoru, ed., *Mao Zedong ji. Bujuan* [Mao Zedong works. Additional volumes] (Tokyo: Sososha, 1986), vol. 9, 101–2.

12. On the early years of the CCP, see Arif Dirlik, *The Origins of Chinese Communism* (New York: Oxford University Press, 1989); Hans J. van de Ven, *From Friend to Comrade: The Founding of the Chinese Communist Party, 1920–1927* (Berkeley: University of California Press, 1991); Hung-Yok Ip, "The Origins of Chinese Communism: A New Interpretation," *Modern China* 20, no. 1 (1994): 34–63; on the Soviet/Comintern role, see Tony Saich, *The Origins of the United Front in China: The Role of Sneevliet*

(Alias Maring (2 vols.) (Leyden: E. J. Brill, 1991); and Clarence M. Wilbur and Julie Lien-ying How, *Missionaries of Revolution: Soviet Advisers and Nationalist China 1920–1927* (Cambridge, Mass.: Harvard University Press, 1989). For a good selection of archival documents coming out of Moscow, see *VKP (b), Komintern i natsionalno-revoliutsionnoe dvizhenie v Kitae: Dokumenty. T. 1: 1920–1925* [The All-Union Communist Party (b), Comintern, and the National-Revolutionary Movement in China: Documents. Vol. 1: 1920–1925] (Moscow: RTsKhIDNI, 1994).

13. By far the best survey of CCP-Soviet relations during the 1927–28 crisis based on Chinese sources is Yang Kuisong, *Zhonggong yu Mosike de guanxi 1920–1960* [Relations between the CCP and Moscow, 1920–1960] (Taipei: Sanmin shudian, 1997), 103–75.

14. The best account is Benjamin Yang, *From Revolution to Politics: Chinese Communists on the Long March* (Boulder, Colo.: Westview, 1990).

15. For CCP domestic strategies, see: Chen Yung-fa, *Making Revolution: The Communist Movement in Eastern and Central China, 1937–1945* (Berkeley: University of California Press, 1986); Kathleen Hartford and Steven M. Goldstein, eds., *Single Sparks: China's Rural Revolutions* (Armonk, N.Y.: M. E. Sharpe, 1989). For Sino-Soviet diplomatic relations during the war against Japan, see John W. Garver, *Chinese-Soviet Relations, 1937–1945* (New York: Oxford University Press, 1988).

16. See, for instance, Mao Zedong to Georgii Dimitrov, November 7, 1940, Rossiiskii tsentr khraneniia i izucheniia dokumentov noveishei istorii, Moscow (RTsKhIDNI), fond (f.) 495, special collection, pp. 182–6 (on the united front); Dimitrov to Stalin, July 18, 1941, RTsKhIDNI, f. 495, opis (op.) 74, delo (d.) 317, pp. 80–1 (on the CCP's reaction to military instructions from Moscow); Mao to Dimitrov, January 2 and 7, 1944, RTsKhIDNI, f. 495, op. 74, d. 342, pp. 4–6 and 8–10 (on the CCP rectification campaign). For CCP documents on this period, see Tony Saich and Benjamin Yang, eds., *The Rise to Power of the Chinese Communist Party: Documents and Analysis* (Armonk, N.Y.: M. E. Sharpe, 1996).

17. See I. Ilichev to Dimitrov, May 31, 1943, RTsKhIDNI, f. 495, op. 74, d. 333, 25–6 (on the CCP Politburo session on the proposition to dissolve the Comintern). On Mao's Soviet policies, see Odd Arne Westad, *Cold War and Revolution: Soviet-American Rivalry and the Origins of the Chinese Civil War* (New York: Columbia University Press, 1993), 57–72.

18. Ibid., 125–6.

19. Ibid., 165–70. See also Hunt, *Genesis,* 159–71.

20. See, for instance, Mao to Filippov (Stalin), November 30, 1947 (on CCP strategy and Soviet support), and Liu Shaoqi to Stalin, June 1949 (report on the situation in China and future CCP-Soviet relations), Tsentr khraneniia sovremennoi dokumentatsii, Moscow (TsKhSD), f. 89, special collection.

21. See Brian Murray, "Western versus Chinese Realism: Soviet-American Diplomacy and the Chinese Civil War," Ph.D. diss., Columbia University, 1995, especially 283–371.

22. We still lack an in-depth study of Soviet assistance to the CCP during the civil war. In general, Soviet aid seems to have been more substantial than either Moscow or Beijing admitted during the Cold War but still far less significant in overall value than the aid provided to the GMD by the United States. Useful overviews of Soviet assistance for the 1947–48 period may be found in the reports in Arkhiv vneshnei politiki Rossiiskoi Federatsii, Moscow (AVPRF), f. 07, op. 21, pa. 21, d. 308.

23. For an insider's view of Stalin's China policy, see Mikhail S. Kapitsa, *Na raznykh paralleliakh: zapiski diplomata* [On different parallels: A diplomat's reports] (Moscow: Kniga i biznes, 1996), 27–55. See also Andrei Ledovskii, "Stalin i Chan Kaishi. Sekretnaia missiia syna Chan Kaishi v Moskvu. Dekabr 1945–Ianvar 1946 g. [Stalin and Chiang Kai-shek. The secret mission of Chiang Kai-shek's son to Moscow. December 1945–January 1946], *Novaiia i noveishaia istoriia* 6 (1996): 100–129.

24. See Andrei Ledovsky, "Mikoyan's Secret Mission to China in January and February 1949," *Far Eastern Affairs* 2 (1995): 72–94 and 3 (1995): 74–90.

25. Mao Zedong to Stalin, January 13, 1949, Arkhiv Prezidenta Rossiiskoi Federatsii (APRF), f. 45, op. 1, d. 330, pp. 100–3. For an English translation of the Mao-Stalin exchanges in early 1949, see *Cold War International History Project Bulletin* 6–7 (Winter 1995/1996): 7, 27–9.

26. Ledovsky, "Mikoyan's Secret Mission," 2 (1995): 85.

27. Liu to Stalin, July 4, 1949, APRF, f. 45, op. 1, d. 328, pp. 48–9. This is the official report from the CCP CC to the CC of the CPSU. It was presented by Liu at a meeting of

the CPSU CC Politburo on July 11, 1949, and first published by Andrei Ledovsky, "The Moscow Visit of a Delegation of the Communist Party of China in June to August 1949," *Far Eastern Affairs* 4 (1996): 64–85. The emphasis is Stalin's. The full text is in the appendix to the present volume, document III.

28. Former Soviet Vice-Foreign Minister Mikhail S. Kapitsa, author's interview, Moscow, September 7, 1992 (hereafter "Kapitsa interview"). For accounts of Liu's visit, see Shi Zhe, *Zai lishi jüren shenbian* [Beside historical giants] (Beijing: Zhongyang wenxian, 1991); Ivan V. Kovalev, "Dialog Stalina s Ma Tsedunom" *Problemy Dalnego Vostoka,* 6 (1991): 83–93; 1–3 (1992): 77–91; Zhu Yuanshi, "Liu Shaoqi 1949 nian mimi fangSu" (Liu Shaoqi's secret visit to the Soviet Union), *Dang de wenxian,* 3 (1991): 77–9.

29. Record of conversation, Stalin–Liu, June 27, 1949, APRF, f. 45, op. 1, d. 329, p. 4.

30. This, indeed, may have been one reason why Mao suggested that he visit "the countries of Eastern and Southeastern Europe" in April 1948 (Ledovsky, "The Moscow Visit," 77).

31. Record of conversation, Mao Zedong–Roshchin, October 16, 1949, AVPRF, f. 07, op. 22, pa. 36, d. 220, pp. 48–51.

32. Record of conversation, Roshchin–Zhou Enlai, November 10, 1949, AVPRF, f. 0100, op. 42, pa. 288, d. 19, pp. 81–5; Andrei Gromyko to Stalin, November 26, 1949, AVPRF, f. 07, op. 22a, pa. 13, d. 198, pp. 32–6.

33. This summary of the 1949–50 Moscow summit is based in part on Sergei N. Goncharov, John W. Lewis, and Xue Litai, *Uncertain Partners: Stalin, Mao and the Korean War* (Stanford, Calif.: Stanford University Press, 1993) and is largely consistent with the findings in that volume. The reminiscences of one of Stalin's main China advisers, Ivan Kovalev, provide a useful, but expectedly one-sided, guide to the talks: Kovalev, "Dialog Stalina s Mao Tszedunem" [Stalin's dialogue with Mao Zedong], *Problemy dalnego vostoka* 6 (1991): 83–93 and 1–3 (1992): 77–91, also useful are the reminiscences of Shi Zhe, Mao's Russian interpreter: *Zai lishi jüren shenbian* [Beside historical giants] (Beijing: Zhongyang wenxian, 1991). The most complete archival holdings on the negotiations are in Vyshinskii's ministerial papers, AVPRF, f. 07, op. 23a–d. These must, however, be supplemented by the available Chinese documents, for instance, in Zhonghua renmin gongheguo waijiaobu and Zhonggong zhongyang wenxian yanjiushi, comps., *Mao Zedong waijiao wenxuan* [Selected Mao Zedong works on foreign affairs] (Beijing:

Zhongyang wenxian, 1994), 117–32, or Zhonggong zhongyang wenxian yanjiushi, comp., *Jianguo yilai Mao Zedong wengao* [Mao Zedong works since the founding of the PRC] (Beijing: Zhongyang wenxian, 1987), vol. 1, 189–267. See also Dieter Heinzig, "The Sino-Soviet Alliance Treaty Negotiations: A Reappraisal in Light of New Sources," paper presented at a CWIHP/Dangdai Zhongguo yanjiusuo conference, Beijing, October 1997.

34. Records of conversation, Stalin–Mao, December 16, 1949, and January 22, 1950, APRF, f. 45, op. 1, d. 329, 9–17 and 29–38; see also Goncharov et al., *Uncertain Partners;* Chen Jian, *China's Road to the Korean War: The Making of the Sino-American Confrontation* (New York: Columbia University Press, 1994).

35. Ledovsky, "Mikoyan's Secret Mission," 88–9; Hu Qiaomu, *Hu Qiaomu huiyi Mao Zedong* [Hu Qiaomu remembers Mao Zedong] (Beijing: Renmin, 1994), 88; Mao to CCP Central Committee, January 3, 1950, in *Mao Zedong waijiao wenxuan,* 122.

36. Records of conversation, Roshchin–Zhou Enlai, November 10, 1949, and Roshchin–Li Kenong, November 17, 1949, AVPRF f. 07, op. 22, pa. 36, d. 220, pp. 52–56 and 67–73. Ambassador Roshchin's conversation with Li, the head of the CCP intelligence services, gives a fairly good overview of Chinese aims in foreign policy prior to Mao's trip. The Chinese priorities were confirmed in the Kapitsa interview and the author's conversations with Vietnamese party historians, Hanoi, January 1996.

37. For further discussion, see comments by Chen Jian, Vojtech Mastny, Odd Arne Westad, and Vladislav Zubok in *CWIHP Bulletin,* 6/7 (Winter 1995/1996): 20–7.

38. See Kathryn Weathersby, "The Soviet Role in the Early Phase of the Korean War: New Documentary Evidence," *Journal of American-East Asian Relations* 2, no. 4 (Winter 1993): 425–58; "To Attack or Not to Attack? Stalin, Kim Il Sung and the Prelude to War," *CWIHP Bulletin* 5 (Spring 1995): 1–9. Both the Russian Foreign Ministry archives (AVPRF, f. 59a) and the archives of the former CPSU Central Committee (TsKhSD, f. 89) have set up consolidated collections of declassified Russian documents on the Korean war.

39. Michael H. Hunt, "Beijing and the Korean Crisis, June 1950–June 1951," *Political Science Quarterly* 107 (Fall 1992): 453–78; Thomas Christensen, "Threats, Assurances, and the Last Chance for Peace: The Lessons of Mao's Korean War Telegrams," *International Security* 17 (Summer 1992): 122–54; and Alexandre Mansourov, "Stalin, Mao, Kim, and China's Decision to Enter the Korean War: September 16–October 15, 1950: New Evidence from the Russian Archives," *CWIHP Bulletin* 6/7 (Winter 1995/1996): 94–107.

40. Kathryn Weathersby, "New Russian Documents on the Korean War," *CWIHP Bulletin* 6–7 (Winter 1995/1996): 30–5; Shu Guang Zhang, *Mao's Military Romanticism: China and the Korean War, 1950–1953* (Lawrence: University Press of Kansas, 1995); Shtykov to Vyshinskii, May 12, 1950, AVPRF, f. 059a, op. 5a, p. 11, d. 3, 100–3. Kathryn Weathersby, who is the leading expert on the new Russian materials on the Korean War, disagrees with the view of Stalin as vacillating on the purpose of his Korean policies in the spring of 1950. "Stalin seems to have made a clear decision in January 1950 that taking South Korea would be feasible and advantageous and he proceeded with the plan." Weathersby, personal communication, October 1996.

41. Mao to Filippov (Stalin), October 2, 1950, APRF, f. 45, op. 1, d. 334, pp. 105–6; see also Mansourov, "Stalin," 99.

42. Mansourov, "Stalin," 103–4; see also Shu Guang Zhang, *Deterrence and Strategic Culture: Chinese-American Confrontations, 1949–1958* (Ithaca, N.Y.: Cornell University Press, 1992), 98–9. On October 12, Stalin had instructed Kim to evacuate North Korea and set up a government-in-exile in the Soviet Union. The next day, after Mao agreed to go to war, Stalin retracted his orders: Fyn Si [Stalin] to Kim Il Sung, October 13, 1950, APRF, f. 45, op. 1, d. 347, pp. 74–5.

43. The best treatment of Chinese strategies during the war is Zhang, *Mao's Military Romanticism.*

44. Evgueni Bajanov, "Assessing the Politics of the Korean War, 1949–51," *CWIHP Bulletin* 6–7 (Winter 1995/1996): 54, 87–91; and Weathersby, "New Russian Documents on the Korean War," ibid., 30–5.

45. Records of conversation, Stalin–Zhou Enlai, August 20, September 3 and 19, 1952, APRF, f. 45, op. 1, d. 329, pp. 54–72, 75–87, and d. 343, pp. 97–103.

46. Record of conversation, Mao–Iudin, May 2, 1956, AVPRF, f. 0100, op. 49, pa. 410, d. 9, pp. 124–30.

47. It is interesting to note, for instance, how Zhou and Liu Shaoqi repeatedly drew a political parallel between the purge of Gao Gang in January 1954 and the Beriia affair in Moscow six months earlier; records of conversation, Liu Shaoqi and Zhou Enlai–Ambassador Pavel Iudin, February 2 and 13, 1954, AVPRF, f. 0100, op. 47, d. 7, pa. 379, pp. 25–35, 36–40.

48. Mao's visit to Moscow was the first time a leader of any unified Chinese state had ever visited another Great Power.

49. See Dmitri A. Volkogonov, *Sem Vozhdei: galeria liderov SSSR* [Seven chiefs: A gallery of Soviet leaders] (2 vols.) (Moscow: 1995), vol. 1, 410–11. The Lüshun base was to be handed over without compensation, while the Chinese would pay in goods deliveries for the takeover of the Manchurian and Xinjiang factories.

50. Record of conversation, Iudin–Zhou Enlai, October 10, 1954, AVPRF, f. 0100, op. 47, pa. 379, d. 7, pp. 77–82.

51. Deborah A. Kaple, *Four Myths about Soviet Involvement in China in the 1950s.* Paper presented at the Cold War International History Project's Conference on New Evidence on Cold War History, Moscow, January 12–15, 1993.

52. The Soviet Foreign Ministry received regular briefings from the Ministry of Education and the KGB on Chinese (and other foreign) students in the Soviet Union; see, for instance, the appendixes to AVPRF, f. 0100, op. 49, d. 4, p. 410.

53. Information from Russian military historians; see also Volkogonov, *Sem Vozhdei,* vol. 1, 411–12. The Russian military archives, at Podolsk outside Moscow, are unfortunately still closed for this period.

54. John Wilson Lewis and Xue Litai, *China Builds the Bomb* (Stanford, Calif.: Stanford University Press, 1988), 39–46. See also Iris Chang, *Thread of the Silkworm* (New York: Basic Books, 1995); David Holloway, *Stalin and the Bomb: The Soviet Union and Atomic Energy, 1939–1956* (New Haven, Conn.: Yale University Press, 1994), especially 354–5. Although the Chinese never received a complete prototype, substantial amounts of technical information and specifications were transferred between early 1955 and mid-1958.

55. For useful overviews, see the quarterly reports of the Cultural Section in the Soviet embassy in Beijing, in AVPRF f. 100 and f. 0100 (referentura po kitaiu). See also the 1954–1955 runs of *People's China,* the official magazine of the Sino-Soviet Friendship Association; the memoirs of Soviet advisers in China, for instance, Nikolai Fedorenko, *Kitaiskie zapisi* [Chinese Reminiscences] (Moscow: Sovetskii pisatel, 1955).

56. When the Soviets hastened to review their conversations with Gao in the wake of his purge, they found no indications of a "special relationship," except Gao's criticizing Bo Yibo's economic policies in a talk with Soviet Vice-Premier Tevosian; see record of conversation, Vice-Premier I. F. Tevosian and Ambassador Iudin–Gao Gang, December 30, 1953, AVPRF, f. 0100, op. 47, pa. 379, d. 7, pp. 3–7.

57. Record of conversation, V. V. Vaskov (Chargé d' affaires)–Mao Zedong, June 16, 1954, AVPRF, f. 0100, op. 47, pa. 379, d. 7, pp. 67–68; Kapitsa interview.

58. Record of conversation, Iudin–Zhou Enlai, January 18, 1954, AVPRF, f. 0100, op. 47, pa. 379, d. 7, pp. 14–17; A. N. Lankov, "Krisis 1956 goda v KNDR" [The 1956 crisis in the People's Democratic Republic of Korea], *Vostok* (1995): 4. On Sino-Soviet cooperation during the Geneva conference, see Molotov to Khrushchev, June 24, 1954, "Ob itogakh Zhenevskogo soveshchaniia" [On the results of the Geneva Conference], draft Central Committee Plenum speech, TsKhSD, CPSU Central Committee Plenum Collection, Nineteenth Congress. The Russian Foreign Ministry archive holds a special fond on the Geneva Conference, AVPRF, f. 0445.

59. Volkogonov, *Sem Vozhdei,* vol. 1, 410–11; Li Wenjing, "Cong Youhao zouxiang polie – Mao Zedong yu Heluxiaofu [From friendship to split – Mao Zedong and Khrushchev], in *Mao Zedong guoji jiaowang lu* [A record of Mao Zedong's international social contacts] (Beijing: Zhonggong dangshi, 1995), 116–28. See also He Di, *Paper or Real Tiger: America's Nuclear Deterrence and Mao Zedong's Response.* Paper presented at a Cold War International History Project conference, Hong Kong, January 1996. The best available collection of Mao's papers relating to the 1954 crisis are in *Jianguo yilai Mao Zedong wengao,* vol. 4; see also *Mao Zedong junshi wenji* [Mao Zedong works on military affairs] (Beijing: Junshi kexue and Zhongyang wenxian, 1993), vol. 6, 357–63.

60. Record of conversation, Mao–Iudin, December 21, 1955, AVPRF, f. 0100, op. 49, pa. 410, d. 9, pp. 11–19; see also Frederick C. Teiwes and Warren Sun, eds., *The Politics of Agricultural Cooperation in China: Mao Zedong, Deng Xihui, and the 'High Tide' of 1955* (Armonk, N.Y.: M. E. Sharpe, 1993).

61. Records of conversation, Mao–Iudin, March 31 and May 2, 1956, AVPRF, f. 0100, op. 49, pa. 410, d. 9, pp. 87–98 and 124–30; Wu Lengxi, *Yi Mao zhuxi* [Recalling Chairman Mao] (Beijing: Xinhua, 1994); Bo Yibo, *Ruogan zhongde juece yu shijian de huigu* [A review of some very important policies and events] (Beijing: Zhongguo zhongyang xuejiao, 1991); Veljko Micunovic, *Moscow Diary* (London: Chatto and Windus, 1980). An unsubstantiated outline of the "secret" speech was reported in *New York Times* on March 16, 1956. An almost complete version was printed in *France Soir* on May 28, 1956.

62. Deng Xiaoping, in his conversations with Soviet leaders in the summer of 1963, provided a useful outline of how the Polish and Hungarian events had influenced Mao's views on the Twentieth Congress. The Soviets had "thrown away Stalin's sword. Now our enemies have taken up the sword and will use it to kill us," Deng quoted Mao as say-

ing in October 1956. See "Zusammenkunft der Delegationen der Kommunistischen Partei der Sowjetunion und der Kommunistichen Partei Chinas im Juli 1963 – unkorrigierte Rohübersetzung" [Meetings of the delegations of the Communist Party of the Soviet Union and the Communist Party of China in July 1963–uncorrected raw translation], Stiftung Archiv der Parteien und Massenorganisationen der ehemaligen DDR im Bundesarchiv (SAPMO-BArch), Berlin, Bestandsignatur DY J IV 2/201, Aktenband 696 [hereafter July 1963-SAPMO-BArch], 75.

63. For Chinese reaction to the Polish and Hungarian events, see AVPRF, f. 0100, op. 49, pa. 410, d. 9. The AVPRF holds records of the CCP Politburo meetings on October 22 and 23, 1956, but these have not yet been declassified.

64. Mao Zedong's conversation with a delegation from the Yugoslav Union of Communists, September 1956, *Mao Zedong waijiao wenxuan,* 260.

65. Mao Zedong's talk at a meeting of city, province, and autonomous region party secretaries, January 27, 1957, ibid., 283.

66. See records of conversation, Iudin–Zhou Enlai, May 22, 1957, and Iudin–Mao, October 11, 1957, AVPRF, f. 0100, op. 50, pa. 423, d. 5, pp. 27–34 and 44–5.

67. For Iudin's conversations with Chinese leaders in the fall of 1957, see AVPRF, f. 0100, op. 50, pa. 423, d. 5.

68. Mao's speech in Moscow, November 14, 1957, *Jianguo yilai Mao Zedong wengao,* vol. 6, 627.

69. For the Soviet reaction, see Kapitsa, *Na raznykh paralleliakh,* 59–60.

70. Record of conversation, Iudin–Mao Zedong, February 28, 1958, AVPRF, f. 0100, op. 51, pa. 432, d. 6, pp. 86–96.

71. Wu Lengxi, *Yi Mao zhuxi;* records of conversations, Iudin–Mao Zedong, March 15 and April 5, 1958, AVPRF, f. 0100, op. 51, pa. 432, d. 6, pp. 86–96, 122–34.

72. Record of conversation, Iudin–Zhou Enlai and Peng Zhen, September 28, 1958, AVPRF, f. 0100, op. 51, pa. 432, d. 6, pp. 170–2; record of conversation, Iudin–Chen Yi, November 30, 1958, AVPRF, f. 0100, op. 51, pa. 432, d. 6, pp. 188–96.

73. See Frederick C. Teiwes, *Politics and Purges in China* (2nd ed.); (Armonk, N.Y.: M. E. Sharpe, 1993), 293–6. Selections from Mao's speeches to this crucial MAC meeting are in *Chinese Law and Government* (Winter 1968–69): 16–21; *Mao Zedong waijiao wenxuan,* 318; *Mao Zedong junshi wenji,* vol. 6, 374–5.

74. Kapitsa interview; an indication of these problems may be found in the meetings in Moscow in June and July 1958 on future Soviet assistance to China; see, for instance, record of conversation, Vice Foreign Minister Kuznetsov–Zhang Weilu, July 11, 1958, and enclosed summary of Chinese requests, AVPRF, f. 0100, op. 51, pa. 431, d. 3, pp. 50–2.

75. Shi Zhe, *Zai lishi jüren shenbian,* 572; see also "Memuari Nikiti Sergeevicha Khrushcheva" [Memoirs of Nikita Sergeevich Khrushchev], *Voprosy istorii* 2 (1993): 90–1.

76. Note from Chinese government to Soviet government, September 22, 1958, AVPRF, f. 0100, op. 51, pa. 431, d. 3, pp. 73–6; Mao Zedong to Zhou Enlai, October 11, 1958, *Jianguo yilai Mao Zedong wengao,* vol. 7, 449–50; Mao speech, December 1959, ibid., vol. 8, 600; record of conversation, Iudin–Chen Yi, November 30, 1958, AVPRF, f. 0100, op. 51, pa. 432, d. 6, pp. 188–96; Soviet statements of September 7 and 19, 1958, in I. F. Kurdiukov et al., eds., *Sovetsko-kitaiskie otnosheniia, 1917–1957: sbornik dokumentov* (Moscow: Vostochnoi literatury, 1959). See also Vladislav M. Zubok, "Khrushchev's Nuclear Promise to Beijing during the 1958 Crisis," *CWIHP Bulletin* 6–7 (Winter 1995/1996): 219, 226–7. For a view underlining Soviet support for China during the crisis, see Mark Kramer, "The USSR Foreign Ministry's Appraisal of Sino-Soviet Relations on the Eve of the Split, September 1959," *CWIHP Bulletin* 6–7 (Winter 1995/1996), 170–85.

77. Kapitsa interview; author's interview with Khrushchev's foreign policy aide and later Soviet ambassador to China, Oleg Troyanovskii, Moscow, September 14, 1992 (hereafter Troyanovskii interview).

78. Mao's writings immediately before and during the 1959 Lushan meetings reveal how he linked his domestic problems with the Sino-Soviet relationship, see *Jianguo yilai Mao Zedong wengao,* vol. 8, 286–430; see also Teiwes, *Politics and Purges,* 301–44.

79. *Jianguo yilai Mao Zedong wengao,* vol. 8, 368. Mao wrote this report and ordered it to be circulated on July 19 in response to a *cri de coeur* from the Chinese embassy in Moscow dated July 2. "Recently, some Russian cadres, especially those who work directly with us, have started commenting on our difficult situation. [They say that] the

Chinese party has made mistakes. Some of our cadres begin to doubt or change their opinion when they listen to them." Chinese embassy, Moscow, to Foreign Ministry and CCP Central Committee, July 2, 1959, *Jianguo yilai Mao Zedong wengao,* vol. 8, 367.

80. The best survey of the Lushan conferences so far available is Li Rui, *Lushan huiyi shilu* [True record of the Lushan meetings] (Beijing: Chunqiu, 1989). See also Teiwes, *Politics and Purges,* 306–35.

81. The Soviet Union on September 9 published a statement not giving support to either of the two sides, over the protest of the Chinese, who had been shown a draft of the statement; John Gittings, *Survey of the Sino-Soviet Dispute: A Commentary and Extracts from the Recent Polemics, 1963–1967* (London: Oxford University Press, 1968), 110–15; record of conversation, Khrushchev–Harriman, June 23, 1959, *Foreign Relations of the United States (FRUS), 1958–1960,* vol. 10, part 1, 277; Troianovskii interview.

82. The best survey of the Mao–Khrushchev meetings on September 30 and October 1 and 2, 1959, yet available is Chen Jian and Yang Kuisong, chapter 8 herein. See also Volkogonov, *Sem Vozhdei,* 413–15. The Soviet records of the conversations, which are not yet declassified, are in APRF, f. 52, op. 1, d. 499, pp. 1–33. See also Zimianin to Malin, October 16, 1959, AVPRF, f. 0100, op. 52, pa. 442, d. 5, p. 52.

83. Mao Zedong notes, December 1959, *Jianguo yilai Mao Zedong wengao,* vol. 8, 599–603.

84. Roderick McFarquhar, *The Origins of the Cultural Revolution. Volume 2: The Great Leap Forward 1958–1960* (Oxford: Oxford University Press, 1983), 293–8; *Hongqi,* April 16, 1960; *Sovietskaia Rossiia,* June 10, 1960.

85. Mao's instructions from information from Chinese historians; Mao Zedong notes, December 1959, *Jianguo yilai Mao Zedong wengao,* vol. 8, 602.

86. Peter Jones and Sian Kevill, comps., *China and the Soviet Union, 1949–1984* (London: Longman, 1985), 19–20.

87. Ibid., 20. See also July 1963-SAPMO-BArch, pp. 128–30.

88. Memorandum of conversation, Chervonenko–Chen Yi, August 4, 1960, AVPRF, f. 0100, op. 53, pa. 454, d. 8, pp. 204–18.

89. For a summary of the Soviet leader's reasons for withdrawing the experts from China, see Frol Kozlov's report to the CPSU Central Committee July 1960 plenum, "Ob itogakh soveshchaniia predstavitelei bratskikh partii v Bukhareste i ob oshibochnykh pozitsiiakh rukovodstva TsK KPK po nekotorym printsipialnym voprosam marksistsko-leninskoi teorii i sovremennykh mezhdunarodnykh otnoshenii" [On the results of the conference of leaders of brotherly parties in Bucharest and on the erroneous positions of the heads of the CCP Central Committee on some main questions of Marxist-Leninist theory and contemporary international relations] (draft), July 13, 1960, TsKhSD, CPSU Central Committee Plenum Collection, Twenty-first Party Congress, especially pp. 62–74.

90. Records of conversation, Chervonenko–Zhou Enlai, August 15 and 23, 1960, AVPRF, f. 0100, op. 53, pa. 8, d. 454, pp. 224–28, 231–38; record of conversation, Leonid Brezhnev–Liu Shaoqi, December 4, 1960, AVPRF, f. 0100, op. 53, pa. 6, d. 453; record of conversation, Mao Zedong–Chervonenko, December 26, 1960, AVPRF, f. 0100, op. 53, pa. 9, d. 454, pp. 98–105. See also reports by Ilia I. Safronov, political counselor at Soviet embassy, Beijing, from August 1960 on Chinese foreign relations after the recall of Soviet experts, summary (n.d.) attached to AVPRF, f. 0100, op. 53, pa. 6, d. 453.

91. Record of conversation, Chervonenko–Zhou Enlai, June 25, 1961, AVPRF, f. 0100, op. 54, pa. 466, d. 8, pp. 119–33; record of conversation, Chervonenko–Deng Xiaoping, September 30, 1961, ibid., pp. 175–8; Zhou Enlai's remarks to a Soviet trade delegation, April 20, 1962, AVPRF, f. 0100, op. 55, pa. 480, d. 6, pp. 109–13. There were rebellions in at least five provinces in China in 1960–61: Teiwes, *Politics and Purges,* 347.

92. Zhou Enlai's talk to the ambassadors from socialist countries, March 8, 1961, AVPRF, f. 0100, op. 54, pa. 466, d. 7, pp. 77–91; record of conversation, Chervonenko–Liu Shaoqi, February 28, 1961, ibid., pp. 67–72, quote on p. 70; record of conversation, Chervonenko–Chen Yi, March 20, 1961, ibid., pp. 120–6, especially pp. 120–1. See also Chervonenko's conversation with the CCP secretary for Yunnan province, Ma Zikun, April 18, 1961, on the effects of the famine in Yunnan, ibid., pp. 199–208.

93. See, for instance, Gittings, *Survey of the Sino-Soviet Dispute,* 105.

94. Chinese foreign ministry note, November 30, 1961, AVPRF, f. 0100, op. 54, pa. 460, d. 2, pp. 11–12.

95. Chinese foreign ministry note, May 18, 1961, AVPRF, f. 0100, op. 54, pa. 466, d. 2, pp. 7–8.

96. Soviet embassy (Beijing) note, AVPRF, f. 0100, op. 55, pa. 480, d. 1, pp. 1, 2.

97. Unnumbered file, attached to AVPRF, f. 0100, op. 55, pa. 480, d. 6, summarizing a December 1962 conversation between a Soviet defense official and General Qiu Chuangcheng, head of the Chinese army special artillery forces.

98. Teiwes, *Politics and Purges,* 375; Zhang Baijia, *Looking at Sino-American Relations during the Cold War from the Chinese Perspective.* Paper presented at a Cold War International History Project conference, Hong Kong, January 1996, 15.

99. Zhang, *Looking at Sino-American Relations,* 16.

100. Record of conversation, Chervonenko–Zhou Enlai, October 8, 1962, AVPRF, f. 0100, op. 55, pa. 480, d. 7, pp. 59–70, details Chinese positions and their request for Soviet aid at the start of the crisis. See also the Soviet appeal to end the fighting, in Record of conversation, Chervonenko–Zhang Hanfu (Chinese vice-foreign minister), AVPRF, f. 0100, op. 55, pa. 480, d. 7, pp. 109–12; and Deng Xiaoping's later comments on the Soviets, in July 1963-SAPMO-BArch, 90.

101. M. Y. Prozumenchikov, *The Influence of the Sino-Indian Border Conflict and the Caribbean Crisis on the Development of Sino-Soviet Relations.* Paper presented at a Cold War International History Project conference, Hong Kong, January 1996, 6–9; Soviet Beijing embassy reports on China and the Cuban crisis, TsKhSD, f. 5, op. 49, d. 530; *Renmin ribao,* December 15, 1962.

102. Gittings, *Survey of the Sino-Soviet Dispute,* 186–7. The Soviet Union had informed China of its overall acceptance of the American proposal already in August 1962. China had then repeatedly warned the Soviet Union against signing a treaty that in any way limited Chinese rights to develop its own nuclear capabilities. On June 9, 1963, just before the beginning of Sino-Soviet negotiations in Moscow, the Soviets had assured the Chinese of their support in this matter; AVPRF, f. 0100, op. 55, p. 480, d. 2. See also Han Nianlong et al., ed., *Diplomacy of Contemporary China* (Hong Kong: New Horizon Press, 1990), 148–50.

103. See, for instance, the views of the British prime minister, Alec Douglas-Home, and President Lyndon Johnson during the prime minister's visit to the United States in February 1964, Public Record Office, PREM 11/4794.

104. Jones and Kevill, *China and the Soviet Union,* 33.

105. Mao Zedong's talk with Venezuelan guests, December 5, 1961, quoted in Yang Kuisong, *On the Causes of the Changes in Mao Zedong's View of the Soviet Union.* Paper presented at a Cold War International History Project conference, Hong Kong, January 1996, 30.

106. It is difficult to say how much of Mao's emphasis on the threat of war in 1964–65 was related to his perception of external circumstances (first and foremost the U.S. intervention in Vietnam) and how much was related to the need to mobilize support for his domestic policies. See, for instance, the CCP Central Committee directive on preparations for war, April 12, 1965, cited in *History of the Chinese Communist Party: A Chronology of Events* (Beijing: Foreign Languages Press, 1991), 316; and Mao's talk to first secretaries of party committees in greater administrative areas, October 10, 1965, cited in ibid., 318.

107. Chen Xiaolu, "Chen Yi and China's Diplomacy," in Michael H. Hunt and Niu Jun, eds., *Chinese Communist Foreign Relations, 1920s–1960s: Personalities and Interpretative Approaches* (Washington, D.C.: Woodrow Wilson International Center for Scholars, Asia Program, n.d. [1994]); Zhang Baojun, "1969 nian qianhou dang dui waijiao lue de zhongda tiaozheng" [Important adjustments in the party's foreign affairs strategy around 1969], *Zhonggong dangshi yanjiu* 1 (1996): 61–7. There are several important debates going on among Chinese scholars on Mao's policies toward the Soviet Union in 1968–69; see, for instance, Niu Jun, *1969 nian Zhong-Su bianjie chongtu yu Zhongguo waijiao zhanlüe de tiaozheng* [The 1969 Sino-Soviet border conflict and changes in China's foreign policy strategy]. Paper presented at a Cold War International History Project/Dangdai Zhongguo yanjiusuo conference, Beijing, October 1997, or Yang Kuisong, *1969: Zhong-Su zhanzheng jijiang baofa?* [1969: Was a Sino-Soviet war about to break out?]. Unpublished.

108. Record of conversation, Mao Zedong–Pham Van Dong, November 17, 1968, in Odd Arne Westad et al., eds., *77 Conversations between Chinese and Foreign Leaders on the Wars in Indochina, 1964–1977,* Cold War International History Project Working Paper (Washington, D.C.: Woodrow Wilson International Center for Scholars, 1998), 142–55.

109. Some of the new research carried out in the People's Republic tends to underline this view; see, for instance, Xue Yu, "Dui liushiniandai ZhongSu lunzhan zhong ruogan wenti de zai sikao" [Rethinking some issues of the Sino-Soviet polemics of the 1960s], *Zhonggong dangshi yanjiu* 2 (1996): 69–78.

1. The Origins of the Sino-Soviet Alliance

Niu Jun

The Sino-Soviet alliance of the 1950s had a long and complex prehistory. It was based on a thirty year relationship between the Soviet and Chinese Communist parties and on the cooperation and conflicts between the leaders of those two parties.

This chapter explores the reasons behind the formation of the alliance, particularly during the five years prior to Mao's departure for Moscow. It studies internal and external factors shaping the alliance, Chinese and Soviet intentions in forming it, and the evolution of Chinese Communist Party (CCP) and Soviet policies. The purpose is to put our new understanding of the alliance and its functions into a historical perspective.

For many years, scholars have studied the alliance and issues related to it. However, during the Cold War period, analysis of the alliance's origins produced more questions than answers. In recent years, because the Chinese government allowed the publication of many historical documents and Russia partially opened the diplomatic archives of the former Soviet Union, historians have begun to reconsider old conclusions. This literature, though still in its infancy, has produced some important works.[1]

By using previously unavailable historical records, these studies have offered many valuable reinterpretations of the motivations of the Chinese and Soviet leaders in formulating and developing policies. By focusing on motives and patterns of action, we are getting closer to seeing the issues of the Sino-Soviet relationship from within, and not only through Western lenses. In sum, the recent opening of historical archives and the appearance of these thought-provoking studies have enabled us to start considering more systematic and critical explanations of the policies of both countries.

The War Against Japan

To understand post–World War II relations between the CCP and the Soviet Union, it is first necessary to review briefly their relationship before and during China's war against Japan in 1937–45. As a branch of the Communist International (Comintern), the CCP from its beginning stood on the side of the international Communist movement led by the Soviet Union and received support and assistance from both the Soviet Union and Comintern. Until the outbreak of the anti-Japanese war, the belief in a common Communist ideology dominated the CCP's relations with the Soviet Union. However, during the war, important changes took place in this relationship.

From 1937 on, the CCP Central Committee (CC) and the Soviet Union/Comintern frequently disagreed over how the CCP should carry out the policy of a united front during the anti-Japanese war. The difference between the CCP and the Soviet Union took the form of intraparty conflicts from the day when Mao's rival, Wang Ming, arrived in Yan'an from Moscow on November 29, 1937.[2] This conflict lasted until the CCP-Guomindang (GMD) battles at Wannan in 1941 in which the CCP suffered great losses. In the Jinnan battle following the Wannan incident, the Soviet military advisor, General I. V. Chuikov, supported GMD attempts to drive CCP troops out of the region. Deeply dissatisfied with this attitude, the CCP leaders criticized the Soviet representative. Mao instructed Zhou Enlai to tell the Soviet advisor "not to speak irresponsibly."[3]

After the outbreak of the Soviet-German war in June 1941, the CCP leaders rejected Moscow's demands that the Chinese Communist forces be redeployed to attack Japanese troops in North China. The Comintern leaders criticized the CCP for this decision, and Wang Ming used the opportunity to restart the debate within the CCP over the validity of Mao Zedong's political line. Because of Mao's gradually increasing importance to the Chinese Communists – as a military strategist, political leader, and symbol – Soviet and Comintern criticism could not change CCP policies at that time. Wang found himself thoroughly defeated in the debate.

As soon as this new confrontation between Mao Zedong and Wang Ming started within the CCP, the differences between Moscow and the CCP headquarters in Yan'an became difficult to manage, even though the Soviet Union and Comintern still backed most aspects of the CCP's political line. The problem was that the starting point of Mao's policy considerations was how to defend the party in a complicated environment, whereas the primary concern of the Soviet Union and the Comintern was how to further Soviet strategies and interests. Once the CCP leaders decided that they could give priority to their own views and concepts, some of their policies necessarily would diverge from Moscow's.

Moreover, the ideological ties between the CCP and the Soviet Union weakened during this period. The policy differences between the two sides made the Soviet and Comintern leaders suspicious as to the nature of the CCP's Marxism. Following Lenin's theory on party-building, they believed that the CCP's rural base had resulted in an excessively large peasant component within the party and that this situation had become a serious ideological problem. During the first years of the anti-Japanese war, the Comintern leaders worried that the CCP's lack of theoretical understanding prevented it from carrying out the united-front policy on which Moscow insisted.[4]

In the early 1940s, as differences in perceptions of the situation in China between the CCP and Moscow deepened, Stalin concluded that the CCP's policies were not merely due to its leaders' inexperience. In typical fashion, Stalin used the categories of Lenin's class struggle theory to trace the origins of the CCP policies. In autumn 1940 he discussed his views of the CCP leaders with General Chuikov, who was on his way to China. Stalin said that the CCP consisted largely of peasants and tended to underestimate the strength of the working class. This inevitably would leave a strong peasant influence on CCP's policies and ideology, which would affect the party's efforts to promote international unity.[5]

In handling the ideological dimension of their relationship with the Soviet Union, Mao Zedong and his associates confronted a very complicated problem. On one hand, the Chinese Communists firmly believed in the principles of Marxism-Leninism and believed that their own policies accorded with them. They showed great respect for Stalin and believed his position on theoretical issues to be authoritative. On the other hand, Chinese Communist leaders had learned from experience that dogmatic adoption of Soviet theory and policies could do great harm to their party both ideologically and organizationally. In terms of theory, unless the CCP modified the basic principles of Marxism and Leninism and "sinified" them, it would not be able to establish ideological guidelines that would suit China's domestic conditions. In organizational terms, unless Mao and his colleagues purged the influence of Wang Ming and his associates, they could not put an end to inner-party conflicts. To Mao and his followers, by the early 1940s the political challenges to Mao's leadership from within the party were already equated with the ultimate failure of the Chinese Revolution.

Mao Zedong launched the Rectification Campaign of 1942 to 1944 to defeat his enemies within the party and to adjust his party's relationship with Moscow. His campaign succeeded: Organizationally, he purged the influence of Wang Ming and his allies; ideologically, he established the authority of Mao Zedong Thought within the party. For Mao, the only inner-party political victory that remained after Rectification was to seek Stalin's acknowledgment that Mao Zedong Thought comported with Marxism-Leninism. Mao believed it crucial to gain Moscow's stamp of approval on the legitimacy of the Chinese Revolution that he led. The Soviet Union was Lenin's home, the birthplace of revolution, the leader of the international Communist movement. The Chinese Communists were idealistic and enthusiastic – and if the Soviets had openly rejected their theory and beliefs, the consequences could have been very damaging.

The Soviet Union significantly influenced CCP policies during the War of Resistance against Japan. However, Moscow's direct contacts with the CCP during the war remained limited. The Soviet Union stayed out of the China theater, and the CCP could not determine when the Soviet Union would join the war in East Asia.[6] Meanwhile, the United States was playing an increasingly important role in China's war efforts and in Chinese domestic politics. This situation compelled the CCP to develop its relations with the United States. In the summer of 1944, with Moscow's acceptance, CCP leaders began to adopt a policy of active cooperation with the United States in China. They hoped to receive aid from Washington in exchange for their military cooperation with the U.S. army.[7]

In sum, during the Sino-Japanese war, the CCP-Soviet relationship weakened substantially compared to what it had been in the 1920s and early 1930s. The Soviet Union, for its part, conducted foreign policy according to its own judgments with little effort to improve ties with the CCP. From the CCP leaders' perspective, while Soviet policies were very important to them, Soviet assistance was limited and not expected to increase soon. Instead, Mao and his associates worried that some of Moscow's instructions damaged the CCP's abilities to fight the Japanese and GMD attacks at the same time.

In the spring of 1945, as the European war neared its end and Moscow signaled its intent to join the war against Japan, the CCP-Soviet relationship began to take a new turn. In February, at Yalta the Soviet Union finally had signed a secret agreement on the question of the Pacific war with the United States and Britain. Consequently, its policy toward China began to take firmer shape.

The Soviets had two objectives in their policy toward China at this time. One was to defeat Japan so as to eliminate its long-term threat to the Soviet border in East Asia. The other was to gain maximum influence in China through military participation in the war and to establish buffer zones along the Soviet border. On the basis of these long-term considerations, Stalin hoped that Chinese politics would be relatively stable and that he could maintain good relations with the GMD government. To achieve this goal, the Soviet Union tried to cooperate with the United States on Chinese issues – including full recognition of the legitimacy of the GMD government – and to use its diplomatic leverage to keep

Jiang Jieshi (Chiang Kai-shek) neutral in the contest between the Soviet Union and the United States. This policy included de facto control of northeast China and limited support to the CCP. However, within its international policy framework, the Soviet Union did not view the CCP as an important factor. The CCP became relevant primarily when Stalin deliberated such questions as how to maintain Chinese political stability and how the party could be used to influence the GMD government.

In contrast to Stalin's passive attitude toward the CCP, the CCP leaders in early 1945 began to reconsider the role the Soviet Union would play in Chinese politics and how to develop their relations with Moscow. The main reason for this reconsideration was the CCP leaders' certainty that the Soviet Union soon would join the war against Japan.[8] Another reason was the sharp deterioration of the CCP's relations with the United States and – by the fall of 1944 – its difficulty in expanding its control southward because of stiff resistance from GMD troops.[9] Under these new circumstances, the CCP leaders sought ways to transform their ties to Moscow into a real alliance.

On April 18, 1945, thirteen days after the Soviet announcement suspending the Soviet-Japanese neutrality treaty, Mao Zedong approved an instruction for the JinChaJi regional party Bureau in North China to prepare for cooperation with the Soviet army. Mao's core idea was to shift the CCP's strategic focus from assisting the landing of U.S. forces on the southeast coast to assisting the Soviet forces in north and northeast China. For this purpose, his order required that in addition to military preparations, CCP organizations should emphasize the Soviet Union's important role in the war against Japan and purge unrealistic expectations about the United States among party cadres.[10] At the CCP Seventh Party Congress that summer, Mao warmly praised the great contributions of the Soviet Union in the war against fascism and claimed that the Pacific question could not be resolved without Soviet participation. He especially emphasized that the Soviet Union was the "best friend of the Chinese people."[11] Against this background, Mao for the first time revealed to the party his long-held plan for control of northeast China after a Japanese withdrawal.[12]

To some degree, it could be said that the congress reaffirmed the CCP policy of seeking cooperation with the Soviet Union. After all, throughout the war against Japan, the CCP viewed Moscow as the main force against imperialism and foreign domination. Mao's speech helped boost morale for the revolutionary ranks, especially at a time when the CCP had come under great pressure from the United States. Still, Mao knew that the CCP could not rely on the Soviet Union to provide it with any substantial assistance.[13] During the congress, Mao cautioned the party to strive for self-reliance and not to expect too much from the Soviet Union, even as he showered praises on the Soviet leadership.[14] Obviously, at that time Mao could not determine how close and how broad his alliance with the Soviet Union would be.

After the Seventh Party Congress, in the summer of 1945, the news from the GMD-Soviet talks in Moscow showed Mao that cooperation would be very limited. On August 3 Wang Ruofei, who had been in charge of CCP foreign relations in Chongqing, reported on the current situation. He outlined the conditions the Soviet Union proposed for its participation in the war against Japan and warned his audience not to place much hope on the negotiations between the GMD government and the Soviet Union. Wang said that it was certain that the two would sign a treaty; although the treaty would serve the interests of both the Soviet Union and the United States, it would not be "a treaty under which the Soviet Union could freely support the CCP against the GMD." However, Wang still expressed the belief that one should not be too pessimistic and argued that there was a limit to the Soviet compromise. First, the Soviet Union would not allow the emergence of a pro-American fascist regime in China in the wake of Japanese defeat. Second, as a Marxist, Stalin could not restrict the CCP's development even though for various tactical reasons he was not willing to provide support to the CCP.[15]

Wang's account of the international situation reflected the views of the CCP CC. The Soviet Union and the CCP shared the same goal of urging the GMD government to introduce democratic reforms and prevent the outbreak of civil war. Also, the Soviet Union was unlikely to attempt to restrict the CCP's struggle for its own political objectives. The key to attaining these objectives was to depend on its own resources while attempting to achieve a long-term alliance with Moscow.

As the war against Japan drew to a close, the CCP-Soviet relationship grew more complicated. The CCP's weight was by no means decisive in the Soviet framework for its China policy, which emphasized Moscow's ties with the United States and the GMD government. By contrast, the question of how to handle its relationship with the Soviet Union had become the key factor in CCP decision making. The CCP had to face the uncomfortable fact that it might be able to obtain only limited Soviet cooperation, since Stalin viewed China as peripheral in the confrontation between capitalism and revolution. But the CCP leaders still firmly believed that the common ideology of the CCP and the Soviet Union would constrain the extent of Soviet compromise with the United States and the GMD in China.

First Encounters

On August 14, 1945, Japan announced its surrender. Within hours Stalin cabled Mao suggesting that the CCP negotiate with the GMD and resolve their differences through mutual compromise.[16] Stalin's cables turned a new page in postwar CCP-Soviet relations.

The problem the Soviet Union faced was how to translate its gains in the secret provisions of the Yalta and Sino-Soviet treaties into firm realities and how to protect its position in the new international structure. Stalin instructed Mao to negotiate so as to fulfill his promises to the United States and the GMD government made during the Yalta and Moscow negotiations. Both Washington and Jiang's government at Chongqing wanted Stalin to use his special relationship with the CCP to compel the party to accept the compromise between the Soviet Union and the United States – that is, to unify China under Jiang Jieshi through political means.

After the Japanese surrender, the CCP leaders tried to estimate the general trends in the relationship between the Great Powers, putting less emphasis on their understanding of the secret deals at Yalta or the Sino-Soviet treaty. The establishment of the global antifascist alliance in 1941–1942 had had a tremendous influence on thinking in Yan'an. During the summer of 1942, Mao made a basic assessment about China's future in the postwar period, according to which the wartime U.S.-Soviet cooperation could be expected to continue after the defeat of the Axis powers. Affected by Great Power cooperation, CCP-GMD collaboration also could continue, and China could develop into a democratic republic, securing at least a period of peace. Although the relationship between the CCP and the GMD and that between the CCP and the United States changed over time, the CCP leaders did not change Mao's 1942 calculation until the end of the war.[17]

According to Mao's assessment, two conditions were necessary for China to avoid civil war: continued cooperation between the Soviet Union and the United States in the postwar period and a better military position for the CCP's forces. When Japan surrendered, CCP leaders still felt that these two conditions were not fully established. Internationally, the Soviet achievements in its war against Germany and its decision to participate in the war against Japan inspired the CCP. At the same time, however, while the United States increased its assistance to the GMD, the CCP could not obtain any direct aid from the Soviet Union. Domestically, the CCP could not yet prevent a GMD attack with its own resources. The Communists therefore took advantage of the sudden announcement of the Japanese surrender and the inability of the GMD forces to reach all areas affected by the surrender to expand their power and influence.

Regarding the relationship between the CCP and the GMD, Mao's main concern was how to prevent Jiang Jieshi from attacking his party. He still believed that the key to preventing an all-out conflict lay in an international compromise between the Soviet Union and the United States, with the two powers together putting pressure on the GMD.[18] However, the American order to let only the GMD government accept the surrender of Japanese troops put the CCP in an unfavorable position. When Jiang invited Mao to go to Chongqing for political negotiations with the GMD, the United States offered guarantees for Mao's personal safety, while Stalin bluntly requested the CCP to give up the armed struggle so as to reach a compromise with Jiang Jieshi. Mao feared that the Soviet policies could expose the CCP to a crushing defeat of the kind inflicted on the party by GMD forces in 1927–1928.[19]

The CCP Politburo eventually accepted Stalin's suggestion for Mao to meet Jiang. In the Politburo discussion, Mao concluded that China to the United States was like Greece to Britain, an object of intervention. "If the Soviet Union supports us, the United States is sure to support Jiang," Mao said. If that happened, war would break out and chances for peace would be minimal. Hence, the Soviet Union could not render public support to the CCP. In this situation China could only take "the French road" – establish "a government led by the bourgeoisie and with proletarian participation."[20] After careful discussion, Yan'an decided to offer quite significant compromises in order to achieve peace through negotiation, for instance by modifying the coalition government plan approved by the Seventh Party Congress.[21]

Even before Mao set off for Chongqing, the CCP Politburo had made a strategic decision to move its forces to the north and to extend its control over the Northeast. This concentration of CCP-held areas would create large revolutionary bases and enable the CCP to continue its rivalry with the GMD. On September 19 the Politburo issued an internal instruction entitled "On Current Tasks and Strategic Arrangements," which outlined its strategy of seizing the Northeast.[22] But Mao's strategic plan for the future implied seeking Soviet support – and as the CCP put its Northeast strategy into practice, the CCP-Soviet relationship took a new turn.[23]

Soviet policy toward China's Northeast also changed after the Japanese surrender. Soviet leaders sought to exploit their military control of northeast China to also achieve political and economic dominance. They already had concluded that the alliance relationship between China and the United States during the war meant that the GMD government would side with the United States in its postwar foreign policy. Moscow, wanting to make the Northeast a buffer zone, in the Sino-Soviet treaty agreed to transfer the region to GMD forces only if Soviet control remained in place.[24] The CCP did not figure in this equation – even in its military planning Moscow did not expect to work with the CCP forces that controlled large parts of northern China and areas close to the Northeast. In mid-August Soviet forces even demanded that the CCP troops sent to meet them provide proof of their status with the GMD. In early September, when CCP units arrived in the suburbs of Shenyang, Soviet forces in control there found it necessary to ask Moscow how to deal with them.[25]

Moscow initially reacted cautiously to the arrival of the CCP forces in the Northeast.[26] Soviet forces at Zhangbei and Shanhaiguan seemed quite friendly toward the CCP, probably due to their long-term ideological education. Nevertheless, the Soviets soon showed a different attitute to military cooperation with CCP troops. For example, at Zhangbei, Soviet commanders refused to cooperate with the CCP forces in taking over important areas.[27] On September 14 the Soviets sent a military representative to Yan'an to request that the CCP not let its forces openly enter the enter the Northeast before the Soviet forces had left and to withdraw those CCP units that had already entered the cities. During his meetings with Liu Shaoqi and CCP military commander Zhu De, the Soviet emissary said that Soviet forces would not interfere with CCP activities in areas not under Soviet military control but agreed to transfer the former anti-Japanese base areas in Rehe and Liaoning to the CCP.[28]

On the whole, the Soviet military hoped to limit CCP activities in the Northeast so as to achieve maximum benefits from the GMD and not encourage further American involvement.[29] Stalin's suspicions of U.S. motives had been further stimulated by the suggestion of the American ambassador to Moscow, Averell Harriman, that the Soviet Union publicly announce that it would follow "Open Door" principles in Manchuria. Together with the failed U.S. attempts at landing on the Liaodong peninsula before the Soviet army reached Dalian, Harriman's remarks undoubtedly exacerbated Soviet doubts about U.S. intentions in the Northeast.[30]

Further clouding the situation, the foreign ministers' conference in London in mid-September among representatives from the United States, the United Kingdom, and the Soviet Union failed to reach agreement on a peace treaty with and control of Japan due to Soviet-American bickering. Meanwhile, U.S. forces began to land in the harbors of north China, and U.S. assistance in transporting GMD forces to the Northeast led the Soviet Union to adjust its policy there in early October. Most important, Moscow now began to support some of the CCP's efforts to seize the region. In particular, the Soviet military suggested to the CCP's Northeast Bureau and the CCP CC that the party send 200,000 to 300,000 troops to Manchuria, where Soviet forces would provide large quantities of military equipment. At the end of October, the Soviet military further encouraged the CCP Northeast Bureau to feel free to carry out its activities in the Northeast, including the dispatch of people to take over industrial cities and industries. Implying that the Soviet military could help the CCP fight the GMD forces, if necessary, the Soviet representative even suggested that it would be best to move the whole CCP leadership to the Northeast.[31]

The sharp changes in Soviet policy had a fundamental influence on CCP strategy. Although the party was eager to take advantage of Soviet participation in the war against Japan to control the Northeast and to set up a base area near the Soviet Union and Mongolia, it hesitated to go all out in carrying out the plan in August due to uncertainty about Soviet policy toward the region. The visit of the Soviet military representative in mid-September had finally enabled CCP leaders to obtain some clarification regarding Soviet policy. They decided that while Moscow's policies set limits to CCP activities, they also provided opportunities. As long as the CCP fully exploited those opportunities, it could acquire a favorable position in the Northeast. And as American and GMD troops entered north China, it became quite urgent for the CCP to get its forces into place in the Northeast. Between September 15 and 19 the CCP CC decided to speed up its efforts to seize Manchuria.[32]

According to the Politburo's strategic plan in mid-September, the Communist troops in the Northeast should be stationed in the east, west, and north, trying to control rural areas and smaller cities not occupied by Soviet forces. The CCP believed that the real opportunity for massive expansion could come only after Soviet forces left the region.[33] At the end of October, as a result of Soviet encouragement, the CCP CC readjusted its strategic plan and decided to "make all-out efforts to dominate the Northeast." To achieve this goal, it prepared to carry out a strategic battle with the GMD forces in south Manchuria and Rehe.[34]

In order to win time to maneuver troops, the CCP Politburo instructed the Northeast Bureau and the CCP delegation in Chongqing to consult with the Soviet Union and seek to postpone the withdrawal of Soviet forces and to prevent GMD landings along the northeastern coast.[35] While the Soviet military replied that postponement of the withdrawal was difficult, it did agree to prevent the GMD from airlifting its forces to Changchun. In addition, the Red Army was ready to supply CCP forces with weapons, communication equipment, and transport. It also permitted CCP forces to conduct activities in areas where GMD forces landed. In Changchun, for instance, the CCP was able to replace all local government officials except the mayor.[36] As the Soviet forces withdrew from Yingkou and Huludao, they helped the CCP occupy these two strategic ports and consequently prevent GMD forces from landing there.

The tighter cooperation between the CCP and Soviet forces in the Northeast had a far-reaching influence on the entire CCP-Soviet relationship. Hoping to counter American pressures and consolidate its own position in the Northeast, a formerly passive Moscow now actively assisted the CCP forces there. This help was vital to the CCP, which could not realize its plan to seize the Northeast and establish large bases there without Soviet acquiescence and support. A common interest in opposing U.S. and GMD attempts to control the Northeast had given a concrete content to the CCP-Soviet alliance. Although the Soviets later readjusted their Northeast policy, the strategic partnership between the CCP and Soviet Union formed during this period in late 1945 was not changed fundamentally until 1949. In this respect, the development of CCP-Soviet relations in the Northeast represented a major turning point and a foundation for the future.

The Soviet Union and the Outbreak of Civil War

The Soviet Union's basic China policy in the immediate postwar period was to keep its agreements with the United States and the GMD government and protect its established positions in the emerging international structure. Fundamental to CCP strategy, on the other hand, was the promotion of revolutionary change in China and in East Asia. Although in most cases the ideologies of the two Communist parties led them to perceive the world in strikingly similar terms, the problems that they had experienced in their cooperation during the first postwar months persisted during the Chinese civil war. Even with the framework of the alliance in place, the divergences in strategic thinking could create serious difficulties.

In mid-November 1945 Jiang Jieshi decided to suspend his negotiations with the Soviet military in the Northeast and obtained U.S. support to attack the CCP in north China and south Manchuria. At the time Moscow estimated that it would take two months for Washington and the GMD to prepare their offensive.[37] Seeking to avoid an immediate confrontation with the United States over the Northeast, Stalin was compelled to draw closer to the GMD.[38] In mid-December he explained to Jiang Jingguo – Jiang Jieshi's son, who was visiting the Soviet Union – that Moscow did not wish to interfere in the struggle between the GMD and the CCP. However, the Soviet leader implied, the GMD government had to maintain neutrality between the United States and the Soviet Union to prevent Soviet support for its enemies.[39]

As the Soviet Union tried to improve its relations with the GMD government, it began to take measures to restrict CCP activities in the Northeast. On November 19 the Soviet military representative told the CCP Northeast Bureau that Moscow already had decided to transfer all the cities along the Changchun railroad to the GMD government and that CCP forces must evacuate areas within 30 miles of the railroad. In addition, CCP forces were not allowed to enter areas where Soviet troops were stationed and could not attack the GMD before Soviet forces left the area. The Soviet representative even declared that the Red Army was ready, if necessary, to use force to expel the CCP.[40] Soon thereafter the Soviet military closed down the local CCP governments and forbade the party from carrying out activities in major cities that interfered with the implementation of the Sino-Soviet treaty that had been concluded the previous summer.[41]

At least temporarily, Stalin had replaced his policy of assisting the CCP to control the Northeast with a diplomatic strategy of direct negotiations with the GMD.[42]

The tactical turnabout in Stalin's policy took the CCP leaders completely by surprise. Mao's strategy of "seizing the Northeast, consolidate north and central China" largely depended on Soviet assistance – and Moscow's policy reversal suddenly seemed to make that strategy worthless. Because of the Red Army's promises to supply weapons to the CCP, many CCP troops had arrived in the Northeast without necessary equipment. When Stalin changed his mind, these troops were literally defenseless. Naturally upset at Soviet behavior, CCP leaders in the Northeast repeatedly asked Yan'an for information and advice.[43]

Before receiving the news from the Soviet military representative, the CCP CC already had noted a change in the diplomatic climate in the Northeast. Believing GMD-Soviet relations to be in crisis and the overall political setting to be still fluid, it advised the Northeast Bureau to be prepared for possible changes in the situation.[44] After learning about the Soviet requests, the CC instructed the Northeast Bureau not to comply. To win time, it should ask the Soviet military to accept continued CCP control over the Jinzhou and Shanhaiguan areas. Finally, it should request the Red Army to postpone for as long as possible the entry of GMD forces into the Northeast.[45] The CCP Politburo still hoped that while their party could not take over all of the Northeast, the Soviet Union would, in the end, help it to seize some of the major cities there.[46]

In their efforts to discern the motivation behind the change in Soviet policy, the CCP Politburo and Northeast Bureau emphasized the struggle between the Soviet Union and the GMD government. They believed that the policy change was an expedient tactical move intended to enable the Kremlin to take the initiative in its diplomatic struggle with the United States and the GMD government.[47] The problem with this assessment was that while it stressed the conflict between the Soviet Union, on one hand, and the United States and the GMD government, on the other, it underestimated Soviet willingness to compromise. Therefore, the CCP Politburo still hoped that the CCP could take over or partially occupy large cities in the Northeast with Soviet assistance.

It was left to the party leaders in the Northeast, who more closely observed Soviet behavior, to provide more systematic thinking on this question. In their report to the Politburo on November 30, Chen Yun, Gao Gang, and Zhang Wentian pointed out that the Soviet Northeast policy's basic goal was to "maintain peace in the Far East and the world." According to them, the change in the Soviet policy served this general aim. Therefore, the CCP should prepare for a long-term struggle and "try to avoid unrealistic dependence on Soviet assistance and blind optimism or pessimism as a result of the increase or decrease of the Soviet aid."[48]

The serious attempts at negotiations with the GMD that Mao and the Politburo engaged in during the first phase of the mission of U.S. mediator George C. Marshall came as a result of the waning of any prospect of Soviet aid. The Chinese Communist leaders recognized that their own limited resources did not allow them to prevent GMD forces from taking over large cities and key communication lines in the Northeast. In late December the CCP Politburo decided to refocus its work in the Northeast on rural areas far from large cities and major communication lines and to establish small but solid base areas there. It also harshly criticized those cadres in the Northeast who still clung to the hope that the Soviets would help the CCP seize the main cities. At the same time, the CCP leadership hoped that negotiations, endorsed by a U.S.-Soviet compromise on China, could prevent Jiang Jieshi from launching an all-out attack.

Mao had expected that the Soviet Union would play a direct role in the negotiations and was surprised and disappointed when Stalin failed to do so. Commenting on the situation, the CCP Politburo said unambiguously: "From the very beginning, China had depended on checks and balances between several states to maintain its independence, that is, using barbarians to deal with barbarians. If China were exclusively controlled by one state, then it would have disintegrated a long time ago."[49] In early January 1946, after being turned down by Stalin, the CCP Politburo explained to the party that it was no longer necessary to seek Moscow's participation, because the Soviets "could ask us to make greater compromises" in order to demonstrate their "fairness."[50]

In early 1946, as the CCP-GMD talks made steady progress, Mao Zedong announced that "the stage of China's peaceful development will begin from here." In Mao's view, the main reason for the change in GMD behavior was the international trend of Soviet-U.S. compromise of which Stalin had advised him.[51] The CCP leaders had learned to design their strategies with a view to adapting them to changing Soviet-U.S. relations. The CCP's continuous adaptation to Soviet policies resulted from this way of thinking, even when these policies restrained the scope of Chinese Communist actions.

The Chongqing negotiations stalled on the issue of Manchuria in late February. At the same time, the Soviet attitude toward the GMD hardened due to the failure of its economic talks with Jiang Jieshi. Seizing the opportunity, the CCP Politburo again strove to have the Red Army transfer some areas under its control to the Chinese Communists. In light of previous experience, the Politburo warned that the Northeast Bureau should obtain clear-cut agreements with the Soviet forces beforehand, because "the Soviet Union could change its attitude toward Jiang again when it resolves the problem of economic cooperation with the GMD government in the future."[52]

It is true that even after altering its Northeast policy in mid-November 1945, the Soviet Union still maintained close relations with the CCP and provided it with secret assistance in the Northeast. However, the CCP leaders felt that the immediate objective of this cooperation was to prevent the United States from entering the area and the GMD government from exclusive domination there. In exchange for minimal Soviet assistance, the CCP cooperated fully with Moscow's China policy.[53]

In the spring of 1946, Soviet-U.S. relations deteriorated rapidly and the Cold War international system began to take shape. As Soviet-U.S. global confrontation intensified, and Stalin's attempts to work with Jiang failed, the Soviet Politburo decided to support the CCP's attempts to control the areas north of Changchun so as to exclude U.S. and GMD influence from the Soviet border zones. On the eve of the Soviet withdrawal, Moscow advised the CCP to "fight without restraint" and accepted the CCP plea for support to occupy Changchun, Harbin, and Qiqiha'er.[54]

Although the Soviet offer of support was exactly what the CCP had hoped for, Mao still warned that the party should consider the effects on the international situation of any offensive actions in the Northeast. In late April, however, as the talks were breaking down and CCP and GMD forces fought for control of Changchun, the chairman wrote top party leaders that he was changing some of his views on the international situation. Mao still saw the Soviet-U.S. compromise as a general trend in the foreseeable future. However, he believed that such a compromise did not mean that people in other countries would follow suit and make corresponding domestic political compromises. Moreover, he argued that a Soviet-U.S. concord could result only from the struggle of world democratic forces against the United States.[55] According to Mao, under conditions of the current Soviet-U.S. confrontation, it was only logical for people of various countries to engage in struggle.

As a result of the GMD offensives and the CCP's new willingness to fight, a full-scale civil war erupted in late June 1946. During its first phase, Mao completed his theoretical adjustment to the new global and regional situation, saying that the center of international politics was not Soviet-U.S. rivalry but rather "the confrontation between American reactionaries and the peoples of the world." Washington's anti-Soviet propaganda, in Mao's view, merely constituted a smokescreen for its domestic problems and external expansion. Before the United States controlled the world's "intermediate zone" of semi-colonized and colonized countries, it could not attack the Soviet Union. Therefore, popular revolutions in that "intermediate zone" played a decisive role in maintaining world peace and defending the Soviet Union. In those circumstances, the CCP's policy was "the policy of war": determined efforts to defeat the GMD offensive in order to carry the Chinese Revolution to victory.[56]

Mao's pronouncements on these issues in 1946–1947 were aimed against those within the party who advocated different interpretations and proposed alternative basic policies. The chairman also attempted to find common ground between his position and that of the Soviet Union, despite their different points of departure. In a theoretical sense, Mao's feat lay in placing the military victory of the Chinese Revolution above the strategic role of the Soviet Union, while making his views closely fit Soviet positions on international affairs.[57]

During the civil war, the Soviet Union repeatedly sought to constrain the CCP out of fear that the Chinese Communists' political and military initiatives might provoke the United States to intervene and lead to Soviet-U.S. conflict. Mao, however, felt that the United States and the Soviet Union by themselves could no longer decisively affect the Chinese political situation and that the CCP therefore should be an ally of Moscow, but not an instrument of its diplomacy and strategy. This view influenced almost all major policy decisions of the CCP Politburo during this period.

Stalin, Mao, and the Civil War

Even though the relationship between the Soviet Union and the CCP had improved substantially by June 1946, no fundamental changes in Soviet East Asian policies ensued as a result. The Soviet leaders believed the CCP forces remained too weak to win the civil war and risked defeat, if not total elimination. The primary task of Soviet diplomacy was to prevent direct U.S. intervention in the Chinese civil war. Moscow therefore used all occasions to condemn U.S. military assistance to the GMD government as intervention in Chinese affairs, while Stalin continued to express his willingness in principle to coordinate policy toward China with the United States. In December 1946 Stalin told James Roosevelt (FDR's son) that the Soviet Union "would like to practice a common policy with the United States on the question of the Far East."[58] In April 1947, in a letter to U.S. Secretary of State Marshall, Soviet foreign Minister V. M. Molotov wrote that by "a common policy" Stalin meant adherence to the agreement reached by the foreign ministers of the three Great Powers in December 1945.[59]

When the CCP leaders decided to use military means to fight the GMD, they also were trying to protect the Chinese Revolution and destroy the existing international system in East Asia centered around the Soviet Union and the United States. Between July and September 1947, the People's Liberation Army (PLA) changed its strategy from defense to offense. In October the CCP Politburo launched the slogan "Defeat Jiang Jieshi and liberate the whole country." In a

CCP CC meeting in December, Mao Zedong repeated the views he had proposed in April 1946, that compromise between the Soviet Union and the United
States did not necessarily mean that people in other countries also must follow
suit and compromise at home. Mao also endorsed Stalin's criticism of the
French and Italian Communist parties for "rightist deviations" and said that the
fundamental reason for the defeat of the revolutionary forces in those countries
was that the two parties had been too devoted to the parliamentary road. He also
praised the policy of Yugoslav Communist Party, arguing that unlike some West
European Communist parties, which had been deceived by the Potsdam and
Yalta agreements, the Yugoslavs had adhered to armed struggle and won. Mao
suggested that one should study the experience of the Yugoslav Communist
Party in its practice of the united front.[60] At the time Mao may not have known
that the past policies of the French and Italian Communist parties had followed
secret Soviet directives. There is, however, some evidence that he intended at
least part of his criticism to warn against a too defensive and passive Soviet foreign policy. While echoing Stalin's new view of both the French and Italian
Communist parties, Mao's comments struck other CCP leaders as encouraging
a more militant attitude in Moscow.[61]

Although the CCP and the Soviet Union had established a solid basis of cooperation in the Northeast and shared interests in opposing U.S. intervention in
the Chinese civil war, the ideological and practical bonds did not obliterate all
differences between the two parties. Stalin is known to have belittled CCP
strength and distrusted the party's leaders.[62] His repeated requests to the CCP to
compromise with the GMD in order to support Soviet diplomacy no doubt irritated Mao. The CCP chairman had many reasons continuously to caution the
party that it should "rely on itself, not on foreign assistance."[63]

Chinese Communist military successes, however, caused Stalin to upgrade
Soviet relations with the CCP. Meeting with Yugoslav leaders on February 10,
1948, Stalin admitted that he had erred in evaluating the Chinese situation. He
said that while the CCP leaders had ostensibly accepted Soviet advice, they had
in fact practiced a different policy – and they had been right.[64] In the spring of
the same year, at the CCP's request, the Soviet Communist Party Central Committee (CPSU CC) decided to assist with repair of railroads in the Northeast.
Unlike previous Soviet actions, the decision came not as a matter of conve-
nience or a consideration exclusively for the Northeast area. In May Stalin told
Ivan Kovalev – the CPSU CC special representative to the CCP – that the Soviet Union should exert itself to help the Chinese party. As long as "the two
countries took the road of socialism, the victory of world revolution was assured."[65]

The CPSU CC decision and Stalin's new views signified an important expansion of Soviet relations with the CCP. If Soviet trade relations with the CCP-controlled areas in the Northeast had been regional and tactical measures, its assistance to the CCP from this time flowed from a strategic consideration. After Soviet experts arrived in the Northeast, they informed the CCP that the Soviet Union would continue to provide aid and would be willing to develop relations with a future CCP government.[66]

The Soviet experts assisted the CCP in repairing the railroads and in training personnel for the CCP military. The rapid restoration of the railways was extremely important; it enabled the CCP Northeast forces to fight and win the Liaoshen campaign. More broadly, the timely Soviet assistance signified an important opportunity for the two sides to develop relations.

Soon after the PLA launched its strategic counteroffensive in mid-1946, CCP leaders began to think about the need to reformulate the party's relations with the Soviet Union. In early 1947, Mao thus proposed to Stalin that he visit Moscow, but his initiative was not followed up during the civil war. Mao's proposal did, however, indicate the CCP's desire to consolidate ties with its Soviet counterpart.[67]

Meanwhile, the CCP Politburo used the Soviet-Yugoslav split as a way of displaying its closeness to Moscow. When the Communist Information Bureau (Cominform) expelled the Yugoslav Communist Party in the summer of 1948,[68] the CCP Politburo quickly passed a resolution backing the Soviet position.[69] The party leadership also launched an education campaign, especially within its Northeast Bureau, to oppose bourgeois nationalism and promote proletarian internationalism.[70] On November 1 Liu Shaoqi published "On Internationalism and Nationalism," pointing out that in the period of fierce struggle between the imperialist and socialist camps, people either stood on one side or the other: Neutrality was not possible. Accordingly, Liu stated that whether or not to side with the Soviet Union was a question of revolution or reaction and of national progress or national degeneration.[71] Through this article, Liu tried not only to unify the party's thinking but also to tell the Soviet Union that the CCP Politburo believed that working out a formal alliance with Moscow was a question of principle. The CCP also wanted to show in practice, through a close relationship with the Soviet military in the Northeast, that its leaders were doing their best to satisfy all Soviet requests. To a large degree, the Northeast Bureau's arrest of several U.S. consular officials in Shenyang reflected Soviet requests.[72]

After the fall of Shenyang on November 2, 1948, the PLA occupied all of the Northeast. Mao judged that "in about another year's time, it [will be] possible to overthrow the reactionary government of the GMD."[73] The PLA's victory in the region not only accelerated the progress of the Chinese Revolution but also effectively promoted the development of the relationship between the Soviet Union and the CCP.

From the winter of 1948–1949 on, Stalin began to take personal control of Soviet policy toward China. In December 1948 Kovalev was recalled to Moscow to report on the rapidly changing Chinese political situation. According to Kovalev, when he returned to China in January 1949, his task already had shifted from providing the CCP with technical assistance to reporting directly to Stalin about CCP policies and leaders. In particular, he was instructed to maintain personal contact between Stalin and Mao.[74] On January 14, 1949, a CPSU Politburo meeting discussed Mao's proposed visit to Moscow. Stalin decided to send Anastas Mikoyan as his commissioner to the CCP CC headquarters in Xibaipo. Obviously Stalin needed to learn more about the CCP and its current policies before deciding on a new China policy.

The confusion created by Stalin's January messages to Mao on negotiations with the GMD were a main reason why Mikoyan was dispatched to Xibaipo so hurriedly. There has been considerable debate among Chinese historians about whether Mikoyan passed on a message from Stalin advising the PLA not to cross the Yangzi River.[75] What we do know is that on January 10, Stalin notified Mao that Moscow had received a message from the GMD requesting that the Soviets, together with the British and Americans, mediate in the civil war. Stalin attached a draft Soviet reply, which said that "the Soviet Government has consistently advocated stopping the Civil War and re-establishing peace in China. However, before agreeing to mediation, the Soviet Government hopes to know whether the other side [i.e., the CCP] will agree to the mediation."

In his message, Stalin told Mao that

> If you [the CCP] were asked about your opinion, you could make the following reply: "The CCP has always supported peace in China. However, China's Civil War was not started by the CCP. It was started by the Nanjing Government which should bear the responsibility for the consequences of the war. The CCP agrees to negotiate with the GMD, but not with those war criminals who started the Civil War. The CCP advocates direct negotiation with the GMD. It does not need foreign mediators to get involved because it believes that such foreign mediation is not acceptable. They use their armed forces and navy to participate in the Civil War against the PLA. Such countries could not be considered neutral and objective in eliminating war in China."

On January 13 Mao replied to Stalin:

> We believe that the Soviet Government should make the following reply to the request of the Nanjing Government's memorandum for Soviet mediation, that is, the Soviet Union has been and still is willing to see China become peaceful, democratic, and united. However, it is Chinese people's own affair as to what means to use to achieve these ends. The Soviet Union follows the principle of non-intervention in other countries' domestic affairs and hence finds it inconvenient to mediate between the two sides of the Civil War.

Mao also told Stalin that the Soviet draft would mislead the United States and other Western countries into believing that involvement in mediation would be "proper." The GMD could exploit the proposed statement and blame the CCP for being "warlike." As to the situation within the CCP, Mao said, accepting the GMD's proposal for negotiations, even if only in principle, could provoke confusion among party members.

Before receiving Mao's reply, Stalin sent off a second telegram, explaining that the purpose of his suggestions was to allow the CCP to seize the political initiative. Upon receiving Mao's telegram on January 13, Stalin argued that he foresaw two scenarios in case the CCP agreed to negotiate: The GMD might refuse to negotiate and therefore would have to take responsibility for continuing the war; or, if the GMD agreed to talk, the CCP could raise prerequisites that the GMD would have to turn down. In both cases the CCP would gain the advantage. But Stalin added that this was merely a suggestion, which the CCP did not have to accept. After Mao agreed in principle to Stalin's analysis in a hastily prepared telegram on January 11, Stalin decided to drop the matter of Soviet involvement in any form of mediation.[76]

It is hard to fathom Stalin's motives in sending these messages. Probably he would have preferred some form of political ending to the civil war, with the Communists in control, as a means to avoid American intervention. At the time, the basic policy of the GMD government led by Li Zongren was to seek a temporary north-south division of China, using the Yangzi River as demarcation line. Although there is little reason to believe that Stalin was out to rescue Li's regime, his behavior put the CCP leaders in a very uncomfortable position.

Mikoyan arrived at Xibaipo on January 31. Over the next three days, Mao and other CCP leaders held extensive talks with him and related details of the CCP's domestic and foreign policies as well as some internal party matters. Mikoyan transmitted Stalin's responses to his Chinese hosts. According to what we know now, the major issues in the bilateral talks included the CCP's strategy and current policy, past problems in the relationship, the Northeast, Xinjiang, and Mongolia, and the reformulation of the relationship after the creation of a CCP-led state.

Mao Zedong presented the military situation to Mikoyan, stressing that the PLA was about to cross the Yangzi River and that the likelihood of U.S. military involvement was very small. After winning the war, the CCP would establish a people's democratic dictatorship. The new government would carry out a pro-Soviet foreign policy and seek Soviet aid in its economic reconstruction. Mikoyan did not object to any of the CCP's principal policies.

In order to make his views plain to the Soviets in preparation for a visit to Moscow, Mao briefed Mikoyan on the history of his struggle against Wang Ming's policies. The fact that Mikoyan was instructed beforehand not to meet with Wang Ming indicates that Stalin wanted to avoid any suspicions regarding his support of Mao and to stay clear of political conflicts within the CCP. Mikoyan transmitted Mao's views on party history to Stalin.

Mao cautiously expressed the hope that the Soviet Union would return the Northeast to full Chinese sovereignty when the new state had been set up. Mikoyan told Mao that Stalin thought the 1945 Sino-Soviet pact unequal. When the CCP took power, the Soviet Union would first sign a Soviet-Japanese peace treaty and then withdraw its forces from Lüshun. If the CCP could not accept this formula, the Soviet Union was willing to withdraw immediately. Mikoyan also expressed Soviet opposition to the Xinjiang independence movement but made clear that the Soviets insisted on keeping Outer Mongolia as an independent state.[77] The talks ended positively for both sides; a Soviet leader had established a personal relationship with Mao, and the two parties found that there were few, if any, concrete issues on which they disagreed. But the main problem of how to work out relations between the new Chinese state and Moscow had not been resolved.

The relationship between Mao and Stalin had been at a low in early 1949 following the Soviet leader's unfortunate meddling just as CCP armies were preparing to cross the Yangzi and defeat the GMD. Although Mikoyan did much to set things right, Soviet leaders could not avoid drawing ideological inferences when formulating their foreign policies and evaluating CCP behavior. The military victories caused Soviet leaders gradually to abandon their previous practice of belittling the CCP's strength. But Stalin still straddled the more fundamental issue: What would political relations between a CCP government and the Soviet Union be like? The Soviet-CCP relationship still had many hurdles to clear. In some ways, the histories of the CCP and the Yugoslav party were similar, and Stalin would have to draw lessons from experience and be cautious in developing relations with an independent-minded and nationalistic CCP. But he could not risk alienating the Chinese Communists over minor matters just as they were taking power.

Stalin's need to avoid minor quibbles explains his willingness to let the CCP conduct its own foreign relations in some areas. In spite of his enduring suspicions of CCP ideological impurity – created in part by the party's attempts to co-operate independently with the United States during and after World War II – Stalin in 1949 believed he could countenance some degree of CCP-U.S. contact without losing control. On March 15 Stalin instructed Kovalev to convey to the CCP that the Soviet Union had no intention of interferring in the CCP's trade with "capitalist countries."[78] In April Stalin told Mao that in order to prevent the United States from dividing China, the CCP should propose to establish diplomatic relations with the United States on the condition that the latter sever its relations with the GMD government.[79]

In early 1949 the CCP leaders began to design the foreign policy of New China. At a Politburo meeting in January, Mao said that the New China "should not be anxious to get diplomatic recognition from the imperialist countries. We want to overthrow them, not to recognize them." China, according to Mao, "should busy itself with discussing the establishment of trade and diplomatic relations with the Soviet Union and other people's democracies."[80] However, no detailed guidelines concerning the new foreign policy were provided. The relevant directives of the Politburo primarily concerned how to deal with the diplomatic missions of Western countries in China.[81]

Mikoyan's visit and the development of the CCP's relations with the Soviet Union prompted the party to make a series of new foreign policy decisions. At the second session of the CC of the Seventh CCP Congress in early March, Mao Zedong warmly praised the Soviet Union for its support and assistance. He said that "the relationship between China and the Soviet Union is a close and brotherly relationship. The Soviet Union and we should stand on the same front. We are allies. We should publicly issue a statement when an appropriate opportunity comes."[82] In his formal report at the conference, Mao in fact announced that the New China would "lean to one side" (toward the Soviets) in its diplomatic relations.[83] This conference signified that the CCP CC was opting for a formal alliance with the Soviet Union.

To the CCP leaders, in a global struggle between the Soviet Union and the United States, any political force must decide on which side it stood. However, political principle was not always diplomatic policy. The New China and the United States could, given time, establish a normal relationship even though it had to be ranked behind that with the Soviet Union. Although never firm in their beliefs on this point, throughout the civil war the CCP leaders tended to believe that the United States did not have the resources to carry out large-scale military intervention and that its aid to the GMD government was limited.[84] The CCP strongly condemned the United States in part to show solidarity with the socialist bloc and in part to promote the anti-imperialist enthusiasm of the Chinese masses. Until uncovering what they viewed as a large subversive operation directed by U.S. intelligence services in Manchuria, which led to the arrest of U.S. consular officers at Shenyang in the winter of 1948–1949, some CCP leaders still felt it was possible to establish diplomatic relations with the United States.[85]

However, CCP leaders reevaluated their aims following the Shenyang incident. In late 1948-early 1949 the party received information from a number of sources, including the Soviets, that the gist of the U.S. China policy was to "create an effective opposition" *within* the new government. Washington would recognize New China, but in return the new Chinese government should contain an opposition party acceptable to the United States and give the United States the right to station troops in Shanghai and Qingdao. Mao Zedong reacted strongly to these messages. He believed the CCP should be on guard and foil the American conspiracy.[86] On December 30 Mao published his article "To Carry Revolution through to the End." He pointed out that U.S. China policy already had changed from purely supporting Jiang Jieshi to continuing its aid to the GMD in its military resistance while trying to organize political opposition within the revolutionary ranks. The CCP and the Chinese people must act to foil this American "political program."[87] On January 8, 1949, the CCP Politburo passed a resolution stressing the two-pronged strategy of the United States and the need to defeat this "imperialist conspiracy."[88]

Nevertheless, after the PLA occupied Nanjing, Mao still permitted officers from the CCP Nanjing Military Area foreign affairs department to hold several talks with U.S. Ambassador John Leighton Stuart to explore the possibilities for establishing ties between New China and the United States. In the talks, Stuart said that Washington could not then recognize the CCP government. He also expressed his hope that the Chinese government would include as many democratic representatives as possible. During the talks, Stuart made no secret of having set up contacts with the CCP to other diplomats.[89]

CCP leaders viewed Stuart's leaking of these contacts as arrogant and diplomatically irresponsible, and it prompted them to be even more cautious in their dealings with the United States. They knew how the Americans and their allies had tried to help the opposition defeat the Communist parties in Eastern Europe and that the primary reason for Communist success in those countries had been the military might of the Soviet Union. Stuart's behavior fitted all too well into this pattern and thereby helped push the Central Committee further toward the Soviet view of the world. Washington, Mao feared, hoped to create internal political turmoil in China while posing as an external military threat. If Stuart's contacts had any effect on CCP foreign policy, then they added a stronger flavor of confrontation with the United States to the CCP's policy of alliance with the Soviet Union.

Civil War to Anti-American War: The Birth of the Alliance

After CCP forces crossed the Yangzi River, the formalization of the Sino-Soviet alliance was only a matter of time, as the Chinese party already had decided to seek such an alliance and Moscow had few reasons to hesitate. But the two sides' willingness to meet and to formalize the ties between them did not mean that problems could be resolved easily. During his final meetings with Mikoyan on February 7, Mao had suggested that the CCP send a high-level delegation to Moscow to seek advice on building a socialist state, to report on the political and military situation in China, and to negotiate further economic aid.[90] In May Mao Zedong asked Liu Shaoqi to head the delegation.

The CCP delegation left for Moscow on June 21 and had its first meeting with Stalin in the evening of June 27. The Soviet leader talked mainly about some issues raised during Mikoyan's visit to China – signing an agreement for a future $300 million loan and providing military assistance in Xinjiang. Liu and other delegation members were alarmed by Stalin's approach, and wondered if he had not been informed of their intention to discuss the overall relationship between the two countries. Liu feared that the CPSU head deliberately avoided discussing issues of paramount importance.

In order to signal the CCP's intentions, Liu decided to provide Stalin with a written report that broadly outlined party policies, including its relationship to Moscow. He notified Beijing of this decision and his reasons for making it. Mao Zedong immediately came to Liu's aid by authorizing the publication of his article, "On the People's Democratic Dictatorship," which openly declared that the New China would "lean to one side."[91] Mao also sent an urgent telegram to the CCP authorities in Nanjing, instructing those in charge of contacts with Leighton Stuart that "we harbor no illusion of the U.S. imperialists ever changing their policy" and calling off all contacts with the U.S. envoy.[92]

On July 11 Liu met with the CPSU Politburo and presented his written report to Stalin. The report dealt with four main problem areas: the current situation of the Chinese Revolution, the political and administrative framework for a new government (including the role of the Political Consultative Conference), the new government's diplomatic policies, and, finally, some issues of future Sino-Soviet relations. It comprehensively outlined the domestic and external policies after the establishment of a new national government and the basic principles the CCP suggested for its relations with the Soviet Union and the CPSU. In the report, Liu stressed that the CCP would accept all directions given by Stalin and the CPSU CC on these issues.[93]

CCP leaders hoped to reach agreement with Moscow on a number of essential questions. They wanted Soviet help and advice in the formation of the new Chinese government and its major policies. They also wanted to achieve consensus with the Soviet Union on the international situation and foreign policy issues, and thereby secure the earliest possible diplomatic recognition from Moscow and other socialist capitals. They wanted Soviet aid to control Xinjiang and liberate Taiwan, agreements on economic and technological assistance, and revisions – or, if possible, a complete renegotiation – of the existing Sino-Soviet treaty.[94]

Stalin readily agreed with the CCP delegation on most questions related to China's domestic policies. Regarding the relationship between the two parties, Stalin stressed that equal and mutually respectful principles should be observed. He said that the victory of the Chinese Revolution was "an achievement of the Chinese Marxists." He called Mao Zedong "a Marxist leader" and said that "the Soviets and Europeans" should learn from the Chinese Communists. He even apologized for interfering in CCP's policymaking in the post–World War II period. In addition, Stalin gave some form of assurance to nearly all CCP requests for economic, technological, and military aid.[95] Stalin's generosity came easy: He knew he had much to make up for *and* that most of the formal agreements would have to wait.

Stalin had, however, much advice on foreign policy questions. On one hand, he stated that the Soviet Union would extend immediate diplomatic recognition to New China in the wake of its establishment. On the other, he encouraged the CCP to take a strong position vis-à-vis the United States and other Western countries and not to establish diplomatic relations with them in a hurry. Regarding the Sino-Soviet treaty signed by the Soviet Union and the GMD, Stalin's attitude was quite complicated. He reaffirmed what Mikoyan had already told Mao Zedong, that the treaty was not an "equal" one, because the Soviet Union was dealing with the GMD and not the CCP at the time of the conclusion of the treaty, and that the problem could be resolved when Mao visited Moscow in the future. At the same time, however, Stalin's attitude on concrete questions such as the stationing of Soviet troops in Lüshun appeared ambiguous at best.[96]

Liu Shaoqi's conversation with Stalin on the PLA's plans to attack Taiwan was even less encouraging to the CCP leaders. Stalin emphatically excluded any possibility that Soviet air and naval forces would participate in such an attack because of the risk of war with the United States. Both before and after the PLA crossed the Yangzi River, Stalin had warned the CCP CC to be vigilant about a possible American military intervention. This time he told Liu that the Truman administration contained some "lunatics" and that the Soviets had to be cautious.[97] The Chinese left with the impression that Stalin would spare no effort to avoid a military showdown with the United States, particularly in Asia – not a welcome position for most Chinese Communists.

In all, however, Liu's Soviet trip was quite successful. It basically completed the preparation for forming an alliance with the Soviet Union on the eve of the People's Republic's founding. Stalin's promise to offer economic, technological, and military assistance and diplomatic recognition to the People's Republic constituted effective support to the CCP both at home and abroad. After Liu's visit to the Soviet Union, the only thing left was for Mao to visit Moscow and conclude the treaty. However, while the abolition of the old Sino-Soviet treaty and the conclusion of a new alliance treaty were both within easy reach in principle, they were difficult to achieve in practice.

The victory of the Chinese Revolution transformed international relations in East Asia. It not only destroyed the international order based on the Yalta agreements and the 1945 Sino-Soviet treaty, but it also forced the established powers to face a new revolutionary state that had arisen from a civil war. In dealing with this new state, previous rules no longer applied, neither for the United States, nor for the Soviet Union. Under the previous order, by coordinating its policy with that of the United States, the Soviet Union had the potential to obtain economic and security advantages in East Asia. When the Chinese Revolution finally succeeded, the Soviet Union had to adjust its policy to the objectives of the Chinese Communists.

Second, the Soviet Union had to reconsider how to manage the benefits it had obtained under the previous international order. During the early Cold War, the strategic benefits to the Soviet Union of concluding an alliance with China were self-evident. Such alliance would not only form a giant security screen in the East for the Soviet Union, but it also would greatly encourage revolutionary movements in Asia. But Moscow also confronted the key problem whether it was willing to abandon the legal and economic rights it had obtained in China's Northeast. On this point, Stalin's attitude did not appear as forthcoming as his endowing Mao with the title of "Marxist leader."

The Chinese leaders' attitude on the question of replacing, or at least greatly modifying, the existing Sino-Soviet treaty also was quite complicated. During their youth, they all had progressed from being patriots, to revolutionaries, and then to devoted believers in communism. One of the most important reasons for them to "take the Russian road" had been the Soviet announcement on two separate occasions in 1919 and 1920 to abandon the territories occupied and the prerogatives grabbed by czarist Russia.[98] To them, "the Russian road" did not only mean abolition of a social system in which people exploit people; it also symbolized the establishment of a new kind of international order. The conclusion of the 1945 Sino-Soviet treaty did not change this belief of the CCP leaders, although they were definitely dissatisfied with the treaty.[99] Whatever praise appeared in CCP newspapers of the 1945 treaty was both limited and tactical – merely applauding its positive significance in maintaining peace in East Asia.[100]

When the CCP leaders decided to conclude an alliance treaty with the Soviet Union, they were not sure of Stalin's attitude. Soviet behavior gave them good reason to doubt whether Moscow actually would practice the "proletarian internationalism" it supported in public. Before the CCP crossed the Yangzi, it told non-Communist allies in China that "some foreign treaties would be abolished; some revised; and some kept."[101] The revision and maintenance was meant only to apply to the Sino-Soviet treaty. Obviously, the CCP leaders did not truly trust the Soviet Union, although they were ready to make some concessions out of more important considerations.

During his Moscow visit, Liu Shaoqi had proposed three alternatives to resolve the problem of the Sino-Soviet treaty: (1) keep the treaty and the new Chinese government would recognize it; (2) abolish the 1945 treaty and establish a new treaty; (3) the two governments exchange memoranda stating that they would maintain the treaty temporarily but would conclude another one at an appropriate time. Liu also mentioned Mongolia and the mining equipment the Soviet Union had removed from the Northeast after the Japanese defeat.[102] However, besides promising to conclude another treaty, Stalin did not clarify his views concerning the principles of the new treaty and other specific questions. The content of the new treaty later became the focus of the talks between Stalin and Mao.

Mao Zedong arrived in Moscow on December 16. That afternoon, however, his first talk with Stalin failed to achieve any concrete results. Stalin stated that the talks were not a proper time to challenge the legitimacy of the 1945 treaty. If Mao thought otherwise, the issue of the Kurile Islands, which the Soviet Union with U.S. support had taken from Japan in 1945, would be reopened. Stalin suggested instead that the two sides issue a statement on Lüshun while committing themselves to a fundational revision of the treaty within two years.[103] After this first talk, Mao questioned whether Stalin really intended to sign a new treaty.

On December 22 Mao proposed two alternatives to Stalin through Kovalev: One was to invite Zhou Enlai to come to Moscow to help resolve the problem of the Sino-Soviet treaty; the other was that both sides merely hold broad discussions about related problems but with no intention to arrive at any agreement.[104] However, during the Mao-Stalin talk on December 24, Stalin avoided mentioning Mao's alternatives. It was obvious that Stalin had *no* intention of solving the treaty issue then. The underlying reason must have been that the Soviet leadership was not prepared to change the status quo in East Asia, including the future of Outer Mongolia.

But by January 2, 1950, the Soviet position evidently had undergone a critical change. When Mao met Molotov and Mikoyan, the Chinese leader began by proposing three alternatives for the Soviet Union: (1) sign a new treaty; (2) through each country's news agencies, issue a brief statement announcing that the two countries had reached agreement on important questions; and (3) issue a common statement outlining the important points in the relations between the two countries. According to the cable Mao sent to Beijing after the conversation, Molotov had immediately stated that the first alternative was the best and suggested inviting Zhou Enlai to visit Moscow.[105] After the talk, accordingly, Mao ordered Zhou to the Soviet capital. But the chairman still had reservations about whether the Soviets would accept a new treaty, believing that Stalin would only agree to make some changes regarding the status of Lüshun and Dalian.[106]

On January 20 Zhou Enlai arrived in Moscow. Within two days Mao, Zhou, and Stalin had decided on the basic content of a new treaty. Then negotiations turned to specific issues. In a January 22 meeting, Mao emphasized that the new treaty should include both an alliance in times of war and a close coordination on all international issues in times of peace. He also stressed how important economic cooperation within the socialist camp was for the future of world revolution. Stalin seconded Mao's emphasis on the strategic nature of the alliance and acknowledged that it would fundamentally transform the balance of power in East Asia. In this light, the two leaders agreed – notwithstanding whatever private misgivings Mao must have had – that the Soviet Union would retain the rights granted to it in northeast China by the GMD in 1945.[107]

Although the documents and recollections currently available to historians are not adequate to reveal the entire negotiating process, we may be reasonably sure that both sides, and especially the Chinese, felt that much had been achieved by the time the treaty was concluded. Both China and the Soviet Union made concessions on some key issues in the treaty, such as on the China Eastern Railway, Lüshun, and Dalian.[108] None of the leaders can have been fully satisfied with the final treaties. But they did manage to come up with agreements that regulated most aspects of the alliance.

On February 14, 1950, the Chinese and Soviet leaders signed the Sino-Soviet Treaty of Friendship, Alliance, and Mutual Assistance. To the Chinese Communists, the alliance was both a goal of their revolution and the only realistic choice they could make in a world of fierce struggle between socialist and capitalist camps. The Soviet choice also reflected both ideological and realist considerations. Stalin did not decide to ally with China merely out of pure practical interest. Although ideology may have played the lesser role, it was not unimportant. On both sides the Sino-Soviet alliance was formed in a process of mutual coordination of immediate purposes and long-term goals.

To both Soviet and Chinese leaders, the Korean War confirmed these fundamentals of the alliance. Although Mao and Stalin did not discuss Korea in detail, the CCP leadership's willingness to conform to Soviet and North Korean plans for reunification became crucial in the relationship between Beijing and Moscow. As these plans progressed in the spring of 1950, Mao was ready to allow China to serve as a supply zone for the operation, even though he regretted the timing of the attack on the South.[109] Based on the evidence we now have, there are no indications of any joint Sino-Soviet planning of military operations before the war began.

Although the timing of the outbreak of the Korean War conflicted with some of the CCP leaders' priorities at home, because of their worldview, they could not refuse aid to their Korean comrades. During the Chinese civil war, the Communist army in northeastern China had received vital assistance from North Korea. Up to 1950, some core units in the People's Liberation Army in Manchuria consisted of ethnic Koreans. These Korean units, transferred to Kim Il Sung's command, would be in the forefront of the attack on the South in June 1950.

Close friends within the military in the North Korean capital Pyongyang almost certainly kept the new Chinese government informed as to Kim's and Moscow's plans for the summer of 1950. But compared to that of Moscow, Beijing's ability to influence North Korean decisions was very limited. The long period of Soviet military occupation of Korea north of the thirty-eighth parallel had secured Moscow's preeminence at all levels of the Pyongyang government. Even had it urgently desired to do so, the CCP could in no way match Moscow's influence. Before the disastrous North Korean defeats in the fall, the Chinese leaders were quite happy to take the backseat on the Korean operations.

That the CCP Politburo – in spite of much doubt and hesitation – ultimately was willing to take China into war against the United States on behalf of the common cause in Korea was final proof that the alliance between Moscow and Beijing worked. As the signing of the Sino-Soviet alliance showed, the victory of the Chinese Revolution had changed both the perceptual and strategic maps of East Asia. The war to reunite Korea followed naturally from these changes and, in turn, helped cement them for almost a decade.

Notes

1. Among the more systematic works are Sergei N. Goncharov, John W. Lewis, and Xue Litai, *Uncertain Partners: Stalin, Mao and the Korean War* (Stanford, Calif.: Stanford University Press, 1993); Odd Arne Westad, *Cold War and Revolution: So-*

viet-American Rivalry and the Origins of the Chinese Civil War (New York: Columbia University Press, 1993); Niu Jun, *Cong Yanan zouxiang shijie: Zhongguo gongchandang dui wai guanxi qiyuan (1935–1949)* [From Yan'an to the world: Origins of the foreign relations of the Chinese Communist Party, 1935–1949] (Fuzhou: Fujian renmin, 1992).

2. At that time, the Comintern found the political line of the CCP Central Committee unsatisfactory and believed it "necessary to send new faces who are familiar with the international situation to help the CCP Central Committee." It was against this background that Wang Ming was sent to Yan'an. See "Jimiteluofu zai Gongchan Guoji zhiweihui mishuchu huiyi shang jiu Zhongguo wenti de fayan" [Dimitrov's talk on the China question in a meeting of the Comintern Executive Secretariat], August 10, 1937, Department of CCP History, Zhongguo renmin daxue, comp., *Gongchan guoji he Zhonggguo geming jiaoxue cankao ziliao* [Teaching reference material on Comintern and the Chinese Revolution] (Beijing: Renmin daxue, 1986), vol. 2, 680.

3. "Zhou Enlai guanyu Jiang Jieshi yaoqiu Huabei wojun peihe zuozhan deng wenti xiang zhongyang de qingshi" [Zhou Enlai's report to the Central Committee on Jiang Jieshi's request for our military support in Huabei], May 10, 1941; "Zhou Enlai guanyu yu Jiang Jieshi tanpan qingkuang xiang zhongyang de baogao" [Zhou Enlai's report to the Central Committee on the progress of the negotiations with Jiang Jieshi], May 11, 1941; "Guanyu Huabei wojun peihe Guomingdang duiRi zuozhan deng wenti de zhishi" [Instructions on our military support to the GMD against Japan in Huabei], May 14, 1941, all in Zhongyang dangan'guan, comp., *Zhonggong Zhongyang wenjian xuanbian* [Collection of CCP Central Committee Documents] (Beijing: Zhongyang dangxiao, 1992), vol. 13, 103, 105, 107–8.

4. "Jimiteluofu zai Gongchan Guoji zhiweihui mishuchu huiyi shang jiu Zhongguo wenti de fayan," 680.

5. Wa Cuikefu [I. V. Chuikov], *Zai Hua shiming: yige junshi guwen de riji* [China mission: Notebook of a military adviser] (Beijing: Xinhua, 1980), 34.

6. As late as August 1944, in a report to the CCP CC, the CCP Southern Bureau still doubted whether the Soviet Union would join the war against Japan and even expressed the belief that Soviet participation was "not necessary." "Nanfang ju tongzhi dui waijiao de yijian ji dui Zhongyang de jianyi" [Views of the comrades of the Southern Bureau about diplomacy and their suggestions to the Central Committee], August 16, 1944, in Nanfangju dangshi ziliao zhengjizu, comp., *Nanfangju dangshi ziliao* [Southern Bureau party history materials] (Chongqing: Chongqing, 1990), vol. 3, 110–17. Mao personally

tried several times to probe the issue of Soviet entry with Moscow's representative in Yan'an, but without success.

7. "Zhongyang guanyu waijao gongzuo de zhishi" [Instructions of CCP Central Committee on diplomatic work], *Zhonggong Zhongyang wenjian xuanji,* vol. 14, 314–8.

8. "Mao Zedong guanyu muqian xingshi ji canjia zhengfu tiaojian zhi Zhou Enlai dian" [Telegram from Mao Zedong to Zhou Enlai on current situation and conditions for joining the government], February 3, 1945; "Zhongyang guanyu fazhan Guomindang tongzhiqu de minzhu yundong gei Wang Ruofei de zhishi" [Instructions of the CCP Central Committee to Wang Ruofei on developing democratic movement in areas under the Guomindang government]; Zhonggong zhongyang tongyi zhanxian bu and Zhongyang dang'anguan, *Zhonggong Zhongyang kangRi minzhu tongyi zhanxian wenjian xuanbian* [Selections of documents of the CCP Central Committee on the National United Front against Japan] (Beijing: Dang'an, 1985), vol. 2, 790, 793–4.

9. In autumn 1944 the CCP CC decided to send troops and a large number of cadres to coastal areas of east China with the aim of cooperating with an American landing and taking over Shanghai, Nanjing, and other major cities. "Zhonggong Zhongyang guanyu Su Zhe Yu Wan fazhan gei Huazhongju de zhishi" [Instructions of the CCP Central Committee to Central China Bureau on developments in Jiangsu, Zhejiang, Henan, and Anhui], October 24, 1944, *Zhonggong Zhongyang wenjian xuanji,* vol. 14, 386–7. Also see telegrams of the CCP CC to Rao Shushi, Zhang Yunyi, and Lai Chuanzhu, November 2, 1944, Chinese Central Archives (hereafter CCA).

10. "Jinchaji fenju jiji peihe Sulian zuozhan zhunbei gongzuo de zhishi" [Instructions of the Jinchaji Branch Bureau to actively prepare to cooperate with the Soviet forces in the war against Japan], April 18, 1945, CCA.

11. Mao Zedong, "Lun xianhe zhengfu" [On coalition government], *Jiefang ribao,* May 20, 1945. Mao Zedong, "Zai Zhongguo Gongchandang di qici quanguo daibiao dahui shang de koutou baogao" [Oral report to the Seventh National Representative Conference of the CCP], *Dang de wenxian* 6 (1993): 18.

12. Mao Zedong, "Zai dangde di qici daibiao dahui shang de jielun" [Conclusions made at the Seventh Congress of the Party], May 31, 1945, in *Mao Zedong zai Qida de baogao he jianghua ji* [Mao Zedong's reports and speeches at the Seventh Party Congress] (Beijing: Zhongyang wenxian, 1995), 182–9. In July 1942 Mao Zedong had telegraphed Liu Shaoqi estimating that the CCP forces probably would move to the Northeast, but he instructed Liu not to tell anyone else about these suggestions. Mao did

not raise the issue again until the Seventh Congress. Mao Zedong, "Shandong you ke-neng chengwei zhanlue zhuanyi de shuniu" [Shandong was likely to be the crossroads of strategic transfer], July 9, 1942, *Mao Zedong wenji* [Collection of Mao Zedong works] (Beijing: Renmin, 1993), vol. 2, 434–5.

13. By this time the CCP CC had already learned about the content of a conversation regarding Soviet policies toward the CCP and GMD between Stalin and U.S. special envoy Patrick Hurley on April 15, 1945. According to the Southern Bureau's report, Stalin told Hurley that the Soviet Union would not provide support to the CCP "He'erli, Sidalin tanhua qingxing" [The content of the talk between Hurley and Stalin], May 7, 1945, CCA.

14. Mao Zedong, "Zai dangde di qici daibiao dahui shang de jielun."

15. "Wang Ruofei tongzhi baogao jilu" [Record of Comrade Wang Ruofei's report], August 3, 1945, no. 6442/1, Archival Section, Department of Party History, Zhongguo Renmin Daxue.

16. So far Stalin's original cables to the CCP's leaders on these issues are not available in Chinese archives. See Zhang Baijia, "Dui Chongqing tanpan yixie wenti de tan-tao" [An exploration of the Chongqing negotiations], *Jindaishi yanjiu* 5 (1993).

17. Mao Zedong, "Lun xianhe zhengfu" [On coalition government], *Jiefang ribao*, May 2, 1945.

18. "Zhongyang guanyu Riben touxiang hou wodang renwu de jueding" [The resolution of the Central Committee on the tasks of the party after the Japanese surrender], August 11, 1945, *Zhonggong Zhongyang wenjian xuanji* [Selection of CCP Central Committee documents], vol. 15, 228–30; "Mao zhuxi zai riben touxiang shi guanyu zhengzhi xingshi de baogao" [Chairman Mao's report on the political situation at the time of Japanese surrender], no. 721/7.1, Archival Section, Department of Party History, Zhongguo Renmin Daxue.

19. Fuladimier Dediyeer [Vladimir Dedijer], *Sunan chongtu de jingli* [The lost battle of J. V. Stalin] (Beijing: Sanlian, 1977), 98. According to Dedijer, Stalin suggested that the CCP should "conclude agreements with Jiang Jieshi on establishing normal relations and dissolve its own military forces." For Stalin's cable and Mao's reactions, see Shi Zhe, *Zai lishi jüren shenbian* [Beside historical giants] (Beijing: Zhongyang wenxian, 1991), 308.

20. "Mao Zedong tongzhi zai zhengzhiju kuoda huiyi shang de fayan" [Mao Zedong's speech at the enlarged meeting of the Politburo], August 23, 1945, *Mao Zedong wenji,* vol. 4, 4–12.

21. On September 14, 1945, Huang Kecheng wrote to the CC disagreeing with the policy of "making greatest possible compromise so as to achieve peace" without first securing some major military victories. On September 20 the CC replied to Huang that it agreed with him and that the strategy of securing the Northeast, which the CC had proposed not long ago, and Huang's views were along the same line; "Huang Kecheng guanyu muqian jushi he zhanlue fangzhen de jianyi" [Huang Kecheng's suggestions concerning current situation and strategy], September 14, 1945; "Zhongyang shujichu dui Huang Kecheng guanyu muqian jushi he zhanlue fangzhen de jianyi de fushi" [Central Committee Secretariat's reply to Huang Kecheng's suggestions concerning current situation and strategy], both in *Zhonggong Zhongyang wenjian xuanji,* vol. 15, 282–5.

22. Liu Shaoqi, "Muqian de renwu yu zhanlue buzhi" [Current tasks and strategic arrangement], *Liu Shaoqi xuanji* [Selected works of Liu Shaoqi] (Beijing: Renmin, 1981), vol. 1, 371–2.

23. Mao Zedong, "Shandong you keneng chengwei zhanlue zhuanyi de shuniu." Mao's suggestion may be related to Stalin's advice. According to Shi Zhe, Stalin had proposed to Mao during this period that the CCP send some of its troops to the border between Mongolia and the Northeast in order to receive weapons and divert the Japanese forces. Shi, *Zai lishi jüren shenbian,* 214–5.

24. *Zhongguo jindai duiwai guanxi shi ziliao xuanji* [Selected materials on the modern history of Chinese foreign relations] (Shanghai: Shanghai Renmin, 1977), part 2, vol. 2, 274.

25. The Chinese versions of relevant Soviet memoirs contain no information about the Soviet military ever considering the question of cooperation with CCP forces. See relevant sections in Ya Mi Huaxiliefusiji [Vasilevskii], *Bisheng de shiye* [The career of my life] (Hong Kong: Sanlian, 1977), part 2; Xie Ma Shijiemianke [S. M. Shtemenko], *Zhanzheng shidai de zong canmou bu* [General command in years of war], (Hong Kong: Sanlian, n.d.) part 2. Also see "Cheng Geng guanyu wo jun yi yu sulian hongjun huishi de baogao" [The report on the meeting of our forces and the Soviet military by Cheng and Geng], August 17, 1945; "Zeng Kelin tan jinjun Dongbei he sibao Linjiang de youguan wenti" [Zeng Kelin on the related questions of entering the Northeast and defending Linjiang], *Dangshi tongxun* 2 (1984).

26. According to Sergei N. Goncharov and others, Soviet leaders worried that the CCP's entrance into the Northeast might damage relations between the Soviet Union and its allies. See Sergei N. Goncharov, John W. Lewis, and Xue Litai, *Uncertain Partners: Stalin, Mao and the Korean War* (Stanford, Calif.: Stanford University Press, 1993), 10.

27. "Guo Liu guanyu hongjun bu peihe wojun xingdong shi zhi Cheng Geng dian" [Guo and Liu's cable to Cheng and Geng on Red Army noncooperation with our activities], August 20, 1945, CCA.

28. "Zhongyang guanyu Dongbei qingkuang ji yu Sujun daibiao tanpan wenti de tongbao" [The Central Committee on the Northeast situation and the negotiations with the Soviet military representatives], September 14, 1945, CCA.

29. Ibid.

30. U.S. Department of State, *Foreign Relations of the United States* [hereafter *FRUS*], 1945, vol. 7. The Far East, China (Washington, D.C.: Government Printing Office, 1969), 973–4.

31. "Jia Yi guanyu choudiao zhuli sanshiwan kongzhi Dongbei zhi Bing Ding dian" [Jia and Yi's cable to Bing and Ding on sending 300,000 troops to control the Northeast], October 5, 1945; "Dongbei ju guanyu yu Sujun jiaoshe jingguo gei Zhonggong Zhongyang de baogao" [The report of the Northeast Bureau to the CCP CC on contacts with the Soviet military], October 8, 1945, both in CCA.

32. "Zhonggong Zhongyang guanyu peibei yibai ge tuan de ganbu jinru Dongbei de zhishi" [Instructions of the CCP CC on sending cadres of 100 regiments to the Northeast], September 15, 1945, CCA; "Zhongyang guanyu queding xiangbei tuijin xiangnan fangyu de zhanlue fangzhen zhi Zhonggong fuyu tanpan daibiao tuan dian" [CC to the CCP delegation to Chongqing on confirming the strategic policy of advancing in the north and defending in the south], September 17, 1945, in *Zhonggong Zhongyang wenjian xuanji,* vol. 15, 278–90; "Muqian renwu he zhanlue bushu" [Current tasks and strategic arrangement], September 19, 1945, *Liu Shaoqi xuanji,* vol. 1, 371–2.

33. "Junwei guanyu zhengduo Dongbei de zhanlue fangzhen yu juti bushu de zhishi" [Instruction of the Military Committee on the strategic policy of seizing the Northeast and concrete applications], September 28, 1945, in *Zhonggong Zhongyang wenjian xuanji,* vol. 15, 299–301.

34. "Zhongyang guanyu jizhong zhuli ju jiangjun denglu gei Dongbei ju de zhishi" [Instruction of the CCP CC to the Northeast Bureau on preventing Jiang Jieshi's forces from landing], October 19, 1945; "Zhongyang junwei guanyu shiyi yuefen zuozhan bushi de zhishi" [Instruction of the Military Committee on military planning in November], November 1, 1945, both in *Zhonggong Zhongyang wenjian xuanji,* vol. 15, 364–5 and 394–6.

35. "Jia Yi dui Bing Ding guanyu yu Zhang Shao xutan qingkuang de baogao de fudian" [Jia and Yi's reply to Bing and Ding regarding the report on further talks with Zhang Shao], October 22, 1945; "Yaoqiu Sulian Hongjun zai liuzhu rehe lianggeyue" [Request the Soviet Red Army to stay in Rehe for another two months], October 25, 1945; "Yu Guomindang huitan fangzhen ji yaoqiu Hongjun huanche" [The policy for negotiations with the GMD and request for postponement in the withdrawal of the Soviet Red Army], October 26, 1945; "Zi Chou guanyu jianjue zhengduo yu kongzhi Dongbei wenti gei Yan Mao de zhishi" [Instruction of Zi and Chou to Yan Mao on firm struggle for the control of the Northeast], October 27, 1945, all in CCA.

36. "Zai bi suo zhi qingkuang" [Information to your area], November 6, 1945, CCA.

37. "Wei Demai zai Hua renwu" [Wedermeyer's mission in China], November 12, 1945, CCA.

38. "*Zhonghua Minguo zhongyao shiliao chubian*" [A preliminary collection of important historical documents of the Republic of China], (Taipei: Yuhua, 1985), vol. 7, part 1, 154–6; Donald G. Gillin and Ramon H. Myers, eds., *Last Chance in Manchuria: The Diary of Chang Kia-Ngau* (Stanford, Calif.: Hoover Institution Press, 1989), 126–7.

39. Jiang Jieshi [Chiang Kai-shek], *Su'er zai Zhongguo* [Soviet Russia in China] (Taibei: Liming wenhua shiye, 1985), 124.

40. "Manzhou buzhun zuozhan" [No fighting in Manchuria], November 20, 1945, CCA.

41. "Dui Manzhou gongzuo de jidian yijian" [A few comments on the work in Manchuria], November 30, 1945, *Chen Yun wenxuan* [Selected works of Chen Yun] (Beijing: Renmin, 1984), 221.

42. For more on Stalin's China policies in 1945–1946, see Westad, *Cold War and Revolution,* chaps. 2 and 3.

43. "Wu Xiuquan tongzhi huiyi lu" [Memoirs of Comrade Wu Xiuquan], *Zhonggong dangshi ziliao,* 2 (1982): 213, 215.

44. "Zai Sujun yuding fangzhen bubian de qingkuang xia congxin bushu liliang" [Redeploy our forces should the Soviet military not change its plan], November 13, 1945; "Zhongyang guanyu Dongbei de gongzuo fangzhen deng gei Dongbei ju de zhishi" [Instructions of the CC to the Northeast Bureau regarding its Northeast policy], November 19, 1945, both in *Zhonggong Zhongyang wenjian xuanji,* vol. 15, 429–30.

45. "Zhongyang guanyu rangchu da chengshi ji Changchun tielu hou kaizhan dong-Man, beiMan gongzuo gei Dongbei de zhishi" [Instruction of the CC to the Northeast regarding the work in east and north Manchuria after the withdrawal from the major cities and the Changchun railroad], November 20, 1945, *Zhonggong Zhongyang wenjian xuanji,* vol. 15, 431–2.

46. "Zhongyang guanyu chechu da chengshi ji zhuyao tielu hou Dongbei de fazhan fangzhen gei Dongbei ju de zhishi" [Instruction of the CC to the Northeast Bureau concerning the policy of development in the Northeast after the withdrawal from the large cities and major railroads], November 28, 1945; "Dongbei ju guanyu chechu da chengshi hou gongzuo renwu de zhishi" [Instruction of the Northeast Bureau on the work following the withdrawal from the major cities], November 26, 1945, both in *Zhonggong Zhongyang wenjian xuanji,* vol. 15, 447–8, 434–6. To the Politburo, one incident appeared to have confirmed this belief. On November 29 Zhang Jia'ao, a key official of the Northeast Headquarters of the GMD government, met with CCP representative Dong Biwu, requesting the CCP to hand over the Beining highway to the GMD. In light of Zhang's request, the CCP Politburo guessed that the gist of Soviet Northeast policy was to prevent U.S. forces from entering the Northeast and, at the same time, to facilitate talks between the CCP and the GMD. Accordingly, it instructed its Northeast Bureau to seek Soviet intervention so as to realize joint takeovers of the large cities in the Northeast by the GMD and the CCP: see "Zhongyang guanyu zai kai tanpan zhimen gei Dong Biwu, Wang Ruofei de zhishi" [Instructions of the CC to Dong Biwu and Wang Ruofei regarding the question of reopening negotiations], December 1, 1945, in Zhongyang tongzhanbu and Zhongyang dang'anguan, comps., *Zhonggong Zhongyang jiefang zhanzheng shiqi tongyi zhanxian wenjian xuanbian* [Compilation of selected documents of the CCP CC on the united front during the war of liberation] (Beijing: Dang'an, 1988), 33; "Zhongyang guanyu Dongbei gongzuo fangzhen yu renwu gei Dongbei ju de zhishi" [Instruction of the CC to the Northeast Bureau on policy and work in the Northeast], December 7, 1945; "Zhongyang guanyu zhengqu wodang zai Dongbei de diwei ji celue wenti gei Dongbei ju de zhishi" [Instruction of the CC to the Northeast Bureau regard-

ing the status of our party and tactical questions], December 8, 1945, both in *Zhonggong Zhongyang wenjian xuanji,* vol. 15, 465–6, 474–5.

47. "Zhongyang guanyu chechu da chengshi ji zhuyao tielu hou Dongbei de fazhan fangzhen gei Dongbei ju de zhishi" [Instruction of the CC to the Northeast Bureau concerning the policy of development in the Northeast after the withdrawal from the large cities and major railroads], November 28, 1945; "Dongbei ju guanyu chechu da chengshi hou gongzuo renwu de zhishi" [Instruction of the Northeast Bureau on the work following the withdrawal from the major cities], November 26, 1945; "Zhongyang guanyu dui MeiJiang douzheng celue de zhishi" [Instruction of the CC on the tactics in the struggle against the U.S. and Jiang Jieshi], all in *Zhonggong Zhongyang wenjian xuanji,* vol. 15, 447–6, 434–6, 455–6.

48. "Dui Manzhou gongzuo de jidian yijian" [A few comments on the work in Manchuria], November 30, 1945, *Chen Yun wenxuan,* 221–4.

49. "Zhonggong Zhongyang gei Chongqing daibiaotun de dianbao" [CCP CC telegram to its delegation in Chongqing], January 3, 1946, CCA.

50. "Zhonggong Zhongyang guanyu Dongbei tingzhan tanpan qingkuang zhi Dongbei ju dian" [CC cable to the Northeast Bureau regarding the talks on armistice in the Northeast], January 3, 1946, CCA.

51. "Zhonggong Zhongyang guanyu tingzhi guonei junshi chongtu de tongzhi" [CCP announcement on ceasing domestic military conflicts], January 10, 1946, *Zhonggong Zhongyang wenjian xuanji,* vol. 16, 15. Mao Zedong, "Guanyu zhengxie chengjiu he dangqian renwu de tanpan" [On the achievement of the political consultative work and the tasks in the current negotiation], *Xinhua ribao,* February 29, 1946.

52. "Zhongyang guanyu Dongbei wenti de zhishi" [CCP CC instructions on Northeast issues], March 5, 1946, CCA.

53. "Zhongyang guanyu dui MeiJiang douzheng celue de zhishi" [CCP CC instruction on the tactics in the struggle against the U.S. and Jiang Jieshi], *Zhonggong Zhongyang wenjian xuanji,* vol. 15, 455–6.

54. "Zhongyang guanyu kongzhi Changchun, Ha'erbin ji zhongdong lu baowei beiMan gei Dongbei ju de zhishi" [CCP CC instruction to the Northeast Bureau on the control of Changchun, Ha'erbin, and the Eastern Railroad and the defense of Northern Manchuria], March 24, 1946, *Zhonggong Zhongyang wenjian xuanji,* vol. 16, 100–1.

Also see "Ke ba wo buzhan Shenyang bu duan dianyuan zuowei tong Guomindang tan-pan ziben" [We can use our not taking Shenyang and not cutting off electricity to that city as a bargaining chip in the negotiations with the GMD], March 18, 1946; "Su xiang Sufang jiaoshe lizheng wo jieguan Chang, Ha, Chi" [Immediately negotiate with the Soviet side to try to gain control over Changchun, Ha'erbin, and Chichiha'er], March 26, 1946; "Peng Zhen guanyu Sujun chejun riqi zhi Li, Huang bing gao Zhongyang" [Cable from Peng Zhen to Li, Huang, and the CC on the date of the withdrawal of the Soviet military], April 3, 1946, all in CCA.

55. *Mao Zedong xuanji*, vol. 4, 1184–5.

56. Ibid., 1193–4; see also "Mao Zedong yu Liu Shaoqi, Zhou Enlai de tanhua" [Conversation between Mao Zedong, Liu Shaoqi, and Zhou Enlai], November 21, 1946, CCA.

57. For a differing analysis, emphasizing Mao's easy adaptation to Soviet policies and views, see Michael Sheng, *Battling Western Imperialism: Mao, Stalin, and the United States* (Princeton: Princeton University Press, 1997), 145–60.

58. *Sidalin wenji, 1934–1952* [Selected works of Stalin, 1934–1952] (Beijing: Renmin, 1985), 518.

59. A. C. Anijin, *Waijiao shi* [Diplomatic history] (Hong Kong: Sanlian, 1983), vol. 5, part 1, 186.

60. "Chen Yi chuanda Mao zhuxi shi'er yue Zhongyang huiyi tanhua" [Chen Yi on the talk of Chairman Mao at the meeting of the Central Committee in December], Archival Section, Department of Party History, Zhongguo Renmin Daxue, no. 6521/2.5.

61. Ibid.

62. After the CCP CC left Yan'an, the Soviet Union had planned to ask the CCP leaders to seek shelter in the Soviet Union. Shi Zhe, *Zai lishi jüren shenbian*, 346.

63. "Chen Yi chuanda Mao zhuxi shi'er yue Zhongyang huiyi tanhua."

64. Dedijer, *Sunan chingtu de jingli*, 98.

65. N. B. Kewaliaofu [Kovalev], "Sidalin he Mao Zedong de duihua" [The dialogue between Stalin and Mao Zedong], *Guowai sheke xinxi*, 21 (1992): 29.

66. Soon after the Soviet expert group arrived in the Northeast, it suggested the CCP Northeast Bureau set up a government there. It also claimed that such a government would receive diplomatic recognition from the Soviet Union and East European countries and that in this way the CCP would be able to obtain more assistance. See "Lin yu Kelei deng de tanhua" [Conversation between Lin and Kelei], June 30, 1948, CCA.

67. There are great discrepancies in Chinese memoirs on Mao Zedong's proposals to Stalin for visiting Moscow. With regard to the reasons for Mao's planned visit, see Shi Zhe, "Mao Zedong zhuxi diyici fangwen Sulian jingguo" [Chairman Mao Zedong's first visit to the Soviet Union], Waijiaobu waijiaoshi bianjibu, ed., *Xin Zhongguo waijiao fengyun* [Diplomacy for the New China] (Beijing: Shijie zhishi, 1990), vol. 1, 8–9; *Nie Rongzhen huiyilu* [Nie Rongzhen's memoirs] (Beijing: Jiefangjun, 1984), vol. 2, 675. Some new information on Mao's proposals can be found in Andrei Ledovsky, "Mikoyan's Secret Mission to China in January and February 1949," *Far Eastern Affairs* no. 2 (1995).

68. *Nansilafu wenti cankao ziliao* [Reference material on Yugoslavia] (Beijing: Shijie zhishi, 1958), 11.

69. "Zhongguo Gongchandang Zhongyang weiyuanhui guanyu xuexi NanGong wenti jueyi de zhishi" [CCP CC instruction on studying the resolution on the question of the Yugoslav Communist Party], July 1, 1948, CCA.

70. "Zhongyang pizhuan Dongbei ju guanyu xuexi NanGong wenti jueyi de zhishi" [CCP CC instruction on referring the resolution of the Northeast Bureau on the study of the question of the Yugoslav Communist Party], August 11, 1948, CCA.

71. For Liu Shaoqi's article, see *Renmin ribao,* November 1, 1948.

72. "Youfang yaoqiu moshou Ying Mei Fa diantai" [The friendly side request confiscation of radio stations of Britain, the U.S., and France], November 16, 1948, CCA.

73. "Zhonggong Zhongyang fuzeren ping Zhongguo junshi xingshi" [The CCP CC leaders' comments on the military situation in China], Department of Party History, Zhongguo renmin daxue, ed., *Zhonggong dangshi jiaoxue cankao ziliao: Jiefang zhanzheng shiqi* [Teaching and reference materials on CCP history: The period of the war of liberation], (Beijing: N.n., n.d. [1979]) vol. 2, 311.

74. Kewaliaofu, "Sidalin he Mao Zedong."

75. At the end of the 1980s, there was much debate on this question among scholars in the People's Republic. For some of the more important works, see Wang Fangming, "Yao shishi qiushi, duli sikao: huiyi Mao zhuxi 1958 nian de yici qinqie tanhua" [Seek truth from facts and develop independent thinking: Recalling a talk with Chairman Mao in 1958], *Renmin ribao,* January 2, 1982; Liu Xiao, *Chushi Sulian banian* [Eight years as ambassador to the Soviet Union] (Beijing: Zhonggong dangshi ziliao, 1986), 4; Yu Zhan and Zhang Guanyou, "Guanyu Sidalin cengfou quanzu wo guo Changjiang de tantao" [Exploring the question whether Stalin did try to prevent us from crossing the Yangzi River], *Dang de wenxian,* 1 (1989); Xiang Qing, "Guanyu Sidalin quanzu jiangfang dajun guojiang zhi wo jian" [My view on Stalin's effort to prevent the PLA to cross the Yangzi River], *Dang de wenxian,* 6 (1989); Chen Guangxiang, "Dui Sidalin ganyu wojun guojiang wenti de tantao" [Exploring the question of Stalin's interference in the effort of our army to cross the Yangzi River], *Dangshi yanjiu ziliao,* 7–8 (1989).

76. Stalin to Mao Zedong, January 10, 1949; Stalin to Mao Zedong, January 11, 1949; Mao Zedong to Stalin, January 13, 1949; Stalin to Mao Zedong, January 14, 1949; Mao Zedong to Stalin, January 14, 1949; Stalin to Mao Zedong, January 15, 1949; *Cold War International History Project Bulletin (CWIHP Bulletin)* 6–7(Winter 1995/1996), 27–9; see also Odd Arne Westad, "Rivals and Allies: Stalin, Mao, and the Chinese Civil War, January 1949," *CWIHP Bulletin* 6–7 (Winter 1995/1996), 7. Yu Zhan and Zhang Guanyou's article quoted Stalin's telegram to Mao on January 10 and Mao's response to Stalin without citation. According to Yu and Zhang, Mao's telegram to Stalin is on January 11. See *Dang de wenxian* 1 (1989): 57–8.

77. Shi Zhe, *Zai lishi jüren shenbian,* 375–85; Ledovsky, "Mikoyan's Secret Mission," 84–92.

78. "Stalin Cable to Kovalev re Trade with Capitalist Countries," March 15, 1949, quoted in Goncharov et al., *Uncertain Partners,* 230–1.

79. "Stalin Cable to Mao re the Principles of Establishing Relations with the United States," April 1949, ibid., 231.

80. Notes on Mao Zedong's address at the Politburo meeting on January 6, 1949, CCA.

81. "Zhongyang guanyu waijiao gongzuo de zhishi" [CCP CC instruction regarding diplomatic work], January 19, 1949, *Zhonggong Zhongyang wenjian xuanji,* vol. 18, 44–9.

82. Mao Zedong, "Zai qijie er'zhong quanhui shang de zongjie" [Summary at the Second Plenary Session of the Central Committee of the Seventh Party Congress], March 13, 1949, CCA.

83. "Zai Zhongguo Gongchandang di qi jie Zhongyang weiyuanhui di er ci quanti huiyi shang de baogao" [Report at the Second Plenary Session of the Central Committee of the Seventh Party Congress], March 5, 1949, *Mao Zedong xuanji*, vol. 4, 1434–5.

84. After the outbreak of the civil war and the CCP's decision to launch an all-out counterattack, CCP leaders repeatedly discussed and rejected the idea that the United States might intervene militarily.

85. "Dongbei ju ying shengming yu Meiguo wu waijiao guanxi" [The Northeast Bureau should issue a public statement to the effect that it does not have diplomatic relations with the United States], November 11, 1948, CCA.

86. Mao Zedong, "Dui 'Leiwen he tanhua zhaiyao' de piyu" [Comments on 'the report about Leiwen and conversation with him'], December 4, 1948, CCA.

87. Mao Zedong, "Jiang geming jinxing daodi" [Carry the revolution through to the end], December 30, 1948, *Mao Zedong xuanji*, vol. 4, 1374.

88. "Muqian de xingshi he dang zai 1949 nian de renwu" [Current situation and the tasks of the party in 1949], January 8, 1949, *Zhonggong Zhongyang wenjian xuanji*, vol. 18, 17–18.

89. "Huang Hua he Situ tanhua neirong" [The conversation between Huang Hua and Stuart], June 7, 1949, CCA. See the discussion of new findings on the "Lost Chance in China" controversy in the Winter 1997 issue of *Diplomatic History*.

90. Ledovsky, "Mikoyan's Secret Mission," 92.

91. *Mao Zedong xuanji*, vol. 4, 1472–3. As early as April 8, in a conversation with Zhang Zhizhong, Mao already had detailed the main viewpoints of the article; see Yu Zhanbang, "Mao Zedong yu Zhang Zhizhong de yici zhongyao tanhua" [An important conversation between Mao Zedong and Zhang Zhizhong], *Zhonggong dangshi ziliao*, 48 (1993): 152–5.

92. "Zhonggong Zhongyang gei Nanjing shiwei he Huadongju de dianbao" [CCP CC to the Nanjing committee and the East China bureau], June 30, 1949, CCA.

93. The full Soviet version of the report, with Stalin's annotations, is in Andrei Ledovsky, "The Moscow Visit of a Delegation of the Communist Party of China in June to August 1949," *Far Eastern Affairs* (Moscow), 4 (1996): 64–85. The Chinese original is "Zhongguo Gongchandang daibiaotun gei Liangong Zhongyang Stalin tongzhi de baogao" [CCP CC delegation's report to CPSU and Stalin], July 4, 1949, CCA. For Chinese discussions of the report, see Shi Zhe, *Zai lishi jüren shenbian,* 398–403, and Zhu Yuanshi, "Liu Shaoqi 1949 nian mimi fangSu" [Liu Shaoqi's secret visit to the Soviet Union], *Dang de wenxian,* 3 (1991): 77–9.

94. In his conversation with Mikoyan, Mao commented that the question of liberating Taiwan was very complicated, because of difficulties in crossing the Taiwan Straits and the danger of American intervention: Shi Zhe, *Zai lishi jüren shenbian,* 380–1. According to Kovalev, in the summer of 1949 Mao Zedong extensively discussed with him the question of liberating Xinjiang and expressed hopes of receiving Soviet assistance on the matter. In addition, Kovalev claims that the CCP had sought Soviet aid to the PLA to liberate Taiwan: N. B. Kewaliaofu [Kovalev], "Sidalin he Mao Zedong de duihua" [The dialogue between Stalin and Mao Zedong], *Guowai sheke xinxi,* 9 (1992): 31 and 21 (1992): 31.

95. According to Kovalev, Stalin did not agree to aid the CCP in liberating Taiwan, because he worried that Soviet involvement migth spark a conflict between the Soviet Union and the United States; Kewaliaofu, "Stalin he Mao Zedong," 21 (1992): 31.

96. Shi Zhe, *Zai lishi jüren shenbian,* 398–403; Zhu Yuanshi, "Liu Shaoqi" 77–9; "Stalin's Remarks to Liu Shaoqi re Creating a Union of Asian Communist Parties," July 1949, quoted in Goncharov et al., *Uncertain Partners,* 232–3; "Yu Sidalin tanhua xiang Zhonggong Zhongyang Mao zhuxi de baogao" [Report to CCP CC and Chairman Mao about conversations with Stalin], July 27, 1949, CCA.

97. Sergei Goncharov, "Stalin tong Mao Zedong de duihua" [The conversation between Stalin and Mao Zedong], *Guoshi yanjiu cankao ziliao,* no. 1 (1993): 75.

98. "Sulian diyi ci duihua xuanyan" [The first Soviet proclamation on China], July 25, 1919; "Sulian di'er ci duihua xuanyan" [The second Soviet proclamation on China], September 27, 1920, both in *Zhonggong dangshi jiaoxue cankao ziliao: dang de chuangli shiqi* [Teaching reference material on CCP history: the period of party establishment], 135–7, 201–3.

99. In his report to the Seventh Party Congress, Mao made a special reference to Soviet proclamations regarding the abolition of all unequal treaties between czarist Russia and China: *Mao Zedong xuanji,* vol. 3, 1085.

100. "Yuandong heping de jishi: zhu ZhongSu youhao tongmeng tiaoyue" [The cornerstone of peace in the Far East: Congratulations to the Sino-Soviet Friendship Treaty of Alliance], *Xinhua ribao,* August 17, 1945; "Zhu zhongsu youhao tongmeng tiaoyue" [Congratulations on the Sino-Soviet Friendship Treaty of Alliance], *Xinhua ribao,* August 27. During this period the CCP official organ, *Jiefang ribao,* published comments on the treaty from Soviet newspapers and did not publish any important comments itself.

101. Zhou Enlai, "Guanyu heping tanpan de baogao" [Report on peace negotiations], April 17, 1949, *Zhou Enlai xuanji* [Selected works of Zhou Enlai] (Beijing: Renmin, 1981), vol. 1, 321.

102. *Hu Qiaomu huiyi Mao Zedong* [Hu Qiaomu remembers Mao Zedong] (Beijing: Renmin, 1994), 550.

103. See Pei Jianzhang, ed., *Zhonghua Renmin Gongheguo waijiao shi (1949–1956)* [The diplomatic history of People's Republic of China, 1949–1956] (Beijing: Shijie zhishi, 1994), 17–18. Unfortunately, it is still not possible to compare the Chinese records of the Stalin-Mao meeting on December 16, 1949, with the Russian record; for the Russian record, see "Conversation between Stalin and Mao, December 16, 1949," *CWIHP Bulletin* 6–7 (Winter 1995/1996): 5–7.

104. "Stalin yu Mao Zedong de duihua" [The dialogue between Stalin and Mao Zedong], *Guowai sheke xinxi* 21 (1992): 32.

105. "Mao Zedong guanyu Zhou Enlai qu Sulian canjia tanpan wenti gei ZhongGong Zhongyang de dianbao" [Cable from Mao Zedong to the CC on Zhou Enlai's visit to the Soviet Union to participate in the negotiations], January 2, 1950, *Jianguo yilai zhongyao wenjian xuanbian* [Selection of important documents since the founding of the PRC], vol. 1, 95–6. For an English translation, see *CWIHP Bulletin* 8–9 (Winter 1997/1998): 228–9.

106. "Mao Zedong guanyu Zhou Enlai qu Sulian canjia tanpan wenti gei ZhongGong Zhongyang de dianbao" [Cable from Mao Zedong to the CC on Zhou Enlai's visit to the Soviet Union to participate in the negotiations], January 3, 1950, ibid., 97. For an English translation, see *CWIHP Bulletin* 8–9 (Winter 1997/1998): 229.

107. Record of conversation between comrade I. V. Stalin and Chairman of the Central People's Government of the People's Republic of China Mao Zedong," January 22, 1950, *CWIHP Bulletin* 6–7 (Winter 1995/1996): 7–9.

108. Mao Zedong, "Guanyu ZhongSu huitan he wenjian qicao qingkuang gei Liu Shaoqi de dianbao" [Cable to Liu Shaoqi on Sino-Soviet talks and the drafting of documents], January 25, 1950, Zhonggong Zhongyang wenxian yanjiushi, comp., *Jianguo yilai Mao Zedong wengao* [Mao Zedong works since the founding of the PRC] (Beijing: Zhongyang wenxian, 1987), vol. 1, 251; for an English translation, see *CWIHP Bulletin* 8–9 (Winter 1997/1998): 235; Pei, ed., *Zhonghua Renmin Gongheguo waijiao shi,* 21–5; "Yu Mao Zedong tanhua jilu" [Record of a talk with Mao Zedong], March 31, 1956, *Guowai ZhongGong dangshi yanjiu,* 2 (1995): 21–2.

109. "Shtykov to Vyshinsky re: Meeting with Kim Il Sung," May 12, 1950, *CWIHP Bulletin* 6–7 (Winter 1995/1996): 38–9.

2. Stalin, Mao, and the End of the Korean War

Kathryn Weathersby

Scholars using the newly released Chinese and Russian archival sources on the Korean War have quite rightly devoted most of their attention to the important questions regarding the outbreak of the war and the dramatic events of the first six months, events that played a pivotal role in escalating and shaping the Cold War.[1] The remaining two and one-half years of the war lack the drama of the early months, as they were marked by stalemate on the battlefield and lengthy and tedious armistice negotiations. However, the more than two-year prolongation of the war caused by the failure of the negotiators to reach an armistice agreement had a significant and long-lasting impact on the development of alliances and perceptions on both sides of the Cold War; thus it requires close examination.

The drawn-out negotiations in Korea, lasting from July 1951 to July 1953, led many within the U.S. government to conclude that negotiations with Communists were useless and even harmful, a perception that contributed to the militarization of U.S. containment policy. In early 1953 newly elected President Dwight D. Eisenhower resolved to terminate the Korean negotiations if a settlement was not reached speedily, and in May the Eisenhower administration threatened to use nuclear weapons against China if the remaining issue at the negotiations, prisoner repatriation, was not resolved soon. For many years after the Korean War, President Eisenhower and Secretary of State John Foster Dulles maintained that Washington's threats to use nuclear weapons against China forced a breakthrough in the negotiations, a claim that had long-lasting impact on U.S. thinking regarding the utility of "nuclear diplomacy."[2]

The prolongation of the war further exacerbated the animosity between the People's Republic of China (PRC) and the United States caused by the fighting. Despite the stalemate at the front, casualties on all sides remained high during the last two years of the conflict. American bombing was, in fact, more intense during the negotiations than in the first year of the war. Furthermore, the American negotiating team's insistence on what the Chinese considered unreasonable and insulting terms persuaded Mao Zedong that the United States was not according the People's Republic the respect it deserved. The chairman therefore concluded that protecting the prestige of China required steadfast resistance to American pressure.

The war's prolongation also meant that the Soviet Union engaged in an intense air war with the United States for more than two years, the only extended confrontation between the armed forces of the superpowers during the Cold War. The story of this air war is only now beginning to emerge,[3] but it appears that, among other important consequences, the capture of downed American fighter planes and bombers contributed significantly to the development of Soviet air force technology. Soviet General Secretary Joseph Stalin apparently used the lengthy war in Korea to gather a broad range of intelligence on American military technology and organization.[4] At the same time, the Korean War provided the United States with the opportunity and rationale for conducting overflights of Soviet and Chinese territory, actions that put considerable pressure on the Soviet Union to speed up the development of effective antiaircraft defense systems.

In a broad sense, the prolongation of the Korean War meant that Stalin spent the last two and one-half years of his life managing a major war with the United States. Among the Communist allies, the Soviet leader had the final say in decisions regarding military and diplomatic strategy during the war, regularly corresponding by telegraph with Chinese and North Korean leaders. Although the Chinese were responsible for the day-to-day management of the war after November 1950, Stalin closely followed the events on the ground, periodically intervening with specific military instructions. Mao Zedong and North Korean leader Kim Il Sung requested and received Stalin's instructions prior to any significant diplomatic move. The Soviet leader also personally negotiated with Mao Zedong over the amounts, delivery schedules, and terms of payment of the massive quantities of armaments and supplies shipped from the Soviet Union to China and Korea as well as the dispatch of significant numbers of Soviet military advisers to both countries.[5]

The new Russian archival sources tend to support the argument that the Korean War served as a substitute for World War III.[6] The parameters for managing a superpower conflict established by the two sides during this war remained in force for the remainder of the Cold War. Similarly, both the Sino-Soviet alliance and the North Atlantic Treaty Organization (NATO), created shortly before war began in Korea, took concrete shape in the course of this lengthy struggle. Thus, on closer inspection, the last two years of the Korean War form a large, complex, and important story. An adequate analysis of why the war lasted for two years after armistice negotiations began requires that we integrate the historical evidence on the strategy of the United States, the United Nations (UN), and the Republic of Korea toward the war, with all the complex international and domestic issues that shaped allied policy, with the new evidence on Soviet, Chinese, and North Korean strategy. We have just begun this formidable task. This chapter, therefore, does not claim to be definitive; instead it attempts to begin analyzing the reasons the war was prolonged by examining the evidence provided by recently released documents regarding the Soviet and Chinese approach to the armistice negotiations, focusing particularly on the evolution of Stalin's attitude toward a negotiated settlement in Korea.

The War and Initial Negotiations

As I have discussed elsewhere, Stalin was surprised and alarmed by the American entry into the war in Korea.[7] Although we have no precise record of his reasons for approving Kim Il Sung's plan to reunify Korea by force, the evidence strongly suggests that considerations of the likely American response were a key factor in Stalin's decision. After the announcement of the Marshall Plan in 1947, the Soviet leader abandoned hopes for partnership with the West and thought increasingly in terms of an eventual conflict with the "imperialist" powers, but he wanted to postpone that confrontation until the Soviet Union had recovered sufficiently from the devastation of World War II. Stalin therefore wished above all to avoid having the action in Korea pull the Soviet Union into military conflict with the United States. Consequently, when the Truman administration abruptly reversed its policy toward the peninsula and committed American armed forces to the defense of the Republic of Korea, Stalin took every measure to distance the Soviet Union from the conflict.[8]

During the first two months of the war in Korea, Stalin instructed Soviet officials to respond positively to British and Indian overtures regarding a peace settlement. He also ordered the Soviet ambassador to the United Nations, Jacob Malik, to return to the Security Council. However, the Soviet Union used Malik's presence at the United Nations more to advance its propaganda campaign against American bombing in Korea than to pursue a negotiated settlement.[9] While conditions on the ground remained favorable to North Korea, Stalin understandably focused primarily on the progress of the fighting, waiting to see whether UN forces would break through the encirclement around Pusan before deciding on a further course of action.

The successful American landing at Inchon on September 15, 1950, and the subsequent disintegration of the Communist Korean People's Army transformed the Korean conflict into a serious military crisis for the Soviet Union. Stalin panicked at the advance of American troops into North Korean territory.[10] In this new, far more dangerous situation, the Soviet leader ordered Malik to pursue possible channels for a negotiated settlement,[11] but his attention was focused overwhelmingly on the difficult and urgent task of finding a way to stop the American advance militarily without drawing the Soviet Union into war with the United States.[12]

The dramatic success of the Chinese People's Volunteers (CPV) in turning back the American advance in November 1950 sharply altered Stalin's approach to the war in Korea. On December 7 the Soviet leadership informed Andrei Vyshinskii, Soviet foreign minister and ranking official in the Soviet delegation to the United Nations, that the draft proposal he had submitted to Moscow about a cease-fire in Korea was "incorrect in the present situation, when American troops are suffering defeat and when the Americans more and more often are advancing a proposal about the cessation of military activity in Korea in order to win time and prevent the complete defeat of the American troops." With the unexpected and no doubt welcome sight of the supposedly fearsome American armed forces retreating before the troops of his junior ally, Stalin ordered Vyshinskii to propose instead that all foreign troops be withdrawn from Korea and that the resolution of the Korean question be left to the Korean people themselves, conditions the United States would surely reject.[13] At this point both Moscow and Beijing were euphoric, and Stalin had every reason to prolong the American disgrace.[14]

In early December representatives of India, Great Britain, and Sweden, along with UN Secretary General Trygve Lie, approached the PRC representative at a UN meeting at Lake Success, with a request that he communicate under what conditions it would be possible to end the military operations in Korea. The Chinese leadership drafted a response repeating the five conditions Premier Zhou Enlai had proposed in July: the withdrawal of all foreign troops from Korea; the withdrawal of American troops from the Taiwan Straits and the territory of Taiwan; the Korean question must be resolved by the Korean people themselves; a representative of the People's Republic must participate in the United Nations and the representative of Jiang Jieshi (Chiang Kai-shek) must be excluded; and if these conditions are accepted, the five Great Powers would convene a conference to sign an armistice.[15]

Before replying, however, Zhou Enlai solicited Stalin's opinion on the proposed terms. The Soviet leader replied that he completely agreed with the proposed conditions for a cease-fire in Korea. "We consider that without the satisfaction of these conditions, military activity cannot be ceased." However, apparently aware that such an extreme position would be tactically disadvantageous, Stalin went on to say that

> we consider that you should not be too open and show all your cards too early in front of the representatives of the three states, who frankly speaking, are spies of the U.S.A. We think that the time has not arrived for China to show all its cards, while Seoul is still not liberated. Moreover, the U.S.A could use China's five conditions to box us on the ear by [making] a UN resolution. It is not necessary to give this advantage to the U.S.A.

Drawing on the diplomatic experience he had by then acquired, Stalin advised Zhou to issue a more subtle statement. The Chinese should say simply that they "would welcome the soonest possible conclusion of the military actions in Korea" and therefore "would like to know the opinion of the UN and the U.S.A with regard to conditions for an armistice." They also should add that

> the delegation from England together with the delegation from the U.S.A, France, Norway, Ecuador and Cuba already introduced into the First Committee [of the General Assembly] of the UN a resolution condemning China, thereby hindering the matter of a settlement of the Korean question. In view of this we will eagerly await the opinion of the UN and the U.S.A about the conditions for a cessation of military actions in Korea.[16]

In accordance with Stalin's recommendation, the Chinese were cool toward the resolution Benegal Rau, head of India's delegation to the United Nations, introduced into the First Committee of the General Assembly on December 12 to create a three-person committee to investigate terms for a cease-fire. At this time Mao Zedong also was unwilling to consider a negotiated settlement, as he was eager to press the advantage the Chinese held on the battlefield. He thus ordered the CPV commander, Peng Dehuai, on December 21 to begin a third offensive, speculating to Peng that in face of this offensive, the Americans might ask for a cease-fire. In such a case, Mao informed Peng, he would demand as a first step toward a cease-fire the withdrawal of U.S. forces south of the thirty-eight parallel.[17]

The third offensive was successful. By January 4, 1951, Chinese and North Korean troops were in possession of Seoul, and by January 8 advance units had reached the thirty-seventh parallel. On January 11, at the point of maximum

Chinese advance, Rau's group at the United Nations introduced its proposal for a negotiated settlement. It called for an immediate cease-fire in Korea, with a promise that foreign troops would withdraw gradually from Korea and that a four-power conference (among the Soviet Union, the United States, the United Kingdom, and the People's Republic) would be convened to settle outstanding East Asian questions, including the Taiwan issue and PRC representation in the United Nations.

Before responding to the UN proposal, Zhou Enlai again turned to Stalin for "advice and consultation," as he phrased it.[18] The Soviet leader agreed that the time had come to lay out their terms. On January 17 Zhou accordingly rejected the UN cease-fire proposal, arguing logically that it was "designed to give U.S. troops a breathing space," and set forth instead harsher conditions: that a seven-power conference be held in China, that the People's Republic be installed in the United Nations at the outset of the negotiations, that all foreign troops be withdrawn from Korea, and that a Great Power conference also discuss the removal of American protection of Taiwan.[19] Although the Indian government was willing to pursue negotiations with the People's Republic on the basis of these terms, the United States could not accept the Chinese conditions; thus discussions of a negotiated settlement were abandoned.

It is not difficult to understand that at this point each of the three Communist allies wanted to press for total victory against American and UN troops. The only cautionary note, as far as we know, came from CPV Commander Peng Dehuai, who was concerned about the logistical difficulties of supplying Chinese troops farther down the peninsula and about the lack of air cover for Chinese and North Korean ground forces.[20] Peng was overruled, however, and despite an unexpectedly strong repulse by UN forces in late January, the Communist allies prepared a large-scale offensive for April 1951, which they believed would be the final campaign.[21] As the CPV commanders phrased it in their mobilization order on April 19, "this is the campaign that will determine the fate and length of the Korean War."[22]

The CPV assessment of the significance of this campaign proved correct, for when the spring offensive of April and May 1951 failed to push UN forces farther south and moreover resulted in very high casualties among Chinese and North Korean troops, the Communist allies decided to pursue a negotiated settlement. Russian sources released thus far do not include records of the initial discussions among the allies regarding opening negotiations, but Chinese documents reveal that on June 2, Mao invited Kim Il Sung to visit Beijing to discuss the new strategy, as Kim was reluctant to abandon hope for a total victory.[23]

While Kim was in Beijing, the Soviet Union took steps toward opening negotiations in Korea. We do not know what communications the three leaders had prior to the Soviet initiative, but on June 5 Jacob Malik informed U.S. diplomat George Kennan in a meeting at Malik's home on Long Island that "the Soviet government wanted peace and wanted a peaceful solution of the Korean question – at the earliest possible moment." He advised the United States to "get in touch with the North Koreans and the Chinese Communists in this matter."[24]

A week later Kim Il Sung and Gao Gang, the CCP Northeast Party Secretary noted for his close ties to the Soviet Union, traveled to Moscow to discuss the new situation with Stalin.[25] The Soviet leader was again concerned about the possibility that the weakened position of the Chinese/Korean forces might endanger Soviet interests by exposing the presence of Soviet Air Force units in Korea. On June 13, 1951, he brusquely admonished his air force representative in Beijing to speed up the training of Chinese and Korean pilots, explaining that

> the Chinese troops will not fight without air cover. Therefore it is necessary to create more quickly a group of eight Chinese air fighter divisions and send them to the front. This is now your main task. Belov can send one division closer to the Chinese border in Manchuria, and two divisions can be held in the rear in North Korea, thus freeing up two airports for the Chinese fighter divisions closer to the front. This is absolutely necessary. It is necessary to arrange matters so that the Chinese rely only on their own aviation at the front.[26]

That day Stalin also reported to Mao the results of his conversations that day with Kim and Gao. "Three questions were raised: First – about an armistice. We recognized that an armistice is now advantageous. Second – about military advisers. If they are very necessary to you, then we are ready to satisfy you. Third – about the delivery of arms for sixteen divisions. There will not be objections from our side." Stalin then relayed to Mao his instructions to Gao and Kim regarding the need to deploy additional air force fighter divisions of MiG-15s and added that

> after the end of the conversation we received information that the Anglo-Americans intend to appeal to you and to the Koreans in the name of the sixteen states fighting against Korea with a proposal about an armistice. But before making this proposal they want to strike a blow against our troops. It is possible that this is just rumors, but it is fully possible and probable that this is not simply rumors, but corresponds to reality. We therefore advise you to hold tight the line of defense and not allow the enemy to advance.[27]

It appears, therefore, that pursuing an armistice was only part of Stalin's approach to managing the Communists' newly weakened position on the battlefield; his primary concern was to strengthen the Chinese People's Volunteers and the Korean People's Army and to prevent a U.S./UN advance.

Mao Zedong's reply to Stalin's telegram, in the form of two telegrams sent the same day, indicates more explicitly that seeking an armistice was primarily a means to avoid a new enemy offensive until the Chinese and North Koreans could reinforce their position. Mao's telegram to Gao and Kim informed them that with regard to an armistice, "we consider it advisable for Korea and China to advance this question today, since in the next two months the Korean army and Chinese volunteer troops must occupy a defensive position." Mao explained that:

> in June and July preparations will be carried out intensively. In August we will carry out a stronger operation. If the enemy does not make a large-scale amphibious landing in our rear, then our goal can be achieved. If the enemy does not send new reinforcements to Korea and does not make an amphibious landing, then in August we will be significantly stronger than now.

However, Mao did not want to take the first step toward entering negotiations, apparently out of concern for China's prestige. He therefore instructed Gao and Kim that it was better that they wait for the enemy to make an appeal and for the Soviet government than to "make an inquiry to the American government about an armistice." He asked both men to decide with Stalin whether it was more advisable for the Soviet government to make an inquiry or for Korea and China to express willingness to open negotiations if the enemy put forth a proposal.[28] As conditions for an armistice, Mao listed restoration of the status quo ante and creation of a neutral zone along the thirty-eighth parallel, the most conciliatory terms the Chinese leader ever advanced. He stated that it was possible to omit the question of PRC representation in the United Nations as a condition "since China can refer to the fact that the UN has in fact become an instrument of aggression, and therefore China does not at the present time attach a special significance to the question of entrance into the UN."[29]

To Stalin, Mao wrote that he "had communicated our opinion on the question of an armistice to Comrade Gao Gang in order for him to relay it to you and receive instructions from you. I won't write about it in detail here." He then focused on the plans for the next offensive, writing that "Comrade Peng Dehuai very much needs Soviet advisers on strategy and tactics. It would be desirable if you could send them as soon as possible. With regard to the participation of 8 fighter divisions in battles, in accordance with your advice, I gave an order to the General Staff to draw up a plan."

Responding to Stalin's admonitions to maintain vigilance at the front, Mao informed him that he had given "an order to Comrade Peng Dehuai that our troops firmly hold the line of defense at the second and third defensive lines and create a new defensive line." Returning to the issue of a future offensive, he explained that "the position at the front in June will be such that our forces will be comparatively weaker than those of the enemy. In July we will be stronger than in June and in August we will be even stronger. We will be ready in August to make a stronger blow to the enemy."[30]

The Communist allies apparently agreed with Mao's suggestion that the Soviet Union take the initiative in pursuing negotiations, for on June 23, 1951, Jacob Malik declared in a scheduled address over the UN radio network that "the Soviet peoples further believe that the most acute problem of the present day – the problem of the armed conflict in Korea – could also be settled. This would require the readiness of the parties to enter on the path of a peaceful settlement of the Korean question."

Retreating from the harsher terms the Chinese had laid out in January, Malik declared that "the Soviet peoples believe that as a first step discussions should be started between the belligerents for a cease-fire and armistice providing for the mutual withdrawal of forces from the 38th Parallel."[31] On June 27, in a meeting with U.S. Ambassador Alan G. Kirk in Moscow, Deputy Foreign Minister Andrei Gromyko confirmed the message communicated in Malik's June 23 speech and suggested that the negotiators should confine the discussions to military matters, avoiding political or territorial considerations.[32]

In the heated debate within the Truman administration that followed Malik's initiative, several officials opposed entering negotiations on the grounds that the Communists were only buying time to reinforce their troops. As Air Force Chief of Staff Hoyt Vandenberg put it, "we are now hurting the communists badly and any respite given them by an armistice would only permit them to build up to start fighting again. . . ."[33] However, due largely to the arguments of Secretary of State Dean Acheson, the United States decided to enter negotiations. Military leaders of both sides opened armistice talks at Kaesong on July 10, 1951. As the talks dragged on without producing an agreement, however, the perception that the Communists were not "sincere" in pursuing a negotiated settlement became increasingly predominant in Washington.

For the broader discussion of the Cold War, it is thus important to establish the motives of the Chinese, Soviets, and North Koreans in entering armistice negotiations in July 1951. Without access to the original documents on the Chinese side, the picture is not entirely clear; in some respects the Russian documents seem to contradict accounts written on the basis of published Chinese documents.[34] At this point, however, it appears from the Russian documentary record that the Chinese leadership viewed armistice negotiations in Korea as one tactic in the ongoing struggle of the People's Republic with the United States and its allies, a struggle that would long outlast the conflict in Korea. As Marxist revolutionaries, Mao and his associates viewed their regime as inherently at war with the United States. Therefore, an armistice in Korea was not pursued to restore the warring parties to a state of normal diplomatic relations. Instead it was sought as an expedient that, if achieved on terms favorable to China, could improve the nation's position for the time being by relieving it of the burden of fighting in Korea.

The party leadership defined China's new policy toward the war as "negotiating while fighting." According to the memoirs of Nie Rongzhen, the acting chief of staff, when the Central Committee met to consider what course to take following the failed fifth offensive of April–May 1951:

> most of the comrades present at the meeting felt that our forces should stop in the vicinity of the 38th Parallel, continue fighting during the armistice talks, and strive to settle the issue through negotiations. . . . Of course, should the war continue, we had nothing to fear and would grow stronger in the fight – but not without difficulty. With Comrade Mao Zedong presiding, the meeting finally endorsed the policy of simultaneously fighting and negotiating, a policy which we conscientiously carried out.[35]

In other words, since the war had become difficult, they would seek to end it through a negotiated settlement. However, if favorable terms could not be achieved, they would continue to fight, despite the cost; Beijing maintained this policy for the remainder of the war.

Mao's telegrams from late June and early July 1951 provide further evidence that he was preparing for future military operations in Korea while simultaneously pursuing a negotiated settlement to the conflict. On June 21 Mao asked Stalin to consider the applications for additional armaments and supplies he had sent via Gao and to deliver these goods from July through the end of the year "so that the various military units in the Korean theater of military operations receive replenishment according to . . . what is advantageous for the conduct of military operations."[36] On June 26 Stalin replied affirmatively to a telegram from Mao that informed him that the government of the PRC intends to send fighter divisions armed with MiG-15s to Korea for participation in the military actions, which will be much better than sending divisions armed with MiG-9 planes. It is therefore necessary in the course of one and a half to two months to retrain the 6th, 12th, and 14th fighter divisions, which are armed with MiG-9s, on MiG-15s, with a calculation of sending them to the front in September 1951.[37]

On June 28 General Stepan Krasovskii, Stalin's representative in Beijing, reported to the Soviet leader that at a meeting on June 27, "Comrade Mao Zedong expressed the opinion that the 6th, 12th and 14th fighter aviation divisions, which have been trained on MiG-9s, must retrain on MiG-15s before being sent to the front. The period of retraining was established as one and one half to two months, so that these divisions could take part in the forthcoming operations in Korea."[38]

On July 2, 1951, eight days before negotiations began, Mao Zedong instructed Peng Dehuai, Gao Gang, and Kim Il Sung that "the period of preparations for and conduct of negotiations with representatives of the enemy will occupy approximately 10–14 days" and asked them during this period

to make every effort to increase the personnel of the front line units and especially to replenish them with arms and ammunition. . . . It is necessary to be prepared for the fact that after the signing of an agreement on cessation of military operations it will be impossible to transfer the aforementioned personnel and armaments. . . . I ask you to think about what could occur after the signing of an agreement on cessation of military operations and be prepared for everything that needs to be done.[39]

The first weeks of the negotiations focused on establishing the agenda and determining the demarcation line that would separate North and South Korea. The UN command first insisted on using the current front line, which ran to the north of the thirty-eighth parallel, as the demarcation line, then made an unreasonable proposal to use a line deep in the Chinese/North Korean rear as the new boundary. This proposal angered and offended the Chinese delegation, who countered with a proposal to designate the thirty-eighth parallel as the demarcation line, since the battle line was constantly shifting north and south of that line. However, a telegram from the Chinese delegation at Kaesong on August 12, addressing the impasse reached on this issue, reveals an assumption that reaching an armistice agreement on acceptable terms would provide time to rebuild Chinese/North Korean forces before renewing the struggle in Korea. The negotiators informed Mao Zedong that having studied, on the basis of the limited materials we have, the general world situation, the needs of our state and the fact that at present Korea cannot continue the war, we think that it is better to think over the question of cessation of military operations at the present front line than to carry on the struggle for the 38th parallel and bring the conference to a breakdown. In connection with this it is necessary to take into consideration that it is possible to gain some concessions from the enemy in the discussion of the proposal about cessation of military operations at the present front line. Thus it will be possible to secure 3–5 years' time for preparation of forces. Of course, if the enemy does not in any way abandon his unfounded proposal, which he is at present insisting on, then we also intend to choose only the path of a schism.[40]

On August 23, 1951, the North Korean and Chinese delegation suspended the negotiations over allegations that UN troops had violated the neutrality of Kaesong.[41] Beijing did not, however, wish a permanent rupture in the talks, apparently still calculating that an armistice was in its favor as long as it was on terms not insulting to China. In Mao Zedong's report to Stalin on August 27, he explained that "if after some period of time the situation will develop so that the enemy wishes to renew the negotiations, then we think that at our own initiative we can propose a way which would lead to a turn in the negotiations and to force the enemy to agree with this."[42]

Stalin also wished the negotiations to continue, but for somewhat different reasons. In response to Mao's telegram, he informed the chairman on August 28 that

we agree with your evaluation of the present condition of the negotiations in Kaesong and with your [policy] line about the necessity of getting a satisfactory answer to the question of the incident provoked by the Americans to pressure the Chinese-Korean side. As before, with regard to this we will proceed from the fact that the Americans have greater need to continue the negotiations. We do not see the use in inviting, according to your initiative, representatives of neutral states to participate in the negotiations as monitors and witnesses during the present period of negotiations. The negative side of this is that the Americans will view it as [an indication] that the Chinese-Korean side has more need to quickly reach an agreement about an armistice than do the Americans. If you are of such an opinion on this question, then you must communicate this to Comrade Kim Il Sung.[43]

Stalin and the Korean Stalemate

After the initial opportunity for a negotiated settlement collapsed in August 1951, Stalin considered it in the Soviet interests for the war to continue, as long as there was no danger that U.S./UN troops would advance into North Korea again. After the war was reduced to a stalemate, it benefited the Soviet Union in several ways. It tied down American forces, rendering the United States less able to engage in military action in Europe; it drained American economic resources; and it caused political difficulties for the Truman administration. It also provided the Soviet Union with a superb opportunity to gather intelligence on U.S. military technology and organization. And the war in Korea created great hostility between the Chinese and Americans and thus tied the People's Republic more firmly to Moscow.

It is true that the North Korean attack on South Korea in June 1950 brought negative consequences to the Soviet Union as it prompted a massive American military buildup, solidified NATO, and made possible the rearmament of Germany. But the outbreak of the war brought about this damage to Soviet interests. By mid-1951 it appeared that Moscow had more to gain than to lose by encouraging the Chinese to continue fighting in Korea. Russian documents indicate that Stalin's main concern regarding the negotiations was to ensure that the Chinese/North Korean side not give an impression of weakness, since the benefits to the Soviet Union would accrue only if the war continued to be a stalemate. However, if the U.S./UN side were to go on the offensive, either militarily or diplomatically, Soviet interests could be harmed.

After the negotiations resumed on October 25, 1951, Stalin repeated the line on the talks he had enunciated in August. Mao Zedong informed Stalin on November 14 that since he expected that the talks would be drawn out for another half year or year, the People's Republic had taken steps

> toward economizing on our human and material forces in the Korean theater of military operations and we are pursuing the tactics of a long, active defense, with the goal of holding the position we presently occupy and inflicting great manpower losses on the enemy, in order to gain victory in the war. . . . It is true that achieving peace as a result of the negotiations is advantageous for us, but we also are not afraid of dragging out the negotiations. Acting thus, we will surely be able to achieve victory. At the same time we will be able successfully to carry out various measures within the country and secure stabilization and further development in the area of politics and the economy.[44]

Stalin replied:

> [W]e agree with your evaluation of the present condition of the negotiations. The entire course of the negotiations for some time past shows that although the Americans are dragging out the negotiations, nonetheless they have more need of rapidly concluding them. This results from the overall international situation. We consider it correct that the Chinese/Korean side, using flexible tactics in the negotiations, continue to pursue a hard line, not showing haste and not displaying interest in a rapid end to the negotiations.[45]

In a telegram to Pyongyang five days later, Stalin revealed his concern for avoiding the appearance of weakness. On November 19 he instructed the Soviet ambassador to North Korea to advise the Koreans that "an appeal by the government of the DPRK [Democratic People's Republic of Korea] to the General Assembly and to the Security Council as it is set forth in your telegram . . . could be evaluated in the present situation, in conditions of blackmail by the Americans, as a sign of weakness on the Chinese/Korean side, which is politically disadvantageous."[46] On December 25, 1951, Deputy Foreign Minister Andrei Gromyko proposed to Stalin that it would be disadvantageous for the Chinese–North Korean command to publish a communiqué exposing the Americans' position in the negotiations (as Andrei Vyshinskii had proposed) because such a communiqué "can be evaluated as a sign of their [the United Nations'] weakness."[47]

On February 3, 1952, Stalin repeated his earlier terse instructions to Mao regarding the negotiations, which apparently were calculated to ensure that the talks would continue. In response to a lengthy telegram laying out the proposed positions of the People's Republic regarding numerous specific negotiating points, Stalin said simply:

> [W]e agree with the plan outlined by you and the evaluation of the course of the negotiations which you give. The firm position taken by you has already given positive results and must force the enemy to make further concessions. We consider that you must make an agreement with the leading comrades of Poland and Czechoslovakia about including their representatives in the commission of observers, and they, of course, will agree with this.[48]

On July 17 Stalin was even more laconic, writing to Mao only that "we consider your position in the negotiations on an armistice to be completely correct. Today we received a report from Pyongyang that Comrade Kim Il Sung also agrees with your position."[49]

In mid-1952, as American bombing of North Korea escalated, Mao Zedong still was willing to continue the war until China secured favorable terms in a settlement. As he explained to Kim Il Sung in a telegram on July 18, "at present, when the enemy is subjecting us to furious bombardment, accepting a provocational and fraudulent proposal from the enemy, which does not signify in fact any kind of concession, is highly disadvantageous for us." Only one negative consequence would follow from rejecting the enemy's proposal, Mao argued: The Korean people and the Chinese people's volunteers would suffer further casualties. However, these sacrifices were strengthening the people of China and Korea and inspiring "the peace-loving peoples of the whole world," which "limits the mobility of the main forces of American imperialism." Furthermore, the Chinese and Korean sacrifice is delaying a new world war because it allows the Soviet Union to "strengthen its reconstruction" and "exercise its influence on the development of the revolutionary movement of peoples of all countries."

Mao went on to inform Kim that the Chinese leadership had concluded that accepting the enemy's proposal "under the influence of its bombardment" would be interpreted as a sign of weakness. Doing so would lead only to "new provocations" that, given the "disadvantageous position" of the Communist forces, would likely result in even greater losses, severe enough that "the whole game will be lost." Instead, Mao maintained that "if we display resolution not to accept the enemy's proposal and to prepare ourselves for a breakdown in the negotiations from the side of the enemy, the enemy surely will not cause a breakdown in the negotiations."

Furthermore, "decisive insistence by our side on our point of view" may lead the enemy to make a new concession. If however, the enemy does not do so or breaks off the negotiations, "we must continue military operations so as to find in the course of the war, which the enemy cannot resolve, a means for changing the present situation." Mao concluded by informing Kim that the Chinese would report their proposal to Stalin and then communicate his opinion to the Koreans.[50]

Zhou Enlai discussed Beijing's proposed strategy toward the armistice negotiations with Stalin the following month, when a Chinese delegation traveled to Moscow to discuss continued economic and military support to the People's Republic. The Russian transcripts of the three discussions between Zhou and Stalin that took place between August 20 and September 19 reveal that the Chinese leaders were by then more eager to reach an armistice settlement than they had been in July. Stalin, on the other hand, continued to press for continuation of the war. Neither leader, however, pursued his goal in a straightforward manner. Instead, reflecting the complexity of the relationship between the two Communist governments, Stalin and Zhou circled warily around the issue of a negotiated settlement in Korea, trying to avoid open disagreement without compromising their individual aims.

Stalin began by framing the prisoner-of-war (POW) issue as a question of whether Mao would give in to the Americans, who were defying international law in their insistence on voluntary repatriation. Zhou replied deftly that the (North) Koreans wanted to accept the American proposal because they wished to end the war but that the Americans were trying to drive a wedge between China and Korea. Zhou added that Mao believed that continuing the war was advantageous because it prevented the United States from preparing for a new world war, an assertion to which Stalin eagerly agreed.

Zhou then stated that they could not yield to the Americans. Stalin, however, by now in a more favorable position, replied that if the Americans "back down a little, then you can accept, assuming that negotiations will continue on questions still unresolved." Zhou parried with a strong statement of agreement, adding that "if the Americans don't want peace, then we must be prepared to continue the war, even if it were to take another year." Zhou also repeated Stalin's analysis that "this war is getting on America's nerves and that the U.S.A. is not ready for a world war." Boosting the revolutionary credentials of the new Communist state, Zhou added that "China, by playing the vanguard role in this war, is helping to stave off the war for 15–20 years, assuming that [our forces] will succeed in containing the American offensive in Korea. Then the U.S.A. will not be able to unleash a third world war at all."

Stalin replied by raising the ante, asserting that the

> Americans are not capable of waging a large-scale war at all, especially after the Korean war. All of their strength lies in air power and the atom bomb. Britain won't fight for America. America cannot defeat little Korea. One must be firm when dealing with America. The Chinese comrades must know that if America does not lose this war, then China will never recapture Taiwan. Americans are merchants. Every American soldier is a speculator, occupied with buying and selling. Germans conquered France in 20 days. It's been already two years, and the U.S.A has still not subdued little Korea. What kind of strength is that? America's primary weapons, [Stalin said jokingly,] are stockings, cigarettes and other merchandise. They want to subjugate the world, yet they cannot subdue little Korea. No, Americans don't know how to fight. After the Korean war, in particular, they have lost the capability to wage a large-scale war. They are pinning

their hopes on the atom bomb and air power. But one cannot win a war with that. One needs infantry, and they don't have much infantry; the infantry they do have is weak. They are fighting with little Korea, and already people are weeping in the U.S.A. What will happen if they start a large-scale war? Then, perhaps, everyone will weep.[51]

Stalin's bombast about America's supposed weakness seems to have been too much for Zhou, however, as the latter abruptly changed his tone, proposing that if the United States

makes some sort of compromises, even if they are small, then they should accept. If America does not agree to return all POWs and proposes a smaller number, then they should accept the offer, under the condition that the question of the remaining POWs will be resolved under mediation by some neutral country, like India, or the remaining POWs transferred to this neutral country until the question is resolved.

Stalin countered with a proposal that if the Americans are holding back a certain percentage of POWs, then North Korea and China would do likewise until a final solution was agreed upon. He also added that if these proposals were unsuccessful, the Chinese could resort to mediation. "The main thing here is to propose a cease-fire," Stalin inconsistently concluded.

Zhou then wrapped up the discussion of the armistice negotiations by outlining three possible strategies.

First – announce from the beginning that they will hold back the same percentage of South Korean and American POWs as the percentage of North Koreans and Chinese held back by America, and leave it at that. Second – resort to mediation by a neutral country. Third – sign an armistice agreement by putting off the POW question and resuming its discussion afterwards.

Without reaching any decision about which of the three strategies to pursue, Zhou turned the discussion to questions of Soviet military assistance to China, arguing that this aid was particularly needed inasmuch as the Chinese government was preparing for the possibility of another two to three years of war.[52]

The same basic dynamic underlaid Zhou's final conversation with Stalin on September 19. The Chinese foreign minister attempted to explore the possibility for a negotiated settlement in Korea without rupturing Beijing's relations with Moscow, while Stalin sought to discourage Chinese agreement to armistice terms but without saying so openly. Stalin began by informing Zhou that the Soviet delegation at the United Nations would reject the proposal advanced by Mexico concerning exchange of POWs, since it conformed to the American position in the negotiations. Instead, the Soviet Union would repeat its call for an immediate cease-fire, withdrawal of all foreign troops, and a political settlement to be reached by "Koreans themselves under the observation of a committee" whose composition could be discussed further. Stalin also informed Zhou that the Soviet delegation would leave "in Mao Zedong's hands" the response to the proposal to withhold temporarily 20 percent of POWs from each side while returning the remaining POWs.

Zhou then raised the question of the third strategy outlined on August 20, asking Stalin's opinion about whether it was possible to accept the proposal then under discussion to transfer POWs to a neutral country so that their fate could be decided separate from an armistice. Stalin answered that the Soviet Union also wanted the return of all POWs, but that "if an agreement cannot be reached on this basis, we cannot deliver the POWs to the UN because the UN is a military participant in the war." Stalin asked Zhou to which country the Chinese proposed to send the prisoners. When Zhou answered with the plausible proposal that India would serve this function, Stalin questioned who would cover the expenses of maintaining the prisoners. Zhou replied rather vaguely that the POWs would "after some time" be transferred to China and then the Chinese and Koreans would cover their expenses.

Stalin admitted that Zhou's proposal could be acceptable but at the same time attempted to dissuade him by cautioning that they "must keep in mind that the Americans will not want to deliver all the POWs, that they will keep some captives, with the intention to recruit them" as spies. Zhou agreed with this warning but nonetheless pressed for a specific strategy with which to end the war, suggesting a cease-fire with resolution of the POW question to come later. He reminded Stalin that he had agreed with this strategy if no agreement were reached about the percentage of POWs to be withheld. Stalin avoided committing himself to this resolution, however. He acknowledged that "this can be considered as one of possible scenarios, but America is not likely to agree to it." Zhou countered by saying that the United States might suggest such a resolution; when Stalin agreed that this would be good, the two turned to other issues.[53] Thus the discussion ended without clear agreement on strategy for ending the war.

According to the records released thus far by the Russian Presidential Archive, Stalin's final instruction to Mao regarding the war in Korea was his puzzling comment on December 27, 1952, before discussing the latest Chinese request for armaments, that Mao's observations about the probability of an American attack in the spring of 1953 reflect the plans of the present American command in Korea, who are operating under the leadership of the Truman government. It is fully possible that these plans will be changed by the Eisenhower government in the direction of less tension on the front in Korea. Nevertheless, you are acting correctly when you count on the worst and proceed from the probability of an attack by the Americans.[54]

In light of the hard line toward communism Eisenhower maintained during the presidential campaign, Stalin's assessment seems illogical; it perhaps reflects his estimation of the general as more "realistic" than the civilian Truman.[55] At any rate, advising the Chinese to prepare for a new American attack served to maintain the status quo in Korea.

Stalin's death on March 5, 1953, resulted in a radical change in the Soviet approach to the Korean War and hence in the position of the Chinese and North Koreans as well, as they were dependent on Soviet support and therefore subordinate to Moscow's directions. Despite the great uncertainty and anxiety within which the new collective leadership operated, it nonetheless moved immediately to bring an end to the war in Korea. On March 19 the Council of Ministers adopted a lengthy resolution on the war, with attached letters to Mao Zedong and Kim Il Sung. In tortuously convoluted language reflecting the great psychological difficulty of altering the policy pursued by Stalin, the resolution declared that

> the Soviet Government has reached the conclusion that it would be incorrect to continue the line on this question which has been followed until now, without making those alterations in that line which correspond to the present political situation and which ensue from the deepest interests of our peoples, the peoples of the USSR, China and Korea. . . .

It went on to outline statements that should be made by Kim Il Sung, Peng Dehuai, the government of the People's Republic, and the Soviet delegation at the United Nations indicating their willingness to resolve the outstanding issues in order to reach an armistice agreement.[56]

The sea change in Moscow that followed Stalin's death was not accompanied, of course, by a corresponding shift within the People's Republic. However, the leadership change in Moscow necessarily affected Chinese strategy since the People's Republic could not pursue the war without continued Soviet support. Furthermore, Russian evidence suggests that the Chinese leadership saw

Stalin's death as an opportunity to bring the war to an end. According to an internal history of the Korean War written by the Soviet Foreign Ministry in 1966, when Zhou discussed plans to end the war while in Moscow for Stalin's funeral, he "urgently proposed that the Soviet side assist the speeding up of the negotiations and the conclusion of an armistice."[57] Thus it appears that Stalin's desire to continue the war had compelled the Chinese to prolong the struggle longer than they wished.

Russian documents also reveal, however, that Mao made a remarkably bellicose statement to an official of the Soviet embassy in Beijing on July 29, after the armistice had been concluded. He declared that

> from a purely military point of view it would not be bad to continue to strike the Americans for approximately another year in order to occupy more favorable borders along the Changan River. Further movement to the south would risk stretching out the flanks in the west and east shore of Korea. In this case the danger of landings in the rear of the Chinese-Korean troops would grow significantly.[58]

This statement may well have been a case of posturing before the Soviets; we must learn the context of the discussion before we can determine the meaning of this statement.

What can we conclude at this point about why the Korean War was prolonged for two years after the opening of armistice negotiations? Unreasonable American demands were partly responsible,[59] as they particularly affected PRC calculations of its needs for international prestige and revolutionary momentum. Mao Zedong apparently would have been willing to reach a negotiated settlement as early as mid-1951 if he could have secured acceptable terms. The failure of the UN command to press their advantage in the summer of 1951 was also a factor. We cannot know, of course, whether a UN offensive would have succeeded, but we do know that following the failed offensive of April/May 1951, the Communist allies considered themselves so vulnerable that they were forced to initiate negotiations in order to buy time.

The leadership of the Democratic People's Republic of Korea apparently wanted to end the war by 1952, but its views were overridden by Beijing and Moscow. Likewise, the Chinese wished to reach a negotiated settlement by late 1952 but were unable to bring Stalin around to their position. On the Communist side, the fundamental factor in prolonging the war appears to have been Stalin's calculation by mid-1951 that it was advantageous to the Soviet Union. Viewed in the perspective of the Soviet international position as a whole, the stalemate in Korea produced several beneficial results. It tied down American forces while providing an excellent opportunity for gathering intelligence on

American military capabilities. It drained American economic resources and weakened the Truman administration. While the Soviet Union was still recovering from World War II, the bloody conflict in Korea made it much less likely that America could begin a full-scale war against it. Although the prolongation of the Korean War taxed Soviet industrial capacities, it deepened the dependence of the People's Republic on Soviet military and economic assistance. It thus lessened the danger that Mao Zedong would follow the path of Marshal Tito in Yugoslavia, an eventuality that ranked among Stalin's greatest fears, second only, perhaps, to a premature war with the United States.

Notes

1. For analyses of the Korean War based on the new evidence from China and Russia, see Chen Jian, *China's Road to the Korean War: The Making of the Sino-American Confrontation* (New York: Columbia University Press, 1994); Sergei N. Goncharov, John W. Lewis, and Xue Litai, *Uncertain Partners: Stalin, Mao and the Korean War* (Stanford: Stanford University Press, 1993); the article and translated documents by Alexandre Mansourov in *Cold War International History Project (CWIHP) Bulletin* 6–7 (Winter 1995/1996): 94–107, 108–19; William Stueck, *The Korean War: An International History* (Princeton: Princeton University Press, 1995); Shu Guang Zhang, *Mao's Military Romanticism: China and the Korean War, 1950–1953* (Lawrence, Kans.: University of Kansas Press, 1995); articles by this author in *CWIHP Bulletin* 3 (Fall 1993): 1, 14–18; 5 (Spring 1995): 1, 2–9; 6–7 (Winter 1995/1996): 30–84; *Journal of American East-Asian Relations* 2, no. 4 (Winter 1993): 425–58.

2. James Sheply, "How Dulles Averted War," *Life* January 16, 1956, 70–2; Dwight D. Eisenhower, *The White House Years: Mandate for Change, 1953–1956* (Garden City, N.Y.: Doubleday and Co., 1963), 179–80. For scholarly analyses of nuclear threats during the Korean War, see Roger Dingman, "Atomic Diplomacy During the Korean War," *International Security* 13, no. 3 (Winter 1988/1989): 50–91; Rosemary Foot, "Nuclear Coercion and the Ending of the Korean Conflict," *International Security* 13, no. 3 (Winter 1988/1989): 92–112.

3. Information about the Soviet air war in Korea was tightly guarded throughout the remainder of the Soviet period, as was all information about Soviet participation in the war. However, a substantial portion of the records on the Korean War in the archive of the Soviet General Staff has been declassified. For the first scholarly examination of these records, see Mark O'Neill, "The Other Side of the Yalu: Soviet Pilots in the Korean War Phase One, November 1950–April 1951," Ph.D. diss., Florida State University, 1996.

4. According to British journalist Paul Lashmar, who conducted extensive research in Russia on Soviet military involvement in the Korean War for a 1996 BBC documentary, "Korea, Russia's Secret War," the Soviets were particularly interested in gaining information on U.S. command and tactical structures from air force prisoners of war. In the spring of 1951, when F-86s replaced F-100s in the air war in Korea, the Soviet Union organized over seventy search teams to find and retrieve equipment from the new planes. Lashmar concluded that at least two F-86 airplanes downed in Korea were taken to the Soviet Union, along with related equipment such as G-suits and radar gun sights. American helicopters, tank equipment, and technology from the B-29 airplane also were transported from Korea to military institutes in Moscow. As the MiG-15 was essentially a World War II–generation airplane, Lashmar concludes that access to the latest American military technology captured in Korea played an important role in the subsequent development of Soviet military capability.

5. For translations of many of the documents that support these claims, see *CWIHP Bulletin* 6–7 (Winter 1995/1996); photocopies of the Soviet documents are on deposit as part of the CWIHP–National Security Archive Russian and East-Bloc Documents Database (READD) at the National Security Archive in Washington.

6. William Stueck, *The Korean War: An International History* (Princeton: Princeton University Press, 1995).

7. Kathryn Weathersby, "The Soviet Role in the Early Phase of the Korean War: New Documentary Evidence," *Journal of American-East Asian Relations* 2, no. 4 (Winter 1993): 425–58.

8. The only explanation the archival record has thus far provided for Stalin's decision to approve Kim's request is his statement to Mao Zedong in mid-May 1950 that because of the "changed international situation" it would be possible to support the plan of "our Korean friends"; see Stalin (Filippov) to Mao, 14 May 1950, trans. in *CWIHP Bulletin* 4 (Fall 1994): 60–1. For texts and discussion of the documents on Soviet decision making regarding an attack on South Korea, see Kathryn Weathersby, "To Attack or Not to Attack? Stalin, Kim Il Sung and the Prelude to War," *CWIHP Bulletin* 5 (Spring 1995): 1–9.

9. Rosemary Foot, *A Substitute for Victory* (Ithaca, N.Y.: Cornell University Press, 1990), 20–4; Stueck, *The Korean War,* 50–84.

10. Weathersby, "Soviet Role in the Early Phase of the Korean War," 458.

11. On September 28 Malik's assistant, Tsarapkin, was instructed to inform an American intermediary named Lancaster that Soviet UN Ambassador Adam Malik would meet with a representative of the U.S. State Department to discuss the situation in Korea. The order specified that "Malik must listen to the State Department representative, and if it becomes obvious that the Americans are making a step toward a peaceful settlement of the Korean question, [he must] tell him that he [Malik] will consider the questions raised in the conversation and will give an answer at the next meeting." Ciphered telegram from Andrei Gromyko, Deputy Minister of Foreign Affairs, to Andrei Vyshinskii in New York. Archive of the President of the Russian Federation (APRF), fond (f.) 3, opis (op.) 65, delo (d.) 827, p. 97.

12. For a discussion of and documents concerning Stalin's communications with Mao Zedong and Kim Il Sung about Chinese entry into the war, see Mansourov's *CWIHP Bulletin* article; Chen, *China's Road to the Korean War;* Goncharov, Lewis, and Xue, *Uncertain Partners.* For Stalin's communications with Kim Il Sung in September and October 1950, see Weathersby, "Soviet Role in the Early Phase of the Korean War."

13. Politburo directive to Vyshinskii, December 7, 1950, Archive of the Foreign Policy of the Russian Federation (AVPRF), f. 059a, op. 5a, [pa.] 11, d. 5, pp. 7–8.

14. Among several exchanges between Moscow and Beijing during this victorious period, one of the most interesting is a telegram Stalin sent to Mao on December 1 thanking him for the information he sent about

> the successful offensive of the Chinese People's Liberation Army [*not* the People's Volunteers] in Korea. Your successes gladden not only me and my comrades in the leadership, but also all Soviet people. Allow me to greet from the soul you and your friends in the leadership, the People's Liberation Army of China and the entire Chinese people in connection with these enormous successes in their struggle against the American troops. I have no doubt that in the war against the up-to-date and well-armed American army the Chinese army will receive great experience in contemporary warfare and will turn itself into a fully up-to-date, well-armed, formidable army, just as the Soviet Army in the struggle with the first-class-armed German army received experience in contemporary warfare and turned into an up-to-date well-equipped army.

APRF, f. 45, op. 1, d. 336, p. 5.

15. Ciphered telegram to Moscow from Soviet Ambassador in Beijing N. V. Roshchin, December 7, 1950, APRF, f. 45, op. 1, d. 336, 17–19; AVPRF, f. 059a, op. 5a, pa. 11, d. 3, pp. 193–5. See also *CWIHP Bulletin* 6–7 (Winter 1995/1996): 51.

16. Ciphered telegram from Deputy Foreign Minister Gromyko to the Soviet ambassador in Beijing, relaying the message from Stalin to Zhou Enlai, December 7, 1950, AVPRF, f. 059a, op. 5a, pa. 11, d. 3, pp. 196–7.

17. Chen Jian, "China's Strategies to End the Korean War," paper presented at the Cold War International History Project conference, Hong Kong, January 1996, 9.

18. Ciphered telegram from Soviet Ambassador Roshchin in Beijing to the Ministry of Foreign Affairs, communicating Zhou's "great thanks to comrade Filippov [Stalin] for the advice and consultation," AVPRF, f. 059a, op. 5a, pa. 11, d. 13.

19. Foot, *A Substitute for Victory,* 29–30.

20. For a discussion of Mao's motives, see Chen, "China's Strategies to End the Korean War," 8–12.

21. In a telegram to Peng Dehuai on January 28, 1951, Mao referred to this campaign as "the last, fifth, operation of decisive importance." For the texts of this telegram and other communications regarding the preparations for the spring 1951 offensive, see the translations by this author in *CWIHP Bulletin* 6 (Winter 1995/1996).

22. Chen, "China's Strategies to End the Korean War," 13, citing Shen Zhonghong and Meng Zhaohui, *Zhongguo Renmin Zhiyuanjun kangMei yuanChao zhanshi,* [A history of the war to resist America and assist Korea by the Chinese People's Volunteers] (Beijing: Junshi Kexue, 1988), 93.

23. Ibid., 13.

24. *Foreign Relations of the United States (FRUS),* 1951, vol. 7, part 1, 507–11.

25. In his telegram to Stalin on June 5 requesting permission for Gao and Kim to travel to Moscow, Mao Zedong asked that they discuss "the financial question, the question of the conduct of military operations directly at the front, the question of the danger of a possible enemy landing on the sea coast in our rear," APRF, f. 45, op. 1, d. 339, p. 23.

26. Ciphered telegram from Filippov [Stalin] to Krasovsky in Beijing, June 13, 1951. APRF, f. 45, op. 1, d. 339, p. 47, and AVPRF, f. 059a, op. 5a, pa. 11, d. 5, p. 33. General Belov was chief of staff for the Soviet First Air Army and commander of the 64th Fighter Air Corps.

27. Ciphered telegram from Filippov [Stalin] to Roshchin in Beijing, for transmission to Mao Zedong, June 13, 1951, AVPRF, f. 059a, op. 5a, pa. 11, d. 5, pp. 31–2. See also *CWIHP Bulletin* 6–7 (Winter 1995/1996): 60–1.

28. This exchange contradicts the conclusion drawn by Rosemary Foot, from a statement by the counselor at the Indian embassy in Beijing, that neither the Chinese nor the North Koreans "were entirely enamored with Malik's peace proposal" of June 23. See Foot, *A Substitute for Victory,* 37.

29. Ciphered telegram from Mao Zedong to Gao Gang and Kim Il Sung, June 13, 1951, AVPRF, f. 059a, op. 5a, pa. 11, d. 5, pp. 35–7. This document and the documents cited in notes 30, 36–50, 54, and 56 are translated in full in *CWIHP Bulletin* 6–7 (Winter 1995/1996): 61–83.

30. Ciphered telegram from Mao Zedong to Filippov [Stalin], June 13, 1951, AVPRF, f. 059a, op. 5a, pa. 11, d. 5, p. 34.

31. *FRUS,* 1951, vol. 7, part 1, 546–7.

32. Ibid., 560–1.

33. Ibid., 567–8.

34. E.g., Chen, "China's Strategies to End the Korean War"; Shu Guang Zhang, *Mao's Military Romanticism,* chap. 8.

35. Nie Rongzhen, *Inside the Red Star: The Memoirs of Marshal Nie Rongzhen* (Beijing: New World Press, 1988), 641.

36. Ciphered telegram from Mao Zedong to Filippov [Stalin], June 21, 1951, APRF, f. 45, op. 1, d. 339, pp. 64–5.

37. Ciphered telegram from Filippov [Stalin] to Krasovsky in Beijing, APRF, f. 45, op. 1, d. 339, p. 81, and AVPRF, f. 059a, op. 5a, pa. 11, d. 5, p. 39.

38. Ciphered telegram from Krasovsky in Beijing to Filippov [Stalin], APRF, f. 45, op. 1, d. 339, pp. 85–6, and AVPRF, f. 059a, op. 5a, pa. 11, d. 5, pp. 40–1.

39. Ciphered telegram from Mao Zedong to Filippov [Stalin] on July 3, 1951, sending him the text of his telegram of July 2 to Peng Dehuai, Gao Gang, and Kim Il Sung, APRF, f. 45, op. 1, d. 339, pp. 14–15.

40. Ciphered telegram from Mao Zedong to Filippov [Stalin] sending him the telegram he received from Li Kenong on August 12, APRF, f. 45, op. 1, d. 341, pp. 56–8.

41. The Chinese and North Koreans claimed that United Nations Command (UNC) aircraft bombed and strafed the conference site on the night of August 22. Two UNC officers immediately investigated the site and reported that the evidence of an attack was inconclusive. The incident remains murky, but Russian documents indicate that, whatever actually happened, the Chinese leadership did believe that UNC aircraft had attacked the negotiation site.

42. Ciphered telegram from Mao Zedong to Filippov [Stalin], August 27, 1951, APRF, f. 45, op. 1, d. 340, 86–8, and AVPRF, f. 059a, op. 5a, pa. 11, d. 5, pp. 51–3.

43. Politburo decision of August 28, 1951, to adopt the following text of Comrade Filippov's answer to Mao Zedong (Protocol #83), APRF, f. 3, op. 65, d. 829, pp. 4–5, and AVPRF, f. 059a, op. 5a, pa. 11, d. 5, pp. 54–5. The telegram was sent to Beijing on August 29, APRF, f. 45, op. 1, d. 340, p. 89.

44. Ciphered telegram from Mao Zedong to Filippov [Stalin], November 14, 1951, APRF, f. 45, op. 1, d. 342, pp. 16–19.

45. Politburo decision of November 19, 1951, approving the attached answer to Comrade Mao Zedong, APRF, f. 3, op. 65, d. 828 [9], pp. 42–3, and AVPRF, f. 059a, op. 5a, pa. 11, d. 5, pp. 64.

46. CC decision of November 19, 1951, to adopt the attached draft instruction to Comrade Razuvaev, APRF, f. 3, op. 65, d. 829, pp. 44–5, and AVPRF, f. 059a, op. 5a, pa. 11, d. 5, pp. 65–6.

47. Note from A. Gromyko to Stalin, December 25, 1951, APRF, f. 3, op. 65, d. 829, pp. 94–7, and AVPRF, f. 059a, op. 5a, pa. 11, d. 5, pp. 76–7.

48. Ciphered telegram to Krasovsky in Beijing from Filippov [Stalin] transmitting text of a message for Mao Zedong, APRF, f. 45, op. 1, d. 342, p. 78, and AVPRF, f. 059a, op. 5a, pa. 11, d. 5, p. 80.

49. Ciphered telegram from Filippov [Stalin] to Krasovsky in Beijing, transmitting a message for Mao Zedong, APRF, f. 45, op. 1, d. 348, 69, and AVPRF, f. 059a, op. 5a, pa. 11, d. 5, p. 89.

50. Ciphered telegram from Mao Zedong to Filippov [Stalin], July 18, 1952, APRF, f. 45, op. 1, d. 343, pp. 72–5, and AVPRF, f. 059a, op. 5a, pa. 11, d. 5, pp. 90–3.

51. Record of conversation between Comrade I. V. Stalin and Zhou Enlai, August 20, 1952, APRF, f. 45, op. 1, d. 329, pp. 54–72. Translated by Danny Rozas, *CWIHP Bulletin* 6–7 (Winter 1995/1996): 10–14.

52. Ibid., 13–14.

53. Record of conversation between Comrade Stalin and Zhou Enlai, September 19, 1952, APRF, f. 45, op. 1, d. 343, pp. 97–103. Translated by Danny Rozas with Kathryn Weathersby, *CWIHP Bulletin* 6–7 (Winter 1995/1996): 17–20.

54. Ciphered telegram from Semenov [Stalin] to Mao Zedong, APRF, f. 45, op. 1, d. 343, pp. 115–16.

55. In discussions on February 17, 1953, with Krishna Menon, Indian ambassador to Moscow, and Saffrudin Kitchlew, chairman of the pro-Soviet Indian Peace Council, Stalin was generally upbeat about the international situation, crediting General Eisenhower with greater realism than the civilian Truman; see Vojtech Mastny, *The Cold War and Soviet Insecurity: The Stalin Years* (New York: Oxford University Press, 1996), 166–7.

56. U.S.S.R. Council of Ministers Resolution, March 19, 1953, APRF, f. 3, op. 65, d. 830, pp. 60–71, and AVPRF, f. 059a, op. 5a, pa. 11, d. 4, pp. 54–65.

57. For the text of this document, see the *CWIHP Bulletin* 3 (Fall 1993): 15–17.

58. Ciphered telegram from Kuznetsov in Beijing to the Foreign Ministry in Moscow, APRF, f. 3, op. 65, d. 830, pp. 187–9, and AVPRF, f. 059a, op. 5a, pa. 11, d. 5, pp. 156–8.

59. For a thorough discussion of the negotiations from the UN side, see Foot, *A Substitute for Victory.*

3. Soviet Advisors in China in the 1950s

Deborah A. Kaple

The Soviet Advisors' Program, an agreement that sent thousands of Soviets to China in the 1950s to assist the Chinese Communists to embark on the socialist path, may be the least studied aspect of the Cold War. Unprecedented in scale and scope, the Advisors' Program was an utterly crucial aspect of both the famous friendship and the infamous split. It is a testimony to the effectiveness of Communist Party secrecy that, forty years later, there is no scholarly, book-length history of this program in any language. Fortunately, the windfall of sources yielded by the collapse of communism in 1989 in the Soviet Union and Eastern Europe provides at least a preliminary understanding of the Sino-Soviet relationship and its problems. This chapter is the beginning of the long process of filling in an important "white spot" of history, that of the role of the Soviet advisors in China in the 1950s.

As outlined in chapters 4 and 6, both the Soviets and the Chinese believed that it was crucially important for their cooperation to be centrally planned, integrating technical, educational, economic, and military support. The political decisions on these plans were taken by the party leaders and often reflected changing aspects of the overall bilateral relationship. The preparation and implementation of the cooperation programs were left to party and state institutions that had to devise ways to fulfill what they understood to be the wishes of their superiors. Ultimately, however, much of the work associated with the programs depended on Soviet specialists, teachers, and advisers who were sent by their institutions to work in China. This chapter centers on them and their experiences.

In attempting to understand the work of the Advisors Program and its impact in China, I have relied on two types of sources. I first read the files of the Communist Party of the Soviet Union Central Committee (CPSU CC), which provide the official, written chronicle of the relationship. These archives, like any in the world, present the researcher with various problems and questions, which are detailed below, so I have augmented the official record with interviews with Soviets who actually worked for the program in China. This often includes both the person who administered the program for the Soviet government and a number of the advisers themselves.

In this chapter, the archival information, the interviews, and advisers' unpublished memoirs are all used to sketch the outlines of the Soviet Advisors' Program. The sources are combined and checked against each other as much as possible, and the result is rather like a bumpy, handmade weaving. Since this is a slightly unusual approach, the next sections detail the problems and opportunities that each source presents.

Sources

The documentary evidence for this chapter comes mostly from the CPSU CC International Department, which oversaw and managed the Soviet Union's relationships with other countries.[1] In using these files extensively, three problems arose.

First, there is the problem of bias and omission. The Communist Party's very structured hold on Soviet society during the 1950s ensured that reports filed to the CPSU CC would be biased. Almost all sources of information in the archives emanated from Communist Party members, whether diplomats, both Soviet and from other socialist countries, government officials, officers of the Committee of State Security (KGB), journalists, members of youth groups, or trade union officials. In the 1950s the Communist Party carefully selected and screened the people it sent abroad, and moreover, all of the chosen understood what could and could not be reported back to the CPSU CC.

The situation is best illustrated by looking at the period we now know as the beginning of the demise of the Sino-Soviet friendship, the mid- to late 1950s. Sometime after 1956, the Chinese began to discuss openly and frankly in the press the problems they had with the "Soviet model" and its implementation. While this type of discussion no doubt bothered the Soviet Communist Party, little evidence of it appears in the Central Committee files from the same period. Instead, the reports filed to the CPSU CC reported "business as usual." It is not clear to researchers whether this indicates a simple lack of honest information on the part of the Central Committee's informants, or whether the files were altered before scholars gained access. In any case, whole periods of time pass without mention in the files, while in other files, memoranda are alluded to but not available.

The second problem with relying on the files of the CPSU CC is the very bureaucratic organization of the Central Committee itself. At various times several committees, departments, and subdepartments existed, all with roughly the same area of responsibility. These administrative divisions slowed communication between departments and involved them in much needless paperwork. Any small problem that needed to be resolved grew cumbersome if it involved the CPSU CC and some department from another interested party, such as the Ministry of Foreign Affairs. In addition, those who worked in the various departments were extremely circumspect and loath to make a decision, which often hampered their bosses' ability to obtain a realistic appraisal of the situation in China.

Third, judging by the organization of the CPSU CC, China was not a major priority in the 1950s. In 1949 the Soviet Union made a big show of recognizing China as the People's Republic of China (PRC). However, within the CPSU CC apparatus, China did not rate the same departmental status as the other people's democracies for several years. China was shelved into departments and subdepartments with other non-Communist countries, while the other people's democracies had a department devoted exclusively to each. In March 1953 the Central Committee International Department was reorganized, and China appeared collectively with Mongolia, Korea, and Japan. Only in May 1957 was China elevated to the status of a people's democracy in the CC apparatus, and by that time the relationship was already deteriorating.[2]

Revelations[3]

Despite their problems, the Communist Party files do expand the existing historical record, which until now has consisted mostly of oft-repeated, CPSU-sanctioned information. For work on the 1950s Sino-Soviet relationship, the Communist Party archives can help to illuminate the historical record in three important areas. These three, which are discussed in detail below, concern the actual beginning of the program, its scope, and the effect of CPSU management on Sino-Soviet relations.

Almost all Soviet sources that document the Sino-Soviet friendship present the decade of the 1950s as a period of Soviet assistance to a needy ally. Recent Western scholarship has postulated that substantive Soviet assistance did not begin until after Stalin's death in 1953. The new work on this period suggests that in most fields, during the first three years of the existence of the People's Republic, the Chinese relied not on Soviet advisors but mostly on books and articles translated from Russian into Chinese.[4] Evidence in the Soviet Communist Party archives seems to confirm this hypothesis, for there is little in the archives about the program until 1954.

The Soviet presence in China increased after the signing of the pact in February 1950,[5] yet few visitors came on long-term civilian advisory missions. The largest single groups were cultural delegations and trade agents, both headed by Soviet Communist Party officials.[6] The Sino-Soviet alliance was not as friendly as both countries wanted the outside world to believe. The relationship between Mao Zedong and Joseph Stalin was fraught with suspicion and hostility, and Soviet assistance to China remained minimal.

With Stalin's death and Nikita Khrushchev's ascent to power, the personal encumbrances of the relationship were lessened, at least for a few years, and the dynamic between the countries altered drastically. A genuine program to help China reconstruct itself with Soviet assistance began, and advisers from nearly all major Soviet ministries arrived in China to begin work. Thus in 1954 began the bulk of the labor for which the Soviet Advisors' Program is remembered, that of building roads, industry, bridges, and factories throughout China.

Also questionable from the Communist Party archives is the Soviet-era assertion that the Soviet Union sent more than 10,000 specialists to China between 1950 and 1959. While this figure is always quoted, without attribution,[7] to demonstrate the seriousness of the Soviet Union's commitment to China, there is no official count of the advisors in China or how many months or years each spent there.[8] (There also have been many Soviet calculations of the economic impact of Soviet assistance to China, yet sources are not clearly cited.)[9]

The archives present evidence of the level and type of Soviet commitment to China during the first quarter of 1954. We can see where the 403 Soviets were placed, for instance, but there is no mention of how long each spent in China. Soviets were working at the following Chinese ministries and administrations:

Advisers	Location
49	Ministry of Fuel Industry
45	Ministry of Heavy Industry
3	Ministry of Construction Work
22	First Ministry of Machine-Building
3	Second Ministry of Machine-Building
9	Ministry of Geology
6	Ministry of Light Industry
2	Ministry of Textile Industry
5	Ministry of Agriculture
4	Ministry of Water Economy (*vodnoe khozyaistvo*)
11	Timber Industry
18	Ministry of Railroads

6	Ministry of Communications
14	"GAS" (interpreters)
8	Gosplan
1	Political-Judicial Committee
1	Ministry of Finance
6	Ministry of Trade
2	All-China Cooperation (*"Kooperatsiya"*)
2	People's Bank
17	Ministry of Health
127	Ministry of Higher Education
13	Ministry of Education
22	Central Committee CCP
3	Ministry of Culture
1	Ministry of Foreign Affairs
2	"NOA" (Spanish language teachers)
1	Committee of the Affairs of Physical Culture and Sport

Of these 403 Soviet specialists in China in early 1954, almost 80 percent (318) were in Beijing; 43 Soviets worked in Harbin, 8 in Shenyang, 7 in Anshan, 4 in Tianjin, 3 in Dalian, 3 in Shanghai, 9 in southern China, and 8 in Urumchi. Broken down very roughly, about 45 percent of the Soviet Advisors worked in industry, transport, and communications; 35 percent worked in educational establishments; and 20 percent were placed in various government and party bureaucracies.[10]

The third aspect of the Sino-Soviet relationship on which the CPSU files shed light is how the management style of CPSU advisers in China affected its relationship with that country. An excellent example of the unintended benefits of reading unexpurgated files is provided by a report filed in 1954[11] by Soviet diplomat Nikolai Fedorenko.[12]

Fedorenko's description allows an inside look at the Advisors' Program and at the scope of Soviet involvement in China. Not surprisingly, the Central Committee's approach to foreign policy was exactly the same as its management in the Soviet Union. In both cases, the CPSU issued centralized directives from above, showed almost complete disregard for those whom its decrees and decisions affected, exhibited a mania for security, and displayed a general lack of supervision of workers at the lower levels.

Fedorenko discusses the inner workings of an unnamed group of high-level bureaucrats, who are referred to as the Senior Soviet Advisors. Following the party habit of issuing decrees from the top, he writes about how the advisers discussed improving the quality of the experts' and technicians' work and establishing closer, more businesslike relations with the leaders of the various Chinese ministries and departments. Then they turned their attention to what they considered China's pressing problems. The deliberation ranged from the role of the Soviet Union in China's first Five-Year Plan, the possibilities for developing several sectors of industry – in particular, copper production, chemical production of coke (*kokskhimicheskaya*), and the production of bulk plastics – to the development of electric power stations.

The senior advisors also discussed the many problems to be solved in various areas in which they thought China particularly weak, such as in project planning (*proektirovanie*) and geological scouting (*razvedki*), which were blamed for slowing down construction in many places. They targeted these areas, plus efforts in the People's Republic in city planning, to expedite work that they had planned for future projects. In other areas they discussed methods to improve the sale of industrial products and ways for creating a single plan for rail and water transport development.

The report stated that the senior advisors listened to an account of Soviet specialists who had been sent to Xinjiang Province to look into the problems of animal husbandry. They also heard a talk detailing the activities of a group of Soviet energy experts in China that discussed various problems and criticisms of their work. The senior advisors then made some suggestions for improvement.

Following the CPSU habit of issuing decrees with little regard for their effect, the report implies that all of these decisions were made by upper-level Soviet advisors, and few, if any, Chinese were involved in the discussions. Not one Chinese participant is mentioned. The report simply states that the Senior Soviet Advisors, after discussing China's various problems, made their recommendations and immediately dispatched them to the heads of the relevant ministries in the People's Republic. The Soviets sent the proposals for what they considered China's most urgent problems immediately to the directors of government administrations. Fedorenko reported that the senior advisors felt that this would guarantee quicker implementation of the suggestions.

Fedorenko also included examples of how well the procedure worked. Evidently this group of Soviets had earlier pinpointed Chinese labor as an area that needed reform. So, according to Fedorenko, in January 1954 the Soviet advisors recommended that the Chinese Communist Party (CCP) CC order its Ministry of Labor, the All-China Federation of Trade Unions, and other relevant ministries to collaborate on labor issues.

According to this account, the Chinese government immediately directed various agencies to work on strengthening labor discipline among Chinese workers and to create a system of payment of wages, social security, and labor protection laws. They were supposed to revamp their labor laws in order to eliminate existing confusion in the system of wages, in particular, to liquidate wage leveling (*uravnilovka*) in the most important sectors and professions. Noting that exaggerations in labor norms had risen more quickly in New China than after the Russian Revolution, the Soviet advisers also suggested that the Chinese correct this.

We do not know yet from the evidence available if this process worked as Fedorenko described. If so, then the ease and directness of response would have astounded CPSU personnel, for they worked in a truly overstaffed, bureaucratic institution. According to the files, sometimes it took months for a CPSU CC department to respond to a simple letter.

The files also illuminate a third characteristic of party management: a fixation on security, which hampered simple communication between the countries and the people, and slowed work down. Those in China who were unfortunate enough to request something from the Soviets found out how time-consuming and difficult the process was. For instance, in April 1954 the Chinese Department of Propaganda and Agitation asked its embassy to request a copy of some speeches by three different heads of departments at the CPSU CC.[13] The speeches appeared to be quite ordinary in their content.[14]

However, the inquiry generated several letters back and forth between Soviet bureaucracies for months, and in the end the Central Committee rejected the request. It said that the first two were merely intended to instruct local workers, that they contained materials only for internal use, and that there were no applications for the Chinese in them. The Central Committee said that the other speech requested, on literature, did not entirely develop the theme, only particular questions, and moreover, it was not typed. So it was not allowed to be sent either. Instead the Chinese were referred to official CPSU articles that had been published in the journals *Party Life* and *Communist*.

The fear of divulging too much hampered the work of Soviet experts who were sent to work in "secret" or "closed" facilities, such as in the development of nuclear power. They experienced many difficulties and uncomfortable situations. A report filed to the Central Committee in 1957 stated that several teachers and educators who were sent in this capacity were never told what they should and should not disclose. Fearing the responsibility of revealing secrets, the report stated, they "doom themselves by remaining passive or saying what the Chinese already long ago knew from newspapers or even the Soviet press."[15]

Finally, the CPSU CC files reveal a myriad of problems that developed due to the party's habit of decentralized supervision. It seems that despite the strict procedures the Central Committee followed in selecting the advisors, checking that they had the correct "standing," and passing them through extensive security checks, once they were in China, its guidance of them all but ended, so there was no real direction where it really counted. The written record alludes to this problem, but it is very evident in the discussions with the actual advisors, which is why they become such an important source.

Finally, for the historian interested in the USSR and China, another possible source of information about the 1950s would seem to be the voluminous Soviet accounts that are available. During the Soviet period, China specialists and ex-advisors did write memoirs about their experiences in China, but they are difficult to use and not totally reliable. With the exception of a few, these accounts are cleaned of any detail and focus on celebrating the Soviet contribution to China.[16] Since Mikhail Gorbachev's time, a couple of brief versions of the workings of the Sino-Soviet relationship of the 1950s have appeared. However, they focus more on the relationship between Mao and Stalin than on the actual work of advisors.[17] The same is largely true of the available Chinese sources.[18]

Interviews as Sources

The fall of communism not only opened archives but made it possible for researchers to talk to the actual participants in formerly secret events of Soviet history. I decided to interview people who had participated in the advisors' program because of my frustration with the Communist Party archives. Too much detail either is not recorded or simply not available to researchers, and I found it impossible to write a history of the program based on the archives alone.

Influenced by my close reading of the archival materials, I first chose to interview Ivan Vasil'evich Arkhipov,[19] who administered the Soviet Advisors' Program for most of its existence. Stalin himself selected Arkhipov to be the top economic advisor in China,[20] and in March 1950 Arkhipov began his association with the People's Republic.[21] The future head of the Soviet Advisors' Program spent almost a year in Beijing, then returned to Moscow as a deputy director of the Ministry of Ferrous Metallurgy until August 1953. After Stalin's death he was sent to China again, this time to direct the Soviet Union's expanded effort to assist in economic reconstruction.[22]

Although talking with Arkhipov was fascinating because of his high status and his knowledge of the party leaders in both China and Russia, he told me no more than I learned by reading the CPSU files. He did not understand the nuts and bolts of the program, nor did he particularly think that the program should be examined as an aspect of the Sino-Soviet relationship. Therefore, I decided to interview those who actually had worked in China as advisors in the 1950s. I advertised in the newspapers *Pravda* and *Moskovskaya Pravda* in February 1993 and located hundreds of willing respondents. After screening all of them, I interviewed thirty. In order to achieve as representative a sample as possible, I selected them on the basis of their profession and length of time spent working in China.

Like the archival sources, these narratives also are somewhat flawed, if only because each person's experience in China was different and unique. The advanced age of the respondents must be taken into account, as must the normal human tendency to present oneself in the most positive light. The same may be said about their personal papers and memoirs, upon which I also rely to some extent.

As central as these advisors were to China's progress and development, it is odd that the CPSU files reveal so little information about them. After all, this organization was in charge of the program. Perhaps these data are contained in other, personal files that have not yet been declassified, but the lack of such information leaves a rather large gap in our understanding of the program. Who were they, how were they chosen at their respective ministries, what was their preparation for going, why did they go, how did they like the Chinese, and what was the relationship between the citizens of this fraternal friendship? For answers to these questions, I will refer to my extensive interviews of former advisors. The professions of these people vary greatly, and include such diverse specialties as biologist, engineer, diplomat, radio announcer, shipbuilder, academic, party cadre, interpreter, and doctor, to name a few.

The Party Summons

Most of the people who were sent to China to work were men in their thirties and forties, and nearly all were Russian by nationality. Some were allowed to take their families along and some were not. This appears to have depended on the status of the advisor. One respondent said that he took his twelve-year-old son and his wife to Harbin with him, but he was not permitted to take his daughter, because only children who were of primary school age were allowed.[23]

Female Soviet advisors were a small minority of those sent, although many wives accompanied their husbands. Only a few spouses worked while in China. One advisor's wife worked at the Soviet consulate in Mukden, first as a librarian, then as an administrator. The advisor explained that they found her a job only because she was also a Communist Party member. Most wives were not party members and therefore did not work. He said, "At that time, it was like this: It wasn't important whether or not a person had a head on his shoulders, the important thing was, do you have a Party card?"[24]

According to almost all accounts, the CPSU was fully in charge of deciding who went to work in China in the 1950s, and the first criterion for any prospective advisor was party membership. It was the main qualification for getting a job abroad at that time. To this day, most of the advisors I interviewed felt that party membership needed to be the most important qualification. First, they insisted that party members could be trusted always. Second, as one said, "with a party member, you could request more sternly than with a nonparty person." Also, one of them explained, party membership was important in that it gave them double access at their jobs. He meant that they could interact not only with their technical counterparts but also with the Communist Party officials who ran the place as well.[25]

Most advisors were summoned by the party organization at work. Often, especially if the person worked in a military-related field, he would be called in for an interview with the CPSU CC. It was a special moment, and most men could recall it in detail even forty years later. One military aviation engineer remembers being summoned there in September 1952. At the meeting, he was told that the CC wanted him to go to China to work in a military arsenal that the Soviets were helping to build in Shenyang. He noted that they did not give him the opportunity to turn the job down.[26]

The man who served as the Beijing bureau chief for *Pravda* for nine years during the 1950s said that the process was begun by filling out a number of forms at work. Then the government did a careful background check on each person as well as his family and relatives. Only if the person passed all these checks was he called to the Central Committee for the meeting and assignment.[27] Another remembers being told that the party announced that it was looking for a person with experience and the right "standing." The person had to be a party member, and most important, he could not have any relatives abroad already. This advisor also felt as if he were given no choice but to go to China.[28] The party demanded and the members accepted.

Although many advisors mentioned that they were pressured into taking the job in China by the Communist Party, almost none of them regretted it later. For one thing, the party compensated its people well for their time abroad. Some claimed to have received at least five times their normal salaries. Much of it was saved for them in Moscow for the duration of their two-year stay. One respondent noted that being in China was wonderful, since there were never any goods available in Russia, neither before nor after the war.[29] In China, the advisors found special stores they could shop in with coupons. One adviser said that he made so much money that he could send a substantial amount of it to his daughter back home to live on.

Preparing for China

Despite the enormous attention the Soviet Communist Party paid to selecting the advisors, for the most part, the men were ill-prepared for what awaited them in China. They were not given reading materials about the situation in China, they knew little about Chinese history, politics, or even the revolution, and none was required to learn even rudimentary Chinese before going.

A few of them prepared by reading on their own. Dmitrii Krivozub, who was an academic, read Mao's articles on the dictatorship of the proletariat before he went. Most, however, were completely unprepared for what they encountered. Aleksandr Chudakov, who worked at a military arsenal in Shenyang, had the typical Soviet reaction to the Chinese people. He remembered thinking how dirty everybody was. He said, "They didn't even know what a bathhouse was." He recollects going to a rural area nearby, where each family "had around eight children," all of whom seemed to be naked, dirty, and snotty. His wife, upon seeing this, resolved to bring soap the next time and hand it out to them. She did this, and right in front of their eyes, they took the soap and began to eat it. "They didn't know what soap was!" he said, shaking his head.

Another, upon arrival in the Manchurian countryside, said about the Chinese villagers: "I first thought that they all looked alike, that they were all very dirty. I guess that I had a very bad first impression. They were poor. They all ate out of the same pot."[30]

Even those people who were sent to teach in Chinese educational institutions were poorly prepared. A report to the Central Committee of July 1957 noted this problem and suggested that in the future, the teachers should be told something about China before they arrived, such as what it was like and what sort of working conditions they would encounter. According to the report, the teachers being sent had not even read the summaries of work in China written by recently returned teachers.[31]

This ignorance on the part of the Soviet advisers inevitably caused friction between the peoples of the two nations. It did not emerge publicly, though, until the early stages of the split, with the Soviet decision to cut back on the number of advisers in China. On September 6, 1958, the Soviets called a meeting with Deng Xiaoping, who at the time was general secretary of the CCP, to give him a letter from the CPSU about decreasing the number of Soviet specialists in China. During the course of the meeting, Deng mentioned that there had been problems due to the advisers' ignorance about internal conditions in China and the peculiarities of the CCP's politics. He said that if the remaining advisers (after some were pulled out) could be better informed, this would help them to "avoid mistakes and more correctly carry out their work."[32]

Who Is in Charge Here?

If the Communist Party chose to send only its best, and screened them carefully, why and how could there be problems? Just as in its control over Soviet society, the Communist Party was best at administering decrees from above, but it often did not trouble itself to check their implementation. In China, this meant that the advisers so carefully chosen were not very well supervised once they arrived. Most of the ex-advisers remember feeling that they were on their own in China.

In most cases, the Soviet advisors found that their workplaces were not well organized. Each handled this differently, of course, but most reported that they simply relied on their past experience and organized the work in China along the same lines. Many of them were pleased with the independence and general lack of supervision. One reported that he liked working in China because he felt free with his time, he respected himself and felt necessary, as if he were doing work that was valuable.[33]

The negative side to this lack of organization, of course, was quality control. Unlike at home in the USSR the advisers were not strictly supervised, nor was there any controlling organization in Moscow that forced the home enterprise or ministry to cooperate as they were supposed to by their agreement.

This lack of support and supervision was problematic and sometimes embarrassing. In November 1955 the secretary of the Central Committee of the Komsomol organization, A. Shelepin, wrote a note to the CC about a youth delegation that had gone to China. He reported in detail about several Soviet advisers he had seen while in China. Many were fulfilling only their technical duties and not worrying about the education of the Chinese with whom they worked. He said that some of them were so poorly informed about their supposed areas of expertise that it was shameful. At a meeting he attended, for example, he was mortified to see that the Soviet who was working as an adviser to China's minister of ferrous metallurgy seemed almost completely ignorant about leading labor methods in the Soviet Union, and he knew nothing at all about the situation of metallurgical factories in China.

He also reported that the Soviets working in a Shanghai shipbuilding factory had said that they were having trouble getting necessary parts and equipment sent to them from their home enterprise. They told him that they had received equipment with necessary parts missing and no technical documentation. They said that the last shipment sent from their Leningrad enterprise included a collective agreement of one of the factories, unneeded bolts, and lots of trash. And they complained that even when they sent questions back to the enterprise, they never received any answers.[34]

We Lived in Nice Soviet Complexes

For all of the rhetoric of friendship and brotherhood, close relationships between Soviets and Chinese were discouraged by both countries. At the work-site level, most respondents described cordial relations. Former advisers reported being pleased at how well the Chinese worked. One respondent said that he thought that it was simply a Chinese national characteristic to work and to set goals and achieve them.[35] Many advisers liked the fact that at the factory or work site, the Chinese, no matter if they were workers, the director, or the head engineer, all wore the same clothing: cotton uniform, cotton cap, and cotton shoes. None of them wore a suit and tie.[36]

At the individual level, most Soviet advisers felt that friendship existed between China and the Soviet Union when they were working there. However, almost all felt that there was a limit to this friendship and that somehow it could not become a personal relationship. Oleg Glazilin, who was an interpreter for a group of geologists looking for uranium, said that even at the peak of friendship between the two countries, the Chinese were outwardly friendly, very much so, but at the same time, inside, somehow, they were on their guard. "We were all the same, well, they were Communists and we were Communists, for God's sake. When I was a student, we were one with, say, the Czechs, the Slovaks, the Poles, and we all went out together in a normal way. But in China, that never happened, in fact, it was the other way around, some sort of estrangement (*otchuzhdennost'*), like some kind of wall stood between us, transparent, invisible, but some kind of wall. . . ."[37]

There was a limit to the personal contact each side had with the other. For one thing, all the Soviet specialists always lived with each other, in a hotel, and they took all their meals together in the hotel's restaurant, no matter what part of China they were in. Some felt this made things easier from the point of view of security,[38] while others felt the reason was to limit real contact with Chinese people.

Some ex-advisers told about times when possible close relationships with a Chinese citizen caused trouble. Most of them blamed this on the Chinese Communist Party. One former adviser said:

> The Chinese treated us honestly, but among the regular people, there were always party leaders who smiled on the outside, but with eyes that were just cold. They controlled everything, restrained everything. I remember being friendly with this young Chinese girl, such a nice girl, and I . . . didn't do anything, didn't even embrace her, we just flirted a little, but then they [the CCP representatives] worked her over until she cried.[39]

Another remembered "a brave Czech woman there," who began seeing a lot of a Chinese man, and who ultimately got into trouble over it from both the Czech and Chinese officials.[40]

All of the advisers spoke of being followed while they lived in China. One said, "Mao gave an order that even if you go to the toilet, the guard must go and stand nearby." This person remembers that under no circumstances were the Soviets allowed to go out alone. It was obligatory that they be followed. He also remembered once leaving his room and realizing a bit later that he had forgotten something. Returning to his room, he saw somebody rooting through his suitcase, but he pretended that he had not seen him and left. Asked why he had pretended, he replied, "Well, because I knew that he was just doing his job, because it was no doubt a worker for state security, I was sure of it. Also, we had been raised in such a country where this was taken as absolutely normal." Continuing, he said, "Our work regime [in China] was absolutely like being in a prison, in general, like a prison with high wages. They didn't let us go anywhere, do anything, without surveillance, and that was it."[41] A journalist in China also recalled that the Soviets were all followed, even openly. The Chinese made journalists submit their questions in advance, in writing. Not long into his term in Beijing, one of the Chinese comrades told him that they were required every week to write a letter about each of the Soviet journalists. He was told that they filed reports on what the Soviets were doing, what kind of questions they were asking, with whom they met, and so on.

One of his fellow Soviet reporters who specialized on China's developing economic transformation had a very unpleasant experience at a factory near Beijing. He was talking to the director about several things, "all within the realm of journalistic interest, nothing more," when suddenly the Chinese comrade who had accompanied him to the factory stuck out his hand, tore the correspondent's notebook from him, and shouted: "You are not allowed to know this or report on this!" He said that the Soviets were embarrassed and did not know what to do. They all simply pretended that there had been no such incident, and the reporter did not ask any more questions.[42]

Not all of the ex-Soviet advisers felt that the constant surveillance as negative. One of them who lived and worked in Harbin said that being accompanied was absolutely necessary. The "guide" helped them find their way and answer questions for them.[43] Most of them needed a guide in any case, since they had not learned any Chinese.

Sino-Soviet Friendship in Question

All of the advisors who were in China after 1956 reported problems on the job as a repercussion of the changing Sino-Soviet relationship at the top. Many Russians who were in China at the time point to Khrushchev's so-called secret speech at the Twentieth Party Congress, at which he denounced Stalin. One highly placed CPSU member who worked at the Foreign Languages Press in Beijing attended the speech in Moscow and sat with Chinese Marshal Zhu De.

After the speech he asked Zhu De how he felt about it, knowing that "of course, without talking with Mao Zedong, he could not give his opinion. But he did say, 'You know, Stalin was the head of the world Communist movement, so he belonged to all [Communist] parties. You criticized him without even consulting with us.' "[44]

Another adviser who was in China in 1956 remembers that the Chinese reaction was severely negative. He said that the cult of Mao was in full flower already and that it appeared to be "a copy, only a Chinese variant, a copy of the Soviet, Stalin cult. . . ." Such a grand, public denunciation made the Chinese uncomfortable, for how could they criticize Stalin's cult and continue building the same for Mao? He said that by this time:

> The Chinese believed in communism, they believed blindly in Mao, blindly completely [believing] that this was god, a living god on earth. I saw how the Chinese people behaved at receptions that Mao was part of, once at a celebration at Tiananmen Square in honor of the founding of the PRC. He was a living god, a living Buddha, and if he said that if you pick up a rock and throw it up into the sky and that it would not fall back down, they said, yes, if Mao said so, it must be so.[45]

Evident problems began to surface between China and the Soviet Union sometime after the secret speech. These were not public, of course, but they were a matter of concern for the CPSU CC. The Chinese began to say that they were not interested in closely copying "the Soviet model." For instance, a report dated July 16, 1957, detailing the work of scientific and technical personnel in China focused on this. It said that the Chinese recently had begun to complain that in their reform of the educational system of the People's Republic, the advisers were simply copying Soviet texts without paying any attention to Chinese characteristics. For example, the Soviets had come in and abolished the traditional Chinese grading system in the schools, replacing it with their own five-point system, which led to problems for those graduating and expecting to graduate.[46]

Perhaps in response to the more vocal Chinese criticism, the Soviet embassy personnel in China began to complain that the Soviet ministries that were selecting and sending advisors were doing a poor job. After 1957, the Advisors' Program seems to have merely become another bureaucratic task for the CPSU CC. The program was no longer such a priority that the Central Committee interviewed each and every prospective applicant.

A dispatch called "Overview of the Work of Soviet Specialists in Science and Technology" illuminated the problems of advisors in China. The report focused on 327 people who were teaching in higher education and technical schools, 24 doctors, 31 consultants and advisers to the Central Chinese ministries and administrations, 14 scientific workers, 17 working in literature and publishing, and 11 translators. The report stated that there had been so many problems with this group that the CPSU organization at the Soviet embassy in Beijing had decided to send many of them back home.

The report complained that the various Soviet ministries and administrations were not paying sufficient attention to the process and were sending poor-quality people to China. The latest arrivals were not at all well prepared, and many of them were doing a bad job. One even broke Chinese law.[47]

Home control over the advisers was, in some cases, almost nonexistent. In reviewing the work of those sent to work in education and other science and technical areas, the same report to the Central Committee complained that the Soviets were sending people who were too old or weak to work in China. Several were sick for a long time, recovered by relaxing while there, and then were sent back to the Soviet Union. Another problem was with the timing. The report stated, with exasperation, that more than once a person had been sent to China to teach for a short period, such as three to six months, only to arrive exactly when the Chinese schools were having their holiday, making the adviser almost useless.[48]

For some reason, the various ministries of the Soviet Union that were supposed to send specialists were dragging their feet, and the Chinese were left expecting people who did not arrive for a long time. A Soviet Council of Minister's decree of July 4 and 9, 1957, was designed to speed the process, but it seemed to accomplish little. In a letter from the Ministry of Foreign Affairs to the CPSU CC, I. Kurdiukov complained that thirty-nine people had been signed up to be sent to China but the cases of thirty-one of them were still stuck in the Committee for Going Abroad (*Komitet po vyezdom za granitsu*). And this occurred after the decree had been promulgated.[49]

Especially surprising were the complaints that the Soviet Ministry of Education was sending advisers without sending supplies, such as books, so that unless the teacher himself thought to bring them, he had nothing to work with. While this complaint surfaced in Central Committee files in 1957,[50] this had been a problem for some years already. One respondent who had been in China in the early 1950s, a medical doctor, said that she remembered that she had very few supplies with which to work. "Mainly, I remember that books were too few. I brought a couple, but very little. We weren't allowed, generally. The problem was our border, not the Chinese border. The Chinese didn't even look at what we Soviets had at the border."[51]

By 1957 a report filed by the Soviet embassy in China noted that overt problems were beginning to surface in the relationship. In an overview of the various political campaigns in China, the report focused on the one that was designed to correct the work style of party cadres. It charted the CCP's progress in its struggle against the "rightists." The report noted that this particular campaign was not organized well and that much damaging information about the Communist Party and about socialism in general had fallen into the hands of these "rightists." This was all by way of explaining why anti-Soviet attacks had been printed recently in the Chinese press. The report worried that although the CCP had increased its measures to educate the Chinese population on "the spirit of Chinese-Soviet friendship" and to teach them about the Soviet experience, still enemy propaganda that circulated news of the "Hungarian events" and the "anti-Soviet speeches of the rightists" had had their influence among some sectors of the population, especially the intelligentsia and students.[52]

The later in the decade that advisers worked in China, the more they felt the growing estrangement between the countries. One remembered that when his group arrived in China in September 1958, the Chinese citizens all stood around and applauded their train, yelling "Hurrah! The Soviet experts are here to help us!" At first, the friendship seemed genuine, for the Chinese were very careful to observe all Soviet holidays and even advisers' birthdays. But in the course of a year, relations had become so strained that the advisers' mail was being intercepted and read, both incoming and outgoing. His group left a year later, in September 1959, and by that time the relationship was at such a low that the Chinese would not even drive them to the train station; one of the Czech specialists drove them.[53]

Of course, not all former advisers felt that external political events weakened the relationship. Some actually felt that there never had been a genuine friendship between the Soviets and the Chinese and that the Chinese had always held back. One ex-adviser said that the Chinese could never truly be friends with anybody, because of "the deeply ingrained habit of theirs to look down on all non-Han people as inferior." He also cited an example of how unappreciative the Chinese were for all that the Soviet Union did for them. He recalled how the Soviets had come in and built a plant for the canning of fruits, vegetables, meats, and fish. They handed hundreds of recipes to the Chinese comrades. Then, when the Chinese took over production, they began to add ingredients to the foods being preserved, and their products were clearly superior to the Soviet ones. When the Soviet side then asked for the improved recipes, the Chinese refused the request.[54]

Most advisers who worked in China after 1956 blamed the internal Chinese political situation for disrupting their work and for ruining the friendship. They felt they experienced unpleasant delays at work and postponements of routine services in their daily lives due to the endless Chinese political campaigns of that time.

One, a teacher at an academy, remembered feeling very frustrated about this because the Chinese would hold long meetings after dinner that he was not allowed to attend. He knew that the officials running it "were working his Chinese colleagues over." He heard about spectacles where a deputy would curse himself in front of the crowd for fouling up work, for being a "semicapitalist," for demanding more than he deserved, and so on.[55] He also found that during his entire time in China, all decisions regarding ordinary issues, such as when to begin the semester, were considered political and could be decided only by the Communist Party committee. The administrators and the teachers had to wait while the CCP discussed everything for them. Because of such delays, sometimes they did not work for days.

The Advisors' Program Reevaluated

The Soviet Advisors' Program in China was indeed grand in its conception, in that it foresaw the complete rebuilding of one society into another in a matter of years. That it did not finish the job it started should be no surprise, for ultimately it was constrained by long-standing mistrust between the respective leaders, problems in coming to a fair and equitable agreement, and difficulties in execution.

The newly opened files of the Central Committee give a new perspective on the Sino-Soviet relationship as seen through the eyes of the CPSU. Clearly, China was not among the highest priorities for that organization until after Stalin's death, for only then did the Soviet Advisors' Program swing into high gear. The archives also reveal that the CC apparatus, which oversaw the Advisors' Program, managed its workers in China in the same way in which it managed Soviet society. This accounts for its style of issuing directives from above, for not always including the Chinese in its major decisions about their own country's development, for its obsession with security, and for its near lack of attention to details at the lowest level, which was exactly where most Soviet advisers worked.

Each of these tendencies runs through the relationship like a leitmotif. In the beginning of the official friendship, problems were ignored or simply not noted, but sometime after 1956, they came into focus as real annoyances and hindrances. The top-down management style became problematic after several incidents in which it was clear that the Soviet decision makers did not have a good idea of the situation in China. Related to this, major decisions were made about China, often without consulting with the Chinese side.

The Soviet proclivity for strict security measures also led to problems, in that advisers had to worry about revealing state secrets and therefore were less effective at communicating with their Chinese comrades than they might have been. And finally, the fact that the Central Committee paid so little attention to the work of Soviet advisers in China led to many uncomfortable predicaments. The CPSU did not seem to be aware that the advisers and technicians represented the Sino-Soviet relationship to the Chinese, so that the Chinese were observing carefully their performance and the interest (or lack thereof) in China of their home institutions.

The new willingness and ability of Russians to speak freely about their lives has added a new dimension to Soviet and Russian studies. In this case, the perspective of those who worked as advisers, technicians, and specialists in China enriches the formal CPSU record of that decade. It was from these people that we learned how the Communist Party's decentralized management style of the advisers in China contributed to difficulties between the two countries. Party membership was one of the most important qualifications for going to China, and all advisers were screened carefully, yet once there, often they were left alone to do as they wanted. The quality of their work seemed to depend on what kind of a person each was. Some gave their all while there, but there were reports of others who did little but relax and enjoy themselves.

The ex-advisers reported that the CPSU did very little to prepare them for their time in China, and as the relationship between the two countries became less friendly in the second half of the 1950s, this ignorance became awkward. The advisers were discouraged from fraternizing with their Chinese comrades, for this was not a relationship like the ones the Soviets had with other Communists, such as those from Poland or Czechoslovakia. According to the ex-advisers, close contact was discouraged officially. Further, they were always housed separately, in large complexes with restaurants, further hindering contacts with Chinese outside of work. Many of them remembered unpleasant incidents regarding those who did try to have a close Chinese friend. All of the advisers reported being followed by Chinese security forces, which also inhibited unmonitored contact.

Sometime after Khrushchev's speech denouncing Stalin in 1956, formerly latent problems in the relationship began to surface. The Central Committee's management style, its habit of neglecting to include the Chinese in major decisions, and its low level of supervision over its workers began to take a toll, and the Chinese began discussing the difficulties in public. And here, the official files illustrate very clearly how ill-equipped the Central Committee was to deal quickly and effectively with such problems. Even when Soviet embassy personnel wrote openly about difficulties, the responses were slow and cumbersome and not always realistic.

The advisers, technicians and experts, working at the lowest level of the alliance were always far removed from the decisions that affected them and usually had little power to alter even their own working situations. The fact that they were all chosen and sent through the Communist Party may even have worked against the success of the friendship, for they all tended to believe that the party knew best. This, of course, discouraged even the most intelligent of them from questioning their government's policies in China.

Almost all Soviets who worked in China in the 1950s feel sympathy for the Chinese and remember their time there as a high point in their lives. Many felt that there was some sort of friendship between the Chinese and Russian people, but it was confined to the lowest level and, in the end, did not matter. Even if there were as many as 10,000 Soviets in China, the friendship could not survive on their good intentions alone. In some fundamental way, the Sino-Soviet friendship, like Soviet society, became an unwitting victim of the CPSU's inability to manage its assets well.

Notes

1. The archives I worked in are the Russian Center for Storage and Study of Documents of Contemporary History [*Rossiiskii tsentr khraneniya i izucheniya dokumentov noveishei istorii,* or RTsKhIDNI], the Storage Center for the Preservation of Contemporary Documents [*Tsentr khraneniia sovremennoi dokumentatsii,* or TsKhSD], and to a lesser extent, the Russian Foreign Ministry Archives [*Arkhiv vneshnei politiki Rossiskii Federatsii*]. Other important organizations, such as the State Committee on Foreign Economic Relations [*Goskomitet po ekonomicheskim sviaziam*], were very involved in China. However, I have tried on several occasions to get access to their files and failed.

2. TsKhSD, fond (f.) 5, opist (op.) 22, roll 4536, no. 969 (February–March 1953), pp. 97–100. See Deborah A. Kaple, "Four Myths about Soviet Involvement in China in the 1950s," paper presented at the Cold War International History Project conference, Moscow, January 12–15, 1993.

3. A more detailed account of new findings is in Kaple, "Four Myths."

4. For a discussion of developments in Chinese industrial management between the years of 1949 and 1953, see Deborah A. Kaple, *Dream of a Red Factory: The Legacy of High Stalinism in China* (New York: Oxford University Press, 1994).

5. For a discussion of the pact and its secret protocols, see Sergei N. Goncharov, John W. Lewis, and Xue Litai, *Uncertain Partners: Stalin, Mao and the Korean War* (Stanford, Calif.: Stanford University Press, 1993), 121–9.

6. The visits of such delegations often were featured in the official magazine of the Soviet-Chinese Friendship Society. See *People's China* (Beijing), 1950–1953.

7. A typical list of Soviet contributions to China can be found in an interview with I. V. Arkhipov in *USSR-China in the Changing World* (Moscow: Novosti Press Agency, 1989), 44–5.

8. It appears that some people were sent for as little as two weeks, others for as long as two years.

9. O. B. Borisov and B. T. Koloskov, *Sovetsko-Kitaiskie otnosheniia 1945–1977gg* [Soviet-Chinese relations, 1945–1977], 2nd ed. (Moscow: Mysl, 1977), especially chapter 2; L. V. Filatov, *Ekonomicheskaia otsenka nauchno-tekhnicheskoy pomoshchi Sovetskogo Soyuza Kitaiu 1949–1966* [An economic evaluation of scientific and technical assistance of the Soviet Union to China, 1949–1966] (Moscow: Nauka, 1980).

10. "An account of the work of Soviet specialist-advisors in the PRC for the first quarter of 1954," TsKhSD, f. 5, op. 28, roll 5113, no. 187 (January–October 1954), 1–97.

11. Ibid.

12. Fedorenko worked with Arkhipov in the early years as his interpreter. About forty years later, he lamented that "The development of relations between the USSR and China was done, inconceivably, without specialists: China specialists, people who knew the history and the contemporary situation of our great neighbor, the spiritual life of the Chinese people," in N. T. Fedorenko, "Stalin i Mao Tszedun" [Stalin and Mao Zedong], *Novatia i noveishatia istoritia* 5 (1992): 98–113, 109.

13. TsKhSD, f. 5, op. 28, roll 5104, no. 138 (January–October 1954).

14. The titles were: "On the tasks of ideological work of party organizations," "Tasks of the department of science and culture of local and party organs in fulfilling the decree of the September plenum of the Central Committee CPSU," and "Soviet literature at the current stage."

15. TsKhSD, f. 5, op. 49, roll 8862, no. 41 (April–December 1957), 146.

16. The best memoir is M. A. Klochko, *Soviet Scientist in Red China,* trans. Andrew McAndrew (New York: Praeger, 1964). Others include A. A. Arsent'ev, *Zvezdy nad Ki-*

taem [Stars over China] (Simferopol': Krymizdat, 1959); N. S. Babin, *Raduga nad Iantszy* [Rainbow over the Yangtze] (Moscow: Sovetskaya rossiya, 1959); N. Fedorenko, *Kitaiskie zapisi* [Chinese reminiscences] (Moscow: Sovietskii pisatel, 1955).

17. Fedorenko, Stalin i Mao Tszedun, 98–113; I. V. Kovalev, "Dialog Stalina s Mao Tszedunom" [Dialogue of Stalin and Mao Zedong], *Problemy dalnego vostoka*, 1/2/3 (1992): 77–91; and ibid., 6 (1991): 83–93.

18. Bo Yibo, *Ruogan zhongde juece yu shijian de huigu* [A review of some very important policies and events] (Zhongguo zhongyang xuejiao, 1991); Wu Xiuquan, *Zai waijiaobu baniande jingli* [Eight years in the Ministry of Foreign Affairs] (Beijing: Shijie zhishi, 1983); *Jianguo yilai Mao Zedong wengao* [Mao Zedong writings since the founding of the PRC], vol. 1 (September 1949–December 1950) (Beijing: Zhongyang wenxian, 1990); Shi Zhe, "Soprovozhdaya Predsedatelia Mao" [Accompanying Chairman Mao], *Problemy dalnego vostoka* 1 (1989): 139–48.

19. He was an engineer and mechanic by profession, and a Communist Party member since the age of twenty. By the time he was thirty-two years old, he was the first secretary of the party in Krivoy Rog, Dnepropetrovsk oblast, in Ukraine.

20. In an interview with Arkhipov on February 23, 1993, in Moscow, I asked him for which government organization he had worked for in China. He answered: "I worked for nobody," and explained later that he had been Stalin's personal emissary.

21. As he tells it, he was called to Moscow from his factory in Ukraine, amid much fear and anxiety during the purges of 1937. It turned out that he had been chosen to move upward quickly in the ranks of the Communist Party.

22. CPSU CC, Registration Blank of CPSU Member, Exchange of Party Documents of 1954. May 23, 1955. From the Collection of Personal Documents on CPSU Members, RTsKhIDNI.

23. Interview with Dmitrii Semenovich Krivozub, Moscow, May 14, 1994.

24. Interview with Aleksandr Vasilevich Chudakov, Moscow, April 6, 1993.

25. Ibid.

26. Ibid.

27. Interview with Aleksei Ivanovich Kozhin, Moscow, March 24, 1993.

28. Krivozub interview.

29. Chudakov interview.

30. Interview with Roza Konstantinova Alfierova, Moscow, March 9, 1993.

31. TsKhSD, f. 5, op. 49, roll 8862, no. 41 (April–December 1957), 146.

32. TsKhSD, f. 5, op. 49, roll 9111, no. 133 (September 6, 1958), 145–7.

33. Krivozub interview.

34. TsKhSD, f. 5, op. 28, roll 5142, no. 308 (October–December 1955), 116–25.

35. Interview with Oleg Konstantinovich Glazilin, Moscow, May 25, 1993.

36. Chudakov interview.

37. Glazilin interview.

38. Chudakov interview.

39. Glazilin interview.

40. Interview with Anatoli Georgevich Voronov and Elizaveta Zakharovna Voronova, Moscow, March 16, 1993.

41. Glazilin interview.

42. Kozhin interview.

43. Krivozub interview.

44. Interview with Vasilii Yakovlevich Sidikhmenov, Moscow, March 15, 1993.

45. Glazilin interview.

46. TsKhSD, f. 5, op. 49, roll 8862, no. 41 (April–December 1957), 124.

47. Ibid., 120–51.

48. Ibid., 147.

49. Ibid., 152.

50. Ibid., 145–6.

51. Alfierova interview.

52. TsKhSD, f. 5, op. 49, roll 8862, no. 41 (April–December 1957), 105–13.

53. Voronov and Voronova interview.

54. Interview with Aleksandr Afanasevich Orlov, Moscow, March 23, 1993.

55. Krivozub interview.

4. Sino-Soviet Military Cooperation

Sergei Goncharenko

None of the topics of the Sino-Soviet alliance has been as difficult to approach as military cooperation. Except for work done by a few Western scholars, this subject was either avoided or neglected for over thirty years. Even over the past few years, when Russian and Chinese scholars have begun to concentrate on general Sino-Soviet relations during the 1950s, the military aspect of the alliance has remained terra incognita.[1] One of the main reasons for this lack of interest has been the lack of reliable materials available for those interested in military affairs. Up until recently, officials in both China and the Soviet Union were uninterested in making all aspects of this sensitive issue public, and access to military archives in both countries remains problematic at best.

Officials feared that any information published on this cooperation could be dangerous to the present security of their countries. This exaggerated fear prevailed during the Cold War in both Beijing and Moscow, when adherence to Communist ideology induced both countries to confront the West. Even during the vigorous campaign of mutual accusations during the 1960s, when many other revealing details and sensitive facts of Sino-Soviet relations were revealed, both sides largely avoided discussing military affairs. It can be argued that, in Russia, only over the past few years have assessments of Sino-Soviet relations of the 1950s stopped bearing political significance.

This chapter reviews the Soviet military assistance to China during the 1950s based on the information that has become available since the collapse of the Soviet Union. The new sources – even if incomplete – show that the transfer of military technology from the Soviet Union to China up to about 1962 was more extensive than was earlier thought and that the cooperation was viewed as a success by both sides, until its usefulness was overtaken by the gradual worsening of political relations in the late 1950s. The sources, mainly from the voluminous records of the Russian Foreign Ministry Archives, also show that the guidelines for transfers of military technology were sometimes surprisingly vague and that those carrying out the military assistance plans – departments of the General Staff or the production centers for arms and technology under the various ministries for industry – often had to reach their own conclusions as to what should be transferred to the Chinese, when, and how.

Background

One effect of the new attention being given to the Sino-Soviet alliance, including its military aspects, is that scholars have become more inclined to believe that the beginning of Sino-Soviet military cooperation during the 1950s was found in 1945, when the Soviet Union liberated Manchuria from Japanese occupation. As Niu Jun notes in chapter 1, Moscow's double-sided policy toward China became quite obvious: Stalin formally recognized the government of Jiang Jieshi (Chiang Kai-shek) while also providing aid to the Chinese Communists.

Stalin's limited cooperation with the Chinese Communist Party (CCP) aimed to make the Communists' armies stronger and to turn them into a force capable of opposing the United States and Japan during the early Cold War. Moscow was afraid that the United States intended to preserve Japan's influence in Manchuria, or to make this strategically important region some kind of U.S.-controlled buffer state.[2]

Arguably, chairman Mao Zedong's usefulness in 1945–1946 added to the CCP's ideological attraction for the Soviets. As the civil war in China commenced in 1946, Moscow contrasted itself and the CCP with the United States and Guomindang (GMD). Although Stalin initially very much doubted the CCP's chances for success, the Soviet Union did help the party create the Manchurian base that later became the "anvil of victory" for the Chinese Communists.[3] Using the Soviet-Chinese treaty of August 14, 1945, and agreements with the GMD on the presence of Soviet troops in Lüshun, Dalian, and on the Chinese-Chanchun Railway, Moscow actually protected northeast China from the intrusion of seaborne GMD troops and thus helped CCP General Lin Biao's rudimentary forces to survive. In 1946 the Soviet Union armed Chinese Communists with Soviet and captured Japanese weapons. It also assisted the CCP with setting up an economic and military infrastructure.

Soviet forces withdrew from Manchuria in May 1946. However, during 1946 and 1947 Lin Biao's army continued to receive modern arms from the Soviet Army. Documents available in Russian archives show that this aid was substantial and included machine-guns, mortars and artillery pieces, tanks, ships of the

Sungai River Fleet, and, ultimately, aircraft.[4] The aid helped to turn the People's Liberation Army (PLA) into a powerful factor that could provide the final victory of the Chinese Revolution.

Arms transfers were accompanied by a movement of regular CCP military units. By mid-December 1945, more than 334,000 troops were in the Northeast; by the second half of October 1947, the number had increased to 465,000. The judgment of Soviet historians, writing in the mid-1980s, that "the Manchurian revolutionary base greatly influenced the political struggle, the course of the civil war and social and economic transformations carried out there in the second half of the 1940s under the influence of the Soviet Union" seems a fair representation of the facts.[5]

It is, of course, impossible to believe this aid was given solely for foreign policy reasons. Moscow knew that its aid was being used mainly to transform the Chinese Communists' army into an offensive-type force capable of undertaking offensive operations in the course of the civil war. Moscow also knew that the ideological affinity between Chinese and Soviet Communists would provide the Soviets with leverage on how the aid was to be used in the future.

In an attempt to create a physical and ideological bridgehead on its East Asian frontiers, the Soviet leadership regarded Mao and the CCP not only as probable allies but also as ideological comrades-in-arms and fellow antagonists of the United States. But Stalin, distrusting Mao's competence as well as his unquestioning loyalty, continued to push the GMD for political and economic concessions. This duality gave Mao reason to accuse Stalin of duplicity as soon as criticism of the former leader had begun in the Soviet capital in the late 1950s. Mao said reproachfully on March 31, 1956, to Pavel Iudin, Soviet ambassador to China:

> In 1947, when the armed struggle against Jiang Jieshi's forces was in full swing, when our troops were winning victory after victory, Stalin insisted upon conclusion of peace with Jiang Jieshi, as he doubted the forces of the Chinese revolution. That lack of faith also remained with Stalin during the first time after the creation of the People's Republic of China, i.e. already after the victory of the revolution.[6]

Nevertheless, despite Moscow's watchfulness, military cooperation between the Soviet Union and the CCP was well under way by 1949. Mao saw the political implications of this aid. In August 1948 he told Dr. A. Y. Orlov, his Soviet physician, that "We have to make sure that our political course completely coincides with that of the USSR." Soviet Politburo member Anastas Mikoyan's visit to Mao in Xibaipo in January–February 1949, made on Stalin's direct orders, furthered that coordination considerably.[7] In a confidential talk with Mikoyan on February 4, Mao assessed the Soviet military aid to the Chinese Communists:

> If there had not been any help from the Soviet Union, we would hardly have been able to gain today's victories. This does not mean that we should not rely upon our own forces. Nevertheless, it is necessary to take into account the fact that the military aid of the Soviet Union in Manchuria, that amounts to one fourth of your total aid, plays quite a considerable role.[8]

Soviet military aid during the civil war created vital psychological conditions for the coming alliance.

Treaties and Bilateral Relations

The 1950 Moscow agreements were set up to provide a legal basis for Sino-Soviet civilian and military cooperation. Both the treaty on friendship and mutual assistance between the Soviet Union and China and the agreement on Lüshun and Dalian contained large military components. According to the treaty, the Soviet Union and China agreed to take all necessary joint measures to prevent any repetition of aggression and breach of peace by Japan or any other state that would directly or indirectly unite with Japan in aggressive acts. In case one party to the treaty was attacked by Japan or its allies, and was thus in a state of war, the other party would immediately render it military or any other assistance with all available means.[9]

With Japan as an ally of the United States, the treaty meant that Moscow acted as a guarantor of the political independence of the People's Republic of China (PRC) and agreed to become a shield in case of possible aggression against China. In addition, the 1950 treaty's protocol established the principles for introduction of Soviet troops and military cargoes on the territory of the People's Republic in case of war in East Asia. This protocol was in force for several years; only in 1957 did the Far Eastern Department of the Soviet Ministry of Foreign Affairs propose to review that particular paragraph of the protocol, as it "was of a one-sided nature."[10]

Under these circumstances, the Soviet leadership could give up a part of the privileges it had acquired from the GMD regime in 1945. The Soviet government gave up its rights on joint management of the Manchurian railways and its properties. Further agreements envisaged the withdrawal of Soviet troops from the jointly used military navy base of Lüshun and its transfer to the Chinese government. But Stalin was in no hurry to withdraw the Soviet troops, and it was left to the post-Stalin leadership to sign an additional document (in October 1954) that confirmed the position of the parties on withdrawal and promised that it would be carried out. As late as 1955 proposals of the People's Republic for the withdrawal of Soviet troops from the Liaodong peninsula languished for several months in Moscow before being implemented in May of that year.[11]

The 1950 agreements also included substantial economic aspects, particularly Soviet credit to the People's Republic in the amount of $300 million. That credit was to be granted over a five-year term in equal portions to cover payments for the deliveries of equipment and machinery from the Soviet Union. The Chinese government agreed to make repayments over ten years, beginning from 1953. The Soviet Union and China also signed a strategically important agreement on construction of a railroad connecting both nations through Mongolia.

The military aspects of this treaty were directed against Japan and the United States, and may be seen to some extent as a mix of the threat perceptions of World War II and the early Cold War. Polarization was the main feature of post-war Asia and was driven largely by Soviet-U.S. rivalry. The Korean War cemented this polarization – on one hand, the common objectives of the Soviet Union and China in the war and their practical military cooperation helped strengthen the alliance; on the other hand, the course of the war reinforced the view that the United States had substantial capabilities for making war even on the Asian continent. Moreover, the U.S.-Taiwan treaty on mutual defense and the creation of the Southeast Asian Treaty Organization (SEATO) in 1954 made the Soviet leaders believe that deepening the alliance with China was their only strategic choice in the region.

For China, the alliance with Moscow thus became a vital security guarantee. The alliance covered Beijing's back and took the People's Republic through the Korean War without the conflict spreading to its territory. After the war, the alliance provided protection and prestige as China shaped its image as a new political force during and after the 1955 Bandung Conference of Afro-Asian newly independent countries.

After Stalin

After Stalin's death in March 1953, Soviet foreign policy went through a series of rapid changes. For the alliance with China, the most important aspect of these changes was the rebirth of Lenin's eastern orientation in foreign affairs, with a special emphasis on China and India.

The policy debate within the Soviet leadership on the approaches to the world outside Europe coincided with a growing uncertainty among Soviet and Chinese military leaders as to the direction of their cooperation. With the end of the Korean War, some higher officers on both sides believed that Sino-Soviet military cooperation had to aim at a higher degree of integration and joint planning. In Moscow in 1953–1954, this debate became part of the more general debate on foreign affairs within the new leadership.

In general policy, two major approaches toward the development of relations with the outside world were in contention. Champions of the first approach, including the Soviet foreign minister, Viacheslav Molotov, while acknowledging the necessity of a "break" in the Cold War, still believed that Soviet foreign policy would have to be based on the idea of continuous and inevitable interbloc struggle. The Soviet Union was vulnerable, the bases of socialism had just been laid, and the party needed to consolidate its leading role in the socialist camp.

Supporters of the second approach, including the CPSU first secretary, Nikita Khrushchev, and the chairman of the USSR Supreme Soviet, Anastas Mikoyan, proceeded from more optimistic estimates and insisted that the European and Asian balance of power was favorable for the socialist camp. Soon after Stalin's death, they began emphasizing the possibility of peaceful coexistence and the existence of "peace zones" in the Third World. This latter understanding attracted serious attention in Soviet diplomacy from 1954 on and was highly relevant with regard to India, for instance. The two approaches battled for supremacy in Soviet foreign policy from 1953 to 1956–1957, and this battle helps explain both the frequently incoherent actions of Soviet diplomacy and its search for new ways to maneuver on the international arena. It was also revealed in full measure in Sino-Soviet military cooperation.

As Khrushchev's dominance grew, the new Soviet leadership commenced to shape up a new course in its relations with China and Yugoslavia, to look for détente in relations with the West, and to reassess its views on the Third World. The leadership counted on Mao's help in keeping the socialist camp stable during this period of foreign policy transformation. Relations between Moscow and Beijing warmed considerably in the very first months after Stalin's death. It is significant that Khrushchev's first foreign trip as leader of the Soviet Union was to China in September 1954.

The Chinese leaders understood that the Soviet Union wanted to use Mao to strengthen its authority in the post-Stalin world and tried to use the opportunity to satisfy China's interests on a large number of issues, primarily economic ones. Already on May 26, 1953, China signed a trade agreement with the Soviet Union on terms quite favorable for Beijing; negotiations over this agreement had long been at a standstill. By establishing a basis for modern Chinese industry, the Soviets also promoted the growth of China's defense power. The Soviet leaders understood well the strategic implications of their economic assistance.

The visit of the Chinese vice-premier, Li Fuchun, to the Soviet Union in May 1953 was also important in this regard. On May 15 Mikoyan and Li signed an agreement on aid to China in the building and reconstruction of 141 large enterprises, with the Soviet Union agreeing to deliver equipment and construction assistance to China by the end of 1959. The list of enterprises included several groups of metallurgic enterprises, nonferrous metals manufacturing enterprises, coal mines, oil refining, motor-car works, tractor plants, and electric power stations. In these negotiations the Chinese obtained several important breakthroughs with regard to Soviet commitments.

The new basic form of military cooperation between the two countries was set out in the Soviet government's memorandum to the People's Republic of August 10, 1954. It said that the Soviet Union was ready to perform design work, to deliver equipment, and to render assistance in construction of fifteen new defense enterprises and to help in construction of the next fourteen new industrial enterprises, including a plant producing up to 600 control devices for antiaircraft missiles per year. The Soviets also agreed to render assistance in design and delivery of equipment for heavy ground and air artillery, including new forms of artillery. In addition, Moscow delivered some of its own draft proposals regarding modernization of separate types of armaments (jet-propelled aircraft MiG-17s, antiaircraft guns, and tank diesel engines).[12] In some cases Chinese plants were able to start production of such improved armaments before the arms industry in the Soviet Union itself.

Khrushchev's visit to China resulted in a series of new agreements. On October 12, 1954, he signed a protocol on increased Soviet equipment deliveries to Chinese industrial enterprises at a cost of more than 400 million rubles and also on rendering assistance in the construction of an additional fifteen enterprises. He also granted the People's Republic another long-term credit of 520 million rubles and signed a joint communiqué on Soviet withdrawal from the Lüshun naval base.[13]

In late 1954 Beijing made a series of other requests to the Soviet Union, among them for assistance in defense and fuel industries and for a group of highly qualified geologists to be sent to the People's Republic. These requests were set out in a letter addressed to Defense Minister Nikolai Bulganin and were passed by Zhou Enlai through the Soviet ambassador. Zhou's office played an important part in coordinating the planning of requests for aid, even if a number of direct channels did exist between Moscow and the individual ministries, not least through Soviet advisers working in Beijing.[14]

After the Twentieth CPSU Congress, in April 1956, Mikoyan visited China and signed new agreements on assistance in the development of advanced industries, including the construction of fifty-five new large enterprises.[15] In his reports to Moscow on the preparations for this visit, Ambassador Iudin noted Beijing's positive reaction to Moscow's new initiatives. Iudin wrote on April 5:

> I visited Mao [on March 31, 1956,] and passed to him the letters of comrade N. S. Khrushchev regarding Soviet aid: 1) in construction of 51 enterprises and 3 scientific research institutes of military industry; 2) in construction of a railway from Urumchi to the Soviet-Chinese border. Mao asked to convey his deep gratefulness to CPSU and the Soviet Government.[16]

China used the aid granted by the Soviet Union to strengthen its defense potential. As the Chinese foreign minister, Chen Yi, put it in a conversation with Iudin on November 22, 1958:

> We in China study the Soviet experience. Socialism in the USSR has already been built, while we are just in the process. Our Army must also study and adopt the rich fighting experience of the Soviet Army. The thing is that if there is a war in the Kuril Islands region, the Soviet Far East will be the front line, while we shall be the home front. At the same time if the war begins in Shandong province, then we shall be the front line, and you will be the home front.[17]

Chen and the other leaders regarded military cooperation with the Soviet Union as a vital component in their efforts to turn China into a powerful state with a developed modern industry. "It is necessary to strengthen ties and cooperation between our armies in time of peace to be ready in case of war," Chen noted a week later. "China is a large but weak country. The Soviet Union has to render China assistance, while listening to some of the points that she makes."[18]

Up until 1958, the Soviet Union was willing to follow this model to a large extent. The main concern of the Soviet leaders was economic: How much could Moscow provide in terms of assistance without harming its own economic development? In terms of military production, therefore, the Soviets preferred to help the Chinese set up enterprises that could help China produce its own sophisticated weapons. This type of military cooperation was rather unusual for Soviet foreign assistance.

The political controversies that in the end destroyed the Sino-Soviet alliance started appearing in the late 1950s. For the military relationship, the most serious difference was the difference in approach to East-West détente. China pressed the Soviet Union to use its leadership and its power for active opposition to the United States and was annoyed when Moscow, quite to the contrary, proclaimed its policy of "peaceful coexistence" with the West. The negative Soviet reactions to the 1958 Taiwan Straits crisis and the 1959 Sino-Indian conflict have to be understood in light of these differences. Assessing these cases in its September 1963 statement, the Soviet government stressed that China had shelled the islands in 1958 without consulting with the Soviet Union, in violation of the 1950 treaty. Moscow also accused China of attempting to torpedo relaxation of global tension by intentionally provoking the border clash with India. Khrushchev believed that China had undertaken these actions expecting Soviet support and that China was seeking to ruin Moscow's détente policy with the United States.[19]

Taiwan and the Conflict with the United States

The military cooperation between the Soviet Union and China was strongly influenced by the war that was continuing between the People's Republic and the Guomindang regime on Taiwan. As the PRC government started to concentrate on the Taiwan issue after the end of the Korean War, Moscow had to decide how far to support Chinese objectives. As long as the United States kept providing security guarantees for the GMD, such Soviet assistance could have started a direct clash with the United States. Under the fragile peace established in Asia after the Korean War, a new outbreak of violence would have represented the Soviet Union in an unfavorable light before the international community. Moreover, at that time the new Soviet leadership loudly proclaimed its course of détente. The détente policy meant that military cooperation with China on this issue would be carried out only secretly, so as not to present the West an opportunity to accuse the Soviets of wishing to unleash a new war.

Throughout the Korean War and in its immediate aftermath, the Soviet Union did supply the Chinese army and its rudimentary navy with amphibious material, such as would be used for landings on the GMD-held offshore islands or on Taiwan itself. But the Soviet General Staff and its advisers in China did not believe that the People's Republic could launch a successful operation against the main islands without several years of preparation and the active involvement of specially assigned Soviet advisers in the planning stages. Even if these conditions were adhered to, the General Staff also realized that Soviet military technology for amphibious operations was still in its infancy and that the Soviet Union could supply little to the PRC that the United States could not easily match with the power it already had in the Taiwan Straits.[20]

The Soviet ambassadors, Iudin especially, kept underlining the international repercussions of a full-scale attack on Taiwan to the Chinese leadership. Chinese officials, on the other hand, felt that they had to reassure the Soviets that no such attacks would be undertaken, even if battles would take place on the smaller GMD-held islands along the Chinese coast. In a conversation with Ambassador Iudin on February 28, 1955, Liu Shaoqi said:

> China's troops can shoot at these islands [Mazu and Jinmen] with our long-range guns, but they have not yet started firing in earnest

upon the islands because in the vicinity of our guns, China does not have railways to deliver arms and ammunition nor airports from where aircraft may support the artillery fire at the islands. At present railroads and airports are being constructed. Let Jiang Jieshi's supporters sit on these islands for a while, and later we shall have them covered so that nobody will be able to run away. If the artillery fire is increased now, they might run away.

Cautious as always, Ambassador Iudin sent the record of the conversation to Moscow but refrained from making any comments of his own.[21]

For Mao and the PRC leaders, the flight of the nationalists to Taiwan caused the struggle to reunify China to be incomplete. After the victory of the 1949 revolution in China, Beijing started to declare the necessity of uniting the country. The Soviets were aware that even though the slogan "Taiwan is an integral part of China" remained the essence of the Chinese approach, China's leaders used the question of Taiwan in different ways. In the mid-1950s it became an important means for tying China to the Soviet Union's nuclear umbrella.

In both Taiwan Straits crises, in 1954–1955 and in 1958, as the United States prepared to repel a PRC attack on Taiwan, the Soviet Union had to evaluate carefully its countermeasures. On both occasions Khrushchev was willing to support China militarily and, if need be, to respond with Soviet forces to an American attack on mainland China. Even though the Soviet leaders had their misgivings about Chinese tactics, they still viewed a credible Soviet nuclear guarantee as being of essential importance both vis-à-vis Washington and in the relationship with Beijing.

On September 19, 1958, Nikita Khrushchev sent a message to President Dwight D. Eisenhower calling on the United States to give up "its aggressive policy, that is constantly creating hot-beds of serious conflicts either in this or that region of the world, and that led to the establishment of an especially tense situation in the Far East at the present time." The message stressed that "nuclear blackmail toward the PRC will intimidate neither us nor the People's Republic of China." It also said that "not only the United States, but our side also possesses nuclear and hydrogen weapons, as well as appropriate means of their delivery, and if the PRC is attacked with such weapons, the aggressor will instantly be repulsed by similar means."[22]

Khrushchev also found it necessary to stress that "attacking the PRC is attacking the USSR" and offered Moscow's version of conflict settlement, which in many ways looked like an ultimatum.

It's necessary to put an end to interference into China's internal affairs. The American navy should be recalled from the Taiwan Straits, and American soldiers should leave Taiwan and go home. There can be no stable peace in the Far East without it. If the U.S. does not do it now, People's China will have no other way out but to banish the armed forces hostile to it from its own territory where a springboard for an attack on the PRC is being created. We are completely on the side of the Chinese Government, the Chinese people. It's their policy that we support and will support.[23]

On September 22, the Soviet position was confirmed in the speech made by the Soviet foreign minister, Andrei Gromyko, at the United Nations General Assembly. Having called for support of India's proposal on the induction of the legitimate government of China into the United Nations, Gromyko said that "the U.S. Government should not treat so lightly the provocations that it started in the Far East, trying to expand aggression against China, including the region of coastal islands. Aggressors should leave Chinese territory, and go where they came from, and do it the sooner the better."[24] Gromyko also said, "China was and still is in China, while the island of Taiwan with coastal islands is an integral part of Chinese territory illegaly captured by the United States and awaiting its liberation."[25]

The tension in the Taiwan Straits and the international attention it attracted pushed Moscow to a more precise formulation of its position on the question of protecting the People's Republic. On September 27 the Central Committee (CC) of the CPSU directed a letter to the CC of CCP, which said that the Soviet Union was ready to render assistance to China in case of an attack of United States or Japan.

> We cannot proceed from a situation in which our enemies can form the illusion that if the PRC is attacked by United States or Japan – the most probable opponents – or by any other state, the Soviet Union will remain as a passive observer. . . . It will be a serious calamity for the whole socialist camp, for the Communist movement, if the U.S.A. lets atomic bombs fall on the PRC and China pays with the lives of its sons and daughters, and, having a dangerous weapon that might not only stop but also defeat our common enemies, we would not render you assistance. . . . As for us, we can say that attacking China means attacking the Soviet Union.[26]

China's immediate reaction to this declaration, made along the channels of interparty communication, was positive, even though the official answer reached Moscow only in the middle of October 1958, after Khrushchev publicly announced that "the Soviet Union will come to the aid of the Chinese People's Republic if it is attacked from the outside. To be more precise, if the U.S. attacks the PRC."[27] Chairman Mao's reply to the CPSU CC dated October 15 was mainly of an ideological nature. It said: "We are deeply touched by your endless devotion to Marxist-Leninist principles and internationalism. On behalf of all the comrades – all CCP members – I express cordial gratitude to you."[28]

Thus Mao secured inclusion of China in the group of countries protected by Moscow's nuclear umbrella. By his actions he had elicited a concrete Soviet commitment to China's defense and thereby strengthened his regime's regional position as well as his influence on Soviet actions. The crisis that he provoked also prompted China to increase its own nuclear program.

Given PRC policies on the Taiwan issue, the Soviet alliance provided the critical support that Mao needed to avert a conflict with the United States. To both Moscow and Beijing, the United States remained a strategic enemy, not least because of its verbal bellicosity on the issue of Taiwan and its support for the GMD. Leaders in both capitals long recalled American statements on "not ruling out" the possibility of using atomic weapons against China and indications that the United States might back GMD vows to recapture the mainland.[29]

Other American policies also forced the Chinese and the Soviets closer together. The embargo on all American exports to China, Hong Kong, and Macao (announced in 1950) and U.S. policies in Japan, Korea, and Indochina meant that the People's Republic found itself almost isolated internationally; thus it was forced to ask ideological allies and Communist countries for help.

Specific Issues of Military Cooperation

According to Russian archival documents, large-scale Sino-Soviet cooperation in building military industries began in early 1955. The Soviet embassy 1955 annual report states that at the end of 1955, the Chinese government officially requested that the Soviets increase and accelerate aid to the People's Republic in a number of industrial and defense construction issues. In a letter to Bulganin dated November 6, 1955, Zhou Enlai requested that 168 Soviet specialists be sent to China to help its defense and fuel industries.[30] Chinese authorities quickly realized that Khrushchev was interested in the creation of a powerful military force in China, and they began to use Moscow's policy in their own interests.

According to Soviet experts, about half of all the equipment delivered from the Soviet Union to China was machinery for integrated enterprises and the defense industry; 95 percent of the total Soviet exports to China consisted of technical equipment, ferrous metals, means of transportation, and oil products – the essentials for building a modern military industry.[31]

The military cooperation between the two countries in the 1950s was one-sided. The Soviet Union was the donor state, while China was the recipient of aid. As the base for China's heavy industry developed in the mid- and late 1950s, Chinese requests for Soviet aid to its military industries became more specific. For instance, in May 1958 Zhou asked Khrushchev to render China technical assistance in the construction of forty-eight projects included in the preliminary list of projects of the PRC's Second Five-Year Plan (all of which required Soviet assistance to complete). Zhou's letter included precise proposals regarding who would design the projects, and he stressed that the most important equipment and machinery for the industrial projects had to be delivered from the Soviet Union. Machinery and equipment set for 1959 delivery would exceed 400 million rubles.[32] The list of projects included enterprises on which China's defense potential depended, among them the aluminium plant in Henan (production capacity of 100,000 tons of aluminium per year), a rare metals plant in Hunan and one in Baotou that processed fifteen rare metals, a special hardware plant with an annual production capacity of 30,000 to 50,000 tons of high-quality wire, a cable factory at a Jiantan military plant producing 50,000 kilometers of cable for defense purposes yearly, precision electrical appliances plants, and power rectifiers plants.[33]

Two months later the PRC government addressed the Soviet government through the Chinese embassy in Moscow with a request for assistance in the construction of several enterprises to produce guided missiles. The enterprises were to be put into operation between 1960 and 1963, along with a number of plants producing devices for those missiles. Actually, the Chinese sought Soviet help in setting up full-scale production of the new Soviet generation of missiles, the most advanced weapons in the Soviet arsenal.[34]

The speed with which defense enterprises in China were to be constructed was so fast that sometimes the Soviets could not keep up. This situation frequently led to failures in the work of Soviet experts. Likewise, the hastily conceived expert missions to China caused havoc in parts of Soviet defense industry, since the necessary staff had to be selected quickly from plants all over the Soviet Union. The Soviet embassy in Beijing collected and reported to Moscow on both Chinese and Soviet accounts on the work of Soviet experts in China. In accordance with the established practice, this information went to the Far East Department of the Foreign Ministry, which then circulated information to appropriate ministries. The Foreign Ministry also coordinated the responses and initiatives from the Soviet side, so that its records give a fairly complete picture even at the level of specific projects in China.

An example related to the military agreements is the correspondence of I. V. Arkhipov, deputy chairman of State Committee on Economic Cooperation, with V. N. Likhachev, deputy head of the Soviet Foreign Ministry's Far East Department in August 1958 on deliveries of "special equipment" (military equipment or weapon prototypes) for the Chinese plant 616, which was engaged in the production of tank engines. According to Arkhipov, difficulties encountered by Soviet designers of these engines caused delays in special equipment deliveries for that plant.[35]

Clearly the capacities of Soviet defense enterprises in the late 1950s could not keep up with the pace of China's defense industry. In his report to the Soviet embassy to China on results of his visit to Soviet-sponsored construction projects in the cities of Baotou and Datong, V. Zharkov, the embassy's first secretary, listed interesting evidence. According to declarations made by Soviet experts, the Soviet Council of Ministers State Committee on Defense Industries was being careless regarding provision of technical documentation to the Chinese recipients. The Soviet diplomat pointed out that sometimes the artillery plant 447 in Baotou received low-quality documentation, which seemed to be collected hurriedly at Soviet plants.[36] Sloppy transport routines often were reported. For instance, there was water inside some of the mixing machines delivered for Jilin's electrode plant, and while in Siberia some of them burst from the frost.[37]

Most hurt by these incidents obviously was the Chinese side, although they also made the work of Soviet experts much more difficult and in some cases caused considerable friction between them and their Chinese colleagues. Zhao Yang, chief engineer of the plant in Jilin, pleaded for the quick arrival of Soviet experts to his plant, telling the Soviets that they should arrive before the agreed date; he was especially insistent that the chief engineer from the Soviet Union arrive more quickly to help the Chinese organize the production after initial mishaps.[38]

In September 1958 the Soviet Council of Ministers adopted a decree on the volume of export of main types of equipment and materials for enterprises that were under construction and planned to be constructed abroad with the Soviet assistance between 1959 and 1965. The plan envisaged that according to the assumed obligations, export volume of equipment and materials for construction of enterprises in China would total 650 million rubles in 1958, 1.160 billion rubles in 1959, 1.082 billion in 1960, 672 million in 1961, 342 million in 1962, 157 million in 1963, and 19 million in 1964.[39] While these plans were never implemented in full, the volumes and the gradual phasing out of this form of Soviet support seems noteworthy.

Soviet Technical Aid to China

A spring 1957 report from the head of the Far East Department of the Soviet Foreign Ministry, I. V. Kurdiukov, provides useful insights into Moscow's technological assistance to China in the 1950s. Kurdiukov pointed out that according to agreements signed between the two countries, it was envisaged that Soviet organizations would deliver engineering equipment for 211 enterprises and 27 separate shops and plants for the total sum of 9.6 billion rubles in export prices. Between 1951 and 1956, 26 enterprises were finished and put into operation in China, 31 enterprises were partially completed, and 17 separate shops and plants were put into operation. Soviet organizations delivered to China equipment costing 8.5 billion rubles; between 1950 and 1956, 5,092 Soviet specialists worked in China, including engineers, workers, and foremen.[40] Enterprises built with Soviet assistance were sometimes equipped with state-of-the-art machinery not yet available at Soviet enterprises.[41]

PRC representatives to the talks with Soviet officials emphasized successes achieved in China with the help of enterprises built with Soviet assistance. In January 1958, for instance, Deputy Premier Bo Yibo said that by the end of 1959, 450 new enterprises would be put into operation, with 57 of them constructed with the help of the Soviet Union. Bo also stated that the number of Soviet-aided enterprises put into operation was in fact larger than indicated in Chinese published documents.[42]

At the same time, the CCP tried to limit the opportunities for any political influence that Soviet specialists might have on their Chinese counterparts. In a talk between Ambassador Iudin and Liu Shaoqi in October 1956, Liu pointed out that serious difficulties had occurred in the work of foreign advisers in the people's democracies, as they were "poorly acquainted with peculiarities of the country they work in. The political recommendations some of these advisers give sometimes lead to negative consequences." According to Liu, some Soviet specialists already had accomplished their tasks in training Chinese staff, and the time had come to discuss their return to the Soviet Union.[43] By 1957 the number of Soviet specialists had been reduced by one-third – by 947 persons in all.[44]

Missile technology was a particularly interesting field of cooperation from a Chinese viewpoint, probably connected to their plans for offensives against Taiwan. On October 7, 1959, a high-speed aircraft (RB-57 D) belonging to the Taiwanese army was shot down by three antiaircraft missiles over Beijing. The aircraft was downed by a Chinese military detachment from an antiaircraft missile complex (C-75). The weapons had been prepared and the personnel had been trained by Soviet military experts. Later, in the 1960s, C-75 complexes were used in Vietnam, and the U.S. Air Force lost many military aircraft because of these weapons.[45]

Several Soviet officers and experts in missile technology served in China in the 1950s. One of the heads of this group was Colonel Alexander Saveliev, a top Soviet specialist, who had been an expert in advanced artillery during the last phase of World War II. He spent almost a year in China in 1958–1959 as chief adviser on battle use of ground-to-ground missiles.

Saveliev headed an independent group of experts and was subordinate only to Army-General Pavel Batov, Chief Military Adviser of the Soviet Union in China. But even this command relationship functioned only in theory: Although he was formally subordinate to Batov, Saveliev's work was considered so important that he could ignore those of the general's orders that did not correspond with instructions received directly from Moscow. Saveliev and his group were supposed to prepare the Chinese as best they could for the use of advanced Soviet missiles, *but* Moscow also instructed him not to pass to China strategic and tactical missiles with an action radius exceeding 1,800 miles. Batov, who was not informed of the decision, kept asking for such weapons for the Chinese.

For most of his mission to China, Saveliev was under direct command of Marshal Nedelin, the deputy Soviet defense minister in charge of special armaments and rocket technology, who from December 1959 headed the new Strategic Missile Corps. It was Nedelin who instructed Saveliev to help the Chinese only regarding SS-2 and SS-1 missiles, the short-range missiles that had just been designed by the famous engineer Sergei Korolev.

The so-called missile group in Beijing was headed by Major Sukhodolskii, a test engineer from the rocket testing base Kapustin Yar. Officers of that group were engaged mainly in introducing the new technology to Chinese military representatives and in work on the testing area that was being constructed in northwest China, in the Gobi Desert. Colonel Saveliev guided that group's activity.

It is impossible to say if the Chinese knew that the Soviets were deliberately holding back some advanced missile technology. On the surface, at least, the PLA expressed gratitude to the Soviet Army for the aid of its specialists. "The USSR seeks to help our army with new, modern weapons. To render assistance in mastering it, the Soviet Army command has sent one of its best missile experts to China," said the PLA deputy chief of staff at a dinner given on the occasion of Colonel Saveliev's arrival.[46]

The Chinese experts carefully studied the Soviet experience with missiles and artillery, including troop structure; Soviet experts recommended that the Chinese take a regiment as the basis for the PLA structure. The Chinese followed that advice; as a result, in a year's time twenty regiments were formed in China with SS-2 and SS-1 missiles.

The Soviet aid was instrumental in equipping China with a fairly advanced system of missile defenses, far above what the Chinese could have managed on their own. But the Soviet Union had no intention of helping China create or deploy modern long-range offensive missile systems. Even during the heyday of

Sino-Soviet cooperation, Soviet leaders believed that it would not be in their interests to give China a forward capacity equaling their own.

Cooperation on Nuclear Science

Nuclear cooperation held a special place in bilateral relations. In March 1956 the Soviet Union, the People's Republic, and nine other socialist countries organized a Joint Institute of Nuclear Research in the small town of Dubna near Moscow. The Soviet Union bore half of the expenses of setting up the institute, while China covered 20 percent. The newly established institute included the nerve centers of Soviet nuclear research, the Institute of Nuclear Research and the Electric and Physical Laboratory of the Soviet Academy of Sciences. The laboratories of the Dubna institute were the best Soviet science could offer; they possessed giant accelerating installations for the study of the atomic nucleus, the world's largest synchrophasotron and synchrocyclotron. Chinese scientists had their first real opportunity to do advanced nuclear research at this institute.

Chinese participation in the programs of the Dubna institute was governed by the April 1955 agreement on Soviet assistance to China in carrying out research in nuclear physics and tests of using nuclear energy for peaceful purposes. According to the agreement, an experimental atomic reactor and accelerators of elementary particles would be designed and delivered to China in 1955–1956; China also would receive, free of charge, scientific and technical documentation related to the atomic reactor and accelerators and assistance in assembling and activating the reactor. The results of this cooperation materialized very soon. On September 27, 1958, not far from Beijing, China's first experimental nuclear reactor (with a capacity of 10,000 kilowatts) was put into operation together with a cyclotron that provided 24 million electron-volts. Marshal Nie Rongzhen, deputy premier of the PRC State Council, said at the opening of the reactor that putting the reactor and cyclotron into operation enabled Chinese industry and agriculture to develop rapidly and would serve as a productive force.[47]

The new Chinese government aimed at becoming a nuclear power, with Soviet assistance. While Mao publicly belittled the effect of nuclear weapons, he and other Chinese leaders argued that China needed such weapons to protect itself against imperialist attacks. During the 1950s, Chinese leaders avoided stating that those weapons must never be used and never discussed nuclear doctrines with the Soviet leaders while Sino-Soviet nuclear cooperation was under way.

Quite early during the Sino-Soviet alliance Soviet leaders started to worry about Chinese views on nuclear war. Mao's speech at the second session of the Eighth CCP Congress in 1956 staggered the Soviets. Mao said:

War will be all right. . . . We should not be afraid of war. If there is war, then there will be those who will be killed. . . . I believe that the atomic bomb is not more dangerous than a large sword. If half of humanity is killed during this war, it will not matter. It is not terrible if only one third of the world's population survives.[48]

The Soviet leaders never seem to have had a clear vision of why China needed nuclear weapons. In the mid-1950s, when the Soviet leaders sought ways to support the CCP's plans for turning China into a socialist state, it seemed that Moscow's assistance to China's own nuclear program would not damage Soviet interests. The 1957 Soviet offer of a sample atomic bomb came at a time when China already had a nuclear program and had started intensive work on nuclear weapons technology. In order to acquire nuclear weapons in the shortest possible time, China made that program a top priority.

By the end of the 1950s, China tried to use the authority of Soviet nuclear weapons to increase its own political weight. This strategy was especially obvious when in May 1958 the Chinese foreign minister, Chen Yi, stressed that China intended to possess nuclear weapons. The Soviet Union supported China during the September–October 1958 crisis over the Taiwan Straits and said that it would not permit an attack on China by the United States and Japan. At the same time, however, Moscow informed Beijing that China could not use threats of Soviet nuclear retaliation to back Chinese political aims in the straits.

The second Taiwan crisis in 1958 led Moscow to reevaluate its attitude toward nuclear-weapon creation in China. Reviewing China's economic potential, Moscow understood that even after the People's Republic created its own nuclear weapons, it would take years for the country to develop a credible nuclear force. Thus, Chinese possession of nuclear weapons would *politically* help to shift the balance of world power in favor of socialism while not threatening Soviet superiority. This attitude did not change until the end of the Sino-Soviet military relationship in the early 1960s, even though Khrushchev started having second thoughts about how outsiders viewed Soviet assistance to Chinese nuclear programs after his visit to Beijing in mid-1958.

In the Soviet-supplied reactor – the only known nuclear installation in that country in 1958 – China could be expected to extract five kilograms of plutonium by the end of 1960, about the amount necessary to manufacture one bomb. Beijing's dependence on Soviet-manufactured enriched uranium for fuel supply for the reactor was probably why the Chinese started looking for their own sources. The enriched uranium used during China's first nuclear test in October 1964 was a product of the gaseous diffusion plant constructed in Lanzhou in Gansu Province with limited Soviet contribution.[49] By the time of the first successful Chinese nuclear explosion in 1964, Soviet-Chinese nuclear cooperation had ceased completely.[50]

Soviet nuclear assistance was withdrawn for three main reasons. First, the Soviet Union, as the only country in the socialist camp to possess nuclear weapons, hesitated to lose that monopoly. Even if there had been no political differences, for Moscow such a development created an unnecessary precedent for polarization between socialist countries. But from 1958–1959 on, Soviet leaders also were worried – although they never stated this openly – that China, attracted by the prospect of its own regional nuclear hegemony, could use its possession of nuclear weapons to blackmail other countries. By 1960 Moscow even feared that Soviet security problems might emerge if China received technology that allowed it to create an atomic bomb. Thus Moscow tried to minimize the risk that China could harm the Soviet Union or its satellites if political relations turned sour.

Nuclear cooperation was undoubtedly the most sensitive and dangerous part of the Sino-Soviet military relationship. Although getting access even to the most basic documentation of these special programs has proven very difficult, we know enough to make us wonder why Khrushchev and his leadership seemed willing to take the extraordinary risks involved in providing another country with nuclear weapons. After all, the United States was never willing to take such risks with any of its allies in Europe – even if Washington accepted and to some degree abetted Great Britain's nuclear weapons program, it never contemplated providing direct assistance in the way the Soviet Union did in China.

Perhaps the most obvious reason why the early Khrushchev leadership was willing to help Beijing to get an atomic bomb was the enthusiasm for socialist construction and technological achievement in Moscow during the mid-1950s. Khrushchev and his close associates believed in the alliance with China in a way that their predecessors never did and in a way that Khrushchev himself later regretted bitterly. During these leaders' first enthusiastic years in power, providing China with nuclear weapons may have seemed a small price to pay for an alliance that would lead two continents into socialism.

Military Cooperation vs. Political Conflict

The 1950s saw very substantial military cooperation between China and the Soviet Union, although few reports of the cooperation reached the open press at the time or have since been reported by historians. In many ways China was dependent on Soviet support to create the foundations of its own armed forces and defense industries. In the postwar period 265 complete enterprises were built in China with technical assistance from the Soviet Union. Industrial enterprises accounted for 243 of them (91.6 percent). Of these only nine were left unfinished when Sino-Soviet cooperation ended.[51] According to the deputy chairman of China's State Planning Committee, Gong Zuoxin, Soviet assistance was involved in about half of all new plants put into operation by the end of 1957.[52]

According to Russian figures, the Soviet Union assisted China in construction of enterprises for 9.4 billion rubles in export prices, with equipment deliveries amounting to 8.4 billion rubles and technical assistance to 1 billion rubles.[53] Thus expenditures on construction of industrial enterprises in China amounted to about 100 billion rubles in Soviet domestic budget terms. Taking into consideration that in 1959, the national income of the Soviet Union totaled approximately 1.3 trillion rubles, construction of enterprises in China accounted for approximately 7 percent of the Soviet annual national income.[54]

It is possible to look at this figure from another angle. In 1960 Soviet authorities decided to begin construction of small apartments worth up to 35,000 rubles each. For the money invested in constructing industrial enterprises in China, the Soviets could have built about 2.6 million such apartments.

About half of all the equipment delivered from the Soviet Union to China was intended for military enterprises and plants. According to Soviet experts, at the end of the 1950s defense expenses amounted to more than one-quarter of the state budget of the People's Republic – 7 billion yuan out of 26.9 billion yuan.[55] Defense was the largest area of expenditure in the PRC budget.

During the frosty Sino-Soviet relations in the 1960s and 70s, Soviet media claimed that the People's Republic would not have survived without Moscow's assistance. China, in turn, disparaged the importance of that aid. The existence of two antipolar views on this question hardly favored the improvement of relations between the countries. But it is telling that even during this period, authors in polemical articles published both in China and the Soviet Union evaded the question of past military cooperation. Now we know that this omission was not accidental – the military cooperation was too important and too sensitive to figure in the polemics. For the Soviet Union, it was a huge gamble that ultimately failed. For China, it was a heritage that proved politically embarrassing but militarily useful as the country took on the role of regional Great Power.

Notes

1. William W. Whitson, ed., *Military and Political in Power in China in the 1970s* (New York: Praeger, 1972), gives a good overview of early Western studies of the field. Western studies and estimates were, however, limited by a narrow database because of

the unwillingness of China and the Soviet Union to provide any records of their cooperation. For more recent surveys, see the introductory chapters in Ellis Joffe, *The Chinese Army after Mao* (Cambridge, Mass.: Harvard University Press, 1987); Gerald Segal, *Defending China* (New York: Oxford University Press, 1987).

2. Sergei Tikhvinskii, *Put kitaia k obedineniiu i nezavisimosti, 1898–1949* [China's road to unification and independence, 1898–1949] (Moscow: Vostochnaia literatura, 1996), 418–19.

3. See Steven I. Levine, *Anvil of Victory: The Communist Revolution in Manchuria, 1945–1948* (New York: Columbia University Press, 1987).

4. Much of the archives on China in the *Rossiiskii tsentr khraneniia i zucheniia dokumentov noveishei istorii* [RTsKhIDNI; Russian Center for the Preservation and Study of Documents of Contemporary History], including the Comintern archives and parts of the archives of the International Department of the CPSU CC, are now available to scholars. In terms of Soviet military support for the pre-1949 CCP, the findings in the archives roughly correspond with Soviet texts from the Cold War period, in spite of their propagandistic nature; see, for instance, O. B. Borisov [Oleg B. Rakhmanin], *The Soviet Union and the Manchurian Revolutionary Base* (Moscow: Progress, 1975), 185; S. L. Tikhvinsky, general ed., *Modern History of China, 1928–1949* (Moscow: Institute of the Far East, 1984), 262. Rakhmanin worked in the Soviet consulate in Harbin from 1946 to 1949.

5. Tikhvinsky, *Modern History of China,* 265.

6. Foreign Policy Archive of the Russian Federation (AVPRF), fond (f.) 0100, opis (op.) 49, papka (pa.) 410, delo (d.) 9, 90.

7. Archive of the President of the Russian Federation (APRF), f. 39, op. 31, pa. 41, d. 1, and f. 3, op. 65, pa. 3, d. 606. Materials on Mikoyan's secret mission to China were selected by Andrei Ledovsky and published in *Problemy dalnego vostoka,* nos. 2 and 3 (1995).

8. APRF, f. 39, op. 1, d. 39, pa. 58.

9. *Pravda,* February 15, 1950.

10. AVPRF, f. 0100, op. 50, pa. 426, d. 29, p. 20.

11. AVPRF, f. 0100, op. 48, pa. 393, d. 9, p. 51.

12. AVPRF, f. 0100, op. 47, pa. 379, d. 5, pp. 90–1.

13. *Pravda,* October 12, 1954.

14. AVPRF, f. 0100, op. 48, pa. 393, d. 9, p. 160.

15. *Pravda,* February 8, 1956; Mikhail S. Kapitsa, *Soviet-Chinese Relations* (Moscow: 1957), 357, 364.

16. AVPRF, f. 0100, op. 49, pa. 410, d. 9, p. 87; for an English translation of Iudin's report, see *Cold War International History Project* (*CWIHP*) *Bulletin* 6–7 (Winter 1995/1996): 164–7.

17. AVPRF, f. 0100, op. 51, pa. 432, d. 6, p. 190.

18. AVPRF, f. 0100, op. 51, pa. 432, d. 6, p. 196.

19. *Pravda,* September 1, 1963.

20. Former Soviet Vice-Foreign Minister Mikhail S. Kapitsa, interview with Odd Arne Westad and others, Moscow, September 7, 1992.

21. AVPRF, f. 0100, op. 49, pa. 410, d. 9, p. 37.

22. *Izvestia,* September 20, 1958.

23. Ibid.

24. *Izvestia,* September 24, 1958.

25. Ibid.

26. AVPRF, f. 0100, op. 51, pa. 432, d. 6, p. 121; see also Vladislav M. Zubok, "Khrushchev's Nuclear Promise to Beijing during the 1958 Crisis," *CWIHP Bulletin,* 6–7 (Winter 1995/1996): 219, 226–7.

27. *Izvestia,* October 7, 1958.

28. AVPRF, f. 0100, op. 51, pa. 432, d. 6, p. 127.

29. See, for instance, *Department of State Bulletin,* May 28, 1951, 848.

30. AVPRF, f. 0100, op. 49, pa. 412, d. 22, p. 129.

31. Ibid., 131.

32. AVPRF, f. 0100, op. 51, pa. 431, d. 3, pp. 40–1.

33. AVPRF, f. 0100, op. 51, pa. 436, d. 42, pp. 9–13.

34. AVPRF, f. 0100, op. 51, pa. 431, d. 3, pp. 50–2.

35. AVPRF, f. 0100, op. 51, pa. 436, d. 42, p. 50.

36. Ibid., 27.

37. AVPRF, f. 0100, op. 49, pa. 412, d. 22, p. 142.

38. AVPRF, f. 0100, op. 51, pa. 436, d. 42, p. 28.

39. Ibid., 53.

40. AVPRF, f. 0100, op. 50, pa. 426, d. 29, pp. 28–32.

41. Kapitsa, *Soviet-Chinese Relations,* 366.

42. AVPRF, f. 0100, op. 51, pa. 432, d. 6, p. 20.

43. AVPRF, f. 0100, op. 40, pa. 410, d. 9, p. 202.

44. AVPRF, f. 0100, op. 50, pa. 426, d. 29, p. 69.

45. *Moskovskii Komsomolets,* April 13, 1995.

46. *Krasnaia Zvezda,* May 13, 1995.

47. *Izvestia,* September 28, 1958.

48. *Pravda,* May 14, 1977.

49. Charles Horner, "The Production of Nuclear Weapons," in Whitson, ed., *Military and Political Power,* 239. See also John Lewis and Xue Litai, *China Builds the Bomb* (Stanford, Calif.: Stanford University Press, 1988).

50. See interview with Zhou Enlai, *New York Times,* May 21, 1970.

51. *Narodnoie khoziaistvo SSSR za 70 let* [USSR economy over 70 years] (Moscow: Finance and Statistics, 1987), 651.

52. *Pravda,* October 2, 1959.

53. AVPRF, f. 0100, op. 50, pa. 426, d. 29, p. 61.

54. Calculated from figures presented by Krushchev in his speech published in *Pravda,* May 6, 1960. In 1959 one ruble in export prices was equal to about 10 rubles in domestic prices.

55. AVPRF, f. 0100, op. 49, pa. 412, d. 22, p. 294.

5. The Sino-Soviet Alliance and the United States

Odd Arne Westad

For the Sino-Soviet alliance, the conflict with the United States was both a co-hesive element and a point of contention. The war against American troops in Korea shaped and cemented the alliance in ways that neither the Soviets nor the Chinese had predicted in 1950. On the other hand, the failure to agree on strat-egy in the global confrontation with Washington fueled the disintegration of the alliance from 1958 on. In this way it makes sense to understand the content of Sino-Soviet friendship primarily as an anti-American alliance – or, at the global level, as an antisystemic alliance – directed against the postwar U.S. presence in Asia and the world capitalist system in which the United States was the domi-nant power.

Although both Soviet and Chinese leaders viewed themselves as locked in an enduring conflict with the United States, their perceptions of the substance of that conflict varied widely. For Mao Zedong and most members of the Chinese leadership, the conflict was about U.S. attempts to dominate their region and about the massive evidence they discovered about the aggressive nature of U.S. imperialism. For the post-Stalin Soviet leaders, the main issues were universal recognition of Moscow's global role and the search for a managed or at least structured conflict with Washington. These differing perceptions spilled over onto other foreign policy issues in the alliance, such as Taiwan, India, Eastern Europe, and the Middle East.[1]

The author wishes to thank Nancy Bernkopf Tucker and Gordon Chang for their helpful comments when this chapter was presented at a conference in Hong Kong in January 1996.

If we choose to regard Sino-Soviet cooperation primarily as an antisystemic alliance directed against the United States and its hegemony in global politics, we need to explain why the alliance broke down just as Washington was solidifying its control of the Asia-Pacific region. How much did U.S. pressure on China contribute to the breakdown? And how did the prospect of conflict with the United States influence the allies' perceptions of each other?

In answering these questions, we need to look more closely at the changing images of U.S. power and intentions within the Soviet and Chinese leaderships. Often these images were very different from Western depictions of its own position and capabilities, and frequently the dominant understandings in Moscow and Beijing were at odds with each other. Although both sets of leaders understood U.S. power within a Marxist framework, they frequently disagreed in their conclusions. Reading through their policy papers, we could easily argue that the limited amount of concrete evidence available in Beijing or Moscow on production, market, and class struggle in the United States, on intercapitalist rivalries, and on the relationship between American capital and the capital of other imperialist countries contributed strongly to these differences.

But the narrow categories for understanding developments in the West did not prevent the two leaderships from constructing broad interpretations regarding the course of American power. On the Soviet side, the Khrushchev leadership from 1957 to 1958 on, under the impression of the integration of West Germany into Western markets and into the North Atlantic Treaty Organization (NATO), and the cautious American response to the 1956–1957 unrest in Eastern Europe, had come to believe that the United States was consolidating its position of dominance in Europe. Contrary to what some scholars have believed, the Soviet sense of its own achievements in the late 1950s was not accompanied by an increased sense of security. Although stressing the deepening impotence of U.S. power outside Europe, Nikita Khrushchev feared that as the domestic successes of socialism grew, American imperialism would become increasingly aggressive and concentrate its main efforts against the Soviet Union and its allies, and even threaten to obliterate the socialist achievements through war. His détente policies were the direct results of this perception.[2]

The Chinese leadership's views of the United States were also uncertain and fluctuating. But in contrast to Khrushchev, Mao Zedong in the late 1950s started to underline American vulnerability, even in military terms. The chairman's reading of the world, especially after the second Taiwan Straits crisis in mid-1958, was that the American position had been undermined by the other main capitalist countries and by nationalist regimes in Asia and Africa. Together with the reignited campaigns for socialism in China, the consolidation of the Communist regimes in Eastern Europe, and the perceived domestic economic problems in the United States, Mao and his followers believed they witnessed a global "anticapitalist wave" that was challenging American hegemony.

The new evidence shows that these differing perceptions played a key role in the breakup of the Sino-Soviet alliance. Just as the parallel perceptions of the United States in the early phase of the alliance provided much of the glue to hold it together, changed perceptions in the later period became a wedge to drive it apart.

The United States and the Formation of the Alliance

During the Chinese civil war, Mao knew that he needed an international alliance of his own to counter the alliance between the Guomindang (GMD) and the United States. He also knew that the Soviet Union was his best choice for an alliance partner, both because of the Marxist-Leninist worldview that both sides professed to and because of the breakdown of Soviet-GMD relations in the spring of 1946. Mao had concluded from his troubled attempts at cooperating with the Soviets in Manchuria after the Japanese surrender that a similar worldview was not enough to keep an alliance between the Chinese Communist Party (CCP) and the Soviets together. He needed to offer Stalin something that Jiang Jieshi (Chiang Kai-shek) would not give: the hope for long-term Soviet influence in China *and* cooperation directed against the United States. These two elements – ideology and availability – together formed the fertile soil from which the alliance grew.[3]

But if the Sino-Soviet relationship during the civil war was the ground from which the alliance sprang, then resentment of the United States was the climate that shaped and nurtured it. To Mao, Washington had proven itself during the last phase of his party's battle with the GMD to be an implacable enemy of the revolution, an enemy that in its search for domination over China would threaten the existence of his government. For Stalin, the United States was the leading country in the imperialist camp and the director of the efforts to deny the Soviet Union its rightful share of global influence after World War II. To his surprise, China became an area in which Stalin could get back at the United States without risking war. The means for doing so was an alliance with the Chinese Communists, even if this was a party that had inconvenienced Stalin at several important junctures and that he therefore distrusted more than most other fraternal parties.[4]

In the final months leading up to the signing of the formal alliance in early 1950 – a period that also saw the establishment of the People's Republic of China (PRC) – both Chinese and Soviets for their own purposes stressed the aggressive intentions of the United States in East Asia. Moscow underlined what it saw as American plans for a rearmament of Japan and economic and military control of Southeast Asia. Mao and the Chinese leaders emphasized that the United States was still plotting to subvert the victory of the Chinese Revolution, by providing support for the GMD remnant on Taiwan and also – and more important – by organizing and funding counterrevolutionary groups on the mainland. To the Chinese, Washington's actions demonstrated the need for creating a formalized Sino-Soviet alliance as soon as possible.[5]

In the written report that the second-ranking leader of the Chinese Party Liu Shaoqi presented to the Soviet Politburo in Moscow on July 11, 1949, he repeatedly stressed the American threat:

> We have always reckoned with the possibility of imperialist armed intervention against the Chinese Revolution. The instructions given to us in this matter by the Soviet Communist Party, which we have accepted in full, have alerted us to give more attention in this regard. . . . Quite possibly, the imperialists would dispatch 100,000 to 200,000 troops for seizing three or four Chinese ports or for committing various acts of sabotage.[6]

American designs to split Moscow and Beijing further underscored the urgency of a meeting between Stalin and Mao to sign a treaty that would powerfully demonstrate to the imperialists Soviet military support for the new Communist regime. Li Kenong – the CCP head of intelligence who served as Mao's messenger to the Soviet ambassador during the first years of the People's Republic – charged in a November 1949 conversation at the Soviet embassy that the Americans had a "plan of changing the CCP to echo the Tito clique" and had strengthened their "efforts in China to undermine Sino-Soviet friendship." Among the main points of imperialist propaganda were, according to Li, accusations that the Soviets were "stealing China's food and resources and attacks on the Sino-Soviet treaty of 1945, characterizing it as an unequal, imperialist treaty as a result of which China lost Guandong and all industrial equipment in Manchuria."[7]

The not-too-subtle duality of Mao's message was not lost on Ambassador Nikolai Roshchin nor on his Moscow superiors and must have been one of the reasons why Stalin was not too eager to see the treaty renegotiated. Yet Stalin probably realized that some changes to the treaty, accompanied by Soviet economic and military aid, were the price that had to be paid to cash in on the advantages a strong Soviet position in China would have in the international power game. There was something halfhearted in the Soviet efforts to postpone a Sino-Soviet summit in the last half of 1949, and when Premier Zhou Enlai made it plain that Mao insisted on being received in Moscow, Stalin did not risk turning down the Chinese leader's self-invitation to the *Vozhd*'s – the "Boss's" – seventieth birthday celebrations.[8]

In the months after the founding of the People's Republic of China, its leaders were much preoccupied with how to meet the American threat. Their main concerns were with U.S.-sponsored domestic subversion, particularly in the cities, which the Chinese Communists, in spite of their military victory, felt unable to control, and with the construction of anti-Communist bases in areas bordering the People's Republic, particularly in Indochina. Mao wanted to reduce the risk of American support for counterrevolution by evicting all Americans – diplomats, missionaries, and businessmen – from China. He also wanted to send People's Liberation Army (PLA) units to Indochina to fight alongside the Vietminh against the French and those GMD remnants that Mao suspected of working for the French and U.S. governments. Indochina, Zhou Enlai explained to the Soviet ambassador, had the highest priority in terms of Chinese military preparations, even higher than the preparations for the liberation of Taiwan.[9]

Mao probably expected to discuss strategy on both these issues during his visit to Moscow. Stalin, however, did not wait for Mao's arrival to reject both proposals. He reiterated his advice from the spring of 1949 that China ought not to reject trade with the United States or other capitalist countries, nor should the new government turn down offers of diplomatic recognition. Stalin also objected strongly to sending PLA units to Vietnam, stressing that neither the timing nor circumstances for such an effort benefited the world Communist movement. It has later been suggested that Stalin's attitude was associated primarily with his view of the political potential of the French left wing in forthcoming elections. In any case, Mao had little of his own foreign policy agenda to discuss with Stalin when the Chinese leader arrived in Moscow on December 16.[10]

What was on Mao's mind when he started his conversations was giving a new shape to Sino-Soviet relations. Mao wanted to formalize his alliance with the Soviet Union in order to secure support from Moscow in case of war with the United States. He also needed Soviet assistance in building China's economy and defense. But in addition to his practical needs, Mao also told Stalin that he wanted something "beautiful" – that is, the abrogation of the 1945 Sino-Soviet treaty that Moscow had signed with Jiang Jieshi and that Mao and his associates regarded as a reminder of the unequal treaties of the past.[11]

Past accounts of the Moscow talks have pointed out that the United States became "the invisible third partner in the Stalin-Mao dialogue."[12] The problem has been *how* the issue of dealing with the invisible player influenced the talks. Some scholars stress Stalin's perfidious strategy of exacerbating Sino-Western tensions in order to increase Chinese dependence on the Soviet Union. It is dif-

169

ficult to find much support for this thesis in the records. Quite to the contrary, Stalin's favorite role during his talks with Mao was that of the cautious statesman who could dictate strategy to his Chinese partners because of his superior understanding of the international situation.

The differing attitudes of Mao and Stalin on how to confront the American enemy were based on differing assumptions of the likelihood of a U.S. attack against their countries. Mao was convinced that an American assault on China would come – he could just not say when it would happen. His chief of intelligence, Li Kenong, visited the Soviet chargé d'affaires, Shibaev on January 16 – just as the two sides were starting serious negotiations in Moscow – and informed the startled diplomat that the CCP "has information . . . that the Americans are going to unleash the new, third World War this June, starting with military actions in the Pacific and making use of Japan, Formosa, and South Korea."[13] Although neither Li nor Mao may have trusted this kind of information, in no way they did consider the prospects unlikely. By informing the Soviets, they prompted the apprehension of an American attack – the very prospect that gave urgency to the Moscow negotiations.

Stalin's perspective was less dramatic with regard to war. The Soviet nuclear test in 1949 and American restraint with regard to Berlin and the Communist victory in China had convinced him that a Soviet-U.S. war could be avoided, at least for the forseeable future. Especially if he was to sign a mutual defense treaty with the People's Republic, he needed to see to it that his Chinese protégées did not on their own provoke a war with Washington. In his first meeting with Mao on December 16, Stalin stressed that concerning Taiwan, the Chinese should not "give [the] Americans an excuse to interfere." "There is no need for you to create conflicts with the British and the Americans."[14] From his dealings with Mao since 1946, Stalin must have realized that he did not need to remind the Chinese of the American threat – it was there already in a much more potent form than could ever be conveyed from abroad.

Initially Stalin was very hesitant to sign an alliance treaty with the People's Republic. He preferred to make revisions to the 1945 treaty that he had signed with the Jiang Jieshi regime, thereby both safeguarding the concessions he had wrested from the Guomindang five years earlier and avoiding unnecessarily provoking the United States by putting the public spotlight on an anti-American alliance. The two main reasons why Mao still got his alliance in the end were first, his increasingly desperate pleads to Andrei Vyshinskii, Vyacheslav Molotov, Anastas Mikoyan, and Ambassador Nikolai Roshchin over the New Year holidays. Many among the Soviet leadership believed that for Mao to leave Moscow without a new treaty would undermine his and his party's position in China. They felt that the Soviet Union needed to do its part to secure its new Communist neighbor, and Mikoyan, among others, suggested to Stalin that there may be ways to set up a new treaty without negative repercussions for the Soviet Union.[15]

Also, Stalin's reading of the signals that came out of Washington during the Sino-Soviet summit helped reduce his hesitancy to negotiate a new agreement. Stalin had Molotov read out aloud to Mao parts of the speech of U.S. Secretary of State Dean Acheson before the National Press Club on January 12. Molotov underlined that Washington wanted to stir up trouble with regard to Sino-Soviet friendship and that Acheson implied that the United States would concentrate on holding on to Taiwan. Mao commented that this was a challenge to which both China and the Soviet Union had to stand up.[16]

The Korean War

The Korean War was a war that nobody but North Korean leader Kim Il Sung and his Pyongyang associates really wanted, but which Stalin brought about as a result of his indecisiveness and precarious judgment. It became the first and only hot war between the United States and another Great Power during the Cold War era and brought with it periods of extraordinary tension and danger, particularly during the first six months. It devastated the Korean peninsula and solidified Mao's control of the Chinese Communist Party, a grip that in the long run would mean at least as much destruction and suffering as the war itself.[17]

The war also anchored the Sino-Soviet alliance in a much more concrete image of the enemy than during the Moscow negotiations – the United States had shown that it was willing to and capable of fighting a war on the Asian mainland. If the United States could intervene in Korea, it also could strike against China if its political leaders decided to do so. For Beijing the Korean War proved that the American threat was real and imminent, an awareness that stayed with the CCP leadership at least up to 1958, although the outcome of the war convinced Mao and most Chinese that China could successfully resist outside intervention in "its" region.

Mao also realized that Soviet aid had contributed to the Chinese ability to fight the United States, although the assistance, at least initially, was far below what the Chinese had hoped for. Since Mao misinterpreted Stalin's prewar diplomatic bungling for revolutionary fervor, he also believed that the war showed the Soviet Union to be "sincere" in its ideological commitments to defend East Asian revolutions. The real significance of Mao's conclusion was of course his realization that the Soviet Union – with its nuclear capabilities – was a powerful permanent deterrent against a direct American attack on China.

To Stalin – after he had recovered from the shock of the powerful U.S. counterattack – the Korean War showed that the Chinese had stronger military capabilities than he had ever expected. This Chinese prowess allowed him to influence the war from the back stage rather than having to face the consequences of giving the go-ahead to Kim's attack. It is quite possible that Stalin was sufficiently impressed with the Chinese performance to plan an upgrading – in terms of economic and technological cooperation – of the alliance during 1952–1953, even though Mao's resistance against ending the war in 1951 had annoyed the Soviet leader.

In practical terms, to both Beijing and Moscow, the war against the United States worked rather well. Already during the first days after the North Korean attack, the two sides discussed how China could assist Kim Il Sung. In a meeting between Ambassador Roshchin and the Chinese head of intelligence, Zhou Dapeng, Zhou described how North Korean forces were being sent to South Korea via ports on the Shandong Peninsula and how Beijing had sent Chinese "specialists" to South Korea to assist the advancing North Korean troops.[18]

The main problem in the latter phase of the war was how to arrive at a cease-fire in a conflict that neither Stalin nor Mao any longer believed that their side could win. During his meetings with Zhou Enlai in Moscow in the summer of 1952, Stalin initially paid lip service to Mao's position from the year before, while underlining that the Chinese and North Koreans should not undertake any offensives and should postpone the prisoner-of-war issues until after an armistice agreement was signed. Stalin knew that the war was taxing China's economy and its resources, and probably had expected that Mao would come around to accept a cease-fire. When that did happen, Stalin's own insistence on controlling the negotiation processes prolonged the war, at least by several months.[19]

The High Point of Sino-Soviet Cooperation

Stalin's death in March 1953 brought with it both a general relaxation of international tension and the prospect for closer Sino-Soviet cooperation. The passing of the increasingly unpredictable dictator left the new Soviet leaders longing for some stability in their foreign relations and an improvement of contacts with the West – interestingly, *all* major contenders for power in the Kremlin seem to have based their ideas on these premises. With Stalin gone, the association between the Soviet Union and China – and between Mao and Stalin's successor – could become more equal, stable, and mutually profitable. The conflict between the blocs seemed headed for a calmer period, one in which the need for inward integration, both East and West, replaced the outward battles of the early Cold War period.[20]

The Geneva conference seemed to symbolize the new spirit of the mid-1950s. A war-weary China not only agreed to Soviet proposals for how to find a peaceful settlement to the Indochina conflict, but Mao also accepted putting Zhou Enlai's diplomatic skills to work in convincing the Vietnamese Communists that a temporary division of their country was in the best interests both of themselves and of world revolution. Moscow concluded that the CCP had lost its appetite for engaging the imperialists at any given chance and thought it a better ally for that.[21]

Mao had three main concerns about the new international climate. First, as a nationalist, he worried that having forced the Vietnamese to accept a division of their country, he also may have to accept the separation of Taiwan from the motherland for a long time to come. Second, he still feared that the United States could launch a surprise attack on China in alliance with Chinese counterrevolutionaries. Third, at least by early 1955 he started to agonize over the fate of domestic social revolution as the CCP regime moved toward normalizing its internal and external state functions.[22]

All these apprehensions may have contributed to Mao's decision in the late summer of 1954 to launch attacks on the small islands that the GMD occupied off the Chinese coast. What prompted the attacks, however, was the Eisenhower administration's negotiations with Jiang Jieshi over a mutual defense treaty. Such a treaty, Mao feared, would separate Taiwan from the mainland permanently and make it a base for U.S. preparations for war against China. It could not stand without challenge. However, the CCP Politburo was very careful in spelling out to its military leaders and to the Soviets that its aims were limited. The purpose of the attacks was to occupy the coastal islands and to "strike against" the U.S.-GMD treaty.[23]

The Soviet leaders did not protest Chinese strategy on the islands issue, although they were baffled by a CCP strategy that they found counterproductive with regard to both the United States and the GMD. In his meetings with Mao in Beijing on September 30 and October 3, 1954, the new Soviet leader, Nikita Khrushchev, accepted Beijing's assurances that the People's Republic would avoid a direct confrontation with Washington at any cost. In January 1955, as the U.S. Seventh Fleet moved in position to defend GMD supply lines to the islands of Jinmen and Mazu, Mao deescalated the crisis by not attempting an assault on them in the wake of the GMD evacuation of the Dachen Islands. Then, in April, Zhou Enlai announced that China was prepared to stop its attacks if the United States was willing to discuss a cease-fire. Based on Soviet sources, it seems that Zhou's statement came just as Moscow was getting ready to tell Beijing to call it quits. The Soviets held back, although their faith in CCP foreign policy, so recently enhanced by the Geneva conference, had been badly shaken.[24]

The period from mid-1955 to mid-1958 was the high point of the Sino-Soviet alliance, a three-year period during which Soviet assistance increased substantially and new areas of cooperation – for instance, in nuclear technology – were opened up. It was also an era of remarkable calm in international affairs in East Asia, probably the only such season of tranquility between 1945 and the end of the Cold War. Mao used this time to radicalize the revolution in China through large-scale collectivization of agriculture and to formulate plans for industrialization that – although much indebted to Soviet models – imagined a pace that would eclipse the Soviet experience.

During this period, Mao gradually revised his perception of an impending American attack against China. The imperialists had accepted cease-fires – albeit of a temporary character – in Korea and Vietnam, and the Taiwan campaign of the People's Republic had taught Washington a lesson, Mao believed. The chairman was very hopeful that the talks that began in Geneva in August 1955 between the United States and China would lead to U.S. concessions with regard to Taiwan as relations between the blocs continued to improve. As long as he still harbored some hope of a settlement with Washington concerning Taiwan, Mao remained a vocal supporter of Khrushchev's policy of international détente. He lauded the Soviet leader's visit to Britain in the spring of 1956, telling Ambassador Pavel Iudin that "with the help of England [we can] make a rapprochement with the United States as well; this is also not hopeless."[25]

The Twentieth Congress of the Communist Party of the Soviet Union (CPSU) in early 1956 made Sino-Soviet relations more complicated and influenced the policies of both countries vis-à-vis the United States. Mao at first responded positively to Khrushchev's criticism of Stalin and the Soviet past, sensing that he finally could vent his own anger at the way he had been treated by the Soviets up to 1950. Although he was annoyed that Khrushchev had not informed the Chinese party in advance (or, for that matter, consulted with him afterward), Mao viewed Khrushchev's speech as giving the CCP latitude to construct its own history and therefore to place himself as a theoreticist and political leader at least on par with the Soviet leader himself. China could take on a new importance in international affairs, inside the Communist bloc and in the East Asian region.

Although Mao's sense of having been liberated from Soviet tutelage persisted, not least in terms of the political experiments he embarked on in the late 1950s, his views of the *effects* of de-Stalinization changed dramatically after the Polish and Hungarian rebellions against Soviet control in the fall of 1956. The East European events fed straight into Mao's fear of U.S.-assisted counterrevolution in China and brought him closer to more "conservative" leaders such as Liu Shaoqi and Deng Xiaoping, who had been more skeptical of Khrushchev's plans than the chairman had been. Mao also interpreted the public criticism against the CCP leadership that came into the open during the 1957 Hundred

Flowers campaign as part of an American-led conspiracy. Together with the lack of progress in the Sino-American talks and the high level of negative U.S. rhetoric directed against China, by late 1957 Mao apparently concluded that any normalization of relations with the United States was out of the question, at least for the time being.[26] The period "from June 1956 to June 1957 were difficult days both in international and domestic affairs," Mao complained to Ambassador Iudin.[27]

During the meeting of Communist parties in Moscow in November 1957, Mao wanted to stress watchfulness and determination against the United States as a way to underline China's need to benefit directly – particularly with regard to Taiwan – from the U.S.-Soviet détente. Mao's main problem then was that he wanted to stress this aspect while generally supporting Soviet foreign policy, and thereby convince the Soviets that supporting China's aims would not endanger their attempts to lessen U.S.-Soviet confrontation. But the Soviet leaders were shocked by Mao's talk about not fearing nuclear war and belittled the chairman's understanding of international relations in conversations with leaders of other fraternal parties. Mao – determined not to be humiliated during his second visit to Moscow – insisted that the Chinese delegates introduce several amendments to the final resolution that reinforced criticism of the United States. The outcome was a compromise, in which the Soviet leaders accepted several of the Chinese suggestions. Mao saw the conference as at least a partial victory and, on his return home, was convinced that he had reinforced his position as a leader of the world Communist movement.

The End of the Alliance

The second offshore islands crisis in 1958 should be understood in terms of the lack of progress in Sino-U.S. relations and the growing Chinese disenchantment with U.S.-Soviet détente. But it was also related to Mao's wish to firm up his position as an authority on international affairs in the Communist movement and to shore up national mobilization for his new economic experiment, the Great Leap Forward.

The timing of the crisis was – interestingly enough – connected to Mao's reading of the international situation and what he viewed as setbacks to the U.S. position in the Middle East. Both within his own party and in talking to the Soviets he used Lebanon as a metaphor for Taiwan: The Arab peoples were dealing a blow to U.S. imperialism in the Middle East, and it was China's duty to join in this battle by attacking the offshore islands. It was a challenge to both Moscow and Washington, indicating that China's claims to Taiwan could be ignored only at their own peril – for Khrushchev at the risk of his leadership of the Communist movement, for Eisenhower at the risk of creating a permanent area of conflict that could be exploited whenever the United States had problems elsewhere.

As in 1954–1955, Mao had no intention of going to war with the United States or of invading Taiwan itself. As often during Mao's career, the shelling of Jinmen and Mazu was a military action with an immediate political purpose. He underestimated, however, the Soviet response to his challenge. For Khrushchev the new Taiwan Straits crisis came on the heels of his "peace offensive" toward Washington and his visit to Beijing in late July 1958, a visit that he undertook to make sure he brought the Chinese onboard in his policies toward the West. Mao did not tell Khrushchev in advance of the Chinese artillery attacks on Jinmen and Mazu – instead the discussions in Beijing centered on Chinese demands for further Soviet aid and on Soviet plans for integrating China further into its system of military preparedness. Although the Soviet side, again, was willing to concede much in terms of economic and technological assistance – although not on the core issue of fully sharing nuclear weapons technology – China strongly objected to the Soviet military plans for a submarine fleet under joint command and construction of shared military communication systems in northern China. In the wake of his visit, Khrushchev viewed the renewed attacks on the islands as a form of coercion by China.[28]

The Soviet reaction after the attacks began on August 23 was very swift. While warning the United States against going to war with China, the Kremlin leveled a barrage of criticism against the Chinese leaders, accusing them of playing into the hands of the enemy and misjudging the international situation. To underline its position, the Soviet Union even withdrew some of its military special advisers from China. Chinese Foreign Minister Chen Yi responded that China would be able to manage the crisis and asked for Soviet assistance in bringing pressure on Washington for a negotiated settlement of the Taiwan issue. After the Warsaw consultations between the two sides began in late September, the Chinese leadership defused the crisis simply by reducing the shelling of the islands. "We could use this method," Mao suggested to Zhou Enlai, "not to fire on even-numbered days, so that Jiang's troops could come out and have some sunshine; this is favorable for protracted war."[29]

The second straits crisis had two main effects on Mao's view of international relations. First, it convinced him that the American threat against China was considerably reduced – "the American capitalists are scared and passive," he wrote in November 1958. He even considered a more flexible tactic against Washington, for instance when he rejected Chen Yi's proposal to publish an article condemning some of U.S. Secretary of State John Foster Dulles's views. "Dulles is ill," Mao said. "Recently the American government has not criticized us very much. It is not suitable to publish this article now."[30]

Mao and other Chinese leaders also felt that they had pushed the Sino-Soviet relationship to the brink and that it was time to take a step back. The chaos created by the policies of the Great Leap Forward contributed to this sense of restraint, as did Mao's subsequent stepping down as head of state in December 1958. At the Twenty-first CPSU Congress in January-February 1959, Zhou Enlai's greetings did not contain any hints of criticism of Soviet-U.S. policies. In his writings, Mao returned to the themes of learning from the Soviet Union and being "modest" in promoting the Chinese experience.[31]

But the lull in Sino-Soviet tensions did not last long. During the second straits crisis in 1958, the Soviet leaders had begun worrying about the possible effects of their nuclear cooperation with China. In late June 1959 Khrushchev chose to inform the Chinese that the Soviet Union was unilaterally scrapping the remaining parts of the program because of its support for a nuclear-free zone in East Asia. A few weeks later, Mao shot back for the first time branding the Soviet leaders' thinking as "right-deviationist" in an inner-party circular. The CCP leadership suspected that the canceling of the nuclear programs had much to do with Khrushchev's forthcoming visit to the United States.[32]

We still do not know if Mao's strong reaction against stepped-up Indian activities along the disputed border with China was related to his suspicions on the outcome of Soviet-U.S. summitry. The Chinese never attempted to enlist their Soviet allies – who had increasingly close relations with the government of Jawaharlal Nehru – as mediators. Just as Mao was assuring Khrushchev that he viewed the forthcoming summit as "a victory for the peaceful Soviet foreign policy," Chinese troops occupied an Indian border post and claimed that India had intruded on Chinese sovereignty. The Chinese actions puzzled Soviet observers, who concluded that Beijing aimed at destabilizing Soviet-Indian relations as a form of punishment for Khrushchev's meeting with Eisenhower. The Soviets decided on strict neutrality in the conflict – a Tass statement pointed out that the Soviet Union "maintains friendly relations with the Chinese People's Republic and the Republic of India."[33]

Immediately after returning to Moscow from the United States, Khrushchev left for Beijing to discuss his U.S. policy and Sino-Indian relations with Mao Zedong. These meetings, of which we still do not have a verbatim record, constituted the final break in personal relations between the two leaders. "To Mao there are no laws, no lasting agreements, no word of honor," Khrushchev concluded in his memoirs. "Khrushchev is very infantile," Mao maintained. "He does not understand Marxism and Leninism [and] he is easily cheated by the imperialists. If he does not correct himself, he will be destroyed some years (eight years) from now. He is afraid of two things: Imperialism and Chinese Communism."[34] In December 1959 Soviet Ambassador Stepan Chervonenko for the first time warned the Chinese that attempts to sabotage Soviet foreign policy would affect all sides of the bilateral relationship.[35]

At the end of 1959, both Mao and the Soviet leaders had concluded that the international position of the United States was weakening. However, they drew opposite tactical conclusions from this observation. Khrushchev wanted to regulate Cold War competition from a position of Soviet bloc strength. He wanted to impress on Western leaders the increasing power and ideological attraction of communism and the need for the West to find practical compromises that would avert nuclear war. Mao, on the other hand, argued to the Soviets and to his own colleagues that this was the time to confront imperialism abroad, especially in the Third World. The socialist cause would suffer considerably, Mao felt, if Communist and anti-imperialist parties did not make use of the "high tide of socialism" to push their enemies back and aim at grabbing state power for themselves. For the chairman, the global trend was consistent with his observations inside China, where the policies of the Great Leap Forward set the pattern for the future, in spite of obstructions and temporary setbacks.

The Chinese policies on Cuba and Vietnam in 1959–1960 show how Mao's thinking came to influence Chinese foreign policy. Mao viewed the victory of the Cuban revolution as another sign of U.S. weakness and a harbinger of similar revolts in other Latin American countries. He instructed the Foreign and Defense ministries to prepare plans for how to best support the Cuban revolution.[36] The attitude of the People's Republic to North Vietnamese plans for armed struggle in the South also went through a sea change in late 1959. While many Chinese shared Moscow's skepticism about the prospects of guerilla warfare against the regime of Ngo Dinh Diem in the early part of the year, by December Beijing had come to support the plans that were in the making in Hanoi for a speedy reunification of Vietnam.[37]

It was Mao's attempts to win over other Communist parties to his views on international affairs that provoked the defining crisis in Sino-Soviet relations in 1960: Angered at Chinese behavior at the Bucharest conference of Communist parties in June, Khrushchev abruptly withdrew most Soviet advisers from China in July and early August. In their conversations with the Soviet ambassador in August, Chinese leaders tried to link the controversy directly to differing views of the United States. China will continue the struggle against the United States, declared Foreign Minister Chen Yi to Ambassador Chervonenko on August 4. "The deep hatred of the Chinese people toward American imperialism . . . will not disappear even in twenty-thirty years."[38]

For the Soviet leaders, too, the relationship to the United States was at the core of their perception of the ideological changes that Mao was promoting inside and outside the People's Republic. In his speech to the CPSU Central Committee in July, in which he summed up the case against the CCP, Khrushchev's second in command, Frol Kozlov, saw a need to push the Chinese onboard if "socialism" was to succeed in its dual task: to expand abroad, especially in Europe and Asia, and to avoid an American nuclear attack while this "final shift in the global correlation of forces" took place. The Chinese, Kozlov claimed, seemed to turn away both from their international obligations and from Marxism-Leninism as a comprehensive way to understand world affairs.[39]

It is interesting that as the Sino-Soviet split deepened in 1960, Mao himself stayed out of view, instead pushing those of his associates who had been critical of his domestic policies and who may have been less inclined to heighten Sino-Soviet tension – men such as Peng Zhen and Deng Xiaoping – to deliver the harshest blows. In his only meeting with the Soviet ambassador that year – a birthday visit on December 26 – Mao tried to keep himself above the fray of the Sino-Soviet confrontation, possibly as an insurance policy in the internal struggle that he perceived existed within his own party. Mao stressed that he was not chairing Politburo meetings any more and that he "practically never speaks at the meetings of the Central Committee." He underlined his support for the compromise documents reached on some issues at a conference of Communist parties in Moscow that fall. "These documents caused a great deal of confusion in Western imperialist circles, among our common enemies," Mao said.[40]

As has been shown, the Sino-Soviet relationship went through a series of brief improvements followed by equally rapid descents in the period from mid-1960 to early 1963. The Cuban Missile Crisis in October 1962 was a hotly disputed topic between the two sides. The Soviet leaders interpreted the Chinese barrage of criticism – first for "adventurism" in deploying the missiles and then for "capitulationism" when withdrawing them – as a sign that China would not be an ally of Moscow if war with the United States did break out. For the Chinese, the main lesson of October was that the Soviet leaders were still trying to dominate other socialist countries by deploying Soviet weapons and forces on their soil. "The missiles were absolutely not necessary for the defense of Cuba," Deng Xiaoping told the Soviet leaders. "When you brought the missiles to Cuba, did you want to help [Cuba] or destroy it? We started to suspect that you wanted to bring this country under your control through deploying your missiles in Cuba."[41]

In terms of Chinese perceptions of Soviet policy, the controversy over international regulations on nuclear weapons proliferation and testing in 1962 and 1963 marked a dividing line. Ever since the Soviets first brought up the issue of a comprehensive agreement with the West on these issues in March 1962, the Chinese had been adamantly opposed to any treaties. In September, after Moscow had informed Beijing of its intention to negotiate a nonproliferation treaty with the United States, Chen Yi replied that the Soviet concern with preventing West Germany from getting nuclear weapons should not lead to preventing socialist countries from getting such weapons: "The defense capabilities of socialist countries should not be limited." On October 20 the Chinese repeated their warnings. The socialist world must seek nuclear superiority, the Chinese note said, not disarmament. "The Soviet comrades have lost their class position in the question of the threat of nuclear war." By refusing to provide China with nuclear weapons, "you betrayed the principle of proletarian internationalism." In the Chinese view, by signing the nonproliferation treaty with the United States in June 1963, Moscow joined Washington's campaign against Beijing.[42]

During the July 1963 meetings between the Soviet and Chinese parties in Moscow, Deng Xiaoping ridiculed any form of cooperation with the United States.

> The United States of America is an imperialist country – the Soviet Union is a socialist country. How can these two countries, which belong to two fundamentally different social systems, coexist; how can they exercise general cooperation? The United States of America exercise deception and trickery toward other imperialist powers. How can one in such a case believe that there can be total unity between an imperialist country, the United States of America, and a socialist country, the Soviet Union? How can one believe that there can be harmonious coexistence between the United States of America and the Soviet Union? This is completely unthinkable and in this relationship one cannot submit to illusions.[43]

Revolutions and Antisystemic Alliances

Having "common enemies" is – as a general concept – not enough to hold alliances together over time. What matters is the combination of individual policy priorities and perceptions of the enemy, entities that both are likely to change over time. Within the NATO alliance and the U.S.-Japan alliance, the policy priorities from all sides changed within a common framework, which was the economic integration brought on by the globalization of the market. This common framework stabilized these alliances, even at times when perceptions of an enemy threat were widely divergent.[44]

Antisystemic alliances such as the Sino-Soviet compact do not have these ties that bind and therefore are more dependent on a common perception of the enemy, of its capabilities, its intentions, and its determination to win. They need a rather complete image of their opponent or opponents, an image created by a fairly synchronic development of perceptions. If they cannot agree on such an image, it will be very difficult to keep alliances of this kind together over time.[45]

This is exactly what happened to the Sino-Soviet alliance in the latter part of the 1950s. Moscow and Beijing could no longer agree on how to interpret American capabilities or intentions. Worldviews that shared many points of reference slowed the process of disintegration, at least up to the time when the dispute became public. In addition, both sides were hesitant to fully embrace their new perceptual positions: Khrushchev was as cautious in viewing détente as Mao was in viewing denunciation and confrontation. But after the second straits crisis in 1958, the divergent views became dogma, and the allies drifted apart.

What role did the conscious "wedge strategies" of the Eisenhower administration play in creating these perceptions? Some historians see Dulles by the mid-1950s as advocating a sophisticated strategy for exploiting Sino-Soviet differences. The gradual heightening of American pressure against the People's Republic led Beijing to make demands for military and economic assistance to which Moscow could not possibly agree. These researchers have concluded that when the Sino-Soviet alliance began to break up, it did so in very much the way Dulles had anticipated several years before.[46]

This, in my opinion, is where the real surprise of the Chinese and Soviet materials come up: The United States was not able to transmit to Beijing its projected image of increasing aggressiveness and determination. On the contrary, in the mid- to late 1950s – starting with the first straits crisis and reaching its climax with the second – Mao believed that the American threat was waning, not increasing, and that China was considerably more secure from an all-out U.S. attack than it had been during the first years of the People's Republic.

It was precisely this perception that enabled the Chinese leader to risk his Soviet alliance by stubbornly pushing for a more belligerent joint strategy against Washington. If Mao had believed that an American attack against his party and his regime was imminent – a view that he held more or less continuously from 1946 until the first straits crisis in 1954–1955 – then risking the alliance that he had fought so hard to get would have been foolhardy, out of style with Mao's strategic view.

But if Mao did not perceive the United States as an imminent threat, why then the need for confrontation? The main issue here was Taiwan and the U.S. blocking of the road to reunification. Mao could not accept a view of the United States that allowed for détente as long as Washington persisted in keeping Taiwan beyond his reach. Reunification had become his main aim in foreign policy, and he forced his views of both the Soviet Union and the United States to conform with his needs to obtain it.

It is interesting that the concrete foreign policy priorities of Mao and much of the Chinese leadership changed over time from voluntarily postponing the conquest of Taiwan for revolutionary gain elsewhere in 1949 to making reunification a vital part of their state-building project in the late 1950s. This instability in foreign policy priorities is common for revolutionary regimes and probably is connected to the leaders' perceptual changes, which occur when the needs of the state surmount those of a movement with international lineages or linkages as its main points of reference. For the People's Republic, the Taiwan issue has been the most powerful symbol of this ideological transformation, from Mao Zedong to Jiang Zemin and beyond.

Notes

1. Gordon Chang provides useful comments on Chinese and Soviet motives in his *Friends and Enemies: The United States, China, and the Soviet Union, 1948–1972* (Stanford, Calif.: Stanford University Press, 1990), although his main focus is on the United States. Constantine Pleshakov includes a skillful discussion of the different emphases in Soviet and Chinese perceptions in his paper for the January 1993 Cold War International History Project (CWIHP) conference in Moscow, "Khrushchev as Counter-Revolutionary: The Taiwan Straits Crisis of 1958 and the Sino-Soviet Schism."

2. For a similar view, see Odd Arne Westad, "Secrets of the Second World: Russian Archives and the Reinterpretation of Cold War History," *Diplomatic History* 21, no. 2 (Spring 1997): 259–72.

3. See Odd Arne Westad, *Cold War and Revolution: Soviet-American Rivalry and the Origins of the Chinese Civil War* (New York: Columbia University Press, 1993).

4. See Sergei Goncharov et al., *Uncertain Partners: Stalin, Mao, and the Korean War* (Stanford, Calif.: Stanford University Press, 1993), 1–35; Chen Jian, *China's Road to the Korean War: The Making of the Sino-American Confrontation* (New York: Columbia University Press, 1994), 9–63. *USSR Ambas in China*

5. Memorandum of conversation, Roshchin–Zhou Enlai, October 31, 1949, Arkhiv vneshnei politiki Rossiiskoi Federatsii (AVPRF), fond (f.) 0100, opis (op.) 42, papka (pa.) 288, delo (d.) 19, pp. 74–7. See also Zhou Enlai's speech at the founding of the PRC foreign ministry, November 8, 1949, *Zhonggong dangshi jiaoxue cankao ziliao (ZDJCZ)* [Teaching reference materials on CCP history] (Beijing: np, nd), vol. 18, 590–2.

6. Liu Shaoqi to Stalin, July 4, 1949, Arkhiv prezidenta Rossiiskoi Federatsii (APRF), f. 45, op. 1, d. 328, quoted in Andrei Ledovsky, "The Moscow Visit of a Delegation of the Communist Party of China in June to August 1949," *Far Eastern Affairs,* no. 4 (1996): 72.

7. Memorandum of conversation, Roshchin–Li Kenong, November 17, 1949, AVPRF, f. 07, op. 22, d. 220, pp. 67–73.

8. Memorandum of conversation, Roshchin–Zhou Enlai, November 10, 1949, AVPRF, f. 0100, op. 42, pa. 288, d. 19, pp. 81–5; Mao Zedong to Wang Jiaxiang, November 9, 1949, *Jianguo yilai Mao Zedong wengao* [Mao Zedong's writings since the founding of the PRC] (Beijing: Zhongyang wenxian, 1987), vol. 1, 131; Andrei Gromyko to Stalin, November 26, 1949, AVPRF, f. 07, op. 22a, pa. 13, d. 198, pp. 32–6.

9. Andrei Ledovsky, "Mikoyan's Secret Mission to China in January and February 1949," *Far Eastern Affairs,* no. 2 (1995): 72–94, and no. 3 (1995): 74–90; memorandum of conversation, Roshchin–Zhou Enlai, November 10, 1949, 54–6.

10. Odd Arne Westad, "Losses, Chances, and Myths: The United States and the Origins of the Sino-Soviet Alliance, 1945–1950," *Diplomatic History* 21, no. 1 (Winter 1997): 105–15; author's interview with Mikhail Kapitsa, Moscow, September 7, 1992; author's notes of conversation with Georgi Kornienko, Oslo, October 2, 1994. See also memorandum of conversation, Shibaev–Li Kenong, December 28, 1949, AVPRF, f. 0100, op. 43, pa. 302, d. 10, pp. 53–6.

11. Shi Zhe, *Zai lishi jüren shenbian* [Alongside giants of history] (Beijing: Zhongyang wenxian, 1991), 438–52.

12. Goncharov et al., *Uncertain Partners,* 104.

13. Memorandum of conversation, Shibaev–Li Kenong, January 16, 1950, AVPRF, f. 0100, op. 43, pa. 302, d. 10, p. 40.

14. Memorandum of conversation, Stalin–Mao Zedong, December 16, 1949, APRF, f. 45, op. 1, d. 331, 9–17; for an English translation, see *Cold War International History Project* (*CWIHP*) *Bulletin* 6–7 (Winter 1995/1996): 5–7.

15. Memorandum of conversation, Roshchin–Mao Zedong, January 1, 1950, AVPRF, f. 0100, op. 43, pa. 302, d. 10, pp. 1–4; memorandum of conversation, Vyshinski–Mao Zedong, January 6, 1950, AVPRF, f. 0100, op. 43, pa. 302, d. 43, pp. 1–5; memorandum of conversation, Molotov–Mao Zedong, January 17, 1950, AVPRF, f. 07, op. 23a, pa. 18, d. 234, pp. 1–7 (for English translations, see *CWIHP Bulletin* 8–9 [Winter 1996/1997]: 227–8, 230–1, 232–4); Kapitsa interview. See also Vyshinski to Stalin, January 5, 1950, AVPRF, f. 07, op. 23d, pa. 306, d. 16, pp. 1–3.

16. Memorandum of conversation, Molotov–Mao Zedong, January 17, 1950, AVPRF, f. 07, op. 23a, pa. 18, d. 234, pp. 1–7.

17. My discussion of the Korean War is based on the recently released Russian materials obtained by the Cold War International History Project through an agreement with the Center for Korean Research at Columbia University and the International Diplomatic Academy, Moscow; deposited at the National Security Archive, Washington, D.C., and on work in progress by Kathryn Weathersby and Chen Jian. Parts of the Korean War documents are translated in *CWIHP Bulletin* 6–7 (Winter 1995/1996): 30–84, 108–19.

18. Memorandum of conversation, Roshchin–Zhou Dapeng, July 4, 1950, AVPRF, f. 0100, op. 43, d. 10, pa. 302, pp. 123–31, and annexed documents.

19. Memorandum of conversation, Stalin–Zhou Enlai, August 20, 1950, APRF, f. 45, op. 1, d. 329, 54–72.

20. See Vladislav Zubok and Constantine Pleshakov, *Inside the Kremlin's Cold War: From Stalin to Khrushchev* (Cambridge: Harvard University Press, 1996), 173–88.

21. Qiang Zhai, "China and the Geneva Conference of 1954," *China Quarterly,* no. 129 (1992): 103–22. See also memorandum of conversation, V. V. Vaskov (chargé d'affaires, Beijing)–Mao Zedong, July 5, 1954, AVPRF, f. 0100, op. 47, pa. 379, d. 7, pp. 69–70. For a look into Zhou's views on China's foreign relations post-Geneva, see his report to the thirty-third session of the standing committee of the Central People's Government on August 11, 1954, in *ZDJCZ,* vol. 20, 358–61.

22. Wang Bingnan, *Zhong-Mei huitan jiunian huigu* [Remembering nine years of Sino-American talks] (Beijing, 1985), 41–2; memorandum of conversation, Vaskov–Mao Zedong, July 16, 1954, AVPRF, f. 0100, op. 47, pa. 379, d. 7, pp. 67–8; Mao Zedong's speech at a meeting of the National Defense Committee, October 18, 1954, *Mao Zedong junshi wenji* [Mao Zedong's collected writings on military affairs] (Beijing: Junshi kexue, 1993), vol. 6, 357–61. See also summary of Mao's remarks during a conversation with a British Labour Party delegation, August 24, 1954, Zhonghua renmin gongheguo waijiaobu and Zhonggong zhongyang wenxian yanjiushi, comps., *Mao Zedong waijiao wenxuan* [Mao Zedong's selected writings on foreign affairs] (Beijing: Zhongyang wenxian, 1994), 158–62.

23. Gordon H. Chang and He Di, "The Absence of War in the U.S.-China Confrontation over Quemoy and Matsu in 1954–1955: Contingency, Luck, Deterrence?" *American Historical Review* 98, no. 5 (December 1993): 1500–24.

24. Memorandum of conversation, Soviet ambassador Pavel Iudin–Zhou Enlai, October 10, 1954, AVPRF, f. 0100, op. 417, pa. 379, d. 9, pp. 77–82. See also Zhou Enlai's statement of December 8, 1954, *ZDJCZ,* vol. 20, 448–51. Information on Mao-Khrushchev talks from Russian archivists. See also memorandum of conversation, Iudin–Mao Zedong, December 12, 1955, and attached summaries, AVPRF, f. 0100, op. 49, pa. 410, d. 9, pp. 17–19.

25. Memorandum of conversation, Iudin–Mao Zedong, December 21, 1955, AVPRF, f. 0100, op. 49, pa. 410, d. 9, pp. 18–19; He Di, "The Most Respected Enemy: Mao Zedong's Perception of the United States," in Michael H. Hunt and Niu Jun, eds., *Toward a History of Chinese Communist Foreign Relations, 1920s–1960s* (Washington, D.C.: Woodrow Wilson International Center for Scholars, Asia Program, 1995), 39–41; memorandum of conversation, Iudin–Mao Zedong, May 2, 1956, AVPRF, f. 0100, op. 49, pa. 410, d. 9, pp. 124–5.

26. Odd Arne Westad, "Mao Zedong and De-Stalinization," forthcoming.

27. Memorandum of conversation, Iudin–Mao Zedong, February 28, 1958, AVPRF, f. 0100, op. 51, pa. 432, d. 6, p. 89.

28. Mao Zedong to Liu Shaoqi et al., June 7, 1958, *Jianguo yilai Mao Zedong wengao,* vol. 7, 265–6; Zhang Weilu (Chinese chargé d'affaires, Moscow) to Vice-Foreign Minister Kuznetsov, July 11, 1958, AVPRF, f. 0100, op. 51, pa. 431, d. 3, pp. 51–2. Joint military communications centers were first suggested by Soviet Minister of Defense Rodion Malinovskii in a letter to his Chinese counterpart Peng Dehuai on April 18, 1958. See also the Chinese version of Mao's talk with Iudin on July 22, 1958, translated in *CWIHP Bulletin* 6–7 (Winter 1995/1996): 155–9.

29. Memorandum of conversation, Iudin–Chen Yi, November 30, 1958, AVPRF, f. 0100, op. 51, pa. 432, d. 6, pp. 188–96; Mao Zedong to Zhou Enlai, October 11, 1958, *Jianguo yilai Mao Zedong wengao,* vol. 7, 449–50; Mao Zedong to Zhou Enlai et al., October 31, 1958, ibid., 479. Soviet Foreign Minister Andrei Gromyko visited Beijing on a secret mission in early September 1958. The records of his conversations are not yet available.

30. Mao Zedong notes, November 1958, *Jianguo yilai Mao Zedong wengao,* vol. 7, 608; Mao Zedong to Chen Yi, February 22, 1959, ibid., vol. 8, 55. Mao generally distinguished between the views of Eisenhower, whom he took to be more moderate, and Dulles, "whose speeches I do not read, because I know in advance what he will say." Memorandum of conversation, Iudin–Mao Zedong, February 28, 1958, AVPRF, f. 0100,

op. 51, pa. 432, d. 6, pp. 89. In limiting the Straits crisis, Mao also made allowance for American politics. On November 2, 1958, he informed Zhou that "I propose that we to-morrow make a big attack, with more than 10,000 shells, all aimed at military targets, to influence the American elections, helping the Democrats to win and beat the Republicans." Mao Zedong to Zhou Enlai, November 2, 1958, *Jianguo yilai Mao Zedong wengao,* vol. 7, 490. See also Mao's comments on a report from the Chinese chargé d'affaires in London dated February 12, 1959, *Jianguo yilai Mao Zedong wengao,* vol. 8, 36–7.

31. Mao Zedong text, February 13, 1959, *Jianguo yilai Mao Zedong wengao,* vol. 8, 38–40.

32. Report from the Chinese embassy in Moscow, circulated on Mao's instructions on July 19, 1959, *Jianguo yilai Mao Zedong wengao,* vol. 8, 368–9.

33. Records of conversations, Chervonenko–Deng Xiaoping and Chervonenko–Zhou Enlai, November 6, 1959, AVPRF, f. 0100, op. 52, pa. 442, d. 7, pp. 104–7, 108–11; Mao to Khrushchev, August 17, 1959, *Jianguo yilai Mao Zedong wengao,* vol. 8, 459–60; Kapitsa interview. (Mikhail Kapitsa still asked, thirty-five years later, "Why didn't they just do the usual thing, fire off some shells in the Taiwan Straits or something like that?"); *Pravda,* September 9, 1959. Steven Hoffmann, in the most comprehensive recent analysis of the Sino-Indian border conflict, believes that China was the aggressive party, both diplomatically and militarily, during the first confrontations in 1959. However, the reasons for the Chinese behavior may well have been connected to the Tibet rebellion rather than Soviet-U.S. relations. *India and the China Crisis* (Berkeley: University of California Press, 1990), 66–84. For a version largely exonerating China, see Xuecheng Liu, *The Sino-Indian Border Dispute and Sino-Indian Relations* (Lanham, Md.: University Press of America, 1994).

34. Jerrold L. Schecter, trans. and ed., *Khrushchev Remembers: The Glasnost Tapes* (Boston: Little, Brown, 1990), 154; Mao Zedong notes, December 1959, *Jianguo yilai Mao Zedong wengao,* vol. 8, 599–603.

35. Memorandum of conversation, Chervonenko–Liu Shaoqi, December 10, 1959, AVPRF, f. 0100, op. 53, pa. 454, d. 8, pp. 1–6.

36. For a summary of these plans, see record of conversation, Chervonenko–Oscar Pino Santos (Cuban ambassador to the People's Republic), January 2, 1961, AVPRF, f. 0100, op. 54, pa. 466, d. 7, pp. 1–3.

37. See, for instance, record of conversation, Chervonenko–Deng Xiaoping, November 6, 1959, AVPRF, f. 0100, op. 52, pa. 442, d. 7, pp. 104–7. See also Mari Olsen, *Solidarity and National Revolution: The Soviet Union and the Vietnamese Communists, 1954–1960* (Oslo: Institute for Defence Studies, 1997).

38. Memorandum of conversation, Chervonenko–Chen Yi, August 4, 1960, AVPRF, f. 0100, op. 53, pa. 454, d. 8, pp. 204–18.

39. Kozlov, "Ob itogakh Soveshchaniia predstavitelei bratskikh partii v Bukhareste i ob oshibochnykh pozitsiiakh rukovodstva TsK KPK po nekotorym printsipialnym voprosam marksistsko-leninskoi teorii i sovremennykh mezhdunarodnykh otnoshenii" [On the results of the conference of leaders of brotherly parties in Bucharest and on the erroneous positions of the heads of the CCP Central Committee on some main questions of Marxist-Leninist theory and contemporary international relations] (draft), July 13, 1960, TsKhSD, CPSU CC Plenum Collection, Twenty-first Party Congress. I am grateful to Vladislav Zubok for drawing my attention to this document.

40. Record of conversation, S. V. Chervonenko–Mao Zedong, December 26, 1960, AVPRF, f. 0100, op. 53, pa. 454, d. 9, pp. 98–105; for an English translation, see *CWIHP Bulletin* 6–7 (Winter 1995/1996): 167–9. Deng may have tried to steer a middle course, at least for a while. In a meeting with Chervonenko in early June, he praised Khrushchev's speech in Paris on May 16, which had "explained the soundness of the position of the countries of the socialist camp led by the Soviet Union." Deng added that he had not yet heard Mao's opinion, since the chairman was absent from Beijing. Record of conversation, Chervonenko–Deng Xiaoping, June 1, 1960, AVPRF, f. 0100, op. 53, pa. 454, d. 8, pp. 165–9.

41. "Zusammenkunft der Delegationen der Kommunistischen Partei der Sowjetunion und der Kommunistichen Partei Chinas im Juli 1963 – unkorrigierte Rohübersetzung" [Meetings of the delegations of the Communist Party of the Soviet Union and the Communist Party of China in July 1963 – uncorrected raw translation], Stiftung Archiv der Parteien und Massenorganisationen der ehemaligen DDR im Bundesarchiv (SAPMO-BArch), Berlin, Bestandsignatur DY J IV 2/201, Aktenband 696 [hereafter July 1963-SAPMO-BArch], 91.

42. Chinese government notes to Soviet government, September 3 and October 20, 1962, AVPRF, f. 0100, op. 55, pa. 480, d. 2, pp. 70–4, 90–102.

43. July 1963-SAPMO-BArch, 190.

44. For good overviews, see Robert Arthur Levine, ed., *Transition and Turmoil in the Atlantic Alliance* (New York: Crane Russak, 1992); Roger Buckley, *U.S.-Japan Alliance Diplomacy, 1945–1990* (Cambridge: Cambridge University Press, 1992).

45. Good insights into these problems can be found in Stephen M. Walt, *The Origins of Alliances* (Ithaca, N.Y.: Cornell University Press, 1997), and Ole R. Holsti, P. Terrence Hopmann, and John D. Sullivan, *Unity and Disintegration in International Alliances: Comparative Studies* (New York: Wiley, 1973). On China, see Odd Arne Westad, "The Foreign Policies of Revolutionary Parties: The CCP in a Comparative Perspective," in Hunt and Niu, eds., *Toward a History of Chinese Communist Foreign Relations.*

46. David Mayers, *Cracking the Monolith: U.S. Policy against the Sino-Soviet Alliance, 1949–1955* (Baton Rouge: Louisiana State University Press, 1986); see also John Lewis Gaddis, *The Long Peace: Inquiries into the History of the Cold War* (New York: Oxford University Press, 1987), 148.

6. Sino-Soviet Economic Cooperation

Shu Guang Zhang

The Sino-Soviet disputes, which had developed largely in secret in the 1950s, became open after 1960. In addition to ideological and political quarrels, the economic aspects deserve a careful reexamination. Such an undertaking is crucial to a better understanding of the disintegration of the Sino-Soviet alliance. How much did the Chinese Communists have to rely on their Soviet comrades? How much did the Sino-Soviet economic relations contribute to the growing tensions in the alliance?

In addressing these questions, most studies of the Sino-Soviet relations have followed two different lines. Some have asserted that the alliance broke down mainly because of Beijing's dissatisfaction with Soviet aid. Soviet grants and loans to China were comparatively small, thus making only modest contributions to China's economic development. This limited Soviet assistance, compared to much larger-scale Soviet aid to other socialist countries, allegedly caused discontent and resentment on the part of the Chinese Communist leadership that consequently served as a potential source of tension in the alliance. On the other hand, however, some have argued just the opposite – that the strains in the alliance stemmed not from Chinese dissatisfaction but from Soviet resentment at the economic burdens imposed by the relationship. Those who hold this view refer to the fact that Sino-Soviet economic relations were essentially disadvantageous to the Soviet Union. To an increasingly distressing extent, especially from the Soviet point of view, Chinese growth was being substituted for Soviet growth, because "Chinese trade meant a forced transfer of resources from growth to consumption, to the extent that they [the Soviets] were not able in return to relocate their resources."[1]

Plausible as they are, however, both arguments provide only partial explanations. While calculations based on purely economic benefits or advantages do matter, a good number of cultural factors, including beliefs, images, perceptions, attitudes, motives, and expectations, prove perhaps more important. After all, an international alliance relationship not only survives and thrives on the premises of state interests, political or economic, but also grows in the hearts and minds of people, political leaders in particular. Interests and feelings often are intertwined, inadvertently affecting one another. The Sino-Soviet alliance experience was no exception.

New China: The Imperatives of State Construction

Based on its perception of external threats to its regime, the Chinese Communist Party (CCP) leadership saw East Asia as an arena of Cold War competition that would require a Sino-Soviet alignment. However, the Chinese wanted to form the alliance as much to balance against their perceived threats as to bandwagon (that is, to ally with a dominant and threatening power).[2]

The foreign policy outlook of CCP paramount leader Mao Zedong deserves special attention. Mao understood realpolitik, or balance of power, fairly well. The postwar international political scene, in his view, evolved into an all-front, long-term struggle between "two camps" – a U.S.-led capitalist one and a Soviet-headed socialist one. Establishing a Communist regime in China in October 1949, he believed that the United States posed a major threat to his nation. This belief derived mainly from what he perceived as a hostile U.S. policy toward the Chinese Communist revolution. Washington had openly supported Jiang Jieshi's (Chiang Kai-shek's) nationalist regime during China's civil war (1946–1949). Despite its failure to undertake a direct, armed intervention in the civil conflict prior to 1949, the United States, Mao feared, might feel compelled or ready to do so in the face of Jiang's impending defeat. Washington's long-term objective, Mao was convinced, was to place China under its control or within its sphere of influence. As to what U.S. leaders could do to achieve this goal, Mao in August 1949 anticipated three possibilities: first, "they could smuggle their agents into China to sow dissension and make trouble"; second, "they could incite the Chinese reactionaries and even throw in their own forces to blockade China's ports"; and third, "if they still long for adventure, they will send some of their troops to invade and harass China's frontiers." All of these scenarios, Mao assured, were "not impossible."[3]

Mao's recondite concerns about U.S. threats led him and his comrades to believe that "leaning" to the Soviet side was essential to China's security. Assessing the postwar international situation at the CCP Politburo meeting on September 8, 1948, Mao pointed out that there existed "the danger of [another world] war." Thus he advocated that "we should assume the task of utilizing the people's force all over the world to prevent it," and priority should be given to the Soviet Union. This was because "the strength of the world democratic force led by the Soviet Union has surpassed that of the [American and British] reactionaries and will continue to grow." If the peace could endure for the next ten or fifteen years, Mao envisioned, world wars might "never happen again," because "if the Soviet Union and Eastern European countries can maintain peace and concentrate on [economic] production during the next ten to fifteen years, the Soviet Union should have elevated its productivity to the level of producing 60,000,000 tons of steel per year. By that time, no one can hope to top it." With three years already passed since the end of World War II, China should waste no time in siding with the Soviet bloc in the "remaining twelve years" of possible peace.[4]

Mao, indeed, wasted little time in persuading Stalin to form an alliance with his regime. With nationwide victory ensured after seizing Nanjing, Jiang's capital, in April 1949, the CCP undertook several steps toward that direction: The CCP's vice-chairman, Liu Shaoqi, secretly visited Moscow in July; Mao openly proclaimed that his country would "lean" to the Soviet side in August; and in December the chairman himself traveled to Moscow with high expectations. To have a serious and comprehensive negotiation over the future Sino-Soviet relationship, he planned to discuss with Stalin "all the [outstanding] issues that our Central Committee is concerned with" or, at least, to "make all our positions clear [to the Soviets]."[5] But Mao's highest priority was to sign a new alliance treaty, of which "the basic spirit . . . should be to prevent the possibility of Japan and its ally [the United States] invading China," and that would "enable us to use it as a big political asset to deal with imperialist countries in the world."[6] That Mao was able to accomplish in Moscow.[7] Mao proclaimed in April 1950 that

> since the foundation of the People's government, one of its significant achievements is the signing of the alliance treaty. . . . [Since] the imperialists still exist in the world, we therefore need friends and allies under this circumstance. . . . Now that the treaty has confirmed the friendship of the Soviet Union and formed the alliance relationship, we will thus have a good hand of assistance if the imperialists prepare to invade us.[8]

At no point, however, did Mao concede that China would have to be a Soviet satellite. Quite the contrary, he expected Moscow to treat his regime as an equal partner. Seeking equality, national integrity, and sovereignty, perhaps much more than balancing external threats, dominated the CCP foreign policy agenda.

This conscious inclination clearly had its roots in the nation's struggles against foreign influence. The Opium War of 1839 to 1842 marked the beginning of Western imperialism in modern China. Since then a major shaping force in China's foreign policy was the search for a way to survive in the new world that had been forcibly thrust upon it by the West. This search involved an extremely hard struggle against the weight of pride, disdain for things foreign, and the inveterate feeling of "national humiliation." The images and symbols of "foreign devils" – foreign gunboats, unequal treaties, international settlements with signs reading "No Chinese and Dogs Allowed" – planted deeply the seeds of distrust and hatred toward foreigners, feelings that stood as monumental reminders of the nation's sufferings and humiliations caused by imperialists. Meanwhile, the search for a path to survival also created new illusions such as "self-strengthening," "learning the superior barbarian technique with which to repel the barbarians," "using the barbarians to control the barbarians," and "forming a united front against foreign invasions." The call for "national liberation" – the recreation of an independent and sovereign China and restoration of the nation's prestige and power in the world – became very appealing to most Chinese people.

It was in the midst of this popular anxiety and aspiration for "a new China [*xinzhongguo*]" that Mao and his revolution had emerged and expanded. Throughout his political career, Mao had taken as his primary goal the radical transformation of Chinese society in order to liberate the nation from imperialist dominance. He and his comrades were determined that the New China should resume its rightful place among the nations. "In order to avoid errors in implementing our foreign policy," a CCP CC order on diplomatic work dated August 18, 1944, had specified, "we must first of all adhere to our principle of nationalism." It further explained:

> In the history of China's foreign relations over the past hundred years, there existed two misunderstandings regarding nationalism. One emerged before the Boxer Rebellion when the anti-foreign sentiment was almost an obsession. The other was seen after the Rebellion when the fear of foreign powers was prevalent. From the May Fourth Movement to the Northern Expedition, this xenophobic sentiment toward foreign countries has been overshadowed by the high tide of nationalism.

These two tendencies, the order pointed out, were erroneous. "To avoid these two mistakes, on the one hand, we should enhance our confidence in and self-respect for our nation by welcoming foreigners to the country; on the other hand, we should know how to work with them in order to learn their advanced experience, but not fear of or fawn on them. This is the correct understanding of nationalism."[9]

This sentimental mind-set underlined CCP attitudes and policies toward the political and economic relationship with the Soviet Union. This relationship, however, constituted for CCP leaders an inevitable paradox: Political independence would require China not to depend on the Soviet Union economically, whereas the enormity of China's economic problems would compel the new regime to seek as much external aid as possible. Finding a balance between obtaining sufficient Soviet economic assistance and avoiding total reliance on the Soviets proved to be one of the gravest challenges the CCP had to deal with in sustaining the alliance relationship.

Aside from security concerns, economic reconstruction became a life-and-death issue for the CCP in its initial years of ruling China. The Communists faced several obvious difficulties. After decades of wars, civil and international, the nation's economy verged on the edge of a total collapse. In 1949, according to rough CCP estimates, China's industrial production was only 30 percent of the nation's best record, with light industry and agriculture no more than 70 percent. The transportation system was hardly functional: More than 5,000 miles of railroads were crippled, 3,200 bridges and 200 tunnels of rail lines were severely damaged; less than 4,000 miles of vehicle roads were barely usable; air and maritime transport capability was close to zero.[10] Moreover, the CCP worried that a possible U.S.-led Western economic embargo would further hamstring the nation's economy. Given China's pro-Soviet stance, Mao earlier had anticipated that the Americans might "throw in their own forces to blockade China's ports." Chen Yun, a top CCP leader in charge of economic reconstruction, believed that it was almost impossible to maintain trade relations with or obtain aid from capitalist countries, because the United States would pressure them "not to buy from or sell to [a Communist] China."[11] The CCP also lacked experience and expertise in handling economic affairs. To reorient his party toward economic reconstruction, Mao told his Politburo in September 1948 that the whole party "must learn how to operate in industry and business." Through education, "propaganda," and "[guideline] articles," Mao stressed, "this task must be fulfilled."[12]

As serious as these difficulties were, however, Mao and his comrades believed that the new regime should not dread them. Mao reasoned that China was a self-sufficient country and its economic rebuilding did not have to rely entirely on external aid and foreign trade. As "scattered, individual agriculture and handicraft, . . . make up 90 percent of the total output of the nation's economy [and the] modern economy accounted [only] for less than 10 percent of China's Gross National Product," he asserted that the principle of "self-reliance" was the key to the CCP's success in economic reconstruction.[13] Mao thus set as "the two basic policies" to guide his regime's economic rebuilding "regulation of capital at home and [state] control of foreign trade."[14] Mao's lieutenant, Zhou Enlai, also made it clear that "most of those materials we need [in economic reconstruction] can be provided by ourselves and some by our friends" and, therefore, there was no need to panic.[15]

The U.S.-led economic embargo was not necessarily a bad thing, the CCP asserted, because it would not only help boost the people's nationalist sentiment against Western imperialism and help the CCP to recruit popular support, but it also would give the CCP ample time to eliminate pro-West elements at home. "Let them [the U.S. and Western capitalist states] blockade us! Let them blockade us for eight or ten years!" Mao declared in 1949. "By that time all of China's problem will be solved. . . . We have come triumphantly through the ordeal of the last three years [of the civil war], why can't we overcome those few difficulties of today? Why can't we live without the United States?"[16] Thus Mao was determined to "make a fresh start" and "sweep the house first and then receive guests." This policy, Zhou Enlai elaborated, was "to clean up the vestiges of imperialist influence [in China] so as not to leave [imperialists] space to operate in the future."[17] Therefore, in order to avoid "being entangled in the shameful diplomatic tradition," the CCP order on foreign affairs on January 19, 1949, stipulated that "we must abolish imperialist privileges in China and safeguard the independence and liberation of China as a nation. This stance is not compromisable." It further specified:

> We do not recognize any embassies, legations, consulates, and other diplomatic agencies of the capitalist countries formerly recognized by the GMD government and which have yet to establish diplomatic relationship with us. . . . We do not formally and legally recognize any foreign investments, economic privileges, and industrial and commercial enterprises conducted and enjoyed by all capitalist countries or individuals. But we should not show any sign at this point that we will forbid, regain, or confiscate them. We will, however, issue an order to forbid foreign investments which infringe upon the sovereignty of the country such as inland water transportation. We will not stop the business of foreign banks but order them to report their capital, accounts, and routine businesses for our ratification later, nor should we deal with insurance companies, particularly the insurance company for maritime transportation. . . . We should not establish or restore hastily normal trade with capitalist countries, such as to sign trade agreements. We only conduct tem-

porary, individual, and lucrative export and import business with these countries at a local level for some needed goods.[18]

This hardly meant, Mao maintained, that China would adopt a "closed-door" policy toward all foreign governments, including the Soviet Union. He saw no reason for Moscow to reject another Communist state's request for economic help; perhaps Moscow would instead treat the CCP regime as an equal. "The Soviet Union and other democratic forces have struggled against the reactionary forces," and more important, "the Soviet policy is not to interfere with any country's internal affair," Mao explained to the Politburo in September 1949.[19] Wishful as it may have sounded, Mao felt that acquiring Soviet aid was highly desirable, if not necessary, so as to resolve the nation's immediate economic problems; at the same time, however, he was clearly wary of Soviet dominance over China. The end result entailed mixed feelings concerning several important aspects of economic relations with the Soviet Union.

The CCP's immediate priority was to establish trade relations with the Soviet Union. As early as August 1946, the CCP's Northeastern Bureau had approached the Soviet authorities at Dalian (Darien) to sell grain (wheat, corn, soybeans) and buy cloth, medicines, and other necessities of daily life so as to stabilize that region's market. The initial endeavor did not work out, because the Soviets would not include cloths in the deal. At the end of 1946, however, scattered, small-scale trade did begin.[20] After as many as fifteen rounds of negotiations in early 1949, the Chinese were able to strike a more comprehensive trade deal with the Soviets.[21] In the summer of that year, the CCP central leadership clearly wanted to enhance trade with the Soviet Union. As a major component of New China's diplomacy, Liu Shaoqi assured Stalin in July, the CCP would "promote [foreign] trade relations with, in particular, the Soviet Union and other new democratic [socialist] countries, but under the premise of equality and mutual benefit."[22] Stalin seemed understanding and supportive. Suggesting that the barter system would be "more appropriate" than "the cash-sale practice of the capitalist world," he promised Liu that his government would compensate for China's losses by bartering low-priced agriculture products for Soviet high-priced machinery.[23]

Encouraged by Stalin's favorable attitude, Mao endorsed his Central Committee's instructions on foreign trade policy on February 16, 1949, which clearly gave priority to trade with the Soviet Union. The instructions stated:

> The basic guideline of our foreign trade policy is that we should export to and import from the Soviet Union and other new democratic countries so long as they need what we are able to offer or they can offer what we need. Only in the situation that the Soviet Union and

other new democratic countries are not in a position to buy from us or sell to us will we do some business with capitalist countries."[24]

In instructions to the North China Bureau and the Tianjin and Beiping City committees on the same day, the Central Committee pointed out that "in order to quickly recover and develop new China's national economy, . . . we should start New China's foreign trade immediately." It directed the setting up of a Bureau of Foreign Trade immediately to administer all foreign trade "in accordance with our needs and capabilities." If possible and necessary, the bureau would send representatives to and establish commercial offices in the Soviet Union and other socialist countries. The bureau was also to consider and decide on:

> (a) the goods that can be imported, or imported with high tariff, or the goods that are banned to import; (b) the goods that can be exported, or exported with high tariff, or the goods that are banned to export; (c) tax rate for imported and exported goods; (d) how to have our domestic production and trade units adjust so as to meet the special requirement of import and export; (e) how to design an import and export plan to meet the needs of import and export and internal domestic economy, to adjust the trade for the purpose of saving foreign currencies, and to decide with which country such trade relationships should be established.

The new government would announce procedures and rules to regulate "domestic and foreign ships entering harbor; berthing at wharf; loading and unloading goods; renting a wharf, going through customs tariff and receiving examination, currency exchange, punishment on smugglers, tax evaders, and violators." In order to increase exports to the Soviet Union, the Central Committee directed all local governments to "pay [special] attention to the production of such important exportable goods as cotton, soy bean, coal, salt, peanut, tobacco, silk, bristles, fur, and other handicraft products."[25]

The Sino-Soviet trade agreement of April 19, 1950, formalized the patterns of trade between the two countries.[26] Having dispersed forever with the "old imperialist trade," the CCP propaganda stressed, New China's foreign trade was "based completely on our country's economic needs" and was under a very "reasonable price system," thus making such a trade "mutually beneficial."[27] However, discontent among the CCP leaders regarding the economic policies existed and grew rather rapidly. As low-price commodities, the Chinese complained, a large amount of Chinese agriculture products and raw materials could be bartered for only a small number of Soviet machines and other industrial goods. Moreover, all the prices were fixed at the time when contracts were signed and thus would not fluctuate according to the world market. Therefore, according to a customs report in 1951, many Soviet items were merely slightly cheaper than comparable items on the world market.[28] Although the CCP leaders kept reminding the Soviet officials of Stalin's promise, they were somewhat disturbed that China did not receive due compensation from the Soviet government.[29]

With regard to economic assistance, the CCP leaders could have asked more from the Soviet Union but chose not to. In early 1950, the Kremlin agreed to provide $300 million in loans over five years at only 1 percent per annum interest. This was what Mao had originally expected. He calculated on January 3, 1950, that "it will be appropriate for our own sake not to borrow too much in [the] next few years."[30] Mao, who came from a Chinese peasant family, believed that loans were debts and that debts ought to be paid back sooner or later. He was also fearful that by providing larger loans, Moscow would be able to expand its influence over China's "domestic" affairs.[31] Pressing economic problems, however, compelled the CCP to take full advantage of the Soviet economic aid. Beijing used the loan to reconstruct energy, machinery, and defense industries mainly in the Northeast (Manchuria). As a first step, it adopted a plan to build or ameliorate a total of fifty projects (later changed to forty-seven) in the spring of 1950; ten were in coal mining, eleven in electric power, three in iron and steel, three in nonferrous metal, five in chemical engineering, seven in machinery, seven in the defense industry, and one in paper manufacturing. As many as thirty-six of these projects were to be located in the Northeast. Complete sets of machines, equipment, materials, and technology would be purchased from the Soviet Union on credit.[32]

Nevertheless, the outbreak of the Korean War and subsequent Chinese intervention shattered plans for the implementation of the planned projects. Only in early 1953, when the war stalemated, did Moscow agree to resume the aid program.[33] More disappointing to the Chinese was the fact that during the war, Beijing had to use a huge portion of the Soviet loan to purchase arms, ammunition, and other military equipment needed to sustain China's military intervention in Korea. As the Soviets failed to send troops to Korea, the Chinese felt that Moscow should not have charged them for the military supplies, which, recalled the former People's Liberation Army (PLA) chief of staff, Xu Xiangqian, were always delayed and often too poor in quality to be of any use.[34] Moreover, the Chinese were annoyed that they were being charged for the rebuilding of the damaged heavy industries in the Northeast – industries the Soviet Red Army had ransacked during its occupation there in 1945 and 1946. Moscow, in fact, should return the captured machines and equipment. The CCP leaders felt that the Soviets were riding roughshod over them.[35]

The CCP leaders faced a more serious challenge to their nationalist sentiments when the Soviets insisted on the establishment of four joint ventures in China. In March 1950 Moscow agreed to assist in China's oil and nonferrous metal manufacturing, but it wanted at least 50 percent of the ownership, share at least 50 percent of the profits, and take charge of the general management. With little bargaining power, China had to accept all these conditions. Shortly thereafter, two other joint venture projects – one on civil aviation, the other on ship manufacturing – came into being with the same terms.[36] These "joint ventures" led the Chinese to suspect that the Soviets were trying to take advantage of China's difficult situation. Remembering how imperial Russia had attempted to expand its economic influence in China, Beijing saw the Soviet leaders continuing to practice the old czarist "imperialism" toward China.[37]

These feelings developed further during the Korean War. As the West intensified its trade embargo against the Soviet bloc, Moscow was in great need of metals such as tin, zinc, tungsten, antimony, aluminum, and molybdenum. At Moscow's request, China shipped all its rare metals to the Soviet Union. In late summer 1952 Beijing also accepted Stalin's demand that China build a rubber plant on the islands of Hainan to help the Soviet bloc to "crash the imperialist blockade" on strategic materials. At the same time, the CCP purchased for the Soviet Union a large amount of badly needed rubber from Sri Lanka.[38] Although Beijing was doing the Soviet Union great favors, the Chinese felt, Moscow did not appear a bit appreciative.

Another issue that stirred resentment concerned Soviet advisors. The CCP leadership initially had high expectations of Soviet expertise. Its regime needed experienced advisors to assist not only in economic reconstruction but in military upgrading. As early as July 1949, Liu Shaoqi submitted a request directly to Stalin that the Soviet Union dispatch to China both economic and military advisors. With Stalin's endorsement, a large number of Soviet military advisors went to China by the end of that year: as many as 878 air force experts went to train PLA pilots, and a total of 90 naval experts arrived to help the PLA establish a modern navy.[39] Shortly afterward, a small pioneer group of Soviet economic experts went to China to "investigate China's needs for economic aid." After Moscow agreed to help China to build forty-seven industrial projects, as many as sixteen advisory groups arrived in 1950. Another twenty-six groups were sent to China's Northeast in the following year, their main mission to design and manage the "reconstruction-aid [yuan jian]" projects.[40]

Chinese enjoyment of the help these Soviet advisors offered was diminished because the Soviet comrades required special privileges in China. In response to Liu Shaoqi's request for the Soviet advisors, Stalin personally stipulated that

> (a) [China] has to guarantee that all the [Soviet] experts will be provided with full living and working conditions, namely, they must be paid reasonably well and supplied with the best possible houses and offices; (b) the spouses of those advisors working in China (even if they choose to stay in the Soviet Union) will be paid by the Chinese government with a certain amount of stipend; when they go to China to visit, the Chinese side must be responsible for their travel and stay; (c) the length of time for the [Soviet] experts to work in China will be determined on the basis of needs and actual circumstances; (d) if the Soviet personnel commit any errors or violates any [Chinese] rules, they will be subject to the Soviet jurisdiction, and the Chinese side has no [legal] authority over [the Soviet people who are working in China].[41]

Stalin repeated these stipulations during his meetings with Mao in Moscow and also stressed that unless China complied with these rules, Moscow would not send advisors. With his staunch determination to abolish the humiliating "imperialistic extraterritoriality" that China had endured in the past, Mao could hardly believe that Stalin would impose such humiliating rules on his regime. He came to believe, his Russian-language interpreter Shi Zhe recalls, that "[although a Georgian,] Stalin's Pan-Russianism is even more strongly expressed than the Russian people. Lenin's criticism of Stalin on this aspect in the past has thus proved absolutely correct." Despite his bitterness, however, Mao chose not to challenge Stalin but to reserve his right to object.[42]

Mao's main desire for an alliance relationship with Moscow was to secure a Soviet commitment to China's security. For economic reconstruction, he understood that China could not – and, perhaps, should not – rely merely on Soviet assistance. To restore and remold the nation's economy, CCP propaganda asserted in March 1950, a combination of three forces would work best: first, "the existing means of production and, especially, the inexhaustible labor [supply] of our country"; second, "the valiant and industrious [Chinese] peasants" whose productivity would "not only guarantee supplies for the cities but provide enough surplus goods to be bartered for the things we need"; and third, "the favorable Soviet loan by which we get a fresh supply of machine parts and equipment."[43] While this was the best that the CCP could hope for, Beijing tried to strike as good a deal as possible with Moscow.

It is more interesting to note that from its outset, economic aspects of the Sino-Soviet alliance already involved strong feelings and bitter images. While expecting the Soviets to treat China as an equal partner in order to build mutually beneficial economic relations, the reality left the CCP leadership confused and disappointed: A chauvinistic Stalin was no better than the imperial czars; primarily concerned about their own interests, the Soviets would not hesitate to take advantage of China's predicament. Yet Beijing authorities, acutely discontent with the Soviet attitude and deeply wary of Soviet intentions, were in no position to demand anything. Instead, they buried their suspicion, dissatisfaction, and resentment deep in their hearts; yet these emotions would slowly but surely come to the surface.

The Rise and Fall of a Sino-Soviet Trade Regime

After the end of the Korean War in July 1953, CCP leaders prepared for an immediate improvement in Sino-Soviet economic relations. With the East Asian international situation more stable than three years earlier, Beijing authorities were eager to speed up the nation's economic reconstruction and improve the country's defense capability. Moreover, to minimize the impact of the Western economic embargo on China, the CCP understood the crucial roles Soviet economic and technological aid would play. Although Stalin's death in March appears to have relieved Mao and his comrades, CCP leaders continued to harbor mixed feelings – anxiety, expectations, misgivings, and vigilance – toward Moscow.

Having sacrificed a great deal in Korea, the CCP believed that China deserved a more favorable aid package from the Soviet Union; in effect, the Soviets owed China for its intervention in Korea. Indeed, China had paid a huge price for its military intervention. As many as twenty-five infantry divisions (73 percent of the PLA forces), sixteen artillery (67 percent), ten armored (100 percent), twelve air force (52 percent), and six guard divisions fought there along with hundreds of thousands of logistical personnel and laborers. A total of more than 2 million combatant and noncombatant Chinese were involved on the battlefield. According to Chinese statistics, the Chinese People's Volunteers consumed approximately 5.6 million tons of war materiel, including the loss of 399 airplanes and 12,916 vehicles. The People's Republic spent more than 6.2 billion yuan on the intervention.[44] All these resources and manpower could have been utilized for China's own economic reconstruction.

Despite the heavy price China had paid, however, CCP leaders seemed euphoric. For the first time in its history, China could claim to have stood up against a major Western power. Only a few decades before, CCP propaganda reminded the Chinese people, a small "united army of eight Western countries" had subdued China (the international intervention of 1900) and 700,000 Japanese troops had conquered most of the country (Japan's invasion in 1937). But in Korea, "after three years of fierce fighting," maintained Peng Dehuai, the commander of Chinese forces in Korea, "the first-rate armed forces of the greatest industrial power of the capitalist world were forced [by the Chinese troops] to stop at where they began [their invasion of North Korea]." To him, this result had proven that "gone forever is the time when the Western powers have been able to conquer a country in the [Far] East merely by mounting several cannons along the coast as in the past hundred years."[45]

Given the success of China's intervention, Beijing authorities felt, the CCP was deserving of Moscow's respect and the Soviets should be more willing to aid China. Foreign Minister Chen Yi recalled later that only after China entered the war had Stalin expressed his "admiration" for the CCP's courage and resolve. Chinese leaders also noticed that the Soviet Union undertook measures to amend its cautious policy of aiding China. During a visit of Chinese Vice-Premier Li Fuchun to Moscow in May 1953, the Kremlin offered to construct defense-related industries for China. With little negotiation, Soviet Vice-Premier Anastas Mikoyan and Li signed an agreement that the Soviet Union would provide technology and complete sets of equipment to build up to 91 projects pertinent to China's defense industry.[46] Mao was pleased with the altered Soviet attitude toward his regime. In his telegram to the Kremlin on September 15, he praised it as "a historically great undertaking" when the two governments achieved an agreement on long-term Soviet assistance after only one round of negotiations. With Soviet technological and economic aid, Mao assured Moscow that "we will industrialize China . . . so that China will play an important role in strengthening the socialist camp."[47]

The radical improvement of Sino-Soviet relations began in October 1954. Shortly after securing control of the Kremlin, Nikita Khrushchev went to China on September 29 and stayed through October 16. Between October 3 and 12, Mao and Khrushchev met several times while other leaders conducted "thorough and comprehensive" dialogues and negotiations concerning the future of Sino-Soviet cooperation. At the end of these meetings, two communiqués – one an assessment of and policy toward the current international situation and one on policy toward Japan – were released. More important, as both sides "exchanged" concerns over the "imperialist economic blockade" and reiterated their determination to "crush" it, the Soviets seemed more ready than ever to assist in China's economic reconstruction.[48]

As a result, Moscow increased its aid to China. In October Khrushchev agreed to provide another long-term loan totaling 520 million rubles. Moreover, he added to the previously agreed "reconstruction-aid" projects fifteen new ones for which the Soviets would supply complete sets of equipment and technical personnel to build China's energy and raw and semifinished materials industries.[49] In March 1955 Moscow and Beijing signed a new aid agreement that stipulated an additional 16 industrial projects that would be funded entirely by the Soviet Union. These new projects would focus on construction of defense-related plants, shipbuilding, and raw and semifinished materials industries. Although some adjustments were made later, for the period under Beijing's First Five-Year Plan (1953–1957), the Soviet Union helped China to build as many as 166 industrial plants.[50] In the 1950s Moscow also helped Beijing to acquire substantial aid from Eastern European countries, including East Germany, Czechoslovakia, Poland, Romania, Hungary, and Bulgaria. These countries agreed to assume the responsibility of constructing 116 completely equipped industrial plants and 88 partially equipped plants.[51]

Industrial and military technology formed an indispensable part of Soviet and Eastern European economic aid to China. Shortly after the Sino-Soviet agreement on technology transfer was signed in October 1954, Beijing obtained similar commitments from Eastern European countries. These agreements enabled China to acquire thousands of technological devices, products, and techniques. While Eastern Europe focused on agriculture and forestry technologies, the Soviet Union was responsible for supplying advanced technologies, including smeltery, ore dressing, petroleum prospecting, locomotive manufacturing, hydraulic and thermal power plants, hydraulic turbine manufacturing, machine tools, high-quality steel manufacturing, and vacuum installations. It is also interesting to point out that China merely compensated the Soviet and East European countries for the costs of blueprint duplication and copying; it paid nothing for the patent rights, and thus obtained these technologies practically for free.[52] In addition, to ensure that the Chinese would master the techniques of production and scientific knowledge, the Soviet and Eastern European states dispatched more than 8,000 advisors and experts to China and received as many as 7,000 Chinese for advanced training and education in the 1950s.[53]

In taking steps to rectify the wrongs Stalin had done to the CCP, the new Soviet leadership also seems to have become sensitive toward Chinese national sentiment. While visiting China in October 1954, Khrushchev expressed his understanding of the CCP's acute sensitivity to issues of sovereignty and independence. He proposed to Mao that the four Sino-Soviet joint ventures established in 1950 to 1951 – oil and nonferrous metal manufacturing plants in Xinjiang and civil aviation and shipbuilding companies in Dalian – become solely Chinese owned and operated. Khrushchev also went one step further by agreeing to the Chinese request that Soviet armed forces begin to withdraw from their naval bases in Lushun (Port Arthur); withdrawal would be completed before May 31, 1955, by which date China would exercise full authority over these bases.[54]

All these developments were very encouraging, and the Chinese leaders welcomed the changed Soviet attitude. However, by the late 1950s the honeymoon of Sino-Soviet cooperation was slowly but surely ebbing away. As the Western trade embargo relaxed, and as CCP's First Five-Year Plan seemingly accomplished a good deal, Beijing became increasingly eager to achieve industrialization and military modernization within as short a time as possible. To fulfill this lofty mission the CCP leaders were expecting steady increases in Soviet economic and technological assistance. Worried about and wary of an emerging powerful China, however, Moscow grew reluctant to meet the Chinese needs. As a result, the deeply rooted but temporarily suppressed suspicion of and misgivings about Soviet "chauvinism" inevitably revived, causing Chinese leaders to reconsider their political policy toward Moscow. Soon disagreements, private complaints, and even personal enmity led to public quarrels and open denunciations. This dynamic made the Sino-Soviet split inescapable by the end of the decade.

The most persistent dynamic driving the escalation of Sino-Soviet conflict was the CCP's aspiration to assert not only national autonomy but an equal-partner status. If the Chinese had hesitated to be assertive in 1950, they felt immensely encouraged by 1957. The First Five-Year Plan created a spectacular advance in industrial output. At the end of the planned period, steel production reached 5.35 million tons; iron, 5.8 million tons; electric power, 19.3 billion kilowatt-hours; coal, 131 million tons; and crude oil, 1.46 million tons.[55] The industrial growth fueled the CCP leadership's ambition for rapid modernization. Addressing the thirtieth session of the Chinese People's Government Council on June 14, 1954, Mao laid out a timetable for China to become an industrial power: It would take China fifteen years to "lay down a foundation," and roughly fifty years to "build a powerful socialist country."[56] Mao reiterated this goal in 1955. Proudly proclaiming that China would soon catch up with the United States, he explained that "America only has a history of 180 years. Sixty years ago, it produced 4 million tons of steel. We are [therefore] only sixty years behind . . . [and] we will surely overtake it."[57] During his visit to Moscow on November 2–21, 1957, the CCP chairman boasted at a meeting with all the other leaders of Communist countries that China would overtake Britain in iron, steel, and other heavy industries in the next fifteen years and would exceed the United States soon thereafter in those areas as well.[58]

Shortly after he returned home, Mao became even more eager to have China outpace Anglo-American industrial strength. In April 1958 he argued that "it probably will not take us as long as we have anticipated to overtake the capitalist powers in industrial and agricultural production." Mao's illusion pushed the central leadership to plan to race past Britain and America; in May Mao assured high-ranking military commanders that "we are quite sure that we will exceed Britain in seven years and overtake the U.S. in ten years."[59] The result of Mao's dreamlike aspiration was the "Great Leap Forward" movement, calling for a 19 percent increase in steel production, 18 percent in electricity, and 17 percent in coal output for 1958. Unduly buoyed by optimism, the CCP leaders kept raising the production targets in hopes of achieving an unprecedented rate of growth.[60]

Beijing, which had expected full support from the Soviet Union, felt disgruntled and discouraged when Moscow kept raising doubts about China's high hopes. In early 1957 the Soviet Far East Economic Committee, in its review of Far Eastern economic development, was bitingly critical of China's economic policies. Agitated by the "several errors [the report made] on China's economic development," Beijing's Foreign Ministry protested in a memorandum to Moscow on March 13, 1957. Referring to the Soviet finding that "China's agrarian collectivization has encountered peasants' opposition," the Chinese argued that "the speed of our country's agricultural collectivization, which has been fully explained by [CCP Vice Chairman] Liu Shaoqi in his report to the [National] People's Congress, completely refutes such a conviction." In discussing China's price problem, the PRC Foreign Ministry found that the Soviet assessment "deliberately distorts and obliterates our basic achievements . . . and instead, exaggerates our isolated weakness and mistakes." The Foreign Ministry memorandum then presented a lengthy explanation of how the draft paper "made errors merely by comparing our published statistics which are to serve different purposes." Given these mistakes, Beijing asserted, the Soviet leaders "could not help but draw erroneous conclusions" about China economic success.[61]

Mao, in particular, was bothered by the Soviet Union's skeptical and critical attitude toward China's economic development. Continuing to look down on the Chinese, he believed, Moscow suspected that an industrialized China would seriously challenge Soviet leadership in the international Communist movement. In a conversation with a Yugoslavian Communist Union delegation in September 1957, Mao vented his bitterness about how Moscow had distrusted the CCP. Stalin had believed, he told his guests, that "there were two Titos in the world: one in Yugoslavia, the other in China, even if no one passed a resolution that Mao Zedong was Tito." Although the CCP had "no objection that the Soviet Union functions as the center [of the world revolution] because it benefits the socialist movement," Mao pointed out that as of this date some people [in Moscow] remain suspicious of whether our socialism can be successfully constructed [in China]. They adhere to the assertion that our Communist Party is a phony one. What can [we] do? These people eat and sleep everyday and then propagate that the Chinese Communist Party is not really a Communist party, China's socialist construction is bound to fail. To them, it would be a bewildering thing if [China] could build a socialist [country]!

Because China's success would cause serious concerns that

China might become an imperialist state, a fourth imperialist state to join America, Britain, and France; [although] at present China has little industry, thus is in no position [to be an imperialist state], [China] will become formidable in one hundred years: Genghis Khan might be brought to life; consequently Europe would suffer again, and Yugoslavia might be conquered!

Mao, however, stressed, that "there is absolutely no chance for revival of the 'Yellow Peril,' " because "the CCP is a Marxist-Leninist Party."[62] He thus asserted that Moscow had no grounds to distrust and defame China.

Given Moscow's persistent distrust of the CCP, Mao became suspicious that the Soviets might have ulterior motives – that they wanted to tighten controls as well as to take advantage of China. During Khrushchev's 1954 China visit, Mao already had bluntly dismissed the possibility that China would be part of the Soviet–Eastern European economic system. After hearing out Khrushchev's proposals for coordinating aid, trade, and production, the CCP chairman stated that "there is no such need, because [such an arrangement] will have no real meaning to China's construction and development." On the contrary, linking itself to the Soviet–Eastern European system "would cause a lot of troubles which might in turn get [China] so much tangled up that [its] progress would be unraveled and blocked."[63]

Beijing believed that the Soviet Union had been counting on China in its efforts to circumvent Western trade restrictions. The second half of the 1950s saw a rapid increase in Soviet exports of manufactured products to China; the Chinese became convinced that Soviet industries would have to depend on China's market.[64] More important, over 30 percent of China's exports to the Soviet Union were of raw materials, especially those of "strategic importance," such as tungsten, tin, antimony, lithium, beryllium, tantalum, molybdenum, magnesium, and sulfur mineral ore and pellets. More than 70 percent of the annual yield of rubber manufactured on China's Hainan Island was being sold to the Soviets at "preferential prices." The Chinese understood that these strategic materials were "indispensable" in Soviet development of missiles and nuclear weapons.[65] Given its special relations with Hong Kong, Sri Lanka, and other non-Communist countries, China, even in the late 1950s, could acquire some materials on the lists of Western trade embargo and conduct *entrepôt* trade on behalf of the Soviet Union. According to Chinese sources, between 1953 and 1957 China imported for the Soviet Union a large amount of rubber, jute, coconut oil, and black pepper worth a total of 330 million yuan. Moreover, the Chinese leaders also believed that their country's agricultural products of rice, beans, peanuts, vegetable oil, salt, beef, pork, mutton, eggs, and fruit, which made up more than 48 percent of its exports to the Soviet Union, were essential to Soviet efforts to survive the Western trade embargo. During the same period, China also had been paying back Soviet loans with gold and hard currencies. Understanding that the Soviets were short of U.S. dollars, by 1958 Beijing had paid Moscow a total of $156 million in cash.[66]

Wary that the Soviets would take more advantage of China, Beijing initiated negotiations with Moscow in July 1956, requesting that Soviets compensate for and rectify their "unreasonable pricing system" and "inequitable payment" in the Sino-Soviet trade. The CCP criticized Moscow for its failure to adhere to the principle of mutual respect and equality, and also expressed "serious" concerns over Soviet "chauvinistic" treatment of the brotherly socialist countries. Under the Chinese pressure, Moscow returned the money it had presumably overcharged China in trade and accepted a "more equitable" pricing and payment system.[67]

Entertaining the old Chinese belief in *li shang wanglai* (courtesy on the basis of reciprocity), CCP leaders felt that they deserved more favorable treatment from Moscow, especially in their development of nuclear weapons. While Khrushchev was in Beijing in 1954, Mao already had probed the possibility that Moscow could help China get the bomb, but the Soviet leader had responded bluntly that China should concentrate on economic reconstruction, "not develop these kinds of weapons." So long as China had Soviet nuclear protection, he asserted, such weapons would be "a huge waste" for China. If China wanted to develop a nuclear energy industry, the Soviet Union "can assist in building a small atomic reactor" for training and scientific research purposes. Evidently disappointed at and skeptical of Khrushchev's offer, Mao replied, "Let us think it over before making any decisions."[68]

Mao soon discovered that the Soviets were willing to extend a nuclear umbrella over China but not to help the Chinese to build an atomic bomb. Moscow had sent a group of geologists to China to prospect for uranium early in 1950 and on January 20, 1955, signed an agreement on a Sino-Soviet joint effort to mine uranium. In response to China's request, the Soviet leaders, late in April of that year, agreed to provide the technology and equipment for the Chinese to construct a heavy-water-moderated reactor and a cyclotron accelerator. They also promised to help the Chinese build a laboratory for nuclear research in August 1958. All these agreements, however, provided that Soviet nuclear technology would be "for peaceful use" only.[69]

The Soviet policy was hardly satisfactory to Beijing, given the CCP's desire to construct its own bomb. In September 1957 Marshal Nie Rongzhen, the vice-premier in charge of military and nuclear industries, led a mission to Moscow to procure Soviet assistance in China's nuclear development. Nie's trip led to the signing of another Sino-Soviet protocol in October; in it the Soviets agreed to provide a training model of an atomic bomb and related equipment. But they deliberately left open exactly what equipment would be delivered, when, and how. When Nie pressed for more definite answers, the Soviet leaders replied that "we are not ready to discuss these issues and we won't be ready in the near future."[70] In August 1958 Moscow did send a delegation to Beijing to make specific arrangements concerning the transfer of Soviet atomic technology. The Chinese leaders, however, found that "the Soviets tried to find all possible excuses not to help us." Although Moscow had dispatched, late in 1957, 102 Soviet missile specialists and two Soviet P-2 short-range ground-to-ground missiles, in fact it never intended to satisfy Beijing's quest for atomic technology and equipment.[71]

Rather than helping the Chinese build an atomic bomb, Moscow, at least in Beijing's view, seemingly intended to incorporate China's coastal defense into its East Asian defense system. On April 18, 1958, in a letter to Peng Dehuai, Marshal Rodion I. Malinovskii, the Soviet minister of defense, suggested "jointly" building a powerful long-wave radio station linking the Chinese navy with the Soviet navy in East Asia. Malinovskii made it clear that the Soviet Union would provide the technology and most of the money needed.[72] Meeting with Mao on July 21, Pavel Iudin, the Soviet ambassador to Beijing, also proposed on behalf of Khrushchev that the Soviet navy would like to establish a joint flotilla of nuclear-powered submarines with China "for a common defense in the Far East." Iudin explained that Russia's coastal conditions were not appropriate for the Soviet navy's newly developed submarines and that China had a long coast and better "harbor conditions for our advanced [nuclear] submarines to demonstrate their strength."[73]

Moscow's proposals led the Chinese leaders to believe that the long-suspected Soviet intention to control China was unfolding. To confront the Soviet "joint radio station" suggestion, Mao instructed the Ministry of Defense on June

6, 1958, that "China must come up with the money to pay for [the financial cost] which must not be covered by the Soviet side." Should the Soviets "take the high-handed [attitude toward us], [we] shall not respond [to their request] and let it drag for a while, or [we] may respond after the central leadership discusses it." No matter how the two governments "settle" this issue, he stressed:

China must shoulder the responsibility of capital investment for this radio station; China is duty-bound in this case. [We] may have to ask for Soviet comrades' help with regard to construction and equipment, but all the costs must be priced and paid in cash by us. [We] may share its use after it is constructed, which ought to be determined by an agreement between the two governments. This is the position of Chinese [government], not purely mine.[74]

On June 12, Mao directed Peng to cable Malinovskii saying that China welcomed the Soviet offers but would accept the Soviet Union's technological assistance only.[75]

Particularly irritated by Iudin's "joint submarine flotilla" suggestion, Mao had a long meeting with him on July 22. "After you left yesterday I could not fall asleep, nor did I have dinner," he told Iudin. "Today I invited you over to talk a bit more so that you can be [my] doctor: [after talking with you], I might be able to eat and sleep this afternoon." Mao immediately focused on the joint nuclear submarine flotilla request. He was agitated particularly by the proposed "joint ownership" and "joint operation," because although "the issue of ownership has long before been dealt with," now it was resurfacing. He concluded firmly:

You never trust the Chinese! You only trust the Russians! [To you] the Russians are the first-class [people] whereas the Chinese are among the inferior who are dumb and careless. Therefore [you] came up with the joint ownership and operation proposition. Well, if [you] want joint ownership and operation, how about having it all – let's turn into joint ownership and operation [all of our] army, navy, air force, industry, agriculture, culture, education? Or, [you] may have all of [China's] more than ten thousand kilometers long coastal line and let us only maintain a guerrilla force. With a few atomic bombs, you think you are in a position to control [us] through joint ownership. Other than [these bombs], what else [do you have] to justify [your request]?

Mao then opened old wounds. "Pressured by Stalin, [we conceded that] the Northeast and Xinjiang became two [Soviet] spheres of influence and four [newly built] plants became jointly owned and operated." Since Khrushchev had these arrangements eliminated in 1954, Mao told Iudin that "we were grateful for that." But, "you [Russians] have never had faith in the Chinese people, and Stalin was among the worst." Stalin regarded the Chinese Communists as "Tito the Second" and treated the Chinese people "as a backward nation." Although "you [Russians] have often stated that the Europeans looked down upon the Russians, some Russians look down upon the Chinese people." Therefore, up to now, "there has never existed such a thing as brotherly relations among all the parties to which [your leaders] merely paid lip service and never meant it; as a result, the relations between parties can still be described as between father and son or between cats and mice." Mao then reminded Iudin that he had raised this issue in private with Khrushchev and other Soviet leaders who "all admitted that such a father-son relationship" should not be tolerated. But, as Mikoyan's congratulatory speech delivered at the CCP's Eighth National Congress had proved, the current Soviet leaders did not want to change that. Hence, "I deliberately refused to attend that day's meeting so as to protest, . . . because, acting as if he was the father, [Mikoyan] regarded China as Russia's son."

Mao explicitly pointed out that Moscow was paying back kindness with ingratitude.

> As for [the differences over] the issue of peaceful evolution, we have never openly discussed [them], nor have we published [them] in the newspapers. Cautious as we have been, we chose to exchange different opinions internally, . . . [because our public criticism of the Soviet leadership] would hurt Comrade Khrushchev's [political position].

With regard to international relations, "we are opposed to any [act] that is harmful to the Soviet Union. We have objected to all the major criticism that the revisionists and imperialists have massed against the Soviet Union." Moreover, China "has held no secrets from you [Russians]. . . . We trust you people, because you are from a socialist country, and you are sons and daughters of Lenin." The CCP leadership even helped Moscow to resolve the Polish dispute. "Once even I have persuaded the Polish people that [we all] should learn from the Soviet Union." But Moscow was taking China's support for granted, Mao asserted.

Moscow, in Mao's view, had never tried to be sensitive to Chinese pride and feelings. "There was a [Soviet] advisor in [our] military academy," he told Iudin, "who, in discussing war cases, would only allow [the Chinese trainees] to talk about those of the Soviet Union, not China's, would only allow them to talk about the ten offensives of the Soviet Army, not [ours] in the Korean War." Defense Minister Peng Dehuai reinforced Mao's allegation by pointing out that some high-ranking Soviet military advisors had "a rude attitude and rough style," and they hardly tolerated any challenge to the Soviet military codes and theories. Mao then became excited and indignant: "Please allow us to talk about [our own war experiences]! For God's sake, we fought wars for twenty-two years; we fought in Korea for three years!" He also advised Iudin and Soviet specialists "to pay more visits to each of our provinces so as to get in touch with the people and obtain firsthand information." Only by doing that would the Soviets be better able to understand the Chinese.

Finally, Mao stressed that he would never accept any Soviet proposition for "a joint ownership." It was his determination that China "won't get mixed with you: we must be independent from one another." These remarks, he told Iudin, "may not sound so pleasing to [your] ear. You may accuse me of being a nationalist or another Tito. My counterargument is that you have extended the Russian nationalism to China's coast." Khrushchev had given up joint ownership of the four plants, "but why in the world do [you Russians] want to build a 'joint ownership' navy now? How would you explain to the rest of the world that you propose to build a 'joint ownership' navy [in China]? How would you explain [that] to the Chinese people?" If Moscow attempted to control China through its economic weapon, Mao asserted, "we won't satisfy you at all, not even [give you] a tiny [piece of our] fingers." Although Beijing had to "refuse to accept [Soviet] aid on [China's submarine construction] for ten thousand years," he assured Iudin that "it still is possible that [we] cooperate on many other affairs; it is unlikely that we would break up. We will, from beginning to the end, support the Soviet Union, although we may quarrel with each other inside the house." Moreover, Moscow did not have to satisfy every CCP request. "Because if you hold back your aid from us, [you] in effect would compel us to work harder [to be self-reliant]; should [we] get everything from you, [in the long run] we will end up in a disadvantageous position." Mao wanted Iudin to report all his comments to Khrushchev: "[Y]ou must tell him exactly what I have remarked without any polishing so as to make him [Khrushchev] uneasy. He has criticized Stalin's [policy] lines but now adopts the same [policies] as Stalin did."[76]

These disputes were not settled until Khrushchev's hastily scheduled visit to Beijing on July 31, 1958. The Soviet leader accommodated the CCP's concerns by confirming that the Soviet Union would provide only loans and technology for building the radio station, which China would own completely. Khrushchev also explained to Mao that Moscow never intended to establish a joint nuclear submarine force in China and that Iudin had passed the wrong message, thus resulting in the "misunderstandings."[77] On October 20, 1958, Liu Xiao, the PRC ambassador to Moscow, reported that the Soviet leadership began to show signs of rectifying its "erroneous" attitudes toward China, thus taking Beijing's positions increasingly seriously. With regard to international situations, Khrushchev on several occasions "underlined the correctness of our position that war must not be feared and peace cannot be begged [for]." The Soviets had "gone one step further in understanding and assessing the important roles that our country has played in international struggle and the experiences that our socialist construction has achieved; . . . in some cases, they gradually incorporate China's experiences [in their economic work]." Moreover, Khrushchev began to "put increasing stress on speeding up [economic] construction to win time." These changes, Liu asserted, were positive; but further changes would "depend upon the interaction of Soviet internal and external forces."[78]

Beijing welcomed these changes and undertook measures to encourage more. Mao endorsed Ambassador Liu Xiao's suggestions of January 13, 1959, that China should be "more considerate" and "take their [Soviet] situations into more serious account so as not to be too imposing"; Chinese leaders "ought not to reveal or criticize Soviet opinions that differ from ours either in the media or to the public"; and "[we] should be more sensible to the Soviet advisors in China and [we] must take a modest attitude toward them."[79] On February 13 Mao added to the "CCP CC Instructions on How to Rectify Arrogant and Imperious Attitudes in Our Dealing with Foreign Relations" that "[we] must emphasize that [we] shall continue to learn all the advanced experiences that suit our conditions from the Soviet Union and other brotherly states."[80] Mao also pointed out in his conversation with the Soviet ambassador and ambassadors of ten other socialist states on May 6 that "all of you are our teachers, but the most important teacher is the Soviet Union" and that China's success in economic construction was in part due to Soviet assistance.[81] In 1959, indeed, Beijing intensified its quest to obtain maximum military-technical aid from Moscow. Despite the CCP's political mistrust of Khrushchev, a good number of Chinese purchase orders and requests for aid and advisors, now available in the Russian Foreign Ministry archives, show that Mao and his comrades seem to have wanted more, not less.[82] The year 1959 also saw the biggest increase in trade between China and the Soviet Union. Amounting to more than 2 billion yuan, which was 5 times more than that in 1950, Sino-Soviet trade made up 48 percent of China's total foreign trade.[83]

Nevertheless, the revival of Sino-Soviet friendship did not last long. Despite its clear need for Soviet aid, the CCP leadership explicitly vowed that China would never imitate Soviet ideas and regulations that ran counter to its cherished revolutionary traditions. In Mao's mind, revolutionary self-reliance and grassroots participation in and support for economic reconstruction, not foreign aid, would guarantee CCP success in resolving any problems, domestic or international.[84] Especially with regard to Western economic sanctions, Mao believed that China had already come out victorious. When asked to comment on the effects of the Western trade embargo during an interview with two Brazilian journalists on September 2, 1958, the CCP chairman replied that it "has not hurt us a bit but has been of great benefit to us." One obvious benefit, Mao explained, was that it helped the Chinese people to do away with "blind faith in foreigners." Getting rid of this "blind faith" was "a matter of immense importance," Mao asserted. "[A]ll countries in Asia, Africa, and Latin America should carry out this task." China would definitely continue to "eradicate this kind of superstition."[85] Mao also admonished against "blind faith in foreigners" at the fifteenth meeting of the Supreme State Conference on September 5 and 8. Addressing the question of what effect the Western economic embargo had on China, he insisted that the embargo "has greatly benefited us, and we don't feel any detrimental effects of the embargo. On the contrary, the embargo has been of enormous benefit to our basic necessities of life including food, clothing, shelter, and transportation [*yi shi zhu xing*] as well as our [economic] construction (iron and steel production)." In his view, the embargo had compelled the Chinese people to "rely on themselves" and to wage the Great Leap Forward. "It is absolutely great that [the embargo] has helped [us] to get rid of the dependent mentality and do away with blind faith [in foreigners]." The longer the embargo lasted, Mao asserted, the more iron and steel China would produce and the stronger China would become, thus ultimately smashing the embargo.[86]

The CCP leaders were dismayed to find out that Moscow had strong doubts about their envisioned achievements. As Ambassador Liu Xiao reported in October 1958, the Soviet leaders "lacked a profound understanding of the application of our Party's strategy and tactics [in economic affairs] and the new thoughts and new practices that have emerged in our [economic] development." Many issues, such as "the People's Communes, China's transformation toward Communism, [the idea of] obtaining food without paying for it, and our current propaganda on Communist ideology," were "incomprehensible" to them.[87] On July 2, 1959, the PRC embassy in Moscow again reported that "recently there have been rumors widely spread among some Soviet cadres, especially those who have had working relations with our country, that China has encountered great difficulties [in its economy], and some yet-to-be-publicized statistics [pertinent to our economy] have been often talked about [by the Soviets]." Ignoring China's "major achievements," these people "merely concentrate on [our] shortcomings" and had concluded that "the Chinese [Communist] Party has committed grave errors." Obviously very concerned about the contents of the embassy's report, Mao added a title to it that read "Some Soviet Comrades Are Criticizing Our Great Leap Forward [Campaign]," and directed his associates to "study [*yan jiu*] this matter."[88]

Mao had long worried that Khrushchev, much like the old czars, would try to dominate China by utilizing the Soviet Union's might. In March 1958, when Khrushchev replaced Nikolai A. Bulganin as Soviet premier, Mao became more concerned that Khrushchev would intensify his control over China once he had consolidated his position in the Kremlin. Mao easily transformed his personal dislike of Khrushchev into political mistrust. At the CCP CC meetings in Lushan in the summer of 1959, the chairman ousted Marshal Peng Dehuai. An important allegation was that Peng and his followers, supported by Khrushchev, had "conspired to topple" Mao's leadership, thereby placing China under Moscow's direct control.[89] A further irritation arose when Khrushchev "suddenly" went to Beijing in late September. At a seven-hour-long meeting with Mao and other top CCP leaders on October 2, the Soviet leader accused Mao of his "risky" policy toward the Taiwan Straits and Beijing's belligerent attitude toward the Sino-Indian territorial dispute. Khrushchev pressured Mao to consider the possibility of an independent Taiwan and adopt a more accommodating policy toward the United States. As minutes of the meeting are still classified, details are unknown. It is hardly surprising, however, that Mao felt bitter because the meeting "severely damaged the Sino-Soviet relations."[90]

Deeply resentful, Mao felt certain that Khrushchev and his policies toward China were becoming an earnest threat to his country's vital national interests. In December 1959 Mao prepared a special meeting with his top associates to discuss the international situation. He vehemently accused Moscow of its constant attempts – he counted a total of ten between 1945 and 1959 – to dominate China. Mao then pointed out that Khrushchev suffered from fatal weaknesses: first, "[he] is very naive, and has so little understanding of Marxism-Leninism that he is easily deceived by imperialists"; second, "he does not understand China to the utmost extent and he refuses to learn; instead, he only trusts a number of false intelligence reports and wags his tongue too freely and, if he does not correct this, he will completely fail in a few years (eight years, maybe)"; third, "he is extremely afraid of China; he is not only fearful of imperialism but also of the Chinese-style Communism, because he is afraid that Eastern European and other [Communist] parties will not trust them but us"; and fourth, "his world view is pragmatism which is subjective idealism, and he is [so] lacking consistency that, whenever he sees an advantage, he will quickly change [his positions]." In Mao's view, all these problems were "historically rooted," and "Lenin didn't have time to remold [these problems]." The chairman was certain that this type of "chauvinism will one day turn to its opposite."[91] At another meeting in the same month, Mao summarized Khrushchev's policies toward China: first, "[he] treats China as Soviet Union's son"; second, "[he] does not want students to surpass masters"; third, "[he always] holds back a trick or two [*liu yishou*]"; and fourth, "[he] is behind subversion [conspiracies against the current CCP leadership]."[92] Hence, in Mao's eyes, Khrushchev lost all his political credibility.

Despite the grievances against Khrushchev, however, Mao did not expect an immediate Sino-Soviet split, nor did he anticipate that Khrushchev would employ economic blackmail against China. But on July 16, 1960, the Soviet Union "suddenly" notified Beijing that all Soviet advisors and experts in China would soon be withdrawn. Without waiting for China's reply, Moscow on July 25 instructed all Soviet advisers and experts to leave China by September 1. At the same time, the Kremlin held back the dispatch of more than 900 experts it had earlier agreed on. Within one month, as many as 1,390 Soviet advisors and experts returned, and Moscow tore up 12 agreements on economic and technologic aid and abrogated more than 200 projects of scientific and technologic cooperation.[93]

The Chinese leaders were shocked and furious. The withdrawal of all the Soviet advisors and experts and abrogation of all the aid projects would damage China greatly: Many priority national defense and high-technology projects had to stop or slow down only partway through. To minimize the potential damage, Beijing in its first response to Moscow on July 31 asked that the Kremlin reconsider its decision, or at least let the experts stay until their contracts expired. On August 4 Vice Premier and Foreign Minister Chen Yi met with the Soviet ambassador to China, pointing out that since the Soviet Union already had caused China to suffer economically, Moscow had to stop "hurting the friendship between the two countries." "We may debate on differences over basic theories of Marxism-Leninism and international issues," Chen said, but "the bilateral [economic] relations should by no means get worse."[94]

Seeing no change in Soviet policy, Beijing began to harden its own. In a series of "diplomatic notes" to the Soviet Foreign Ministry in August and September, the CCP attacked Moscow for "seriously violating the common laws and rules guiding the relationships among the socialist countries"; China would never be intimidated by "socialist-imperialist blackmail."[95] Meeting with a high-ranking Soviet delegation in September, CCP Secretariat-in-General Deng Xiaoping explicitly pointed out:

> The CCP will never accept the father-and-son relationships between
> parties or governments. Your withdrawal of experts has inflicted
> damages upon us, thus causing us a great deal of difficulty, and hav-

ing adverse effects on our country's economic construction, especially those economic and foreign trade plans that will have to be rearranged. The Chinese people are prepared to swallow these losses, and determined to make up for the losses with our own hands and build our own nation.[96]

The Sino-Soviet split thus became a reality.

Economic Relations and the Causes of the Split

Inevitable friction arising from economic relations was one of the most persistent dynamic characteristics of the Sino-Soviet rift; economic conflicts constituted a contributing factor to the Sino-Soviet split. Was it because the economic relations benefited one side more than the other so much that the unsatisfied partner had to withdraw? Or was it because, as some scholars claimed, Mao was determined that "China should become a superpower" politically and economically whereas the Soviet leadership was determined "to prevent it"?[97] Or were other factors to blame?

Rational considerations, or cost-effect calculations, were not as significant as culture-bound irrational factors. Clearly, cultural thought patterns – myths as well as reason and images as well as reality – formed the core of Chinese Communist policy toward Sino-Soviet economic relations. There can be little doubt that the economic relations forged an interdependent pattern. In that, both sides more or less gained: Whereas China acquired badly needed aid, technology, expertise, and industrial products, the Soviet Union penetrated China's market, established an external channel to obtain materials subject to the Western embargo, and would, in the long run, be able to incorporate China into the economic system of the Soviet-led Eastern Bloc. The economic interdependency should have gratified both sides.

Nevertheless, Beijing's discontent and antagonism toward Moscow derived largely from how its leaders *perceived* and *felt* about their ally. Given their strong sentiment about "foreign devils" and "national humiliations," the CCP leaders hardly could let go of their memories of the century-long Russian "chauvinism." Ideological similarities, shared security concerns, and mutual economic interests failed to make the Chinese less sensitive to or more tolerant of "Russian arrogance." With old grievances against Stalin unresolved, conditions attached to the Soviet aid, trade on an allegedly unequal basis, Soviet advisors' special privileges in China, Moscow's reluctance to offer advanced (especially atomic) technology, dubious "joint ventures," and, most of all, harsh and open criticism of China's economic policies – all led the Chinese leaders to suspect that, like the old czars, the Soviet leaders continued to look down on the Chinese and aspired to control and take advantage of China. Mao felt this most acutely of all. In addition to his extreme nationalism, he easily let his own emotions and feelings interfere with policymaking and frequently turned personal dislike into political mistrust.

China's power aspiration certainly was a factor. Seriously concerned about American threats, the CCP leadership felt obliged to acquire a formidable power status within the shortest possible time. Moreover, hardly immune from an inferiority complex as a result of China's impotence in facing foreign challenges in the past, Mao and his associates persistently hoped to restore China's rightful place in the socialist bloc, if not the entire international community. To reach these goals, Mao had to undertake rapid industrialization and military modernization, of which iron, steel, and atomic weapons were the prominent symbols of Great Power status. The accomplishment of these goals invariably depended on Moscow's extensive economic and technological aid, which, Mao believed, the Kremlin had every reason to offer, for an industrialized and powerful China would enhance the socialist camp's strength. Hence the CCP leadership adopted labor-intensive, extremist economic policies for rapid development: the First Five-Year Plan, the People's Communes, and most of all, the Great Leap Forward. Clearly, the Soviet leadership saw the postwar period from a rather different angle and had distinctively different expectations of China's modernization efforts. When Moscow attempted to modify Beijing's "premature advance," "irresponsible behavior," and "reckless policies," the CCP tended to see the Soviet policies through the lens of traditional foreign interference and intimidation.

It is sheer exaggeration to assert that, from the outset, the People's Republic wanted to become a superpower. In its relations with the Soviet Union, the best that Beijing hoped for was to become an equal partner; anything less would not be acceptable. Cognizant of the long-held notion that China was a country with vast land, rich resources, and a nation of intelligent and hardworking people, Mao and his associates never doubted that China could survive economically by being self-sufficient and self-reliant. Although valuing Soviet economic and technological aid, in due time the Chinese leaders became too optimistic about their success and too sensitive to their pride to adopt a flexible stance toward Moscow. It is evident that the Chinese leaders held an *ethnocentric* view of foreign affairs. They were strongly inclined to see the whole material world through the prism of their own experience, images, memories, and, sometimes, aspirations. Thus it was more likely for them to mold their perception of external threat to fit their own strategy than to adapt their strategy to an adversary's behavior. While accusing Khrushchev of not understanding Chinese culture and of refusing to learn about China, Mao never asked himself how much he understood Russian culture or how his lack of understanding of Russian thought processes might foster misperception, miscalculation, and ultimately friction.

It is interesting to note that, in the end, Khrushchev employed economic weapons to cope with Beijing's challenge. How and why did he choose to do so? What objectives did he intend to achieve? How effective did he believe his "economic blackmail" could be? A succinct answer to these questions has yet to be found. And perhaps a more interesting question is: How great an effect did the Western embargo against China have in causing the Sino-Soviet split? These questions deserve a more comprehensive study than what this chapter has aimed at. Such an undertaking would have to be an international history with an analytic focus on the use of economic sanctions in pursuit of foreign policy goals – an interesting and important phenomenon of twentieth-century international relations.[98]

Notes

1. These views are best summarized in Alexander Eckstein, *Communist China's Economic Growth and Foreign Trade: Implications for U.S. Policy* (New York: McGraw-Hill, 1966), 136–7.

2. See, in particular, Stephen M. Walt, *The Origins of Alliance* (Ithaca, N.Y.: Cornell University Press, 1987), chaps. 1–3; Robert Jervis and Jack Snyder, eds., *Dominoes and Bandwagons: Strategic Beliefs and Great Power Competition in the Eurasian Rimland* (New York: Oxford University Press, 1991), intro.

3. Mao Zedong, "Address to the Preparatory Meeting of the New Political Consultative Council," *Selected Works of Mao Tse-tung* (Beijing: Foreign Languages Press, 1971), vol. 4, 469. For how Mao's concerns about the U.S. threat evolved, see Zhang Shuguang, *Deterrence and Strategic Culture: Chinese-American Confrontation, 1949–1958* (Ithaca, N.Y.: Cornell University Press, 1992), 14–21.

4. Speech, Mao Zedong, at the Meeting of the Politburo of the Central Committee, September 8, 1948, *Dang de wenxian* [Party documents], no. 5 (1989): 3–6.

5. Mao's telegram to the CCP Central Committee, January 5, 1950, *Jianguo yilai Mao Zedong wengao* [Mao's manuscripts since the founding of the People's Republic of China] (hereafter *Mao wengao*), vol. 1, 215; for an English translation, see *Cold War International History Project (CWIHP) Bulletin* 8–9 (Winter 1996/1997): 229–30.

6. Mao's telegram to the CCP CC, January 2, 1950, *Mao wengao*, vol. 1, 213; See also *CWIHP Bulletin* 8–9 (Winter 1996/1997): 228–9.

7. When the negotiations started, the Soviets seemed unwilling to accommodate all the Chinese demands. One great difficulty for Chinese Prime Minister Zhou Enlai was to obtain a clear commitment from the Soviet Union to assist China if it was invaded, an objective he regarded as the key to an alliance treaty. The first Soviet-drafted version of the treaty stated that if one side was invaded by a third party, the other side "is supposed to [*de yi,* in Chinese] offer assistance." To Zhou this was not sufficient because it did not make clear the binding liability of a military alliance. He exerted all his efforts to get a clarified version out of the Soviets: "is supposed to" was to become "must devote all its efforts" [*jiejin quanli,* in Chinese]. It took quite a while for Zhou and his aides to bargain over this with the Soviets. The Chinese were happy with the final text, however, which provided that "if one side is attacked by a third party, the other side must devote all its efforts to provide military and other assistance." Wu Xiuquan, *Zai Waijiaobu banian* [My eight years in the Ministry of Foreign Affairs, January 1950–October 1958] (Beijing: Shijie Zhishi, 1983), 8–9.

8. Mao Zedong's speech at the sixth meeting of the Central People's Government Council, April 11, 1950, *Mao wengao,* vol. 1, 291.

9. CCP CC, Instruction on Diplomatic Affairs, August 18, 1944, *Zhonggong zhongyang wenjian xuanji* [Selected documents of the CCP CC], vol. 14, 314–18.

10. *Dangdai Zhongguo jiben jianshe* [China today: Capital construction] (Beijing: Zhongguo shehui kexue, 1989), vol. 1, 4–5.

11. Mao Zedong, "Address to the Preparatory Meeting of the New Political Consultative Council," *Selected Works,* vol. 4, 469; Chen Yun, "To Overcome Serious Financial and Economic Difficulties," *Chen Yun wengao xuanbian, 1949–1956* [Selected works and manuscripts of Chen Yun] (Beijing: Renmin, 1984), 2.

12. Speech, Mao Zedong, at the meeting of the Politburo of the Central Committee, September 8, 1948, *Dang de wenxian,* no. 5 (1989): 15.

13. Mao, "Report to the Second Plenary Session of the Seventh Central Committee of the CCP" and "On the People's Democratic Dictatorship," *Mao Zedong xuanji* [Selected works of Mao Zedong] (Beijing: Renmin, 1960), 1432–4, 1479–80.

14. Ibid., 1434, 1436.

15. Zhou, "The Present Financial and Economic Situation and Relations between the

Different Aspects of New China's Economy," December 21–23, 1949, *Zhou Enlai xuanji* [Selected works of Zhou Enlai] (Beijing: Renmin, 1984), vol. 2, 10–11.

16. Mao, "Farewell, [John] Leighton Stuart," *Mao Zedong xuanji,* 1500.

17. Zhou, "The Principles and Tasks of Our Diplomacy," *Zhou Enlai xuanji,* vol. 2, 85–7.

18. CCP CC, "Instruction on Foreign Affairs," January 19, 1949, *Zhonggong zhongyang wenjian xuanji,* vol. 18, 44–9.

19. Speech, Mao Zedong, at the meeting of the Politburo of the CC, September 8, 1949, *Dang de wenxian,* no. 5 (1989): 11.

20. Report, Northeast Trading Company to the Finance and Economy Commission, CCP Northeast Bureau, [n.d.] 1947, Northeast Finance and Economy Commission Papers, file 5065, 1–2, Liaoning Provincial Archives, Shenyang, China.

21. Northeast Finance and Economy Commission, "A Final Decision on the Trade Negotiation with the Soviet Union," 1949, Northeast Finance and Economy Commission Papers, file 5077, Liaoning Provincial Archives, Shenyang, China.

22. Report, Liu Shaoqi to Stalin, July 1949, cited in Shi Zhe, *Zai lishi juren shenbian* [Together with historical giants] (hereafter *Shi Zhe memoirs*) (Beijing: zhongyang wenxian, 1991), 402.

23. Ibid., 409.

24. The CCP CC to North and Northeast Bureaus, February 16, 1949, *Zhonggong zhongyang wenjian xuanji,* vol. 14, 559.

25. CC Resolution, "Foreign Trade [Policy]," ibid., vol. 18, 560–3.

26. Trade agreement between the People's Republic of China and the Soviet Union, April 19, 1950, *Zhonghua renmin gongheguo tiaoyue ji* [The collection of treaties and agreements between the PRC (and foreign countries)], ed. Ministry of Foreign Affairs (Beijing: Faxue, 1951), 47.

27. Di Chaoba, "The Modes and Implications of Sino-Soviet Economic Relations," *Renmin ribao*, April 12, 1950, 2.

28. "Report on Our Trade with the Soviet Union at Each Port for 1950–1951," cited in Meng Xianzhang, ed. *ZhongSu maoyishi ziliao* [Historical materials on Sino-Soviet trade] (Beijing: Zhongguo duiwai jingzi mooyi, 1991), 556–69.

29. *Shi Zhe memoirs,* 409.

30. Mao's telegram to the CCP CC, January 3, 1950, *Mao wengao,* vol. 1, 213; see also *CWIHP Bulletin* 8–9 (Winter 1996/1997): 229.

31. *Shi Zhe memoirs,* 17.

32. *Dangdai zhongguo jiben jianshe,* vol. 1, 14–15.

33. Ibid., 16–17.

34. Wang Linsheng and Chen Yujie, eds., *Zhongguo de duiwai jingji guanxi* [China's foreign economic relations] (Beijing: Beijing renmin, 1982), 9; *Shi Zhe memoirs,* 519; Xu Xiangqian, *Lishi de huigu* [To recall the history] (Beijing: Jiexangjun, 1987), vol. 2, 797–805.

35. *Dangdai Zhongguo jiben jianshe,* vol. 1, 16; *Shi Zhe memoirs,* 449.

36. *ZhongSu maoyishi ziliao,* 553–6.

37. *Shi Zhe memoirs,* 447.

38. Ibid., 522–3.

39. Chen Jian, *China's Road to the Korean War: The Making of the Sino-American Confrontation* (New York: Columbia University Press, 1994), 76–7.

40. *Dangdai Zhongguo jiben jianshe,* vol. 1, 16; *Shi Zhe memoirs,* 415.

41. *Shi Zhe memoirs,* 415.

42. Ibid., pp. 446–7.

43. Di Chaobai, "The Great Implications of the Sino-Soviet Agreement on Loans," *Renmin ribao*, March 2, 1950, 2.

44. *KangMei yuanChao zhanzheng* [The war to resist the U.S. and aid Korea] (Beijing: Zhongguo shehui kexue, 1990), 332–3; *Dangdai Zhongguo jundui de junshi gongzuo* [China today: The military affairs of the Chinese army] (Beijing: Zhongguo shehui kexue, 1989), vol. 1, 512; Xu Yan, *Diyici jiaoliang: KangMei yuanChao Zhanzheng de lishi huigu yu fansi* [The first encounter: Historical retrospection and review of the war to resist U.S. aggression and aid Korea] (Beijing: Zhongguo guangbo dianshi, 1990), 322–3.

45. Peng's speech at the twenty-fourth session of the Central People's Government Council, *Peng Dehuai junshi wenxuan* [Selected military works of Peng Dehuai] (Beijing: Zhongyang wenxian, 1988), 445.

46. Yao Xu, "A Brilliant Decision to Resist U.S. Aggression and Aid Korea," *Danshi yanjiu* [Studies of CCP history], no. 5 (1980): 13; *Dangdai Zhongguo duiwai maoyi* (Beijing: Dangdai Zhongguo, 1992), 258–9; *Dangdai zhongguo jiben jianshe,* vol. 1, 52–3.

47. Telegram, Mao to the Soviet Government, September 15, 1953, *Mao wengao,* vol. 4, 331–2. For a brief discussion of the Sino-Soviet relations in the post–Korean War period, see John Gittings, *The Role of the Chinese Army* (London: Oxford University Press, 1967), 119–31.

48. *Renmin Ribao,* October 12, 1954, 1.

49. *Dangdai Zhongguo jiben jianshe,* vol. 1, 52–3.

50. Ibid.

51. Ibid.

52. Ibid., 56–7.

53. Ibid., 54.

54. *Shi Zhe memoirs,* 570–1.

55. The statistics are cited in Bo Yibo, *Ruogan zhongda juece yu shijian de huigu* [My recollections of decision making on several important policies and events] (Beijing: Zhongyang dang'on, 1993), vol. 1, 295–6. For discussion of the "economic miracles"

after the Korean War, see Ruan Jiaxin, "The War to Resist America and Aid Korea and the Rise of the New China," *Junshi shilin* [History of military affairs], no. 6 (1993): 13–19.

56. Mao Zedong's speech at the thirtieth session of the CPGC, June 14, 1954, *Mao wengao*, vol. 4, 505–6.

57. Excerpts of Mao's speeches in March and October 1955 and August 1956 are cited in Huang Xiangbing, "How the Policy of 'Overtaking Britain and Catching Up with America Was Formed in Late 1950s," *Dangshi yanjiu ziliao* [Materials and studies of CCP history], no. 4 (1988): 22.

58. Ibid. Also see Bo Yibo, *Ruogan zhongda juece*, vol. 2, 691–2.

59. Ibid., 692–8.

60. Immanuel C. Y. Hsu, *The Rise of Modern China,* 4th ed. (New York: Oxford University Press, 1990), 655–7.

61. Memorandum, PRC Foreign Ministry to the USSR Embassy to Beijing, March 13 1957, Archives of Foreign Policy of the Russian Federation (AVPRF), fond. (f.) 100, opis (op.) 50, papka (pa.) 423, delo (d.) 4; for an English translation, see *CWIHP Bulletin* 6–7 (Winter 1995/1996): 159–60.

62. Minutes, Mao's conversation with a Yugoslavian Communist Union delegation, Beijing, [undated], September 1957, *Mao Zedong waijiao wenxuan* [Selected works of Mao Zedong on foreign affairs] (Beijing: Zhongyang wenxian, 1993), 251–62; for an English translation, see *CWIHP Bulletin* 6–7 (Winter 1995/1996): 148–52.

63. *Shi Zhe memoirs,* 580–1.

64. *Dangdai Zhongguo duiwai maoyi,* 259.

65. Ibid., 259; *Dangdai Zhongguo waijiao* [China today: Diplomacy] (Beijing: Zhongguo shehui kexue, 1987), 31.

66. *Dangdai Zhongguo duiwai maoyi,* 260.

67. *Dangdai Zhongguo waijiao,* 29.

68. *Shi Zhe memoirs,* 572–3.

69. *Dangdai Zhongguo hegongye* [China today: Nuclear industry] (Beijing: Zhongguo shehui kexue, 1987), 20–1.

70. Ibid., 19–22.

71. Ibid., 32.

72. Malinovskii's letter to Peng Dehuai, April 19, 1958, cited in *Dangdai Zhongguo waijiao,* 112.

73. Minutes, Mao–Iudin meeting, July 21, 1958, ibid., 113. Mao clearly stated that "first of all we ought to establish a principle, that is, we will be mainly responsible to the program only with your assistance."

74. Mao's instructions concerning the Soviet request on establishing a special long-wave radio station near China's coast, June 7, 1958, *Mao Zedong waijiao wenxuan,* 316–17.

75. Peng to Soviet Ministry of National Defense, June 12, 1958, *Dangdai Zhongguo waijiao,* 113.

76. Minutes, Mao–Iudin meeting, July 21, 1958, *Dangdai Zhongguo waijiao* 114; minutes, conversation between Mao and Ambassador Iudin, July 22, 1958, *Mao Zedong waijiao wenxuan,* 322–33; for an English translation of the latter, see *CWIHP Bulletin* 6–7 (Winter 1995/1996): 155–9.

77. Minutes of Mao-Khrushchev talks, July 31, 1958, *Dangdai Zhongguo waijiao,* 114.

78. Memorandum, Liu Xiao to Ministry of Foreign Affairs, October 20, 1958, in *Mao wengao,* vol. 7, 486–7.

79. Memorandum, Liu Xiao to Ministry of Foreign Affairs, January 13, 1959, in *Mao wengao,* vol. 8, 5–6.

80. Instructions, Mao Zedong, February 13, 1959, *Mao wengao,* vol. 8, 41–2.

81. Speech, Mao Zedong, at the meeting with the delegation of eleven ambassadors, May 6, 1959, *Mao wengao,* vol. 8, 248–9.

82. Memorandum, "Request for 54 More Advisers," PRC Foreign Ministry to Soviet Embassy to Beijing, December 29, 1958; memorandum, "Request for 13 Soviet Advisers on Intelligence and Confidential Works Related to National Defense," PRC Foreign Ministry to Soviet Embassy to Beijing, January 27, 1959; memorandum, "Request to Extend the Terms of 195 Soviet Military Advisers," PRC Foreign Ministry to Soviet Embassy to Beijing, June 24, 1959; memorandum, "Request for 8 Soviet Advisers on P-2 Missiles," PRC Foreign Ministry to Soviet Embassy to Beijing, September 22, 1959; memorandum, "Request to Extend the Terms of 23 Soviet Advisers on Advanced Military Technology," PRC Foreign Ministry to Soviet Embassy to Beijing, November 23, 1959; all in AVPRF, f. 0100, op. 52, p. 442, d. 3.

83. *Dangdai Zhongguo duiwai maoyi,* 259.

84. For this point, see John Lewis and Litai Xue, *China's Strategic Seapower: The Politics of Force Modernization in the Nuclear Age* (Stanford, Calif.: Stanford University Press, 1994), 3–4.

85. Minutes of conversation, Mao and two Brazilian journalists, September 2, 1958, *Mao wengao,* vol. 7, 373–4.

86. Speeches, Mao Zedong, at the fifteenth meeting of the Supreme State Conference, September 5 and 8, 1958, ibid., 387–9.

87. Memorandum, Liu Xiao to Ministry of Foreign Affairs, October 20, 1958, ibid., 487.

88. Embassy in Moscow to Foreign Ministry, July 2, 1959, enclosed in Mao's instruction, July 19, 1959, ibid., vol. 8, 367.

89. Speech outline, Mao at the enlarged meeting of the Central Military Commission, September 11, 1959, ibid., 523; speech outline, Mao at the CCP Politburo meeting on the international situation, December 1959, ibid., 600.

90. *Dangdai Zhongguo waijiao,* 115–16; for an internal Soviet assessment of the

meeting, see Mikhail Suslov's report to December 1959 CPSU Plenum, excerpted in *CWIHP Bulletin* 8–9 (Winter 1996/1997): 244, 248, 259–62.

91. Speech, Mao Zedong, at the CCP Politburo meeting on the current international situation, December 1959, *Mao wengao,* vol. 8, 599–602.

92. Speech, Mao Zedong, at a meeting in Hangzhou, December [undated] 1959, ibid., 604.

93. *Dangdai Zhongguo waijiao,* 117–18. Unfortunately, documents concerning why Khrushchev chose to adopt a policy of economic blackmail against China are yet to be made available. However, for a Soviet letter explaining the action, see *CWIHP Bulletin* 8–9 (Winter 1996/1997): 246, 249–50.

94. *Dangdai Zhongguo waijiao,* 117–18.

95. Diplomatic note, PRC Foreign Ministry to Soviet Foreign Ministry, August 13, 1960, AVPRF, f. 0100, op. 2, pa. 453; diplomatic note, PRC Foreign Ministry to Soviet Foreign Ministry, September 20, 1960, ibid.; diplomatic note, PRC Foreign Ministry to Soviet Foreign Ministry, October 24, 1960, ibid.

96. *Dangdai Zhongguo waijiao,* 118.

97. William E. Griffith, ed., *Sino-Soviet Relations, 1964–1965* (Cambridge, Mass: MIT Press, 1967), 4.

98. See, for example, D. Losman, *International Economic Sanctions: The Cases of Cuba, Israel, and Rhodesia* (Albuquerque, N.M.: University of New Mexico Press, 1979); Barry E. Carter, *International Economic Sanctions: Improving the Haphazard U.S. Legal System* (Cambridge: Cambridge University Press, 1989); Margaret P. Doxey, *International Sanctions in Contemporary Perspective* (London: Macmillan, 1987); Makio Miyagawa, *Do Economic Sanctions Work?* (New York: St. Martin's Press, 1992); David A. Baldwin, *Economic Statecraft* (Princeton, N.J.: Princeton University Press, 1985); M. P. Doxey, *Economic Sanctions and International Enforcement* (London: Macmillan, 1980); M. P. Doxey, "Do Sanctions Work?" *International Perspectives* (July–August 1982): 13–15; Richard C. Porter, "Economic Sanctions: The Theory and the Evidence from Rhodesia," *Journal of Peace Science* 3, no. 2 (Fall 1978): 93–110; Harry R. Strack, *Sanctions: The Case of Rhodesia* (Syracuse, N.Y.: Syracuse University Press, 1978); James Barber and Michael Spicer, "Sanctions against South Africa – Options for the West," *International Affairs* 55, no. 3 (July 1979): 385–401.

7. Nikita Khrushchev and Sino-Soviet Relations

Constantine Pleshakov

In Moscow, on July 25, 1963, representatives of the Soviet Union, the United States, and Great Britain signed a partial nuclear test-ban treaty – the first tangible agreement of the new East-West détente. Six days later Beijing labeled the treaty a "dirty fraud" aimed at preserving the nuclear monopoly.[1] The Sino-Soviet confrontation over nuclear proliferation took place less than six years after Soviet First Secretary Nikita Khrushchev promised to help the Chinese build a nuclear bomb. In the summer of 1963, Communist Moscow was allying with the Western capitals to deter the nuclear appetite of Communist Beijing. The whole traditional Cold War landscape had been transformed; global politics was now more than just two camps opposing each other, and communism itself was becoming as diversified as the human race.

The 1963 conflict proved that the Cold War pattern of the 1950s – with the red hammer and sickle occuping the heartland of Eurasia – was no more. The Soviet hammer no longer united the continent from Central Europe to Southeast Asia; divorced from the Chinese sickle that covered the arc of Eurasia's eastern coast, the symbol had become geopolitically impaired, its loose end getting stuck somewhere in the backwoods near Vladivostok. And the breakdown of the symbol's geopolitical meaning was accompanied by a breakdown in the coherence of ideology: The Soviet hammer of industrial socialist society was now divorced from the sickle of the Chinese peasant revolution.

Geopolitics and Ideology: Symbiosis Sovieticus

The interaction of geopolitics and ideology in Soviet foreign policy is instrumental for understanding both its basic presumptions and its concrete decision making. Up until the mid-1960s, ideology had always played a primary role in Soviet foreign policy, contrary to what is often argued. But ideology was never separated from geopolitics; rather they were united in a stable and paradigmatic symbiosis.[2] Geopolitics and ideology were "mutually promotive" for the Kremlin. Any geopolitical breakthrough (i.e., newly extended control over space) meant expansion of Soviet ideology in the country won through realpolitik or war, as was the case with Eastern Europe in 1945 to 1948, when the countries of the Baltic–Black Sea belt were first occupied by the Red Army and then supplied with ideologically immaculate pro-Soviet regimes. Any major influx of Soviet ideology into a foreign country automatically strengthened the geopolitical stand of the Soviet Union in that area of the world (as in the case of Spain in the mid-1930s).

This mode of interaction between geopolitics and ideology, born in the early 1920s after the collapse of Soviet expectations of an immediate world revolution, had reached its maturity during Stalin's reign in the 1930s and 1940s. Vladimir Lenin had regarded the geoideological paradigm as a temporary retreat: The security needs and the international prestige of Soviet Russia could not be established in any other way. Although Lenin would have preferred direct revolutionary action, he was prepared to wait for the necessary social discord to occur. Joseph Stalin, to the contrary, found the duet of realpolitik and ideology very appealing, not least because of his distrust of unrestrained mass movements. He enthusiastically used these two swords to promote the growth of the Soviet empire.

The post-Stalin generation of the Soviet elite, separated from any revolutionary momentum by bureaucratic institutions and their own growing pragmatism, started to introduce innovations into Stalin's model of geoideological interaction. While under Stalin geopolitics and ideology were more or less equal partners, the ideological motivations had started to decrease by late 1950s, and for the leadership under Leonid Brezhnev, from October 1964 on, ideology was already limp. Yet all major expansionist moves of the later Soviet Union, up until the late 1980s, were still based on a weakened but nevertheless substantial interaction of imperial territorial expansionism and ideological proselytism.

Nikita Khrushchev was the last Soviet leader who was captivated by the classical Stalin paradigm; hence his inconsistent foreign policy. His exotic cocktail of nuclear age realism and revolutionary idealism, calculating brinkmanship and a utopian view of the future of humankind, can be explained only by the ideological luggage that Khrushchev was left by his predecessors. Khrushchev pursued the global triumph of socialism through projecting Soviet power abroad with an eagerness that dwarfed Stalin's halfhearted postwar efforts. But since Khrushchev was much more convinced of the coming political victory of socialism in the capitalist countries than Stalin ever was, he saw no reason for a permanent state of conflict with the West, and used his first years in power to prepare a policy of limited détente. Yet Khrushchev's attempts to be both a leader of a great power and a supreme priest of ideology – "Communist #1" in his own terms – proved to be exceedingly difficult during the 1950s and early 1960s.[3] The Soviet tribulations during the Cuban Missile Crisis is just one example. Sino-Soviet relations fit the same pattern. Khrushchev's ideological estrangement from China contributed to the loss of Soviet geopolitical presence in the country, and the geopolitical devaluation of the Sino-Soviet alliance led in turn both the Kremlin and the Chinese leadership compound at Zhongnanhai to overt and acid polemics. Thus the geopolitical divorce facilitated a complete ideological breakup.

Stalin's Legacy

Stalin's mixed record of dealing with China left a complex legacy for his successors.[4] After almost twenty years of vacillating on how best to gain influence within the politics of his giant neighbor, Stalin in February 1950 finally got some tangible results for his efforts: spheres of interest in Outer Mongolia, Chinese Central Asia (Xinjiang), and Manchuria that he believed to be secure. However, Stalin's successors were aware of the dubious nature of his legacy in dealings with Beijing.

For Khrushchev, the legacy of Stalin's China policy was extremely ambiguous. He regretted that under Stalin the Soviets had thrust themselves into China like Western-style colonizers.[5] The arrogance shown by the Kremlin's viceroys in China troubled Khrushchev, particularly since he also knew of the personal tensions between Mao Zedong and Stalin, both during the years of civil war in China and at the early stage of the existence of the People's Republic of China (PRC) from 1949 to 1952.[6] The new Soviet leader found that the Soviet Union's geopolitical dominance in Manchuria and Xinjiang, obtained through Stalin's personal involvement during the civil war and in the early stages of the revolutionary state, could not be a lasting phenomenon: There was just too much coercion in the relationship.[7]

The secret protocols and agreements from 1950 concerning the political, military, and economic preeminence of Moscow in those two areas clouded the Sino-Soviet relationship,[8] and Khrushchev already in 1954 decided that they had to go. As a result of Stalin's personal involvement, the Soviet control over those areas was regarded as a matter of strategic state interest: Even the Soviet embassy in China had no idea what was going on in the Soviet agencies stationed in Xinjiang, since the area was controlled "directly from the Center."[9]

The Soviet protectorate in northern China did not survive Stalin's death. Khrushchev stressed his belief in the alliance with China by yielding control of the Soviet military, political, and economic spheres of interest there. His 1954 concessions included not only the naval bases of Lüshun and Dalian but also the Changchun Railway, regarded by the Soviets as the most efficient railway of China, carrying around 40 percent of its goods traffic.[10] Khrushchev also accepted Mao Zedong's cleansing of the ranks within his own party in the immediate post-Stalin era; among others, Mao killed the northeastern Communist leader Gao Gang, whom the chairman suspected of being able to manipulate Soviet support in his own interest.[11]

At the same time, although loaded with problems, Stalin's legacy in China contained much of value for Khrushchev. The Chinese ideological admiration for the Soviet Union, originating in the Comintern years between 1921 and 1943, looked promising as a future framework of the alliance. Cooperation between Moscow and Beijing, at least for the short term, also had been ensured by the Korean War, which had formed a blood bond. In global geopolitical terms, the Soviet Union and the People's Republic constituted a continental challenge to the oceanic might of the United States. In those many moments in which Khrushchev and Mao forgot the realities of the nuclear age, there seemed to be parity between the United States and the Sino-Soviet bloc in terms of traditional geopolitics: The former was invincible as an oceanic power and the latter as a continental alliance. Even though Khrushchev's perception of both geopolitics and ideology evolved during his years in power, his challenge was always to rescue the foundations of the Sino-Soviet relationship laid under Stalin – to mend the alliance and therefore make it more useful to Moscow.

Stabilization: 1954–1956

Khrushchev's policy toward China underwent a number of distinct stages, reflecting the shifts in his approach to world affairs in general. The years 1954 to 1956 were definitely the period of stabilization of bilateral relations, both with China and, in a somewhat different way, with the East European "people's democracies." There was also Marshal Tito's breakaway from the Soviet Union, which was very much on Khrushchev's mind in mid-1950s. He privately accepted Stalin's responsibility for the breakup with Yugoslavia and intended to prevent such happenings in the eastern flank of the "socialist camp."[12]

Any breakaway inside the camp was bad in ideological terms: Tito's example, for instance, was demonstrating that communism was actually not a universal phenomenon, remaining the same in any country wherever applied. Yugoslavia's independent survival proved that communism could be national, taking into account local specifics and also becoming independent from the center of world communism: Moscow. That was a heresy that could threaten not only the global position of the Soviet party, but also Khrushchev's domestic and international standing.

Khrushchev also had to consider the geopolitical consequences of the defections from the Soviet bloc. Yugoslavia's breakaway was bad enough, with the Eastern Bloc deprived of an outlet to the Mediterranean. In spite of Stalin's efforts between 1939 and 1946, the Black Sea straits (Bosphorus and Dardanelles) had remained Turkish. However much Stalin had wanted to give the Soviet state naval access to the Mediterranean, he failed even to preserve the alliance with Yugoslavia, the only chance to break the oceanic blockade of the Soviet Union in the southwest. Trouble with China could have even graver consequences.

The Soviet interest in Sino-Soviet border areas highlighted the mix of Marxist ideology with a form of geopolitical "ideology": By ousting capitalist competitors from these areas, the Soviet Union assured reliable security for the territorial core of the empire – the Slavic lands. By the mid-1950s a new threat to the Soviet Union in Asia – the United States – was exerting pressure on Moscow from two flanks, Europe and the North Pacific. Moscow had little space for geopolitical maneuvering, since the major threat was embodied by the same power in the West and in the East. With no anti-American ally in the Western camp available, and with the Marxist concept of "interimperialist tensions" outdated, Khrushchev could not hope to divide the Western camp as Stalin had done between 1939 and 1945. The only option was to consolidate the Soviet continental stronghold, making Eurasia's heartland an invincible fortress. This uninterrupted control over immense space was possible only with China holding the eastern semicircular bastion of Eurasia in the security interests of the whole bloc. A paramount task was also to keep the United States away from the oceanic periphery of Eurasia in as many areas as possible, so that the Americans would have fewer geopolitical strongholds and springboards on the continent.

Holding the Americans back in Korea was one of these joint Soviet-Chinese tasks. But even more important to Khrushchev and Mao was a possible American challenge from the south. The 1954 Geneva accords on Indochina stabilized the south for the time being, while reserving the possibility that the leftist revolutionary movements of the region could be assisted through Chinese territory in the future. Thus for several reasons China had become indispensable to Moscow's strategy of continentalism – making Eurasia's heartland unattainable to U.S. control.

Stalin had promised much but given little economic aid to China. Despite generous rhetoric, Stalin always remained stingy. He seems to have believed that northern China could become a Soviet treasure chest. Rare nonferrous metals such as beryllium and lithium were already coming from there; Stalin hoped that rich oil depositories could be found too.[13]

Khrushchev reversed Stalin's plans and initiated large-scale economic interaction between the two countries, much of it in the form of Soviet aid, some in the form of loans or barter agreements that the Chinese paid for up to 1965. These adjustments were undertaken during Khrushchev's visit to China in 1954. This trip was like a debutante ball for Khrushchev as a leader. For the first time he was making strategic foreign policy decisions in a direct dialogue with a prominent foreign leader. The visit set the tone for the period of stabilization of Sino-Soviet relations.[14]

Throughout 1954 to 1957 Khrushchev sought to make Beijing feel comfortable within the confines of the Soviet bloc. Krushchev's decision in early 1955 to support the Chinese nuclear energy program for "peaceful purposes" was part of this campaign.[15] Of course he understood that the step meant rapid Chinese progress toward attaining the atomic bomb. But unlike Stalin, Khrushchev was willing to build a nuclear relationship with the People's Republic comparable to that which the United States had with Britain.

The "new," revamped Sino-Soviet alliance had a real potential for being a long-term success. Even Khrushchev's criticism of Stalin at the Twentieth Party Congress of the Communist Party of the Soviet Union (CPSU) in February 1956 did not weaken cooperation at first. Mao may have been troubled by the implications of Khrushchev's speech in terms of revolutionary theory. But much more important was the chance the congress gave Mao to express his own personal grievances about the way Stalin had tried to manage and manipulate China; he accused the late Soviet dictator of imperialism.[16]

Abortive Adjustment: 1957–1959

The year 1957 was the turning point in Khrushchev's China policies. From mid-1957 on, the new Soviet leader attempted to adjust Sino-Soviet relations to fit his new priorities: a global Soviet-bloc military policy *and* détente with the West. Having vanquished his political rivals inside the Kremlin (the "antiparty group" of Stalin's lieutenant Viacheslav Molotov and other old-timers) in July 1957, Khrushchev embarked on a revision of the standard Soviet approach to world affairs.

Some of these innovations had been introduced to the doctrine as early as the Twentieth CPSU Congress, but for a while the traditionalists inside the party prevented Khrushchev from transferring into practical policymaking his theoretical innovations: Peaceful coexistence with the West was possible. World War III could be prevented. Leftist parties did not necessarily have to come to power through a violent revolution. The Soviet Union could expand its power without risking attack from the outside.

The complete defeat of the diehard Stalinists such as Molotov was made possible by Khrushchev's getting the support of the party/state apparatus. Soviet elites, nurtured by Stalin, had grown up to be a Frankenstein for Stalinism, and the personal dictatorship could be replaced with a dictatorship of the apparatus. In terms of its organization, power in the Soviet state was diverging dramatically from the increasingly personalized control of Mao Zedong in China.

The real trouble in the Sino-Soviet relationship began when Khrushchev wanted Mao to move in his direction on foreign affairs and defense issues just as Mao's skepticism about Soviet internal developments peaked. Although inconsistent, Khrushchev's foreign policy lacked revolutionary appeal, while Mao still saw revolution abroad as a vital part of his concept of foreign policy. Besides, already in early 1950s the two societies were very different: The revolution in the Soviet Union was already bureaucratized and less violent than in China, where between November 1950 and July 1951, 500,000 people were shot.[17] Mao and Khrushchev were dealing with two societies at different stages of revolution. Mao's was still to undergo the highest point of the revolutionary tide with the Great Leap Forward and the Cultural Revolution, whereas many of Khrushchev's backers were already tired of the physical effects of revolution and longed for domestic stability.

Just as in 1954, Khrushchev was too clever a policymaker not to combine a degree of acceptance of the Chinese Communist Party's policies with his request for support on foreign affairs in 1957–1958. In spite of his resentment of Mao's interference in East European affairs after the Polish and Hungarian crises of 1956, Khrushchev quickly abandoned his attempts to "correct" China's *domestic* revolution, even though his advisors told him that land reform and rectification were clear deviations from the Soviet model (which they hardly were in basic terms; they were just asynchronous). In 1957–1958, Khrushchev attempted to use the same approach to China that he had used in Poland, where Wladyslaw Gomulka had been allowed to take the lead on domestic matters. In light of the experience of the East European crises, Mao's revolutionary zeal must have struck Khrushchev as a lesser problem.

But some accord on international issues seemed essential to Khrushchev: China was crucial for maintaining the continental Eurasian socialist stronghold. In October 1957, after the successful launching of the two Soviet Sputniks and the world's first intercontinental ballistic missile (ICBM), Khrushchev sanctioned an agreement with China on sharing nuclear arms and missile technology as part of a Kremlin attempt to integrate China in the Soviet military strategy.[18]

That implied delivering vast amounts of technological information to China, such as a sample medium-range ballistic missile minus its atomic warhead, a G-class ballistic missile submarine without its missiles, and TU-16 jet fighters. Chinese nuclear scientists were trained at the Joint Institute for Nuclear Research at Dubna.[19] Soviet atomic weapons experts went to China, as did leading Russian theoretical nuclear physicists. Soviet geologists were dispatched to the People's Republic to locate deposits of nuclear raw materials.[20]

However, when Mao went to Moscow in November 1957 (immediately after the nuclear deal), Khrushchev was to learn that the results of the nuclear concord were counterproductive. Mao became so enthusiastic about the forthcoming nuclear prominence of the Sino-Soviet alliance that he publicly urged Khrushchev to cancel the peaceful coexistence approach.[21] Mao repeated that advice during Khrushchev's visit to China in July 1958. The ideology of mature socialism in the Soviet Union pursued stability; the ideology of revolutionary (young) socialism in China advocated change. Mao was unhappy about Khrushchev's détente, just as Lenin had been upset by the Kremlin's forced retreat to realpolitik in 1922. Both Khrushchev and Mao regarded their respective ideologies – those of stability and change – as truly Marxist imperatives that should have been shared by the other side of the Eurasian axis.

To make the matters worse, Khrushchev was simultaneously behaving like a dove and a hawk. Thus in his dealings with Mao Zedong, Khrushchev attempted to reach two rather contradictory goals. On one hand, Mao had to agree to lessening tensions with the West, for brinkmanship could happen only under Moscow's immediate control. Khrushchev's concern about the consequences of nuclear war was ambiguous but real. On the other hand if Khrushchev was ambivalent about his own policy of détente, Mao increasingly regarded it as harmful, both for ideological and for political reasons. Mao intended to consolidate society by mobilization against an external threat, much as Stalin had attempted to do in the 1930s. He believed that the international revolutionary movement (especially in the Third World) would prosper from Cold War instability. For Mao, Washington was an enemy; how could he possibly embrace détente when the United States was supporting Taiwan vs. the People's Republic? Finally, Khrushchev's deeper involvement in dialogue with the Western powers could in principle lead to a situation when Chinese policies would be discussed with Mao absent – and a repetition of Great Power agreements á la Yalta was the last thing Mao wanted.

In spite of his stance on détente, Khrushchev sought a practical way to involve China in the Soviet bloc's military activities. Détente or not, the global geopolitical challenge of the United States had to be met. Khrushchev planned to secure peace through power, and China was geopolitically instrumental for his objective. However, the problem was to develop a fixed and mutually agreeable plan for how to employ the Chinese potential in the area.

Paradoxically enough, the Sino-Soviet alliance, the prominence of which was pronounced so pompously by the Kremlin and the Zhongnanhai and so deeply feared in Washington, Tokyo, and Taibei, was deprived of any concrete regional meaning beyond its own borders in the mid-1950s. True, together the Soviet Union and China controlled Eurasia's heartland. But they were doing that automatically, just by virtue of having a common border. No particular and deliberate East Asian agenda for strategic cooperation existed – after the partnership of the Korean War, the Soviet Union and China had failed to devise a common framework for security and the expansion of socialism in the region.

Shared ideological values by themselves could not hold the alliance together. An alliance void of any concrete strategic cooperation soon becomes very fragile. Such strategic hollowness also raises the question whether so-called shared values are genuinely shared. Khrushchev was right in trying to fill the alliance with concrete cooperation. But his means for doing so turned out to be disastrous.

Khrushchev ruled out any attempts to integrate the Soviet and Chinese armies. He was skeptical of landmass armies and decided in 1959 to reduce the Soviet army by one-third.[22] He also saw few possibilities of concrete regional political cooperation. Moscow did not try, for instance, to push China toward extending the bloc's control over Indochina. Khrushchev was not sure whether he could afford a major offensive in the Third World.

But Khrushchev had one plan for the alliance up his sleeve: a naval plan. Basically a continental power, by the late 1950s the Soviet Union had found itself endangered by the nuclear oceanic capacity of the United States. Just like Russia before and after the Soviet era, the Soviet Union was oceanically challenged. Yet the only time when the country suffered a defeat because of its naval disability was during the Russo-Japanese War of 1904–1905. In all other conflicts – whether the two world wars or the Napoleonic Wars – the nation had found the Eurasian heartland to be protective as a womb.

But nuclear age geopolitics made the traditional continental invincibility of the Soviet Union seem problematic. The missiles and aviation launched from the seas in the mid-1950s had started to look like a "winning weapon." The United States had successfully established its missile bases along the western oceanic periphery of Eurasia, in Britain, Italy, and Turkey. Nuclear-powered Polaris submarines with submarine-launched ballistic missiles cruised the seas.[23] All components of the American strategic triad – the Minuteman missile, Polaris submarine, and B-52 bomber – benefited from overseas bases, but for the submarines the U.S. oceanic capacity was crucial and the challenge from the American-controlled ocean needed a symmetric Soviet response.

Obsessed with missiles, Khrushchev believed traditional navies to be expensive, old-fashioned, and ultimately useless scrap.[24] Thus Stalin's "battleship concept" of a navy was abandoned.[25] A "submarine" concept emerged, with the American Polaris viewed as the major threat to Soviet security.[26] Khrushchev foresaw a glorious future for missile-carrying submarines and firmly believed them to be the "basis" of sea power.[27] His defense minister, Admiral S. G. Gorshkov, preached submarines, aircraft carriers, and amphibious forces.[28] A blue-water navy as the way to gain "dominance at sea" was the punchline of the Soviet leader's public and private approach.[29]

Yet the Soviet Union was lagging behind the United States in all these types of armament. In 1955 the Soviet submarine fleet was totally conventionally powered and armed.[30] The Soviet blue-water navy, to say nothing about "dominance at sea," was curtailed by the lack of overseas naval bases. Having yielded naval bases in Manchuria in 1954, four years later Khrushchev decided to press Mao to proceed with naval cooperation.

China was the only Soviet ally with a strategically important and long coastline and the only major ally in the Pacific. The two existing Soviet naval bases in the Pacific – Petropavlovsk and Vladivostok – were virtually useless. Petropavlovsk had to rely upon supplies by surface ships, a link easily interrupted by an adversary in case of war. Vladivostok was locked in the Sea of Japan,[31] with its straits (La Perouse, Tsugaru, and Tsushima) controlled by the U.S. fleet.[32] Khrushchev did not like the exposed position of Vladivostok, the major submarine base, at all when he saw it in 1954 after his trip to China and believed that the base had to be moved.[33] To make things worse, one of the other three Soviet fleets (the Black Sea) had been permanently constrained by the 1936 Montreux Convention, which limited the passage of warships through the Turkish-controlled Bosporus straits.[34] Khrushchev believed that the Soviet Union had to free itself from being locked in Eurasia's heartland. Therefore he stationed twelve diesel submarines in Albania in 1958; in case of war, the squadron was to attack U.S. aircraft carriers in the area.[35] But the North Pacific remained the primary problem on the naval agenda.

In July 1958 Khrushchev, visiting China for the second time, wanted to discuss two major naval issues with Mao Zedong: a radio communications station on Chinese territory for Soviet submarines in the Pacific and Indian oceans and a joint Sino-Soviet submarine fleet, with China donating the ports and the Soviet Union the vessels. Mao indignantly refused. He suggested that China could build its own joint long-range radio station if given Soviet equipment and technology. A joint fleet was also possible – if the Soviets were willing to cede command over the warships to Chinese captains.[36] The Chinese also rejected the Soviet proposal to start cooperation in antiaircraft defenses.[37] Khrushchev had foolishly chosen forms of cooperation that would stimulate Mao's sense of being the underdog in the alliance. As Mao had told the Soviet ambassador, Pavel Iudin, in June 1958, when he had pushed Khrushchev's plan: "You never trust the Chinese! You only trust the Russians! [To you] the Russians are first-class people, while the Chinese are among the inferior who are dumb and careless."[38]

Mao's overall impression was that Khrushchev was trying to tie his hands and feet. He was proud of his resistance and called it "sticking a needle" up Khrushchev's ass.[39] But he also must have been struck by the fact that Khrushchev suggested China advocate peaceful coexistence and at the same time planned to use China's geopolitical potential for improving Moscow's position vis-à-vis the United States – in Mao's view, a double-standards policy.

Moscow was outraged by Mao's retort. Soviet elites believed that Beijing was "too preoccupied" with the "sovereignty and independence" of China.[40] Thus by defending his strategic independence, Mao, in Moscow's eyes, was violating the basic tenets of "Communist internationalism." Khrushchev had his own secret concern: If Mao Zedong was unwilling to cooperate in the naval sphere, suspecting Moscow of intending to violate China's sovereignty, what would happen when Khrushchev would have to bring up the problem of the command of joint nuclear forces?

During the 1958 Jinmen and Mazu crisis, Mao pursued goals unacceptable to Khrushchev. Mao wanted to reassure the nation that he was taking his role as a reunifier of China seriously and was making this symbolic gesture to prove that Taiwan was indeed a part of China.[41] On the other hand, he wanted to probe how deep was Khrushchev's commitment to the course of détente with the United States. At the beginning of the crisis, Mao said that if Khrushchev wanted to improve relations with Washington, China would congratulate him with its guns by bombarding the Taiwanese offshore islands. "Let's get the United States involved, too. Maybe we can get the United States to drop an atom bomb on Fujian. . . . Let's see what Khrushchev says then."[42]

Whether Khrushchev had been informed about the coming attack on Jinmen and Mazu remains unclear. Some evidence suggests that in principle Khrushchev knew about the planned operation.[43] However, for the Soviet embassy in Beijing, the attack had come out of the blue; Ambassador Iudin believed that the top Soviet leadership had not been informed either.[44] In any event, until the new Soviet foreign minister, Andrei Gromyko, was hastily dispatched to China, the Soviet leaders definitely had had absolutely no idea what goals the Chinese side was pursuing during the crisis.[45] It took Mao only one hour on September 5 to agree to the Soviet foreign minister's visit: He knew that the difficult explanation to Moscow would have to come anyway.[46] Zhou Enlai asked Gromyko to inform Khrushchev plainly that during the crisis, the Chinese leaders had deliberately provoked the rage of the Americans upon China, were ready to sustain all harsh counterreactions "up to atomic bombings and the destruction of our cities," and expected the Soviet Union to come to China's rescue during the decisive phase of the conflict.[47]

As a result, Khrushchev faced Chinese ridicule and threats to both his strategic détente plan and his tactical muscle-building. Mao proved unwilling to embrace Khrushchev's ideology of stability and his concurrent strategy of leasing China's coastline for geopolitical maneuvering. The disagreements between Mao and Khrushchev had become so basic that in 1959 the Kremlin ceased all aid to the Chinese nuclear program.

In September 1959, after a visit to the United States that he regarded as a diplomatic breakthrough, Khrushchev announced the unilateral reduction of the Soviet armed forces. (Even earlier, in March 1958, Soviet nuclear testing had been unilaterally suspended.)[48] Pursuing primarily propaganda goals and not intentionally weakening the Soviet military buildup, Khrushchev was still sending a message to the West that he was serious in his détente advances.

Nevertheless, the Soviet leader made one last personal attempt to get the Chinese onboard. Immediately after his autumn trip to the United States and his Camp David talks with President Dwight D. Eisenhower – whom he liked and believed (at the time, at least) to be a sincere champion of peace – Khrushchev tried to discuss foreign policy with Mao in Beijing. This time Khrushchev's renewed enthusiasm about détente and his inability to understand Mao's reservations further aggravated the situation. Khrushchev never could appreciate Mao's need to establish his reputation as a unifier of the country – an essential image of any new Chinese ruler – by military expeditions against the separatists on Taiwan. Khrushchev told Mao that he should not worry about Taiwan, for the great Lenin himself had let the Russian Far East be independent for a while. It was also unnecessary, Khrushchev argued, to clash with India, referring to the August 25 Chinese occupation of the frontier post of Longju.[49] The same great Lenin had had to tolerate the loss of Russian territories after the civil war – and later the territories had been won back.[50] The atmosphere of the summit was darkened also by the Peng Dehuai episode: Khrushchev had met Marshal Peng Dehuai, the Chinese defense minister, earlier that year, and Peng allegedly had conferred with him on the ideological rectitude of Mao's domestic policies. But the pro-Soviet Peng was replaced by Lin Biao two weeks before Khrushchev visited Beijing in late September 1959 – a slap in the face for the Soviet leader.[51] No understandings whatsoever were reached in Beijing at what turned out to be the last meeting between Nikita Khrushchev and Mao Zedong.

Breakup: 1960–1964

By late 1959 it was obvious to the Kremlin that the concrete difficulties in Sino-Soviet relations were not ad hoc nuisances but the manifestation of basic ideological disagreements between the two parties. By April 1960 a consensus had emerged among Soviet foreign policy elites that the ideological deviations of the Chinese comrades were going too far, especially after the leading Chinese journal, *Hongqi,* published the article "Long Live Leninism!" They felt it was time to punish the Chinese leadership by publishing in the Soviet press authoritative articles on the theory of contemporary Marxism-Leninism.[52] Up to a point the ideological warfare went hand in hand with the deterioration of state relations.[53]

The Kremlin was amazed to note how great the ideological differences between Moscow and Beijing were. Not only were the Chinese unwilling to embrace the course of peaceful coexistence and underline the potential for disarmament, but they were uncompromisingly against any détente with the United States. With respect to relations with capitalist countries, the conflict with India showed that Mao opposed the Soviet Union's foreign policy in toto. The Chinese asserted that world war was inevitable and insisted on preserving the violent course of the revolutionary movement. Mao's adventurist economic policy had resulted in widescale starvation. All in all, to Moscow, Chinese policy indicated a classic leftist deviation from Marxism-Leninism.[54] Mao's unwillingness to let the Soviets control China's coast by establishing naval bases added injury to the theoretical insults.[55]

In Sino-Soviet relations of the early 1960s, geopolitical disagreements strengthened ideological differences, while the latter undermined the fundamentals of the geopolitical alliance. This fatal interaction of geopolitical and ideological factors led to the final split between the two powers. But the timing of the split was ironic. First, the basic ideological disagreement was actually on the pace and methods of promoting the socialist cause. Due to Khrushchev's détente, this disagreement took the form of an argument on how to deal with the imperialist powers and whether peaceful coexistence was a revisionist deviation from Marxism-Leninism. Second, starting about 1960, Khrushchev, while accusing Mao of revolutionary adventurism, had himself started promoting revolutions in the Third World. Encouraged by the stabilization of Soviet positions domestically and internationally, Khrushchev believed that he could afford to push rivalry with the West in the huge zone of national liberation movements that he saw as booming in Asia, Africa, and Latin America. But by 1961 Khrushchev saw China as a rival, not an ally, in developing these policies.

In early summer 1960, the Chinese leaders launched a quiet campaign that might have triggered Khrushchev's decision for a complete break with China.

In their talks with the Soviets and East Europeans, the Chinese leaders started maintaining that the only way the Soviet Union could secure global peace was to transfer nuclear weapons to China and other socialist countries.[56] Nothing could have hurt Khrushchev more. Not only did the Chinese still insist on sharing Soviet nuclear secrets, they also were trying to whet the nuclear appetites of other socialist countries. In August the Kremlin withdrew its advisors and technicians from China.

As Khrushchev proceeded with the de-Stalinization of the Soviet Union – with the twenty-second CPSU Party Congress in October 1961 taking an unprecedented anti-Stalinist stand – the Chinese started a propaganda campaign that defended Stalin, Mao's bête noir from five years earlier.[57] The Chinese leaders began clearly ignoring any foreign policy actions by Soviet leaders.[58]

By mid-1962 the Soviet leadership had come to see China as a possible geopolitical threat even along the common border in Central Asia. In 1961–1962 at least 60,000 Chinese Muslims had crossed the Sino-Soviet border, fleeing the violence and famine of the new upsurge of Mao's revolution.[59] The specter of a new great game emerged: the fight between Moscow and Beijing for influence among the Central Asian peoples divided by the Sino-Soviet border. It was the first hint of the great territorial dispute that was to come during the 1960s.

But in spite of the unrest at the border, the Soviet leaders seem to have been unprepared for Mao's raising of the issue of territorial claims, aiming at lands acquired by imperial Russia and its successor, the Soviet Union, in East Asia, Siberia, and Central Asia. At least in the first phase of the new border dispute, the Kremlin acted with restraint, although its fears of the consequences of the Chinese claims were obvious. Boundary negotiations between the People's Republic and the Soviet Union started in February 1964. In July, talking to a Japanese Socialist Party delegation, Mao upped the ante by raising the issue of "Outer Mongolia": the Mongolian People's Republic, since 1924 a vassal of Moscow.[60] The geoideological divergence between Communists in Moscow and Beijing, having begun under Stalin as a dispute on how to make socialist revolution in an Asian peasant society and Soviet "rights" in Manchuria, by 1964 had divided the world's leftist movement into pro-Moscow and pro-Beijing factions and raised the question of a complete geopolitical repartition in the East.

Khrushchev had been alerted to the possibility of a strategic military rivalry between Moscow and Beijing as early as 1961. The sole Chinese ally worldwide – Albania in the Mediterranean – had banned Soviet submarines from its bases at that time.[61] In the summer of 1962, Khrushchev decided to deliver a dozen MiG-21s to India, a new foe of China after the October 1959 border clashes.[62]

The successful October 1962 Chinese offensive in Ladakh laid the foundations for a Soviet-Indian anti-Chinese entente. The Soviet policy of befriending China's neighbors had started, a policy that would culminate in February 1979, when Moscow supported Vietnam during the Sino-Vietnamese border war.

Because of his failure in China, Khrushchev had to rely solely on Soviet efforts in his naval strategies. By the time he was ousted from power in 1964, new Soviet submarines carrying submarine-launched ballistic missiles (SLBMs) had begun patrolling the Atlantic and a new fleet to defend the SLBM submarines had been created.[63] But his strategy of seeking overseas bases had failed, a fact that seriously weaked the Soviet Union in its global military rivalry with the United States. In the process of seeking what ultimately eluded him, Khrushchev had done his part to ruin the Soviet alliance with the world's most populous country. Whatever strategic successes his successors could claim, they could not put that alliance back together again.[64]

Notes

1. Gordon H. Chang, *Friends and Enemies: The United States, China and the Soviet Union, 1948–1972* (Stanford, Calif.: Stanford University Press, 1990), 249.

2. Such is the point of view of the authors of an excellent book on Stalin and Mao: Sergei N. Goncharov, John W. Lewis, and Xue Litai, *Uncertain Partners: Stalin, Mao and the Korean War* (Stanford, Calif.: Stanford University Press, 1993), 219. It is indisputable that certain acts of Soviet foreign policy were purely geopolitical. But with the exception of the *force majeur* situation of World War II from 1939 to 1945, ideology was never downplayed by the Kremlin until the Brezhnevites came to power in 1964. See also the analysis of "revolutionary imperial paradigm" in Constantine Pleshakov and Vladislav Zubok, *Inside the Kremlin's Cold War* (Cambridge, Mass.: Harvard University Press, 1996).

3. Ernst Neisvestny's talk at Khrushchev Centenary Conference, Brown University, Providence, R.I., December 3, 1994.

4. For an analysis of Stalin's attempts to use realpolitik in East Asia in 1945 to avoid conflict with the United States, see Odd Arne Westad, *Cold War and Revolution: Soviet-American Rivalry and the Origins of the Chinese Civil War, 1944–1946* (New York: Columbia University Press, 1993), 31–56.

5. *Khrushchev Remembers: The Last Testament,* ed. Strobe Talbott (London: Andrew Deutsch, 1974), 240.

6. "Doklad o vneshnei politike pravitelstva Kitaiskoi Narodnoi Respubliki i o vnu-tripoliticheskom i ekonomicheskom polozhenii Kitaya za 1 polugodie 1951 goda" [Report on the foreign policy of the leadership of the People's Republic of China and on the domestic, political, and economic situation in China in the first half of 1951], Archive of Foreign Policy, Russian Federation (AVPRF), fond (f.) 022, opis (op.) 4, papka (pa.) 41, delo (d.) 57, pp. 22–7. Hereafter "Doklad . . . 1951."

7. *Khrushchev Remembers,* 239–44.

8. Report, B. Beshchev to V. M. Molotov, January 19, 1950, AVPRF, f. 022, op. 3, p. 21, d. 39.

9. "Doklad . . . 1951," 10. As late as January 26, 1950, in one of the last attempts to check Soviet control, Zhou Enlai gave Soviet Foreign Minister Andrei Vyshinskii a Chinese draft of an agreement on Lüshun, Dalian, and the Changchun Railway emphasizing Chinese sovereignty. According to that draft, the Soviet side was to decline any rights on Lüshun, Dalian, and the Changchun Railway; Soviet troops were to be withdrawn from China after signing a peace treaty with Japan, or, if a peace treaty would not be signed, in three years after the signing the Sino-Soviet treaty. Yet Stalin, having exerted pressure upon Mao, insisted on the tough Soviet draft of the protocols. Vyshinski to Stalin, January 26, 1950, AVPRF, f. 022, op. 3, pa. 21, d. 39, pp. 36–9.

10. "Doklad . . . 1951," 8.

11. Ambassador Xue Mouhong's speech at Woodrow Wilson International Center for Scholars, Washington, D.C., January 31, 1995. Already in May 1951 Gao Gang had told Soviet diplomat Andrei M. Ledovsky that he had to be cautious in his dealings with the Soviets, for it was not recommended to mix with them. "Doklad . . . 1951," AVPRF, f. 022, op. 4, pa. 41, d. 57, p. 21.

12. *Khrushchev Remembers,* 181.

13. "Doklad . . . 1951," 10.

14. AVPRF, fond sekretariata t. Gromyko A. A., op. 7, pa. 102, d. 30, pp. 5, 7.

15. Edward E. Rice, *Mao's Way* (Berkeley: University of California Press, 1972), 150.

16. Goncharov et al., *Uncertain Partners,* 122.

17. "Doklad . . . 1951," 18.

18. Rice, *Mao's Way,* 150.

19. Lowell Dittmer, *Sino-Soviet Normalization and Its International Implications, 1945–1990* (Seattle: University of Washington Press, 1992), 185.

20. Otchet posolstva SSSR v Kitaiskoi Narodnoi Respublike za 1958 god, Center for the Storage of Contemporary Documentation (TsKhSD), Moscow, f. 5, op. 49, pa. 247, d. 134. Hereafter "Otchet . . . 1958."

21. *Khrushchev Remembers,* 255.

22. Craig R. Nation, *Black Earth, Red Star: A History of Soviet Security Policy, 1917–1991* (Ithaca, N.Y.: Cornell University Press, 1992), 223.

23. Ibid., 213.

24. *Khrushchev Remembers,* 257.

25. Edward Wegener, *The Soviet Naval Offensive* (Annapolis, Md.: Naval Institute Press, 1975), 22–3.

26. Ibid., 26–7.

27. *Khrushchev Remembers,* 33. For an analysis of the controversy surrounding Khrushchev's "naval revolution," see George E. Hudson, "The Soviet Naval Doctrine and Soviet Politics, 1953–1975," *World Politics* 29 (1976): 98–104.

28. S. G. Gorshkov, *The Sea Power of the State* (Oxford: Pergamon Press, 1979), 156.

29. Ibid., 229–34.

30. Bradford Dismukes, James M. McConnell, eds., *Soviet Naval Diplomacy* (New York: Pergamon Press, 1979), 16.

31. See Wegener, *The Soviet Naval Offensive,* 49.

32. Herve Coutau-Begarie, *La puissance maritime sovietique* [Soviet naval power] (Paris: Economica, 1983), 17.

33. *Khrushchev Remembers,* 24.

34. See Barry M. Blechman, *The Control of Naval Armaments: Prospects and Possibilities* (Washington, D.C.: Brookings Institution, 1975), 32–3.

35. Dismukes and McConnell, *Soviet Naval Diplomacy,* 18.

36. Li Zhisui, *Private Life of Chairman Mao* (London: Chatto and Windus, 1994), 261.

37. "Otchet . . . 1958," 92.

38. Record of conversation, Mao–Iudin, July 22, 1958, Zhonghua renmin gongheguo waijiaobu and Zhonggong zhongyang wenxian yanjiushi, comps., *Mao Zedong waijiao wenxuan* [Mao Zedong selected works on foreign affairs], (Beijing: Zhonggong wenxian, 1994), 322; for an English translation, see *Cold War International History Project (CWIHP) Bulletin* 6–7 (Winter 1995/1996): 155–9.

39. Li, *Private Life of Chairman Mao,* 261–2.

40. "Otchet . . . 1958," 92.

41. Record of conversation N. Sudarikov–Zhou Enlai, September 5, 1958, TsKhSD, f. 5, op. 49, d. 131, p. 4.

42. Li, *Private Life of Chairman Mao,* 262.

43. *Khrushchev Remembers,* 258.

44. "Otchet . . . 1958," 84.

45. On September 5 Zhou Enlai told Soviet diplomat Sudarikov that Beijing was "just going to inform" Moscow on its motivations. Record of conversation N. Sudarikov–Zhou Enlai, September 5, 1958, 1.

46. Ibid., 8.

47. Record of conversation, N. Antonva–Zhou Enlai, September 10, 1958, TsKhSD, f. 5, op. 49, d. 131, p. 3.

48. Nation, *Black Earth, Red Star,* 233–4.

49. Peter Jones and Sîân Kevill, comps., *China and the Soviet Union* (New York: Facts on File, 1985), 13–14.

50. Ambassador Xue Mouhong's speech.

51. Jones and Kevill, *China and the Soviet Union,* 13–14.

52. "Ob osnovnykh momentakh vnutrennei zhizni, vneshnei politiki KNR i sovet-sko-kitaiskikh otnoshenii" [On the basic elements of domestic life, foreign policy of the PRC and Soviet-Chinese relations], April 12, 1960, TsKhSD, f. 5, op. 49, d. 340–2, p. 28.

53. "Otchet posolstva SSSR v Kitaiskoi Narodnoi respublike za 1962 god" [Annual report of the USSR embassy in the People's Republic of China for 1962], TsKhSD, f. 5, op. 49, d. 536, p. 232.

54. "Politicheskoie pismo posolstva SSSR v KNR za II kvartal 1960 g.," TsKhSD, f. 5, op. 49, d. 340–2, pp. 19, 53–4, 56, 59, 69, 70.

55. "Otchet . . . 1958," 92.

56. "Politicheskoie pismo posolstva SSSR v KNR za II kvartal 1960 g.," TsKhSD, f. 5, op. 49, ed. khr. 134, p. 68.

57. "Iz besed s mestnymi sovetskimi i kitaiskimi grazhdanami vo vremya ko-mandirovki v g. Dalny (December 26–31, 1961)" [Concerning conversations with local Soviet and Chinese citizens on a recent official visit to Dalian], TsKhSD, f. 5, op. 49. d. 535, p. 1.

58. "Ob usloviyakh raboty sovetskikh uchrezhdeny i sovetskikh predtsavitelei v KNR v 1961 g." [On the working conditions for Soviet institutions and Soviet officials in the PRC in 1961], TsKhSD, f. 5, op. 49, d. 535, p. 3.

59. "Politicheskoie pismo posolstva SSSR v KNR za II kvartal 1962 goda" [Political report of the USSR embassy in the PRC for the second quarter of 1962], 37.

60. Dittmer, *Sino-Soviet Normalization,* 189–90.

61. Dismukes and McConnell, *Soviet Naval Diplomacy,* 20.

62. Dittmer, *Sino-Soviet Normalization,* 172.

63. See Robert G. Weinland, "The Evolution of Soviet Requirements for Naval Forces: Solving the Problems of the Early 1960s," *Survival* 26 (1984): 22–3.

64. For a description of the initial period of uncertainty and attempts to mend the alliance, see Jones and Kevill, *China and the Soviet Union,* 60–1.

8. Chinese Politics and the Collapse of the Sino-Soviet Alliance

Chen Jian and Yang Kuisong

No other event during the Cold War contributed so much to changes in perceptions of the Communist powers as the rise and fall of the Sino-Soviet alliance. Emerging in the late 1940s and early 1950s, the "brotherly solidarity" between the People's Republic of China (PRC) and the Soviet Union was claimed to be "unbreakable" and "eternal." But by the latter part of the decade, serious disputes began to develop between Chinese and Soviet leaders, causing the alliance to decline and then to collapse in the early 1960s. In the years that followed, the hostility between the two countries rose so far that it led to a bloody border war in 1969. In the 1960s and 1970s, the total confrontation between the two countries became a basic element of international affairs.

What, then, were the causes underlying the rise and demise of the Sino-Soviet alliance? Scholars may answer this question in many ways. This chapter, with the insights gained from newly available Chinese source materials,[1] reinforced by fresh Russian documents,[2] adopts a *domestic-oriented* approach. Without ignoring the merits of other interpretations, especially those emphasizing the role played by China's security concerns and international ideological commitments, this chapter argues that China's alliance policy toward the Soviet Union was *always* an integral part of Chairman Mao Zedong's grand plans for transforming China's state, society, and international outlook. While security concerns and socialist internationalism conditioned the rise and fall of the alliance, it was Mao's efforts to define and redefine the mission and scope of his "continuous revolution" that constituted the central theme of Chinese politics during his era (1949 to 1976) and that shaped Beijing's attitude toward China's alliance with the Soviet Union.

The Meaning of the "Lean-to-One-Side" Approach

On June 30, 1949, Mao Zedong issued his famous "lean-to-one-side" state-ment. In a long article entitled "On People's Democratic Dictatorship," he an-nounced the special relationship of the New China with the Soviet Union. He said that the People's Republic must:

> Externally, unite in a common struggle with those nations of the world which treat us as equal and unite with the peoples of all coun-tries. That is, ally ourselves with the Soviet Union, with the People's Democratic Countries, and with the proletariat and the broad masses of the people in all other countries, and form an international united front. . . . We must lean to one side.[3]

What was the meaning of Mao's extraordinary choice of terms? The content was obviously linked to the long-term revolutionary policy of the Chinese Com-munist Party (CCP) of attaching itself to the international "progressive forces" led by the Soviet Union. By the late 1940s, CCP leaders clearly perceived the postwar world as divided into two camps, one headed by the Soviet Union and the other by the United States, and regarded their revolution as a part of the So-viet-led international proletarian movement.[4] Mao's statement was consistent with this view of the postwar world structure.

But the lean-to-one-side approach also grew out of the CCP's assessment of the serious nature of the threat from Western imperialist countries, especially from the United States, to the completion of the Chinese revolution. As the CCP neared final victory in China's civil war in 1949, Mao and his fellow CCP lead-ers became very much concerned about the prospect of direct U.S. intervention in China.[5] Although the American military did not intervene directly during the latter phase of the civil war, CCP leaders, given their belief in the aggressive and evil nature of Western imperialism, continued to view the Western capitalist countries in general and the United States in particular as dangerous enemies. In the eyes of Mao and his comrades, "it was the possibility of military interven-tion from imperialist countries that decided the necessity of China allying itself with socialist countries."[6]

In addition to these ideological commitments and security concerns, though, Mao's lean-to-one-side decision must be understood in the context of his deter-mination to maintain and enhance the inner dynamics of the Chinese Commu-nist revolution at the time of its nationwide victory. The final goal of Mao's Chi-nese Revolution, as the CCP chairman himself repeatedly emphasized, was the transformation of China's "old" state and society and the destruction of the "old" world in which, as Mao and his comrades viewed it, China had been a hu-miliated member during modern times. Mao never concealed his ambition that his revolution should finally turn China into a land of universal justice and equality, while at the same time, through presenting the experience of the Chinese Revolution as a model for other "oppressed nations" in the world, China would reestablish its central position in the international community.

In 1949, when the Chinese Communist revolution approached nationwide victory, Mao and his comrades understood that the New China would have to meet such challenges as establishing and consolidating a new revolutionary regime and reviving China's war-worn economy. But what concerned the CCP chairman the most was how to prevent the revolution from losing its momentum. In his New Year's message for 1949, Mao called upon his party "to carry the revolution through to the end," by which he meant not only the thorough destruction of the Guomindang (GMD) regime but also the promotion of the revolution toward its higher, post-takeover stage.[7] Throughout 1949 he repeatedly warned against imperialist plots to sabotage the revolution from within either using the "sugar-coated bullet" to shoot down the weak-willed Communists or dividing the revolutionary camp by applying the "doctrine of means" to confuse the distinction between revolution and counterrevolution.[8] Mao stressed that "after the destruction of the enemies with guns, the enemies without guns are still there, and they are bound to struggle desperately against us." He therefore warned the party: "If we fail to pay enough attention to these problems, if we do not know how to wage the struggle against them and win victory in the struggle, we shall be unable to maintain our political power, we shall be unable to stand on our feet, we shall fail."[9]

It was to create momentum for China's continuous revolution that the CCP leadership made three fundamental decisions on New China's external relations, what Zhou Enlai referred to as "making a fresh start," "cleaning the house before entertaining guests," and "leaning to one side."[10] These three decisions were closely interconnected. While the first two represented Mao's and his comrades' determination not to be influenced by the legacy of "old" China's diplomatic practice, the last one reflected Mao's conviction that an alliance with the Soviet Union would help destroy any remaining illusions among the Chinese people, especially the intellectuals, of the utility of assistance from Western capitalist countries. Because the Soviet Union had been the first socialist country in the world and had established the only example for building a socialist and Communist state and society, Mao's continuous revolution had to learn from the Soviet experience. In this regard, the argument of Zhang Baijia, a leading Chinese scholar in Chinese diplomatic history, certainly makes good sense:

> Contrary to the prevalent view, Mao treated the "lean-to-one-side" concept as a grand strategy to influence the Party's foreign *and* do-

mestic policies. The key question Mao tried to answer by introducing the lean-to-one-side approach was how to define the general direction of New China's development.[11]

Not surprisingly, despite the fact that the development of the CCP-Soviet relations had been tortuous during the Chinese revolution, Mao and the CCP leadership made genuine efforts to strengthen their relations with Moscow when the party was winning China's civil war. From late 1947 Mao actively prepared to visit the Soviet Union to "discuss important domestic and international issues" with Stalin.[12] From January 31 to February 7, 1949, Mao and other CCP leaders received Anastas Mikoyan, a Soviet Politburo member and Joseph Stalin's representative, at Xibaipo, then CCP headquarters, and introduced him to the party's strategies and policies. As the first major contact between top CCP and Soviet leaders in many years, Mikoyan's visit proved to be the first step toward a new mutual understanding and cooperation between the CCP and the Soviet Union.[13] In May and June 1949 the CCP kept the Soviets well informed of the meetings between CCP foreign relations official Huang Hua and John Leighton Stuart, U.S. ambassador to China.[14]

From late June to mid-August 1949, Liu Shaoqi, the CCP's second most important leader, visited Moscow. During meetings with Soviet leaders, Stalin promised Liu that the Soviet Union would give the Chinese Communists substantial political, military, and other material support. Moreover, the Soviets and the Chinese discussed the "division of labor" between them in promoting the world revolution and reached a general consensus: While the Soviet Union would remain the center of the international proletarian revolution, promoting Eastern revolution would become primarily China's duty. Liu's visit promoted Sino-Soviet strategic cooperation, making Mao and his fellow CCP leaders more confident in dealing with the international problems facing revolutionary China.[15]

The CCP's efforts to achieve a strategic alliance with the Soviet Union culminated in December 1949–February 1950 with Mao's visit to the Soviet Union. The contacts during the visit, however, were uneasy. During Mao's first meeting with Stalin on December 16, the Soviet leader asked him what he hoped to achieve from his visit. Mao, according to his interpreter's recollections, first replied that he wanted to "bring about something that not only looked nice but also tasted delicious" – an obvious reference to his wish to sign a new Sino-Soviet treaty.[16] However, Stalin greatly disappointed Mao by initially emphasizing that it was not in Moscow's or Beijing's interests to abolish the 1945 Sino-Soviet treaty he had signed with the GMD.[17] Mao's visit was at a deadlock for almost three weeks before the Soviets relented.[18] Chinese Premier Zhou Enlai arrived in Moscow on January 20 to negotiate the details of the new alliance treaty, which was signed finally on February 14, 1950. The Chinese, however, had to agree to allow the Soviets to maintain their privileges in China's Northeast and Xinjiang[19]; in exchange, the Soviets agreed to provide more military and other material support to China, including taking the responsibility of providing air defense to coastal areas of the People's Republic.[20]

Mao's feelings when he left Moscow to return to China must have been complicated. On one hand, he had reasons to celebrate the signing of the Sino-Soviet alliance treaty. The alliance would greatly enhance the People's Republic's security, and, more important, it would strengthen the CCP's position to promote the revolution at home: With the backing of the Soviet Union, Mao and his comrades were in a powerful position to wipe out the political, economic, social, and cultural legacies of the old China and carry out China's state-building and societal transformation on the CCP's terms. It was not just rhetoric when the CCP chairman, after returning to Beijing, told his comrades that the making of the Sino-Soviet alliance would help the CCP to cope with both domestic and international threats to the Chinese revolution.[21]

On the other hand, however, Mao could clearly sense that a divergence persisted between Stalin and himself. Stalin's raw use of the language of power put Mao off. Mao's wish to discuss revolutionary ideals and the Communists' historical responsibilities came to nothing. Mao never enjoyed meeting Stalin face to face, and he was extremely sensitive toward Stalin treating him, the revolutionary leader from the "Central Kingdom," as the inferior "younger brother."[22] The signing of the Sino-Soviet treaty made the lean-to-one-side approach the cornerstone for PRC foreign relations, yet, because of the way it was worked out, the future development of Sino-Soviet relations was bound to be uneasy.

The Alliance and China's Entry into the Korean War

The first major test for the Sino-Soviet alliance came just eight months after it had been established, when, in October 1950, the CCP leadership decided to dispatch Chinese troops to enter the Korean War. From Beijing's perspective, such a test not only allowed Mao and his comrades to define more specifically the alliance's utility for China's national security; it also provided them with a valuable opportunity to better understand how the alliance would serve Mao's continuous revolution projects. China's Korean War experience, consequently, would profoundly influence both Mao's concerns about the future of the Chinese Revolution and the future development of the Sino-Soviet alliance.

As revealed by new Russian and Chinese sources, the Korean War was, first of all, North Korean leader Kim Il Sung's war, which he initiated on the basis of his judgment (or misjudgment) of the revolutionary situation existing on the

Korean peninsula.[23] Stalin initially feared that such a war could result in direct military conflict between the Soviet Union and the United States, and he did not endorse Kim's plans of unifying his country by military means until the end of January 1950, when U.S. Secretary of State Dean Acheson's statement of excluding Korea from America's western Pacific defense perimeter appears to have convinced him that direct U.S. military intervention in the peninsula was unlikely.[24] In the months prior to the outbreak of the Korean War, the Soviet Union provided large amounts of military aid to the Korean Communists, but Stalin had reservations on two key issues. First, he never made the commitment to use Soviet military forces in Korea. Second, he insisted that Kim travel to Beijing to consult with Mao Zedong, so that the Chinese Communists would share responsibility for Kim's war preparations.[25]

Mao and the CCP leadership faced a dilemma on the Korean issue. Since the remaining Nationalist forces were still occupying Taiwan, Mao and his comrades were reluctant to see a war to break out in Korea; they worried that that might complicate the situation in East Asia and jeopardize the CCP's effort to liberate Taiwan.[26] Yet, because Mao and his comrades were eager to revive China's central position on the international scene through supporting revolutionary movements in other countries (especially in East Asia), and because between the Chinese and North Korean Communists there existed profound historical connections, it would have been inconceivable for Mao to veto Kim's plans to unify his country through a revolutionary war.[27] From 1949 to 1950, in meeting North Korean leaders (including Kim Il Sung in mid-May 1950), Mao made it clear that the CCP supported the Korean revolution but hoped that the Koreans would not initiate the invasion of the South until the Chinese People's Liberation Army (PLA) had seized Taiwan.[28] In the meantime, during Mao's 1949–1950 visit to the Soviet Union, the CCP chairman shared with Stalin his belief that it was unlikely that the United States would involve itself in a revolutionary civil war in East Asia, thus enhancing Stalin's determination to back Kim's plans to invade the South.[29] Further, from summer 1949 to spring 1950, the Chinese sent 50,000 to 70,000 Korean-nationality PLA soldiers (with weapons) back to Korea.[30] As a result, Mao virtually gave Kim's plan to invade the South a green light.

The Korean War erupted on June 25, 1950. U.S. President Harry Truman quickly decided to come to the rescue of Syngman Rhee's South Korean regime and to dispatch the Seventh Fleet to "neutralize" the Taiwan Straits, which changed the Korean War into an international crisis. Chinese leaders quickly decided to postpone the invasion of Taiwan and to focus on dealing with the crisis in Korea.[31] On July 13 the CCP leadership formally established a Northeast Border Defense Army, the main task of which was to prepare for military intervention in Korea in case the war turned against North Korea.[32] By early August over 260,000 Chinese troops had taken up positions along the Chinese-Korean border.[33] On August 18 Mao set the end of September as the deadline for these troops to complete preparations for military operations in Korea.[34]

Beijing based its handling of the Korean crisis on the assumption that if China entered the Korean War, the Soviet Union would honor its obligations in accordance with the Sino-Soviet alliance treaty and provide China with all kinds of support, including ammunition, military equipment, and air cover for Chinese land forces. Early in July, when the Chinese leaders informed Stalin of the decision to establish the Northeast Border Defense Army, Stalin supported it and promised that if the Chinese troops were to fight in Korea, the Soviet Union would "try to provide air cover for these units."[35] In the following weeks the Soviets accelerated military deliveries to China, and a Soviet air force division, with 122 MiG-15 fighters, entered China's Northeast (Manchuria) to help with air defense there.[36] All of this must have enhanced Beijing's belief that China's entry into the Korean War would warrant substantial Soviet military support.

When the course of war reversed after U.S. troops landed at Inchon on September 15, however, Stalin's attitude regarding Soviet military assistance changed. He became more determined than ever to avoid a direct military confrontation with the United States. In a telegram to Chinese leaders dated October 1, Stalin pointed out that the situation in Korea was grave and that without outside support, the Korean Communist regime would collapse. He thus asked the Chinese to dispatch their troops to Korea. It is noticeable, however, that he did not mention what support the Soviet Union would offer China, let alone touch on the question of Soviet air support.[37]

At this time, serious differences in opinions already existed among top Chinese leaders on whether China should enter the war. Mao favored dispatching troops to Korea. On October 2 he personally drafted a long telegram to respond to Stalin's request, informing Stalin that the Chinese leadership had decided "to send a portion of our troops, under the name of [Chinese People's] Volunteers, to Korea, assisting the Korean comrades to fight the troops of the United States and its running dog Syngman Rhee." Mao summarized the reasons for this decision, emphasizing that even though China's intervention might cause a war between China and the United States, it was necessary for the sake of the Korean and Eastern revolutions. Mao also made it clear that in order to defeat the American troops in Korea, China needed substantial Soviet military support as well as air cover for Chinese land forces.[38]

Mao, however, apparently failed to dispatch this telegram, probably because of the divided opinions among top CCP leaders.[39] According to Russian archival documents, Mao sent a note to Nikolai Roshchin, the Soviet ambassador to China, late on October 2, informing him and the Soviet leadership that because dispatching Chinese troops to Korea "may entail extremely serious consequences," including "provoking an open conflict between the United States and China," many leaders in Beijing believed that China should "show caution" in entering the Korean War. Mao therefore told Stalin that the Chinese leadership had not reached the decision to send troops to Korea.[40]

Over the ensuing two weeks, the Sino-Soviet alliance underwent a major test. Before October 7 (when he informed Kim of the communication), Stalin cabled the Chinese leadership, advising Beijing that for the sake of China's security interests as well as in the interests of the world proletarian revolution, it was necessary for China to send troops to Korea. Indeed, Stalin even introduced a thesis that may be called the Communist version of domino theory, warning Mao and his comrades that Beijing's failure to intervene could result in grave consequences first for China's Northeast, then for all China, and then for the entire world revolution. Again and ironically, however, Stalin did not mention how the Soviet Union would support China if Chinese troops did enter operations in Korea.[41]

Although it is not clear precisely when Stalin's message reached Beijing and what impact it had on deliberations there, we do know that by October 7, Chinese leaders had made the decision to enter the war. From October 3 to 6 the CCP leadership held a series of strictly secret meetings to discuss the Korean issue. Although most CCP leaders had opposed, or at least had reservations about, dispatching troops to Korea, Mao used both his authority and his political insights to secure the support of his colleagues for the decision to go to war.[42] On October 8 Mao Zedong formally issued the order to establish "Chinese People's Volunteers" forces with Peng Dehuai as the commander[43] and informed Kim Il Sung of the decision the same evening.[44]

But, to strengthen China's bargaining position in pursuing Soviet military support, Mao decided to "play tough with" Stalin.[45] On October 10–11 Zhou Enlai, who had traveled from Beijing to the Soviet Union, met with Stalin at the latter's villa on the Black Sea. Zhou, according to Shi Zhe, did not tell Stalin that China would send troops to Korea but persistently led the discussion to Soviet military support, especially air cover, for China. Stalin agreed to provide China with substantial military support but explained that it was impossible for the Soviet air force to engage in fighting over Korea until two to two and a half months after Chinese land forces entered operations there.[46]

In view of this situation, on October 12 Mao again ordered Chinese troops to halt preparations for entering operations in Korea.[47] The next day the CCP Politburo met again to discuss China's entry into the Korean War. Pushed by Mao, the Politburo confirmed that entering the war was in the fundamental interests of the Chinese revolution as well as the Eastern revolution. Mao then authorized Zhou Enlai, who was still in Moscow, to inform Stalin of the decision. At the same time, Mao instructed Zhou to continue to "consult with" the Soviet leaders, to clarify whether they would ask China to lease or to purchase the military equipment that Stalin agreed to provide, and whether the Soviet air force would enter operations in Korea later.[48]

On October 17, the day Zhou returned to Beijing, Mao again ordered the troops on the Chinese-Korean border to halt their movements. The next day, when Mao was convinced that the Soviet Union would provide China with all kinds of military support, including air cover in a later stage of the war, he finally ordered Chinese troops to enter the Korean War.[49]

Mao Zedong was always the central figure in the process of deciding whether to intervene in Korea. Early in July 1950 it was Mao who proposed the establishment of the Northeast Border Defense Army. In August Mao twice set up deadlines for completion of China's preparations for military operations in Korea. During the first three weeks of October, when the CCP leadership made the final decision, Mao was almost the only person who consistently favored intervention. Using both his reasoning and his authority, he convinced his comrades that China had to enter the conflict even without direct Soviet air cover at first.

The concerns over safeguarding China's physical security certainly played an important role in bringing Chinese leaders in Beijing to the decision to enter the war. Yet factors more complicated than these narrowly defined "security concerns" dominated Mao's conceptual world. When Chinese troops entered the Korean War, Mao meant to pursue a glorious victory over the American-led UN forces, which, he hoped, would transform the challenge and threat posed by the Korean crisis into added energy for enhancing Communist control of China's state and society as well as promote the international prestige and influence of the People's Republic.

This was why at the same time when Mao and his comrades were considering entering the Korean War, the CCP leadership started a Great Movement to Resist America and Assist Korea, with "beating American arrogance" as its central slogan. The party used every means available to stir the "hatred of the U.S. imperialists" among common Chinese, emphasizing that the United States had long engaged in political and economic aggression against China, that the declining capitalist America was not as powerful as it seemed, and that a confrontation between China and the United States was inevitable.[50] When the Chinese troops were crossing the Yalu River to Korea in October 1950, a nationwide campaign aimed at suppressing "reactionaries and reactionary activities" emerged in China's cities and countryside.[51] All of this indicates that China's entrance into the Korean War must be understood as part of Mao's efforts to mobilize the population to promote his grand programs for continuing the Chinese Revolution.

Mao's already ambivalent feeling toward Stalin must have been further complicated during the first three weeks of October. Because Mao needed to use the Korean crisis as a means to increase domestic political mobilization, he should have welcomed Stalin's constant push for China to enter the war as well as his promise, even if late, that the Soviet Union would provide China with ammunition, military equipment, and eventual air cover. Stalin's promises strengthened Mao's own ability to gain his party leadership's approval of the war decision. However, Stalin's behavior of always putting the interests of the Soviet Union ahead of anything else demonstrated to Mao the limits of Stalin's "proletarian internationalism." Mao also worried about Stalin's fears of a direct Soviet-U.S. confrontation. In comparison, Mao's decision to rescue the Korean and Eastern revolutions at a time of real difficulties strengthened his sense of moral superiority, of being able to help others out, even if the Soviet "elder brother" could not. As a result, a seed for the future Sino-Soviet split was sown during the first test of the Sino-Soviet alliance.

The Alliance and China's Korean War Experience

During the three years of China's intervention in Korea, the relationship between Beijing and Moscow was strengthened. Mao Zedong consulted with Stalin on almost all important decisions. In December 1950 and January 1951, when Mao and his comrades made the decision to order Chinese troops to cross the thirty-eighth parallel, Beijing maintained daily communication with Moscow and received Stalin's support.[52] In May–June 1951, when Chinese leaders in Beijing were considering adopting a new strategy to end the war, one that would shift their policy emphasis from fighting to negotiation, they had extensive exchanges of opinions with Stalin and did not make the decision until the strategy was fully backed by Moscow.[53] After 1952, when the armistice negotiations at Panmunjom hit a deadlock on the prisoner-of-war issue, Beijing consulted with Moscow and concluded that the Chinese/North Korean side would not compromise on this issue until its political and military position had improved.[54]

As far as the foundation of the Sino-Soviet alliance is concerned, Mao's decision to send Chinese troops to Korea seemed to have enhanced Stalin's confidence in his comrades in Beijing as genuine proletarian internationalists. During the war years, the Soviet Union provided China with large amounts of ammunition and military equipment. Units of the Soviet air force, based in Manchuria, began to engage in defense of the transportation lines across the Chinese–Korean border as early as November 1950 and began operations over the northern part of North Korea in January 1951.[55] In the meantime, Stalin became more willing to commit Soviet financial and technological resources to China's economic reconstruction; during the war years, the Soviet Union's share in China's foreign trade increased from 30 percent (in 1950) to 56.3 percent (in 1953).[56] In retrospect, it would have been virtually impossible for China to have fought the Korean War without the alliance with the Soviet Union.

The Soviet support was crucial for Mao's plans for his revolution. Indeed, China's involvement in the Korean War stimulated a series of political and social upheavals in the country that would have been inconceivable during the early stage of the new republic. In the wake of China's entrance into the war, the Communist regime found itself in a powerful position to penetrate into almost every area of Chinese society through intensive mass mobilization under the banner of "Resisting America and Assisting Korea." During the three years of war, three nationwide campaigns swept across China's countryside and cities: the movement to suppress counterrevolutionaries, the land reform movement, and the "Three Antis" and "Five Antis" movements.[57]

When the war ended in July 1953, China's society and political landscape had been transformed: Resistance to the new regime had been destroyed; land had been redistributed and the landlord class had been eliminated; those Communist cadres whom Mao believed had lost the revolutionary momentum had been either "reeducated" or removed from leading positions; the national bourgeoisie was under the tight control of the Communist state; and the "petit-bourgeoise" intellectuals had experienced the first round of Communist reeducation. Consequently, the CCP effectively strengthened its organizational control of Chinese society and dramatically increased its authority in the minds of the Chinese people.

These domestic changes were further facilitated by the fact that during the war, the Chinese troops successfully forced the U.S./UN forces to retreat from the Chinese-Korean border to the thirty-eighth parallel, something that allowed Beijing to call its involvement in Korea a great victory. Mao and his comrades thus believed that they had won a position from which to claim that international society – friends and foes alike – had to accept China as a Great Power. Consequently Mao, as the mastermind of the war decision, began to enjoy political power inside China with far fewer checks and balances than before. His international victory made him more confident and enthusiastic and convinced him of the necessity of undertaking a series of new steps to transform China. Mao had good reason to be thankful for the Sino-Soviet alliance during the Korean crisis.

Yet, on another level, the Chinese experience during the Korean War also ground away at some of the cement that kept the Sino-Soviet alliance together. The extreme pragmatism Stalin had demonstrated in his management of the Korean crisis, especially in his failure to commit Soviet air support to China during the key weeks of late September and early October 1950, revealed the superficial nature of the Soviet dictator's "proletarian internationalism." What really hurt Mao and his comrades, however, was the Soviet request that China pay for all the military support Beijing had received during the war, which thereby added to China's long-term economic challenges.[58] To the Chinese, Stalin's stinginess made the Soviets seem more like arms merchants than genuine Communist internationalists.

Although China's Korean War experience made Beijing more dependent on Moscow, psychologically Mao and his fellow Chinese leaders enhanced their sense of moral superiority vis-à-vis their comrades in Moscow. Stalin's death in March 1953 further hardened this feeling. As will be discussed later, this subtle change in Mao's and his comrades' view of themselves would have a crucial impact upon the fate of the Sino-Soviet alliance.

The Alliance's Golden Years

For a period of several years after Stalin's death, Sino-Soviet cooperation developed smoothly. The Soviets offered the Chinese substantial support to assist the economic reconstruction of the People's Republic as well as to promote its international position. From September 29 to October 12, 1954, Communist Party of the Soviet Union (CPSU) First Secretary Nikita Khrushchev led a top-level Soviet party and governmental delegation to visit China to participate in celebrations of the fifth anniversary of the republic's founding. During this visit, the Soviets signed a series of agreements with the Chinese, including returning to China Soviet military bases in Lüshun (Port Arthur), together with its equipment, giving up Soviet shares in four Sino-Soviet joint ventures,[59] providing China with loans totaling 520 million rubles, and offering technological support to China in initiating or upgrading 156 key industrial projects for the First Five-Year Plan of the People's Republic.[60] In April 1955 the Soviet Union and China signed an agreement under which Moscow provided Beijing nuclear technology, purportedly for peaceful purposes.[61] It seemed that Khrushchev and the new Soviet leadership were willing to establish a more productive cooperative relationship with their Chinese comrades.[62]

Chinese leaders in Beijing also demonstrated solidarity with Khrushchev and the new Soviet leadership on a series of important domestic and international issues. When the Soviet leaders made the decision to purge Lavrentii Beriia, Stalin's chief of the secret police, and when Khrushchev became first secretary of the CPSU, the CCP leadership quickly offered their support. In the meantime, on such important Soviet foreign policy issues as the formation of the Warsaw Pact Organization, the establishment of diplomatic relations between the Soviet

Union and West Germany, the signing of a peace treaty with Austria, and the improvement of relations with Yugoslavia, Beijing provided Moscow with timely and firm support.[63]

On important international issues, Chinese and Soviet leaders carefully consulted with each other to coordinate their strategies and policies. A revealing example in this regard was Beijing's and Moscow's management of the Geneva Conference of 1954. Before the conference, Zhou Enlai twice visited Moscow to hold a series of meetings with Soviet leaders, which resulted in well-coordinated Sino-Soviet strategies toward the Korean and Indochina questions that were to be discussed at the conference.[64] At Geneva, the Chinese and the Soviet delegations exchanged opinions and intelligence information on a daily basis. When the Vietnamese Communists hesitated before accepting the temporary division of their country along the seventeenth parallel, both the Chinese and the Soviets pressured their comrades, convincing them that such a solution was in the interests of both the Vietnamese revolution and the cause of world peace. In this sense it is fair to say that the conference's final settlement of the Indochina issue should be attributed to the cooperation between Zhou Enlai and Viacheslav Molotov.[65] The years of 1954 to 1955, in retrospect, should be regarded as a golden age of the Sino-Soviet alliance.

The continuous enhancement of the alliance during this period reflected, to some degree, Moscow's and Beijing's strategic concerns. From a Soviet perspective, these were the years that Khrushchev and his comrades slowly began to rid themselves of Stalin's shadow. Khrushchev, who had just emerged as top Soviet leader and needed time to consolidate the leadership role, certainly understood that the support from China was vital for him.[66]

Beijing, on the other hand, also needed Moscow's assistance. The CCP leadership was adjusting China's domestic and international policies after the Korean War ended. Domestically, in 1953–1954 the Central Committee was contemplating the introduction of the First Five-Year Plan as well as liberating the GMD-controlled Taiwan either peacefully or, if necessary, by military means. Internationally, after five years of being excluded from the international community, Beijing's leaders (including Mao at that time) were eager to escape China's international isolation.[67] Under these circumstances, especially considering that China's socialist reconstruction had to learn from the Soviet model, political, military, and economic support from the Soviet Union became highly valuable. In other words, the specific needs of China's revolution at this stage were well served by the Sino-Soviet alliance.

A vague undercurrent of disagreement and distrust, however, continued to exist between Chinese and Soviet leaders. In retrospect, even during the heyday of Sino-Soviet solidarity, Mao and his comrades were never comfortable with the junior partner's role China had to play in its relations with the Soviet Union. As they would explain later, Mao and his comrades felt a deep sense of inequality in their dealings with the Soviets, and particularly with Stalin.[68] To make Beijing a real equal partner with Moscow was the constant aim of Mao and his fellow Beijing leaders. After Stalin's death, as we shall see, Beijing's pursuit of an elusive "equality" would cause friction with the new Soviet leadership.[69]

Related to the discomfort over "inequality" were the potential tensions between Moscow's dominance in the international Communist movement and Beijing's aspirations for recognition of its experience as a central part of the "world revolution." Such international recognition would have a positive effect on Mao's plans for the Chinese Revolution. When Stalin was alive, Mao and his comrades had to respect his authority and yield to his reputation; with Stalin gone, Mao became increasingly reluctant to acknowledge the authority of his much younger and, in his eyes, less sophisticated successor, Nikita Khrushchev.

One outstanding example of the problems existing between Beijing and Moscow during this time could be found in Mao's management of the Gao Gang affair. Gao was a CCP Politburo member and the vice chairman of the PRC Central Government. Mao and other Politburo members believed Gao had been close to Moscow since his days as the CCP leader in the Northeast. Beginning in December 1953, Gao became the target of a series of escalating attacks within the CCP leadership. He was labeled a "conspirator who intended to split the Party" and was reported to have committed suicide in August 1954.

It is now believed that Gao Gang's purge was the result of a long-standing conflict between him and other top CCP leaders, especially Liu Shaoqi and Zhou Enlai, and probably was not directly related to his presumed close ties with the Soviets.[70] However, the timing of the purge was important and revealing. Although the tensions between Gao Gang and Liu Shaoqi had existed for years, Mao did not decide to take Liu's side to criticize Gao until after Stalin's death. Despite Gao's close relations with the Soviets, the CCP did not keep Moscow abreast of what was happening to him. Gao died two weeks before Mao informed the Soviet leaders officially that Gao had committed "serious crimes in trying to split the Party" on September 1, 1954.[71] Ignoring Moscow's "right to know" (if not "right to lead") in this way would have been inconceivable if Stalin had been alive, or if genuine trust had existed between the Chinese and Soviet leaders.

Accumulated Tension

A turning point came in February 1956, when the CPSU held its Twentieth Congress. Several Chinese sources claim that the CCP delegation attending the congress, headed by Zhu De and Deng Xiaoping, was not invited to the closed-door session at which Khrushchev made his secret speech attacking Stalin and that the Soviets did not provide the Chinese with a copy of it. Both assertions seem doubtful based on recent Russian archival evidence.[72] The main reason for the subsequent anger of Mao and his fellow CCP leaders was, in any case, that no attempt had been made to consult them *in advance of* Khrushchev's fateful speech. They felt deeply offended by their Soviet comrades' way of handling this matter.[73]

From mid-March to early April 1956, Mao chaired several CCP Central Secretariat meetings to discuss Khrushchev's speech. At the first of such meetings, convened on the evening of March 17, Mao set the tone for the discussion, pointing out that Khrushchev's speech not only "exposed the problems" *(jie le gaizi)* but also "made a mess" *(tong le louzi).*[74] In accordance with these two fundamental points, Mao and his comrades discussed the messages contained in the Soviet leader's speech and reached several basic conclusions on how to assess them. They believed that Khrushchev's criticism of Stalin's mistakes had shattered the myth that Stalin and the Soviet Union had always been correct and would thus contribute to "correcting Stalin's mistakes as well as the erroneous tendency of treating other parties as inferiors within the international Communist movement."

Within this context, Mao Zedong summarized the mistakes Stalin had committed during the process of the Chinese Communist revolution. He mentioned that during the early stage of China's War of Resistance against Japan, Stalin supported Mao's chief rival Wang Ming's "rightist" policy of "putting the interests of the united front above the interests of the Communist Party," and that after the end of the War of Resistance, he forced the CCP not to fight against the Guomindang's anti-Communist civil war plot. The chairman also recalled that during his visit to the Soviet Union from December 1949 to February 1950, Stalin was reluctant to sign a new alliance treaty with the People's Republic. Not until after Chinese volunteers entered the Korean War, he observed, did Stalin begin to regard the CCP as a genuine Communist Party devoted to true proletarian internationalism.[75]

Despite Stalin's mistakes, the CCP chairman emphasized, he should still be regarded as a "great Marxist-Leninist revolutionary leader." Mao told his comrades that Stalin should be evaluated on historical merit:

> The realization of Communism is an extremely difficult task as there exists no example [for the Communists] to follow. . . . During the process of fulfilling this arduous task, it is impossible that mistakes would not be committed. This is because what we are doing is some-

thing that no one has tried in the past. I thus always believe [the Communists would] inevitably commit mistakes. The fact that Stalin has committed many mistakes should not be taken as a surprise. Comrade Khrushchev will commit mistakes. The Soviet Union will commit mistakes. And we will also commit mistakes.[76]

Therefore, Mao concluded, in making an overall assessment of Stalin as a historical figure, it was necessary to adopt a "seventy-thirty ratio" methodology – that is, acknowledge that achievements should account for 70 percent of Stalin's career and mistakes for only 30 percent.[77]

As a result of these discussions, Mao and his comrades decided to make public China's view on de-Stalinization, in order to clarify the confusion prompted by Khrushchev's speech. Considering that the Soviets had not formally published Khrushchev's speech and that de-Stalinization was still a developing process, the CCP leadership decided to promulgate the party's official view through the editorial board of *Renmin ribao* (People's Daily). On April 5, 1956, *Renmin ribao* published a lengthy editorial entitled "On the Historical Experience of Proletarian Dictatorship," arguing that Stalin, in spite of all his "serious mistakes," still needed to be respected as a "great Marxist-Leninist."[78]

Mao's dialectical or ambivalent initial response to de-Stalinization reflected his mixed feelings toward Stalin and the Soviet model of socialism. Since the early days of the People's Republic, the experience of Stalin's Soviet Union had been an example for the CCP's own designs for China's state-building, societal transformation, and economic reconstruction. While Mao and his comrades were unwilling to copy completely the "Stalin model," several basic elements of it – such as the tight central control of economic planning, the emphasis on developing heavy industry and defense industry, the control of the rural population through collectivization processes, and the top leader's authority over the party and the government – had penetrated into the CCP's own political philosophy.

In exploring a Chinese path of continuous revolution, Mao criticized the "Stalin model" in many respects, but he also found that the model offered him valuable grounds on which to establish basic understandings of several fundamental relationships with which he and his party had to deal in China.[79] Indeed, the Stalin model provided Mao and his comrades with an important reference for developing a "Chinese-style" socialist and Communist society. Thus Mao had reasons not to negate completely Stalin's historical role in the international Communist movement.

Mao's response to de-Stalinization also reflected China's changing political situation and his perception of it in the mid-1950s. In a sense, Mao's continuous revolution was his own great enterprise, which resulted from his views about how to transform China into a land of universal justice and equality. In 1955–1956 this great enterprise had reached a turning point, causing potential tensions between the CCP chairman and many of his prominent colleagues. On one hand, the introduction of the First Five-Year Plan, the successful completion of agricultural cooperativization in the countryside, and the advancement of the socialist transformation of industry and commerce in the cities combined to convince Mao that the continuous revolution should be elevated to a higher stage, one that would accelerate China's economic development and its development into a socialist and Communist society.[80]

On the other hand, many members of the CCP leadership – Zhou Enlai and Chen Yun in particular – believed it essential to maintain balanced economic development and societal transformation, and that "adventurism" (*maojin*) should be opposed.[81] Although this potential divergence between Mao and his comrades would not surface fully until late 1956 and 1957, the chairman already realized in early 1956 that China's Communist elite did not always comprehend the direction of his train of thought, let alone follow it.[82] As a result, he increasingly felt that one of the best guarantors of his continuous revolution was his own leadership role.

This, in turn, conditioned his response to de-Stalinization in two important respects. First, his criticism of the Soviet leader focused on the construction of a narrative about his resistance to Stalin's erroneous interference in the Chinese Revolution, enhancing the myth that he himself had been the representative of eternal correctness. Second, he adopted a unique approach toward the "cult of personality" issue. In his initial response toward de-Stalinization, Mao generally avoided sharp criticism of Stalin's personality cult. With the radicalization of China's political and social life in 1957–1958, he made it clear that he had no intention of opposing personality cults in general and his own personality cult in particular. It is not surprising that Ke Qingshi, a CCP Politburo member with close ties to the chairman, would openly argue that "it is all right to worship Chairman Mao to the extent of having a blind faith in him."[83] Mao agreed, saying that he favored distinguishing "correct" from "incorrect" personality cults.[84]

Mao's response to de-Stalinization also revealed his changing perception of his own position in the international Communist movement after Stalin's death. Indeed, now Mao, consciously or unconsciously, behaved with a stronger sense of superiority. On March 31, 1956, Mao Zedong had one of the first of his many long monologues with Pavel Iudin, the Soviet ambassador to China, in which he systematically expressed his overall view on criticism of Stalin. Again, Mao reviewed the history of Stalin's relations with China, emphasizing that the late Soviet leader had committed serious mistakes during all stages of the Chinese Revolution; in particular, Mao said, Stalin had failed to treat his Chinese comrades as equals. In a more general discussion about how to evaluate Stalin, though, the chairman argued that "the simple fact that the population of the Socialist Camp had grown from 200 million to 900 million speaks for itself" – that is, in an over-all sense, "Stalin, without doubt, is a great Marxist, a good and honest revolutionary."[85] In another long monologue-style conversation with Anastas Mikoyan on April 6, the CCP chairman again reviewed the "serious mistakes" committed by Stalin toward the Chinese Revolution and argued that in an over-all sense, "Stalin's achievements surpass his mistakes" and that it was thus necessary to have a "concrete analysis" as well as a "comprehensive evaluation" of the Stalin issue.[86]

Through these talks, Mao delivered several crucial messages to the Soviets. First, he conveyed to Khrushchev and his fellow Soviet leaders his idea of the proper tone for criticizing Stalin. Despite all of Stalin's "serious mistakes," the chairman advised his Soviet comrades that it was wrong to condemn him completely and that continuing to hold high his banner was in the interests of both the Soviet Union and the international Communist movement. Second, by criticizing Stalin's wrongdoings toward the Chinese Communist revolution, especially his failure to treat his Chinese comrades as "equals," Mao meant to remind Khrushchev and his fellow Soviet leaders that they should not repeat the same mistake and that a new pattern of Sino-Soviet relations, one based on the principle of "equality" (as Mao himself defined the term), should be established between Beijing and Moscow. Third, in a more fundamental sense, Mao revealed his new method of handling relations with Moscow; with Stalin's death, Mao felt that he should have a greater voice on questions concerning not only matters between Beijing and Moscow but also the fate of the entire international Communist movement. When Mao was discoursing on Stalin's mistakes and achievements, he made it clear that it was he, not the Soviet leaders, who now occupied the morally superior position to direct the course of the world proletarian revolution.

Within this context Mao endeavored during 1956 to make known his views on the Stalin issue to Communist leaders from other parts of the world. On June 28, 1956, in a conversation with the Romanian ambassador to China, Mao reiterated that Communists should not be surprised by Stalin's mistakes. "After all," the chairman said, "good things exist in the world together with bad things. This has been so since ancient times, and will continue to be so in the future. This is why we need to, and can, transform the world."[87] In September 1956, in a meeting with a Yugoslav Communist Union delegation attending the CCP's Eighth National Congress, Mao repeated his story about the "serious mistakes" Stalin had committed toward the Chinese Revolution, yet he also argued that achievements should be regarded as the main Soviet experience during Stalin's era.[88] On these occasions, indeed, the CCP chairman acted as if he had become the "new emperor" of the international Communist movement.

Consequently, by late 1956, China's relations with the Soviet Union experienced a significant change: Although in public Mao continued to maintain that Moscow remained the center of the socialist camp, he really believed that it was he who was more qualified to dictate the principles underlying relations between and among socialist countries. This seeming reversal of the relationship between Beijing and Moscow was demonstrated most clearly in the responses of the two countries to the Polish and Hungarian crises in late 1956.[89]

To Mao and his fellow CCP leaders, the crises emerging in Poland and Hungary were not of the same nature. While they believed that both crises had resulted from Soviet big-power chauvinism, they saw the crisis in Poland as basically anti-Soviet and the one in Hungary (after initial uncertainty) as essentially anti-Communist. Therefore, when Moscow informed Beijing that it planned to intervene militarily in Poland on October 19–20,[90] the CCP leadership held an urgent meeting to discuss the situation. They concluded that if the Soviets were to use military forces to solve the Polish issue, they would be intervening in Poland's internal affairs.[91]

Early on the morning of October 23, Mao summoned Ambassador Iudin to his quarters and requested that he inform Moscow urgently that China would severely protest any Soviet intervention in Poland's internal affairs.[92] From October 23 to 31 a high-ranking CCP delegation headed by Liu Shaoqi and Deng Xiaoping traveled to Moscow to consult with the Soviet leaders about the Polish (and, it turned out, Hungarian) crisis. Largely because of the pressure from the Chinese, reportedly, Khrushchev and his fellow Soviet leaders not only decided not to use force to solve the Polish question, but also agreed to issue (on October 30, 1956) a "Declaration on Developing and Enhancing the Friendship and Cooperation between the Soviet Union and other Socialist Countries," in which Moscow promised to follow a pattern of more equal exchanges with other Communist states and parties.[93] Mao and his comrades regarded this as Beijing's success.

In comparison, Mao's and the CCP leadership's attitude toward the Hungarian crisis was very different. Although they initially believed that the origins of the crisis lay in Moscow's failure to treat the Hungarians as equals, they were alarmed when anti-Communist riots began to spread all over Hungary. On October 30, after receiving Liu's and Deng's report from Moscow that the Soviet leaders were planning to withdraw their troops from Hungary, Mao chaired a meeting of top CCP leaders at which it was decided to oppose Moscow's abandonment of Hungary to reactionary forces.[94] Liu, following instructions from Beijing, met with Khrushchev and other Soviet leaders on the same day, informing them that it was the Chinese leaders' belief that Soviet withdrawal would be a betrayal of the Hungarian people and that it would put the Soviet leaders on the stand as "historical criminals."[95] The next day, it is reported, Khrushchev told Liu and other members of the Chinese delegation on their way to the airport that the Soviet leadership would use military force to suppress the "reactionary revolt" in Hungary.[96] Four days later the Soviet Red Army's attack on Budapest began.

Beijing's tough attitude toward the Hungarian crisis reflected Mao's persistent belief that "class struggle continued to exist in a socialist country."[97] The crisis, in turn, further strengthened Mao's determination to promote China's continuous revolution, especially in the fields of politics and ideology. In the wake of the Hungary crisis, Mao initiated in early 1957 the Hundred Flowers campaign to encourage intellectuals to help the CCP "correct its mistakes." But when some intellectuals criticized the party, an Anti-Rightist movement began to sweep across China, branding over 300,000 intellectuals (many of whom never said anything against the party) as "rightists," a label that would effectively shut their mouths and ruin their careers. As a result, Mao and the CCP established absolute control over China's "public opinion."[98]

Related to the Anti-Rightist movement, Mao started an equally important yet less well known (at least in the West) political offensive within the CCP leadership aimed at those of his comrades who had opposed "adventurism" in handling China's socialist construction in 1956 and early 1957. The main target was Zhou Enlai. Beginning in late summer 1957, Mao claimed that Zhou had committed serious mistakes in emphasizing the utmost importance of achieving balanced development in China's economic reconstruction. The chairman told his comrades that he favored "adventurism," even at the risk of breaking up the balance in economic development, as it would accelerate China's transformation into a socialist and Communist society. The chairman distrusted the premier to such an extent that he even considered removing Zhou and replacing him with Ke Qingshi.[99] The outcome of the Hungarian incident, in retrospect, complicated Chinese politics while at the same time pushing Mao's continuous revolution to enter a more radical stage.

Their perception of their contributions to the resolution of the Polish and Hungarian crises also strengthened the Chinese leaders' belief in their more prominent position in the international Communist movement, while at the same time justifying Beijing's critical attitude toward the seemingly less sophisticated Soviet leadership. On January 7–18, 1957, Zhou Enlai visited the Soviet Union, Poland, and Hungary.[100] In his report summarizing the visit, he commented extensively on the Soviet leadership's lack of sophistication in managing the complicated situation both within the Soviet Union and in Eastern Europe.[101] In several internal speeches, Mao Zedong discussed how the CCP diverged from the Soviet leaders, charging that Khrushchev and his comrades had abandoned not only "the sword of Stalin" but also, to a large extent, "the sword of Lenin."[102] In the wake of Khrushchev's de-Stalinization and the Polish and Hungarian crises, the potential tensions between Beijing and Moscow deepened.

Yet Sino-Soviet relations seemed to develop smoothly in 1956–1957. While the Soviet Union continued to provide China with extensive economic and military assistance, China offered open support for preserving the Soviet Union's leading position in the international Communist movement. In November 1957 Mao Zedong visited Moscow to attend celebrations for the fortieth anniversary of the October Revolution of 1917. At a meeting of leaders of Communist and workers' parties from socialist countries, Mao called on the socialist camp to recognize the Soviet Union's leadership role. On one occasion the CCP chairman used a metaphor to describe the relations between himself and Khrushchev, saying that the flower of Khrushchev was more beautiful than the flower of Mao Zedong.[103] Beneath this high-profile rhetoric, however, ran an undercurrent of disagreement and distrust. It was at the Moscow meeting that Mao emphasized that the Communists should not be frightened by the prospect of a nuclear war started by the imperialists but should realize that such a war, although carrying a high price, would bring the imperialist system to its final conclusion.[104]

These statements obviously worried Khrushchev and his fellow Soviet leaders. From Mao's perspective, Khrushchev's emphasis on the necessity and possibility of "peaceful coexistence" with Western imperialist countries was exceedingly dubious. Indeed, even Mao's endorsement of the Soviet Union's leading position in the international Communist movement could be understood as an indication of potential conflict – such an endorsement implied that Mao and revolutionary China now occupied a higher moral position than the Soviet Union. All of this meant that a storm was gathering between Beijing and Moscow.

From Tension to Crisis

The year 1958 was pivotal in the history of the People's Republic as it witnessed one of the most important episodes of Mao's continuous revolution: the Great Leap Forward. In January 1958 Mao chaired two meetings attended by central and provincial party leaders in Hangzhou and Nanning. At both meetings the chairman continued his criticism of the mistake of "opposing adventurism" committed by Zhou Enlai's State Council in previous years, labeling it "a mistake concerning principles, which has damaged the revolutionary vigor of 600 million [Chinese] people." He further warned Zhou that he had reached the verge of becoming a rightist – the distance, the chairman said, was "only 50 meters."[105] Facing Mao's repeated criticism, Zhou Enlai acknowledged at the Nanning conference that "as far as the mistake of 'opposing adventurism' is concerned, I should take the main responsibility."[106]

On January 31 Mao Zedong summarized the discussions at the two conferences in an important document entitled "Sixty Articles on Work Methods"; in it he attempted to be as explicit as the political situation allowed in defining the mission of his continuous revolution:

> Continuing revolution. Our revolutions come one after another. The seizure of political power in the whole county in 1949 was soon followed by the antifeudal land reform. As soon as the land reform was completed, the agricultural cooperativization followed. Then the socialist transformation of private-owned industry and commerce and handicraft occurred. The three socialist transformations, that is, the socialist revolution in the field of the ownership of means of production, will be completed by 1958, and will be followed by the socialist revolution on the political and ideological fronts. . . . [We are] now preparing to make a revolution in the technological field, so that [we may] overtake Britain in fifteen or more years.[107]

In this text Mao set up the overall purpose of the Great Leap Forward, the campaign that was to sweep across China's cities and countryside a few months later.

From March 8 to 26 Mao chaired another Central Committee working conference, in Chengdu, and further escalated his criticism of "opposing adventurism." The chairman claimed that "adventurism is a Marxist way and 'opposing adventurism' is an anti-Marxist way." He announced that "we shall continue to commit to adventurism in the future." On March 25 Zhou Enlai, on the verge of political defeat, made a more comprehensive self-criticism.[108] In addition to dealing with his own domestic mistakes, Zhou devoted a large portion of the self-criticism to his "conservative and rightist tendency" in handling the foreign relations of the People's Republic in previous years. He admitted that the Foreign Ministry's work under his direction had neglected the necessary struggle in dealing with nationalist countries, had maintained a kind of wishful thinking concerning imperialism (especially toward Japan and the United States), and had failed to conduct necessary criticism of the revisionist policies of other socialist countries. He particularly mentioned that while it was plausible to learn from the experience of the Soviet Union, it was a mistake to copy it completely.[109]

Zhou's self-criticism clearly showed that profound interconnections existed between the domestic and international aspects of Chinese politics in the late 1950s. Following Mao's ideas, the CCP leadership at the Chengdu conference decided to revise radically China's economic development plans, so that "it would catch the right opportunity to surpass Britain in a period even shorter than fifteen years."[110] The Great Leap Forward followed as a consequence of the party's implementation of these aims.

It was at this crucial juncture of Mao's continuous revolution that the potential tensions between China and the Soviet Union became an inner Chinese political problem. First there was Moscow's suggestion of establishing communication systems for the Soviet navy in China. In November 1957, during the visit of China's defense minister, Peng Dehuai, to the Soviet Union, the two sides reached an agreement that they would cooperate closely on developing naval and air forces in the East Asia.[111] In a letter dated April 18, 1958, Soviet Defense Minister Rodion Malinovskii proposed to Peng that in order to communicate with the Soviet Union's submarines in the Pacific area, the Soviet high command and the Chinese Ministry of Defense cooperate over a four-year period in constructing a long-wave radio transmission center and a long-wave radio receiving station specially designed for long-distance communication. The Soviet Union would cover 70 percent of the construction costs.[112] Mao came to consider these plans as a threat to China's sovereignty and integrity. He decided to accept building the stations but to pay all the expenses and to have exclusive ownership. Following Mao's instructions, Peng responded to Malinovskii on June 12, informing him that the Chinese government "agrees to the construction of high-power long-wave radio stations, and welcomes the technological assistance from the Soviet Union." However, Peng emphasized that "China will cover all expenses, and the stations will be jointly used by China and the Soviet Union after the completion of their construction." Peng proposed that the two governments sign a formal agreement along these lines.[113]

On July 11 the Soviet Union provided a draft agreement for the construction of the radio stations. Probably without understanding the nature of Beijing's request for exclusive ownership, the Soviets still insisted that the stations should be jointly constructed and managed by China and the Soviet Union. The Chinese responded with several suggestions for revision: China would take the responsibility for constructing the stations and they would belong to China; China would purchase the equipment it was unable to produce from the Soviet Union and would invite Soviet experts to help construct the station; and after the station's completion, it would be used jointly by China and the Soviet Union.[114]

Before the radio station issue was settled, a second dispute in the military field emerged, this one concerning the establishment of a joint Soviet-Chinese submarine flotilla. Already in late 1957, Soviet military and naval advisers in China had indicated to the Chinese that they could purchase new naval equipment from the Soviet Union. On June 28, 1958, Zhou Enlai wrote to Khrushchev, requesting that the Soviet Union provide technological assistance for China's naval buildup, especially the designs for new-type submarines.[115]

On July 21 Iudin called on Mao Zedong. Speaking on behalf of Khrushchev, Iudin said that the geography of the Soviet Union made it difficult for the Soviet navy to take full advantage of the new submarines. Because China had long coastlines and good natural harbors, the Soviets proposed that China and the Soviet Union establish a joint submarine flotilla. Mao Zedong told the ambassador that "first, we should make clear the guiding principle. [Do you mean that] we should create [the fleet] with your assistance? Or [do you mean] that we should jointly create [the fleet], otherwise you will not offer any assistance?" Mao emphasized that he was not interested in creating a Sino-Soviet "military cooperative."[116]

The next day Mao summoned Iudin to his quarters for a lengthy and very emotional conversation. Mao surveyed the history of the relations between the CCP and the Soviet Union, criticizing the fact that the Soviets had always treated their Chinese comrades from a stand of "big power chauvinism." He then repeatedly emphasized that the essence of the Soviet proposals of establishing long-wave radio stations and a joint submarine flotilla lay in Moscow's attempt to control China. The chairman angrily claimed that "you may accuse me of being a nationalist or another Tito, but my counter argument is that you have extended Russian nationalism to China's coast." Throughout the talk, Iudin seemed like the head of a foreign (or "barbarian") tribute mission who was receiving the teachings of the Chinese "son of heaven." As with many of Mao's meetings with Iudin, the chairman presented a near monologue, and the Soviet ambassador had few opportunities to respond. When the conversation was approaching its end, Mao told Iudin to "report all my comments to Comrade Khrushchev," emphasizing that "you must tell him exactly what I have said without any polishing."[117]

Alarmed by Iudin's report, Khrushchev traveled to Beijing from July 31 to August 3, meeting four times with Mao and other Chinese leaders. At the first meeting Khrushchev endeavored to explain to Mao that the Soviets had no intention of controlling China. On the radio station issue, he emphasized that it was the "personal opinion" of Malinovskii, rather than the decision of the Central Committee of the Communist Party of the Soviet Union (CPSU), to construct "jointly" the long-wave station. He agreed that the Soviet Union would provide financial and technical support for establishing the station but would let the Chinese own it. On the joint fleet issue, Khrushchev explained that Iudin might not have accurately conveyed the message from Moscow, emphasizing that the Soviets were more than willing to treat their Chinese comrades as equals. Mao Zedong, however, would not easily buy Khrushchev's explanations, claiming that "big-power chauvinism" did exist in the Soviet attitude toward China.[118] After four days' intensive meetings, on August 3 Malinovskii and Peng, representing the Soviet and Chinese governments, signed an agreement on the construction of long-wave stations and the dispatch of Soviet experts to China.[119] Yet the psychological gap between the Chinese and Soviet leaders, especially between Mao and Khrushchev, persisted.[120] Mao would later recall that "the overturning of [our relations with] the Soviet Union occurred in 1958, that was because they wanted to control China militarily."[121]

Mao's harsh reaction to these two issues reflected his increasing sensitivity toward questions concerning China's sovereignty and equal status vis-à-vis the Soviet Union. Underlying this sensitivity, though, was a strong "victim mentality" that characterized Chinese revolutionary nationalism during modern times. This mentality had been informed by the conviction that the political incursion, economic exploitation, and military aggression of foreign imperialist countries had undermined the historical glory of Chinese civilization and humiliated the country. Consequently, it became natural for the Chinese Communists, in their efforts to end China's humiliating modern experiences, to suspect the behavior of *any* foreign country as being driven by ulterior, or even evil, intentions. Although the Soviet Union was a Communist country, when Mao claimed that Khrushchev and his Kremlin colleagues intended to control China, he apparently had equated them with the leaders of Western imperialism.

That the explosion of Mao's suspicion and distrust of Soviet "chauvinist intentions" toward China came in the summer of 1958, rather than earlier, should be understood in the context of the chairman's criticism of "opposing adventurism" within the CCP leadership. Indeed, reading the transcripts of Mao's talks with Iudin and Khrushchev, one gets an impression that was quite similar to many of the chairman's inner-party speeches throughout late 1957 and early 1958. In both circumstances, Mao believed that he had absolute command of the truth; and, in these monologues, the chairman became accustomed to teaching others in critical, often passionate, terms. Indeed, when Mao was turning his own revolutionary emotion into the dynamics for the Great Leap Forward, it is not surprising that he had the same offensive-oriented mood in dealing with his Soviet comrades.

When Khrushchev arrived in China at the end of July 1958, the leaders in Beijing already had decided to begin large-scale shelling of the GMD-controlled Jinmen (Quemoy) island off the coast of Fujian Province.[122] In determining the timing of the shelling, the chairman hoped that it would not only confront international imperialism and call attention to the issue of Taiwan being part of the People's Republic but also help stimulate the rising tide of the Great Leap. While the shelling would be accompanied by an anti-Jiang Jieshi (Chiang Kaishek) and anti-U.S. campaign – with "we must liberate Taiwan" as its central slogan – Mao did not have an established plan to invade Taiwan or to involve China in a direct military confrontation with the United States.[123] What he needed was a sustained and controllable conflict, one that would enhance popular support for his radical transformation of China's polity, economy, and society. In the chairman's own words, spoken at the peak of the Taiwan Straits crisis, "besides its disadvantageous side, a tense [international] situation could mobilize the population, could particularly mobilize the backward people, could mobilize the people in the middle, and could therefore promote the Great Leap Forward in economic construction."[124]

Mao did not, however, inform Khrushchev of his tactical plans while meeting him in Beijing.[125] When the PLA began an intensive artillery bombardment of the island on August 23, the Soviet leaders were at a loss to interpret China's aims. In the following two months, several hundred thousand artillery shells exploded on Jinmen and in the waters around it. The Eisenhower administration, in accordance with its obligations under the 1954 U.S.-Taiwan defense treaty, reinforced U.S. naval units in East Asia and used U.S. naval vessels to help the Nationalists protect Jinmen's supply lines.

The leaders of the Soviet Union, fearing the possible consequences of Beijing's actions, sent Deputy Foreign Minister Andrei Gromyko on a secret visit to Beijing in early September to inquire about China's reasons for shelling Jinmen. At this time the Chinese leaders said that the shelling was designed to attract the world's attention to the Taiwan question and to divert American strength from other parts of the world (especially the Middle East), but not as a step leading to the invasion of Taiwan, let alone to provoke a direct confrontation with the United States.[126] Only after receiving these explanations from Beijing did the Soviet government issue a statement on September 8 to show its solidarity with the Chinese. However, a real fissure between Beijing and Moscow had already opened.[127]

With the rapid development of the Great Leap Forward in China, this gap widened further. In the fall and winter of 1958, tens of thousands of people's communes, which, with their free supply system, were supposed to form the basic units of a Communist society, emerged in China's countryside and cities. In the meantime, millions of ordinary Chinese were mobilized to produce steel from small backyard furnaces in order to double the nation's steel production in one year's time. Khrushchev and his comrades were confused by what was happening in China. While thousands of Soviet advisors there issued warnings about the possible negative economic consequences of the Great Leap, the officially controlled Soviet media avoided making any public reference to the Chinese plans. During a meeting with U.S. Senator Hubert Humphrey, Khrushchev even dismissed the people's communes as "reactionary."[128] The Soviet reaction offended Mao deeply, intensifying his belief in the Soviet leaders' lack of political wisdom and revolutionary vigor, Khrushchev in particular.[129] The foundation of the Sino-Soviet alliance had been severely damaged.

Further Deepening of the Crisis

In 1959 the relations between Moscow and Beijing reached a low point. The negative effects of the Great Leap Forward began to be felt in Chinese economy. From the spring of 1959, the rural population increasingly resisted the slogan of a "continuous leap forward." China's industrial production began to decrease.[130] What made the situation more complicated for Beijing was that in March, an anti-Chinese and anti-Communist rebellion erupted in Tibet. Although the rebellion itself was quickly suppressed, it caused new tensions between China and India, countries that, since the early 1950s, had maintained friendly relations. International pressure on Beijing seemed to strengthen.[131]

With Mao Zedong's continuous revolution facing its most serious challenge since the establishment of the People's Republic, Khrushchev and the other Soviet leaders seemed willing to add to Beijing's misfortune. On June 20 the CPSU informed the CCP that because of the Soviet-U.S. negotiations at Geneva to ban nuclear weapon tests, it was difficult for Moscow to provide China with assistance on nuclear technology. If the Western countries learned that the Soviet Union had agreed to share its nuclear secrets with China, the Soviet leaders explained, "it is possible that the efforts by socialist countries to strive for peace and the relaxation of international tensions would be jeopardized." The Soviets thus told the Chinese that they would no longer honor some of their obligations set up in the agreement signed with the Chinese on October 15, 1957, and would not provide Beijing with atomic bomb prototypes and technical data for producing the bomb.[132] Mao Zedong regarded this as an indication of Moscow's attempt to put pressure on the CCP and especially on himself.[133] Consequently, relations between Beijing and Moscow worsened.

The escalating crisis in the Sino-Soviet alliance coincided with the intensification of tensions within the CCP leadership in the wake of the Great Leap. In July 1959 top CCP leaders gathered at Lushan to discuss the consequences of the Great Leap Forward and strategies to deal with them. Peng Dehuai, who had just returned from a visit to the Soviet Union and East European countries, wrote to Mao on July 14 to propose that the party leadership should "overcome petit bourgeois enthusiasm" and carefully evaluate the "losses and achievements" of the Great Leap.[134] The chairman, sensing that Peng's letter might pose a serious threat to both his continuous revolution programs and his position as China's indisputable leader, responded fiercely. He claimed that Peng had long been a careerist and that his "total negation" of the Great Leap aimed to overturn the party's general line for socialist reconstruction and to overthrow the party's top leadership. Using his authority and power, the chairman converted the Lushan conference into a denunciation of Peng's "antiparty plot." Peng, in turn, lost his position as China's defense minister after the conference.[135] The Lushan conference represented a crucial step toward Mao's initiation of the Great Proletarian Cultural Revolution.

It is noticeable that when Peng Dehuai became the main target of criticism and denunciation during and after this conference, many CCP leaders connected the defense minister's letter to Mao to Peng's visit to the Soviet Union and his meetings with Khrushchev. Those who followed Mao repeatedly asked whether Peng Dehuai's "intentional attack" against Mao and the party had an "international background," meaning the support of the Soviets. Although Peng categorically denied any such connections, Mao and other party leaders, including Liu Shaoqi – who himself would later be labeled "China's Khrushchev" – persistently claimed that at Lushan, Peng acted as a "Soviet agent."[136]

The divergence between China and the Soviet Union became public for the first time in August 1959, when a border conflict occurred between China and India. In spite of China having maintained friendly relations with India throughout the 1950s, New Delhi's acceptance of the Tibetan Dalai Lama's exile government in spring 1959 caused severe tension between the two countries. On September 9 the Soviet media issued a statement expressing "regret" at the conflict between India and China. To Mao and his comrades, this statement, which failed to stand clearly on Beijing's side, indicated that Moscow "had virtually adopted a policy to support India's position."[137]

On September 30, Khrushchev, after extensive conversations with President Eisenhower in the United States, arrived in Beijing to participate in celebrations of the People's Republic's tenth anniversary. The same evening he made a forty-minute speech at the state banquet held by Chinese leaders at the newly completed Great Hall of the People. Without paying any attention to the mood of his Chinese hosts, Khrushchev emphasized the "Camp David" spirit, which, according to him, would contribute to the relaxation of tensions between East and West. In Mao's eyes this was a real offense – how could the Soviet leader bring such a topic to an occasion that was supposed to be devoted to celebrating the victory of the Chinese Revolution? When Khrushchev mentioned that "it is unwise to use military means to test the stability of the capitalist system," Mao believed that the Soviet leader meant to insult him and revolutionary China.[138]

It was against this background that Khrushchev and other members of the Soviet delegation had an important meeting with Mao and other Chinese leaders on October 2.[139] This meeting was supposed to offer an opportunity for Chinese and Soviet leaders to find ways to remedy the divergence between them, but it quickly degenerated into vitriolic debates. At the beginning of the meeting, Khrushchev delivered a message from President Eisenhower to the Chinese leaders, which requested that China release two American pilots who had been detained by the Chinese. Mao Zedong immediately denied the request, telling Khrushchev that these Americans would be released eventually but certainly not immediately after the Soviet leader's visit.

The meeting then turned to the Taiwan issue. Khrushchev criticized the Chinese for having adopted a policy of adventurism in handling the Taiwan crisis in 1958 and was particularly upset with Beijing's failure to inform Moscow of its intentions in shelling Jinmen. To show Mao and his fellow Chinese leaders that it was necessary to make compromises with the enemy, Khrushchev lectured about history, quoting Lenin's establishment of the Far Eastern Republic as a buffer between Soviet Russia and Japan as an example. The Chinese leaders angrily rebutted Khrushchev's claims, claiming that not to use force in Taiwan had been an American position and that Khrushchev wanted to acquiesce to Washington's plot of creating "two Chinas."[140]

Khrushchev then shifted the conversation to Beijing's policy toward India. He declared that Beijing was wrong in trying to solve the disputes with New Delhi by military means. He also challenged the sovereignty claim of the People's Republic over certain areas along the unsettled Chinese-Indian border, calling Beijing unwise to be competing with India over "a few square kilometers of barren land." These statements angered the Chinese. Zhou Enlai ridiculed Khrushchev for his "inability to tell right from wrong." Marshal Chen Yi, China's foreign minister, angrily reproached Khrushchev, saying that while it was necessary for socialist countries to unite with nationalist countries, it was a mistake for the former to yield to the latter's wrongdoings. Chen in particular singled out the Soviet statement of September 9 concerning the Chinese-Indian border conflict as "a huge mistake."[141]

At this point the meeting deteriorated into complete disorder. Leaders of both sides attacked their alliance partners. On one occasion Khrushchev complained that "Mao Zedong sternly criticized our Party face to face with Comrade Iudin last year, and we tolerated it, but we will not tolerate [it] now." The meeting ended in discord.[142]

During Khrushchev's stay in Beijing he also advised Mao that the CCP's criticism of Peng Dehuai was groundless, and he urged Mao to restore Peng to his former position. This advice of course did Peng no good. Instead, Mao was further convinced that Peng's "antiparty plot" was instigated by the Soviets. In an inner-party speech two months later, Mao identified Peng's action at Lushan as "a coup attempt supported by [his Soviet] friends."[143] The CCP Central Committee passed formal decisions to claim that Peng's antiparty activities were related to a foreign "plot" to overthrow the party leadership headed by Mao Zedong.[144]

Khrushchev left China on October 4, 1959. On his way back to Moscow he stopped at Vladivostok and made a public speech there on October 6. He talked about his recent visits to the United States and China, and praised the "brotherly solidarity" between Moscow and Beijing as a cornerstone for world peace. It was difficult at the time for a general audience to detect that serious discord had developed between Chinese and Soviet leaders.[145] However, Mao and his comrades in Beijing read the message contained in the speech carefully and found that Khrushchev had claimed that "it was unwise to behave like a bellicose cock and to long for war." The Chinese leaders believed that Khrushchev was preparing to go public in his criticism of them.[146] The CCP chairman now saw little chance to avoid a serious confrontation with the "revisionists" in Moscow.

Breakdown

As the 1960s began, a growing chasm had emerged between Beijing and Moscow. The prospect of future Sino-Soviet relations was further damaged by Khrushchev's belief that putting more pressure on the Chinese would enable him to take advantage of the potential differences between Mao and his comrades, forcing Mao to change his course of action. Without understanding Mao's confrontational, challenge-oriented character, Khrushchev, in July 1960, just as China was being deeply affected by the disastrous aftermath of the Great Leap Forward, recalled all Soviet experts from China and drastically reduced material and military aid to Beijing.[147]

Moscow's decision to recall the Soviet experts weakened China's ability to deal with the extraordinary difficulties brought on by the Great Leap. Still, Khrushchev's order was not necessarily unwelcome from Mao's perspective. The disastrous consequences of the Great Leap Forward had shaken the myth of Mao's infallibility, weakening for the first time the chairman's leadership of the party and state. Beginning in 1960 the CCP leadership – with Mao by his own will relegated to the "second line" – adopted a series of moderate and flexible domestic policies designed for economic recovery and social stability. Mao could clearly sense that both his grand enterprise – the continuous revolution – and his own position as leader were at stake.

Mao used the recall of Soviet experts as a convenient excuse to make the Soviets the scapegoat for the Great Leap Forward's disastrous consequences.

Moreover, in the conflict with the Soviets, the chairman found one of the long-term weapons he badly needed to enhance the much-weakened momentum of his continuous revolution. In the early 1960s Mao repeatedly used the conflict with Moscow to claim that his struggle for true communism was also a struggle for China's national integrity. As far as Chinese politics is concerned, the growing confrontation with Moscow made it more difficult for those of Mao's comrades who disagreed with some of the chairman's radical ideas to challenge him.[148]

There is a striking similarity between the new patterns that emerged in China's domestic politics and in external relations in the early and mid-1960s. On one hand, Mao, especially after 1962, repeatedly argued that in order to avert a Soviet-style "capitalist restoration," it was necessary for the Chinese party and people "never to forget class struggle," pushing the whole country toward another high wave of continuous revolution. On the other hand, Mao personally initiated the great polemic debate between the Chinese and Soviet parties, claiming that the Soviet party and state had fallen into the "revisionist" abyss and that it had become the duty of the Chinese party and the Chinese people to hold high the banner of true socialism and communism.[149]

Mao's wrecking of the Sino-Soviet relationship did not happen without challenge within the CCP leadership. In February 1962 Wang Jiaxiang, head of the CCP's International Liaison Department, submitted to the party's top leadership a report on China's international polices. He argued that the strategic goal of China's foreign policy should be the maintenance of world peace, so that it would be able to focus on socialist construction at home. He particularly emphasized that "it is necessary [for China] to carry out a foreign policy aimed at easing international tension, and not exacerbate [the tension]."[150]

Wang's views received the consent (if not the active support) of several party leaders, including Liu Shaoqi and Deng Xiaoping. Mao, understandably, was upset. The CCP chairman characterized Wang's ideas as an attempt to be conciliatory toward imperialists, revisionists, and international reactionaries, while at the same time reducing support to those countries and peoples fighting against the imperialists. Mao stressed that the policy of "three reconciliations and one reduction" came at a time when some leading CCP members (as it would turn out, he had Liu and Deng in mind) had been frightened by the international reactionaries and were inclined to adopt a "pro-revisionist" policy line at home. He emphasized that his policy, by contrast, was to fight against the imperialists, revisionists, and reactionaries in all countries and, at the same time, to promote revolutionary developments at home and abroad.[151] Those of Mao's colleagues who might have doubts about these ideas of the chairman's yielded to his argument without a fight.

With the continuous radicalization of China's political and social life, the relationship between Beijing and Moscow rapidly worsened. Even Khrushchev's fall from power in October 1964 could not turn around the trend of deteriorating relations. In the meantime, Mao linked his widespread domestic purges during the Cultural Revolution to the "antirevisionist" and "anti–social-imperialist" struggles on the international scene, labeling Liu Shaoqi, the major target of his purge during the Cultural Revolution, "China's Khrushchev." Consequently, until the last days of his life, Mao made the rhetoric of antirevisionism (after 1969, anti–social-imperialism) central slogans in mobilizing China's people to sustain his continuous revolution. The Soviet Union, accordingly, became China's worst enemy. Not until the mid- and late 1980s, when Mao's continuous revolution had long been abandoned in China, would Beijing and Moscow move toward normal state relations.

Notes

1. Chinese archives are still largely closed to scholars. Yet in recent years many valuable sources related to Sino-Soviet relations have appeared, including memoirs, selected party documents and leaders' works, and official and semiofficial histories based on archival sources. Among these sources, the most important ones include *Jianguo yilai Mao Zedong wengao* [Mao Zedong's manuscripts since the formation of the People's Republic], 11 vols. covering 1949 to 1965 (Beijing: Zhongyang wenxian, 1987–95); *Mao Zedong waijiao wenxuan* [Selected diplomatic papers of Mao Zedong] (Beijing: Zhongyang wenxian, 1994); *Zhou Enlai Waijiao wenxuan* [Selected diplomatic papers of Zhou Enlai] (Beijing: Zhongyang wenxian, 1990); Shi Zhe, *Zai lishi jüren shenbian* [Together with historical giants] (Beijing: Zhongyang wenxian, 1992); Shi Zhe, *Feng yu gu: Shi Zhe huiyilu* [High peak and deep valley: Shi Zhe's memoirs] (Beijing: Hongqi, 1992); Liu Xiao, *Chushi sulian banian* [Eight years as ambassador to the Soviet Union] (Beijing: Zhonggong dangshi ziliao, 1986); Pei Jianzhang, *Zhonghua renmin gongheguo waijiaoshi, 1949–1956* [A diplomatic history of the People's Republic of China, 1949–1956] (Beijing: Shijie zhishi, 1994); Han Nianlong et al., *Dangdai zhongguo waijiao* [Contemporary Chinese diplomacy] (Beijing: Zhongguo shehui kexue, 1987). For English translations of key documents for the period 1944 to 1950, see Shuguang Zhang and Chen Jian, eds., *Chinese Communist Foreign Policy and the Cold War in Asia: New Documentary Evidence* (Chicago: Imprint Publications, 1996).

2. Many of these documents have been translated into English and are available in the *Cold War International History (CWIHP) Bulletin* published by the Cold War International History Project at the Woodrow Wilson International Center for Scholars, Washington, D.C.

3. Mao Zedong, "On the People's Democratic Dictatorship," *Mao Zedong xuanji* [Selected works of Mao Zedong] (Beijing: Renmin, 1992), vol. 4, 1477.

4. See, for example, Lu Dingyi, "Explanations of Several Basic Problems Concerning the Postwar International Situation," *Jiefang ribao* [Liberation daily], January 4, 1947; Liu Shaoqi, "On Internationalism and Nationalism," *Renmin ribao* [People's daily], November 7, 1948.

5. Mao Zedong, "The Current Situation and the Party's Tasks in 1949," January 8, 1949; Mao Zedong, "Plans to March to the Whole Country," May 23, 1949; both in *Mao Zedong junshi wenxuan* [Selected military papers of Mao Zedong], (Beijing: Jiexangjun, 1981), 328, 338.

6. Han Nianlong et al., *Dangdai Zhongguo waijiao*, 4.

7. In the 1940s, Mao Zedong divided the Chinese Communist revolution into two stages: the stage of new democratic revolution and the stage of socialist revolution. During the first stage, the revolution had to overthrow the rule of the bureaucratic-capitalist class, wipe out foreign influence, eliminate remnants of feudal tradition, and establish a Communist-led regime. The second stage of the revolution would transform China's state and society, laying the foundation of China's transition into a socialist and later Communist society. In 1949, he was thinking about leading the revolution into its higher second stage. See Mao Zedong, "The Chinese Revolution and the Chinese Communist Party," and "On New Democracy," *Mao Zedong xuanji* [Selected works of Mao Zedong], (Beijing: Renmin, 1965), vol. 2, 626–47, 656–72; Mao, "On People's Democratic Dictatorship," ibid., vol. 4, 1473–86.

8. See, for example, Mao Zedong, "Report to the Second Plenary Session of the Seventh Central Committee," *Mao Zedong xuanji*, vol. 4, 1439–40; Zhou Enlai, "Report on Problems Concerning Peace Talks," *Zhou Enlai xuanji* [Selected works of Zhou Enlai] (Beijing: Renmin, 1984), vol. 1, 318.

9. Mao Zedong, "Report to the Second Plenary Session of the Seventh Central Committee," *Mao Zedong xuanji*, vol. 4, 1425–6.

10. See Zhou Enlai, "Our Diplomatic Policies and Tasks," *Zhou Enlai waijiao wenxuan*, 48–51; see also Han Nianlong et al., *Dangdai Zhongguo waijiao*, 4–5; Pei Jianzhang, *Zhonghua Renmin Gongheguo waijiaoshi*, 2–4.

11. Zhang Baijia, "The Shaping of New China's Diplomacy," *Chinese Historians* 13–14 (1994): 62.

12. Andrei Ledovsky, "Mikoyan's Secret Mission to China in January and February 1949," *Far Eastern Affairs* (Moscow) 2 (1995): 72–94, esp. 75–7; Shi Zhe, *Zai lishi juren shenbian,* 370–2.

13. See Shi Zhe (trans. Chen Jian), "With Mao and Stalin: The Reminiscences of a Chinese Interpreter," *Chinese Historians* 5, no. 1 (Spring 1992): 45–56. For a Soviet account of the visit, see Ledovsky, "Mikoyan's Secret Mission," 72–94. It is interesting and important to note that the Chinese and Soviet accounts of this visit are highly compatible.

14. See S. Tikhvinsky, "The Zhou Enlai 'Demarche' and the CCP's Informal Negotiations with the Americans in June 1949," *Problemy Dalnego Vostoka* 3 (1994).

15. For a more detailed account of Liu's visit to the Soviet Union, see Shi Zhe (trans. Chen Jian), "With Mao and Stalin: The Reminiscences of Mao's Interpreter, Part II: Liu Shaoqi in Moscow," *Chinese Historians* 6, no. 1 (Spring 1993): 67–90; Zhu Yuanshi, "Liu Shaoqi's Secret Visit to the Soviet Union in 1949," *Dangde wenxian* 3 (1991): 74–81.

16. Shi Zhe, *Zai lishi jüren shenbian,* 436. In the Soviet minutes of this conversation, however, this statement was not included. See "Conversation between Stalin and Mao, Moscow, December 16, 1949," *CWIHP Bulletin* 6–7 (Winter 1995/1996): 5–7. We believe that a possible answer to this discrepancy could lie in the cultural differences between Chinese and Soviet interpreters. For a discussion, see Chen Jian, "Comparing Russian and Chinese Sources: A New Point of Departure for Cold War History," ibid., 21.

17. Telegram, Mao Zedong to Liu Shaoqi, December 18, 1949, in Zhang Shuguang and Chen Jian, eds., *Chinese Communist Foreign Policy and the Cold War in Asia,* doc. no. 2.41; conversation between Stalin and Mao, Moscow, December 16, 1949, *CWIHP Bulletin* 6–7 (Winter 1995/1996): 5–7.

18. Telegrams, Mao Zedong to the CCP CC, January 2, 3, and 5, 1950, in Zhang and Chen, eds., *Chinese Communist Foreign Policy and the Cold War in Asia,* doc. nos. 2.45 and 2.46. See also "More on Mao in Moscow," *CWIHP Bulletin* 8–9 (Winter 1996/1997): 223–36.

19. For plausible discussions of the signing of the Sino-Soviet alliance, see Sergei

Goncharov, John W. Lewis, and Xue Litai, *Uncertain Partners: Stalin, Mao and the Korean War* (Stanford, Calif.: Stanford University Press, 1993), chap. 4 (which we believe is the best chapter of the book); Pei Jianzhang, *Zhonghua renmin gongheguo waijiaoshi,* 16–27.

20. During Mao's visit to the Soviet Union, China ordered 586 planes, including 280 fighters, 198 bombers, and 108 trainers and other planes. From February 16 to March 5, 1950, a mixed Soviet air defense division, following the request of the PRC government, moved into Shanghai, Nanjing, and Xuzhou, to take responsibility for the air defense of these areas. From March 13 to May 11 this Soviet division shot down 5 GMD planes in the Shanghai area, greatly strengthening Shanghai's air defense system. Han Huanzhi and Tan Jinjiao, *Dangdai Zhongguo jundui de junshi gongzuo* [Military affairs of contemporary Chinese army] (Beijing: Jiexangjun, 1989), vol. 2, 161; Wang Dinglie, *Dangdai Zhongguo kongjun* [Contemporary Chinese air force] (Beijing: Jiexangjun,1989), 78–9, 110.

21. Mao Zedong's address to the Sixth Session of the Central People's Government Council, April 11, 1950, *Jianguo yilai Mao Zedong wengao,* vol. 1, p. 291.

22. Mao later would repeatedly recall that during his meetings with Stalin from December 1949 to February 1950, Stalin did not trust him and failed to treat him equally. See, for example, his statements to the Soviet ambassador in Beijing in 1956 and 1958 in *CWIHP Bulletin* 6–7 (Winter 1995/1996): especially 155–6, 165–6.

23. We now know that in 1949 and early 1950, Kim Il Sung made extensive efforts to convince Stalin that there existed a real revolutionary situation on the Korean peninsula, so that he would get Stalin's support for his plans to unify Korea by military means. See, for example, Kathryn Weathersby, "Korea, 1949–1950: To Attack, or Not to Attack? Stalin, Kim Il Sung, and the Prelude to War," *CWIHP Bulletin* 5 (Spring 1995): 1, 2–9.

24. For a more detailed discussion, see Goncharov et al., *Uncertain Partners,* chap. 5.

25. For Stalin's discussions with Kim Il Sung, see Weathersby, "Korea, 1949–1950"; see also "New Russian Documents on the Korean War," trans. Kathryn Weathersby, *CWIHP Bulletin* 6–7 (Winter 1995/1996): 36–9.

26. Mao Zedong, however, did not believe that the Americans would intervene directly in a revolutionary civil war in Korea. For a more detailed discussion, see Chen Jian, *China's Road to the Korean War: The Making of the Sino-American Confrontation* (New York: Columbia University Press, 1994), 88–90.

27. For a more detailed discussion of the relationship between Chinese and North Korean Communists prior to the Korean War, see ibid., 106–13.

28. For a discussion, see Chen Jian, "Why and How China Entered the Korean War: In Light of New Evidence," paper prepared for an international conference entitled "The Korean War: An Assessment of the Historical Record," July 24–25, 1995, Georgetown University, Washington, D.C., 10–12.

29. For a more detailed discussion, see Chen Jian, *China's Road to the Korean War,* 87–8.

30. See ibid., pp. 110–11; see also Bruce Cumings, *The Origins of the Korean War* (Princeton, N.J.: Princeton University Press, 1990), vol. 2, 363.

31. Xiao Jinguang, *Xiao Jinguang huiyilu* [Xiao Jinguang's memoirs] (Beijing: Jiexangjun, 1990), vol. 2, 8, 26.

32. Mao Zedong to Nie Rongzhen, July 7, 1950, *Jianguo yilai Mao Zedong wengao,* vol. 1, 428; Han Huanzhi and Tai Jinqiao et al., *Dangdai zhongguo jundui de junshi gongzuo* [Military affairs of contemporary Chinese armed forces] (Beijing: Zhongguo shehui kexue, 1988), vol. 1, 449–50.

33. Chen Jian, *China's Road to the Korean War,* 137.

34. Telegram, Mao Zedong to Gao Gang, August 18, 1950, *Jianguo yilai Mao Zedong wengao,* vol. 1, 499; see also telegram, Mao Zedong to Gao Gang, August 5, 1950, ibid., 454.

35. Telegram, Stalin to Soviet Ambassador in Beijing (N. V. Roshchin) with message for Zhou Enlai, July 5, 1950, *CWIHP Bulletin* 6–7 (Winter 1995/1996): 43.

36. See Chen Jian, *China's Road to the Korea War,* 156; see also telegram, Filippov (Stalin) to Zhou Enlai, August 27, 1950, *CWIHP Bulletin* 6–7 (Winter 1995/1996): 45.

37. Telegram, Stalin to Mao Zedong and Zhou Enlai, October 1, 1950; see *CWIHP Bulletin* 6–7 (Winter 1995/1996):114. Stalin dispatched this telegram after the UN forces crossed the thirty-eighth parallel and Kim Il Sung requested direct Soviet and Chinese intervention in the war.

38. Telegram, Mao Zedong to Stalin, October 2, 1950, *Jianguo yilai Mao Zedong wengao,* vol. 1, 539–40. The text of the telegram published in this volume is abridged. For citation and discussion of the parts that are not included, see Chen Jian, *China's Road to the Korean War,* 177–8.

39. The telegram is in Mao's own handwriting. There is no doubt that this is a genuine document and that its contents reflected Mao's thinking. But the facts that this telegram is not found in Russian archives and that another version of Mao's message to Stalin does exist point to the possibility that although Mao had drafted the telegram, he may not have dispatched it. In actuality, the original of this telegram is different from many of Mao's other telegrams in format: While other telegrams usually (but not always) carry Mao's office staff's signature indicating the time when the telegram was dispatched, this telegram does not. It is therefore possible that Mao drafted this telegram but did not dispatch it to Stalin. This was probably because of the difference of opinions that existed among top CCP leaders, and because Stalin had failed to clearly commit Soviet military support, air cover in particular, to China. See Shen Zhihua (trans. Chen Jian), "The Discrepancy between the Russian and Chinese Versions of Mao's 2 October 1950 Message to Stalin on Chinese Entry into the Korean War: A Chinese Scholar's Reply," *CWIHP Bulletin* 8–9 (Winter 1996/1997): 237–42.

40. Telegram, Roshchin in Beijing to Stalin, October 3, 1950, conveying October 2, 1950, message from Mao to Stalin, *CWIHP Bulletin* 6–7 (Winter 1995/1996): 114–15.

41. Letter, Fyn Si (Stalin) to Kim Il Sung (via Shtykov), October 8 [7], 1950, *CWIHP Bulletin* 6–7 (Winter 1995/1996): 116. Stalin cited the text of his message to Beijing in this letter.

42. For a detailed discussion of these meetings, see Chen Jian, *China's Road to the Korean War,* chap. 5; see also Zhang Xi, "Peng Dehuai and China's Entry into the Korean War," *Chinese Historians* 6, no. 1 (Spring 1993): 8–16.

43. "Mao Zedong's Order to Establish the Chinese People's Volunteers," October 8, 1950, *Jianguo yilai Mao Zedong wengao,* vol. 1, 543–4.

44. Telegram, Mao Zedong to Kim Il Sung, October 8, 1950, ibid., 545; see also Chai Chengwen and Zhao Yongtian, *Banmendian tanpan* [Panmunjom negotiations] (Beijing: Jiexangjun, 1989), 84.

45. This is the term used by Shi Zhe, Mao Zedong's and Zhou Enlai's Russian-language interpreter, in describing Sino-Soviet relations in October 1950. Interviews with Shi Zhe, August 1992.

46. For a more detailed discussion based on Shi Zhe's recollections, which is checked against other Chinese sources, see Chen Jian, *China's Road to the Korean War,* 197–200.

47. Telegram, Mao Zedong to Peng Dehuai, Gao Gang, and others, October 12, 1950, *Jianguo yilai Mao Zedong wengao,* vol. 1, 552.

48. Telegram, Mao Zedong to Zhou Enlai, October 13, 1950, ibid., 556. The telegram published in *Mao Zedong wengao* is abridged. The citation here is based on the original of the telegram, kept at the Chinese Central Archives in Beijing. For a more comprehensive discussion of this telegram and the meeting from which it resulted, see Chen Jian, *China's Road to the Korean War,* 200–3.

49. Telegram, Mao Zedong to Peng Dehuai, Gao Gang, and others, October 17, 1950; telegram, Mao Zedong to Deng Hua, Hong Xuezhi, Han Xianchu, and Xie Fang, October 18, 1950, *Jianguo yilai Mao Zedong wengao,* vol. 1, 566–8; see also Zhang Xi, "Peng Dehuai and China's Entry into the Korean War," 27–8.

50. *Weida de kangMei yuanChao yundong* [The great movement to resist America and assist Korea] (Beijing: Renmin, 1954), 7–8.

51. See State Council and Supreme People's Court, "Instructions on Suppressing Reactionary Activities," issued on July 23, 1950, in *Jianguo yilai zhongyao wenxian xianbian* [Selected important documents since the founding of the People's Republic] (Beijing: Zhongyang wenxian, 1992), vol. 1, 358–60; see also Zhang Min, "A Survey of the Struggle to Suppress Reactionaries in the Early Years of the PRC," *Dangde wenxian* [Party documents], no. 2 (1988).

52. For Russian documentary evidence on this issue, see "New Russian Documents on the Korean War," *CWIHP Bulletin* 6–7 (Winter 1995/1996): 47–53.

53. Beijing reached the decision to come to the negotiating table after extensive consultation with Stalin, who approved it in a meeting with Gao Gang and Kim Il Sung in June 1951. For a more detailed discussion, see Chen Jian, "China's Strategies to End the Korean War," paper presented to an international conference entitled "New Evidence on the Cold War in Asia," organized by the Cold War International History Project (CWIHP), Hong Kong University, January 9–12, 1996; see also Shi Zhe, *Zai lishi jüren*

shenbian, 505–9; "New Russian Documents on the Korean War," *CWIHP Bulletin* 6–7 (Winter 1995/1996): 59–66.

54. Beijing maintained daily telegraphic communication with Moscow during the armistice negotiations. Indeed, Beijing's leaders even forwarded copies of correspondence between Chinese negotiators at Panmunjom and the leaders in Beijing to Stalin to keep him abreast of developments. Copies of these and other Russian documents on the Korean War obtained by CWIHP are available for research at the National Security Archive at George Washington University in Washington, D.C. For examples of these communications, see "New Russian Documents on the Korean War," 66–84.

55. When and how the Soviet air force entered operations in Korea has been a confusing question for scholars in recent years. While some scholars, basing their discussion on information provided by Russian recollections and documents, believe that this occurred as early as November 1950, others, following the insights gained from Chinese sources, argue that the Soviet air force began operations in Korea in January 1951. We believe that the key here is to make a distinction between operations for the purpose of defending China's Northeast (Manchuria) and the transportation lines across the Chinese-Korean border, especially the bridge over the Yalu River, and operations designed for supporting Chinese–North Korean land forces fighting in Korean territory. While the former did happen as early as November 1950 (as an inevitable extension of defending the air space of China's Northeast), the latter did not occur until January 1951.

56. Han Nianlong et al., *Dangdai Zhongguo waijiao,* 28–30; Pei Jianzhang, *Zhonghua Renmin Gongheguo waijiaoshi,* 40–1.

57. The "Three Antis" movement was designed to oppose corrupt Communist cadres; the "Five Antis" movement was aimed at the national bourgeoisie "who should not be destroyed at this stage but who needed to be tightly controlled by the power of the people's state." For discussions of these movements, see Frederick C. Teiwes, "Establishment and Consolidation of the New Regime," in Roderick MacFarquhar and John K. Fairbank, eds., *The Cambridge History of China* (Cambridge: Cambridge University Press, 1987), vol. 14, 88–91.

58. During the war years, the Soviet Union provided China with military equipment for 64 army divisions and 22 air force divisions, which placed China in a debt totaling 3 billion old rubles (about US$ 650 million); China did not pay off this debt (plus interest) until 1965. See Xu Yan, *Diyici jiaoliang* [The first test of strength] (Beijing: Zhongguo guang bo dianshi, 1990), 31–2.

59. In March 1950 and July 1951, the Chinese and Soviet governments had signed four agreements, establishing a civil aviation company, an oil company, a nonferrous and rare metal company, and a shipbuilding company jointly owned by the two countries. Stalin in the last years of his life refused to allow the Chinese to establish full ownership over the companies, but Khrushchev agreed. See Han Nianlong et al., *Dangdai Zhongguo waijiao,* 26–7.

60. Ibid., 27–8.

61. Li Jue et al., *Dangdai Zhongguo he gongyue* [Contemporary China's nuclear industry] (Beijing: Zhongguo shehui kexue, 1987), 20.

62. Even Mao himself later acknowledged that "the first time I met with Comrade Khrushchev, we had very pleasant conversations . . . and established mutual trust." Cited from Li Danhui, "The Evolution of Sino-Soviet Relations," *Dangshi yanjiu ziliao,* 6 (1995). Still, Chinese sources report that when Khrushchev requested to visit historic sites in Lüshun dedicated to Russian generals who had participated in the Russo-Japanese War of 1904, the CCP leaders politely yet firmly turned him down. Liu Guoxin, chief ed., *Zhonghua Renmin Gongheguo lishi changbian* [A draft history of the People's Republic of China] (Nanning: Guangxi Renmin, 1994), vol. 1, 117.

63. Pei Jianzhang, *Zhonghua renmin gongheguo waijiaoshi,* vol. 1, 35–7.

64. For two detailed accounts about Zhou Enlai's visits to Moscow before the Geneva Conference, see Shi Zhe, *Zai lishi jüren shenbian,* 539–44, and Li Lianqing, *Da waijiaojia Zhou Enlai: shezhan rineiwa* [Great diplomat Zhou Enlai: The Geneva debate] (Hong Kong: Tiandi tushu, 1994), 13–33. See also Chen Jian, "China and the First Indo-China War, 1950–1954," *China Quarterly* 133 (Spring 1993): 106–7.

65. For discussions of Sino-Soviet cooperation at the Geneva Conference, see Zhai Qiang, "China and the Geneva Conference of 1954," *China Quarterly* 129 (March 1992); Chen Jian, "China and the First Indo-China War," 106–10.

66. This was the view of the CCP leadership. See Li Yueran, *Waijiao wutai shang de xin Zhongguo lingxue* [New China's leaders on the diplomatic scene] (Beijing: Jiexangjun, 1989), 52–3.

67. For discussions, see Han Nianlong et al., *Dangdai Zhongguo waijiao,* chap. 8.

68. See, for example, Mao's talks with the delegation of the Yugoslav Communist

League, September 1956, in Zhang Shuguang and Chen Jian, trans. and eds., "The Emerging Disputes between Beijing and Moscow: Ten Newly Available Chinese Documents, 1956–1958," *CWIHP Bulletin* 6–7 (Winter 1995/1996): 148–51.

69. One of the authors has argued elsewhere that Mao's definition of "equality" was a metaphor that reflected his perception of China's unequal exchanges with foreign countries in the modern era. The implicit aspect of Mao's pursuit of equality was that revolutionary China was in a position to define the international standard of equality. In this sense, China's approach reflected a Chinese superiority mentality. See Chen Jian, *China's Road to the Korean War*, 42–3.

70. For good accounts of the Gao Gang affair, see Frederick Teiwes, *Politics at Mao's Court: Gao Gang and Party Factionalism* (Armonk, N.Y.: Sharpe, 1990); Lin Yunhui et al., *Kaige xingjing de shiqi* [The period of triumphant advance] (Zhengzhou: Henan Renmin, 1989), 319–35.

71. Telegram, Mao Zedong to the CPSU CC, September 1, 1954, *Jianguo yilai Mao Zedong wengao,* vol. 4, 537–8.

72. Shi Zhe, *Zai lishi jüren shenbian,* chap. 20; Wu Lengxi, *Yi Mao zhuxi* [Recalling Chairman Mao] (Beijing: Xinhua, 1994), 2–3; Liu Xiao, *Chushi sulian, banian,* 18. These Chinese sources differ on whether the Soviets provided the CCP delegation with a copy of Khrushchev's speech after the secret session. While Shi recalls that the CCP was given a copy the day after the speech was given, Wu Lengxi claims that the Chinese did not know about the contents of the speech until the Xinhua News Agency received the issue of the *New York Times* in which it was published. The *Times* did not, however, as Wu claims, publish the speech on March 10, but almost three months later, on June 4. According to the archival sources now available, it seems that Shi Zhe's recollection is correct. On March 31, 1956, when meeting Soviet ambassador to China Pavel Iudin, Mao Zedong mentioned that "the members of the Chinese delegation who had attended the 20th Congress . . . had brought a copy of Comrade Khrushchev's speech regarding the cult of personality." See Mao's conversation with Iudin, March 31, 1956, *CWIHP Bulletin* 6–7 (Winter 1995/1996): 327.

73. Mao Zedong and other CCP leaders later complained repeatedly that Khrushchev's secret speech came as a surprise to the CCP and other Communist parties. See Cong Jin, *Quzhe fazhan de suiyue,* 327.

74. See Wu Lengxi, *Yi Mao zhuxi,* 4. Wu Lengxi was then director of the New China News Agency and editor-in-chief of *Renmin ribao, [People's daily],* and attended sev-

eral Politburo Standing Committee meetings discussing the de-Stalinization issue. Mao would repeat the same claim in many later speeches.

75. Ibid., 5–7. Mao would repeat the same narrative on many other occasions, see, for example, Mao Zedong, "Speech at the Tenth Plenum of the Eighth CC," September 24, 1962, Stuart Schram, ed., *Chairman Mao Talks to the People: Talks and Letters: 1956–1971* (New York: Pantheon Books, 1974), 191.

76. Cited from Wu Lengxi, *Yi Mao zhuxi,* 6.

77. Ibid., 5–10.

78. *Renmin ribao,* April 5, 1956. The timing of publishing the article was chosen intentionally, as a high-ranking Soviet delegation headed by Mikoyan would arrive in Beijing on April 6, 1956. See Wu Lengxi, *Yi Mao zhuxi,* 10.

79. Mao's most famous deliberation in this regard was reflected in his article "On the Ten Great Relationships," in *Mao Zedong xuanji,* vol. 5, 267–88. For an English translation that was based on an early version of the article, see Schram, ed., *Chairman Mao Talks to the People,* 61–83.

80. In the winter of 1955–1956, Mao wrote the preface and over 100 pieces of editor's notes for a volume entitled *The Socialist High Tide in China's Countryside,* arguing that it was necessary and possible to accelerate the realization of a socialist society in China. See *Jianguo yilai Mao Zedong wengao,* vol. 5, 484–576.

81. Li Ping, *Kaiguo zongli Zhou Enlai* [The first premier Zhou Enlai], (Beijing: Zhonggong dangxiao, 1994), 354–8.

82. According to Li Ping, at one Politburo conference in late April 1956, Zhou Enlai had a face-to-face dispute with Mao: While Mao favored increasing construction investment by 2 billion yuan so that the speed of China's socialist construction would be accelerated, Zhou opposed it, arguing that this could cause tension in commodity supply as well as the overgrowth of the urban population. Zhou even told Mao that his conscience as China's premier would not allow him to yield to Mao's ideas. Mao felt very offended and left Beijing soon after the conference. See ibid., 356.

83. Cong Jin, *Quzhe fazhan de suiyue* [The years of tortuous advance] (Zhengzhou: Henan Renmin, 1989), 117.

84. Mao Zedong, "Speech Outlines at the Chengdu Conference," March 10, 1958, *Jianguo yilai Mao Zedong wengao,* vol. 7, 113.

85. Odd Arne Westad, "Mao on Sino-Soviet Relations: Two Conversations with the Soviet Ambassador," *CWIHP Bulletin* 6–7 (Winter 1995/1996): 164–9.

86. Zhou Wenqi and Zhu Liangru, *Teshu er fuzha de keti: gongchan guoji, Sulian he Zhongguo gongchandang guanxi biannian shi, 1919–1991* [A special and complicated subject: A chronological history of the relations between the Comintern, the Soviet Union, and the Chinese Communist Party] (Wuhan: Hubei Renmin, 1993), 500.

87. Minutes, Mao Zedong's conversations with the Romanian ambassador to China, June 28, 1956, *Mao Zedong waijiao wenxuan,* 240–1.

88. "The Emerging Disputes between Beijing and Moscow: Ten Newly Available Chinese Documents," *CWIHP Bulletin* 6–7 (Winter 1995/1996): 148–52.

89. In October 1956, following the suppression four months earlier of an uprising in Poznan, Polish Communists elected a new Politburo of the Polish United Workers Party excluding pro-Soviet, Stalinist leaders. Further, the Poles requested Moscow to recall Marshal Konstantin Rokossovskii, a Russian who had been Poland's defense minister since 1949. In the meantime, beginning on October 22–23, an anti-Communist revolt erupted in Hungary. Consequently, on November 1, Imre Nagy, Hungary's new prime minister, announced that his country would withdraw unilaterally from the Warsaw Pact, maintain neutrality in bloc politics, and adopt a multiparty democracy. Three days later the Soviets invaded to crush the revolution. For translations of important recently released Soviet bloc materials on these events, see the articles and documents published in *CWIHP Bulletin* 5 (Spring 1995): 1, 22–57; *CWIHP Bulletin* 6–7 (Winter 1995/1996): 153–4, 282; *CWIHP Bulletin* 8–9 (Winter 1996/1997): 355–410; also see papers presented at the conference "Hungary and the World, 1956: The New Archival Evidence," September 26–29, 1996, Budapest, Hungary, organized by the National Security Archive, the Institute for the History of the 1956 Hungarian Revolution, and CWIHP.

90. On October 19 the CPSU CC dispatched a telegram to the CCP CC, informing it that because of the serious situation in Poland, Moscow was planning to send troops to solve the crisis. The Soviets solicited Beijing's advice on this matter. See Wu Lengxi, *Yi Mao zhuxi,* 11.

91. Ibid., 11–12.

92. Pei Jianzhang, *Zhonghua renmin gongheguo waijiao shi*, 61–2; Wu Lengxi, *Yi Mao zhuxi*, 12–13.

93. Shi Zhe, *Feng yu gu: Shi Zhe huiyilu*, 122–3; Zhou Wenqi and Zhu Liangru, *Teshu er fuzha de keti*, 502–3; Pei Jianzhang, *Zhonghua Renmin Gongheguo waijiao shi*, 62. China's precise influence on Soviet decision making during the Polish and Hungarian events is the subject of investigation by several scholars working in Chinese, Russian, and Polish sources, including the present authors, L. W. Gluschowski (University of Toronto), Mark Kramer (Harvard University), Vladislav Zubok (National Security Archive), and Odd Arne Westad (Norwegian Nobel Institute/London School of Economics). Results are slated to appear in the *CWIHP Bulletin*.

94. Wu Lengxi, *Yi Mao zhuxi*, 14.

95. Shi Zhe, *Feng yu gu: Shi Zhe huiyilu*, 119–23; Wu Lengxi, *Yi Mao zhuxi*, 14–15.

96. Zhou Wenqi and Zhu Liangru, *Teshu er fuzha de keti*, 503; Wu Lengxi, *Yi Mao zhuxi*, 15.

97. Wu Lengxi, *Yi Mao zhuxi*, 16–17.

98. The "Hundred Flower Campaign" and the "Anti-Rightist Movement" are both complicated historical events, and scholars have different understandings of Mao's real intentions in initiating the former. But they all agree that these two events were relate to the Hungarian crisis. For a plausible discussion of these two events, see Merle Goldman, "The Party and the Intellectuals," in MacFarquhar and Fairbank, eds., *The Cambridge History of China*, vol. 14, 242–58.

99. Zhou Enlai expressed his willingness to resign as premier, but because of the opposition of other members of the CCP leadership, his resignation did not materialize. See Li Ping, *Kaiguo zongli Zhou Enlai*, 362–3.

100. *Zhou Enlai waijiao huodong dashiji, 1949–75* [A chronology of Zhou Enlai's foreign policy activities, 1949–1975] (Beijing: Shijie zhishi, 1993), 183–7.

101. Report, "My Observation on the Soviet Union," Zhou Enlai to Mao Zedong and the CCP leadership, January 24, 1957 (trans. Zhang Shuguan and Chen Jian), *CWIHP Bulletin* 6–7 (Winter 1995/1996): 153–4.

102. Zhou Wenqi and Zhu Liangru, *Teshu er fuzha de keti*, 504.

103. Mao Zedong, "Speeches at the Moscow Conference of Communist and Workers' Parties," November 14, 16, and 18, 1957, *Jianguo yilai Mao Zedong wengao,* vol. 6, 625–44.

104. Ibid., 635–6.

105. Li Ping, *Kaiguo zongli Zhou Enlai,* 360–1; Shi Zhongquan, *Zhou Enlai de zuoyue fengxian,* 329; Cong Jin, *Quzhe qianjin de suiyue,* 111–12.

106. For the main portion of the text of Zhou Enlai's self-criticism at the Nanning conference, see Xin Ziling, *Mao Zedong dazhuan* [A grand biography of Mao Zedong] (Hong Kong: Liwen, 1993), vol. 4, 102–5.

107. Mao Zedong, "Sixty Articles on Work Methods (Draft)," January 1958, *Jianguo yilai Mao Zedong wengao,* vol. 7, 51.

108. Li Ping, *Kaiguo zongli Zhou Enlai,* 361–2.

109. Authors' interviews with participants at the conference.

110. For a detailed account of the Chengdu conference, see Roderick MacFarquhar, *The Origins of the Cultural Revolution, Vol. 2: The Great Leap Forward, 1958–1960* (New York: Columbia University Press, 1983), 33–50; for a plausible Chinese account, see Cong Jin, *Quzhe qianjin de suiyue,* 112–21. However, neither author touches upon Zhou's self-criticism on his "conservative mistakes" in handling the foreign relations of the People's Republic.

111. Liu Guoxin et al., *Zhonghua Renmin Gongheguo lishi changbian* [An extended history of the People's Republic of China] (Nanning: Guangxi Renmin, 1994), vol. 2, 40.

112. Han Nianlong et al., *Dangdai Zhongguo waijiao,* 112–13.

113. Report, Peng Dehuai to Mao Zedong and the CCP Central Committee, June 5, 1958, *Mao Zedong waijiao wenxuan,* 634.

114. Han Nianlong et al., *Dangdai Zhongguo waijiao,* 113.

115. Zhou Wenqi and Zhu Liangru, *Teshu er fuzha de keti,* 512–13; Han Nianlong et al., *Dangdai Zhongguo waijiao,* 113.

116. Zhou Wenqi and Zhu Liangru, *Teshu er fuzha de keti,* 513; Han Nianlong et al., *Dangdai Zhongguo waijiao,* 113–14; Liu Guoxin et al., *Zhonghua Renmin Gongheguo lishi changbian,* vol. 2, 41.

117. Minutes, conversation between Mao Zedong and Ambassador Iudin, July 22, 1958, *Mao Zedong waijiao wenxuan,* 322–33; for an English translation (by Zhang Shuguang and Chen Jian), see *CWIHP Bulletin* 6–7 (Winter 1995/1996): 155–9.

118. Zhou Wenqi and Zhu Liangru, *Teshu er fuzha de keti,* 513–14; Han Nianlong et al., *Dangdai Zhongguo waijiao,* 114.

119. Han Nianlong et al., *Dangdai Zhongguo waijiao,* 114; Zhou Wenqi and Zhu Liangru, *Teshu er fuzha de keti,* 514; Liu Guoxin et al., *Zhonghua Renmin Gongheguo lishi changbian,* vol. 2, 41.

120. Khrushchev was so upset that he said at the end of the meeting: "Comrade Mao Zedong, the NATO countries have no problem in mutual cooperation and supply, and we even cannot reach agreement on such a matter!" Liu Guoxin et al., *Zhonghua Renmin Gongheguo lishi changbian,* vol. 2, 41.

121. Cited from Cong Jin, *Quzhe qianjin de suiyue,* 350.

122. Letter, Mao Zedong to Peng Dehuai and Huang Kecheng, July 27, 1958, in "Mao Zedong's Management of the Taiwan Crisis of 1958: Chinese Recollections and Documents," trans. and annot. by Li Xiaobing, Chen Jian, and David L. Wilson, *CWIHP Bulletin* 6–7 (Winter 1995/1996): 215–16.

123. Ibid., 208–18.

124. Mao Zedong's speech to the Supreme State Council, September 5, 1958, ibid., 216–18.

125. While meeting Khrushchev on the evening of September 30, 1959, Mao explained to the Soviet leader that "we did not discuss this issue [the Taiwan issue] at that time [Khrushchev's visit to Beijing in July-August 1958]. We did not mention it to you because we only had the intention, but had not made the final decision. We did not anticipate that the shelling would cause such a storm." Cited from Shi Zhongquan, *Zhou Enlai de zuoyue fengxian,* 370. In November 1958, speaking at an inner-party meeting, Mao said that "at the Sino-Soviet talks [from July 31 to August 3, 1958] . . . nothing was mentioned about the Taiwan situation." Mao Zedong, "Record of Talks with Directors

of Various Cooperative Areas," November 30, 1958, *Mao Zedong sixiang wansui* [Long live Mao Zedong thought] (no pub., 1969), 255.

126. Wei Shiyan, "The Truth of Gromyko's Conversation with Chairman Mao Zedong on the Taiwan Issue," in Pei Jianzhang et al., *Xin Zhongguo waijiao fengyun* (Beijing: Shijie zhishi, 1991), 135–8; Han Nianlong et al., *Dangdai Zhongguo waijiao,* 115; Zhou Wenqi and Zhu Liangru, *Teshu er fuzha de keti,* 515; Liu Guoxin et al., *Zhonghua Renmin Gongheguo lishi changbian,* vol. 2, 45.

127. Zhou Wenqi and Zhu Liangru, *Teshu er fuzha de keti,* 515.

128. Allen Whiting, "The Sino-Soviet Split," in MacFarquhar and Fairbank, eds., *Cambridge History of China,* vol. 14, 500.

129. See, for example, Mao Zedong, "Speech Outlines on International Situation," December 1959, *Jianguo yilai Mao Zedong wengao,* vol. 8, 599–602. In this speech, Mao angrily criticized Khrushchev's "unwitting" and "naive" attitude toward the Great Leap Forward. In another letter Mao wrote: "The Khrushchevs oppose or are dubious about these three things: letting a hundred flowers bloom, the people's communes, and the Great Leap Forward. I think they are in a passive position, whereas we are in an extremely active position." Letter, Mao Zedong to Wang Jiaxiang, August 1, 1959, *Jianguo yilai Mao Zedong wengao,* vol. 8, 391.

130. Cong Jin, *Quzhe fazhan de suiyue,* 180–1.

131. "Materials on the Tibet Rebellion," *Zhonggong dangshi jiaoxue cankao ziliao* [Reference materials for teaching CCP history] (Beijing: Guofang daxue, 1986), vol. 23, 23–40.

132. Cong Jin, *Quzhe qianjin de suiyue,* 352; Zhou Wenqi and Zhu Liangru, *Teshu er fuzha de keti,* 516.

133. Liu Guoxin et al., *Zhonghua Renmin Gongheguo lishi changbian,* vol. 2, 71–2.

134. The best account of the Lushan conference is Li Rui, *Mao Zedong mishu sheji: Lushan huiyi shilu* [The hand-taken notes of Mao Zedong's secretary: A factual record of the Lushan conference], rev. ed. (Zhengzhou: Henan Renmin, 1994).

135. For discussions of Mao's criticism of Peng at the Lushan conference, see Li Rui, *Mao Zedong mishu sheji: Lushan huiyi shilu.*

136. For the criticism of Peng Dehuai being a "Soviet agent" during and after the Lushan conference, see Cong Jin, *Quzhe fazhan de suiyue,* 305; Shi Dongbing, *Lushan zhen mianmu: Peng Dehuai fandang shijian jiemi* [Lushan's true face: Exposing the secrets behind "The Peng Dehuai anti-party clique" incident] (Hong Kong: Honglong, 1994), chap. 59; the compilation group of Peng Dehuai's biography, *Yige zhenzheng de ren: Peng Dehuai* [A true man: Peng Dehuai] (Beijing: Renmin, 1994), 292–4.

137. Zhou Wenqi and Zhu Liangru, *Teshu er fuzha de keti,* 517. Mao Zedong later complained that "in September 1959 during the Sino-Indian border dispute, Khrushchev supported Nehru in attacking us and Tass issued a communiqué." See Mao Zedong, "Speech at the Tenth Plenum of the Eighth Central Committee," in Schram, *Chairman Mao Talks to the People,* 190; also related findings in *CWIHP Bulletin* 8–9 (Winter 1996/1997): 251–69, esp. 251–2, 259–62.

138. Cong Jin, *Quzhe fazhan de suiyue,* 352; see also Mao Zedong, "Speech," in Schram, *Chairman Mao Talks to the People,* 190–1.

139. On the Chinese side, the participants included Liu Shaoqi, Zhou Enlai, Zhu De, and Chen Yi. See Cong Jin, *Quzhe fazhan de suiyue,* 352.

140. Liu Guoxin et al., *Zhonghua Renmin Gongheguo lishi changbian,* vol. 2, 64.

141. Cong Jin, *Quzhe fazhan de suiyue,* 353.

142. The Chinese version of the transcript of this important meeting is still closed at the Chinese Central Archives. The account of the meeting provided here is based on the following sources: Zhou Wenqi and Zhu Liangru, *Teshu er fuzha de keti,* 517–18; Cong Jin, *Quzhe fazhan de suiyue,* 354; Liu Guoxin et al., *Zhonghua renmin gongheguo lishi changbian,* vol. 2, 64–5. The Russian transcript exists in the Archive of the President of the Russian Federation (APRF) and has been cited by the late historian Dmitrii Volkogorov, but as of late 1999 it had not become openly available.

143. Mao Zedong, "Speech Outlines on International Situation," December 1959, *Jianguo yilai Mao Zedong wengao,* vol. 8, 600.

144. Cong Jin, *Quzhe fazhan de suiyue,* 305–7.

145. The Chinese embassy to the Soviet Union wrote a detailed report about the speech to Beijing on October 9, 1959. See *Jianguo yilai Mao Zedong wengao,* vol. 8, 564–5.

146. Zhou Wenqi and Zhu Liangru, *Teshu er fuzha de keti,* 518–19; Liu Guoxin et al., *Zhonghua Renmin Gongheguo lishi changbian,* vol. 2, 65.

147. Han Nianlong et al., *Dangdai Zhongguo waijiao,* 116–19; Cong Jin, *Quzhe qianjin de shinian,* 364; see also Chen Jian, "A Crucial Step toward the Breakdown of the Sino-Soviet Alliance: The Withdrawal of Soviet Experts from China in July 1960," *CWHIP Bulletin* 8–9 (Winter 1996/1997): 246, 249–50.

148. In the wake of the Great Leap Forward, many top CCP leaders began to have serious doubts about Mao's radical plans to transform China's state and society, but they seldom questioned the wisdom of Mao's radical foreign policy.

149. Cong Jin, *Quzhe qianjin de suiyue,* 505–24.

150. Li Cheng, chief ed., *Zhonghua Renmin Gongheguo shilu* [A factual history of the People's Republic of China] (Changchun: Jilin Renmin, 1994), vol. 2, 2nd part, 656–7.

151. Cong Jin, *Quzhe qianjin de suiyue,* 576–7, 579.

Appendix

Appendix

Some Documents on Sino-Soviet Relations, 1948 to 1963

We include a brief document appendix with this volume to illustrate terms, concepts, and issues in the Sino-Soviet relationship and how these developed over time during the period of the alliance. In order to understand how the alliance functioned, it is important to grasp the main terms the protagonists themselves used to describe their relationship. It is also necessary to have at least some insight into how Soviet and Chinese leaders used specific concepts – both of a Marxist and a more general origin – to discuss the present and to plan the future. And it is essential to have some idea about what mattered in the bilateral relationship – which issues were important and which were not so important – in terms of both domestic priorities and international affairs.

By including some documents, we do not intend to argue for any specific interpretations or to come up with "proof" in old debates about chronology or the roles of individual leaders. The time is long passed when access to single documents (or parts thereof) from Soviet or Chinese archives could be transformed into sensational scholarly publications. The chapters in this collection show how wide the source base now is and, it is hoped, how the questions we ask have to be reoriented to suit this sudden availability of a historical record. So that the documents are seen in conjunction with the interpretative essays in the volume, we have chosen to avoid excessive annotations and to include only a brief identification of each document and notes to identify individuals and institutions mentioned therein.

I. Telegram, Stalin to Mao Zedong, April 20, 1948

Documents I and II are part of the 1947–1948 discussion on political strategy in China between Stalin and the CCP leadership. Although the Chinese Communists communicated frequently with Moscow by coded radio messages, Stalin obviously took his time in replying to some of the more general points that Mao had raised. One reason for the delay in this case may have been the fluid military situation in the Chinese civil war, in which the People's Liberation Army went on the offensive in the winter of 1947/48. Another reason may have been Mao's somewhat unfortunate reference to Yugoslavia, a country with which Moscow's relations were rapidly deteriorating during the spring of 1948. The text also set out Stalin's view of a CCP victory in China as part of the "bourgeois-democratic stage" of the Chinese revolution. In document II, Mao repeated his request to visit the Soviet Union, a request that Stalin had agreed to "in principle" already in February 1947. But in early May 1948 Stalin called the visit off, believing that Mao's presence was needed in China. Stalin also turned down a similar request by Mao in the late fall of 1948.

To Terebin[1] to be passed to Mao Zedong.

We have received both letters from Comrade Mao Zedong from November 30, 1947, and March 15, 1948. We could not react to them immediately because we were checking some information necessary for our answer. Now that the facts are verified, we can answer both letters.

First. The answer to the letter of November 30, 1947. We are very grateful for the information from Comrade Mao Zedong. We agree with the assessment of the situation given by Comrade Mao Zedong. We have doubts only about one point in the letter, where it is said that "In the period of the final victory of the Chinese revolution, following the example of the USSR and Yugoslavia, all political parties except the CCP should leave the political scene, which will significantly strengthen the Chinese revolution."

We do not agree with this. We think that the various opposition parties in China which are representing the middle strata of the Chinese population and are opposing the Guomindang clique will exist for a long time. And the CCP will have to involve them in cooperation against the Chinese reactionary forces and imperialist powers, while keeping hegemony, i.e., the leading position, in its hands. It is possible that some representatives of these parties will have to be included into the Chinese people's democratic govern-

[1] Also known as Orlov or Zhelepin; Soviet military intelligence agent who was in charge of radio communications between Mao and Stalin during the Chinese civil war.

ment and the government itself has to be proclaimed a coalition government in order to widen the basis of this government among the population and to isolate imperialists and their Guomindang agents. It is necessary to keep in mind that the Chinese government in its policy will be a national revolutionary-democratic government, not a Communist one, after the victory of the People's Liberation Armies of China, at any rate in the period immediately after the victory, the length of which is difficult to define now.

This means that nationalization of all land and abolition of private ownership of land, confiscation of the property of all industrial and trade bourgeoisie from petty to big, confiscation of property belonging not only to big landowners but to middle and small holders exploiting hired labor, will not be fulfilled for the present. These reforms have to wait for some time.

It has to be said for your information that there are other parties in Yugoslavia besides the Communists which form part of the People's Front.

Second. The answer to the letter from Comrade Mao Zedong from March 15, 1948. We are very grateful to Comrade Mao Zedong for the detailed information on military and political questions. We agree with all the conclusions of Comrade Mao Zedong given in this letter. We consider as absolutely correct Comrade Mao Zedong's thoughts concerning the creation of a central government of China and including in it representatives of the liberal bourgeosie.

With Communist greetings
Stalin

Source: Arkhiv prezidenta Rossiiskoi Federatsii (APRF), fond (f.) 39, opis (op.) 1, delo (d.) 31, 43–4.

II. Telegram, Mao Zedong to Stalin, April 26, 1948

Comrade Stalin,

1. I have received the letter of April 20. Completely agree with it.
2. Our Central Committee has already moved to an area near Shijiazhuang in Hebei province. It has merged and united with the working committee of the CC which used to consist of Liu Shaoqi, Zhu De, [and] Dong Biwu.
3. We passed through the northern part of Shanxi province and the northwestern part of Hebei province, where we met and had conversations with the comrades from the JinSui subbureau of the CC CCP and the comrades from the JinChaJi bureau of the CC CCP as

well as with the masses. On our way we saw that the work with rectifying party ranks, carrying out land reform, reconstruction, and development of agriculture and industry, work on supplying the fronts, on helping victims of various disasters, work with non-party progressive gentry and so on had moved in the right direction.

Leftist tendencies, which came into being in the provinces during the two years following the Japanese capitulation, have already been thoroughly corrected. A new work spirit can be felt everywhere.

4. I decided to move forward my visit [to] the USSR. I am planning to leave the Fobin district (100 km to the north from Shijiazhuang) in Hebei province in the beginning of the month and under cover of troops to cross the railway Beiping [Beijing]-Kalgan [Zhangjiakou] (the Guomindang has concentrated around 100,000 troops on this railway). Possibly, I'll be able to arrive in Harbin in the beginning or in the middle of July. Then, from Harbin – to you.

I will be accompanied by Comrade Ren Bishi, member of the Political Bureau of the CC CCP. He has been to the USSR more than once, [he] knows Russian. On my arrival at Harbin I am planning to invite to go with me another member of the Politbureau, Comrade Chen Yun. He is now in charge of industry and labor movement in Manchuria; he was in the USSR in 1936.

Besides them, I'll have with me two secretaries and several cipher officers and radio operators.

I have organized such a big group for my trip to the USSR because I will ask for advice and guidance from the comrades in the CC VKP(b)[2] on political, military, economic, and other important questions; besides, if you agree, we are planning to conduct studies in the USSR on military, economic, governmental, and party questions.

Besides, if possible, I would like to travel to the countries of Eastern and Southeastern Europe in order to study the work of the people's front and other kinds of work.

We are planning to travel for one to three months. If you agree with this plan, we will act according to it. If not, then, of course, there is only one way out – to come by myself.

5. My health is not good. I hope that the two Russian doctors who live here (one of them can speak Chinese) will accompany me to the USSR and then return here with me. Terebin's radio station will go with us ("to be in touch on the way" [he] said but did not write. Terebin). On arrival in Harbin, we will leave the radio station there.

Please indicate to me whether we can do this.

Mao Zedong

Source: APRF, f. 39, op. 1, d. 31, 45–6.

[2] All-Union Communist Party (bolsheviks), (after 1954 Communist Party of the Soviet Union [CPSU]).

III. Liu Shaoqi's Report to the CPSU CC Politburo, July 4, 1949

Since Mao did not get Stalin's permission to come to the Soviet Union, the CCP chairman instead sent his deputy, Liu Shaoqi, as head of a delegation that paid an almost two-month-long visit to Moscow in the summer of 1949. Document III is the report that Liu Shaoqi presented to the CPSU Politburo on July 11, 1949. The report was originally drafted by Liu in Beijing before departure, discussed among a number of CCP Politburo members, and revised by Mao Zedong. After arrival in Moscow, and especially after the first conversation with Stalin on June 28, Liu made several changes to the report. All of these changes were agreed to by Mao. Stalin received a copy of the text on July 4. Stalin's handwritten notes on the report are given in italics. The underlinings are all Stalin's.

To the Central Committee of the Soviet Communist Party, Comrade Joseph Stalin. We are sending you the enclosed report.

Liu Shaoqi, head of the delegation of the Central Committee of the Communist Party of China, July 4, 1949.

1. The Present Situation of the Chinese Revolution
The revolutionary war of the Chinese people has already been won by and large, and it is to culminate in complete victory shortly.

By the end of May 1949 the People's Liberation Army had occupied 2.9 million square kilometers of the country's richest regions making up 30 percent of China's territory (30 percent because Xinjiang, Qinghai, and Tibet occupy a large part of the country's territory). The territory liberated by the People's Liberation Army is populated by 275 million people, or 57 percent of China's total population. The People's Liberation Army has occupied 1,043 cities, including such major cities as Shanghai, Nanjing, Beiping [Beijing], Tianjin, and Wuhan, or 51 percent of China's 2,000 cities from country towns up.

In the course of its three-year combat operations the People's Liberation Army has destroyed 5.59 million Guomindang troops. At the present time the Guomindang army, including the personnel of the logistics services, is only about 1.5 million strong, of whom only 200,000 may be considered battleworthy. On the other hand, according to the latest data, the People's Liberation Army is 3.9 million strong. Its four field armies have 2.4 million combatants, with the rest of the personnel being distributed among military districts, local troops, the armies of the Chief Command, military institutions, and military schools. The <u>air force has 7,500</u> and the <u>navy has 7,700.</u> *(Airmen, are there? Sailors, are there?)*

This summer and autumn the People's Liberation Army will be able to clear the provinces of Fujian, Hunan, Jiangxi, and Shaanxi, and in the winter it will be able to liberate the provinces of Guangdong, Guangxi, Yunnan, Guizhou, Sichuan, Xikang, Gansu, Ningxia, and Qinghai. Thereby the hostilities against the Guomindang will be terminated in the main. To be liberated yet will then be Formosa [Taiwan], Hainan island, Xinjiang, and Tibet. The issue of Tibet should be resolved by political means and not by the military option. Formosa, Hainan, and Xinjiang will be liberated next year. Since part of the Guomindang forces on the island of Formosa might take our side, the liberation of Formosa could take place even earlier than the above date. We would like to liberate Xinjiang as soon as possible were it not for the great obstacle of clearing the enemy from the route to Xinjiang and getting traffic moving along it. Another great difficulty is the shortage of required transport (traveling from Gansu to Xinjiang, one must cover a great distance passing through desolate areas devoid of food supplies and drinking water). If we can overcome these difficulties, we could liberate Xinjiang much sooner.

Alongside military victories we also have political victories. The American imperialists and Jiang Jieshi's Guomindang are now completely isolated. All democratic parties and groups are on our side. The popular masses are warmly greeting the People's Liberation Army and coming out against the imperialists and the Guomindang. We believe there could now be no doubt about the victory of the Chinese Revolution. Yet because of the constraints imposed on the operations of our troops by roads and terrain, some time will yet be needed for us to score a complete victory. We have always reckoned with the possibility of imperialist armed intervention against the Chinese Revolution. The instructions given to us on this matter by the Soviet Communist Party, which we have accepted in full, have alerted us to pay more attention in this regard. Although we have not slackened our caution with respect to the probability of imperialist armed intervention, yet, judging by the current international situation, there can be no possibility for the imperialists to dispatch troops more than a million strong for a massive intervention in China. Such moves on their part could only delay the ultimate victory of the Chinese Revolution but they are unable to annihilate or stall the Chinese Revolution. On the contrary, they would put the imperialists in a very awkward position.

Quite possibly, the imperialists would dispatch 100,000 to 200,000 troops for seizing three or four Chinese ports or for committing various acts of sabotage. Considering the possibility of such actions, we have made certain preparations. Since we have no navy or air force, we have no naval defenses. A possible armed attack by the imperialists may pose difficulties to us and may cause damage to us, but our armed forces will not suffer a defeat. Such actions on the part of the imperialists will make the Chinese people and its army rise against the imperialists, and they will drive out the interventionist forces.

Therefore, we believe that should we act properly, the imperialists might not venture upon direct military intervention in China. We must be careful not to give the imperialists pretexts for carrying out open armed intervention in China. Simultaneously, we must wipe out the imperialist agents, the remnants of the Guomindang forces, as soon as possible, which in its turn would confront the imperialists with greater difficulties should they risk armed intervention in China.

It is highly probable that the imperialists will resort to a policy of blockade against the Chinese Revolution. In fact, they have already embarked on it. Such a policy will present certain difficulties for us, especially in shipping and foreign trade, but it will be unable to delay the early victory of the Chinese Revolution.

The victories of the Chinese people in the revolutionary struggle are taking place after the Second World War when the world proletariat and the people's democratic forces, the Soviet Union in particular, are giving assistance to the Chinese people, which is a decisive condition for the Chinese people's victories. The Communist Party of China is using these conditions. The Chinese Revolution has experience in the successful organization of a single anti-imperialist national front, the experience of an agrarian revolution, of the long conduct of armed struggle in rural areas, of the siege of cities and of their subsequent seizure. The Chinese Revolution has the experience of waging illegal and legal struggle in cities and of combining these struggles with the operations of our armed forces. Finally, we have gained experience in building a Marxist-Leninist Communist Party in a country like China. All this experience might be useful for other colonial and semicolonial nations.

2. The New Political Consultative Council and the Central Government
The revolutionary war in China has culminated in victory by and large, and it will culminate in ultimate victory in the near future. Our further task consists in ending the war the faster, in clearing from the country the leftovers of Jiang Jieshi's Guomindang, in rehabilitating and developing the national economy as soon as possible, and in learning to build and govern the country.

We have decided to <u>convene in August a new Political Consultative</u> Conference and set up a coalition government. At present we are active in carrying out preparatory work. The new PCC is being convened not only by the Communist Party alone or by several parties, it is being convened by all democratic parties, people's organizations, representatives of ethnic minorities, and representatives of Chinese citizens living abroad – altogether by twenty-three organizations that have joined up in preparing the convocation of the PCC. Democratic and unaffiliated public figures are quite satisfied with such a method.

A Preparatory Committee on PCC Convocation has already been set up. It comprises 134 members, among them 43 Communists, 48 progressive figures who will certainly support us, 43 centrists, with 12 centrists with rightist leanings among them. The progressives include 15 undercover Communists. The leadership of the Preparatory Committee is securely with the Communist Party. A standing presidium of 21 has been set up within the Preparatory Committee. Leadership in this presidium has likewise been secured for the Communist Party.

The Preparatory Committee has decided to admit to the forthcoming PCC yet another 14 democratic parties and groups that could send 142 representatives. There will be 102 delegates in the PCC from various districts, 60 from the army, and 206 from mass popular organizations, ethnic minorities, and Chinese citizens resident abroad. All told, 45 organizations will be represented in the PCC by 510 delegates. The Communists will make up a majority.

We believe that the PCC of China is a suitable organizational form for a single national front in the Chinese Revolution, a form that is well known to the popular masses. Therefore, we are preparing to let the PCC continue as a standing body, and on the local level, where necessary, local PCCs will be established.

At the PCC we intend to adopt a common political program which will be adhered to by all parties, groups, and organizations. The PCC will elect a <u>Central Government,</u> draft and publish a declaration, approve the new national anthem, emblem, and flag. *(But* will *there also be provincial governments?)*

The organizational composition of the new Central Government has not yet been determined. Besides the Military Council, the new Central Government, its cabinet of ministers, will also include: a Financial and Economic Committee, a Committee on Culture and Education, an Administrative and Juridical Committee (this committee will be concerned with matters of state security, internal affairs, and justice); also to be established are ministries for railways, agriculture, forestry, trade, metal industry, textiles, fuels, communications and roads, the post, telegraph, etc. <u>Comrade Mao Zedong has been nominated chairman of the central government,</u> and Comrade Zhou Enlai prime minister. *(What's that:* president *in fact?)* Comrades Liu Shaoqi and Ren Bishi will not be within the government.

We perceive the nature of the new democratic state and the nature of new government in China in this way:

This state is a people's democratic dictatorship based on the class alliance of the workers and peasants under the guidance of the proletariat.

This dictatorship is directed against the imperialists, feudal forces, and <u>bureaucratic capital.</u> *(What is "bureaucratic capital"?)*

The working class is the leading force of this dictatorship. The working class in alliance with the peasantry and the revolutionary intelligentsia constitutes the core of this dictatorship. Simultaneously, being drawn in every way into participation in this dictatorship are the petty bourgeoisie, the liberal bourgeoisie, their representatives, and political groups that can cooperate with us. Such is the organizational pattern of this dictatorship.

There is no need to explain that the people's democratic dictatorship is not a dictatorship of the bourgeoisie, but it is not a dictatorship of the proletariat either. *(Yes!)*

The people's democratic dictatorship in China has certain points in common with "the democratic dictatorship of the workers and peasants," or what Lenin said with reference to the Revolution of 1905–1907. Yet it has a certain distinction as well.

What they have in common is that guidance is exercised by the proletariat and that the basis of this dictatorship is an alliance of workers and peasants. However, the people's democratic dictatorship in China also encompasses representatives and political groups of the liberal bourgeoisie who wish to fight against imperialism, feudalism, and bureaucratic capital. Herein lies the distinction. *(Yes!)* The point is that China is a semicolonial state and that during the revolution and after its victory we shall still need concerted action by all forces in the struggle against imperialism and its agents. *(Yes!)* Another point is in the specifics of the Chinese national bourgeoisie. This is quite in keeping with what Comrade Stalin said in 1926 in his speech at a meeting of the China Commission of the Comintern Executive Committee when he pointed out that a revolutionary government in China would be a "predominantly anti-imperialist government."

In form, the people's democratic dictatorship in China is a regime of people's congresses, but it is not another form of the regime of bourgeois parliamentarism. It comes closer to the regime of Soviets, but is distinct from dictatorship of the proletariat in the form of Soviets, for representatives of the national bourgeoisie are within the people's congresses. *(Yes!)* The people's democratic dictatorship in China has its internal and external contradictions, and it has to wage an internal and external struggle.

The so-called external contradiction and the external struggle mean that the dictatorship has contradictions with imperialism, feudalism, bureaucratic capital, with the remnants of the Guomindang forces and thus has to wage a struggle against them. These contradictions will continue to be fundamental contradictions and a fundamental struggle for a relatively long period after the overthrow of the Guomindang government.

The internal contradiction and the internal struggle mean that within this dictatorship there are contradictions and a struggle among various social classes and various parties and groupings. These contradictions and this struggle will be intensifying in the future, but they will be of secondary importance, compared with the external contradictions, for a fairly long period.

Some people say that "after the toppling of the Guomindang rule or after the completion of land reform the contradictions between the proletariat and the bourgeoisie will immediately become fundamental contradictions and the struggle between the workers and the capitalists will instantly come to the forefront as the main struggle." We consider this interpretation of the problem erroneous because should this government direct its main fire against the bourgeoisie, this would mean it was a dictatorship of the proletariat or was growing into one, and such policies would push the national bourgeoisie, still capable of cooperating with us, away from us into the imperialist camp. Pursuit of this policy in China <u>at the present time would be tantamount to a dangerous adventurist policy.</u> *(Yes!)* Last February Comrade Andreev [Anastas Mikoyan] in a talk with Mao Zedong approved the policy of the CCP [Chinese Communist Party] in enlisting support from the national bourgeoisie, and then the Central Committee of the Soviet Communist Party likewise pointed to the need for us to draw support from the national bourgeoisie. We fully agree with these instructions.

With the overthrow of the Guomindang government the contradictions between labor and capital will persist as an objective phenomenon, and will intensify. Therefore, the working class should wage a corresponding struggle with the bourgeoisie. It is thus that the interests of the working class and the people's democratic dictatorship could be safeguarded. But simultaneously we still have to work toward an appropriate compromise agreement and a bloc with the national bourgeoisie in order to concentrate forces against the external enemy and also to overcome China's backwardness. *(Collective agreements excluding strikes.)*

From now on and until complete nationalization of national capital many measures will have to be carried out which will take a long time. The length of this period will depend on various conditions of the international and domestic situation. We believe this job may take from ten to fifteen years.

The people's democratic dictatorship in China will effect the country's unification. This would mean great progress for China. The country's unification will occur under the leadership of the proletariat. Yet because of China's backwardness, its underdeveloped road system, the presence in the past of spheres of imperialist influence and remnants of feudal division, China still lacks an integrated economy. Therefore, at present we are compelled to vest local governments with fairly broad rights of self-government so as to stimulate activity and initiative on the local level. *(Local provincial governments, will be?)* <u>We consider it wrong and harmful to carry into effect a system of excessive centralism.</u> *(Yes!)*

We would like Comrade Stalin and the Central Committee of the Soviet Communist Party to point out to us whether our views expounded above are correct.

The majority of the leading figures of the Chinese democratic parties and groups have already arrived in Beiping [Beijing]. There are over ten such democratic parties and groups in China. These are small organizations engaged in political activity. The total membership of all these parties and groups does not exceed 30,000. Among them, the Democratic League alone has 20,000 members. This league wields a relatively strong influence among a part of the intelligentsia. These parties and groups are not active among workers and peasant masses. They are organizationally weak and lack inner cohesion. For example, all these parties and groups were unable to present a list of their representatives for participation in the PCC because of mutual discord. Lists of their representatives could be drawn up only after the CCP had conveyed its opinion to them concerning candidacies. Yet each democratic party and group has several leading figures who, thanks to their long record of political activity in China, have some influence among the popular masses. Their party organizations are held together by these leading personalities only. Each party and each group has three categories of persons, rightists, leftists, and centrists.

The remaining Guomindang officials and imperialist agents are trying in every way to sneak into these democratic parties and groups so as to secure a legal status for themselves. We have given a serious warning to these parties and groups in this regard. All these parties and groups are at one only in waging a struggle against Jiang Jieshi, the Guomindang, and the imperialists. Yet some of their members had maintained ties with imperialist elements in the recent past and broken off these ties but quite recently. On the land reform, a part of them shares the CCP stand with reservations, and on the question of relations with the USSR, some of them are showing outright nationalist trends. All democratic parties and groups are officially adopting a program worked out by the Communist Party and officially stating their readiness to give support to the CCP as the main leader. Apart from the imperialist agents, Jiang Jieshi's Guomindang, China has no other political party of the national bourgeoisie in its consummate form. China has no such reactionary bourgeois parties yet as those in European countries. *(But what about the group of compradores?)* In China's practical political life, the mass popular organizations that will be involved in the PCC are playing a substantial role. Some of these organizations already have a large membership and are attracting ever more new members. In the past these organizations were playing an important role in the struggle against the American imperialists and Jiang Jieshi. In future they are bound to play an even more important role. Most of these organizations accept CCP guidance or else are fully controlled by the CCP. Beside the All-China General Association of Trade Unions set up long ago, representatives of women's, students', and youth organizations recently held congresses, which set up the All-China Democratic Association of Women, the Youth League for New Democracy, and the All-China Association of Students. Since Chinese youth used to have a great number of various organizations, these have been merged into local and all-China youth associations that are promoting the cause of youth movement unification. The Guomindang trade unions, youth organizations, the Youth League of Sun Yat-sen's Three Principles, and the Guomindang women's organizations are now illegal with the Guomindang's defeat and are rapidly breaking up, with their leaders having fled or ceased their activities. Some of the progressive elements in their midst had made common cause with the CCP even before the Guomindang's defeat. The Chinese Federation of Labor with Zhu Xiufan at the head, still leading a segment of the working masses, has already merged with the All-China General Association of Trade Unions. Last February we received instructions from the Central Committee of the Soviet Communist Party on the need of stepping up work among the workers, civil servants, youth, and women. We agree with these instructions. This work is well under way in all cities. However, since formerly there was a long break in this activity, it has become necessary to retrain personnel for carrying it on. Today each organization is running schools for educating the personnel in which the student classes are from several hundred to several thousand each. Consequently, so far we have been unable to carry out this work with much promptitude. We would like to have several experienced Soviet comrades arrive in China for assistance in doing this work.

In the near future all-China congresses of cultural, educational, and scientific workers will be convened in Beiping [Beijing] who will set up professional organizations of their own on an all-China level. They will operate under CCP guidance.

3. External Relations

We fully agree with the latest instructions from the Central Committee of the Soviet Communist Party concerning foreign policy issues, foreign trade, and loans.

At the present time, as the imperialists have suffered a setback in their policy of giving all-out support to the Guomindang in the struggle against the Chinese Revolution, they are using the following methods with the aim of continuing their struggle against the Chinese Revolution:

1. They are continuing to give support to the Guomindang and other potential forces in the struggle against the Chinese Revolution.

2. They are taking all measures to infiltrate the revolutionary camp so as to disintegrate it and cause damage to the Chinese Revolution.

3. They are going out of their way to disturb relations between the Chinese Revolution and the USSR, and also with the world Communist movement.

4. They are trying in every possible way to show that they seek rapprochement with the CCP and, simultaneously, are striving to lure the CCP onto the path of rapprochement with the imperialist states.

We are clearly aware of these imperialist schemings, and we have sufficient experience in combating them. We shall never let these imperialist schemings succeed. On all these issues we have already warned the democratic parties and groups, and urged vigilance from the people.

The Chinese Revolution should work consistently to destroy imperialist domination in China in the military, political, economic, and cultural fields. This goal is set in the resolutions of the Second Plenary Meeting of the CCP Central Committee, and it is inviolable. In districts being occupied by our troops, the military and political domination of the imperialists ends after the overthrow of the Guomindang. Their economic and cultural influence has also been weakened significantly. However, there still are economic enterprises and cultural institutions directly controlled by the imperialists. Their diplomats and correspondents still remain. The tactics and method of actions on all these issues merit attention.

We believe that now and in the future we should adhere to the following principles in our foreign policy:

1. Waging a struggle against the imperialist states with the aim of achieving complete independence for the Chinese people.

2. In international affairs, siding with the USSR and the countries of new democracy, fighting against the threat of a new war, safeguarding peace and democracy throughout the world.

3. Making use of the differences among the capitalist countries and contradictions within these countries. *(Yes.)*

4. Promoting China's commercial relations with foreign states, above all, with the USSR and the people's democracies on the principle of equality and mutual benefit.

We lack the latest data on capital investments of the imperialist countries in China. According to Japanese data of 1936, Britain, the U.S., France, Germany, Italy, and Belgium had a total of $1.828 billion in investments. Of this sum $1 billion belonged to Britain, 220 million to the U.S., 210 million to Germany and Italy; 500 million was in railway and political loans, 450 million was invested in foreign banks and financial institutions, 380 million was in export-import trade, and 360 million was invested in mining and other industries. However, after Japan's defeat, the investments of Japan, Germany, and Italy in China were confiscated. *(By whom?)* Britain, France, and Belgium have lost some of their investments in China, while the capital investments made by the U.S. have increased a little. At the present time, foreign states own enterprises, banks, insurance-companies, export-import offices, seagoing vessels, wharves, and warehouses. The companies of Kailan collieries with an annual output of 4 million tons of coal (in which Britain has half of the capital), the tobacco factories in Tianjin and Shanghai, the American electric power station in Shanghai, and some other utilities are of some importance. The other foreign-owned enterprises in China are of no great importance, neither are industrial and mining businesses run by the imperialists. While applying certain essential restrictions, we still permit by and large the economic enterprises owned by the imperialists to continue their work in China. *(What restrictions?)* However, some imperialists have already withdrawn their capital assets from China or else they would rather take a wait-and-see stand. Thus far we have not decided at what particular moment and by what particular methods the issue of imperialist investments in China is to be resolved – whether they should be confiscated or dealt with in some other way. Today we are very busy with military matters and other work, and have not got down to this issue. Nevertheless, we must be ready with a solution.

Imperialist countries have their propaganda setups and cultural institutions in China. According to available data, apart from the newspapers, magazines, and news agencies,

Britain and the U.S. alone have 31 universities and specialized schools, 32 religious educational institutions, 29 libraries, 26 cultural organizations, 324 high schools, 2,364 elementary schools, 3,729 religious missions, 93 religious organizations, 147 hospitals, and 53 philanthropic organizations.

The CCP Central Committee has decided to stop the publication of the existing foreign newspapers and magazines and discontinue the activity of foreign news agencies and correspondents. This decision is being carried out locally. But since in Shanghai the imperialists still have in their hands a few economically vital facilities, the CCP Central Committee has approved the proposal of our Shanghai comrades to refrain for the time being from action on the above-mentioned decision; but we are getting ready to carry it out in the future. With regard to the schools and hospitals owned by imperialist countries in China, we still allow them to continue their activity provided they abide by our laws. But we shall not permit the opening of new schools and hospitals in China. In the future, once we are able to run these educational institutions and hospitals by ourselves, we shall take them over.

We allow foreign religious organizations to continue their activity provided they observe our laws, but simultaneously we are carrying out antireligious propaganda. The lands of religious missions and churches are confiscated and distributed with the consent of the believers. *(Yes.)* The land owned by other foreign institutions and organizations is also confiscated and distributed.

We do not recognize diplomats of foreign states in China and regard them as foreign residents. As a result of our policy on this issue the people see that China has already risen and that the CCP does not fear the imperialists. Besides, this enables us to avoid much trouble, for members of democratic parties and groups no longer dare maintain relations and meet diplomats from imperialist countries, and even common people dare not meet these foreigners from the imperialist countries.

Diplomats representing imperialist countries in China are turning to us with requests and trying to establish relations with us in order to obtain de facto recognition. No one in Chinese history has ever dared to pursue a policy toward foreigners in China the like of which we are pursuing. But, as a consequence, foreign residents, feeling all kinds of inconveniences, are turning to us in great numbers with requests for permission to leave China. Simultaneously, we are also experiencing certain inconveniences in this connection. In the territory of liberated China there are about 120,000 foreign residents, of whom more than 65,000 live in Shanghai alone. In Manchuria there are 54,000 foreigners, the larger part of them being Soviet citizens, with the Japanese coming second.

Right after the formation of a new central government will come the question of establishing official diplomatic relations with foreign states and of our participation in the UN and other international organizations and at international conferences. Probably for some period of time imperialist states will be ignoring us or will put forward conditions with strings attached, in exchange for any recognition they would grant us. What should our policy be on this issue? *(Discriminatory. He who does not recognize China should not be given any easy terms in trade with China (a crisis in the U.S. will compel the U.S. to value trade with China). Use Chinese merchants for this purpose.)* Naturally we shall not accept conditions that might hamper our actions, but should we take active steps to gain recognition from these states and thus secure a legitimate position for carrying out international activity? But, on the other hand, had we not better wait and not hurry to gain recognition from these states? *(Yes! Better not hurry.)* Had we not better get down to purging our domestic front to avoid trouble? *(Yes!)* After the formation of a new government in China will the USSR and the new democracies give early recognition to the new government of China even if imperialist countries ignore us in their policy? *(Yes.)* If imperialist countries adopt a policy of granting recognition to the new government in China, we will be ready then to establish diplomatic relations with these countries and would like the USSR to recognize us before other countries do.

We are going to revise every treaty and every agreement that the Guomindang government has signed with foreign states. In this way we shall adhere to the following principle: We are prepared to recognize and act on all the treaties which are in the interests of Chinese people, peace and democracy throughout the world, that is, UN status, the Cairo Declaration, the Treaty of Friendship and Alliance between China and the USSR. But we are prepared to abrogate all the treaties harmful to the interests of the Chinese people, peace and democracy throughout the world, that is, the treaty on trade and high seas navigation between China and the U.S. We are going to recognize some treaties upon adequate amendments. *(Yes.)*

After foreign states have recognized new China, we are going to take part in the work of the UN and other international organizations, especially in various international organizations having to do with Japan. In our policy in international relations we shall certainly be at one with the USSR, and we have already made some elucidations to this effect to the democratic parties and groups. *(Yes!)* Some nonpartisan people criticized our policy for its pro-USSR slant, but Comrade Mao Zedong told them that our policy would be leaning toward the USSR, for it would be an error should we not stand together with the USSR in the struggle against the imperialist front but take a middle road. Upon such elucidations all democratic parties and groups, jointly with the CCP, signed and published a statement against the North Atlantic Pact. We would like to get instructions from the Soviet Communist Party and Comrade Joseph Stalin on various foreign policy issues.

4. Soviet-Chinese Relations

The strong friendship between the great peoples of the USSR and China is of paramount importance for our two countries and the entire world. It is crucial particularly for the independence of China and its constructive development. The CCP Central Committee is fully awake to the importance of this matter. The CCP shall stint no effort in the cause of strengthening the friendship between our two peoples.

The Soviet-Chinese Treaty of Friendship and Cooperation has been of great use to the Chinese people. The new government of China will accept this treaty, and this will be a still greater contribution for the benefit of the peoples of China and the USSR, especially for the Chinese people. We fully desire to accept this treaty. While establishing their diplomatic relations, the USSR and new China will have to give closer attention to this treaty. In general, they could act with regard to this treaty according to one of the following three options:

1. The new government of China will state its complete acceptance of this treaty as valid, without any amendments whatsoever.

2. Proceeding from the original text of the treaty, representatives of both governments will conclude a new treaty of friendship and alliance between the USSR and China which, in conformity with the new situation, would be amended in style and substance.

3. Representatives of the governments of both countries will exchange notes to the effect that the present treaty temporarily remains what it is but state that they are prepared to revise it at an opportune moment.

Which of the above three variants is best? *(Settle the issue upon Mao Zedong's arrival in Moscow.)*

Some persons from democratic parties, students, and workers raised the issues about the Soviet troops stationed in Port Arthur, about the independence of Mongolia, and about the removal by the Soviet Union of machinery from Manchuria. *(From Manchuria we have removed Japanese capital but partially, far from completely.)*

We gave the following explanations to these people.

If, being unable to defend our coast by ourselves, we had not agreed to have Soviet troops stationed in Port Arthur, we would have helped the imperialists that way.

On the issue of the Mongolian People's Republic, we said that the Mongolian people, in keeping with the principle of national self-determination, had demanded independence and thus we ought to recognize Mongolia's independence. But if the MPR wished to join China, we would welcome that. It is the Mongolian people alone that has the right to decide on this issue. *(Yes.)*

On the issue of the removal by the Soviet Union of machinery from Manchuria we said that these machines had belonged to the Japanese, and that the Soviet Union had taken this equipment as war booty for use at home for socialist construction. Another consideration was that this equipment might get into the hands of the Chinese reactionary party that could use it in its struggle against the Chinese people. The USSR was absolutely right in doing that.

Are these explanations of ours correct?

We would like to settle as soon as possible matters related to establishing postal, telegraph, railway, and air services with the USSR and, also, we would like to set up a joint Soviet-Chinese air company. How is this to be done? *(Yes. We shall help.)*

How will it be best to establish relations with the people's democracies of East Europe and to trade with them? *(By means of direct negotiations with them.)*

Having for a long time stayed in the countryside waging guerrilla war, we, therefore, have a poor knowledge of external affairs. Today we are to govern such a large state, steer economic construction, and carry on diplomatic activity. We yet have a good deal to learn. Of great significance in this respect are instructions and assistance to us from the Soviet Communist Party. We are badly in need of these instructions and of this assistance. Besides the sending of Soviet experts to China for assistance to us, we would like to have Soviet teachers sent to China for lecturing and to have delegations sent from China to the USSR for firsthand acquaintance and learning. Besides, we would like to send students for a course of education in the USSR. *(Yes.)*

On the question of relations between the Soviet Communist Party and the CCP, Comrade Mao Zedong and the CCP Central Committee maintain the following:

The Soviet Communist Party is the main headquarters of the international Communist movement, while the Communist Party of China is only a single-front headquarters. The interests of a part should be subordinated to international interests and, therefore, the CCP submits to decisions of the Soviet Communist Party, though the Comintern is no longer in existence and the CCP is not within the Information Bureau of European Communist Parties. *(No!)* If on some questions differences should arise between the CCP and the Soviet Communist Party, the CCP, having outlined its point of view, will submit and will resolutely carry out decisions of the Soviet Communist Party. *(No!)* We believe it is necessary to establish the closest mutual ties between the two parties, exchange appropriate authorized political representation so as to decide questions of interest to our two parties and, besides, achieve better mutual understanding between our parties. *(Yes!)*

Comrade Mao Zedong wishes to visit Moscow, but now he cannot arrive in Moscow in secret, and he has to wait for the USSR and China to establish diplomatic relations before he could visit Moscow legally. We ask for advice as to when Mao Zedong could come to Moscow and how to best do that. *(Yes. Late in 1949 upon establishment of diplomatic relations.)*

We ask for instructions on the above questions.

We fully agree with the conditions which Comrade Joseph Stalin has set concerning the Soviet Union's loan to China amounting to $300,000,000, and we are grateful to the Soviet Union for its aid to the Chinese people. *(But what about silver?)*

We wish the Soviet Communist Party's Central Committee and Comrade Stalin not to hesitate in giving instructions to the CCP and in criticizing its work and policy.

Source: APRF, f. 45, op. 1, d. 328, 11–50. The translation is based on Andrei Ledovsky's in the Russian journal *Far Eastern Affairs,* no. 4, 1996, 70–85, but amended according to the original document.

IV. Record of Conversation, Stalin and Mao Zedong, December 16, 1949

Documents 4–7 show different stages of Mao Zedong's visit to Moscow in the winter of 1949/50. Document 4 is Mao's first conversation with Stalin, which took place in the Kremlin in the evening of December 16, right after the arrival of the Chinese delegation. Document 5 is Mao's conversation with the Soviet ambassador to China, Nikolai Roshchin, who had accompanied him to Moscow. Mao often used Roshchin as a sounding board for how to approach the Soviet leaders. Document 6 is one of Mao's telegrams to the CCP Politburo. Writing on January 2, Mao was probably too optimistic about Stalin's change of mind, but, as shown in Document 7, real negotiations did get going after Zhou Enlai's arrival on January 20.

After an exchange of greetings and a discussion of general topics, the following conversation took place:

Mao Zedong: The most important question at the present time is the question of establishing peace. China needs a period of three to five years of peace, which would be used to bring the economy back to prewar levels and to stabilize the country in general. Decisions on the most important questions in China hinge on the prospects for a peaceful future. With this in mind the CC CCP [Central Committee of the Communist Party of China] entrusted me to ascertain from you, Comrade Stalin, in what way and for how long will international peace be preserved.

Stalin: In China a war for peace, as it were, is taking place. The question of peace greatly preoccupies the Soviet Union as well, though we have already had peace for the past four years. With regards to China, there is no immediate threat at the present time: Japan has yet to stand up on its feet and is thus not ready for war; America, though it screams war, is actually afraid of war more than anything; Europe is afraid of war; in essence, there is no one to fight with China, not unless Kim Il Sung decides to invade China? Peace will depend on our efforts. If we continue to be friendly, peace can last not only five to ten years, but twenty to twenty-five years and perhaps even longer.

Mao Zedong: Since Liu Shaoqi's return to China, CC CCP has been discussing the treaty of friendship, alliance, and mutual assistance between China and the USSR.

Stalin: This question we can discuss and decide. We must ascertain whether to declare the continuation of the current 1945 treaty of alliance and friendship between the USSR and China, to announce impending changes in the future, or to make these changes right now. As you know, this treaty was concluded between the USSR and China as a result of the Yalta Agreement, which provided for the main points of the treaty (the question of the Kurile Islands, South Sakhalin, Port Arthur [Lushan], etc.). That is, the given treaty was concluded, so to speak, with the consent of America and England. Keeping in mind this circumstance, we, within our inner circle, have decided not to modify any of the points of this treaty for now, since a change in even one point could give America and England the legal grounds to raise questions about modifying also the treaty's provisions concerning the Kurile Islands, South Sakhalin, etc. This is why we searched to find a way to modify the current treaty in effect while formally maintaining its provisions, in this case by formally maintaining the Soviet Union's right to station its troops at Port Arthur while, at the request of the Chinese government, actually withdrawing the Soviet armed forces currently stationed there. Such an operation could be carried out upon China's request.

One could do the same with CCR [Chinese Changchun Railroad, which traverses Manchuria], that is, to effectively modify the corresponding points of the agreement while formally maintaining its provisions, upon China's request. If, on the other hand, the Chinese comrades are not satisfied with this strategy, they can present their own proposals.

Mao Zedong: The present situation with regard to CCR and Port Arthur corresponds well with Chinese interests, as the Chinese forces are inadequate to effectively fight against imperialist aggression. In addition, CCR is a training school for the preparation of Chinese cadres in railroad and industry.

Stalin: The withdrawal of troops does not mean that the Soviet Union refuses to assist China, if such assistance is needed. The fact is that we, as Communists, are not altogether comfortable with stationing our forces on foreign soil, especially on the soil of a friendly nation. Given this situation anyone could say that if Soviet forces can be stationed on Chinese territory, then why could not the British, for example, station their forces in Hong Kong, or the Americans in Tokyo? We would gain much in the arena of international relations if, with mutual agreement, the Soviet forces were to be withdrawn from Port Arthur. In addition, the withdrawal of Soviet forces would provide a serious boost to Chinese Communists in their relations with the national bourgeoisie.

Everyone would see that the Communists have managed to achieve what [Nationalist Chinese leader] Jiang Jieshi could not. The Chinese Communists must take the national bourgeoisie into consideration. The treaty ensures the USSR's right to station its troops in Port Arthur. But the USSR is not obligated to exercise this right and can withdraw its troops upon Chinese request. However, if this is unsuitable, the troops in Port Arthur can remain there for two, five, or ten years, whatever suits China best. Let them not think that we want to run away from China. We can stay there for twenty years even.

Mao Zedong: In discussing the treaty in China we had not taken into account the American and English positions regarding the Yalta Agreement. We must act in a way that is best for the common cause. This question merits further consideration. However, it is already becoming clear that the treaty should not be modified at the present time, nor should one rush to withdraw troops from Port Arthur.

Should not Zhou Enlai visit Moscow in order to decide the treaty question?

Stalin: No, this question you must decide for yourselves. Zhou may be needed in regard to other matters.

Mao Zedong: We would like to decide on the question of Soviet credit to China, that is, to draw up a credit agreement for $300,000,000 between the government of the USSR and China.

Stalin: This can be done. If you would like to formalize this agreement now, we can.

Mao Zedong: Yes, exactly now, as this would resonate well in China. At the same time it is necessary to resolve the question of trade, especially between the USSR and Xinjiang, though at present we cannot present a specific trade operations plan for this region.

Stalin: We must know right now what kind of equipment China will need, especially now, since we do not have equipment in reserve and the request for industrial goods must be submitted ahead of time.

Mao Zedong: We are having difficulties in putting together a request for equipment, as the industrial picture is as yet unclear.

Stalin: It is desirable to expedite the preparation of this request, as requests for equipment are submitted to our industry at least a year in advance.

Mao Zedong: We would very much like to receive assistance from the USSR in creating air transportation routes.

Stalin: We are ready to render such assistance. Air routes can be established over Xinjiang and the MPR [Mongolian People's Republic]. We have specialists. We will give you assistance.

Mao Zedong: We would also like to receive your assistance in creating a naval force.

Stalin: Cadres for Chinese navy could be prepared at Port Arthur. You give us people, and we will give you ships. Trained cadres of the Chinese navy could then return to China on these ships.

Mao Zedong: Guomindang supporters have built a naval and air base on the island of Formosa [Taiwan]. Our lack of naval forces and aviation makes the occupation of the island by the People's Liberation Army [PLA] more difficult. With regard to this, some of our generals have been voicing opinions that we should request assistance from the Soviet Union, which could send volunteer pilots or secret military detachments to speed up the conquest of Formosa.

Stalin: Assistance has not been ruled out, though one ought to consider the form of such assistance. What is most important here is not to give Americans a pretext to intervene. With regard to headquarters staff and instructors we can give them to you anytime. The rest we will have to think about. Do you have any assault landing units?

Mao Zedong: We have one former Guomindang assault landing regiment unit which came to join our side.

Stalin: One could select a company of landing forces, train them in propaganda, send them over to Formosa, and through them organize an uprising on the isle.

Mao Zedong: Our troops have approached the borders of Burma and Indochina. As a result, the Americans and the British are alarmed, not knowing whether we will cross the border or whether our troops will halt their movement.

Stalin: One could create a rumor that you are preparing to cross the border and in this way frighten the imperialists a bit.

Mao Zedong: Several countries, especially Britain, are actively campaigning to recognize the People's Republic of China. However, we believe that we should not rush to be recognized. We must first bring about order to the country, strengthen our position, and then we can talk to foreign imperialists.

Stalin: That is a good policy. In addition, there is no need for you to create conflicts with the British and the Americans. If, for example, there will be a need to put pressure on the British, this can be done by resorting to a conflict between Guangdong province and Hong Kong. And to resolve this conflict, Mao Zedong could come forward as the mediator. The main point is not to rush and to avoid conflicts.

Are there foreign banks operating in Shanghai?

Mao Zedong: Yes.

Stalin: And whom are they serving?

Mao Zedong: The Chinese national bourgeoisie and foreign enterprises which so far we have not touched. As for the foreigner's spheres of influence, the British predominate in investments in the economic and commercial sectors, while the Americans lead in the sector of cultural-educational organizations.

Stalin: What is the situation regarding Japanese enterprises?

Mao Zedong: They have been nationalized.

Stalin: In whose hands is the customs agency?

Mao Zedong: In the hands of the government.

Stalin: It is important to focus attention on the customs agency as it is usually a good source of government revenue.

Mao Zedong: In the military and political sectors we have already achieved complete success; as for cultural and economic sectors, we have as yet not freed ourselves from foreign influence there.

Stalin: Do you have inspectors and agents overseeing foreign enterprises, banks, etc.?

Mao Zedong: Yes, we have. We are carrying out such work in the study and oversight of foreign enterprises (the Kailan mines, electric power plants and aqueducts in Shanghai, etc.).

317

Stalin: One should have government inspectors who must operate legally. The foreigners should also be taxed at higher levels than the Chinese.

Who owns the enterprises mining wolfram [tungsten], molybdenum, and petroleum?

Mao Zedong: The government.

Stalin: It is important to increase the mining of minerals and especially of petroleum. You could build an oil pipeline from Lanzhou in the west to Chengdu and then transport fuel by ship.

Mao Zedong: So far we have not decided which districts of China we should strive to develop first – the coastal areas or those inland – since we were unsure of the prospects for peace.

Stalin: Petroleum, coal, and metal are always needed, regardless of whether there be war or not.

Can rubber-bearing trees be grown in southern China?

Mao Zedong: So far it has not been possible.

Stalin: Is there a meteorological service in China?

Mao Zedong: No, it has not been established yet.

Stalin: It should be established.

We would like to receive from you a list of your works which could be translated into Russian.

Mao Zedong: I am currently reviewing my works which were published in various local publishing houses and which contain a number of errors and misrepresentations. I plan to complete this review by spring of 1950. However, I would like to receive help from Soviet comrades: first of all, to work on the texts with Russian translators and, secondly, to receive help in editing the Chinese original.

Stalin: This can be done. However, do you need your works edited?

Mao Zedong: Yes, and I ask you to select a comrade suitable for such a task, say, for example, someone from CC VKP(b).

Stalin: It can be arranged, if indeed there is such a need.

Also present at the meeting: Comrades Molotov, Malenkov, Bulganin, Vyshinskii, [Soviet translator N. T.] Fedorenko, and [Chinese translator] Shi Zhe (Karskii). Recorded by Comrade Fedorenko.

Source: APRF, f. 45, op. 1, d. 329, pp. 9–17. Translation by Danny Rozas.

V. Record of Conversation, Soviet Ambassador to Beijing Nikolai Roshchin and Mao Zedong, in Moscow, January 1, 1950

Following the orders of the USSR Minister of Foreign Affairs, Comrade [Andrei] Vyshinskii, on January 1 [I] visited the chairman of the People's Central Government of the People's Republic of China, Comrade Mao Zedong. After an exchange of New Year greetings and other formalities, a friendly and warm conversation took place, during which Comrade Mao Zedong related the following.

During the past few days he received a report from Beijing that the governments of Burma and India expressed their readiness to recognize the government of the People's Republic of China. The position of the Chinese government on this matter is as follows: to inform the governments of Burma and India that if they are sincere in their wishes to mend diplomatic relations with the People's Republic of China, first they must completely break all ties with Jiang Jieshi, unconditionally refuse any kind of support and assistance to this regime, making it into an official declaration. Under the condition that the governments of these countries accept the aforementioned proposals of the Chinese government, the Indian and Burmese governments may send their representatives to Beijing for negotiations.

Comrade Mao Zedong pointed out that there is also information which states that in the very near future England and other countries of the British Commonwealth will evidently take steps toward recognizing the People's Republic of China.

Touching upon the military situation in China, Comrade Mao Zedong pointed out that as of now all of the main Guomindang forces on the mainland of China have been crushed. In the Sichuan and Xinjiang provinces approximately 400,000 Guomindang troops were taken prisoner and switched to the side of the People's Liberation Army. For the remainder of the Hu Zongnan[3] cluster, numbering 30,000–40,000 persons, all the routes for retreating to Tibet and to the south have been cut off. They will be destroyed in the very near future. In Yunnan there are also up to another 30,000 persons scattered to the southwest from Kunming in separate groups of Guomindang followers, but their fate has been decided.

Mao Zedong requested to transmit the following information concerning his health condition and his plans for further stay in Moscow to the leaders of the Soviet government:

"My health condition – says Mao Zedong – has improved after a two-week resting period. For the last four days I have been sleeping eight hours a day with no problems, without taking special sleeping medication. I feel much more energetic, but when going for

---

[3] GMD general, commander of the remaining GMD forces in western China.

a walk, I cannot remain out in the fresh air for more than a quarter of an hour – I get dizzy. With regard to this, I intend to rest one more week in total peace and completely restore a normal sleeping pattern."

Further he pointed out that following the weeklong rest period he would like to visit Comrades Shvernik,[4] Molotov, Voroshilov, Beriia, Malenkov, Vasilevskii,[5] and Vyshinskii. These visits will have to take the nature of ordinary conversations. He will not talk about any specific topics nor discuss any business matters. There must be one visit per day, they must not be very lengthy, and he thinks that the best time for them would be after 5–6 P.M.

During the same time period he would like to meet with I. V. Stalin to discuss business matters. After completing the discussion concerning business matters, during the remainder of the stay he intends to place a wreath at Lenin's mausoleum, see the subway system, visit a few collective farms, attend theaters, and with that finish his stay in Moscow.

Comrade Mao Zedong emphasized that he refrains from visiting factories, meetings with large audiences, and giving public speeches, because it is tiring to his health and may, once again, disturb his sleeping pattern and provoke a relapse of spells of dizziness. Previously he intended to visit different places in the Soviet Union, but presently, due to his health condition, he refrains from traveling around the Soviet Union, because there is a long trip home ahead of him. Upon leaving Beijing he intended to stay in the USSR for three months, however, presently the circumstances of [his] work in China are forcing him to reduce the length of his stay to two months. Keeping in mind the eleven-day [train] travel to Beijing, he intends to leave Moscow at the end of January, counting on being in Beijing on February 6.

After listening to all of Comrade Mao Zedong's announcements, I stated that I will report all of his wishes to the government the very next day.

Further I asked Comrade Mao Zedong if he is aware of the proposal made by the Soviet government in November [1949], to hand over a few hundred Japanese army officers to the Chinese government, in order to bring them to justice for crimes and atrocities which they committed while stationed in China.

Comrade Mao Zedong stated that he was aware of this even prior to his departure from Beijing, but because they were busy with preparations for the trip to Moscow, the Chinese government was not able to look into this matter seriously. His point of view on this matter is as follows: As a matter of principle, the Chinese government will take these criminals and will put them on trial for all their deeds. However, taking into consideration that presently the attention of the Chinese people is concentrated on the

[4] Nikolai Shvernik, chairman of the Supreme Soviet.

[5] Aleksander Vasilevskii, minister of Armed Forces.

events surrounding the elimination of the final remnants of the Guomindang and that the Chinese court system has not yet been ironed out, the Chinese government cannot begin the trial process without preparing the population for it, because it will not have a proper political effect.

Besides, the Chinese government must at the same time prepare the trials against the Guomindang military criminals.

Taking into consideration all of this – says Mao Zedong – I suppose that we will be able to take the military criminals from Soviet territory after six months. I ask the Soviet government to keep these criminals for the first six months of 1950 on its territory and, if possible, to collect more information on them for the trial. In the beginning of the second half of the year we will take them and will put them on trial.

On this the business discussion was concluded. Following the discussion Comrade Mao Zedong invited me to the table to have dinner together with him. I accepted the invitation.

The conversation was translated by Shi Zhe (Karskii).

After parting with Comrade Mao Zedong, I remained to wait for the car with Karskii. The latter informed me that Comrade Mao Zedong has been feeling much better for three days already. He sleeps fine, without taking medication, jokes, is cheerful and talkative with everyone, but, the same as before, cannot be out in the fresh air for long. He still gets spells of dizziness. Comrade Mao Zedong firmly decided to rest another week and not travel anywhere. On January 2 a conference of doctors will take place.

Source: Arkhiv vneshnei politiki Rossiiskoi Federatsii (AVPRF), f. 0100, op. 43, papka (pa.) 302, d. 10, pp. 1–4. Document provided by O. A. Westad; translated by Daniel Rozas.

VI. Telegram, Mao Zedong to Chinese Communist Party Central Committee, January 2, 1950

Central Committee:

(1) Our work here has achieved an important breakthrough in the past two days. Comrade Stalin has finally agreed to invite Comrade Zhou Enlai to Moscow and sign a

new Sino-Soviet Treaty of Friendship and Alliance and other agreements on credit, trade, and civil aviation. Yesterday, on January 1, a decision was made to publish my interview with the Tass correspondent, and it is in the newspapers today (January 2), which you might have already received. At 8:00 P.M. today, Comrade Molotov and Comrade Mikoyan came to my quarters to have a talk, asking about my opinions on the Sino-Soviet treaty and other matters. I immediately gave them a detailed description of three options: (a) To sign a new Sino-Soviet Treaty of Friendship and Alliance. By taking this action, we will gain enormous advantages. Sino-Soviet relations will be solidified on the basis of the new treaty; in China, workers, peasants, intellectuals, and the left wing of the national bourgeoisie will be greatly inspired, while the right wing of the national bourgeoisie will be isolated; and internationally, we may acquire more political capital to deal with the imperialist countries and to examine all the treaties signed between China and each of the imperialist countries in the past. (b) To publish through the news agencies of the two countries a brief communiqué stating that the authorities of the two countries have exchanged opinions on the old Sino-Soviet treaty and other issues, and have achieved a consensus, without mentioning any of the details. In fact, by doing so we mean to put off the solution of the problem to the future, until a few years later. Accordingly, China's foreign minister Zhou Enlai does not need to come here. (c) To sign a statement, not a treaty, that will summarize the key points in the two countries' relations. If this is the option, Zhou Enlai will not have to come either. After I have analyzed in detail the advantages and disadvantages of these three options, Comrade Molotov said promptly that option (a) was good and that Zhou should come. I then asked: "Do you mean that the old treaty will be replaced by a new one?" Comrade Molotov replied: "Yes." After that we calculated how long it would take for Zhou to come here and to sign the treaty. I said that my telegram would reach Beijing on January 3, and that [Zhou] Enlai would need five days for preparations and could depart from Beijing on January 9. It would take him eleven days by train [to travel to Moscow], so he could arrive in Moscow on January 19. The negotiation and the signing of the treaty would need about ten days, from January 20 to the end of the month. Zhou and I would return home in early February. Meanwhile we also discussed the plans for my sightseeing outside [my quarters and Moscow], and we decided that I would visit Lenin's tomb, travel to Leningrad, Gorky, and other places, and make tours of such places as an ordinance factory, the subway (Molotov and Mikoyan recommended these two items), and a collective farm. We also discussed the problem of my meeting with various Soviet leaders (so far I have not left my quarters to pay an individual visit to any of them).

(2) Please finish all the preparations [for Zhou's departure] in five days after you receive this telegram. I hope that [Zhou] Enlai, together with the minister of trade and other necessary aides, and with the necessary documents and materials, will depart from Beijing for Moscow by train (not by air) on January 9. Comrade Dong Biwu will assume the

post of acting premier of the Government Administration Council. The news should not be publicized until Zhou has arrived in Moscow.

(3) Are the above-stated arrangements feasible? Will five days be enough for you to finish the preparations? Does [Zhou] need one or two more days for preparation? Is it necessary for Comrade Li Fuchun or other comrades to come to offer assistance? Please consider them and report to me in a return telegram.

Source: *Jiangguo yilai Mao Zedong wengao* [Mao Zedong's works since the founding of the PRC] (Beijing: Zhongyang wenxian, 1987), vol. 1, 211–12. Translated by Shu Guang Zhang and Chen Jian.

VII. Record of Conversation, Stalin and Mao Zedong, January 22, 1950

After an exchange of greetings and a short discussion of general topics, the following conversation took place:

Stalin: There are two groups of questions which must be discussed: The first group of questions concerns the existing agreements between the USSR and China; the second group of questions concerns the current events in Manchuria, Xinjiang, etc. I think that it would be better to begin not with the current events, but rather with a discussion of the existing agreements. We believe that these agreements need to be changed, though earlier we had thought that they could be left intact. The existing agreements, including the treaty, should be changed because war against Japan figures at the very heart of the treaty. Since the war is over and Japan has been crushed, the situation has been altered, and now the treaty has become an anachronism. I ask to hear your opinion regarding the treaty of friendship and alliance.

Mao Zedong: So far we have not worked out a concrete draft of the treaty, only a few outlines.

Stalin: We can exchange opinions, and then prepare an appropriate draft.

Mao Zedong: Judging from the current situation, we believe that we should strengthen our existing friendship using the help of treaties and agreements. This would resonate well both in China and in the international arena. Everything that guarantees the future prosperity of our countries must be stated in the treaty of alliance and friendship, including the necessity of avoiding a repetition of Japanese aggression. So long as we show interest in the prosperity of our countries, one cannot rule out the possibility that the imperialist countries will attempt to hinder us.

Stalin: True. Japan still has cadres remaining, and it will certainly lift itself up again, especially if Americans continue their current policy.

Mao Zedong: Two points that I made earlier are cardinal in changing our future treaty from the existing one. Previously, the Guomindang spoke of friendship in words only. Now the situation has changed, with all the conditions for real friendship and cooperation in place.

In addition, whereas before there was talk of cooperation in the war against Japan, now attention must turn to preventing Japanese aggression. The new treaty must include the questions of political, economic, cultural, and military cooperation. Of most importance will be the question of economic cooperation.

Stalin: Is it necessary to keep the provision, stated in article 3 of the current Treaty of Friendship: ". . . This article shall remain in force up until that time when, by request of both High Participants in the Treaty, the United Nations is given the responsibility of preventing any future aggression on the part of Japan"?

Mao Zedong: I do not believe it is necessary to keep this provision.

Stalin: We also believe that it is unnecessary. What provisions do we need to specify in the new treaty?

Mao Zedong: We believe that the new treaty should include a paragraph on consultation regarding international concerns. The addition of this paragraph would strengthen our position, since among the Chinese national bourgeoisie there are objections to the policy of rapprochement with the Soviet Union on questions of international concern.

Stalin: Good. When signing a treaty of friendship and cooperation, the inclusion of such a paragraph goes without saying.

Mao Zedong: That's right.

Stalin: To whom shall we entrust the preparation of the draft? I believe that we should entrust it to [Andrei] Vyshinskii and Zhou Enlai.

Mao Zedong: Agreed.

Stalin: Let us move over to the agreement on the Chinese Changchun Railway [CCR]. What proposals do you have on this question?

Mao Zedong: Perhaps we should accept as the guiding principle the idea of making practical changes concerning the CCR and the Port Arthur agreements, while legally continuing them in their present state?

Stalin: That is, you agree to declare the legal continuation of the current agreement, while, in effect, allowing appropriate changes to take place.

Mao Zedong: We must act so as to take into account the interests of both sides, China and the Soviet Union.

Stalin: True. We believe that the agreement concerning Port Arthur is not equitable.

Mao Zedong: But changing this agreement goes against the decisions of the Yalta Conference?!

Stalin: True, it does – and to hell with it! Once we have taken up the position that the treaties must be changed, we must go all the way. It is true that for us this entails certain inconveniences, and we will have to struggle against the Americans. But we are already reconciled to that.

Mao Zedong: This question worries us only because it may have undesirable consequences for the USSR.

Stalin: As you know, we made the current agreement during the war with Japan. We did not know that Jiang Jieshi would be toppled. We acted under the premise that the presence of our troops in Port Arthur would be in the interests of Soviet Union and democracy in China.

Mao Zedong: The matter is clear.

Stalin: In that case, would you deem the following scenario acceptable: Declare that the agreement on Port Arthur shall remain in force until a peace treaty with Japan is signed, after which the Russian troops would be withdrawn from Port Arthur. Or perhaps one could propose another scenario: Declare that the current agreement shall remain in place, while in effect withdrawing troops from Port Arthur. We will accept whichever of these scenarios is more suitable. We agree with both scenarios.

Mao Zedong: This question should be thought through. We agree with the opinion of Comrade Stalin and believe that the agreement on Port Arthur must remain in force until a peace treaty is signed with Japan, after which the treaty shall become invalid and the Soviet soldiers will leave. However, we would like for Port Arthur to be a place for military collaboration, where we could train our military naval forces.

Stalin: The question of Dalny [Dalian]. We have no intention of securing any Soviet rights in Dalny.

Mao Zedong: Will Dalny remain a free port?

Stalin: Since we are giving up our rights there, China must decide on its own the question of Dalny: Will it remain a free port or not? During his time Roosevelt insisted that Dairen [Dalian] remain a free port.

Mao Zedong: So the preservation of the free port would be in the interests of America and Britain?

Stalin: Of course. It's a house with open gates.

Mao Zedong: We believe that Port Arthur could serve as a base for our military collaboration, while Dalny could serve as a base for Sino-Soviet economic collaboration. In

Dalny' there is a whole array of enterprises that we are in no position to exploit without Soviet assistance. We should develop a closer economic collaboration there.

Stalin: In other words, the agreement on Port Arthur will remain in force until a peace treaty is signed with Japan. After the signing of the peace treaty the existing agreement shall become invalid and the Russians shall withdraw their troops. Did I sum up your thoughts correctly?

Mao Zedong: Yes, basically so, and it is exactly this which we would like to set forth in the new treaty.

Stalin: Let us continue the discussion of the CCR question. Tell us, as an honest Communist, what doubts do you have here?

Mao Zedong: The principal point is that the new treaty should note that joint exploitation and administration will continue in the future. However, in the case of administration, China should take the lead role here. Furthermore, it is necessary to examine the question of shortening the duration of the agreement and to determine the amount of investment by each side.

Molotov: The conditions governing the cooperation and joint administration of an enterprise by two interested countries usually provide for equal participation by both sides, as well as for alteration in the appointment of replacements for management positions. In the old agreement the administration of the railroad belonged to the Soviets; however, in the future we think it necessary to alternate in the creation of management functions. Let's say that such an alternation could take place every two to three years.

Zhou Enlai: Our comrades believe that the existing management of CCR and the office of the director ought to be abolished and a railroad administration commission be set up in their place; and that the offices of the commission chairman and of the director should be replaced by Chinese cadres. However, given Comrade Molotov's proposals, this question requires more thought.

Stalin: If we are talking about joint administration, then it is important that the replacements for the managing position be alternated. That would be more logical. As for the duration of the agreement, we would not be against shortening it.

Zhou Enlai: Should we not change the ratio of capital investment by each side, by increasing the level of Chinese investment to 51 percent, instead of the current requirement for parity?

Molotov: This would go against the existing provision for parity.

Stalin: We do indeed have agreements with the Czechs and the Bulgarians which provide for parity and equal footing for both sides. Since we already have joint administration, then we might as well have equal participation.

Mao Zedong: The question needs to be further examined, keeping in mind the interests of both sides.

Stalin: Let us discuss the credit agreement. We need to officially formalize that which has already been agreed to earlier. Do you have any observations to make?

Mao Zedong: Is the shipment of military arms considered a part of the monetary loan?

Stalin: This you can decide yourself: We can bill that toward the loan, or we can formalize it through trade agreements.

Mao Zedong: If the military shipments are billed toward the loan, then we will have little means left for industry. It appears that part of the military shipments will have to be billed toward the loan, while the other part will have to be paid with Chinese goods. Can't the period of delivery of industrial equipment and military arms be shortened from five to three to four years?

Stalin: We must examine our options. The matter rests in the requisition list for our industry. Nevertheless, we can move the date that the credit agreement goes into effect to January 1, 1950, since the shipments should begin just about now. If the agreement specified July 1949 as the time for the commencement of the loan, the international community would not be able to understand how an agreement could have been reached between the Soviet Union and China, which at the time did not even have its own government. It seems that you should hasten somewhat to present the requisition list for industrial equipment. It should be kept in mind that the sooner such a list is presented, the better for the matter at hand.

Mao Zedong: We believe that the conditions of the credit agreement are generally favorable to China. Under its terms we pay only 1 percent interest.

Stalin: Our credit agreements with people's democracies provide for 2 percent interest. We could, says Comrade Stalin jokingly, increase this interest for you as well, if you would like. Of course, we acted under the premise that the Chinese economy was practically in ruin.

As is clear from the telegrams that we have received, the Chinese government intends to use its army in the reconstruction of its economy. That is very good. In our time we also made use of the army in our economic development and had very good results.

Mao Zedong: That's right. We are drawing on the experience of our Soviet comrades.

Stalin: You raised the question of China receiving a certain amount of grain for Xinjiang?

Mao Zedong: Wheat and textile.

Stalin: For this you need to come up with the necessary requests that include numbers.

Mao Zedong: Very well, we shall prepare these.

How shall we proceed with the trade agreement?

Stalin: What is your opinion? Up until now we have only had a trade agreement with Manchuria. We would like to know what sort of a situation we should look forward to in the future: Will we be signing separate agreements with Xinjiang, Manchuria, and other provinces, or a single agreement with the central government?

Mao Zedong: We would like to have a single, central agreement. But in time Xinjiang may have a separate agreement.

Stalin: Just Xinjiang; what about Manchuria?

Zhou Enlai: A separate agreement with Manchuria can be ruled out, since in the agreement with the central government China's obligations would in essence be fulfilled by shipments made from Manchuria.

Stalin: We would like the central government to sanction and take the responsibility for the agreements with Xinjiang or Manchuria.

Mao Zedong: The agreement with Xinjiang must be signed in the name of the central government.

Stalin: Right, since [a] provincial government might not take many things into account, whereas things are always clearer to the central government.

What other questions do you have?

Mao Zedong: At the present time the main question is economic cooperation – the reconstruction and development of the Manchurian economy.

Stalin: I think that we will entrust the preparation of this question to Comrades Mikoyan, Vyshinskii, Zhou Enlai, and Li Fuchun.[6]

Any other questions?

Mao Zedong: I would like to note that the air regiment that you sent to China was very helpful. They transported 10,000 people. Let me thank you, Comrade Stalin, for the help and ask you to allow it to stay a little longer, so it could help transport provisions to Liu Bocheng's troops,[7] currently preparing for an attack on Tibet.

Stalin: It's good that you are preparing to attack. The Tibetans need to be subdued. As for the air regiment, we shall talk this over with the military personnel and give you an answer.

The meeting took two hours.
Present at the meeting were Comrades Molotov, Malenkov, Mikoyan, Vyshinskii,

[6] Li Fuchun, member of the PRC State Council Finance and Economics Committee.

[7] Li Bocheng, People's Liberation Army general, commander of the Second Field Army.

Roshchin, Fedorenko; Mao Zedong, Zhou Enlai, Li Fuchun, Wang Jiaxiang, Chen Boda, and Shi Zhe (Karskii).

Source: APRF, f. 45, op. 1, d. 329, 29–38. Translated by Danny Rozas.

VIII. Record of Conversation, Stalin and Zhou Enlai, September 19, 1952

Zhou Enlai visited the Soviet Union from 15 August to 24 September 1952, primarily to discuss the conditions for a ceasefire in Korea. The tone of the conversation which follows is typical for meetings between Chinese and Soviet top leaders up to the mid-1950s: The Soviets provided the orientation and advice which set the course of the alliance, while the Chinese very much appeared to be junior partners.

Stalin, opening the conversation with the Mexican proposal concerning the exchange of prisoners of war (POWs), says that we agree with Mao Zedong that the Mexican proposal is not acceptable, since it conforms with America's position at the negotiations in Korea. If Mexico comes forward with its proposal at the UN, the USSR delegation will reject this proposal as not conducive to the cessation of the war in Korea and will strive toward the following:

1. Immediate cessation of military activities of the involved parties on land, sea, and air.

2. Return of all POWs to their native land in accordance with international standards.

3. Withdrawal of foreign armies, including the Chinese volunteer units, from Korea in the course of two to three months; a peaceful settlement of the Korean issue in the spirit of Korean unification, conducted by Koreans themselves under the observation of a committee with participation of the immediately concerned parties and other countries, including those which did not take part in the Korean War.

He adds that the question of which and how many countries should take part in this committee can be further discussed and decided.

Regarding the proposal of temporary withholding of 20 percent of POWs from each side, and the return of the remaining POWs, the Soviet delegation will not involve itself with this proposal, which will be left in Mao Zedong's hands.

Zhou Enlai asks: What is your opinion concerning the possibility of the Chinese government entering into a nonaggression pact with India and Burma? Mao Zedong thinks such a pact would be expedient.

Stalin answers that we support Comrade Mao Zedong's opinion. Of course, there are and there will not be any obstacles here. Zhou Enlai asks: Is it possible to delay the introduction of the second position, to wait two to three weeks?

Stalin answers that this is Mao Zedong's business. If Mao Zedong wants, we can introduce in the Assembly (UN General Assembly) the discussion of the second position concerning the percentage of withheld POWs.

Zhou Enlai introduces a question about the third position – the possibility of transferring POWs to neutral countries so that their subsequent fate can be decided separately. He says that this is talked about in the international community, and asks whether Comrade Stalin considers it possible to support this position.

Stalin answer that we want the return of all POWs. This also concurs with the Chinese position. If an agreement cannot be reached on this basis, we cannot deliver the POWs to the UN because the UN is a military participant in the war; he asks: In China's opinion, which country will the captives be sent to?

Zhou Enlai answers: Mao Zedong entrusted me to say that we had in mind India. Stalin asks who will be responsible, in this case, for the expense of maintaining POWs. It seems, every involved party?

Zhou Enlai answers that if the POWs are transferred to India, then after some time they will be transferred from India to China, and then the Chinese and Korean parties will pay for the maintenance of Chinese and Korean POWs.

Stalin says that this proposal can be acceptable, but we must keep in mind that the Americans will not want to deliver all the POWs, that they will keep some captives, with the intention to recruit them. This was the case with our POWs. Now we are capturing several of our POWs a day who are being sent over by America. They are withholding POWs not because, as they say, the POWs do not want to return – America often refers to this – but so that they could use them for spying.

Zhou Enlai concedes that this is precisely so.

He introduces the following scenario: to cease fire and resolve the issue of POWs later. He reminds that Comrade Stalin agreed with this, if no agreement is reached regarding the percentage [of POWs] withheld.

Stalin acknowledges that this can be considered as one of possible scenarios, but America is not likely to agree to it.

Zhou Enlai says that perhaps America will suggest this in the [General] Assembly.

Stalin: This would be good.

Zhou Enlai says that in the last discussion Comrade Stalin suggested that China take initiative in creating a continental or regional UN. He asks whether there would be any other instructions regarding this matter.

Stalin answers that he continues to hold his previous point of view. In addition he says that, besides the current UN, it is necessary to create separate organizations for Asia, Europe, etc., not in lieu of the UN, but parallel to the UN. Let America create an American organization, Europe, a European one, Asia, an Asian one, but parallel to the UN, not contrary to the UN.

Zhou Enlai says that China has no interest in the UN and obviously it is necessary to take initiative in creating a continental organization.

Stalin emphasizes that UN is an American organization and we should destroy it, while keeping up the appearance that we are not against the UN; we should conduct this with an appearance of respect to the UN, without saying that it should be destroyed, weakened, but in reality weaken it. He reminds that during the war Churchill suggested the creation of a continental UN, but America opposed this. We quietly observed the debate, but then Britain rejected its position and we supported the proposal regarding the creation of the UN.

Zhou Enlai asks whether there will be letters concerning this matter from Comrade Stalin to Mao Zedong.

Stalin explains that it will be better without a letter. He sees that Zhou Enlai is taking notes and he fully trusts him.

Zhou Enlai mentioned the Peace Congress in Beijing, scheduled in the end of September, saying that now it will be necessary to move the congress to the beginning of October. He adds that China is striving for the participation of Japan and India in this congress.

Stalin asks if Pakistan will participate.

Zhou Enlai agrees that Pakistan should participate as well and that Pakistan representatives are invited, but the Pakistan government is not issuing them passports. As for India, a part of the Indian delegation has already arrived, and the Japanese delegation will arrive via Hong Kong.

Stalin says further that we should aim for China to have the principal role [in the congress], because:

1. The initiative in assembling the congress belongs to China.

2. It will be better this way, because the USSR is only partly located in Asia, and China is entirely in Asia, therefore it should have the principal role.

Zhou Enlai asks what specific actions will be taken by our delegation.

Stalin answers: Peace.

Zhou Enlai talks about Nehru's proposal concerning the conference of five countries – the Soviet Union, China, England, France, and USA.

Molotov explains that this was a proposal of the Committee of the National Congress Party.

Stalin says that this proposal should be supported.

Zhou Enlai emphasizes that at such a conference India, it goes without saying, will speak [in agreement] with England, but, it would seem, that it would be advisable to utilize this proposal.

Stalin agrees with this.

Zhou Enlai says that in connection with the publication of the note about Port Arthur, the position which the PRC should take with regard to Japan is completely clear. The PRC should indicate that Japan does not wish the conclusion of a peace agreement with China and the Soviet Union.

Stalin adds – and is preparing for aggression. He underscores that our position was not directed against the Japanese people.

Zhou Enlai raises the question of Formosa [Taiwan]. He says that since the Japanese government has concluded an agreement with Jiang Jieshi, it thus has confirmed that it is ignoring the interests of the Chinese people. This excludes the possibility of concluding a peace agreement. So long as a peace agreement exists with Formosa, a peace agreement between the PRC and Japan is not possible.

Stalin emphasizes that the note on Port Arthur was directed against America and not against the Japanese people. America maintains a [naval] fleet around Taiwan and exploits Taiwan. He affirms the correctness of Zhou Enlai's point of view on the impossibility of a peace agreement with Jiang Jieshi, and indicates that the fact of the signing of an agreement by Japan with Jiang Jieshi only worsens its [Japan's] position.

Zhou Enlai asks: What will be the further development of events with regard to Germany?

Stalin says that it is difficult to forecast. It seems America will not support German unification. They plundered Germany; if the West Germany and East Germany unite, then it will not be possible to plunder Germany any longer. That is why America does not want German unification.

Zhou Enlai says in his opinion, even though America is rebuilding the military forces of West Germany and Japan, hoping to use them, this weapon can turn against them.

Stalin says that it is quite possible, even though the German government will be controlled by nationalists, Hitler's followers.

Zhou Enlai shifts to the situation in Xinjiang. He says that the work in Xinjiang is generally going well and that agricultural reforms are being instituted there. But there are also some leftist excesses, which manifest themselves in unlawful confiscation of domestic animals, in the domain of religion, and the reduction of interest rates and land lease. To eliminate these excesses the CC [Central Committee] Plenum was assembled, which released Wang Zhen[8] from the office of Secretary of Xinjiang CC CCP [Chinese Communist Party] subbureau, and a group of CC members was directed to take care of

[8] Wang Zhen, PLA general, commander and political commissar of the Xinjiang Military District to July 1952.

the excesses. In general discontent was eliminated, and cases of defection, including those to USSR territory, have been halted.

Stalin says that the excesses resulted from the desire to obtain land and domestic animals faster, confiscating both from the rich.

Zhou Enlai notes that as soon as the rumors about reforms had spread, the hostile elements began to slaughter domestic animals.

Stalin notes that similar incidents took place at a certain time in our experience as well. It is necessary to hurry up with the reform. If the agricultural reform is not instituted, such looting will continue to occur.

Zhou Enlai explains that the agricultural reform is being instituted in crop farming regions, and redistribution and excesses connected with it [are occurring] in the animal farming regions. Since animal herders participated in the redistribution, the Chinese government has decided to improve their condition, which should improve the general condition as well.

Stalin says: Of course, it is up to you.

Zhou Enlai says that according to the Liu Shaoqi report, two representatives from the Indonesian Communist Party should arrive at the Nineteenth [Party] Congress, and he asks whether it would be timely to discuss party issues in Moscow with them.

Stalin says that it is difficult to tell yet. It depends on whether they will address the CC. He points out that when the representatives from the Indian Communist Party arrived, they asked us to help in determining the party policy, and we had to do it, even though we were busy.

Zhou Enlai reports that the Japanese comrades should arrive as well, and it is likely they will also want to discuss party issues.

Stalin answers that older brothers cannot refuse their younger brothers in such a matter. He says that this should be discussed with Liu Shaoqi, who has substantial experience, and [it should be] clarified how the Chinese comrades perceive it.

Zhou Enlai points out that Liu Shaoqi intends to bring with him appropriate material, in order to discuss a number of questions.

Stalin notes that if the Chinese comrades want to discuss these issues, then of course we will have no contradictions, but if they do not want it, then we will not have to discuss anything.

Zhou Enlai answers that the Chinese comrades will definitely want to talk.

Stalin answers that, in this case, we shall find the time.

Zhou Enlai says that it is possible that the comrades from Vietnam will also arrive.

Stalin notes that the Vietnamese comrades are our friends and will be our welcome guests.

Zhou Enlai, ending the conversation, says they would like to receive instructions concerning all these issues.

Stalin asks: Instructions or suggestions?

Zhou Enlai answers that from Comrade Stalin's perspective perhaps this would be advice, but in their perception these would be instructions.

Stalin notes that we give only advice, convey our opinion, and the Chinese comrades may accept it or not; instructions, on the other hand, are mandatory.

Zhou Enlai repeats that from the Chinese perspective these are instructions, most valuable instructions. He notes that they do not accept these instructions blindly, but consider it necessary to understand and accept them deliberately.

Stalin emphasizes that we know China too little, and that is why we are cautious in giving instructions.

Zhou Enlai says that Comrade Stalin certainly is well familiar with the particular issues they are addressing, and asks again whether there will be any instructions.

Comrade Stalin answers that our advice is this: We should remember that England and America will try to place their people into the apparatus of the Chinese government. It does not matter if they are American or French. They will work to undermine, try to cause decay from within, could even commit such crimes as poisonings. That is why we must be alert. He says we should keep this in mind. Here – these are all the instructions.

Zhou Enlai says that these are very valuable instructions. He agrees that not only Americans, English, and French can commit such treacheries, but they also push the Chinese into it.

Stalin adds: Their agents from the [Chinese] national bourgeoisie.

Molotov, returning to the question of military credit, the payment for weapons for sixty Chinese divisions, asks whether he understood Zhou Enlai correctly the last time, that the cost of deliveries for sixty divisions is not related to the military credit, granted by the Soviet government to China from February 1, 1951, according to the agreement. The deliveries of weaponry for sixty Chinese infantry divisions will be paid in [the] full amount according to the credit, granted in a special agreement between China and the Soviet Union.

Zhou Enlai answers that Comrade Molotov understood him absolutely correctly, and again asserts that the weapon supplies for sixty Chinese divisions have to be paid in full, according to the rates established for countries other than China, and not in half.

Stalin says that in this case we should sign a special agreement.

He mentions the gifts presented to Soviet representatives by the Chinese government, and notes that there have been very many gifts.

Zhou Enlai explains that they could not present gifts to Comrade Stalin for the seventieth anniversary [of Stalin's birth]. They attended the museum of gifts, saw the gifts sent by other countries, and they feel they must make up for what they were not able to do before.

Stalin says that we also would like to present the Chinese delegation automobiles made in USSR. He says that we have automobiles "ZIS," smaller than "ZIM," but very beautiful, and we would like to present you with these "ZISs."

Then he mentions the question concerning Song Qingling.[9]

Zhou Enlai says that he is working on getting her closer to him, that she is gradually shifting from bourgeois ideology to our side, that she comes out with good articles based on our ideology. She says that Song Qingling is very proud of being the winner of the International Stalin Peace Award.

The conversation started at 10:30, ended at 12:30.

Also present: Comrades Molotov, Malenkov, Beriia, Mikoyan, Bulganin, Vyshinskii; Li Fuchun, Zhang Wentian,[10] Su Yu,[11] Shi Zhe.

Source: APRF, f. 45, op. 1, d. 343, pp. 97–103. Translated by Danny Rozas with Kathryn Weathersby.

IX. Record of Conversation, Soviet Beijing Ambassador Pavel Iudin and Mao Zedong, March 31, 1956

This document records one of several conversations between Mao Zedong and Soviet leaders after the CPSU Twentieth Party Congress in which Mao described his relationship to Stalin. Mao's evaluation of Stalin went through a remarkable transformation during 1956 – from welcoming Khrushchev's criticism in the spring to being highly critical of it after the Polish and Hungarian events in the fall.

Today I visited Mao Zedong and gave him Comrade Khrushchev's letter about the assistance which the Soviet Union will provide: (1) in the construction of fifty-one enterprises and three scientific research institutes for military industry, (2) in the construction of a railroad line from Urumqi to the Soviet-Chinese border. Mao Zedong asked me to send his deep gratitude to the CC CPSU [Central Committee of the Communist Party of the Soviet Union] and the Soviet government.

Further I said that I had wanted to visit him (Mao Zedong) in the very first days following my return to Beijing and to tell about the work of the Twentieth Congress of the

[9] Song Qingling, widow of GMD founder Sun Yat-sen and sister-in-law of Jiang Jieshi.

[10] Zhang Wentian, PRC ambassador to Moscow.

[11] Su Yu, general, deputy chief of the PRC General Staff.

CPSU and, in particular, about Comrade Khrushchev's speech at the closed session regarding the cult of personality. Mao Zedong responded that because of his illness he had found it necessary to put off the meeting with me. Mao Zedong said that the members of the CCP [Chinese Communist Party] delegation who had attended the Twentieth Congress had told him something about the work of the congress and had brought one copy of Comrade Khrushchev's speech regarding the cult of personality. That speech has already been translated into Chinese and he had managed to become acquainted with it.

During a conversation about I. V. Stalin's mistakes Mao Zedong noted that Stalin's line on the China question, though it had basically been correct, in certain periods he, Stalin, had made serious mistakes. In his speeches in 1926 Stalin had exaggerated the revolutionary capabilities of the Guomindang, had spoken about the Guomindang as the main revolutionary force in China. In 1926 Stalin had given the Chinese Communists an instruction about the orientation to the Guomindang, having viewed it as a united front of the revolutionary forces of China. Stalin said that it is necessary to depend on the Guomindang, to follow after that party, i.e., he spoke directly about the subordination of the Communist Party of China to the Guomindang. This was a great mistake which had held back the independent work of the Communist Party of China on the mobilization of the masses and on attracting them to the side of the Communist Party.

Through the Comintern, Mao Zedong continued, Stalin, having become after the death of V. I. Lenin the de facto leader of the Comintern, gave to the CC CCP a great number of incorrect directives. These mistaken and incorrect directives resulted from the fact that Stalin did not take into account the opinion of the CCP. At that time Wang Ming,[12] being a Comintern worker, met frequently with Stalin and tendentiously had informed him about the situation in the CCP. Stalin, evidently, considered Wang Ming the single exponent of the opinion of the CC CCP.

Wang Ming and Li Lisan,[13] who represented the CCP in the Comintern, tried to concentrate the whole leadership of the CCP in their own hands. They tried to present all the Communists who criticized the mistakes of Wang Ming and Li Lisan as opportunists. Mao Zedong said they called me a right opportunist and a narrow empiricist. As an example of how the Comintern acted incorrectly in relation to the Communist Party of China, Mao Zedong introduced the following.

Under the pretext that the Third Plenum of the CC CCP, while considering the coupplotting errors of Li Lisan, had not carried the successive criticism of these mistakes to

[12] Wang Ming (Chen Shaoyi), rival of Mao Zedong in the 1930s, lived in the Soviet Union after 1955.

[13] Li Lisan, head of the CCP in the late 1920s, lived in the Soviet Union from 1931 to 1945, deputy head of the All-China Federation of Labor after 1949, deputy director of the CCP CC Industrial and Communications Work Department. Died during the Cultural Revolution.

its conclusion and allegedly so as to correct the mistakes of the Third Plenum of the CC CCP, the Comintern after three to four months had sent to China two of its own workers – [Pavel] Mif and Wang Ming – charged with the task of conducting the Fourth Plenum of the CCP. Nonetheless the decisions of the Fourth Plenum of the CC CCP made under the pressure of Mif and Wang Ming were in fact more ultra-leftist that Li Lisan's line. In them it was stated that it is necessary to move into the large cities, to take control of them, and not to conduct the struggle in rural regions. In the decisions of the Fourth Plenum of the CC CCP there was permitted such, for example, a deviation that in the Soviet regions of China which were blockaded by the Guomindang even the petty trading bourgeoisie was liquidated and all kinds of internal trade was stopped. As a result of this policy the Chinese Red Army, which in 1929 was comprised of 300,000 fighters, was reduced by 1934–1935 to 25,000, and the territory which made up the Soviet regions of China was reduced by 99 percent. CCP organizations in the cities were routed by the Guomindang and the number of Communists was reduced from 300,000 to 26,000 people. The Soviet regions were totally isolated from the remaining part of the country and remained without any products, even without salt. All this caused serious discontent among the population of the Soviet regions.

As a result of the ultra-leftist policy of Wang Ming, the more or less large regions which remained under CCP leadership were mostly in North China (the provinces of Shaanxi, Gansu, [and] Ningxia), to which Wang Ming's power did not extend. Wang Ming, backed by the Comintern, essentially managed it so that the 8th and 4th armies removed themselves from subordination to the CC CCP.

Wang Ming and his successors saw the Guomindang as the "young power," which absorbs all the best and will be able to gain a victory over Japan. They spoke against the independent and autonomous policy of the Communist Party in the united front, against the strengthening of the armed forces of the CCP and revolutionary bases, and against the unification of all strata of the population around the policy of the CCP. Wang Ming's supporters tried to replace the genuinely revolutionary program of the CCP, which consisted of ten points, with their own six-point program, the author of which was Wang Ming, although this was, in the essence of the matter, a capitulationist program. In conducting this whole program Wang Ming, backed by the Comintern and in Stalin's name, spoke as the main authority.

Wang Ming's supporters, taking advantage of the fact that they had captured a majority in the Southern Bureau of the CC CCP in Wuhan, gave incorrect directives to the army and to the local authorities.

So, for example, once, to our surprise, said Mao Zedong, even in Yanan the slogans of the CCP which were posted on the walls of the houses were replaced, on Wang Ming's order, with slogans "about a stable union with the Guomindang," etc.

As a result of the serious ideological struggle and the great explanatory work following the Seventh Congress of the Communist Party, especially in the last four years, the majority of Communists who made left or right errors acknowledged their guilt. Wang Ming at the Seventh Congress also wrote a letter with acknowledgment of his mistakes, however he then once again returned to his old positions. All of the former activity of Wang Ming, Mao Zedong said, which was carried out under the direct leadership of the Comintern and Stalin, inflicted a serious loss to the Chinese Revolution.

Characterizing the Comintern's activity overall, Mao Zedong noted that while Lenin was alive he had played the most prominent role in bringing together the forces of the Communist movement, in the creation and consolidation of the Communist parties in various countries, in the fight with the opportunists from the Second International. But that had been a short period in the activity of the Comintern. Consequently, to the Comintern came "officials" like [Grigorii] Zinoviev, [Nikolai] Bukharin, [Losif] Piatnitskii, and others, who, as far as China was concerned, trusted Wang Ming more than the CC CCP. In the last period of the Comintern's work, especially when Dimitrov worked there, certain movements were noticed, since Dimitrov depended on us and trusted the CC CCP, rather than Wang Ming. However, in this period as well, not just a few mistakes were made by the Comintern, for example, the dissolution of the Polish Communist Party and others. In this way, said Mao Zedong, it is possible to discern three periods in the activity of the Comintern, of which the second, longest period brought the biggest loss to the Chinese Revolution. Moreover, unfortunately, precisely in this period the Comintern dealt most of all with the East. We can say directly, commented Mao Zedong, that the defeat of the Chinese Revolution at that time was, right along with other reasons, also the result of the incorrect, mistaken actions of the Comintern. Therefore, speaking openly, noted Mao Zedong, we were satisfied when we found out about the dissolution of the Comintern.

In the last period, continued Mao Zedong, Stalin also incorrectly evaluated the situation in China and the possibilities for the development of the revolution. He continued to believe more in the power of the Guomindang than of the Communist Party. In 1945 he insisted on peace with Jiang Jieshi's supporters, on a united front with the Guomindang and the creation in China of a "democratic republic." In particular, in August 1945 the CC CCP received a secret telegram, for some reason in the name of the "VKP (b)" (in fact from Stalin), in which it was insisted that Mao Zedong travel to Chongqing for negotiations with Jiang Jieshi. The CC CCP was against this journey, since a provocation from Jiang Jieshi's side was expected. However, said Mao Zedong, I was required to go since Stalin had insisted on this. In 1947, when the armed struggle against the forces of Jiang Jieshi was at its height, when our forces were on the brink of victory, Stalin insisted that peace be made with Jiang Jieshi, since he doubted the forces of the Chinese Revolution. This lack of belief remained in Stalin even during the first stages of the formation of the PRC, i.e., already after the victory of the revolution. It is possible that Stalin's lack of trust and suspiciousness were caused by the Yugoslavian events, particularly since at that time, said Mao Zedong with a certain disappointment, many conversations took place to the effect that the Chinese Communist Party was going along the Yugoslav path, that Mao Zedong is a "Chinese Tito." I told Mao Zedong that there were no such moods and conversations in our party.

The bourgeois press around the world, continued Mao Zedong, particularly the right socialists, had taken up the version of "China's third way," and extolled it. At that time, noted Mao Zedong, Stalin, evidently, did not believe us, while the bourgoisie and laborites sustained the illusion of the "Yugoslav path of China," and only Jiang Jieshi alone "defended" Mao Zedong, shrieking that the capitalist powers should not in any circumstance believe Mao Zedong, that "he will not turn from his path," etc. This behavior of Jiang Jieshi is understandable, since he knows us too well, he more than once had to stand in confrontation to us and to fight with us.

The distrust of Stalin to the CCP, Mao Zedong continued further, was apparent also during the time of Mao Zedong's visit to the Soviet Union. One of our main goals for the trip to Moscow was the conclusion of a Chinese-Soviet treaty on friendship, cooperation, and mutual assistance. The Chinese people asked us whether a treaty of the USSR with the new China will be signed, why until now legally there continues to exist a treaty with the supporters of the Guomindang, etc. The issue of the treaty was an extremely important matter for us, which determined the possibilities for the further development of the PRC. At the first conversation with Stalin, Mao Zedong said, I brought a proposal to conclude a treaty along government lines, but Stalin declined to answer. During the second conversation I returned once again to that issue, showing Stalin a telegram from the CC CCP with the same type of proposal about a treaty. I proposed to summon Zhou Enlai to Moscow to sign the treaty, since he is the minister of foreign affairs. Stalin used this suggestion as a pretext for refusal and said that "it is inconvenient to act in this way, since the bourgeois press will cry that the whole Chinese government is located in Moscow." Subsequently, Stalin refrained from any meetings with me. From my side there was an attempt to phone him in his apartment, but they responded to me that Stalin is not home, and recommended that I meet with [Anastas] Mikoyan. All this offended me, Mao Zedong said, and I decided to undertake nothing further and to wait it out at the dacha. Then an unpleasant conversation took place with [I. V.] Kovalev and [N. T.] Fedorenko, who proposed that I go on an excursion around the country. I sharply rejected this proposal and responded that I prefer "to sleep through it at the dacha." Some time later, continued Mao Zedong, they handed me a draft of my interview for publication which had been signed by Stalin. In this document it was reported that negotiations are being held in Moscow on concluding a Soviet-Chinese treaty. This already was a significant step forward. It is possible that in Stalin's change of position, said Mao Zedong, we were helped by the Indians and the English, who had recognized the PRC in January 1950. Negotiations began right after this, in which Malenkov, Molotov, Mikoyan, Bulganin, Kaganovich, and Beriia took part. During the negotiations, at Stalin's initiative there was undertaken an attempt by the Soviet Union to assume sole ownership of the Chinese

Changchun (i.e., Harbin) Railway. Subsequently, however, a decision was made about the joint exploitation of the Chinese Changchun (i.e., Harbin) Railway, besides which the PRC gave the USSR the naval base in Port Arthur, and four joint stock companies were opened in China. At Stalin's initiative, said Mao Zedong, Manchuria and Xinjiang were practically turned into spheres of influence of the USSR. Stalin insisted on the fact that in these regions only Chinese people and Soviet citizens be permitted to live. Representatives of other foreign states, including Czechs, Polish people, and Englishmen who were living permanently in those regions, should be evicted from there. The only ones whom Stalin skipped over through his silence were Koreans, of whom there are counted one and a half million in Manchuria. These types of pretensions from Stalin's side, said Mao Zedong, were incomprehensible to us. All this also was fodder for the bourgeois press and representatives of capitalist states. In fact, continued Mao Zedong, in the course of the negotiations around this treaty, there was the most genuine trading going on. It was an unattractive way to pose the issue, in which Stalin's distrust and suspicion of the CCP was clearly expressed.

We are glad to note, said Mao Zedong, that the Chinese Changchun (i.e., Harbin) Railway and Port Arthur have been returned to China, and the joint stock companies have ceased to exist. In this part of the conversation Mao Zedong stressed that Khrushchev did not attend these negotiations and that Bulganin's participation in them was minimal. Stalin's distrust of the CCP was apparent in a number of other issues, including Kovalev's notorious document about anti-Soviet moods in the leadership of the CCP. Stalin, in passing this document to the CC CCP, wanted, evidently, to stress his mistrust and suspicions.

Over the course of the time I spent in Moscow, said Mao Zedong, I felt that distrust of us even more strongly and therefore I asked that a Marxist representative of the CC CPSU be sent to China in order to become acquainted with the true situation in China and to get to know the works of the Chinese theoreticians, and simultaneously to examine the works of Mao Zedong, since these works in the Chinese edition were not reviewed by the author in advance, while the Soviet comrades, counter to the wish of the author, insisted on their publication.

Mao Zedong reminded me that upon my (Iudin's) arrival in China he had persistently and specially recommended to me to complete a trip around the whole country. In relation to this I told Mao Zedong about a conversation which I had with Stalin, in the presence of several members of the Politburo, upon my return from the trip to China. Stalin at that time asked me whether the ruling Chinese comrades are Marxists. Having heard my affirming response, Stalin said, "That's good! We can be calm. They've grown up themselves, without our help."

Mao Zedong noted that in the very posing of this question Stalin's distrust of the Chinese Communists was also made apparent. Important things which, evidently, to some extent strengthened Stalin's belief in the CCP were your (Iudin's) report about the journey to China and the Korean War performance of the Chinese People's Volunteers.

In such a way, said Mao Zedong, if we look historically at the development of the Chinese Revolution and at Stalin's attitude to it, then it is possible to see that serious mistakes were made, which were especially widespread during the time of the Comintern's work. After 1945, during the period of the struggle with Jiang Jieshi, because of the overestimation of the forces of the Guomindang and the underestimation of the forces of the Chinese Revolution, Stalin undertook attempts at pacification, at restraining the development of the revolutionary events. And even after the victory of the revolution Stalin continued to express mistrust of the Chinese Communists. Despite all that, said Mao Zedong, we have stood firmly behind the revolutionary positions, for if we had permitted vacillations and indecisiveness, then, no doubt, long ago we would not have been among the living.

Then Mao Zedong moved on to a general evaluation of Stalin's role. He noted that Stalin, without a doubt, is a great Marxist, a good and honest revolutionary. However, in his great work in the course of a long period of time he made a number of great and serious mistakes, the primary ones of which were listed in Khrushchev's speech. These fundamental mistakes, said Mao Zedong, could be summed up in seven points:

1. Unlawful repressions.

2. Mistakes made in the course of the [world] war, moreover, in particular in the beginning, rather than in the concluding period of the war.

3. Mistakes which dealt a serious blow to the union of the working class and the peasantry. Mao Zedong observed that this group of mistakes, in particular the incorrect policy in relation to the peasantry, was discussed during Comrade Khrushchev's conversation with Zhu De in Moscow.

4. Mistakes in the nationality question connected to the unlawful resettlement of certain nationalities and others. However, overall, said Mao Zedong, nationality policy was implemented correctly.

5. Rejection of the principle of collective leadership, conceit, and surrounding himself with toadies.

6. Dictatorial methods and leadership style.

7. Serious mistakes in foreign policy (Yugoslavia, etc.).

Mao Zedong further stressed a thought to the effect that overall in the Communist movement great victories were won. The single fact of the growth of the Socialist camp from 200 million people to 900 million people speaks for itself. However, in the course of successful forward advance in some certain countries, in some certain parties these or other mistakes arose. Mistakes similar to these and others, he said, can arise in the future too. I [Iudin] observed that it would be better not to repeat mistakes like Stalin's. To this Mao Zedong answered that, evidently, there will be these types of mistakes again. The appearance of these mistakes is entirely explicable from the point of view of dialectical materialism, since it is well known that society develops through a struggle of contradictions, the fight of the old with the new, the newborn with the obsolete. In our consciousness, said Mao Zedong, there are still too many vestiges of the past. It lags behind the constantly developing material world, behind everyday life.

In our countries, continued Mao Zedong, much has come from the former, capitalist society. Take, for example, the issue of the application of corporal punishments to the accused. For China too, this is not a new issue. Even in 1930 in the Red Army during interrogations, beatings were broadly applied. I, said Mao Zedong, at that time personally was a witness to how they beat up the accused. Already at that time a corresponding decision was made regarding a ban on corporal punishment. However, this decision was violated, and in Yanan, it is true, we tried not to allow unlawful executions. With the creation of the PRC we undertook a further struggle with this ugly manifestation.

It is entirely evident, continued Mao Zedong, that according to the logic of things during a beating the one who is being beaten begins to give false testimony, while the one who is conducting the interrogation accepts that testimony as truth. This and other vestiges which have come to us from the bourgeois past will still for a long time be preserved in the consciousness of people. A striving for pomposity, for ostentatiousness, for broad anniversary celebrations, this is also a vestige of the psychology of bourgeois man, since such customs and such psychology objectively could not arise among the poorest peasantry and the working class. The presence of these and other circumstances, said Mao Zedong, creates the conditions for the arising of those or other mistakes with which the Communist parties will have to deal.

I [Iudin] observed that the main reason for Stalin's mistakes was the cult of personality, bordering on deification.

Mao Zedong, having agreed with me, noted that Stalin's mistakes accumulated gradually, from small ones growing to huge ones. To crown all this, he did not acknowledge his own mistakes, although it is well known that it is characteristic of a person to make mistakes. Mao Zedong told how, reviewing Lenin's manuscripts, he had become convinced of the fact that even Lenin crossed out and rewrote some phrases or other in his own works. In conclusion to his characterization of Stalin, Mao Zedong once again stressed that Stalin had made mistakes not in everything, but on some certain issues.

Overall, he stressed that the materials from the congress made a strong impression on him. The spirit of criticism and self-criticism and the atmosphere which was created after the congress will help us, he said, to express our thoughts more freely on a range of issues. It is good that the CPSU [Communist Party of the Soviet Union] has posed all these issues. For us, said Mao Zedong, it would be difficult to take the initiative on this matter.

Mao Zedong declared that he proposes to continue in the future the exchange of opinions on these issues during Comrade Mikoyan's visit, and also at a convenient time with Comrades Khrushchev and Bulganin.

Then Mao Zedong got distracted from this topic and getting greatly carried away briefly touched on a few philosophical questions (about the struggle of materialism with idealism, etc.). In particular he stressed that it is incorrect to imagine to oneself Communist society as a society which is free from any sort of contradictions, from ideological struggle, from any sort of vestiges of the past. In a Communist society too, said Mao Zedong, there will be good and bad people. Further he said that the ideological work of China still to a significant extent suffers from a spirit of puffery [nachetnichestva] and clichés. The Chinese press, in particular, still cannot answer to the demands which are presented to it. On the pages of the newspapers the struggle of opinions is lacking, there are no serious theoretical discussions. Because of insufficient time Mao Zedong expressed a wish to meet with me again to talk a little specifically about issues of philosophy. At the end of the discussion I [Iudin] inquired of Mao Zedong whether he had become acquainted with the *Pravda* editorial about the harm of the cult of personality, a translation of which was placed in [*Renmin Ribao*] on March 30. He responded that he still had not managed to read through that article, but they had told him that it is a very good article. Now, said Mao Zedong, we are preparing for publication in *Renmin Ribao* a lead article which is dedicated to this issue, which should appear in the newspapers in the coming week. Beginning on March 16, he noted jokingly, all the newspapers in the world raised a ruckus about this issue – China alone for the time being is silent.

Then I briefly told Mao Zedong about the arrival in the PRC of sixteen prominent Soviet scholars and about the beginning of the work of a theoretical conference dedicated to the Twentieth Congress, which is opening today in the club of Soviet specialists. Soviet and Chinese scholars will deliver speeches at the conference.

Mao Zedong listened to these thoughts with great interest. The conversation continued for three hours. Mao Zedong was in a good mood, and joked often.

The Deputy Head of the Administration of Affairs of the CCP Yang Shankun, the Chief of the CC CCP Translation Bureau Shi Zhe, and Counselor of the USSR Embassy in the PRC T. F. Skvortsov attended the conversation.

Source: AVPRF, f. 0100, op. 49, pa. 410, d. 9, pp. 87–98. Translated by Mark Doctoroff.

X. Mao Zedong, Speech on Sino-American and Sino-Soviet Relations, January 27, 1957

Mao Zedong often gave impromptu speeches on various topics to various audiences, even on sensitive topics such as foreign relations. This is an excerpt from his speech

at a meeting of first secretaries of CCP committees at the provincial, city, and au-
tonomous region level from early 1957. Mao spoke right after receiving Zhou Enlai's
report on his visit to the Soviet Union and several East European countries in January
1957.

[Let me] talk about U.S.-China relations. At this conference we have circulated a copy
of the letter from [Dwight D.] Eisenhower to Jiang Jieshi. This letter, in my view, aims
largely at dampening the enthusiasm of Jiang Jieshi and, then, cheering him up a bit. The
letter urges [Jiang] to keep calm, not to be impetuous, that is, to resolve the problems
through the United Nations, but not through a war. This is to pour cold water [on Jiang].
It is easy for Jiang Jieshi to get excited. To cheer [Jiang] up is to continue the hard, un-
compromising policy toward the [Chinese] Communist Party and to hope that internal
unrest would disable us. In his [Eisenhower's] calculation, internal unrest has already occurred and it is hard for the Communist Party to suppress it. Well, different people observe things differently!

I still believe that it is much better to establish diplomatic relations with the United
States several years later than sooner. This is in our favor. The Soviet Union did not form
diplomatic relations with the United States until seventeen years after the October Revolution. The global economic crisis erupted in 1929 and lasted until 1933. In that year
Hitler came to power in Germany whereas Roosevelt took office in the United States.
Only then was the Soviet-American diplomatic relationship established. [As far as I can
anticipate,] it will probably wait until when we have completed the Third Five-Year Plan
that we should consider forming diplomatic relations with the United States. In other
words, it will take eighteen or even more years [before we do so]. We are not anxious to
enter the United Nations either. This is based on exactly the same reasoning as why we
are not anxious to establish diplomatic relations with the United States. The objective of
this policy is to deprive the U.S. of its political assets as much as possible, so that the
U.S. will be placed in an unreasonable and isolated position. It is therefore all right if [the
U.S.] blocks us from the United Nations and refuses to establish diplomatic relations with
us. The longer you drag on [these issues], the more debts you will owe us. The longer the
issues linger there, the more unreasonable you will appear, and the more isolated you will
become both domestically and in face of international public opinion. I once told an
American in Yanan that even if you United States refused to recognize us for one hundred years, I simply did not believe that you United States could refuse to recognize us
in the one hundred and first year. Sooner or later the U.S. will establish diplomatic relations with us. When the United States does so and when Americans finally come to visit
China, they will feel deep regret. It is because by then, China will become completely
different [from what it is now]: the house has been thoroughly swept and cleaned, "the

four pests"[14] have altogether been eliminated; and they can hardly find any of their "friends." Even if they spread some germs [in China], it will have no use at all.

Since the end of the World War II, every capitalist country has suffered from instability which has led to disturbance and disorder. Every country in the world is disturbed, and China is no exception. However, we are much less disturbed than they are. I want you to think about this issue: Between the socialist countries and the imperialist countries, especially the United States, which side is more afraid of the other after all? In my opinion, both are afraid [of the other], but the issue is who is afraid more. I am inclined to accept such an assessment: The imperialists are more afraid of us. However, such an assessment entails a danger, that is, it could put us into a three-day-long sleep. Therefore, [we] always have to stress two possibilities. Putting the positive possibility aside, the negative potential is that the imperialists may become crazy. Imperialists always harbor malicious intentions and constantly want to make trouble. Nevertheless, it will not be that easy for the imperialists to start a world war; they have to consider the consequences once war starts.

[Let me] also talk about Sino-Soviet relations. In my view, wrangling [between us] will continue. [We shall] never pretend that the Communist parties will not wrangle. Is there a place in the world where wrangling does not exist? Marxism itself is a wrangling-ism and is about contradiction and struggle. Contradictions are everywhere, and contradictions invariably lead to struggle. At present there exist some controversies between China and the Soviet Union. Their [the Soviets'] ways of thinking, behavior, and historical traditions differ from ours. Therefore, we must try to persuade them. Persuasion is what I have always advocated as a way to deal with our own comrades. Some may argue that since we are comrades, we must be of the same good quality, and why in the world is persuasion needed among comrades? Moreover, persuasion is often employed for building a common front and always targeted at the democratic figures, and why is it employed toward Communist Party members? This reasoning is wrong. Different opinions and views do exist even within a Communist Party. Some have joined the party, but have not changed their mind-set. Some old cadres do not share the same language with us. Therefore, [we] have to engage in heart-to-heart talks with them: sometimes individually, sometimes in groups. In one meeting after another we will be able to persuade them.

As far as I can see, circumstances are beyond what persons, even those occupying high positions, can control. Under the pressure of circumstance, those in the Soviet Union who still want to practice big-power chauvinism will invariably encounter dif-

[14] In traditional China, flies, bedbugs, rats, and mosquitos; in the 1950s, "local tyrants," "enemy agents," "members of reactionary parties," and "heads of secret societies."

ficulties. To persuade them remains our current policy and requires us to engage in direct dialogue with them. The last time our delegation visited the Soviet Union, [we] openly talked about some [controversial] issues. I told Comrade Zhou Enlai over the phone that, as those people are blinded by lust for gain, the best way to deal with them is to give them a tongue-lashing. What is [their] asset? It involves nothing more than 50 million tons of steel, 400 million tons of coal, and 80 million tons of oil. How much does this count? It does not count for a thing. With this asset, however, their heads have gotten really big. How can they be Communists [by being so cocky]? How can they be Marxists? Let me stress, even ten times or a hundred times bigger, these things do not count for a thing. They have achieved nothing but digging a few things out of the earth, turning them into steel, thereby manufacturing some airplanes and automobiles. This is nothing to be proud of! They, however, turn these [achievements] into huge burdens on their back and hardly care about revolutionary principles. If this cannot be described as being blinded by lust for gain, what else could this be? Taking the office of the first secretary can also become a source for being blinded by lust for gain, making it easy for one to be out of one's mind. Whenever one is out of his mind, there must be a way to bring him back to his senses. This time Comrade [Zhou] Enlai no longer maintained a modest attitude but quarreled with them and, of course, they argued back. This is a correct attitude, because it is always better to make every [controversial] issue clear face to face. As much as they intend to influence us, we want to influence them too. However, we did not unveil everything this time, because we must save some magic weapons [in reserve]. Conflict will always exist. All we hope for at present is to avoid major clashes so as to seek common ground while reserving differences. Let these differences be dealt with in the future. Should they stick to the current path, one day, we will have to expose everything.

As for us, our external propaganda must not contain any exaggeration. In the future, we shall always remain cautious and modest, and shall tightly tuck our tails between our legs. We still need to learn from the Soviet Union. However, we shall learn from them rather selectively: only accept the good stuff, while at the same avoiding picking up the bad stuff. There is a way to deal with the bad stuff, that is, we shall not learn from it. As long as we are aware of their mistakes, [we] can avoid committing the same mistakes. We, however, must learn from anything that is useful to us and, at the same time, we must grasp useful things all over the world. One ought to seek knowledge in all parts of the world. It would be monotonous if one only sticks to one place to receive education.

Source: Zhonghua renmin gongheguo waijiaobu and Zhonggong zhongyang wenxian yanjiusuo, eds., *Mao Zedong waijiao wenxuan* [Selected Mao Zedong works on foreign affairs] (Beijing: Zhongyang wenxian, 1994), 280–3.

XI. Record of conversation, Mao Zedong and Soviet Ambassador to Beijing Pavel Iudin, July 22, 1958

In the summer of 1958, with the Great Leap Forward well underway in China, Mao sensed a trend toward a global revolutionary upswing. His criticism of the Soviet leaders for ignoring these developments grew harsher and his fears of getting his new policies shackled by Soviet influence within China became more acute. Mao was particularly fearful of Soviet influence within the military. At a meeting of the Central Committee's Military Committee, which ended the day the recorded conversation with Iudin took place, Mao had criticized many of his generals for "systematic dogmatist errors" and for "following a bourgeois military line." Therefore, Iudin's airing in a meeting with Mao on July 21 of Soviet ideas about the creation of a joint Sino-Soviet submarine fleet could not have come at a worse time. The Soviet leaders were horrified when learning of Mao's fury, especially since they had intended the suggestions for naval cooperation as a response to numerous Chinese requests in the spring of 1958 for assistance with naval technology, the most recent in a letter from Zhou Enlai on June 28, 1958.

After you left yesterday I could not fall asleep, nor did I have dinner. Today I invite you over to talk a bit more so that you can be [my] doctor: [After talking with you], I might be able to eat and sleep this afternoon. You are fortunate to have little difficulty in eating and sleeping.

Let us return to the main subject and chat about the issues we discussed yesterday. We will only talk about these issues here in this room! There exists no crisis situation between you and me. Our relationship can be described as: nine out of ten fingers of yours and ours are quite the same with only one finger differing. I have repeated this point two or three times. You haven't forgotten, have you?

I've thought over and again of the issues that were discussed yesterday. It is likely that I might have misunderstood you, but it is also possible that I was right. We may work out a solution after discussion or debate. It appears that [we] will have to withdraw [our] navy's request for [obtaining] nuclear-powered submarines [from the Soviet Union]. Barely remembering this matter, I have acquired some information about it only after asking others.[15] There are some warmhearted people at our navy's headquarters, namely, the Soviet advisers. They asserted that, now that the Soviet nuclear submarines have been developed, we can obtain [them] simply by sending a cable [to Moscow].

[15] Mao referred to Zhou Enlai and Peng Dehuai who were present during this discussion.

Well, your navy's nuclear submarines are of a [top] secret advanced technology. The Chinese people are careless in handling things. If we are provided with them, we might cause you trouble. The Soviet comrades have won victory for forty years, and are thus rich in experience. It has only been eight years since our victory and we have little experience. You therefore raised the question of joint ownership and operation. The issue of ownership has long before been dealt with: Lenin proposed the system of rent and lease which, however, was targeted at the capitalists.

China has some remnant capitalists, but the state is under the leadership of the Communist Party. You never trust the Chinese! You only trust the Russians! [To you] the Russians are the first-class [people] whereas the Chinese are among the inferior who are dumb and careless. Therefore [you] came up with the joint ownership and operation proposition. Well, if [you] want joint ownership and operation, how about having them all – let us turn into joint ownership and operation our army, navy, air force, industry, agriculture, culture, education. Can we do this? Or, [you] may have all of China's more than ten thousand kilometers of coastline and let us only maintain a guerrilla force. With a few atomic bombs, you think you are in a position to control us through asking for the right of rent and lease. Other than this, what else [do you have] to justify [your request]?

Lushan [Port Arthur] and Dalian [Dalny] were under your control before. You departed from these places later. Why [were these places] under your control? It is because then China was under the Guomindang's rule. Why did you volunteer to leave? It is because the Communist Party had taken control of China.

Because of Stalin's pressure, the Northeast and Xinjiang became [a Soviet] sphere of influence, and four jointly owned and operated enterprises were established. Comrade Khrushchev later proposed to have these [settlements] eliminated, and we were grateful for that.

You [Russians] have never had faith in the Chinese people, and Stalin was among the worst. The Chinese [Communists] were regarded as Tito the Second; [the Chinese people] were considered as a backward nation. You [Russians] have often stated that the Europeans looked down upon the Russians. I believe that some Russians look down upon the Chinese people.

At the most critical juncture [of the Chinese Revolution], Stalin did not allow us to carry out our revolution and opposed our carrying out the revolution. He made a huge mistake on this issue. So did [Grigory Y.] Zinoviev.

Neither were we pleased with [Anastas] Mikoyan. He flaunted his seniority and treated us as if [we were] his sons. He put on airs and looked very arrogant. He assumed the greatest airs when he first visited Xibaipo in 1949[16] and has been like that every time

[16] Dispatched by Stalin, Mikoyan secretly visited Xibaipo from January 31 to February 7, 1949, and held extensive meetings with Mao Zedong and other CCP leaders.

he came to China. Every time he came, he would urge me to visit Moscow. I asked him what for. He would then say that there was always something for you to do there. Nevertheless, only until later when Comrade Khrushchev proposed to hold a conference to work out a resolution [concerning the relationship among all the Communist parties and socialist states] did [I go to Moscow].[17]

It was our common duty to commemorate the fortieth anniversary of the October Revolution. Up to that time, as I often pointed out, there had existed no such thing as brotherly relations among all the parties because, [your leaders] merely paid lip service and never meant it; as a result, the relations between [the brotherly] parties can be described as between father and son or between cats and mice. I have raised this issue in my private meetings with Khrushchev and other [Soviet] comrades. They all admitted that such a father-son relationship was not of European but Asian style. Present were Bulganin, Mikoyan, and [M. A.] Suslov. Were you also at the meeting? From the Chinese side, I and Deng Xiaoping were present.

I was unhappy with Mikoyan's congratulation speech which he delivered at our Eighth National Congress and I deliberately refused to attend that day's meeting as a protest. You did not know that many of our deputies were not happy with [Mikoyan's speech]. Acting as if he was the father, he regarded China as Russia's son.

China has her own revolutionary traditions, although China's revolution could not have succeeded without the October Revolution, nor without Marxism-Leninism.

We must learn from the Soviet experiences. We will comply with the commonly accepted principles, especially the nine principles stated in the "Moscow Manifesto."[18] We ought to learn from all the experiences whether they are correct or erroneous. The erroneous lessons included Stalin's metaphysics and dogmatism. He was not totally metaphysical because he had acquired some dialectics in thinking; but a large part of his [thoughts] focused on metaphysics. What you termed as the cult of personality was one [example of his metaphysics]. Stalin loved to assume the greatest airs.

Although we support the Soviet Union, we won't endorse its mistakes. As for [the differences over] the issue of peaceful evolution, we have never openly discussed [these differences], nor have we published [them] in the newspapers. Cautious as we have been, we choose to exchange different opinions internally. I had discussed them with you before I went to Moscow. While in Moscow, [we assigned] Deng Xiaoping to raise five

[17] Mao attended the Moscow conference of leaders of Communist and worker's parties from socialist countries in November 1957, on the occasion of the fortieth anniversary of the Russian October Revolution.

[18] The "Moscow Manifesto" was adopted by the Moscow conference of leaders of Communist and workers' parties from socialist countries in November 1957.

[controversial] issues. We won't openly talk about them even in the future, because our doing so would hurt Comrade Khrushchev's [political position]. In order to help consolidate his [Khrushchev's] leadership, we decided not to talk about these [controversies], although it does not mean that the justice is not on our side. With regard to intergovernmental relations, we remain united and unified up to this date which even our adversaries have conceded. We are opposed to any [act] that is harmful to the Soviet Union. We have objected to all the major criticism that the revisionists and imperialists have massed against the Soviet Union. The Soviet Union has so far done the same thing [for us]. When did the Soviets begin to trust us Chinese? At the time when [we] entered the Korean War. From then on, the two countries got closer to one another [than before] and as a result, the 156 aid projects came about. When Stalin was alive, the [Soviet] aid consisted of 141 projects. Comrade Khrushchev later added a few more.

We have held no secrets from you. Because more than one thousand of your experts are working in our country, you are fully aware of the state of our military, political, economic, and cultural affairs. We trust your people, because you are from a socialist country, and you are sons and daughters of Lenin.

Problems have existed in our relations, but it was mainly Stalin's responsibility. [We] have had three grievances [against Stalin]. The first concerns the two Wang Ming lines. Wang Ming was Stalin's follower. The second was [Stalin's] discouragement of and opposition to our revolution. Even after the dissolution of the Third International, he still issued orders claiming that, if we did not strike a peace deal with Jiang Jieshi, China would risk a grave danger of national elimination. Well, for whatever reason, we are not eliminated. The third was during my first visit to Moscow during which Stalin, [V. M.] Molotov, and [Lavrenti] Beriia personally attacked me.

Why did I ask Stalin to send a scholar [to China] to read my works?[19] Was it because I so lacked confidence that I would even have to have you read my works? Or was it because I had nothing to do myself? Not a chance! [My real intention] was to get you over to China to see with your own eyes whether China was truly practicing Marxism or only half-hearted toward Marxism. Upon your return [to Moscow] you spoke highly of us. Your first comment to Stalin was "the Chinese [comrades] are truly Marxists." Nevertheless Stalin remained doubtful. Only when [we entered] the Korean War did he change his view [about us], and so did East European and other brotherly parties drop their doubts [about us].

It appears that there are reasons for us to be suspect: "First, you opposed Wang Ming; second, you simply insisted on carrying out your revolution regardless of [our] opposi-

---

[19] Before becoming Soviet ambassador to China, Iudin was in China from July 1950 to January 1951 and July to October 1951, participating in the editing and translation of Mao Zedong's works.

tion; third, you looked so smart when you went all the way to Moscow desiring Stalin to sign an agreement so that [China] would regain authority over the [Manchurian] railroad." In Moscow it was [I. V.] Kovalev who took care of me with [N. T.] Fedorenko as my interpreter.[20] I got so angry that I once pounded on the table. I only had three tasks here [in Moscow], I said to them, the first was to eat, the second was to sleep, and the third was to shit.

There was a [Soviet] adviser in [our] military academy who, in discussing war cases, would only allow [the Chinese trainees] to talk about those of the Soviet Union, not China's, would only allow them to talk about the ten offensives of the Soviet Army, not [ours] in the Korean War. Please allow us to talk about these cases! [Can you imagine] he wouldn't even allow us to talk about [our own war experiences]! For God's sake, we fought wars for twenty-two years; we fought in Korea for three years! Let [me ask] the Central Military Committee to prepare some materials concerning [our war experiences] and give them to Comrade Iudin, of course, if he is interested.

We did not speak out on some [controversial] issues because we did not want to cause problems in the Sino-Soviet relations. This was particularly true when the Polish Incident broke out. When Poland demanded that all of your specialists go home, Comrade Liu Shaoqi suggested, in Moscow, that you withdraw some. You accepted [Liu's] suggestion which made the Polish people happy because they then tasted some freedom. At that time we did not raise our problems with your specialists [in China] because, we believe, it would have caused you to be suspicious that we took the advantage [of your crisis situation] to send all the specialists home. We will not send your specialists home; we will not do so even if Poland does so ten more times. We need Soviet aid. Once I have persuaded the Polish people that [we all] should learn from the Soviet Union, and that after putting the antidogmatism campaign at rest, [they] ought to advocate a "learn from the Soviet Union" slogan. Who will benefit in learning from the Soviet Union? The Soviet Union or Poland? Of course, it will benefit Poland more.

Although we shall learn from the Soviet Union, we must first of all take into account our own experiences and mainly rely on our own experiences.

There should be some agreed limits on the terms of [Soviet] specialists. For instance, there have never been restrictions on your chief advisers in [our] military and public security branches, who can come and go without even notifying or consulting with us in advance. Presumably, if you leave your post, is it all right that another ambassador be sent [to China] without discussing it with us? No, absolutely not! How much informa-

---

[20] I. V. Kovalev, Stalin's representative to China from 1948 to 1950, accompanied Mao Zedong to visit the Soviet Union in December 1949–February 1950; N. T. Fedorenko, a Soviet sinologist, in the early 1950s served as the cultural counselor at the Soviet embassy in Beijing.

tion could your advisers to our ministry of public security obtain if they merely sit there totally uninformed by their Chinese colleagues?

Let me advise you [and your specialists] to pay more visits to each of our provinces so as to get in touch with the people and obtain firsthand information. This have I mentioned to Comrade Iudin many times: if not ten thousand times, at least one thousand times!

With some exceptions, though, most of the [Soviet] specialists are of a good quality. We have also made mistakes before: We did not take the initiative to pass on information to the Soviet comrades. Now we must correct these mistakes by adopting a more active attitude [toward the Soviet comrades]. Next time [we] ought to introduce to them China's general line. If the first time [we] fail to get the information through, [we] will try a second time, third time, and so forth. Indeed, it was [your] proposition for establishing a "cooperative" on nuclear submarines which led to these remarks. Now that we've decided not to build our nuclear submarines, we are withdrawing our request [for obtaining submarines from the Soviet Union]. Otherwise, we would have to let you have the entire coast, much larger areas than [what you used to control in] Lushan and Dalian. Either way, however, we will not get mixed up with you: We must be independent from one another. Since we will in the end build our own flotilla, it is not in our interest that [we] play a minor role in this regard.

Certainly [the arrangements] will be totally different in war time. Your army can operate in our [land], and our army can move to your places to fight. If your army operates on our territory, however, it must be commanded by us. When our army fights in your land, as long as it does not outnumber your army, it has to be directed by you.

These remarks of mine may not sound so pleasing to your ear. You may accuse me of being a nationalist or another Tito. My counter argument is that you have extended Russian nationalism to China's coast.

It was Comrade Khrushchev who had eliminated the four joint enterprises. Before his death, Stalin demanded the right to build a plant to manufacture canned food in our country. My response was that [we] would accept [the demand] as long as you provide us equipment, help us build it, and import all the products [from us]. Comrade Khrushchev praised me for giving [Stalin] a good answer. But why in the world do [you Russians] want to build a naval "cooperative" now? How would you explain to the rest of the world that you propose to build a naval "cooperative"? How would you explain to the Chinese people? For the sake of struggling against the imperialists, you may, as advisers, train the Chinese people. Otherwise, you would have to lease Lushan and other [ports] for ninety-nine years; but your "cooperative" proposal involves the question of ownership, as you propose that each side will own fifty percent of it. Yesterday you made me so enraged that I could not sleep at all last night. They (pointing at other CCP leaders present) are not angry. Only me alone! If this is wrong, it will be my sole responsibility. (Zhou Enlai: Our Politburo has unanimously agreed upon these points.)

If we fail to get our messages through this time, we may have to arrange another meeting; if not, we may have to meet every day. Still, I can go to Moscow to speak to Comrade Khrushchev; or we can invite Comrade Khrushchev to come to Beijing so as to clarify every issue.

(Peng Dehuai: This year Soviet Defense Minister Malinovskii cabled me requesting to build a long-wave radio station along China's coast to direct the [Soviet] submarine flotilla in the Pacific Ocean. As the project will cost a total of 110 million rubles, the Soviet Union will cover 70 million and China will pay 40 million.)

This request is of the same nature as the naval "cooperative" proposal which [we] cannot explain to the people. [We] will be put in a politically disadvantageous position if [we] reveal these requests to the world.

(Peng Dehuai: Petroshevskii [a Soviet military adviser] also has a rude attitude and rough style. He is not very pleased because some of our principles for army building do not completely follow the Soviet military codes. Once at an enlarged CMC meeting, when Comrade Ye Fei from the Fujian Military District pointed out that, as the Soviet military codes were basically to guide operations on flatlands, and as Fujian [province] had nothing but mountains, the Soviet codes were not entirely applicable [to Fujian's reality]. Very upset at hearing this, Petroshevskii immediately responded: "You have insulted the great military science by the great Stalin!" His remarks made everyone at the meeting very nervous.)

Some of the above-mentioned [controversial] issues have been raised [by us] before, some have not. You have greatly aided us but now we are downplaying your [role]; you may feel very bad about it. Our relationship, however, resembles that between professor and student: the professor may make mistakes, do not you agree that the student has to point them out? Pointing out mistakes does not mean that the [student] will drive the professor out. After all the professor is a good one.

You are assisting us to build a navy! Your [people] can serve as advisers. Why would you have to have fifty percent of the ownership? This is a political issue. We plan to build two or three hundred submarines of this kind.

If you insist on attaching political conditions [to our submarine request], we will not satisfy you at all, not even give you a tiny [piece of our] finger. You may inform Comrade Khrushchev that, if [he] still [insists on] these conditions, there is no point for us to talk about this issue. If he accepts our requirement, he may come [to Beijing]; if not, he does not have to come, because there is nothing for us to talk about. Even one tiny condition is unacceptable [for us]!

When this issue is involved, we will refuse to accept your aid for ten thousand years. However, it is still possible for us to cooperate on many other affairs; it is unlikely that we would break up. We will, from beginning to the end, support the Soviet Union, although we may quarrel with each other inside the house.

While I was in Moscow, I once made it clear to Comrade Khrushchev that you did not have to satisfy every one of our requests. Because if you hold back your aid from us, [you] in effect would compel us to work harder [to be self-reliant]; should we get everything from you, we will end up in a disadvantageous position.

It is, however, extremely important for us to cooperate politically. Because, if we undermine your political positions, you will encounter considerable problems; the same is true with us: if you undermine our [political] positions, we will be in trouble.

In wartime, you can utilize all our naval ports, military bases, and other [facilities]. [In return] our [military] can operate in your places including your port or bases at Vladivostok and shall return home when war is over. We may sign an agreement on wartime cooperation in advance which does not have to wait until war breaks out. Such an agreement must contain a stipulation that our [forces] can operate on your territory; even if we might not do so, such a stipulation is required, because it involves the issue of equality. In peacetime, however, such an arrangement cannot be accepted. In peacetime, you are only to help us construct [military] bases and build armed forces. We would not have accepted [your] proposition for building a naval "cooperative" even if it had been during Stalin's time. I quarreled with him in Moscow!

Comrade Khrushchev has established his credibility by having the [previous] "cooperative" projects eliminated. Now that such an issue involving ownership is raised again, we are reminded of Stalin's positions. I might be mistaken, but I must express my opinion.

You explained [to me] yesterday that [your proposition] was based on the consideration that [Russia's coastal] conditions were not as good for nuclear submarines to function fully as China's, thus hamstringing future development of nuclear submarines. You can reach [the Pacific] Ocean from Vladivostok through the Kurile Islands. The condition is very good!

What you said [yesterday] made me very uneasy and displeased. Please report all my comments to Comrade Khrushchev: You must tell him exactly what I have said without any polishing so as to make him uneasy. He has criticized Stalin's [policy] lines but now adopts the same policies as Stalin did.

We will still have controversies. You do not endorse some of our positions; we cannot accept some of your policies. For instance, your [leadership] is not pleased at our policy regarding "internal contradictions among the people," and the policy of "letting a hundred flowers bloom and a hundred schools of thought contend."

Stalin endorsed the Wang Ming line, causing the losses of our revolutionary strength up to more than ninety percent. At the critical junctures [of our revolution], he wanted to hold us back and opposed our revolution. Even after [we] achieved victory, he remained doubtful about us. At the same time, he boasted that it was because of the direction of his theories that China's [revolution] succeeded. [We] must do away with any superstition about him. Before I die, I am prepared to write an article on what Stalin had done to China, which is to be published in one thousand years. (Iudin: The Soviet central leadership's attitude toward the policies of the Chinese central leadership is: it is completely up to the Chinese comrades how to resolve the Chinese problems, because it is the Chinese comrades who understand the situation best. Moreover, we maintain that it is hasty and arrogant to judge and assess whether or not the CCP's policies are correct, for the CCP is a great party.)

Well, [we] can only say that we have been basically correct. I myself have committed errors before. Because of my mistakes, [we] had suffered setbacks, of which examples included Changsha, Tucheng, and two other campaigns.[21] I will be very content if I am refuted as being basically correct, because such an assessment is close to reality.

Whether a [joint] submarine flotilla will be built is a policy issue: only China is in a position to decide whether we should build it with your assistance or it should be "jointly owned." Comrade Khrushchev ought to come to China [to discuss this issue] because I have already visited him [in Moscow].

[We] should by no means have blind faith in [authorities]. For instance, one of your specialists asserted on the basis of a book written by one [of your] academy scholars that our coal from Shanxi [province] cannot be turned into coke. Well, such an assertion has despaired us: We therefore would have no coal which can be turned into coke, for Shanxi has the largest coal deposit!

Comrade Xining [transliteration], a Soviet specialist who helped us build the Yangzi River Bridge [in Wuhan], is a very good comrade. His bridge-building method has never been utilized in your country: [You] never allowed him to try his method, either to build a big or medium or even small-sized bridge. When he came here, however, his explanation of his method sounded all right. Since we knew little about it, [we] let him try his method! As a result, his trial achieved a remarkable success which has become a first-rate, world-class scientific invention.

I have never met with Comrade Xining, but I have talked to many cadres who participated in the construction of the Yangzi River Bridge. They all told me that Comrade Xining was a very good comrade because he took part in every part of the work, adopted a very pleasant working style, and worked very closely with the Chinese comrades. When the bridge was built, the Chinese comrades had learned a great deal [from him]. Any of you who knows him personally please convey my regards to him.

---

[21] Mao commanded these military operations during the CCP-Guomindang civil war in 1927–1934.

Please do not create any tensions among the specialists regarding the relations between our two parties and two countries. I never advocate that. Our cooperation has covered a large ground and is by far very satisfactory. You ought to make this point clear to your embassy staff members and your experts so that they will not panic when they hear that Comrade Mao Zedong criticized [Soviet leaders].

I have long before wanted to talk about some of these issues. However, it has not been appropriate to talk about them because the incidents in Poland and Hungary put your [leadership] in political trouble. For instance, we then did not feel it right to talk about the problem concerning the experts [in China].

Even Stalin did improve himself: He let China and the Soviet Union sign the [alliance] treaty, supported [us] during the Korean War, and provided [us] with a total of 141 aid projects. Certainly these achievements did not belong to him but to the entire Soviet central leadership. Nevertheless, we do not want to exaggerate Stalin's mistakes.

Source: *Mao Zedong waijiao wenxuan*, 322–33

XII. Head of the Soviet Foreign Ministry's Far Eastern Department, Mikhail Zimyanin, on Sino-Soviet Relations, September 15, 1959

Before Nikita Khrushchev's visit to Beijing in October 1959, Soviet Foreign Minister Andrei Gromyko ordered the head of his ministry's Far Eastern department, Mikhail Zimyanin, to prepare a comprehensive report on Sino-Soviet relations since 1950. Khrushchev was given the report on September 28, on the flight back to Moscow from his visit to the United States. Khrushchev arrived in Beijing on September 30. This is the final part of Zimyanin's report.

The victory of the people's revolution in China and the establishment of the Chinese People's Republic marked the start of a qualitatively new stage in relations between the peoples of the Soviet Union and China, based on a commonality of interests and a unity of goals in constructing a socialist and Communist society in both countries. . . .

When discussing the overall success of the development of Soviet-Chinese relations during the first three years after the formation of the PRC, we must not overlook several negative features of these relations connected with the violation of the sovereign rights and interests of the Chinese People's Republic, as reflected in bilateral agreements signed between the Soviet Union and PRC, including, for example, agreements to prohibit foreigners from entering Manchuria and Xinjiang (February 14, 1950), to establish Soviet-Chinese joint-stock companies, and to set the rate of exchange for the ruble and yuan for the national bank (June 1, 1950), as well as other such documents.

Beginning in 1953, the Soviet side took measures to eliminate everything that, by keeping the PRC in a subordinate position vis-à-vis the USSR, had impeded the successful development of Soviet-Chinese relations on the basis of full equality, mutuality, and trust. Over time, the above-mentioned agreements were annulled or revised if they did not accord with the spirit of fraternal friendship. The trip to China by a Soviet party and state delegation headed by Comrade N. S. Khrushchev in October 1954 played an important role in the establishment of closer and more trusting relations. As a result of this visit, joint declarations were signed on Soviet-Chinese relations and the international situation and on relations with Japan. In addition, a communiqué and additional agreements were signed on: the transfer to the PRC of the Soviet stake in Soviet-Chinese joint-stock companies responsible for scientific-technical cooperation, the construction of a Lanzhou–Urumchi–Alma Ata railroad, the construction of a Tianjin–Ulan Bator railroad, and so forth.

The Twentieth Congress of the CPSU [Communist Party of the Soviet Union] was of exceptionally great importance for the further improvement of Soviet-Chinese relations. It created an atmosphere conducive to a more frequent and more amicable exchange of candid views. The Chinese friends began to speak more openly about their plans and difficulties and, at the same time, to express critical comments (from a friendly position) about Soviet organizations, the work of Soviet specialists, and other issues in Soviet-Chinese relations. The CCP CC [Chinese Communist Party Central Committee] fully supported the CPSU's measures to eliminate the cult of personality and its consequences. It is worth noting, however, that the CCP CC, while not speaking about this directly, took a position different from ours when evaluating the activity of J. V. Stalin. A bit later the Chinese comrades reexamined their evaluation of the role of J. V. Stalin, as reflected in Mao Zedong's pronouncements when he was visiting Moscow. For example, he said: ". . . Overall, in evaluating J. V. Stalin, we now have the same view as the CPSU." In a number of discussions Mao Zedong gave a critical analysis of the mistakes of J. V. Stalin.

Soon after the Twentieth CPSU Congress, a campaign was launched in China to combat dogmatism, and a course was proclaimed to "let a hundred flowers bloom." In connection with this the Chinese press began, with increasing frequency, to express criticism of specific conditions and of works by Soviet authors in the fields of philosophy, natural history, literature, and art. This inevitably gave strong impetus to hostile statements by rightist forces who denounced the Soviet Union and Soviet-Chinese friendship. The rightists accused the Soviet Union of failing to uphold principles of equality and mutuality, and they alleged that Soviet assistance was self-interested and of inferior quality.

They also asserted that the Soviet Union had not provided compensation for equipment taken from Manchuria, and they insisted that the Soviet Union was extracting money from China in return for weapons supplied to Korea, which were already paid for with the blood of Chinese volunteers. In addition, they lodged a number of territorial demands against the USSR.

The airing of these types of statements during the struggle against rightists can in no way be justified, even if one takes account of the tactical aims of our friends, who were seeking to unmask the rightists and deliver a decisive rebuff against them for all their statements. It is also worth noting that the Chinese friends, despite crushing the rightist elements, did not offer any open condemnation of statements expressed by them about so-called territorial claims on the USSR. The Soviet government's declaration of October 30, 1956, was received with great satisfaction in China.[22] In January 1957 a government delegation headed by Zhou Enlai visited the Soviet Union, leading to the signature of a joint Soviet-Chinese declaration. The declaration emphasized the complete unity of the USSR and PRC as an important factor in unifying the whole socialist camp, and it exposed the groundlessness of far-fetched claims about a "struggle between the CPSU and CCP for the right to leadership of world Communism." In accordance with the declaration, the Soviet Union devised and implemented concrete measures aimed at the further development of Soviet-Chinese friendship and cooperation on the basis of equality, mutual interest, and complete trust.

In 1957 a series of consultations took place between the CPSU CC and the CCP CC on common, concrete matters pertaining to the international situation and the Communist movement. The Chinese friends actively participated in the preparations and conduct of the Moscow conference of officials from Communist and workers' parties in November 1957. While the Chinese delegation was in Moscow, Mao Zedong spoke approvingly about the positive experience of such consultations and the constant readiness of the Chinese comrades to undertake a joint review of these and other matters.

The steps to reorganize the management of the national economy in the USSR were greatly welcomed in the PRC. The CCP CC fully supported the decisions of the June [1957] and other plenary sessions of the CPSU CC, although the Chinese press did not feature an official commentary or reactions to the decisions of these sessions. After details about the activity of the Anti-Party faction had been explained to the CCP CC, the friends began to speak more resolutely about these matters. "If Molotov's line had prevailed within the CPSU," Mao declared in Moscow, "that would have been dangerous not only for the USSR, but for other socialist countries as well."

Taking account of the divisive activity of revisionists and the surge of imperialist propaganda, which tried to use several ideological campaigns in China in 1957 – and, in par-

[22] Declaration endorsing the principle of equality in relations between the Soviet Union and other Communist countries.

ticular, the campaign to "let a hundred flowers bloom" as well as the publication of a work by Mao Zedong "On the Question of Correctly Resolving Contradictions among the People" – to provoke a schism in relations between the Soviet Union and PRC, the leadership of the CCP CC and the government of the PRC emphasized the close unity of the socialist camp and the leading role of the CPSU among Communist and workers' parties. Mao Zedong stated this very definitively in his speech to Chinese students attending Moscow State University (November 1957), and he spoke about it at length with officials from Yugoslavia and also during meetings that PRC government delegations had with delegations from Poland and other countries of the socialist camp. In 1959 the CCP CC, having reexamined the proposal of the CPSU CC to clarify its formula about the leading role of the Soviet Union in the socialist camp, again affirmed that this formula must be preserved in the future.

The durability of Soviet-Chinese relations and the role of Soviet-Chinese friendship gained new strength as the international situation deteriorated in the Middle East and also in connection with the provocations by the USA around the Taiwan Straits in the summer of 1958. The most important political event that year in Soviet-Chinese relations, which had an enormously positive influence on the development of the whole international situation, was the July-August meeting in Beijing between Comrades N. S. Khrushchev and Mao Zedong. During an exchange of views they considered a number of matters pertaining to Soviet-Chinese relations and, in particular, questions of military cooperation. The speech by Comrade N. S. Khrushchev, including his statement that an attack on the PRC would be regarded as an attack on the Soviet Union itself, was fervently greeted with expressions of gratitude and approval in China. The government of the PRC displayed great satisfaction at our assurance about our readiness to launch a nuclear strike in retaliation for a nuclear strike against China. In turn, the Chinese government declared that the PRC will come to the assistance of the USSR in any part of the globe if an attack is carried out against it.

The letter from Comrade N. S. Khrushchev, and a variety of reports from the CPSU CC – about the provision of assistance to the PRC to continue strengthening its defense capability, about a reduction in the number of Soviet specialists in the PRC and the elimination of the network of Soviet "advisor-consultants," about the CPSU CC's views of the Yugoslav Communist League's draft program, and about other matters – had important political benefits.

The results of the CPSU's Twenty-first Congress provided a great boost to the practical activity of the CCP in overseeing socialist construction in the country. It is worth noting that after the publication of the report by Comrade N. S. Khrushchev at the CPSU's Twenty-first Congress and during the proceedings of the Congress, the Chinese friends, while giving a generally positive evaluation of the achievements of socialist construction in the USSR, made almost no mention of the theoretical portions of the report by Comrade N. S. Khrushchev and said that those portions related only to the practice of socialist and Communist construction in the USSR.

In a similar vein, the provisions adopted at the Second Session of the CCP's Eighth Congress (May 1958) regarding a struggle against "blind faith" and regarding the need to foster sentiments of national pride among the people, as well as some preliminary success in implementing the "Great Leap Forward," caused a number of cadre workers in the PRC to take on airs. They began excessively emphasizing China's uniqueness and displaying a guarded attitude toward Soviet experience and the recommendations of Soviet specialists. Some began declaring that the Soviet Union had stayed too long at the socialist stage of development, while China was moving valiantly ahead toward communism. The Chinese press quite actively featured criticism of the socialist principles implemented in the USSR for the distribution of material goods in accordance with one's labor, for the compensation of labor on a job-by-job basis, and so forth. Some authors essentially argued that communes were incompatible with kolkhozes.

Later on, after studying materials from the Congress and after numerous mistakes arose during the establishment of the peasant communes and during the implementation of the "Great Leap Forward," the CCP began to display a more proper understanding of matters considered by the Twenty-first Congress, such as the question of the significance of creating a material-technical base and increasing the productivity of labor for the construction of socialism, the question of the role of the principle of material incentives and labor distribution under socialism, and other questions. The CPSU's position in offering a principled explanation of a number of Marxist-Leninist precepts and laws of the building of socialism and communism, which were ignored in China during the implementation of the "Great Leap Forward" and the establishment of communes (see the report and speech by Comrade N. S. Khrushchev at the Twenty-first Congress and the speeches that followed), helped the Chinese comrades to evaluate the situation correctly and to begin rectifying the mistakes and shortcomings that had arisen. The statement by Comrade N. S. Khrushchev about the permanent foundations of Soviet-Chinese friendship swept the rug out from under imperialist and Yugoslav revisionist propaganda, which was intended to sow mistrust between our countries and provoke a deterioration of Soviet-Chinese relations. . . .

An analysis of Soviet-Chinese relations over the past decade confirms that relations of fraternal amity and fruitful cooperation have been established on a lasting basis and are growing wider and stronger with every passing year. These relations are a decisive factor in the further growth of the might and cohesion of the world socialist camp and in the consolidation of world peace and the security of nations.

Source: Report to CC CPSU, "Vnutripoliticheskoe, ekonomicheskoe i mezhdunarodnoe polozhenie KNR," Tsentr khraneniia sovremennoi dokumentatsii (TsKhSD), f. 5, op. 30, d. 307, 49–79. Obtained and translated by Mark Kramer.

XIII. Record of Conversation, Soviet Beijing Ambassador Stepan Chervonenko and Chinese Foreign Minister Chen Yi, August 4, 1960

This document is an excerpt of the record of the first meeting between a Chinese leader and the Soviet ambassador to Beijing after Moscow's decision to withdraw its advisers from China in July 1960. Chen Yi had returned to Beijing from the annual CCP leadership summer meetings in Beidahe to meet with the ambassador. Before leaving Beidahe, Chen had consulted both with Mao Zedong and Zhou Enlai, but had been given no specific instructions on what to tell Chervonenko.

I [Chervonenko] visited Chen Yi in the Ministry of Foreign Affairs of the PRC on my own initiative and made the following verbal statement:

"It has became known to the embassy that the Chinese organizations who employ Soviet specialists have been giving talks to them. During these talks the notes are read which the governments of the USSR and the PRC have exchanged confidentially on the issue of the recall of Soviet specialists from the PRC, while the specialists are not informed beforehand about the aims of their invitation to such talks. Some of the specialists were told by responsible Chinese officials (up to deputy minister level) that the organizing of the readings had been ordered by the government of the PRC.

"The embassy considers these actions of the Chinese side not only as illegitimate, but also as aimed at unprovoked substitution of the functions of the Soviet organizations concerning their specialists working abroad. Moreover, there is no necessity in these actions because all Soviet specialists working in the PRC have been informed about the decision of the Soviet government concerning their recall from the PRC.

"The embassy cannot help noting the unusual, willful nature of the actions of the Chinese organizations in relation to the Soviet specialists and has to establish that their drawing in the above-mentioned talks has the goal of spreading doubts about the recall of the specialists and [in] this way creating contradictions between the Soviet people working in the PRC and the government of the Soviet Union.

"In connection with these tactless, clearly unfriendly actions toward the Soviet government and the Soviet people working in the PRC, the embassy considers it its duty to call the attention of the Ministry of Foreign Affairs of the People's Republic of China to the inadmissibility of such actions in the relations between our countries and expects that the corresponding Chinese organizations will be given orders to stop and prevent in future such actions toward the Soviet people."

Having heard that statement, Chen Yi said that he would like to give an answer to it. He said that the very event – the recall of the Soviet specialists – had been created by the Soviet side and had a very big political importance. The decision to recall all Soviet specialists which number approximately 1,400 to 1,500 persons has been made without consultations with the Chinese side, unilaterally. The Chinese side was informed about the recall on July 16, and without waiting for our (Chinese) answer their departure has started. At the present moment big groups of the specialists have already left China. The Soviet specialists work in sixteen towns and in 500 to 600 Chinese organizations. And despite the fact that "machinery works there," they all are being recalled. Chen Yi said that the Soviet Union did not pay attention any more to China being a fraternal country, [it] ignored obligations taken according to the Treaty and the agreements. The recall of the specialists – "this is a big event, which will shake the whole China."

He further stated that they had not reproached the embassy in the past, were not reproaching it at the moment, and would not reproach for the organizing of the departure of the specialists, because it had the right to implement the decision of its government. We (the Chinese) will not guess what kind of work the embassy has conducted with the specialists. You have your own rights here and we should not call your attention to anything. But this issue has at least an unusual nature in the relations between our countries, because this is a unilateral action of the Soviet Union.

Chen Yi said that the fact of the recall of the Soviet specialists could not be hidden. By September 1 all specialists will have been sent from China. The whole world will know and this will be also "a big event, which will shake the whole world." Our two countries are the great states, which always cooperated with each other. He stressed that he was saying this not on behalf of the Minister for Foreign Affairs and not as a representative of the Communist Party of China. "I am a little person and will not assess the actions of the Soviet government. I would ask you to understand us correctly. The sudden and decisive steps of the Soviet government cause big economic losses for our enterprises. A split in a friendship – this is serious." Chen Yi again stressed that everything said was his own opinion and declared that the official position of the Chinese side would be presented soon.

Chen Yi stated that it was impossible even to think that our countries could be unfriendly, could live without friendship. Of course we [the Chinese] are in a very difficult situation because of the recall of the specialists. But we will try to restore this friendship. "Brothers still remain brothers." You have had no capitalists, landowners, exploiting classes for a long time, you have only the working class, peasantry and the revolutionary intelligentsia. . . .

Chen Yi said, laughing: "You see, you have wanted to see Chen Yi and he has received you, although he knew that the discussion would concern the specialists, and could have charged his deputy with that problem." Having stressed that he was speaking not on behalf of the party and the government, but considered this an exchange of views between friends, he said that if the Soviet and the Chinese Communists would discuss such trifles, that discussion would have no end. We must step aside from these small questions and put the emphasis on the main problems. But you and I cannot solve them, so I am expressing only my own opinion. Ambassador Iudin, chargé d'affairs Antonov worked in the PRC, now Chervonenko works here. All these comrades have been received and talked to by deputy ministers, ministers, deputy premiers, the premier, Liu Shaoqi, Mao Zedong. But the ambassador of the PRC to the USSR cannot meet even with a deputy foreign minister of the USSR and talks just with a deputy head of the corresponding department of the Ministry of Foreign Affairs of the USSR. Chen Yi stressed again: "with a deputy head of the department. From this one can see – continued he – to what extent our friendship has deteriorated. The main thing is the existence of disagreements between our parties; if they are resolved, other questions will be resolved as well." But at the talks between Peng Zhen and F. R. Koslov[23] in Moscow and N. S. Khrushchev in Bucharest unity was not achieved, [neither was it] at the meeting of the fraternal parties in Bucharest. Our party signed the communiqué [from that meeting], but with certain reservations. "As a Communist I hope, and our party hopes, that all these disagreements will be solved during the next meeting."

Having expressed agreement with the opinion that the specialists emphasized the growth of China's power in order not to give a pretext for hostile propaganda in connection with their departure, Chen Yi declared that during the last year some partial and trifling disagreements between the CCP [Chinese Communist Party] and the CPSU [Communist Party of the Soviet Union] "has become known to others. And this is not China's fault." In any case, according to his words, up to 1958 there were no such cases as now, but beginning from 1959 there have been more and more of them. He stressed that the fact that they read the two notes to the specialists was not known to anybody.

Coming back to the question of readings of the notes, Chen Yi repeated, that "at the bottom of all this are your sudden actions – unilateral, illegal, violating the treaty and the agreements, breaking friendship" and that it was not fair to blame only the Chinese side. Disagreements on some theoretical questions can be fully settled through consultations and such actions should be avoided for the sake of comradely friendship. We can accept your reproach for the illegitimate unfriendly actions, if you accept that your actions have been unilateral, illegitimate, sudden.

Chen Yi said that he did not want to say much, because all the questions would be raised at the meeting of fraternal parties, but considered it necessary to say that [only] once, in 1948, we (the Soviet Union) had undertaken such action (the recall of specialists) against Yugoslavia. . . .

[23] Frol Koslov, first deputy chairman of the USSR Council of Ministers and secretary of the CC CPSU.

Chen Yi continued: I am thinking about another side of the problem. You have undertaken two actions – have closed down the journal and have recalled the specialists.[24] I don't know what will be next. But we are still brothers, the friendship between our parties was established long ago – in Lenin's time. The Chinese side will not undertake any actions against you. Our only task is to give appropriate explanations. Chen Yi again expressed surprise why the Soviet side, while undertaking large-scale political actions against the Chinese side, was "indifferent toward them" and at the same time reproached the Chinese. "We are not Yugoslavia," he said. "If you want to treat us as Yugoslavia, then we will not accept it."

After that Chen Yi began to talk about the deep hatred of the Chinese people toward the American imperialism, this hatred "will not disappear even in twenty to thirty years." Without reacting to our remark that the Soviet people felt no less hatred toward the American imperialism than the Chinese people, Chen Yi declared that "we will continue this struggle, even if you undertake the third, the fourth, the fifth, and other actions against us." He said that the situation in China was at the moment better than during the guerrilla war. And we (the Chinese) will never lose faith in the Soviet country, in the Soviet Communist Party, which was created by great Lenin and is the legacy of great Lenin.

Chen Yi again mentioned "a third action" and said that as the Minister for Foreign Affairs he was ready for that. But at the same time he expressed the opinion that it would have been good if those events have become the turning point and the situation didn't deteriorate further. He said that we (the Soviet Union) had an advantage there. You (the Soviet Union) have greater power and less difficulties than we. You have the right to help or not to help us, to recall or not to recall the specialists. We (the Chinese) don't have these rights. Our only advantage lies in the fact that we have a little more people. Of course, the recall of the specialists will cause little damage to you and great damage to us.

After that Chen Yi again started to talk about the reading of the notes, trying to reduce the whole problem to the dissatisfaction of the Soviet side with the very method of the reading. I said that the problem should not be artificially complicated, and stressed that the elementary rules of tact did not demand discussion.

Chen Yi agreed with me, but immediately declared that neither were our methods "very good" and that "you began," referring to the fact that since the border conflict with India the Soviet press had started to present regularly materials criticizing China. Chen Yi expressed satisfaction with the frank exchange of opinions.

Source: AVPRF, f. 0100, op. 53, pa. 454, d. 8, pp. 204–18; excerpted. Provided by O. A. Westad; translated by Olga Baeva.

[24] At the same time as recalling its experts, the Soviet government also banned the Moscow journal *Druzhba,* published by the Sino-Soviet Friendship Association and withdrew support from its Beijing counterpart, *SuZhong youhao.*

XIV. Record of Conversation, Chervonenko and Mao Zedong, December 26, 1960

This document records what was probably the last the meeting between Mao and a Soviet representative during the Sino-Soviet alliance. The Moscow conference of Communist parties, which had ended in the late fall of 1960, had produced a short-lived compromise between the Soviet and Chinese positions on theoretical issues, and Mao seemed eager to avoid taking any personal blame for any further deterioration in relations.

According to the instructions of the Center, I [Chervonenko] visited Mao Zedong today.

In the name of the CPSU CC [Communist Party of the Soviet Union Central Committee] and Comrade N. S. Khrushchev personally, I congratulated Mao Zedong on his sixty-seventh birthday and wished him good health, long life, and fruitful work. Mao Zedong was very impressed by this warm attention from the CPSU CC and Comrade N. S. Khrushchev. He was deeply moved, and, without concealing his emotions, he most warmly expressed his thanks for the friendly congratulations and wishes. Mao Zedong stated that it is a great honor for him to receive these high congratulations on his birthday. He asked to give his warmest thanks to Comrade N. S. Khrushchev and wished him, personally, as well as all the members of the CPSU CC Presidium, good health and big and fruitful accomplishments in their work. Then, on Mao Zedong's initiative, we had a conversation. He told me that the Chinese leaders have to work a lot now. "As for myself – he mentioned – I am now working much less than before. Though – Mao Zedong went on – I mostly work eight hours a day (sometimes more), the productivity is not the same as it used to be." His comprehension of the material studied is less effective, and the necessity arose [for him] to read documents printed in large characters. He mentioned in this connection that "this must be a general rule that people of advanced age are in an unequal position to the young as regards the efficiency of their work."

Mao Zedong then emphasized that his resignation from the post of the chairman of the PRC had lessened the load of state activities on him. Speaking about this he mentioned that at the time when he had submitted this proposal he had been supported only by the Politburo members, while many members of the CCP CC [Chinese Communist Party Central Committee] had objected. "There was even more disagreement among the rank-and-file Communists." By now, he said, everybody was supporting this decision.

As he continued talking about his work and the activities of the leadership of the CCP CC, Mao Zedong said that for several years, practically from 1953–1954 he was not chairing the Politbureau meetings any more. He said that from 1956 on Liu Shaoqi is in charge of all the routine activities of the Politbureau, while he is taking part in some of the meetings from time to time. Mao Zedong mentioned that he personally is usually working and consulting mostly with the members of the Permanent Committee of the CCP CC Politbureau. Sometimes specially invited persons also take part in the meetings of the Permanent Committee.

Then Mao Zedong said that on some occasions he takes part in the enlarged Politbureau meetings.

Leading party executives from the periphery are usually invited to these meetings, for instance, the secretaries and deputy secretaries of the CCP CC bureaus from certain regions, the secretaries of the CCP Provincial Committees. Mao Zedong said that he now practically never speaks at the CCP CC plenums, and even at the CCP Congress he just delivers a short introductory speech. His resignation from the post of the chairman of the republic gave him also an opportunity to refrain from participating in the work of the Supreme State Conference. However, he mentioned in this connection [that he] systematically stud[ies] the documents and materials (before they are adopted) of the most important party and state conferences and meetings.

Mao Zedong agreed with my statement that in spite of a certain redistribution of authority between the CCP CC leaders he (Mao Zedong) still has great responsibilities in the leadership of the party and the country. He said that he still often has to work at night. "The principal workload is connected with the reading of numerous documents and materials." Twice a day, for instance, he said, "they bring me two big volumes of routine information on international affairs, which of course it is necessary to look through to keep updated, not to lose contact with life."

In the course of the conversation I mentioned that the rapidly developing international affairs demand constant attention and timely analysis. I stressed the outstanding significance of the Moscow Conference where the recent international developments were submitted to deep Marxist-Leninist analysis.

Mao Zedong agreed with this statement and quickly responded to the topic, saying: "The Moscow Conference was a success, it was thoroughly prepared, and the editing commission, which included the representatives of twenty-six parties, worked fruitfully." Foreign representatives, he went on, are often puzzled and ask why was the conference so long. Mao Zedong said that they apparently do not have a full understanding of the real situation, when it took more than ten days for each of the representatives of eighty-one parties to deliver his speech. Then there were repeated speeches, not to mention the work on the documents themselves. He stated: "It is very good that there were arguments and discussions at the conference. This is not bad."

Then, agreeing with my statement on the deep theoretical character of the documents of the Moscow Conference, Mao Zedong added that these documents caused a great confusion in the Western imperialist circles, among our common enemies.

During the conversation, I gave a brief review of the work to popularize the results of the Moscow Conference in the Soviet Union, to study the conference's documents within the political education network.

In his turn Mao Zedong told me that the study of the Moscow Conference documents is also being organized by the CCP. As for the summarizing of the conference's results, the CCP CC has not yet sent any precise instructions on this question to the provinces.

Then he told me that the CCP CC Plenum will take place in January 1961 (the last plenum was in April 1960), where the CCP CC delegation at the Moscow Conference will present its report. It is planned to adopt a short plenum resolution on this question, expressing support of the Moscow Conference's decisions. Apart from the results of the conference the January plenum of the CCP CC will also discuss the economic plan of the PRC for 1961.

After that Mao Zedong told me that there are certain difficulties in the PRC which make it impossible to elaborate a perspective plan, "and we also lack the experience for this." At first, he went on, the CCP CC wanted to work out a plan for the three remaining years of the second Five-Year Plan. However, 1960 is already over. So it was decided to make separate plans for the two remaining years of the Five-Year Plan. He said that the current plan of economic development for the first quarter of 1961 exists and is practically put into implementation.

For my part I told him about the favorable conditions for planning achieved in the Soviet Union, of the adoption of the economic plan and budget for 1961 by the Supreme Council of the USSR. Expressing a critical opinion of the lag with the adoption of economic plans in the PRC, Mao Zedong said that the plan for 1960, for instance, was adopted only in April 1960, and on some occasions plans were adopted by the sessions of CAPR [Chinese Assembly of People's Representatives] only in June-July. He explained it by the lack of sufficient experience in the PRC. I told Mao Zedong of the forthcoming plenum of the CPSU CC, of the serious attention paid by the party and government to the problems of agricultural development in the Soviet Union, including some special features of the forthcoming plenum, where the most important questions of further increase of agricultural production will be discussed and resolved.

Mao Zedong said that the CCP CC is now also "specializing" in agriculture. Increasing the attention to this question, he continued, "we are even thinking about narrowing the industrial front to some extent." Explaining this idea he said that it is about a certain lowering of the scale of capital investments into the industrial production, including some branches of heavy industry; capital investments into the construction of public buildings will also be cut.

In the course of the conversation he briefly mentioned the bottlenecks of the PRC's industry, pointing, for instance, at the mining and coal industry, and the transport as well, talked about the interconnection of these industries, their influence on the development of many other branches (steel production, etc.).

Returning to the problem of agriculture, he emphasized that the lack of appropriate attention to this most important field of the PRC's economy, as well as to the development of the light industry, would make it impossible to satisfy the requirements of the population for foodstuffs, clothing, and consumer goods. Our own experience, Mao Zedong went on, persuaded us that "organizing the production of living plants and animals is much more difficult than the production of lifeless items – metals, ore, coal, etc." He stated jokingly that "the dead will not run away from us and can wait."

In the course of the conversation Mao Zedong repeatedly stressed that after the revolution in the PRC the material requirements of the Chinese population have been steadily growing. So the CCP must seriously contemplate these problems and the way to overcome the difficulties that arise. Of course, it is not the difficulties only that matter. Even when we have successes, new problems and tasks are appearing all the same. He stated in this connection that even in 300 to 400 years new problems will be still arising, demanding to be solved, "no development will be possible without them."

I shared with Mao Zedong some of the impressions from my trip around the Soviet Union together with the Chinese delegation headed by Liu Shaoqi, stressing the significance of the trip for the strengthening of friendship and solidarity between the USSR and the PRC.

Mao Zedong actively supported this part of the conversation. He said that in China they are very happy with this visit, "it is very good that it took place." Both our peoples, he said with emphasis, demanded such an action to be taken. "By making this decision, the Central Committees of both parties satisfied the demands of both peoples."

I told him as if jokingly that many republics of the USSR, Ukraine for instance, were however "displeased" that the Chinese delegation was not able to visit them. He said, laughing, that this protest should be addressed to the members of the delegation, for instance to Yang Shankun,[25] who is present here at the conversation, as the Politburo had no objections against prolonging the visit. I noted in the same tone that the Chinese friends had disarmed the "displeased" Soviet comrades, saying that it was not their last visit to the Soviet Union. So, Mao Zedong said, one can maintain that they owe you.

When he broadened the topic of the usefulness of these meetings and visits I told him that during the trip of the Chinese delegation Soviet citizens had repeatedly asked to give him (Mao Zedong) their best wishes and expressed their hope that he will also come to the Soviet Union when he finds it convenient, visit different cities, enterprises, collective farms, especially that he had had no chance to get better acquainted with the country during his previous visits. He reacted warmly and stated that he "must certainly find the time for such a visit."

Then Mao Zedong told that in China he is criticized by the functionaries from the periphery, who are displeased that he has not been able yet to visit a number of cities and regions – Xinjiang, Yunnan, Guizhou, Tibet, Taiyuan, Baotou, Xian, Lanzhou, etc. These workers, he said, used to call me "the Chairman for half of the Republic," and when I resigned from this post in favor of Liu Shaoqi, they started to call me "the Chairman of the CCP for half of the country."

[25] Yang Shankun, CCP CC secretary for party organization.

In the final part of the conversation Mao Zedong returned to the notion of his alleged retirement from active state and party work, saying half jokingly that now "he will wait for the moment when he will become an ordinary member of the Politburo." I have not consulted anybody in the party on this matter, he mentioned, even him, Mao Zedong said, pointing at Yang Shankun, you are the first whom I am telling about my "conspiracy."

I expressed assurance that the members of the CCP will apparently not agree to such a proposal from Mao Zedong. Then, he said jokingly, I will have to wait until everybody realizes its necessity; "in several years they will have mercy for me."

The conversation lasted more than an hour in an exceptionally cordial, friendly atmosphere. When it was over Mao Zedong came to see us to our car. Bidding us a warm farewell, he once again asked to give his warm greetings to Comrade N. S. Khrushchev and the members of the CPSU CC Presidium and most sincere thanks for their congratulations and warm wishes.

Candidate member of the CCP CC Secretariat Yang Shankun, the functionaries of the CCP CC apparatus Yan Minfu and Zhu Jueren, Counselor Minister of the USSR Embassy in the PRC N. G. Sudarikov and the counselor of the embassy O. B. Rakhmanin were present at the conversation.

Source: AVPRF, f. 0100, op. 55, pa. 454, d. 9, pp. 98–105. Translated by Maxim Korobochkin.

XV. Record of Conversation, Chervonenko and Zhou Enlai, June 25, 1961

This meeting between Premier Zhou and the Soviet ambassador took place in the wake of the disasters of the CCP's "Great Leap Forward," during which millions of Chinese had starved to death as a result of the party's policies. The Soviet Union had provided significant food-aid to China in the spring of 1961, and Deng Xiaoping and Zhou Enlai had worked to stabilize Sino-Soviet relations during the famine. The document is excerpted.

In connection with a commission from the Center, I [Chervonenko] was received by Zhou Enlai today at 9 o'clock in the evening. He said that Mao Zedong wasn't able to receive me because he had been suffering from angina for the whole last month. Liu Shaoqi was given the task to prepare a report for the meeting on the occasion of the fortieth anniversary of the CCP. He is now released from all his other duties and works on the report – is "condemned to hard labor," "we have enslaved him" – added Zhou Enlai in jest.

For my part I congratulated Zhou Enlai on the approaching fortieth anniversary of the CCP.

Zhou Enlai thanked me and said that it had been decided not to celebrate that event very widely. A ceremonial anniversary meeting would be held and a report would be published. He added, as if explaining why such a decision had been made, that there was quite a strained internal situation in the country. There is a very serious drought. The situation will be worse than last year. The number of provinces suffering from the drought continues to grow. The summer harvest will be gathered in soon. It is already clear that this year's harvest of grain crops will be 10 million tons less in comparison with the last year. Last year's summer harvest was 30 million tons, this year's yield will be only little more than 20 million tons.

I asked about the planned harvest of grain crops.

Zhou Enlai said that only the summer harvest was meant. And the plan for this year has been set at last year's level. A summer harvest makes up a big share – one-fifth of an annual yield. A crop of 160 million tons was gathered in last year. Judging by this summer's harvest, the same number will hardly be achieved this year.

He continued that the spring sowing had not yet been finished in some regions of the country. It concerned especially the central provinces – the northern part of Anhui province and Henan and Jiangsu provinces – where rice planting hadn't been finished because of drought. In Shandong, Henan, Hebei, Shanxi, [and] Liaoning provinces, and in inner Mongolia the summer harvest of wheat had been gathered in, but because of a strong drought it was impossible to start sowing. The situation was better in places where water was supplied mechanically, but in places where it was done manually, the situation was difficult. Besides there was no water in many wells.

According to the forecasts of the weather bureau, heavy showers are expected in northern provinces in July and August. Currently, it is raining too much in the region to the south from Yangzi.

I asked whether there was a possibility to find a way out of the situation. Zhou Enlai told me that it was planned to increase the area with drought-resistant crops (batat, etc.) and to carry out other measures.

He mentioned that a number of sister nations had their own problems in connection with natural calamities. We, the socialist countries, have to work hard in order to strengthen the agricultural base. I agreed with this point of view.

I said further that I had a commission from the CC CPSU to pass over to Mao Zedong the stenographic record of N. S. Khrushchev's talks with [President John F.] Kennedy in Vienna. Having given a gist of these talks, I passed the material to Zhou Enlai.

Zhou Enlai thanked me and mentioned that "the Western sources give various interpretations of the meeting in Vienna. Of course, we cannot take all of these sources seriously." Zhou Enlai didn't express other opinions concerning that question.

During our further discussion, I said to Zhou Enlai that I was going to Moscow in the beginning of July and would like to discuss some questions, if he had time. Zhou Enlai gladly agreed with this.

I said I had got a good impression of the big work on fulfillment of the decisions of the Nineteenth CC CCP [Central Committee Chinese Communist Party] Plenum, which was being done in provinces and in the local units. I asked him to tell me, if possible, what large-scale measures were planned for the nearest future, in particular in connection with the perspectives of the discussion on the national economy planning for the coming years, and also about the assessment of the fulfillment of the decisions of the Nineteenth CC CCP Plenum concerning internal questions. I asked whether any other steps in the direction of putting in order the People's Communes were considered, except for those that had already been taken.

Zhou Enlai said that the CC CCP had recently conducted a "working meeting" (apparently, an enlarged session of the Politbureau with participation of the CC CCP members and province leaders), which considered internal questions.

After three years of the Great Leap and two years of natural calamities we are thinking to conduct a certain regulation of the overall national economic plan, sticking to the course of "regulation, consolidation, increase, and replenishment." The aim of this course is "to liquidate certain disproportions which came into existence as a result of the Great Leap." This means bringing a proper correlation between agriculture, heavy and light industries, and removing disproportions which have been created. The question is about regulating the interrelations between town and country.

Zhou Enlai said that the reasons for the emergence of the disproportions had to be stated. Natural calamities have to be pointed out among the objective reasons. Because of them a drop in production of agricultural products and industrial crops happened. This adversely affected providing the industry with raw materials and the urban population with objects of consumption. On the other hand, subjective reasons have to be noted. The three red banners – the basic line, the Great Leap, and People's Communes – are new phenomena, which were born on Chinese soil and are based on Chinese practice. These new phenomena helped to achieve new success but also created a new situation. Zhou Enlai continued that they hadn't had enough experience and had been culpable of a certain roughness, of shortcomings, and errors in the work.

Zhou Enlai mentioned that such things (shortcomings, errors, etc.) took place not only in the countries where the dictatorship of the proletariat had won, but were also typical of bourgeois and feudal societies. He said further: "We in China use the experience of the Soviet Union and other sister nations, but we also have a zigzag development, because everything new that appears on the Chinese soil inevitably gives rise to roughness, errors. That is why this regulation is necessary. Things that we do differ, of course, radically from what the exploiter classes do. They do everything in the interests of minority, but we [do it] in the interests of majority. That is why we, supported by the great mass of the population, will be better able to overcome the shortcomings."

Zhou Enlai said that it also had to be pointed out that cadre had rested content with the success of the three-year period and as a result their work suffered from omissions and shortcomings. After the shortcomings in the work began to be revealed and corrected last year, cadre were able to comprehend and realize them. So, each phenomenon has two sides in its development. The victory is won, but if no one pays attention any longer, it can contain the seeds of errors and shortcomings. If errors are committed and work suffers from shortcomings – pay attention to them and then they will be eliminated. K. Marx and V. I. Lenin talked about this. "In case of a victory, don't be intoxicated by it, in case of defeat – don't give up."

Zhou Enlai mentioned that it wasn't possible to master this rule completely. Theory needs to be tested by practice. One has to experience much oneself and to store own knowledge. This thesis applies both to a class as a whole and to individual workers. He added that to all appearances, the report on the fortieth anniversary of the CCP would dwell on it. . . .

He said he would like to stress that they considered training of cadre and party-organizational activities to be the main point in their work. Using a Chinese formula, this idea can be expressed according to the "three-words principle": "(1) leadership, (2) training, [and] (3) education."

Each political aim can be achieved only through the cadre on different levels. The cadre must realize all the depth of these aims, only then they will be able to transmit everything correctly to the people. You have been accumulating experience during forty-four years. We have been doing it only twelve years.

I mentioned in jest that together that was fifty-six years.

Zhou Enlai answered kindly that China was repeating the experience of the Soviet Union in many ways, so it was not correct to sum up merely arithmetically.

Zhou Enlai proceeded with his thought and said that the democratic revolution had taken twenty-eight years. During this period, much educational work had been conducted with cadre. Only twelve years have passed since the victory of the revolution. That is why not enough work has been done in the sphere of cadre training.

As regards general trends, we can learn from our sister nations. But as far as specific measures are concerned, we can learn only from our own experience. And this experience has two sides: the right one and the mistaken one, the successful and the unsuccessful. It is necessary to be able to generalize experience in good time.

For my part I mentioned that it was impossible to be a leader without this ability. I added that it wasn't enough to have a course, it was necessary to provide for it organizationally.

Zhou Enlai agreed with me and, continuing this thought, said that it wasn't enough to have the CC leadership and the CC course. This course had to be carried out through cadre to masses, to be tested by them, and only then to be converted into a concrete practice. He concluded that to put it briefly, they were accomplishing such deeds as their ancestors didn't achieve.

I expressed agreement with his point of view and said that I would like to point out one feature. From my numerous conversations and observations during my travels in the country, I had got the impression that the knowledge of concrete matters, [a] kind of professionalism was the most critical problem for the local cadre. As a rule, these persons had gone through a great school of struggle, they were politically devoted, but obviously had a poor knowledge of the specific work they were asked to do. I gave some concrete examples from my own observations during my travels in the country and expressed my point of view that maybe it would have been advisable to give these questions major importance to the state and party as a whole, to open special schools for such cadre and this way to give them opportunity to professionally master a concrete duty. I referred to the experience of our country in this field at different stages of the building of socialism.

Zhou Enlai answered that he considered that remark as a very correct one. He continued that during the last twelve years the socialist revolution and socialist construction were going on simultaneously, interweaving with each other. That is why in many spheres the personnel had not been paying enough attention to studies. But that also pointed to the fact that we hadn't educated them enough. Zhou Enlai spoke critically about himself at this point. He said that he had been a prime minister for twelve years, but in discussions he could speak more on political problems than on specific questions. He added that he was sincere in saying that.

For my part I mentioned that Comrade Zhou Enlai was too modest.

He repeated that he had been talking about it sincerely. Further Zhou Enlai said that the main trends, the main sides of economic construction were not quite clear to him. To master them, to understand them – that was the task. He went on and said that they frequently didn't foresee, but got to know the general trends in the process of work. Obviously, he said, the Communist Party had to go through that process.

During the meeting with Zhou Enlai, I, on a commission from the Center, informed him about the forthcoming signing of the Soviet-Korean treaty. Zhou Enlai said that they in China heartily approved the signing of that treaty and in advance congratulated Soviet and Korean comrades on their success.

On a commission from the Center, I asked about the Chinese comrades' opinion concerning a possible date of L. I. Brezhnev's visit to the PRC in accordance with the invitation extended by Liu Shaochi in Moscow. I did so in a careful way and used an appropriate moment (when the conversation turned to the exchange of a number of governmental delegations and to the visits to the PRC of many foreign guests). Zhou Enlai said that the embassy would be informed about this issue during the coming days.

In the course of our conversation, Zhou Enlai said that in accordance with the invitation from the CC CCP,[26] ten Chinese comrades were planning to come on holiday to the USSR. But he also said that the main Chinese leaders couldn't accept our invitation because they were too occupied by internal problems in the country.

Zhou Enlai said, for example, that he himself had not been on holiday during the three years of the "Great Leap," even after his illness in 1959.

In this connection he informed me that a decision of the last "working meeting" the CC CCP "recommended me to work half a day for reasons of health, but this decision I am unable to implement in practice."

I said that he systematically broke that decision and, obviously, wouldn't be able to stick to it in the future. Zhou Enlai said that, unfortunately, this was true.

The conversation lasted more than two hours in a relaxed and friendly atmosphere. The head of the first sector of the department on relations with brotherly parties of the CC CCP Ye Husheng, the CC CCP staff workers Yan Minfu and Zhou Zhucheng, as well as the Counselors of the Embassy O. B. Rakhmanin and F. V. Mochulskii were present.

Source: AVPRF, f. 0100, op. 54, pa. 466, d. 8, pp. 119–33, excerpted. Obtained by O. A. Westad; translated by Olga Baeva.

XVI. Records of Conversations, Chervonenko and Deng Xiaoping, March–April 1962

These are two brief excerpts from conversations between Deng Xiaoping and the Soviet ambassador, which took place at a time when Deng and other CCP leaders made a last attempt at restoring some form of stability to Sino-Soviet relations. Several such exploratory meetings were held in Beijing between February and early June 1962. During the Beidahe meetings in the summer of 1962, Mao Zedong criticized those leaders who had believed that it could be possible to find some areas of cooperation with the Soviet Union.

MARCH 1

At the beginning of the meeting, Deng Xiaoping and CC CCP [Central Committee Chinese Communist Party] Secretariat candidate member Yang Shangkun were cautiously

[26] Almost certainly a typing error in original; "CPSU" makes more sense.

reserved, noticeably nervous, and evidently ready to receive a document of a different character.[27]

[Deng said] ". . . we draw your attention to the fact that your letter talks about the necessity of improving relations with Albania. In the end, the larger party should take the initiative on such issues. Issues of prestige do not exist for a large party and a large country. In the past we had disagreements with other parties and we have experience in resolving them, as we told Comrade Khrushchev. As we told you earlier, we have experience in relations with Korea. The CPSU [Communist Party of the Soviet Union] has much experience in relations with Poland. For this reason, given a desire to improve relations, of course, a resolution will be found. . . ."

The meeting, which continued for about an hour and a half, took place in an even, calm tone. After the Chinese comrades had acquainted themselves with the contents of the CC CPSU's letter, their reservations disappeared; they acted more freely and cordially. In parting with us, Deng Xiaoping said: "Your letter calls for solidarity – and that is good."

APRIL 9

On April 5, in keeping with instructions from the Center, I turned to the CC CCP with a request to meet with Mao Zedong, or with a person to be named by him, in order to inform the Chinese side of the negotiations of Comrade A. A. Gromyko with [U.S. Secretary of State] D[ean] Rusk on the German issue. After a silence lasting for four days, they replied to us that Deng Xiaoping had been instructed by the CC CCP to meet with the ambassador.

I visited Deng Xiaoping in the CC CCP building. In connection with Deng Xiaoping's question about my trip to Moscow, I told him in detail about the work of the March plenum of the CC CPSU. Deng Xiaoping then handed me a letter from the CC CCP of April 7, 1962, which is an answer to the CC CPSU letter of February 22, 1962.

Since these letters by the CC CCP are long, Deng Xiaoping stated that he would not read it out. The basic content of the letter of the CC CCP to the CC CPSU, he continued, is that, no matter what, the CPSU and the CCP must close ranks and, in a spirit of unity, resolve their problems. . . .

Source: AVPRF, f. 0100, op. 55, pa. 480, d. 6, pp. 43–9, 100–4. Translated by Benjamin Aldrich-Moodie.

[27] Chervonenko presented the CC CPSU's letter to fraternal parties on relations with Albania.

XVII. Records of Meetings of the CPSU and CCP Delegations, Moscow, July 5–20, 1963[28]

The final document is an excerpt from the records of several secret meetings between So-viet and Chinese leaders in Moscow in the summer of 1963. The Soviets had agreed to the meetings as a last attempt to find common ground with the Chinese, and the Soviet Politburo had prior to the meetings decided to reduce anti-CCP propaganda and to re-sume aid to China if some form of agreement was reached. At the meetings, however, both sides presented their views in ways which gave little hope for compromise. The fi-nal meeting, on July 20, 1963, broke up with no agreements, not even on where and when to continue the discussions. In effect, this was the last meeting between top leaders of the two sides during the alliance. In the fall of 1963 the CPSU and the CCP attacked each other publicly in massive propaganda efforts. On July 25, 1963, the CCP Politburo cir-culated a report that stressed the need to intensify the revolution on the ideological and cultural fronts.

JULY 8

Deng Xiaoping: By law, obviously, Comrade Grishin[29] should not object to our work-ing?

Grishin: Today is a work day. I don't know what Liu Ningyi[30] thinks.

Kang Sheng:[31] Liu Ningyi is silent, which means that he agrees.

Deng Xiaoping: Well, as for today, perhaps I should speak?

Suslov: Please, [go ahead]. . . .

[Speech by the CCP delegation head Comrade Deng Xiaoping]

First of all, I want to announce that our delegation at the request of the CC [Central Committee] of our party came to this meeting in Moscow of representatives of the CCP [Chinese Communist Party] and USSR with the sincere intention of removing discord and strengthening unity. . . .

. . . It can be said with all candor that a whole series of disagreements of a fundamen-tal character which exist today in the international Communist movement started at the Twentieth Congress of the CPSU [Communist Party of the Soviet Union].

---

[28] The Chinese delegation was headed by Deng Xiaoping; the Soviet delegation by Mikhail Suslov.

[29] Viktor Grishin, chairman of the Soviet Council of Trade Unions and candidate member of the CC CPSU Politburo.

[30] Liu Ningyi, head of the All-China Foundation of Trade Unions.

[31] Kang Sheng, CCP head of intelligence, secretary of the CCP CC.

In the past we never spoke about this openly, because we were taking into account the situation you were in. We only mentioned that the disagreements which have arisen in the past few years in the international Communist movement were provoked by the violation of the Declaration of 1957 by comrades from several fraternal parties. . . . We have always considered and still consider that the Twentieth Congress of the CPSU put forward positions on the issues of war and peace, peaceful coexistence and peaceful transition which went against Marxism-Leninism. Especially serious are two issues: the issue of the so-called peaceful transition and the issue of the full, groundless denunciation of Stalin under the pretext of the so-called struggle with the cult of personality. . . .

Here I want just briefly to say the following: A criticism of some errors by Stalin is necessary; taking off the lid, so to speak, and ending superstition is a good thing. However, this criticism must be correct both from the point of view of principles and from the point of view of methods.

Since the Twentieth Congress of the CPSU, the facts demonstrate that the full, groundless denunciation of Stalin is a serious step undertaken by the leading comrades from the CPSU with the aim of laying out the path to the revision of Marxism-Leninism on a whole series of issues. . . . After the Twentieth Congress of the CPSU, as a consequence of the so-called struggle against the cult of personality and the full, groundless denunciation of Stalin, a wave of anti-Soviet and anti-Communist campaigns was provoked around the whole world. . . . The most prominent events which took place in this period were the events in Poland and Hungary.

We have always considered and still consider that in resolving the issues connected with the events in Poland, the CPSU took a position of great-power chauvinism, trying to exert pressure on the Polish comrades and to subordinate them to itself by means of coercion and even tried to resort to military force. We consider that such a method is not only evidence of great-power chauvinism in relation to fraternal countries and to fraternal parties, but also evidence of adventurism.

Following this, the counterrevolutionary rebellion in Hungary took place. The Hungarian events by their character differ from the events in Poland. In resolving the issues associated with the events in Poland, which were issues of an internal order between fraternal parties and fraternal countries, the comrades in the CPSU resorted to coercive methods, even trying to resort to military force.

And what position did the CPSU take in regard to the counterrevolutionary revolt in Hungary? The leadership of the CPSU at one time tried to leave socialist Hungary to the mercy of fate. You know that at that time we spoke out against your position on the matter. Such a position was practically tantamount to capitulation. The course and details of these two events are well known to you and to us. I do not want to dwell on them. . . . After the Twentieth Congress of the CPSU, beginning in 1956, at meetings of an internal kind, the leading comrades of our party criticized your errors in a moderate form more than once. In his statement Comrade Suslov said that we kept quiet for seven years. There are no grounds for [saying] that. In fact, both on the issue of Stalin and on the issue of the form of transition, that is, peaceful transition, the leaders of the CCP presented their views more than once to the leaders of the CPSU. And these views are well known to you. Back in April 1956, Comrade Mao Zedong stated our opinion on the issue of Stalin in a discussion with Comrade Mikoyan and also after that, in a discussion with Ambassador Comrade Iudin.

Comrade Mao Zedong emphasized that it is incorrect to think that "Stalin's errors and contributions are divided into equal halves"; "whatever happened, all the same Stalin's contributions are greater than his errors. One must evaluate it as follows, that his contributions make up 70 percent, and his mistakes 30 percent. It is necessary to make a concrete analysis and to give an all-around assessment. . . ." In October 1956, Comrade Zhou Enlai also stated our views about Stalin in a discussion with Comrade Ponomarev,[32] who was then a member of the CPSU delegation present at the Eighth Congress of our [CCP] party. In discussion with Comrade Ponomarev, Comrade Zhou Enlai criticized the mistakes by comrades from the CPSU: first, "no preliminary consultation was carried out with fraternal parties"; second, "an all-around historical analysis was completely lacking" in relation to Stalin; third, the leading comrades from the CPSU "lacked self-criticism." These are the three points which Comrade Zhou Enlai talked about.

On October 23, 1956, Comrade Mao Zedong again talked with Comrade Iudin about the issue of Stalin. Comrade Mao Zedong then said that it was necessary to criticize Stalin, but that in relation to the methods of criticism we hold a different opinion, and [we] also hold a different opinion about some other issues. Comrade Mao Zedong also said that you had completely renounced such a sword as Stalin, and had thrown away that sword. As a result, enemies had seized it in order to kill us. That is the same as if, having picked up a stone, one were to throw it on one's own feet.

On November 30, 1956, Comrade Mao Zedong again received Comrade Iudin and in a conversation with him said that the basic course and line in the period of Stalin's leadership was correct and that one must not treat one's comrade like an enemy.

On January 18, 1957, in Moscow, at the fifth discussion with the government delegation of the Soviet Union, Comrade Zhou Enlai touched on the events in Hungary, noting that the counterrevolutionary revolt in Hungary was connected, on the one hand, with some mistakes committed by Stalin when resolving issues of mutual relations between fraternal parties and fraternal countries, and, on the other hand, was connected with mistakes committed by the leadership of the CPSU in its criticism of Stalin. In discussion Comrade Zhou Enlai again set out the aforementioned three points on this issue to the

[32] Boris Ponomarev, head of the International Department of the CC CPSU Secretariat.

leadership of the CPSU: the lack of an all-around analysis, the lack of self-criticism, and the lack of consultation with the fraternal countries.

Both Comrade Mao Zedong on the October 29, 1957, on the eve of his departure for Moscow, in a conversation with Comrade Iudin, and Comrade Zhou Enlai during the Twenty-second Congress of the CPSU in 1961, in a conversation with Comrade Khrushchev, stated our opinion on the issue of Stalin.

It should be further noted that when the events in Poland arose, Comrade Liu Shaoqi, heading the delegation of the CCP, arrived in Moscow for negotiations, during which he also talked about the issue of Stalin and criticized comrades from the CPSU for committing the same mistakes during the events in Poland, [those] mistakes of great-power chauvinism which took place during Stalin's leadership as well. . . . From that very time, you, considering that your internal problems have already been resolved, started to direct the cutting edge of your action against Marxism-Leninism against fraternal parties defending the principles of Marxism-Leninism and began to engage in activities directed against the CCP, against the PRC, and these activities are of a serious character.

What has been done by you over this period? Let us cite some of the facts, so as to make things clear.

From April to July of 1958 the CPSU put to China the issue of the creation of a long-wave radar station and a joint fleet, trying thereby to bring China under its military control. But we guessed your intentions and you were not able to attain your goals.

Following that you started both in statements and in actions to carry out anti-Chinese activities in an intensified manner. You continually spoke out attacking the internal policies of the CCP, in particular on the People's Communes. By way of example one can refer to the conversation by Comrade Khrushchev with the American Congressman [Hubert] Humphrey in December 1958 and to the speech by Comrade Khrushchev in a Polish agricultural cooperative in July 1959.

In June 1959 you unilaterally annulled the agreement on rendering help to China in developing a nuclear industry and in producing atom bombs.

Following this, on September 9, 1959, TASS made an announcement about the incident on the Chinese-Indian border and displayed bias in favor of the Indian reaction, making the disagreements between China and the Soviet Union clear to the whole world for the first time.

In November of that year Comrade Khrushchev openly accused China of having acted "stupidly" and "regrettably" in a conversation with a correspondent of the Indian daily *New Age.*

At the last meeting at Camp David which was held in September 1959, Comrade Khrushchev began to preach to the whole world about a "world without arms, without armies, without wars," made the leader of American imperialism (look good in all sorts of different ways), considered peaceful coexistence the task of all tasks, and propagandized the idea that, supposedly, the American-Soviet friendship decides the fate of humanity.[33] All of this practically signified a sermon to the effect that the nature of imperialism had already changed, that Marxism-Leninism was already obsolete.

During this very period you started to propagandize the so-called "spirit of Camp David" everywhere. Incidentally, [President Dwight D.] Eisenhower did not recognize the existence of any "spirit of Camp David."

During this very period you, counting on some "spirit of Camp David," clutched at the straw extended by Eisenhower and began mounting attacks upon China in your statements without restraint.

On September 30, 1959, in his speech at a banquet held by us on the occasion of the tenth anniversary of the creation of the PRC, Comrade Khrushchev stated that one must not test the firmness of a capitalist power with force.

On October 6, 1959, in his speech in Vladivostok, Comrade Khrushchev stated that allegedly we were looking for war, like cocks for a fight.

On October 31, 1959, in his report to the session of the Supreme Soviet of the USSR, Comrade Khrushchev said that some, similarly to Trotsky, want "neither war nor peace."

On December 1, 1959, in his speech at the Seventh Congress of the Hungarian Socialist Workers' Party, Comrade Khrushchev demanded "a checking of watches." In that same speech he stated that "if the leadership of this or that country becomes conceited, then that can play into the hands of the enemy."

In February 1960 during the meeting of the Political Consultative Council of the participating countries of the Warsaw Pact, Comrade Khrushchev spoke rudely using an expression like "old galoshes." Meanwhile, the CC CPSU in its oral presentation to the CC CCP accused China of committing such mistakes as a "narrowly nationalist approach" and of acting on "narrowly nationalist interests," in relation to the issues of the Indian-Chinese border.

The meaning of all these statements and speeches is understood by you and by us, and also by our enemies. . . . In such circumstances we could not remain silent any longer. We published three articles "Long Live Leninism!" and others, in which we defended Marxism-Leninism and the Moscow Declaration, and exposed some revisionist and opportunist views to criticism. But in these three articles, we as before directed the brunt of our struggle for the most part against imperialism and Yugoslav revisionism without open criticism of comrades from the CPSU. Following this, such events occurred as the intrusion of the American "U-2" plane into USSR air space, the collapse of the meeting of the heads of government of the four powers in Paris, and the collapse

---

[33] Khrushchev and Eisenhower met at the U.S. president's country retreat (Camp David) during the Soviet leader's visit.

of the entirely nonexistent so-called "spirit of Camp David." All of this proved the error of the views of our comrades from the CPSU and the correctness of our views. . . .

In June 1960 in Bucharest, the leadership of the CPSU mounted a sudden attack on the CCP, disseminated the Informational Note of the CC of the CPSU which contains an all-around attack on the CCP, and organized a campaign by a whole group of fraternal parties against us. . . .

On July 16, 1960, the Soviet side unilaterally decided to withdraw between July 28 and September 1 over 1,300 Soviet specialists working in China. Over 900 specialists were recalled from [extended] business trips and contracts and agreements were broken. . . .

On August 25, 1962, the Soviet government informed China that it was ready to conclude an agreement with the USA on the prevention of the proliferation of nuclear weapons. In our view, you were pursuing an unseemly goal in coming to such an agreement, namely: to bind China by the hands and feet through an agreement with the USA.

After India started a major attack on the border regions of China in October 1962, the Soviet Union began to supply India with even larger quantities of military matériel, to do its utmost to give [India] an economic blood transfusion, to support [Jawaharlal] Nehru by political means, and to spur him on in the struggle against China.

Your position on the issues of the Indian-Chinese border conflict received praise from the United States. The U.S. Assistant Secretary of State [Averell] Harriman, said: "I consider that the maintenance of relations that are as friendly as possible between India and Moscow serves its own interests well and also serves our interests well." Harriman made this statement on December 9, 1962. Further, on December 18, 1962, in conversation with a Japanese correspondent, Harriman also stated that the USA wanted to see the Soviet Union help India in the matter of supporting its defense capabilities.

On the issue of Chinese-Indian relations you went too far. With all [bad] intention, you spoke out together with [President John F.] Kennedy and Nehru against China. Where then did the spirit of proletarian internationalism, which existed under Lenin and Stalin, go?

In October 1962 there was a crisis in the region of the Caribbean Sea. During these events, we consider that you committed two errors: in shipping the missiles to Cuba you indulged in adventurism, and then, showing confusion in the face of nuclear blackmail from the USA, you capitulated.

People understandably ask why you began to ship missiles to Cuba. In this regard we have our own experience. Judging by our experience, your actions in this regard remind us in their character of your efforts to develop a long-wave radar station and a joint fleet in China. For Cuba's defense no missiles are necessary at all. And so, in shipping missiles to Cuba, did you want to help her or to ruin her? We have become suspicious that you, in shipping missiles to Cuba, were trying to place her under your control.

You failed to consult with fraternal countries on such an important issue. You daily speak about the danger of thermonuclear war. But in the given case you rashly played with nuclear weapons.

You justify your actions by saying that you wanted to obtain some sort of "promise" from the USA, and you say that you truly received such a "promise." But what are the facts? The facts are that under threat from the United States you were obliged to remove your missiles. By all sorts of means you tried to convince Cuba to agree to so-called international inspection, which encroaches upon their sovereignty and constitutes interference in their internal affairs. Besides that, you also conduct propaganda among the peoples of the world, convincing them to believe in some sort of promise by Kennedy, and thereby you make American imperialism look good.

In his letters to Kennedy of October 27 and 28, 1962, Comrade Khrushchev wrote: "You are working toward the preservation of peace" and "I express my satisfaction and recognition of your manifestation of a sense of moderation and an understanding of the responsibility which now rests on you for the preservation of peace in the whole world."

But the question remains did the USA in the end give some sort of promise? Let us look at [U.S. Secretary of State Dean] Rusk's statement of January 11, 1963. Rusk stated: "To whatever extent President Kennedy took on obligations not to encroach on Cuba at the moment of the Cuban crisis, these obligations have not come into force." He further said: "In general no such obligations exist. . . ."

At the congresses of these parties another strange phenomenon was observed: On the one hand at these congresses they attacked the CCP and completely removed the Albanian Workers' Party, and on the other hand, they forcibly dragged the Titoist clique in Yugoslavia into the ranks of the international Communist movement and tried to rehabilitate that clique. In addition, at the Congress of the Socialist Unity Party of Germany, there was noise, whistling, and stamping right at the time when our representative subjected Yugoslav revisionism to criticism on the basis of the Moscow Declaration by citing the Moscow Declaration verbatim.

What do the facts we have cited above, which took place after the Twenty-second Congress of the CPSU, testify to? These facts testify to the fact that comrades from the CPSU have taken further steps to create a split in the ranks of the international Communist movement and, moreover, have done so in an increasingly sharp, increasingly extreme form, in an increasingly organized [way], on an increasingly large scale, trying, come what may, to crush others.

I would like to note that using such methods is a habitual affair for you. You began using such methods as far back as the Bucharest Conference. During the bilateral meeting between the representatives of our two parties in 1960, I said that it was fortunate that Comrade Peng Zhen went to the Bucharest meeting; he weighs approximately 80 kilograms, and for that reason he endured; if I had gone, and I weigh only a bit over 50 kilograms, I could not have endured. After that it was just as well that Comrade Wu

Xiuquan, who weighs more than 70 kilograms, went to the GDR, and was able to en-dure.[34] Frankly speaking, such methods do not help matters. You cannot prove by such methods that you are in the right; you cannot prove that the truth is on your side. Quite the opposite; the use of such methods is an insult to the glorious Marxist-Leninist party.

Ponomarev: And Comrade Grishin weighs 70 kg. After all, this started before Bucharest, in Beijing. That was the start of and the reason for the Bucharest Conference.

Deng Xiaoping: I understand you.

Peng Zhen: Wait. You will have [your] time; you will be able to say as much as you want then. We are ready to hear you out. . . .

Deng Xiaoping: I have already taken five hours in my statement, and on that I end it. Are we going to continue the session today, or will we continue it tomorrow?

Suslov: We propose a break until the day after tomorrow, at 10 A. M. We must acquaint ourselves with your statement.

Deng Xiaoping: We agree. Who will speak the day after tomorrow, you or we?

Suslov: By the order it will be our turn.

Andropov:[35] By the principle: we, you, we, you.

Deng Xiaoping: That is Comrade Andropov's invention. . . .

JULY 10
[Suslov speaks for the delegation today.]

Again, as in 1960, you are putting in motion the practice, which has already been con-demned by Communist parties, of personal attacks on Comrade N. S. Khrushchev. Such a practice in the past did not provoke anything but indignation in any true Communist, and will do the same now.

Comrade N. S. Khrushchev is our recognized leader. Reflecting the collective will of the CC CPSU, he has gained unlimited authority for himself in our party, in the country, in the whole world through his selfless devotion to Marxism-Leninism and through his truly titanic struggle to build communism in the USSR, to preserve peace in the whole world in defense of the interests of all working people. . . .

For obviously demagogic ends you are trying to connect the decisions of the Twenti-eth Congress with the well-known events in Poland and also with the counterrevolution-

[34] The Chinese leaders had complained that they were not given enough to eat during the meetings in Bucharest and Berlin. They also claimed that the Soviet plane that brought them back to Beijing had no food on board.

[35] Iurii Andropov, ambassador to Hungary, 1956, secretary of the CPSU CC, later head of the Committee for State Security, KGB.

ary revolt in Hungary in 1956. . . . We do not plan to examine these issues anew. We will simply note the complete groundlessness of your assertions to the effect that the decisions of the Twentieth Congress led to the counterrevolutionary revolt in Hungary. One of the reasons for those events, as is shown by materials of the fraternal parties, comes from the errors of the previous leadership of Hungary connected with Stalin's actions: elements of unequal rights in the relations between socialist countries which took place during that period by the fault of Stalin. How could the Twentieth Congress, which abolished these elements of unequal rights and fully restored the principle of respecting national sovereignty, be reason for dissatisfaction on the part of the Hungarian people?

You are now trying to accumulate capital by speculating on these events and by proving that allegedly the Soviet Union committed errors, and that by your interference you almost managed to save the situation.

This is a strange and monstrous accusation to lay at the feet of the CPSU and a more than strange pretension on the part of the Chinese leaders. Did our country not pay with thousands of its sons' lives in order to preserve the socialist order in fraternal Hungary; did it not come to the aid of the friendly Hungarian people in its difficult hour? . . .

Throughout the whole period of existence of the PRC, the CC of the CPSU and the Soviet government invariably gave help to China in creating and strengthening the defense of the country. The twenty-four defense enterprises built with the technical assistance of the Soviet Union were the basis for the creation of corresponding branches of Chinese industry. Another thirty-three defense enterprises are being built. At one time, sixty infantry divisions were equipped with arms and military-technical property supplied from the USSR, and from 1955–1956 the modernization of the Chinese army with more modern types of armaments and matériel was carried out. In past years our country has given the PRC a large quantity of technical and technological documentation by which China was able to organize the production of MiG-17, MiG-19, MiG-21-F, and TU-16 airplanes, MI-4 helicopters, "air-to-air," "ground-to-air," "ground-to-ground," "air-to-ground," and "ship-to-ground" missiles, naval matériel, submarines, and craft of various types. The Soviet Union helped the PRC develop the basis for a nuclear industry. . . .

Some words on the issue you raised about the so-called joint construction of a naval fleet. Comrade Deng Xiaoping stated that apparently our party tried to stick China with the joint construction of a naval fleet and that by doing so we allegedly encroached upon the sovereignty of the PRC. Comrade Deng Xiaoping, after all, you were present at the discussion between Comrade Khrushchev and Comrade Mao Zedong on July 31, 1958, and took part in it. Have you really forgotten the following statement made by Comrade Khrushchev in the course of the conversation: "Never have we at the CC of the CPSU even had the thought of jointly building a fleet. You know my point of view. During Stalin's reign I was against the 'joint companies.'" Later, N. S. Khrushchev announced: "We considered it necessary to talk about the issue of building a fleet, but we neither thought about or considered it necessary to construct a joint factory or a joint fleet." In response to this Comrade Mao Zedong stated that: "If it is so, then all the dark clouds have dispersed." There is no issue, but you have brought it up again today. What do you need it for? . . .

We would also like to remind our forgetful Chinese comrades about some facts and about the assistance the USSR has given to the economic development of the PRC. Do not the 198 modern industrial enterprises built with the technical assistance of the Soviet Union, the scientific-research institutes which it set up, and the technical cadres trained in the USSR bear witness to the commitment by the CPSU to fraternal friendship with People's China? Up until 1959 almost a half of all the cast iron was produced, more than half of all the steel was smelted, and more than half of the rolled iron was made in the metallurgical enterprises constructed in China with help from the USSR. Such new branches of industry as the automobile, the tractor, and the aviation industry have been developed in China with the help of the Soviet Union. The Soviet Union gave the PRC 21,000 sets of scientific-technical documentation, including more than 1,400 plans of whole enterprises . . . .

Deng Xiaoping: Perhaps tomorrow we rest for a day? The day after tomorrow we will speak according to his principle. (He turns to Comrade Andropov.)

Suslov: Fine, until ten o'clock, yes?

Deng Xiaoping: Fine, we agree. . . .

JULY 12

[Deng Xiaoping speaks for the delegation today.]

Under the influence of your nonrevolutionary line on peaceful transition, the People's Socialist Party of Cuba at one time descended to attacking the armed struggle led by Comrade Fidel Castro, calling it "putschism," "adventurism," and "terrorism." It accused Comrade Castro of saying that the armed struggle led by him was a "total mistake" "caused by a petty-bourgeois nature, and that its leaders do not rely on the masses." It even openly demanded of Comrade Castro that he renounce "putschistic activities" and "the erroneous path of armed struggle, leading to a rupture with the people."

Under the influence of your nonrevolutionary line on peaceful transition, the Algerian Communist Party from 1957 fully renounced armed struggle and, moreover, began to propagandize the "dangers" of national-liberationist war, advocating the attainment of independence through compromise, and in doing so wasted its place in the political life of the country.

Under the influence of your nonrevolutionary line on peaceful transition, the Communist Party of Iraq renounced the correct line, which it at one time had implemented, and began dreaming about the realization of a peaceful transition in Iraq. This led the revolution in Iraq to serious failures and to defeat. During the counterrevolutionary coup of

February 8, 1963, the Communist Party of Iraq found itself in a condition of complete unpreparedness and suffered heavy losses. . . .

JULY 13

[Comrade Ponomarev will speak today for our delegation.]

Comrades, yesterday we heard the second address by the head of the Chinese delegation. Our delegation cannot hide the fact that we came out of the meeting feeling deep sorrow and distress. Of course, this was not because the address allegedly contained criticism, which is what Deng Xiaoping had in mind when he talked about "bitter, but necessary medicine." We Communists are steadfast people, and more than once have [we] come across not only groundless criticism but also malicious slander.

No, that was not what left us with a bitter taste. The second address by Comrade Deng Xiaoping confirmed our worst fears, formed toward the end of his first speech. It is becoming clearer and clearer that the delegation of the CC of the CCP came here not to find agreement and to eliminate our differences. Your design, evidently, is different – to bring a whole load of [?] to Moscow, to dump it on us, to do everything, not shying away from any tactics, to defame the policies of the CPSU and thereby further worsen the relations between our two parties and countries. . . .

You fabricated an undoubted falsehood to the effect that the USSR did not aid the Algerian people's war of liberation. Here are the facts. In the most decisive period of the war, from 1960 to 1962, we supplied free to the People's Liberation Army of Algeria 25,000 rifles, 21,000 machine guns and submachine guns, 1,300 howitzers, cannons, and mortars, many tens of thousands of pistols and other weapons. Over 5 million rubles' worth of clothes, provisions, and medical supplies were supplied to Algeria by Soviet social organizations alone. Hundreds of wounded from the People's Liberation Army of Algeria were saved and treated in the Soviet Union. Soviet wheat, sugar, butter, conserves, condensed milk, etc., streamed into Algeria.

Finally, Fabrication Number 5. You again and again repeat your lies about Soviet policy toward Poland, Hungary, and Cuba. Who are you [to set yourselves up] as judges in these matters, if the party and governmental leaders of these three countries fully, decisively, and publicly for the whole world reject your insinuations and declare to you that it is impermissible for representatives of a Communist Party to try and split the USSR, Poland, and Hungary through fabrications? Comrade Fidel Castro in speeches in the USSR and on returning [to Cuba] clearly described the internationalist policies of the CPSU. By the way, why didn't you publish these speeches? They would have shown the Chinese people that your position during the Caribbean crisis was erroneous and contradicted the interests of the Cuban, Soviet, and Chinese peoples. . . .

Andropov: As for you, you long ago ceased any sort of consultation with us. In 1958, the Chinese side did not inform us in a timely fashion about its intentions to carry out the shelling of the coastal islands in the Taiwan Straits which was carried out soon after

Comrade N. S. Khrushchev left Beijing. According to the later admission of Comrade Mao Zedong, during Comrade N. S. Khrushchev's presence in Beijing the Chinese comrades had already decided on this operation and had prepared it, but you did not consider it necessary to inform the Soviet government about it. Despite this, during a dark hour for the Chinese government, the head of the Soviet government informed the U.S. President Eisenhower that an attack on China would be taken as an attack on the Soviet Union.

Over the last several years the government of the PRC has completely failed to inform the government of the USSR about the Chinese-American negotiations that have been going on since 1955 at the ambassadorial level in Warsaw. Judging by the press reports, over 100 meetings were held there. Since May 1958 you have twice sharply changed your political course on relations with Japan, and, in both cases, despite the Treaty of 1950, you did so without consulting with us. . . .

Kang Sheng: In your criticism of Stalin, you do not take the position of seeking the truth and do not use methods of scientific analysis, but resort to demagogy, slander, and abusive language.

Comrades from the CPSU call Stalin "a murderer," "a criminal," "a bandit," "a gambler," "a despot like Ivan the Terrible," "the greatest dictator in the history of Russia," "a fool," "shit," "an idiot."

All of these curses and swear words came from the mouth of Comrade N. S. Khrushchev.

Trying to justify Comrade N. S. Khrushchev, in your address of July 10 you stated that allegedly he gave Stalin an "objective and all-around assessment," that allegedly he adhered to the "heart of the matter." Is this not the same as telling cock-and-bull stories with your eyes shut? Frankly speaking, we cannot understand at all why the leadership of the CPSU feels such a fierce hatred for Stalin, why it uses every kind of the most malicious abuse, why it attacks him with more hatred than it shows its enemies?

From your statements it emerges that allegedly the great Soviet people lived for thirty years under the tyranny of "the greatest dictator in the history of Russia." Can it really be that such a great leader who for many years enjoyed the general recognition of the Soviet people really turned out to be "the greatest dictator in the history of Russia"? Can it really be that the experience of the first state in the world to be a dictatorship of the proletariat, which the Soviet people [then] shared with the peoples of the whole world, has been the Soviet people's experience of existence in the conditions of tyranny under some "dictator"?

From what you have said it appears as if the first socialist country in the world was built thanks to the fact that a "fool" headed the leadership. Can it really be that the achievements of the national economy and the development of the latest technology in the Soviet Union during several decades have been attained under the leadership of some sort of "fool"? Can it really be that the basis for the development of nuclear weapons and missile technology in the Soviet Union has been laid down under the leadership of some sort of "fool"?

From what you have said it appears as if the supreme commander of the great Soviet Army turns out to have been some sort of "idiot." Can it really be that the great victory of the Soviet Army during World War II was won under the command of some sort of "idiot"?

From what you have said it appears as if the great CPSU was in the position of having some sort of "bandit" at the head of its leadership for thirty years. Can it really be that the CPSU which for a long time had the love and respect of the revolutionary peoples of the whole world had a "bandit" as its great leader for several decades?

From what you have said it appears as if the ranks of the international Communist movement which grew and became stronger from year to year were under the leadership of some sort of "shit." Can it really be that Communists of all countries considered some sort of "shit" to be their flag-bearer for several decades?

From what you have said it appears as if the great proletarian leader for whom imperialists and reactionaries of different countries felt fierce hatred for a long time has turned out to be all-in-all some sort of "gambler." Can it really be that the Soviet people and the revolutionary peoples of all countries struggling against imperialism and reaction considered their teacher some sort of "gambler"? . . .

Comrades, you, so to speak, having picked up the stone, have thrown it on your own feet. How can you treat Stalin in such a way? Your actions in this regard not only go counter to historical reality, but also put you in a very awkward position. In depicting Stalin as such a bad man, you also blacken the entire leadership of the Soviet state and the CPSU; and, at the same time, as comrades who then took part in the leadership of the state and the party, you cannot justify yourselves by saying that you do not carry your portion of responsibility for the "crimes" you talk about.

Let us take, for example, Comrade Khrushchev. He heaped all of the errors of the period of Stalin's leadership, especially the excesses committed on the issue of counterrevolutionary elements, on Stalin alone while he presented himself as being completely clean. Can this really convince people? If the memory of men is not too short, they will be able to recall that during Stalin's leadership Comrade Khrushchev more than once extolled Stalin and the policy he was then carrying out of struggling with counterrevolutionary elements.

Comrade Khrushchev constantly praised Stalin, calling him "a close friend and comrade-in-arms of Lenin," "a very great genius, teacher, great leader of humanity," "a great Marshal of victories," "a friend of peoples in his simplicity," "one's own father," and so on and so on.

On June 6, 1937, in his report at the fifth party conference of the Moscow oblast', Comrade Khrushchev said: "Our party will mercilessly crush the band of betrayers and traitors, will wipe all the Trotskyist-rightist carrion from the face of the earth. . . . The guarantee is the unshakable leadership of our CC, the unshakable leadership of our great leader, Comrade Stalin. . . . We will annihilate our enemies without a trace to the last one and will scatter their ashes in the wind."

Later, for example on June 8, 1938, while speaking at the fourth party conference of the Kiev oblast', Comrade Khrushchev said: "Yakiry, balitskie, liubchenki, zatomskie,[36] and other bastards wanted to bring Polish nobles to the Ukraine, wanted to bring German fascists, landowners, and capitalists here. . . . We have destroyed quite a few enemies, but not all. For that reason one must keep one's eyes open. We must firmly remember the words of Comrade Stalin, that as long as capitalist encirclement exists, they will send spies and provocateurs to us. . . ."

Frankly speaking, on the issue of criticism and self-criticism you are inferior to Stalin. Having made mistakes, Stalin sometimes still practiced self-criticism. For instance, Stalin gave some mistaken advice relating to the Chinese Revolution. After the victory of the Chinese Revolution, he recognized his mistakes before Chinese comrades and friends. And how are you acting? You know well that you slough off all of your mistakes onto others and ascribe all successes to yourself. . . .

Suslov: Our delegation states a decisive protest against the distortion, falsification, and slanders made in relation to the leadership of our party and to Comrade N. S. Khrushchev, against our party and the decisions of its congresses. The delegation of the CPSU also states its protest against the sort of propaganda that has begun in the last few days on Beijing radio. We consider that the entire responsibility for these actions rests with the leadership of the CCP. . . .

Deng Xiaoping: Comrade Suslov has expressed some sort of protest. If we are talking about protest, then we have an even greater basis for voicing even more protests. . . .

Already two weeks have gone by since our meeting began. At the meeting both sides stated their views. Although as of yet it has been difficult to attain a unity of both sides' views right away, still, a frank exposition of views by both sides in this circle where the representatives of the two parties have been meeting is very useful for mutual under-standing, for gradually finding a common language, for searching out a way to eliminate disagreements and strengthen cohesion. For that reason we consider that it serves as a good start . . . our delegation is introducing a proposal temporarily to adjourn the current meeting; the representatives of the CCP and the CPSU, both sides, can continue their meeting at another time. The time and place of the next meeting will be set through a con-sultation between the Central Committees of our two parties. . . .

Our delegation once again expresses the sincere hope of our party that we and you will not spare our efforts toward an all-around, repeated, and most careful discussion of the

[36] Peter Iakir, V. A. Balitskii, Iridor Liubchenko, Vladimir Zatomskii, Ukrainian Com-munists who were killed on Stalin's orders during the 1930s purges. Reference here is to their names in plural form.

disagreements existing between our parties. If a single meeting is not enough for this, it is possible to hold a second meeting, and if two meetings do not suffice, a third can be held. . . .

JULY 20

Deng Xiaoping: In conclusion I would like to say a few words.

However great the disagreements between us may be, we hope that we can gradually find a way to eliminate those disagreements, since unity between us is very important.

Despite the fact that in the course of the discussion both our sides have stated more than a few views with which the other side does not agree, and despite the fact that you have said that our statements are not pleasant to the ear, and that we have also said that your statements are not pleasant to the ear, despite all of this, our current meeting will serve as a good start. Moreover, we have agreed with you to publish a communiqué on the continuation of our meetings. We consider this a good thing.

We have come to the agreement that it is necessary to continue our meetings and that the time and place of the next meeting will be agreed by the Central Committees of our parties.

Here I would like to express in passing the following hope of ours: If your delegation, if the CC of the CPSU agrees, then we would like to invite the delegation of the CPSU to Beijing for the continuation of the meeting. That issue, of course, could be agreed upon separately.

Suslov: This is also a question for discussion between our Central Committees.

Finished. Will I see you [later] today?

Deng Xiaoping: At six?

Suslov: Yes, at six.

Source: Stiftung Archiv der Parteien und Massenorganisationen der ehemaligen DDR im Bundesarchiv (SAPMO-BArch), JIV 2/207 698, 187–330 (in Russian). Obtained by Vladislav Zubok; translated by Benjamin Aldrich-Moodie.

Contributors

Chen Jian is associate professor of history at Southern Illinois University at Carbondale. He is the author of *China's Road to the Korean War: The Making of the Chinese-American Confrontation* (1994) and numerous articles on China's external relations during the Cold War period. His new book, *Mao's China in the Cold War,* is forthcoming in 1999.

Sergei Goncharenko is senior researcher at the Institute of World Economy and International Relations (IMEMO), Russian Academy of Sciences, Moscow. He is a specialist in the history of the People's Republic of China, Sino-Soviet/Russian relations, and Southeast Asian history. He recently has published several works in Russian on Russia and East Asia in the 1990s.

Deborah A. Kaple received her Ph.D. in sociology from Princeton University. She is the author of *Dream of a Red Factory: High Stalinism in China* (1994) and the editor of the *World Encyclopedia of Political Systems and Parties* (forthcoming). She is currently a freelance writer and teaches in the Princeton University Writing Program.

Niu Jun is senior researcher at the Institute of American Studies, Chinese Academy of Social Sciences, Beijing. He has published several books in Chinese on CCP foreign policy and Sino-American relations, most recently *Cong Yan'an zou xiang shijie: Zhongguo gongchandang dui wai guanxi qiyuan (1935–1949)* [From Yan'an to the world: Origins of the foreign relations of the Chinese Communist Party 1935–1949] (1992).

Constantine Pleshakov is an independent scholar and writer living in Moscow. His most recent book in English is *Inside the Kremlin's Cold War: From Stalin* *to Khrushchev* (1996), coauthored with Vladislav M. Zubok. He is now finishing a book on the Romanov dynasty in exile (with John Curtis Perry).

Kathryn Weathersby is an independent scholar living in Washington, D.C. She has pioneered the study of the international history of the Korean War through the use of Russian archives and has published a number of articles on the topic. She is now working on a book on the Soviet Union and the Korean War.

Odd Arne Westad was director of research at the Norwegian Nobel Institute, and is now reader in International History at the London School of Economics. He is the author of a number of books and articles on Cold War history, including *Cold War and Revolution: Soviet-American Rivalry and the Origins of the Chinese Civil War, 1944–1946* (1994) and, most recently, *The Fall of Détente: Soviet-American Relations during the Carter Years* (1997).

Yang Kuisong is senior research fellow at the Institute of Modern History, Chinese Academy of Social Sciences. A leading authority on the history of the Chinese Communist Party, he has written and published widely on the CCP's external relations. His most recent major publication is *Zhonggong yu Mosike de guanxi* [The Chinese Communist Party's relations with Moscow] (1996).

Shu Guang Zhang is professor of diplomatic history at the University of Maryland. He is the author of *Deterrence and Strategic Culture: Chinese-American Confrontations, 1949–1958* (1992) and *Mao's Military Romanticism: China and the Korean War, 1950–1953* (1995), and coeditor (with Chen Jian) of *Chinese Communist Foreign Policy and the Cold War in Asia, 1944–1950: Documentary Evidence* (1996). He is currently writing an international history of the Western embargo against China in the 1950s.

Index

Acheson, Dean, 98, 171, 251
adventurism, 238, 262, 265, 266–8
advisers. *See* Soviet advisers
agriculture, collectivization of, 17, 26–7, 174, 204, 261, 262
aircraft, 16, 27, 28, 96, 100, 143, 147
Albania, 26, 235, 239
antiadventurism, 238, 262, 265, 266–8
antiaircraft systems. *See* missiles
anti-Japanese war. *See* Sino-Japanese war
antileftism, 6. *See also* revisionism
antirevisionism, 277. *See also* revisionism
Anti-Rightist movement, 265, 289n98
Anti-social-imperialism, 277
anti-Stalinism. *See* de-Stalinization
antisystemic alliance, 2, 165–6, 167–8
Arkhipov, Ivan V., 124, 137n12, 138nn19, 20, 21, 153–4
armaments, 35n22, 55, 56, 142–4, 147, 148, 149, 152–7. *See also specific types*
armies. *See* Chinese People's Volunteers; Korean People's Army; Northeast Border Defense Army; PLA; Soviet Red Army

balance of power, 190–1
Bandung Conference, 145
bandwagon effect, 190
Batov, Pavel, 156
Beriia, Lavrentii, 1, 15, 257
border issues: Chinese Muslim border crossings, 239; Sino-Indian 1959 dispute, 23–4, 43n81, 177, 186n33, 213, 273, 293n137; Sino-Indian 1962 dispute, 27–8, 45n100; Sino-Soviet dispute, 239; Sino-Vietnamese dispute, 240; Soviet buffer zones, 8, 29, 50, 142–3; Soviets on Sino-Indian disputes, 23–4, 28, 43n81, 45n100, 148–9, 213, 237, 273, 274, 293n137
Bo Yibo, 155
Brezhnev, Leonid, 25, 26, 29
Bucharest conference (1960), 25, 178
Bulganin, Nikolai A., 147, 152, 213

Camp David spirit, 273
Castro, Fidel, 28
CCP CC (Chinese Communist Party Central Committee): anti-Zhou Enlai campaign, 265, 266–8, 289n99 (*See also specific subjects);* Eighth Congress,

232; Soviet advisers on, 127, 129, 131, 133–4; Soviet disrespect of, 209–10; Soviet influence on, 17; xenophobia of, 192. *See also* Chinese Revolution
Chinese Muslims, 239
Chinese Nationalist Party, 142, 150. *See also* GMD
Chinese People's Volunteers (CPV), 93, 95, 200, 252, 253
Chinese Revolution, 18–19, 20–1, 23, 24, 26–7, 29, 49–50, 256; adventurism/anti-adventurism in, 262, 265, 266–8; CCP disagreements about, 30, 262, 266–7, 272–3, 287n82; and class struggle, 29, 49, 265, 276; collectivization of agriculture in, 17, 26–7, 174, 204, 261, 262; and continuous revolution, 246, 247–9, 261–2, 265, 267, 276; counterrevolution in/subversion of, 18–19, 68, 167–8, 169, 173, 174–5, 190, 254–5, 256; and human capabilities, 3, 211–12; and imperialistic influences, 194–5, 247, 248; and people's communes, 271–2; status reports, 301–13, 369–75. *See also* Anti-Rightist movement; Cultural Revolution; Five Antis movement; Great Leap Forward; Great Movement to Resist America and Assist Korea; Hundred Flowers campaign; Three Antis movement
Chinese students, 16, 39n52
Chuikov, I. V., 48, 49
class struggle, 29, 49, 265, 276
collectivization of agriculture, 17, 26–7, 174, 204, 261, 262. *See also* Great Leap Forward
Comintern, 6–7, 48–9
communes, people's, 271–2
communications systems, 27, 176, 235–6, 268–70, 291n120

Communist International (Comintern), 6–7, 48–9
Communist Korean People's Army, 93
Communist Party, Chinese. *See* CCP
Communist Party of the Soviet Union. *See* CPSU
containment, 90
continentalism, 229, 230, 232, 234
continuous revolution, 246, 261–2, 265, 267, 276. *See also* Chinese Revolution
counterrevolution, 18–19, 167–8, 169, 174–5, 254–5, 256
CPSU (Communist Party of the Soviet Union): depersonalization of control, 232; foreign policy disagreements, 145–6; Stalinists defeated, 20, 231–2; threats to, 229–30; Twentieth Party Congress, 18, 174, 231, 259–60; Twenty-second Party Congress, 26, 147, 177, 239. *See also specific subjects*
cult of Mao, 131
cult of personality, 131, 262, 336. *See also* de-Stalinization
Cultural Revolution, 29–30, 192, 232, 273, 276. *See also* Chinese Revolution

Dachen Islands, 173
Dalian, 55, 73, 144, 229, 241n9
Democratic People's Republic of Korea. *See* Korean War
Deng Xiaoping, 174, 180, 187n40, 260; on advisers, 127; on agreements, 214–15; on Cuban Missile Crisis, 179; on détente, 276; in negotiations, 20, 26, 28, 374–5, 376–90; and Polish and Hungarian uprisings, 264–5
de-Stalinization, 239; CCP CC on, 239, 260–1, 261–4, 286nn72, 73, 287nn74, 75, 78; Khrushchev on, 18–19, 130–1,

revolutionary support, 238. *See also*
CCP-GMD hostilities; Chinese civil
war; Korean War; Sino-Japanese war;
Taiwan Straits
crisis
Soviet-GMD treaty (1945), 7, 52, 54, 66,
70, 71–3, 142, 168, 169, 249
Soviet-Indian relations, 146, 177, 239–40
Soviet military affairs, 91, 153–4,
280n20, 284n55; military intelligence,
27, 91; oceanic access, 207, 230,
234–6, 240; reductions in army, 234,
237; submarine capabilities, 234–6.
See also CCP-GMD hostilities; Chinese civil war; Korean War; Sino-
Japanese war; Sino-Soviet military cooperation; Soviet Red Army; Taiwan
Straits crisis
Soviet Red Army, 7, 144–5, 197–8, 234,
237, 265. *See also* Chinese civil war
Stalin, Joseph, 31; on advisers, 199; on
avoidance of war, 92, 170; on CCP-
GMD hostilities, 52–3, 54, 77n13; on
Chinese Revolution, 49; on compensation for China's losses, 195; death of,
14, 15, 145, 172; on Eisenhower, 108,
116n55; on geopolitics/ideology, 227,
228, 240n4; on international relations,
330–2, 333; on Korean and civil wars,
329–35; on Mao, 70, 142, 167; underestimation of CCP, 8, 51, 142, 171–2;
on U.S. weaknesses, 105–6. *See also*
de-Stalinization; Korean war; *specific
subjects*
starvation, 26–7
Strategic Missile Corps. (Soviet), 156
Stuart, John Leighton, 68–9, 249
students, Chinese, 16, 39n52
submarines, 176, 207, 234–6, 239–40,
268–9

subversion, 68, 167–8, 173, 174, 190. *See
also* counterrevolution
Sudarikov, N., 243n45
Sukhodolskii, Major, 156
Sungai River Fleet, 142–3
Suslov, Mikhail, 28, 376–90

Taiwan, 145, 149. *See also* Taiwan Straits
crisis
Taiwan Straits crisis, 17–8, 21–4; crisis
of 1954–1955, 150, 173; crisis of 1958,
148–52, 158–9, 175–6, 236–7, 243n45,
270–2, 274, 291n125
Third World revolutions/liberation movements, 31, 238
Third World War, 24, 91–2, 105–6, 110,
170, 190–1
Three Antis movement, 256, 284n57
three-thirds system, 6
Tibet rebellion, 27–8, 272
Tito, Marshal, 229
trade. *See* Sino-Soviet economic relations
transportation systems and vehicles, 143,
145, 147, 148, 193
Treaty of Friendship. *See* Sino-Soviet
Treaty of Friendship
Truman, Harry, 251
Twentieth Party Congress (CPSU), 18,
174, 231, 259–60
Twenty-second Party Congress (CPSU),
26, 147, 177, 239

United Nations (UN), 13, 109, 151, 256.
See also Korean War
U.S. affairs and policies: foreign policies,
90, 152, 166, 168, 171, 175; subversion
of Chinese Revolution, 68, 167–8, 173,
174, 190; support of GMD/Jiang
Jieshi/Taiwan, 55, 56, 57, 145, 149,
150–1, 152, 171, 271; U.S. Air Force,